P9-CCQ-805

Favorite Recipes® of America

SALADS

including appetizers

FAVORITE RECIPES PRESS,
Louisville,

TABLE OF CONTENTS

FAVORITE RECIPES PRESS, INC. © MCMLXVI

Post Office Box 18324
Louisville, Kentucky 40218

INTRODUCTION

Americans love salads. In fact, many wouldn't think of serving a meal without a salad. In some homes, salads make up the main part of the meal, while other homemakers use salads as appetizers, meat accompaniments or even desserts.

Americans are weight conscious and salads just seem to be the natural light food for weight watchers—even though some salads can be rich and hearty. Salads are usually easy to prepare and are great for days when the homemaker is busy and doesn't have much time to devote to preparing a meal.

In this collection you will find desserts galore—the pages are packed with recipes for fruit, vegetable, meat, green and molded salads—plus those from foreign lands.

The recipes in this "Salads" edition of FAVORITE RECIPES OF AMERICA were selected from the more than 50,000 recipes in my files to represent regional cookery at its very best. Recipes from southern, eastern, western and northern areas of the country are represented in this edition.

These favorite American recipes were home tested by hundreds of cooks across the nation just like yourself. Each recipe was endorsed by the homemaker whose name appears under the recipe. You'll treasure the many recipes in this collection which will become *your* favorites.

Mary Anne Richards
Staff Home Economist
Favorite Recipes Press, Inc.

ABBREVIATIONS

Teaspoon	tsp.	Large	lge.
Tablespoon	tbsp.	Package	pkg.
Cup	c.	Square	sq.
Pound	lb.	Dozen	doz.
Ounce	oz.	Pint	pt.
Medium	med.	Quart	qt.

MEASUREMENTS

3 tsp. = 1 tbsp.
2 tbsp. = ⅛ c.
4 tbsp. = ¼ c.
8 tbsp. = ½ c.
16 tbsp. = 1 c.
5 tbsp. + 1 tsp. = ⅓ c.
12 tbsp. = ¾ c.
4 oz. = ½ c.
8 oz. = 1 c.
16 oz. = 1 lb.
1 oz. = 2 tbsp. fat or liquid

2 c. fat = 1 lb.
2 c. = 1 pt.
2 c. sugar = 1 lb.
⅝ c. = ½ c. + 2 tbsp.
⅞ c. = ¾ c. + 2 tbsp.
2 pt. = 1 qt.
1 qt. = 4 c.
A few grains = Less than ⅛ tsp.
Pinch = As much as can be taken between tip of finger and thumb
Speck = Less than ⅛ tsp.

CAN CONTENTS

Average Contents	*Can Size*
1 c.	8 oz.
1¾ c.	No. 300
2 c.	No. 1 tall
2½ c.	No. 2
3½ c.	No. 2½
4 c.	No. 3

SALAD MAKING TERMS AND DEFINITIONS

BEAT	To make a mixture smooth or to introduce air by using a brisk, regular motion that lifts the mixture over and over
BLANCH	To parboil in water for a minute, or to pour boiling water over food and then drain it almost immediately
BLEND	To thoroughly mix two or more ingredients
CHILL	To refrigerate until thoroughly cold
CHOP	To cut into pieces with a sharp knife
CREAM	To work one or more foods until mixture is soft and creamy
CUT	To divide food materials with a knife or scissors
DICE	To cut into cubes
FLAKE	To break into small pieces with a fork
FOLD	To combine by using two motions, cutting vertically through the mixture and turning over and over by sliding the implement across the bottom of the mixing bowl with each turn
GARNISH	To decorate. For example, to decorate a fish salad with hard-cooked eggs or parsley
GRATE	To cut food into minute bits by rubbing on a grater
GRIND	To cut food into tiny particles by putting through a grinder
MARINATE	To let food stand in a marinade—usually an oil-acid mixture such as French dressing
MINCE	To cut or chop into very small pieces
MIX	To combine ingredients in any way that evenly distributes them
PARE	To cut off the outside covering

SALAD MAKING TERMS AND DEFINITIONS

PEEL	To strip off the outside covering
SCALD	To heat milk to just below the boiling point
SHRED	To cut finely with a knife or sharp instrument
SLIVER	To slice into long, thin strips
STIR	To mix food materials with a circular motion for the purpose of blending or securing uniform consistency
TEAR	To break or tear into bite-sized pieces
TOSS	To lightly blend food ingredients
WHIP	To beat rapidly to produce expansion due to the incorporation of air as applied to cream, egg and gelatin dishes

Choosing the Right Salad . . .

. . . is important because salads are always in good taste for most any meal. Without salads many meals would be incomplete. Salads offer variety, food values and often that bit of color needed to perk up an otherwise drab menu.

The uses of salads are almost as varied as the kinds of salads from which to choose. Most often salads are served in medium-size portions as accompaniments to meals, and are light rather than heavy. Small bits of tart fruit or seafood arranged on a bed of greens are appetite-teasers and are often used as the first course of a meal.

Hearty salads . . . those that contain meat, seafood or poultry with fresh raw or cooked vegetables . . . are a meal in themselves and are used as main dishes. Cheese and eggs also make good bases for tasty main dish salads.

A Good Rule of Thumb . . .

. . . to remember when choosing a salad is that a light rather than a heavy, rich salad goes better with hearty meals. Tart salads are especially good with seafoods. Hot or hearty salads make good main dishes and fruit salads may be used as appetizers, desserts or meat accompaniments.

For Simply Successful Salads . . .

. . . choose pleasing combinations of ingredients with contrasts in color, texture, form and flavor. Experiment with color, but use only foods with pleasing color combinations that don't clash.

. . . experiment with soft and firm food textures. Try fruits and vegetables mixed for a different and delightful taste treat.

. . . prepare ingredients carefully. Use only chilled, crisp greens. When using fruits, drain thoroughly on absorbent paper. Drain vegetables in a sieve.

. . . sprinkle lemon juice on fruits, vegetables, meat, poultry, fish and seafood to enhance the flavor and keep the food from turning brown.

. . . cut or tear foods into pieces that are large enough to tell what they are, yet small enough to handle easily. Avoid cutting salad greens. Cutting tends to make them wilt faster.

. . . keep hot salads hot, not lukewarm, and cold salads icy cold.

. . . use the correct dressing. But don't drown salads. Too much dressing will result in a soggy, limp product. Add dressings at the last possible moment. If salads stand too long in their dressings, they tend to lose their crispness and are unattractive.

. . . prepare salads just before serving for a crisp, fresh look and taste. Serve on chilled plates.

. . . toss salads lightly to prevent bruising and discoloration. Don't overmix.

. . . arrange salads attractively, but avoid a fixed, rigid look. Make sure the greens don't extend over the edge of the plate. Never crowd a too-large salad on a too-small plate.

. . . serve salads daily, but aim for variety.

Your Salad Bowl . . .

. . . deserves good care, regardless of the type you choose to show off your salad. Some of the choices of salad bowls are wood, silver, ceramic, stainless steel, clear glass, plastic, china, aluminum, pottery or pyrex.

No matter what type of bowl you choose for your salad showcase, each type needs a little extra care. A silver bowl is truly elegant for serving a salad on those special occasions, but you must protect the silver by using a glass liner. Toss the salad first in the glass bowl, then place the glass bowl in the silver one for serving.

Ceramic salad bowls are cheery and great for daily or family use. Stainproof ceramic bowls require very careful handling to prevent chipping. Cermamic salad bowls come in wonderful colors and a variety of shapes—some designed for a specific purpose such as a tomato-shaped bowl for a vegetable salad or a melon-shaped one for fruit salad.

Stainless steel bowls are sleek and modern looking. It's never necessary to polish these bowls and they may be used for all types of salads—tossed, fruit, vegetable, molded, hot or cold.

Handle china carefully or you'll be apt to chip it if you toss your salad too hard. As with silver, a glass liner should be used in an aluminum salad bowl. Toss the salad in the glass bowl, then place the glass bowl in the aluminum bowl.

Clear glass salad bowls are perfect for showing off a fresh fruit salad or mixed greens. Glass bowls are relatively inexpensive and easy to care for. Ovenproof glass bowls are essential for those hot salads. Hearty, delicious hot salads may be prepared, heated and served in these wonderful stainproof bowls. For an added touch, slip the bowl into wicker or stainless steel holder before putting on the table.

A fine wooden bowl is the popular choice of most folks. The very hard woods such as olive, maple or teak make the best bowls because the hard woods don't absorb so much dressing. Wash your wooden salad bowl with a damp cloth—no soap—and dry at once. Never soak a wooden salad bowl in water.

Almost Every Salad Creation . . .

. . . starts with greens, whether they be used as a salad bed or mixed for the salad itself. Brighten your salads and make them sing with new-to-you salad greens such as romaine, endive, water cress, chicory, escarole, spinach, kale, celery leaves, Swiss chard or beet, mustard, turnip and dandelion greens. Try mixing them with the old familiar standbys, head or leaf lettuce, for added vitamin richness and a zesty tang.

To make sure that the salad bed is eaten, sprinkle with dressing just before the salad is arranged on the top. Keep the bed small and never let the greens extend over the edge of the plate.

In General, All Greens . . .

. . . should be young and crisp, clean, green and tender. Avoid greens that have yellow or withered leaves or that have red, rusty streaks or spots. These discolorations are harmless, but make unattractive salads.

When choosing greens remember that the darker salad vegetables offer larger amounts of vitamins A and C and are richer in iron than the paler ones.

Select crisp lettuce, such as iceberg, that is firm and heavy for its size. If the lettuce is to be used for cups, choose a loose head. Leaf lettuce should have pale green leaves and a firm core.

Select chicory, endive and escarole that have a few dark, tough outer leaves. The inner leaves are more likely to stay crisp longer and have a better flavor. Spinach should have dark, small tender leaves. A good sign of toughness is coarse stems.

When selecting celery, make sure that the stalks are solid and thick, yet brittle enough to snap easily. Stalks that are medium in length are usually best. Avoid celery with cracked stalks and dry brown spots. Test the stalk to see if it is firm by gently pressing it.

ESCAROLE has large, broad leaves that shade from deep green on the outside to butter yellow in the center. Its edges look ruffled. It is sturdy and crisp and has a slightly bitter taste.

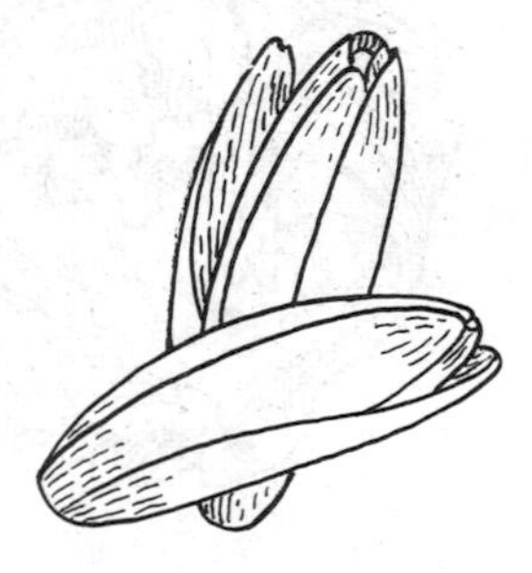

FRENCH OR BELGIAN ENDIVE is light green, almost white. Its head is compact, 5 to 6 inches long. It has a slightly bitter taste.

ROMAINE OR COS is lettuce with an elongated head and stiff leaves. The leaves are coarse but sweet. They keep well. The dark outer leaves shade to almost white at the root end. The lighter inner leaves are particularly tender and flavorful.

BIBB LETTUCE is a small, crisp, cup-shaped lettuce with a distinctive color and flavor. The leaves are a deep rich green that blend to whitish green toward the core.

BOSTON LETTUCE is loosely headed with oily feeling leaves. It is not expecially crisp. The outer leaves are a deep dark green and the inner leaves shade to almost white. It is very perishable and should be used the day it is purchased.

ICEBERG LETTUCE is the best known and most available lettuce on the market. Heads are firm, heavy and crisp textured. The cores are small. Leaves are medium green on the outside and shade to pale green in the center.

LEAF LETTUCE is an unheaded type of lettuce. It has light green, loosely bunched leaves with ragged edges.

CHICORY OR CURLY ENDIVE has a large head with long, ragged leaves. It has a slightly bitter flavor.

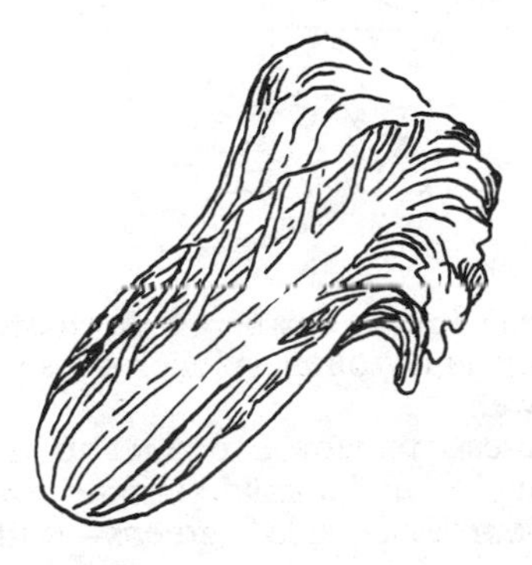

CHINESE OR CELERY CABBAGE has a long, oval head that is firm, fresh and well blanched.

SPINACH LEAVES are slightly tart and tangy.

WATER CRESS is an aquatic plant sold in bunches. The leaves are small, oval and mildly pungent.

PREPARING GREENS FOR SALADS

A salad is good only if the greens are fresh and crisp instead of watery and wilted. And, how you wash greens makes a difference in their texture . . . and the texture of the salad.

Rinse greens carefully under cool running water to remove any outside grit. Remove any discolored or wilted leaves. Remove tough outer leaves. If these outer leaves aren't bruised, shred them for use in sandwiches or as salad beds. These outer leaves, although not as tender as the inner ones, are especially rich in vitamins and minerals.

To rid greens of bugs, add 4 tablespoons of salt to each gallon of water for washing. Rinse the greens well; shake off excess water or drain well. Place in refrigerator to crisp.

Just before making the salad, remove the greens from the crisper and finish washing them.

To wash iceberg lettuce, cut out the core with a sharp knife to separate the leaves. Hold the lettuce with the cored side up under running water. Run cold water into the opening. The leaves will separate. Shake off excess water and dry thoroughly.

Separate romaine, endive, escarole and leaf lettuce, leaf by leaf, washing each well. Dry thoroughly. Wash chicory and young spinach in several changes of water to remove all grit. Dry well.

Open and pick over bunches of water cress, parsley and mint to remove all dead and tough stems. Wash thoroughly under cold running water. Drain well and store loosely—apart from other salad greens—with stems down in a covered jar in the refrigerator.

DRYING GREENS . . .

. . . is very important. This job must be done very gently because some greens are tender and will bruise easily. Shake off excess water after washing. Spread the greens out on a fresh clean tea towel or paper towel. Roll up loosely and put into the refrigerator until it's time to prepare the salad.

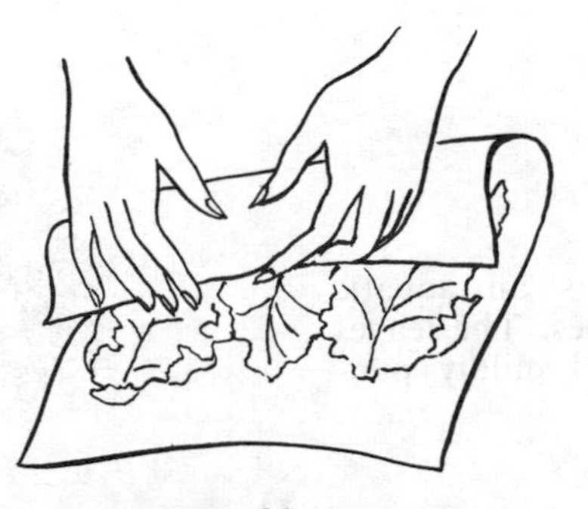

SELECTING FRUITS FOR SALADS

FRUIT	HOW TO SELECT	STORAGE
APPLES	Avoid those that are soft to the touch or that have shriveled skins.	Keep in a cool place. Apples may be refrigerated.
BANANAS	Should be plump and firm with a bright yellow skin, or, when fully ripe, flecked with brown. Avoid those that are green-tipped.	Store at room temperature. Refrigerator storage stops ripening and impairs flavor.
BERRIES	Should be bright, clean, plump, fully colored and fragrant. Avoid overripe, soft berries with leaking juice.	Very perishable. Pick over carefully and spread out before refrigerating. Wash just before using. Use as soon as possible.
CITRUS FRUITS	Choose those that are firm and heavy for their size, with fine textured skins. Avoid those that have a puffy skin (except tangerines.)	Store in a cool, dark, dry place or refrigerate.
CHERRIES	Choose those that are plump, firm and bright and have stems attached. Stain will indicate they are overripe.	Wash and store in the refrigerator.
GRAPES	Should be plump with fresh good color and firmly attached stems. If stems are brittle, bunches will "shatter" easily.	Store in refrigerator for as short a time as possible.
MELONS	Should have a fragrant aroma, be unbruised. A ripe melon will be soft near the stem and will give a little. Thump watermelons and if they give a hollow, not dull, thudding sound, they are ripe.	Store at 70° F. to ripen. Refrigerate before serving.
PEACHES	Should be plump, firm, smooth-skinned and have a good color (whitish or yellowish with a reddish blush). Avoid those that are shriveled or very green.	Very perishable. Handle gently and refrigerate.
PEARS	Should be smooth surfaced and well shaped. Firm to fairly firm, but not hard. Avoid those that are rotted or bruised at stem or blossom end.	Store in a cool, dry, dark place. If hard, ripen at room temperature.
PINEAPPLE	Should be fragrant, dark orange-yellow in color, heavy to feel. Avoid those with discolored areas or soft watery spots. To test for ripeness, pull one of the leaves at the top. It should pull out easily.	Keep in cool place.
PLUMS	Choose plump, dark ones that are soft but not mushy. Avoid those that are shriveled or brownish.	Keep in refrigerator.

PREPARING FRUITS FOR SALADS

A fruit salad is delicious at any time. And most fruit salads are pretty because of the rainbow of colors found in the fruits. To make your fruit salads even more eye appealing, tuck away these suggestions for future use.

MELON BALLS

Use a melon ball tool, or scoop fruit out with a ½ teaspoon measuring spoon. Pile mixture of watermelon and cantaloupe balls back into a scooped out watermelon shell.

PINEAPPLE

Use your pineapple for a centerpiece for several days, then put it to use as a salad and the shell as a salad server.

A. Pineapple Basket

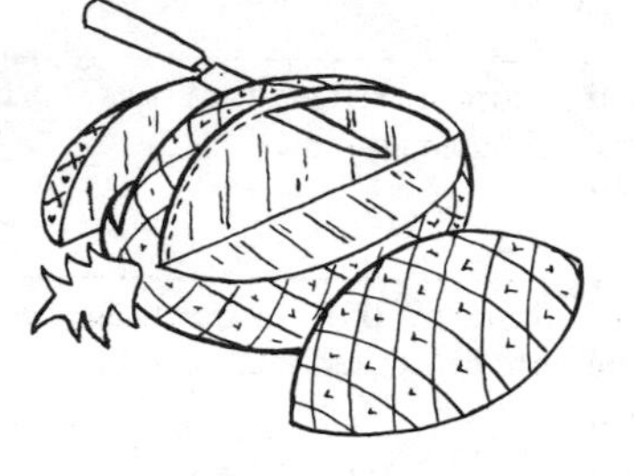

At the right of the center of the pineapple, make a vertical cut to the core. Repeat the same cut on the left to form a handle 1-inch wide.

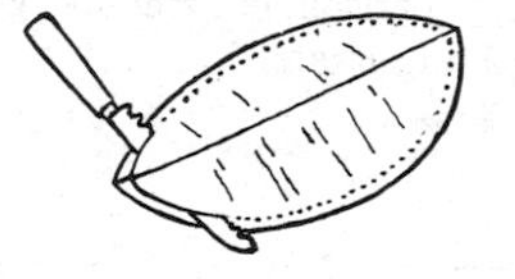

Cut from sides to center to free wedges. Remove the fruit from the cut out wedges.

Remove fruit from under the handle. Using a grapefruit knife, remove the fruit from the basket. Dice pineapple and mix with other fruits. Pile into pineapple basket for serving.

B. Individual Pineapple Servers

Cut pineapple into lengthwise quarters, cutting evenly through the crown and core.

Remove fruit in one piece with curved knife, cutting just under core of each quarter.

Slice fruit. Alternate pieces of fruit under strip of core so they extend alternately. If desired, other fruits may be alternated with the pineapple strips.

C. Luau Pineapple

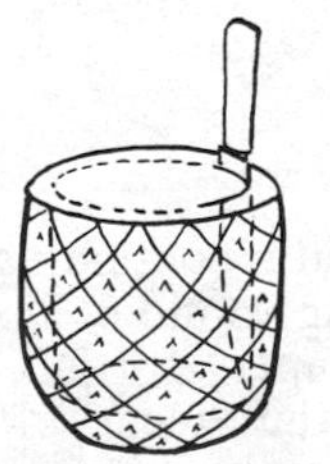

Cut off top of pineapple about 1½ inches down. Cut inside of pineapple leaving ½ inch inside rind, to within 1 inch of the bottom.

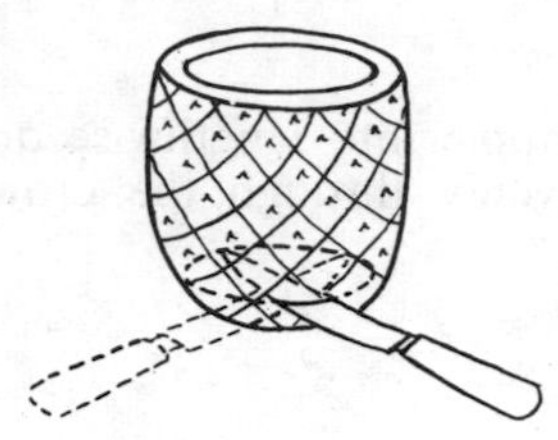

Insert a knife about 1½ inches up from the bottom, pointing the rind opposite. Draw the knife along the rind to the right. Turn the knife and repeat to sever fruit on the left.

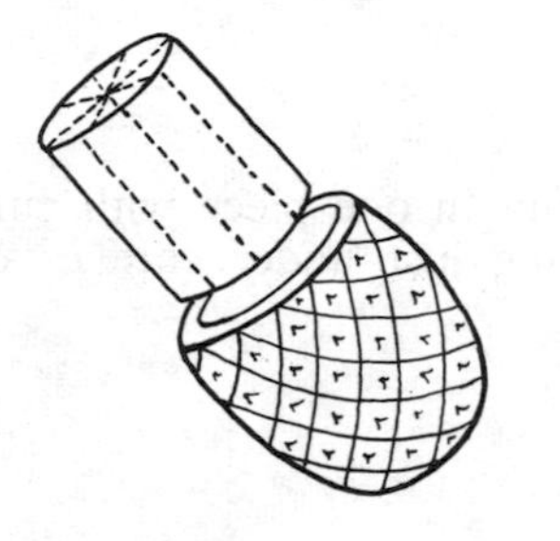

Remove fruit from shell. Cut fruit in wedges or spears and replace in pineapple shell. Or, if desired, cut the hollow shell crosswise to form a bowl that will hold about 2 cups of salad dressing.

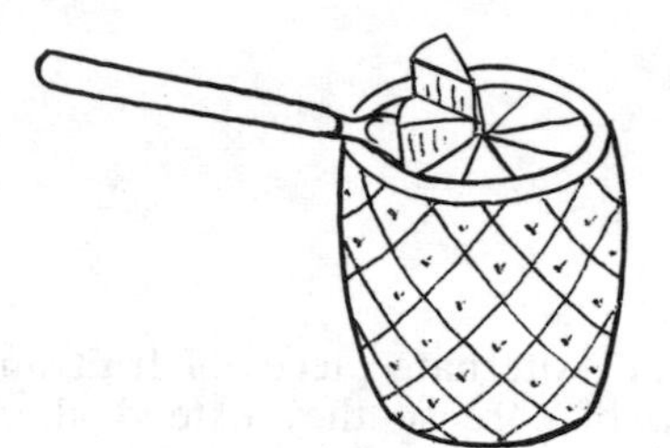

Set shell filled with dressing on a large serving plate or tray. Let guests help themselves to the dressing from the pineapple shell.

CITRUS FRUITS

A. Round and Round Method

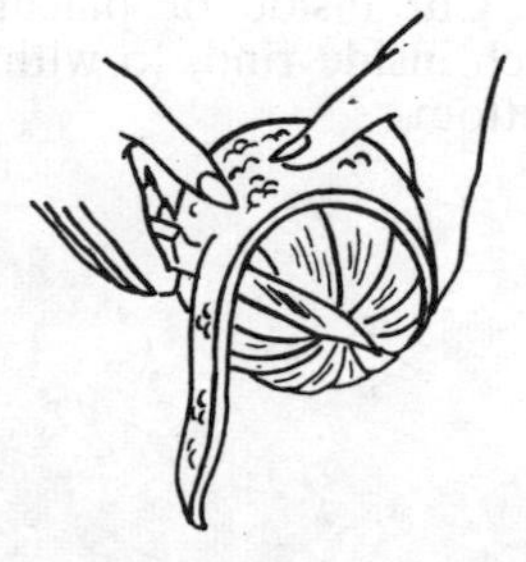

Cut the peel away in a continuing spiral with a slight sawing motion. Don't remove the white inner portion which clings naturally to the "meat." It's rich in vitamins and minerals.

B. Basketball Method

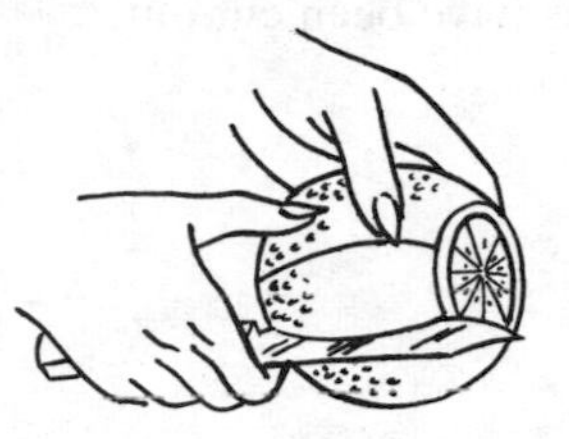

With a sharp knife slice off the stem end of the fruit. Score the peel with a knife so it looks like the sections on the outside of a basketball. Don't cut down into the meat. Pull the peel away with your fingers, again leaving the white inner portion which clings to the meat.

C. Cartwheels

Use them peeled for salads—unpeeled for garnishes. Slice fruit crosswise in desired thickness. For halfwheels, cut cartwheels in two parts.

D. Sections

Peel fruit. Cut sections halfway between segment walls so that the membrane is in the center of the meat.

E. Segments

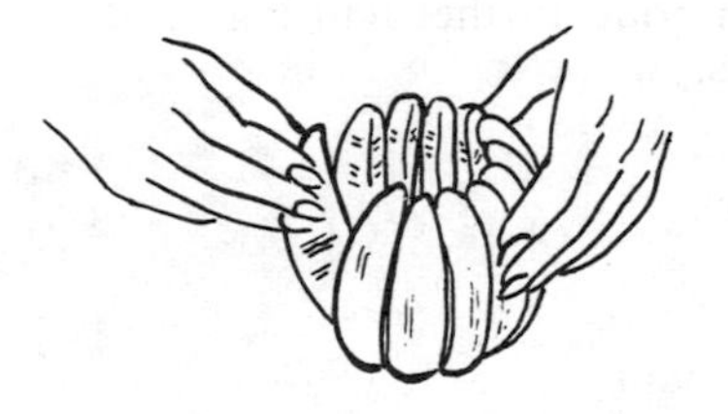

Peel fruit. Gently separate into natural sections.

F. Shells

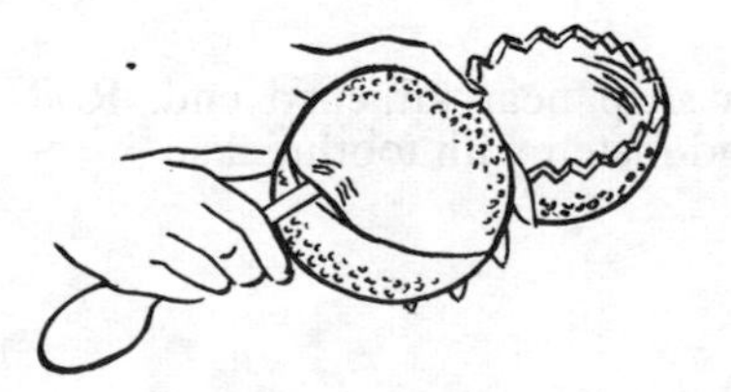

Score fruit around middle with a knife point. Peel away from the fruit with a spoon handle. Edges may be notched with scissors if desired.

For a swirling edge fringe, cut top edge at an angle with a sharp knife after fruit sections have been cut out.

FANCY CITRUS BASKETS

Cut ¼-inch wide strip around the top of an orange or grapefruit half, leaving a 1-inch strip on each side uncut. Cut down through membrane to free the strips.

A. Bow

Cut the ¼-inch strip as directed above. Cut each strip at center and fold back. Fasten with toothpicks.

B. Handles

Pull together at top the two ¼-inch strips, without further cutting. Fasten with picks.

C. Spirals

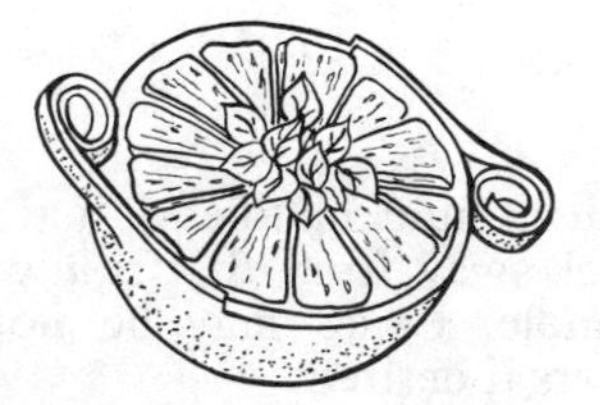

Cut each strip near attached end. Roll tightly and fasten with toothpicks.

MOLDING A MASTERPIECE

Stars, crescents, bunnies, fish, rings—all of these special molds are available for congealed salads. Round, square, oval and oblong molds may also be found on the market.

One of the most popular of all molds is the ring mold. Its popularity is based on the fact that the ring mold is so versatile. The center may be filled with fruits, jelly, vegetables, cheese or a bowl of dressing.

Don't overlook the possibility of using the most common utensils in your kitchen for molding salads. Custard cups, muffin pans, cake tins, ice cube trays, empty coffee cans and even paper cups make effective molds.

There's Really Little Magic . . .

. . . involved in making a perfect molded salad. These simple suggestions will help you turn out a masterpiece every time.

. . . to avoid diluting the gelatin mixture, drain frozen or canned fruits thoroughly before adding. Or, substitute syrup from the fruits as a part of the liquid for added flavor.

. . . chill gelatin until it is the consistency of unbeaten egg whites before adding fruits and vegetables. If they are added to the gelatin mixture before it is this consistency, they will sink to the bottom of the mold and won't be distributed throughout the gelatin.

. . . carefully fold the fruits and vegetables into the thickened gelatin to distribute them evenly.

. . . to mold different flavors or colors in layers, chill each layer until set before adding the next one.

. . . for a stay-put garnish in a molded salad, arrange the design—such as a ring of cucumber slices—on a layer of partially set gelatin. Chill, then pour another layer of gelatin over the design. Chill until firm.

. . . to keep bubbles in a carbonated beverage that is used as the liquid in a gelatin salad, pour the beverage down the side of the bowl. Stir with an up and down motion.

. . . gelatin mixtures usually require from two to four hours to set in the refrigerator. They'll congeal faster if they are in small individual molds.

. . . for a quick chill, place gelatin mixture in freezing compartment for 10 minutes. Or, set the bowl in ice water and stir the gelatin mixture until it starts to thicken. If mixture becomes too solid, remelt over boiling water.

MOLDING AND UNMOLDING GELATIN SALADS

For success in molding and unmolding a layered or ribbon salad, use heavy duty aluminum foil. Tear off long strips of the foil and cross them in the bottom of a loaf pan. Mold salad layers according to recipe directions. When salad is congealed, lift the foil strips to loosen the firm gelatin. Unmold very carefully and pėel off foil.

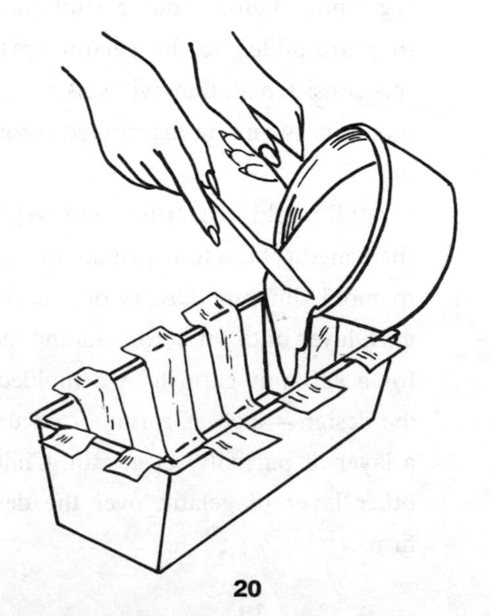

For salads molded in fancy or plain molds, try these suggestions for unmolding.

Dip mold in warm, but not hot, water to the depth of the gelatin. Loosen around the edge with the tip of a paring knife.

Rinse the serving dish with cold water. Don't dry the plate so the gelatin will slide easily if it needs to be centered on the plate.

Place the serving dish on top of the mold and turn upside down. Shake gently, holding serving dish tightly to the mold. Remove mold carefully.

If the gelatin does not unmold rapidly, repeat the process.

In A Dither . . .

. . . about chilling gelatin mixtures to the right consistency? Different recipes will call for different degrees of chilling the gelatin mixtures.

When a recipe calls for chilling a mixture to "slightly thicker than unbeaten egg whites," it means that the gelatin will dribble unevenly from a spoon when chilled to the proper degree of coldness.

For whipped cream mixtures, the gelatin mixture should be chilled so it is thick enough to mound slightly when dropped from a spoon.

Gelatin mixtures will pour from a spoon in an unbroken stream when "chilled to the consistency of unbeaten egg whites." This is the consistency usually required for simple gels and chiffons.

FREEZING SALADS

A boon to the hurried homemaker is the salad which can be frozen and served later. It may be prepared days in advance of serving time and still be fresh and delicious.

Salads which freeze best are those with a base of cream cheese, cottage cheese or whipped cream. Those which contain large amounts of mayonnaise or salad dressing tend to separate if frozen.

In general, salads which are frozen in refrigerator ice trays are best suited for freezing.

Be sure that salads that are to be frozen and left in the freezer for any length of time are packaged in moisture-vaporproof containers. Limit storage time for frozen salads. Don't store them in the freezer for more than three months. In serving these salads, remember that frozen salads are generally better if they are served before they are completely thawed.

Salad Dressings Are Like . . .

. . . the icing on a cake—the varieties are almost endless. And, just as icings add that extra taste appeal to cakes, dressings do the same for salads.

If a salad looks attractive, it's no problem to get guests to take that first bite. But it's the dressing that makes the salad disappear. But, a note of warning! Never soak or drown a salad in dressing. Too much dressing will result in a soggy, limp product. Add dressings just before serving for a better salad flavor and crisp texture.

There's No Definite Rule . . .

. . . when it comes to choosing a dressing for a salad. But there are guideposts to follow.

Tangy French dressings are used to marinate vegetables and to toss with greens. Use tart or sweet dressings for fruit salads.

Mayonnaise and salad dressing combinations enhance meat, seafood, egg and molded salads. Cooked dressings just naturally go with greens and vegetables, and sour cream dressings add zip to fruit and vegetable salads.

DRESSING DICTIONARY

French Dressing

. . . is a mixture of oil, vinegar and seasonings. Clear French dressing separates and must be thoroughly shaken before it is used. Creamy French dressings are homogenized and will stay mixed.

Mayonnaise

. . . is smooth and creamy. It is made by beating oil very slowly into seasoned vinegar and egg. It is mildly flavored and can be used with additional seasonings.

Cooked Dressing

. . . has a cooked white sauce and egg base. It is fluffy, creamy and has a zippy flavor.

Fine salad oil is essential to good dressings. Choose either corn, cottonseed, olive, peanut or soy oil, or a blend of these. Never use mineral oil . . . it may rob the body of important vitamins.

Lemon juice gives a tangy accent to dressings. Fresh, frozen or canned . . . it not only adds zip and tartness, but vitamin C as well. Use lemon juice interchangeably with vinegar.

Vinegar comes in many exciting flavors. Choose from one or several of these:

CIDER vinegar is a good all-purpose vinegar for salads and dressings.

MALT vinegar has a rich flavor and gives added zest to dressings.

TARRAGON vinegar has a herb fragrance which is wonderful in salads and dressings.

WINE vinegar is made from select table wines and adds flavor to dressings.

BASIL, HERB AND SPICE OR MIXED HERB vinegar is used lightly in salad dressings or on cooked greens, slaws, etc.

GARLIC WINE vinegar is used instead of garlic in salads and dressings.

A Garnish On A Salad . . .

. . . is the finishing touch. A garnish has two functions—to decorate and to add to the taste of the food it decorates.

A garnish is not the center of attraction and should be kept small. The garnish should provide contrast and added interest to a salad, but should never be gaudy. Never over garnish a salad, especially if it is served buffet-style. Guests may end up with no salad, just garnish.

Choose salad plates carefully. The dish, as well as the salad and the garnish, is important to the attractiveness of a salad. Always leave some plate showing to provide a frame for the salad.

Use your imagination when arranging a salad on a plate. Often the way a salad is placed on the serving plate is all the garnish that is needed.

CHOOSING A GARNISH

TYPE OF SALAD	GARNISH
Tossed Green	Apples, artichoke bottoms, avocado, bacon, cheese, meat, eggs, citrus fruit, grapes, olives, radishes, seafood, cold cooked vegetables, croutons, nuts

TYPE OF SALAD	GARNISH
Tossed Vegetable	Anchovies, bacon, Bleu cheese, capers, eggs, grated lemon rind, nuts, pickle relish, sardines, dill pickles, pimento
Poultry	Asparagus tips, avocado, cranberry jelly, fruit, olives, nuts, water cress, dill, mint, parsley
Fruit	Cheese, cheese spreads, nuts
Meat, Seafood	Fruit, cheese, cucumbers, olives, tomatoes, pickles, mushrooms

GLAMOROUS GARNISHES

Celery Curls

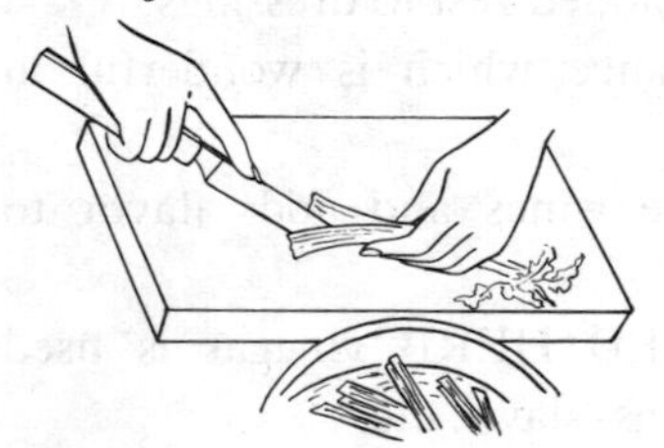

Cut celery stalks into short pieces. Slice ends in narrow lengthwise strips. Both ends may be slit if desired. Place cut celery in ice water to crisp.

Carrot Curls

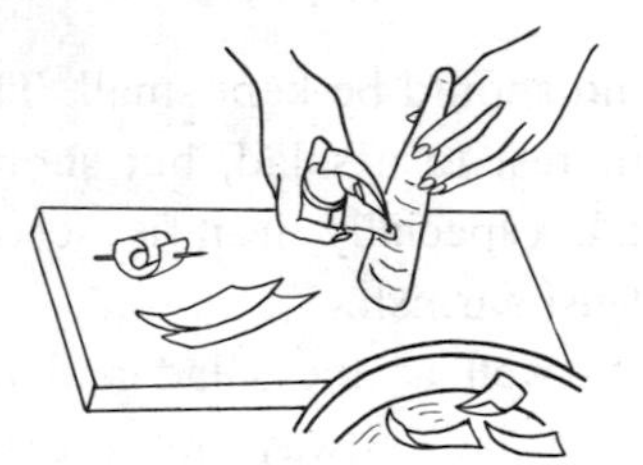

Scrape raw carrots to remove tough outer skin. Use potato peeler to make thin strips down the length of the carrots. Roll up strips and secure with toothpicks. Place in ice water until crisp and curled.

Scored or Fluted Cucumbers

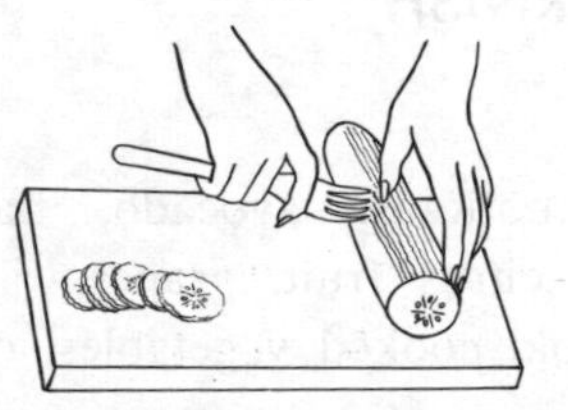

Cut off end of cucumber. Peel if the cucumber is tough. Leave young cucumber unpeeled for added color. Pull the tines of a fork firmly down the length of the cucumber. Cut into thin slices and chill in the refrigerator.

Radish Roses

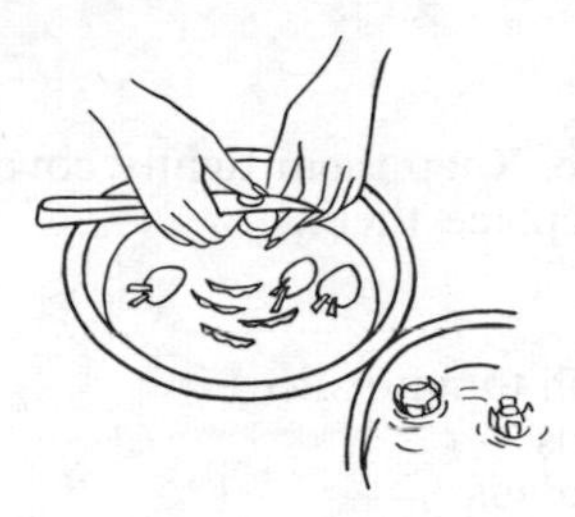

Using a sharp knife, cut off the radish root. Leave some of the stem and leaves. Thinly slice around the radish from stem to root end. Place in ice water. Don't try to separate or spread the "petals" apart. The ice water will cause them to "bloom."

Tomato Flowers

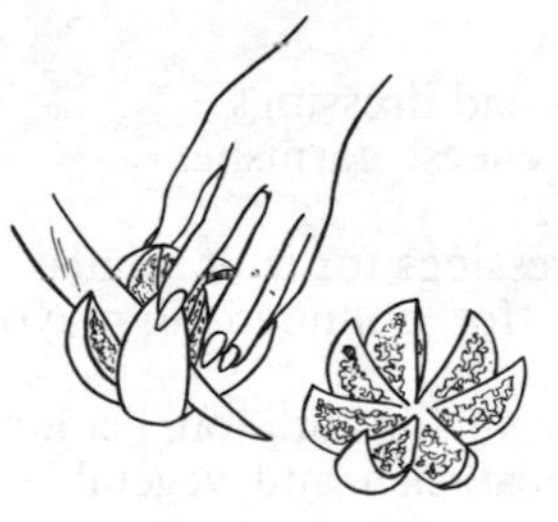

Using a sharp knife, cut the tomato into wedges, making sure that it is not cut completely through. Lightly spread wedges apart.

Citrus Fruit Flowers

Cut unpeeled fruit into eighths, slicing almost to the bottom. Spread wedges gently apart.

Citrus Fruit Twists

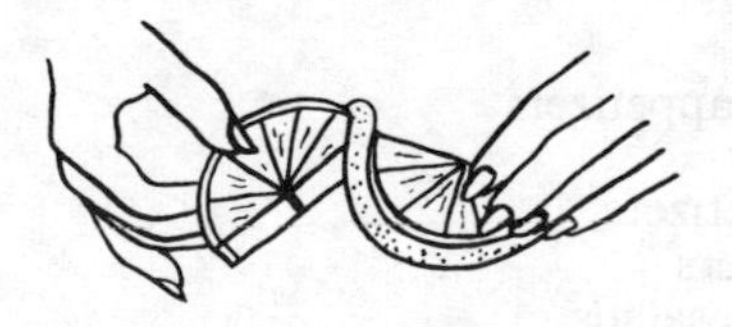

Cut unpeeled fruit into thin slices. Cut through one side of the peel. Twist.

HERB, SPICE, CHEESE AND BLEND CHART

Never store seasonings above or near the stove. Keep them tightly covered. When seasonings lose their delicate aroma, replace them.

HERBS:	USE WITH:
Basil	Tomato salads, fresh tomato slices
Caraway	Coleslaw, beet salads
Dill seed	Coleslaw, potato salads
Majoram	French dressing, fresh tomato slices, meat salads
Oregano	Potato or tuna salads
Rosemary	French dressing or mayonnaise for chicken or potato salads
Savory	Tossed salads
Thyme	French dressing marinade for diced chicken

SPICES:	USE WITH:
Allspice	Fruit salads, fruit salad dressings
Cinnamon	Tomatoes, cottage cheese garnishes
Ginger	Pear salads
Mace	Whipped cream dressings for fruit salads
Mustard	Mixed with water for commercial mayonnaise or French dressing
Paprika	Add to oil and vinegar for additional color
Cayenne pepper	Salad dressings, meat, fish and vegetable salads

BLENDS:	USE WITH:
Seasoning salt	Substitute for salt in oil and vinegar dressings
Italian dressing	French dressing, tossed green salads
Apple pie spice	Waldorf salads
Curry powder	French dressing for chicken salads
Salad lift	Add to oil and vinegar for French dressing or stir into prepared salad dressing
Pickling spice	Beet salads
Herb seasoning	Sliced cucumbers, sliced tomatoes, French dressing

CHEESE	USE WITH:
American Cheddar	Tossed salads, dressings, appetizers
Bleu (blue)	Tossed salads, dressings, appetizer spreads
Brick	Salads, appetizers
Camembert	Fruit salads, appetizer spreads
Cottage	Fruit, vegetable salads
Cream	Fruit, vegetable salads, dressings, appetizer spreads
Gorgonzola	Salads, dressings
Gouda	Appetizers
Muenster	Raw vegetable appetizers
Provolone	Appetizers
Roquefort	Dressings, appetizers
Ricotta	Salads, appetizers
Swiss	Fruit, vegetable salads

SALAD CALORIE CHART

FOOD	AMOUNT	CALORIES
CHEESE		
Blue mold (Roquefort type)	1 oz.	105
Cheddar or American		
Ungrated	1 1-in. cube	70
Grated	1 c.	455
Cheddar, process	1 oz.	105
Cheddar cheese foods	1 oz.	28
Cottage cheese (from skim milk)		
Creamed	1 oz.	30
Uncreamed	1 oz.	25
Creamed	1 c.	240
Uncreamed	1 c.	195
Cream cheese	1 c.	105
	1 tbsp.	55
Swiss	1 oz.	105
MEAT, POULTRY, FISH, SHELL-FISH, RELATED PRODUCTS		
Bacon, broiled or fried crisp	2 slices	95
Chicken, cooked:		
Flesh and skin, broiled, boneless	oz.	185
Canned, boneless	3 oz.	170
Pork, cured, cooked		
Ham, smoked, lean and fat	3 oz.	290
Luncheon meat		
Cooked ham, sliced	2 oz.	170
Canned, spiced or unspiced	2 oz.	165
Crab meat, canned or cooked	3 oz.	90
Salmon, pink, canned	3 oz.	120
Shrimp, canned, meat only	3 oz.	110
Tuna, canned in oil, drained, solids	3 oz.	170
NUTS, PEANUTS, RELATED PRODUCTS		
Almonds, shelled	1 c.	850
Brazil nuts, broken pieces	1 c.	905
Cashew nuts, roasted	1 c.	770
Coconut		
Fresh or shredded	1 c.	330
Dried, shredded, sweetened	1 c.	345
Peanuts, roasted, shelled		
Halves	1 c.	840
Chopped	1 tbsp.	50

SALAD CALORIE CHART (Continued)

FOOD	AMOUNT	CALORIES
Peanut butter	1 tbsp.	90
Pecans		
Halves	1 c.	740
Chopped	1 tbsp.	50
Walnuts, shelled		
Black or native, chopped	1 c.	790
English or Persian, halves	1 c.	650
English or Persian, chopped	1 tbsp.	50
VEGETABLES AND VEGETABLE PRODUCTS		
Beans		
Lima, immature, cooked	1 c.	150
Snap, green, cooked in small amount of water	1 c.	25
Snap, green, canned, solids and liquids	1 c.	45
Beets, cooked, diced	1 c.	70
Cabbage		
Raw, finely shredded	1 c.	25
Raw, coleslaw	1 c.	100
Cooked	1 c.	40
Cabbage, celery or Chinese		
Raw, leaves and stem, 1-in. pieces	1 c.	15
Cooked	1 c.	25
Carrots		
Raw, whole, 5½ x 1 in.	1 carrot	20
Grated	1 c.	45
Cooked, diced	1 c.	45
Cauliflower, cooked, flower buds	1 c.	30
Celery, raw		
Stalk, large outer, 8 x 1½ in. at root end	1 stalk	5
Pieces, diced	1 c.	20
Cucumber, 10 oz., 7½ x 2 in.		
Raw, pared	1 cucumber	25
Raw, pared, center slice, ⅛-in. thick	6 slices	5
Endive, curly (including escarole)	2 oz.	10
Lettuce, headed, raw		
Head, loose leaf, 4-in. diameter	1 head	30
Head, compact, 4¾-in. diameter, 1 lb.	1 head	70
Leaves	2 large or 4 small	5
Mushrooms, canned, solids and liquids	1 c.	30

SALAD CALORIE CHART (Continued)

FOOD	AMOUNT	CALORIES
Onions		
Mature, raw 2½-in. diameter	1 onion	50
Mature, cooked	1 c.	80
Young, green, small, without tops	6 onions	25
Parsley, raw, chopped	1 tbsp.	1
Peas, green		
Cooked	1 c.	110
Canned, solids and liquids	1 c.	170
Canned, strained	1 oz.	10
Peppers, sweet, raw, about 6 per lb.		
Green pod without stem and seeds	1 pod	15
Red pod without stem and seeds	1 pod	20
Canned, pimentoes, medium	1 pod	10
Potatoes, medium, about 3 per lb.		
Peeled after boiling	1 potato	105
Peeled before boiling	1 potato	90
Potato chips, medium, 2-in. diameter	10 chips	110
Radishes, raw, small, without tops	4 radishes	10
Sauerkraut, canned, drained, solids	1 c.	30
Tomatoes, raw, about 3 per lb.	1 tomato	30
Tomato juice, canned	1 c.	50
Tomato catsup	1 tbsp.	15
FRUIT AND FRUIT PRODUCTS		
Apples, raw, 2½-in. diameter, about 3 per lb.	1 apple	70
Apple juice, fresh or canned	1 c.	125
Applesauce, canned		
Sweetened	1 c.	185
Unsweetened	1 c.	100
Apricots		
Raw, about 12 per lb.	3 apricots	55
Canned, in heavy syrup, halves and syrup	1 c.	220
Dried, uncooked, 40 small halves	1 c.	390
Dried, cooked, unsweetened, fruit and liquid	1 c.	240
Avocados, raw		
California varieties, 10 oz. 3⅓ x 4¼ in., peeled and pitted	½ avocado	185
Florida varieties, 13 oz., 4 x 3 in., peeled and pitted	½ avocado	160
½-in. cubes	1 c.	195
Bananas, raw, 6 x 1½ in.	1 banana	85

SALAD CALORIE CHART (Continued)

FOOD	AMOUNT	CALORIES
Blackberries or blueberries, raw	1 c.	85
Cantaloup, raw, about 1⅔ lb.	½ melon	40
Cherries		
Raw, sour, sweet, hybrid	1 c.	65
Canned, sour, red, pitted	1 c.	105
Cranberry sauce, sweetened, canned or cooked	1 c.	550
Cranberry juice cocktail, canned	1 c.	140
Dates, pitted, cut	1 c.	505
Figs		
Raw, small, about 12 per lb.	3 figs	90
Dried, large, 2 x 1 in.	1 fig	60
Fruit cocktail, canned in heavy syrup, solids and liquids	1 c.	195
Grapefruit, raw, medium, 4¼-in. diameter		
White	½ grapefruit	50
Pink or red	½ grapefruit	55
Grapefruit sections, raw, white	1 c.	75
Grapefruit juice		
Fresh	1 c.	95
Canned, unsweetened	1 c.	100
Canned, sweetened	1 c.	130
Grapes, raw		
American type (slip skin)	1 c.	70
European type (adherent skin)	1 c.	100
Grape juice, bottled	1 c.	165
Lemons, raw, medium, 2⅕-in. diameter	1 lemon	20
Lemon juice		
Fresh	1 c.	60
	1 tbsp.	5
Canned, unsweetened	1 c.	60
Lemonade concentrate, frozen, sweetened		
Undiluted, 6-oz. can	1 can	430
Water added	1 c.	110
Lime juice, fresh or canned	1 c.	65
Oranges, raw		
Navel, California (winter) 2⅘-in. diameter	1 orange	60
Other varieties, 3-in. diameter	1 orange	70
Orange juice, fresh		
California, Valencia, summer	1 c.	120
Florida varieties	1 c.	110

SALAD CALORIE CHART (Continued)

FOOD	AMOUNT	CALORIES
Orange juice, canned, unsweetened	1 c.	120
Orange juice concentrate, frozen		
Undiluted 6-oz. can	1 can.	330
Water added	1 c.	110
Orange and grapefruit juice, frozen concentrate		
Undiluted 6-oz. can	1 can	330
Water added	1 c.	110
Papayas, raw, ½-in. cubes	1 c.	70
Peaches		
Raw, whole, about 4 per lb.	1 peach	35
Raw, sliced	1 c.	65
Canned, yellow fleshed, solids and liquids	1 c.	65
Canned, syrup pack, heavy, halves or slices	1 c.	200
Dried, uncooked	1 c.	420
Dried, cooked, unsweetened, 10-12 halves and 6 tbsp. liquid	1 c.	220
Frozen, 12-oz. carton	1 carton	265
Peach nectar, canned	1 c.	115
Pears		
Raw, 3 x 2½-in. diameter	1 pear	100
Canned, solids and liquids, heavy syrup	1 c.	195
Pear nectar, canned	1 c.	130
Pineapple		
Raw, diced	1 c.	75
Canned, syrup pack, solids and liquid		
Crushed	1 c.	205
Sliced, slices and juice	2 sm. or 1 lge. and 2 tbsp. juice	95
Pineapple juice, canned	1 c.	120
Raisins, dried	1 c.	460
Raspberries, red:		
Raw	1 c.	70
Frozen, 10-oz. carton	1 carton	280
Strawberries:		
Raw, capped	1 c.	55
Frozen, 10-oz. carton	1 carton	300
Frozen, 16-oz. can	1 can	485
Watermelon, raw, wedge 4 x 8-in.	1 wedge	120

SALAD CALORIE CHART (Continued)

FOOD	AMOUNT	CALORIES
GRAIN PRODUCTS		
Macaroni, cooked until tender	1 c.	155
Noodles, egg, cooked	1 c.	200
Rice, cooked:		
Parboiled	1 c.	205
White	1 c.	200
Spaghetti, cooked until tender	1 c.	155
FATS AND OILS		
Oils, salad or cooking:		
Corn	1 tbsp.	125
Cottonseed	1 tbsp.	125
Olive	1 tbsp.	125
Soybean	1 tbsp.	125
Salad dressings		
Bleu cheese	1 tbsp.	90
Commercial, plain, mayonnaise type	1 tbsp.	60
French	1 tbsp.	60
Home cooked, boiled	1 tbsp.	30
Mayonnaise	1 tbsp.	110
Thousand Island	1 tbsp.	75
MISCELLANEOUS ITEMS		
Beverages, carbonated:		
Ginger ale	1 c.	80
Cola type	1 c.	105
Gelatin, dry:		
Plain	1 tbsp.	35
Dessert powder, 3-oz. pkg.	½ c.	325
Gelatin dessert salad, ready to eat:		
Plain	1 c.	155
With fruit	1 c.	170
Olives, pickled:		
Green	7 jumbo	65
Ripe	7 jumbo	85
Pickles, cucumber:		
Dill, large, 4 x 1¾-in.	1 pickle	15
Sweet, 2¾ x ¾-in.	1 pickle	20
Sherbet, factory packed	1 c.	235
Vinegar	1 tbsp.	2

JIFFY SALAD GUIDE

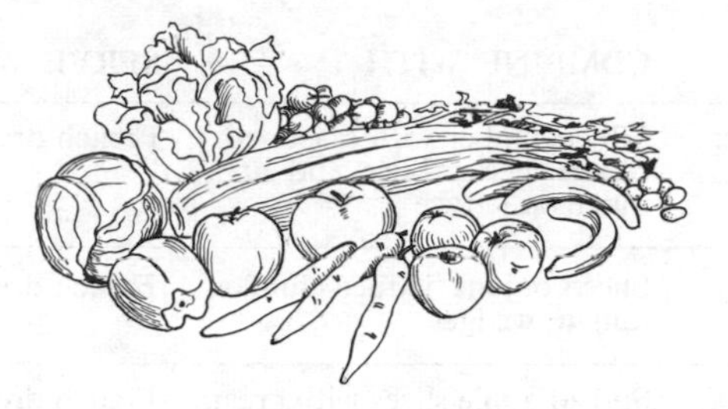

VEGETABLES

START WITH	COMBINE WITH	SERVE WITH
Shredded cabbage	Chopped onion, thinly sliced carrots	Olive French dressing
Shredded cabbage	Chopped green pepper, chopped pimento	Garlic French dressing, dash of Tabasco
Shredded cabbage	Drained pineapple chunks	Fluffy cream dressing with extra salt to taste
Shredded cabbage	Salted peanuts	French dressing
Shredded cabbage	Chopped celery, chopped parsley	Thousand Island French dressing
Shredded cabbage	Unpared, diced red apples, broken nut meats	Cooked mayonnaise with extra salt to taste
Shredded cabbage	Minced green pepper, minced onion	Celery seed French dressing
Tomatoes, cut in eighths	Chopped onion, capers	Celery seed French dressing
Tomatoes, sliced	Sliced cucumber	Garlic French dressing
Tomatoes, cut in very thin vertical slices	Minced parsley, minced green onions, freshly ground black pepper	Onion French dressing
Tomatoes, sliced	Avocado, pared and cut into strips	French dressing
Tomatoes, sliced	Cottage cheese	Chive French dressing
Tomatoes, centers removed	Diced cooked chicken	Creamy French dressing
Cucumber, sliced	Green onions, sliced or sweet onions, sliced	French dressing
Cucumber, sliced	Sliced tomatoes	Garlic French dressing
Cucumber, sliced	Sliced radishes, green pepper strips	Onion French dressing
Cucumber, chopped	Chopped onion, hearts of lettuce	Creamy French dressing

FRUIT

START WITH	COMBINE WITH	SERVE WITH
Cucumber, with center removed	Fill cucumber with seasoned cream cheese. Slice and arrange on lettuce	French dressing
Cucumber, sliced	Sliced onions, lettuce chunks, tomato wedges	French dressing
Red apples, sliced	Spread apple slices with cream cheese	French dressing
Red apples, sliced	Grapefruit sections	Fruit dressing
Apple wedges, cooked in cinnamon candy syrup	Avocado, pared and sliced	French dressing
Apples, diced	Halved raw cranberries, diced celery	Creamy French dressing
Apples, diced	Diced celery, orange sections	Mayonnaise
Apples, diced	Chopped celery, nuts, seeded Tokay grapes	French dressing
Crushed pineapple	Chopped cucumber, lettuce	Mayonnaise
Pineapple chunks (fresh or canned)	Melon balls	Mint French dressing
Pineapple chunks (fresh or canned)	Sliced bananas, diced celery	Cooked dressing
Sliced pineapple (fresh or canned)	Prunes, stuffed with cream cheese	French dressing
Sliced pineapple (fresh or canned)	Grapefruit sections, orange sections	Fruit dressing
Sliced pineapple (fresh or canned)	Cream cheese, chopped nuts	French dressing
Sliced pineapple (fresh or canned)	Peach halves, cottage cheese	Creamy French dressing
Bananas, sliced	Red apples, sliced	Fruit dressing
Bananas, sliced	Shredded cabbage	Mayonnaise with prepared mustard added
Bananas, sliced	Orange and grapefruit sections	Honey French dressing
Bananas, sliced	Pineapple slices, red berries	French dressing
Bananas, sliced lengthwise	Spread with peanut butter; press slices together. Slice crosswise. Sprinkle with chopped salted peanuts.	Creamy French dressing

RECIPE FOR PICKLE-CHEESE PINEAPPLE ON PAGE 38

CHEESE BALL

½ lb. Velveeta cheese
3 sm. pkg. cream cheese
1 square Bleu cheese
1 med. onion, minced
1 c. chopped parsley
1 c. chopped pecans

Run Velveeta cheese through grinder or mash with fork. Mix cheeses, onion, 1/2 cup parsley and 1/2 cup nuts; chill. Shape into balls; roll in remaining nuts and parsley. Bring to room temperature 1 hour before serving.

Mrs. Bettie Plack
Peoria, Ill.

CHEESE BALL

2 glasses Old English cheese
1 glass Bleu cheese
1 8-oz. pkg. cream cheese
1 clove of garlic, mashed
1 sm. onion, chopped
2 dashes Worcestershire sauce
Chopped walnuts
Chopped parsley

Blend cheeses and seasonings; chill. Form two balls; roll in walnuts and parsley. Serve with assorted crackers or potato chips.

Ola Baker
Ridge Farm, Ill.

CHEESE BALL PICK-ME-UPS

1 8-oz. pkg. cream cheese
1 4-oz. pkg. Bleu cheese
1 5-oz. jar Old English cheese
1 6-oz. roll smoked cheese
1 tsp. monosodium glutamate
Dash of salt
¼ tsp. garlic powder or 1 clove of garlic, crushed
1 tbsp. Worcestershire sauce
⅛ tsp. Tabasco sauce
1 c. finely snipped parsley
1 c. finely chopped pecans
Pretzel sticks

Soften cheeses to room temperature. Blend well with monosodium glutamate, salt, garlic and sauces. Add 1/3 cup parsley and 1/2 cup pecans; blend. Chill cheese mixture until easy to handle. Form into 1-inch balls and roll in reserved parsley-nut mixture. Refrigerate. May be stored for several days. Insert a pretzel stick in each cheese ball just before serving. Yield: 90 balls.

Mrs. Lura Lee Davis
Sweetwater, Tex.

CHEESE LOGS

1 lge. pkg. cream cheese
½ lb. pimento cheese, grated
½ lb. sharp cheese, grated
½ lb. Cheddar cheese, grated
2 c. pecans, chopped
1 onion
2 cloves of garlic
2 pimentos, chopped
Red pepper to taste
Salt to taste
Paprika

Soften cream cheese; add remaining cheeses and pecans. Grind onion, garlic and pimentos together; blend with cheese mixture, pepper and salt. Form three logs; roll in paprika. Wrap with waxed paper; store in freezer. Thinly slice; serve on crackers.

Mrs. Abe Daigle
Lafayette, La.

CHEESE-OLIVE COCKTAIL SNACK

1 c. grated medium Cheddar cheese
¼ c. butter
½ c. flour
¼ tsp. red pepper, ground
Salt to taste
25 med. stuffed green olives

Combine all ingredients except olives; blend until smooth and creamy. Mold mixture around each olive. Bake at 400 degrees for 10 to 12 minutes. Yield: 25 servings.

Kate Cullum
Batesburg, S.C.

COCONUT-CRANBERRY-CHEESE BALLS

1 8-oz. pkg. cream cheese, softened
3 tbsp. whole cranberry sauce, well drained
½ tsp. grated orange rind
⅛ tsp. salt
Flaked coconut

Combine all ingredients except coconut; chill slightly. Shape into bite-sized balls; roll in flaked coconut. Yield: 40 servings.

Mrs. Elaine N. Blake
Whiteville, N.C.

CREAM CHEESE BALL

1 16-oz. pkg. cream cheese
1 c. cottage cheese
2 ½-oz. Roquefort cheese
¼ lb. sharp Cheddar cheese, grated
2 tbsp. Worcestershire sauce
1 sm. onion, grated
¼ tsp. grated garlic
1 tbsp. monosodium glutamate
1 or 2 dashes Tabasco sauce
½ tsp. seasoned salt
1 c. finely chopped parsley
1 c. finely chopped pecans

Mix all cheeses and seasonings with one-half the parsley and pecans. Mold in round greased mold. Mix remaining parsley and pecans; pat on outside of ball. Chill for 24 hours. Serve with crackers or corn chips.

Mrs. P. H. Loh
Morrilton, Ark.

EXOTIC HORS D' OEUVRES

¼ c. grated sharp Cheddar cheese
¼ c. chopped ripe olives or pickle relish
1 med. onion, grated
½ tsp. curry powder
Mayonnaise
English muffins

Combine all ingredients except muffins with enough mayonnaise to moisten; spread on muffins. Broil until slightly browned and bubbly. Cut into serving pieces.

Helen V. Childs
Covington, Va.

FROZEN LOG

½ lb. yellow sharp cheese
8 slices bacon
½ tsp. Worcestershire sauce
2 sm. onions
1 tsp. dry mustard
2 tsp. mayonnaise

Put all ingredients through food chopper; blend well. Roll into a log the size of a 50-cent piece; freeze. Slice and place on bread rounds, crackers or split English muffins. Broil until browned; serve.

Mrs. Mary Evans
San Antonio, Tex.

GARLIC-CHEESE ROLL

½ lb. Cheddar cheese, grated
1 3-oz. pkg. cream cheese, softened
1 sm. clove of garlic, finely chopped
1 tsp. salt
¼ c. chopped pecans
Paprika
Round salted crackers

Combine cheeses, garlic and salt; blend in pecans. Form into roll the diameter of round crackers. Roll on waxed paper sprinkled with paprika; wrap. Chill overnight. Slice; serve on crackers. Yield: 10-12 servings.

Mrs. Cary King, Sr.
Tullos, La.

GOURMET CHEESE SPREAD

1 lb. Edam cheese
1 slice onion, ground
1 tbsp. Worcestershire sauce
½ tsp. mustard
½ tsp. horseradish
Salt and pepper to taste
Garlic salt to taste
Cream

Slice top of cheese round about 2 inches from top. Hollow out center, forming a bowl. Combine mashed cheese with all remaining ingredients. Add enough cream to obtain spreading consistency. Place mixture in shell. Serve with assorted crackers.

Mrs. LeJeune McCracken
Arlington Hall Sta., Va.

LIPTAUER CHEESE

1 8-oz. pkg. cream cheese
2 oz. Roquefort cheese
¼ c. butter
2 tbsp. chopped parsley
2 tbsp. anchovies, cut into ¼-in. strips
1 tsp. capers
1 tsp. finely minced onion
½ tsp. caraway seed
3 tbsp. sour cream
1 tsp. lemon juice

Blend cheeses and butter; add all remaining ingredients. Place in buttered mold or shape cheese into roll in waxed paper. Refrigerate for a day or two before serving. NOTE: Whole cheese mold may be covered with chopped parsley.

Mrs. William Southworth
Sunbury, O.

OLIVE TARTS

2 c. finely grated sharp natural American cheese
½ c. soft butter
1 c. sifted flour
¼ tsp. Tabasco sauce
½ tsp. salt
1 tsp. paprika
36 small stuffed olives

Blend cheese with butter; stir in flour, Tabasco sauce, salt and paprika. Wrap 1 teaspoon mixture around each olive, covering completely. Arrange on baking sheet or flat pan; freeze firm. Pack in freezing bags or cartons. Spread out on baking sheet when ready to use. Bake at 400 degrees for 15 minutes. Serve hot.

Photograph for this recipe above.

LULU PASTE

2 eggs, slightly beaten
3 tbsp. vinegar
3 tbsp. sugar
¼ tsp. salt
¼ tsp. pepper
2 pkg. cream cheese
1 tbsp. chopped onion
2 tbsp. chopped pepper

Combine eggs, vinegar, sugar, salt and pepper. Cook over low heat until thickened, stirring constantly; cool. Add cream cheese, onion and pepper. Serve on crackers or bread.

Ruth McLaughlin
New London, O.

PICKLE-CHEESE PINEAPPLE

2 8-oz. pkg. cream cheese, softened
½ c. grated process Swiss cheese
½ c. grated process Cheddar cheese
½ c. peanut butter
½ c. sweet pickle relish
Sweet gherkins

Combine cheeses, peanut butter and pickle relish; blend. Chill thoroughly. Shape into ball. Garnish with sweet gherkin slices and strips to resemble a pineapple. Serve as a spread for rye bread, as desired.

Photograph for this recipe on page 35 .

ROQUEFORT ROLLS

2 3-oz. pkg. cream cheese
⅛ lb. Roquefort cheese
2 tbsp. finely chopped celery
1 tbsp. finely chopped onion
Dash of cayenne pepper
Salad dressing
1 ½ c. finely chopped walnuts

Blend cheeses; add celery, onion, cayenne and salad dressing. Form into tiny rolls or balls. Roll in nuts; chill. Yield: 16-20 rolls.

Mrs. Jo Frances Weimar
Alto, Tex.

SPICY CHEESE ROLL

½ lb. mild American Cheddar cheese, grated
1 4-oz. pkg. cream cheese
1 sm. triangle Roquefort cheese
½ c. finely chopped pecans
1 tsp. Worcestershire sauce
Dash of ground red pepper
Garlic salt or ground cloves to taste
Salt and black pepper to taste
Paprika or curry

Blend all ingredients except paprika; roll into slender long rolls. Coat with paprika or curry; refrigerate. Thinly slice and serve.

Mrs. Richard J. Dunham
Indianapolis, Ind.

THREE-WAY CHEESE TREAT

BASIC CHEESE BASE:
1 ½ lb. cream cheese
1 ½ lb. Cheddar cheese, grated
¼ c. milk

Blend cheeses with milk. Divide mixture into three portions to be used as base for caraway, anchovy and coffee loaves.

CARAWAY LOAF:
4 tbsp. caraway seed
1 tbsp. horseradish
1 tbsp. Worcestershire sauce

Thoroughly blend all ingredients with one portion of the basic cheese base. Shape into a long loaf; chill for 4 hours or until firm. Slice. May be served on crackers.

ANCHOVY LOAF:
2 oz. anchovy paste

Thoroughly blend anchovy paste with another portion of the basic cheese base. Shape into long loaf; chill for 4 hours. Slice. May be served on crackers.

COFFEE LOAF:
1 tbsp. instant coffee
2 tbsp. sugar

Thoroughly blend coffee and sugar with remaining portion of basic cheese base. Shape into long loaf; chill until firm. Slice. May be served on crackers.

Ann Williams
Angier, N.C.

CLAM-CHEESE LOG

1 8-oz. pkg. cream cheese
1 tbsp. lemon juice
1 tsp. mustard
1 tsp. Worcestershire sauce
2 tbsp. chopped parsley
2 tbsp. finely chopped onion
1 4-oz. can pimento
2 7 ½-oz. cans minced clams
⅓ c. finely crushed saltines
½ c. finely chopped pecans

Soften cream cheese to room temperature; blend in lemon juice, mustard, Worcestershire sauce, parsley and onion. Drain and chop pimento. Drain clams; mix with pimento and saltine crumbs. Blend into cheese mixture; shape into 8-inch roll. Coat with chopped nuts; chill thoroughly.

Mrs. Jerald A. Peters
Sault Sainte Marie, Mich.

AVOCADO APPETIZER

¼ sm. watermelon
1 pt. lime sherbet
1 lge. avocado, peeled and sliced
1 12-oz. bottle 7-Up

Make melon balls of watermelon. Alternate small scoops of lime sherbet, melon balls and avocado slices in chilled parfait glasses or sherbet glasses. Pour 7-Up over mixture immediately before serving.

Mrs. Lyn Hartbauer
Eaton, Colo.

AVOCADO COCKTAIL

2 lemons
3 avocados, peeled and diced
1 c. catsup
2 tsp. Worcestershire sauce
1 c. half and half

Squeeze lemons over avocados; refrigerate for 1 hour. Drain lemon juice; place avocados in cocktail glasses. Combine all remaining ingredients; cover avocados with mixture. Chill until ready to serve. Yield: 8 servings.

Mrs. Raphael J. Polk
Nevada City, Calif.

AVOCADO COCKTAIL

2 avocados, diced
2 hard-cooked eggs, diced
3 green onions, minced

Combine avocados, eggs and onions; chill.

SAUCE:
¼ c. mayonnaise
2 tbsp. catsup
Juice of 1 lemon
1 tbsp. Worcestershire sauce
Salt and pepper to taste
Juice of 1 orange

Thoroughly blend all ingredients; fold into chilled avocado mixture just before serving. Garnish with parsley or sliced olives. Yield: 4 servings.

Mrs. Lawrence D. Townsend
Encinitas, Calif.

BANANA CANAPES

2 ripe bananas
½ c. lemon juice
¼ c. finely chopped nuts

Cut bananas into small pieces 1/2 to 3/4-inches long; dip into lemon juice. Roll in nuts to coat well. Insert cocktail picks and place in airtight container to freeze. Yield: 4-6 servings.

Mrs. Jeanne C. Shirley
Wynnewood, Okla.

BANANA-COCONUT ROLLS

½ pt. sour cream
1 tsp. lemon juice
1 tbsp. honey
4 ripe bananas, peeled and cut into 1-in. cubes
Flaked or toasted coconut

Mix sour cream with lemon juice and honey. Coat banana cubes with sour cream mixture; roll bananas in coconut. Serve on toothpicks or bamboo skewers.

Sara Skandera
The Dalles, Oreg.

BLACK-EYED SUSANS

1 lb. sharp cheese
½ lb. margarine
1 tsp. salt
3 c. flour
½ tsp. red pepper
1 ½ lb. pitted dates
Pecan halves
Sugar

Cream cheese with margarine; add salt, flour and pepper. Work dough well; press against outside of bowl. Cut into strips; stuff each date with pecan half. Wrap dough around dates with each end of date showing; roll in sugar. Bake at 300 degrees until slightly browned. Store in covered container. Yield: 100 servings.

Mrs. J. W. Ferguson
Pelham, N.C.

CINNAMON DROP- FRUIT CUP

1 No. 2 can fruit cocktail
3 tbsp. hot cinnamon candies
1 10-oz. pkg. frozen strawberries, thawed

Drain fruit cocktail; reserve juice. Heat and dissolve candies in drained juice. Pour over fruit cocktail and chill. Just before serving, add thawed strawberries. NOTE: May be garnished with coconut, nuts or a cherry. Yield: 8 servings.

Mrs. Dwayne Herman
Brinsmade, N.D.

CLUB APPETIZER

2 qt. crushed pineapple
1 lb. sugar
3 in. stick cinnamon
1 qt. finely chopped apples
Green or red food coloring

(Continued on next page)

Drain syrup from pineapple; reserve syrup. Add sugar and cinnamon to syrup. Cook for 10 minutes; remove cinnamon and cool. Add apples, pineapple and coloring; stir well. Serve chilled in frosted glasses. Yield: 12-18 servings.

Mrs. Ruth S. Riale
Bloomsburg, Pa.

CRANBERRY ICE

1 qt. cranberries
1 qt. water
3 c. sugar
Juice of 1 lemon
2 egg whites, stiffly beaten

Cook cranberries in water until berries all pop. Strain just until skins remain; add sugar and lemon juice. Cool. Fold egg whites into cranberry mixture; pour into tray. Freeze until mushy. Beat thoroughly and return to freezer; freeze until stiff. Serve as an appetizer with turkey dinner. Yield: 24 servings.

Mrs. J. Russell Anderson
Fremont, Nebr.

CRANBERRY PINK FLUFF

1 pkg. lemon flavored gelatin
1 c. hot water
1 c. cranberry juice cocktail
2 egg whites

Dissolve gelatin in hot water; stir in cranberry juice. Chill until slightly thickened. Beat egg whites until stiff but not dry. Gradually pour cranberry mixture over egg whites, beating until foamy. Pour into individual sherbet glasses. Mixture will separate into red and pink layers. Chill for 4 hours. Yield: 4 servings.

Mrs. James Potter
Tomah, Wisc.

FROZEN FRUIT CUP

1 c. fruit cocktail or cut up fruit
½ c. seedless grapes
½ c. watermelon balls
1 bottle ginger ale, chilled
Mint leaves

Mix fruits; place in ice cube tray. Pour ginger ale over fruit; freeze for 1 hour and 30 minutes to 2 hours or until mixture is mushy. Serve in small sherbet glasses garnished with mint leaves. Yield: 8 servings.

Abbie E. Nordstrom
Edmonds, Wash.

FRUIT COCKTAIL

1 can frozen pineapple chunks, thawed
1 can Mandarin orange sections
1 pkg. frozen mixed fruit
2 tbsp. orange curacao cordial

Mix fruits; keep chilled until ready to serve. Add curacao just before serving. Yield: 6 servings.

Mrs. Ada B. Dobson
Macomb, Ill.

FRUIT KABOBS

½ grapefruit
Fresh or frozen melon balls
Whole strawberries
Pineapple chunks
Bananas

Place grapefruit half, cut-side down, on plate or tray. Place fruit on skewers and stick into grapefruit. NOTE: Makes attractive centerpieces for breakfast or brunch.

Mrs. Ralph Shipman
Paris, Tex.

BROILED GRAPEFRUIT

1 grapefruit
2 tbsp. brown sugar
2 Maraschino cherries

Halve grapefruit. Cut around each section and remove center. Sprinkle 1 tablespoon brown sugar on each half; place a cherry in each center. Broil about 3 inches from heat until all sugar melts and edge of grapefruit turns a delicate brown. Serve immediately.

Mrs. Genevieve Snyder
Denver, Pa.

GRAPEFRUIT CONVERSATION PIECE

1 lge. firm grapefruit
Cocktail sausages

Cut a hole in one end of grapefruit just large enough to hold a sterno lamp. Place on a small platter and surround with real or artificial leaves. Thrust wooden picks through cocktail sausages and stick into grapefruit. Let guests broil their own sausages over lamp.

Mrs. Carol Hawkins
Turlock, Calif.

GRAPES IN MINTED GINGER ALE

Green grapes
1 ½ c. ginger ale
4 or 5 mint leaves or sprigs

Place 10 to 15 green grapes in sherbet glass; pour 1/4 to 1/2 cup ginger ale over grapes. Add a sprig of mint. Yield: 4-5 servings.

Nancy Hickcox
Burlington, Vt.

SEEDLESS GRAPES IN SOUR CREAM

Seedless grapes
Sour cream
Brown sugar

Stem grapes; wash and dry well. Coat grapes with sour cream; place in refrigerator until serving time. Roll in brown sugar; serve with lettuce or as an appetizer.

Loraine Burtch
Champaign, Ill.

FROZEN PEACHES

9 c. sugar
3 cans frozen orange juice
1 crate fresh peaches, washed and blanched

Combine sugar and orange juice; stir. Slice peaches into sugar and orange mixture; mix lightly until all peaches are covered. Freeze.

Mrs. Lawrence E. Urbanski
Wrenshall, Minn.

PINEAPPLE SLUSH

1 No. 2 can crushed pineapple
1 6-oz. can frozen orange juice
1 6-oz. can frozen lemon juice
4 or 5 bananas, mashed
1 c. sugar
1 12-oz. can ginger ale

Blend all ingredients; freeze. Stir several times during freezing. NOTE: May be topped with Maraschino cherry. Yield: 12 servings.

Mrs. Donald F. Christensen
Lyons, Nebr.

PLEASINGLY PLUMP PRUNES

1 1-lb. pkg. dried prunes
1 c. raisins
1 lemon, sliced
6 whole cloves
1 stick cinnamon
3 7-oz. bottles lemon-lime carbonated beverage

Combine all ingredients in bowl; cover and refrigerate for two days. Serve with whipped cream, if desired.

Mrs. Violet Shaffner
Marshall, Ill.

BACON APPETIZER

1 jar peanut butter
1 bottle catsup
1 pkg. soda crackers
1 pkg. bacon

Blend peanut butter and catsup to spreading consistency. Spread one side of each cracker with mixture. Place crackers on cookie sheet; top with a piece of bacon. Broil under low heat until bacon is crisp and brown. Serve hot.

Clara S. Stillwell
Northport, N.Y.

BACON BITS

20 slices bread
2 tbsp. melted butter
1 c. grated sharp cheese
2 egg whites
⅔ c. chopped green peppers
1 tsp. chopped parsley
½ tsp. salt
Dash of pepper
3 slices bacon, finely chopped

(Continued on next page)

With 2-inch cookie cutter, cut twenty bread rounds. Toast one side under broiler. Brush untoasted side with melted butter. Fold cheese into stiffly beaten egg whites; add green peppers, parsley, salt and pepper. Spoon mixture onto buttered side of bread rounds. Sprinkle tops with bacon. Broil 4 or 5 inches from heat for 10 minutes or until bacon browns and cheese melts. Yield: 20 servings.

June L. Schwar
Millersville, Pa.

BACON 'N' ONION APPETIZER

½ lb. bacon
⅓ c. brown sugar
1 sm. jar cocktail onions

Cut bacon slices into thirds; dip one side in brown sugar. Wrap bacon pieces with sugar side in, around cocktail onions. Secure with toothpick. Broil for 2 minutes on each side. May be served hot. Yield: 10 servings.

Mrs. Jeanne Clark
Flint, Mich.

BACON WRAPPED OLIVES

1 pkg. thinly sliced bacon
1 jar lge. stuffed olives

Cut each slice of bacon in half; wrap each olive with one-half slice of bacon. Secure with toothpicks. Broil until bacon is crisp, turning once during the broiling period.

Mrs. Shirley A. Randall
Port Edwards, Wisc.

BEEF STUFFED MUSHROOMS

1 ½ lb. medium mushrooms
1 lb. lean ground beef
¼ c. mayonnaise
1 tbsp. mustard
½ tsp. sugar
1 tbsp. minced onion
1 tbsp. chopped parsley
2 tsp. salt

Remove stems from mushrooms; wash caps in salted water. Broil mushroom caps, rounded-side down, for 3 minutes. Combine all remaining ingredients; shape into balls which fit mushroom caps. Place in caps. Broil about 2 inches from heat for 5 to 8 minutes. Serve hot. Yield: 25 servings.

Phyllis J. Hill
Phoenix, Ariz.

BURGER BALLS

1 lb. hamburger
1 can vegetable soup, condensed
½ onion, finely chopped
1 c. soft bread crumbs
1 egg, slightly beaten
Salt and pepper to taste

Blend all ingredients well. Shape into 1-inch balls. Place meat balls on broiler rack. Bake at 450 degrees for 10 minutes. Spear on toothpicks; serve as hot appetizer.

Alicia Hampton
Naples, Tex.

CRISPY HAM BITS

½ c. cooked ham, ground
¼ c. grated cheddar cheese
¼ c. tomato soup
1 tbsp. minced onion
¼ tsp. horseradish
¼ tsp. mustard

Combine all ingredients. Spread on crackers. Broil 3 inches from heat for 3 to 5 minutes or until slightly browned. Serve hot.

Marcelle T. Montminy
Manchester, N.H.

HAMMED-UP DIAMONDS

2 sticks instant pie crust mix
1 4 ½-oz. can deviled ham

Prepare pie crust mix according to package directions. Roll out into 14 x 12-inch oblong; place on ungreased baking sheet. Spread one-half of the pastry with deviled ham; fold plain pastry over filled half. Cut into diamond shapes. Bake at 450 degrees for 10 to 12 minutes or until browned. Serve warm. Yield: 3-4 dozen.

Mrs. Donald H. Charlton
Two Rock Ranch Sta., Calif.

HAM-FILLED CREAM CHEESE PASTRY

½ lb. margarine, softened
2 3-oz. pkg. cream cheese, softened
2 c. sifted flour
½ tsp. salt
Ham spread

Mix margarine and cream cheese; add flour and salt. Refrigerate for at least 1 hour; roll out. Cut with round tumbler; fill with 1 teaspoon ham spread. Fold over; pinch edges. Bake at 375 degrees for 15 minutes.

Viola Jaaksi
Detroit, Mich.

HAPPY HAMWICHES

1 pkg. refrigerated biscuits
1 4½-oz. can deviled ham
1 tbsp. chili sauce
2 tbsp. minced onion
4 slices cheese

Flatten biscuits into 3 1/2-inch rounds. Blend deviled ham, chili sauce and onion; spread one-half the biscuits with mixture. Top with cheese and remaining biscuit rounds. Bake at 470 degrees for 8 to 10 minutes. Yield: 5 servings.

Mrs. Sarah Van Tuinen
Selma, Ala.

LAMB ROLLS

1 3-oz. pkg. cream cheese, softened
½ tsp. salt
⅛ tsp. black pepper
1 tbsp. lemon juice
2 tbsp. minced green onion
1 c. cooked diced lamb
2 c. prepared biscuit mix
⅔ c. milk
1 c. sour cream (opt.)

Blend cheese with seasonings, lemon juice, onion and lamb. Prepare biscuit mix with milk as directed on package. Pat out into four rounds 1/8-inch thick. Divide meat filling onto rounds; pull dough over filling. Crimp edges to hold filling in place. Bake on greased baking sheet at 425 degrees for 20 minutes. Brush with melted butter to keep crust soft. Top with sour cream.

Bessie L. Mills
Los Angeles, Calif.

LITTLE PIZZAS

1 pkg. refrigerator biscuits
½ can tomato paste
Oregano
1 pkg. sausage links
1 c. shredded Cheddar cheese

Roll each biscuit to 4-inch diameter. Place on baking sheet; spread with tomato paste. Sprinkle with oregano. Add about six penny-sized pieces of sausage to each biscuit; sprinkle with cheese. Bake at 450 degrees for 5 minutes. Serve hot. Yield: 10 servings.

Mrs. Diane M. Brown
Grayville, Ill.

APPETIZER MEAT BALLS

¾ lb. ground beef
¼ lb. ground pork
¾ c. rolled oats
¼ c. finely chopped water chestnuts
¼ tsp. Worcestershire sauce
½ c. milk
½ tsp. onion salt
½ tsp. garlic salt
Few drops Tabasco sauce
Margarine

Blend all ingredients; form into about 75 small balls. Brown well in margarine; drain on paper towels.

SWEET SOUR SAUCE:
1 c. sugar
¾ c. vinegar
¾ c. water
1 tsp. paprika
½ tsp. salt
3 tsp. cornstarch
1 tbsp. water

Combine sugar, vinegar, water, paprika and salt; cook for 5 minutes. Add cornstarch mixed with water; cook until thickened, stirring constantly. Simmer for 30 minutes. Serve warm. Yield: 15 servings.

Mrs. George Green
Lincoln, Nebr.

ROLLMOPS OF PORK

1 pkg. pork roll slices
1 3-oz. pkg. cream cheese, softened
1 lge. dill pickle

Spread each slice of pork roll with cream cheese. Slice pickle into eight slices lengthwise. Place a pickle slice in the center of each pork slice; roll tightly. Fasten with toothpicks; refrigerate. To serve, slice across roll. May be frozen. NOTE: Beef roll may be substituted for pork. Yield: 4 servings.

Marianne Weston
Huntington Sta., N.Y.

SAUERKRAUT BALLS

½ lb. ham
½ lb. pork
½ lb. corned beef
1 med. onion, chopped
Pinch of parsley
2 c. flour
1 tsp. dry mustard
1 tsp. salt
2 c. milk
2 lb. sauerkraut
Flour
1 egg, beaten
Bread crumbs

Grind meats together twice; combine with onion and parsley. Fry until brown. Sift dry ingredients; add to meat mixture alternately with milk. Cook together until fluffy; cool. Fold in sauerkraut; put entire mixture through food chopper twice. Mix thoroughly; roll into small balls. Dredge in flour; dip into beaten egg. Roll in bread crumbs; fry in deep fat until browned. NOTE: These may be frozen after frying and reheated in oven at 325 degrees for 20 minutes. Yield: 12-15 servings.

Mrs. Marie J. Hanrahan
Delphi, Ind.

SAUSAGE CRESCENTS

1 can refrigerated crescent dinner rolls
16 brown 'n' serve sausages

Halve crescent triangles. Place a brown and serve sausage on each small triangle; roll up. Place on ungreased baking sheet. Bake at 375 degrees for 10 to 13 minutes or until golden brown. Yield: 16 servings.

Mrs. Harriet Gerou
Beaverton, Mich.

STEAK TARTAR

1 lb. ground tenderloin or sirloin steak
1 egg
¼ c. capers
¼ c. minced onion
1 tsp. salt
Pepper to taste
Few drops Worcestershire sauce

Combine all ingredients. Shape into a ball; garnish with parsley and additional capers. Serve with crackers or party breads. Yield: 12 servings.

Mrs. B. Goldberg
Harrisburg, Pa.

TARTELETTES AU FROMAGE

3 eggs
2 c. light cream
Salt and pepper to taste
Cayenne pepper to taste
1 c. grated Swiss cheese
1 tbsp. melted butter
⅔ c. cooked diced ham
12 partially baked tart shells

Beat eggs with cream. Add salt, pepper and cayenne pepper; strain. Add cheese and butter. Place a spoonful of ham in each tart shell; fill shells with custard mixture. Bake at 350 degrees for 15 minutes or until custard is set. Serve warm. Yield: 12 servings.

Mary Lou Thomas
Wauseon, O.

TERIYAKI APPETIZERS

½ c. soy sauce
2 tbsp. brown sugar
1 clove of garlic
1 tsp. cracked ginger root
1 ½ lb. round steak

Combine soy sauce, sugar, garlic and ginger root. Cut steak into 1/2-inch cubes; add to soy sauce mixture. Let stand overnight. Remove meat; cook quickly in Hibachi and serve on toothpicks. Yield: 6-8 servings.

Donna Franquemont
Asheboro, N.C.

CHEESE TURKS

¾ c. cooked finely diced turkey
½ lb. sharp cheese, grated
½ lb. butter, softened
1 c. nuts, chopped
2 c. flour
¼ tsp. red pepper
1 tsp. Worcestershire sauce

Combine turkey and cheese with butter; add all remaining ingredients. Shape into 1-inch balls. Bake on ungreased cookie sheet at 250 degrees for 20 minutes. Yield: 4 dozen.

Mrs. W. T. Bradshaw
Canton, Ga.

CHICKEN-NUT PUFFS

1 ½ c. finely chopped cooked or canned chicken
⅓ c. chopped toasted almonds

(Continued on next page)

1 c. canned or fresh chicken broth
½ c. salad oil or chicken fat
2 tsp. seasoned salt
⅛ tsp. cayenne
1 tsp. celery seed
1 tbsp. parsley flakes
2 tsp. Worcestershire sauce
1 c. flour
4 eggs

Combine chicken with almonds. Blend chicken broth, oil or fat, seasoned salt, cayenne, celery seed, parsley flakes and Worcestershire sauce; bring to a boil. Add flour; cook over low heat, beating rapidly, until mixture leaves sides of pan and forms a smooth compact ball. Remove from heat; add an egg at a time. After each addition, beat with a spoon until mixture is shiny. Stir in chicken mixture. Drop 1/2 teaspoonful of mixture at a time onto greased baking sheet. Bake at 450 degrees for 10 to 15 minutes. Serve hot. Yield: 20-25 servings.

Mrs. Mary A. Moore
Stephenville, Tex.

CHICKEN SALAD PUFFS

½ c. water
¼ c. butter
½ c. sifted flour
2 eggs
2 c. cooked diced chicken
1 c. sliced celery
¾ c. olive chunks
⅓ c. mayonnaise
1 tbsp. lemon juice
1 tsp. grated onion
¼ tsp. Worcestershire sauce
⅛ tsp. black pepper
Salt to taste

Combine water and butter; heat to boiling. Add flour; stir over direct heat until mixture forms a ball that follows spoon around the pan. Remove from heat; add an egg at a time. Beat vigorously until well blended after each addition. Drop in four mounds onto ungreased baking sheet. Bake in preheated 400 degree oven for 45 to 50 minutes. Cool on wire rack. Combine chicken, celery and olives. Blend in all remaining ingredients; mix lightly with chicken mixture. Split puffs; fill with chicken mixture. NOTE: Flour mixture may be baked in tiny amounts for canapes.

Mrs. Rubye R. Hill
Thomson, Ill.

JELLIED APPETIZER CUBES

2 envelopes unflavored gelatin
1 c. water
1 13-oz. can consomme
2 tsp. lime juice
1 can chicken consomme
⅛ tsp. curry powder
⅛ tsp. salt

Soften gelatin in water; heat until gelatin dissolves, stirring constantly. Pour equal amounts of gelatin into two 9 x 9 x 2-inch pans. Stir consomme and lime juice in one pan; stir chicken consomme, curry and salt into remaining pan. Chill both mixtures for about 2 hours or until firm; cut into 1/2-inch cubes. Spoon consomme cubes into six small bowls; top each with chicken consomme cubes. Garnish with lime slices. Yield: 6 servings.

Esther M. McNulty
Tomah, Wisc.

POULTRY MEAT BALLS

8 slices very dry bread
2 lge. onions
2 cloves of garlic (opt.)
½ c. butter or margarine
6 c. finely chopped cooked chicken or turkey
4 tbsp. Worcestershire sauce
½ tsp. ground cardamom
2 tsp. salt
1 tsp. pepper
¼ tsp. red pepper
2 tbsp. flaked or finely chopped fresh parsley
3 eggs, well beaten

Place bread, onions and garlic in blender; blend until very fine. Saute bread mixture in butter or margarine until light brown. Remove from heat; blend in all remaining ingredients. Shape into 1-inch meat balls. Fry in deep fat at 375 degrees until golden brown. Yield: 24 balls.

Mrs. Danis Hilliard
Adams City, Colo.

ANCHOVY SPREAD

1 sm. pkg. cream cheese
1 can flat anchovies, cut
½ med. Bermuda onion
½ c. sour cream
Dash of Worcestershire sauce

Blend all ingredients thoroughly with fork. Serve as spread for crackers. Thin with additional sour cream for use as a dip. Yield: 20-25 servings.

Mrs. George B. Carty
Tamassee, S.C.

BROILED CLAMS

12 med. cherrystone or soft shell clams
Salt to taste
Paprika to taste
Cayenne pepper to taste
Finely chopped green pepper
Finely chopped red pimento
12 slices bacon, cut into clam-sized pieces
Lemon sections

Prepare shallow baking pan with crumbled aluminum foil. Firmly arrange clams on foil to steady them while cooking. Season each clam with salt, paprika and cayenne pepper. Add a pinch of green pepper, pimento and bacon pieces. Place pan about 4 inches from broiler; broil until bacon has cooked. Remove bacon; place in warm dish. Broil clams for 5 to 6 minutes longer. Serve in shell. Garnish with bacon and lemon sections. Yield: 4 servings.

Ruth Adams
Claymont, Del.

CLAM PUFFS ON TOAST

1 3-oz. pkg. cream cheese
2 tbsp. heavy cream
1 c. minced clams
¼ tsp. dry mustard
1 tbsp. Worcestershire sauce
¼ tsp. salt
½ tsp. grated onion or onion juice

Combine all ingredients. Heap mixture on toast rounds and broil. Serve hot. Yield: 6 servings.

Mrs. Joseph Kawulok
McClellan AFB, Calif.

CRAB MEAT AND GRAPEFRUIT

1 No. 2 can grapefruit sections, chilled
1 6-oz. can crab meat, chilled
1 c. mayonnaise
1 tbsp. vinegar
1 tsp. lemon juice
2 tbsp. catsup
1 drop Tabasco sauce

Drain grapefruit. Flake crab meat; remove boney tissue. Alternate grapefruit sections and crab meat in chilled cocktail glasses. Mix all remaining ingredients; pour over grapefruit and crab meat just before serving. Yield: 8-10 servings.

Mrs. Marion G. Stewart
Montpelier, Miss.

HOT CRAB MEAT PUFFS

1 c. mayonnaise
1 c. flaked crab meat
2 egg whites, stiffly beaten
Toast rounds
Paprika

Fold mayonnaise and crab meat into egg whites. Season to taste; pile on toast rounds. Sprinkle with paprika. Broil for 3 minutes or until puffy and lightly browned.

Mrs. Erma Manning
Doddsville, Miss.

HOT OYSTER BALLS

1 pt. oysters, drained
1 tsp. grated onion
1 tsp. minced parsley
1 c. soft bread crumbs
¼ tsp. salt
¼ tsp. pepper
Dash of Tabasco sauce or pinch of cayenne
Pinch of mace
2 eggs
2 tbsp. butter
Fine dry bread crumbs

Pour boiling water over oysters; drain well. Finely chop. Add onion, parsley and bread crumbs; season to taste. Blend with 1 beaten egg and butter; chill. Shape into tiny balls; roll in remaining beaten egg and fine crumbs. Fry in deep hot fat at 360 degrees until browned; drain on absorbent paper. Serve hot on toothpicks.

Mrs. Joe Pierson
Natchitoches, La.

BARBECUED OYSTERS

24 oysters, seasoned
Butter or cooking oil
¼ c. lemon juice
1 c. steak sauce
2 tbsp. Worcestershire sauce
2 oz. cooking Sherry
2 tbsp. flour
3 tbsp. cold water

Coat oysters in flour. Grill on lightly buttered grill or in heavy skillet until crisp and browned on both sides. Sprinkle with butter or cooking oil while grilling. Combine lemon juice, steak sauce, Worcestershire sauce and cooking Sherry; heat thoroughly but do not boil. Blend 2 tablespoons flour into cold water; stir into sauce. Cook until thickened, stirring constantly. If sauce is too thin, add more steak sauce; if too thick, or highly seasoned, add more Sherry. Insert toothpick in each oyster.

(Continued on next page)

Place on hot serving dish and dress with sauce. If any sauce remains, it may be strained, reheated and used again.

Mrs. W. I. Davis
Houston, Tex.

PINEAPPLE SHRIMP--LUAU LEIS

1 14-oz. can chunk pineapple
2 tbsp. soy sauce
2 tbsp. lemon juice
1 tbsp. salad oil
1 tsp. dry mustard
24 lge. cleaned cooked shrimp
Finely chopped Macadamia nuts
Flaked coconut

Drain pineapple; reserve juice. Blend 1/4 cup pineapple juice, soy sauce, lemon juice, oil and mustard. Pour over shrimp; cover and let stand for 30 minutes. Soak eight bamboo skewers in water. Alternate 3 shrimp and 4 pineapple chunks on each skewer. Brush on remaining marinade. Place on rack or in shallow pan. Broil 2 to 3 inches from heat, turning and basting, for 3 to 5 minutes or until hot and lightly browned. Sprinkle four skewers with nuts and four with coconut. Yield: 8 servings.

Mrs. Mary Ann Seidler
Colby, Wisc.

CUCUMBER-SHRIMP CANAPES

1 8-oz. pkg. cream cheese
2 tbsp. milk
1 tsp. mayonnaise
1 lge. loaf white bread
2 med. cucumbers, thinly sliced
1 can small shrimp

Blend cream cheese, milk and mayonnaise. Cut rounds of bread; spread with cream cheese mixture. Place cucumber slice on top. Dot with cream cheese. Place 1 shrimp on each dot. Yield: 4 1/2 dozen canapes.

Mrs. Harold L. Townes
Ft. Sheridan, Ill.

DONIE'S SHRIMP

2 tbsp. white wine vinegar
6 tbsp. olive oil
1 tbsp. paprika
4 tbsp. creole mustard
½ tsp. pepper
½ tsp. hot pepper sauce
Salt to taste
1 c. finely diced celery hearts
½ white onion, finely chopped
¼ c. finely chopped green pepper
2 hard-cooked eggs, chopped
Chopped parsley
1 lb. shrimp, cooked and cleaned

Combine vinegar, oil, paprika, mustard, pepper, pepper sauce and salt; blend well. Add celery, onion, green pepper, eggs and parsley. Blend together; add shrimp. Cover and place in refrigerator for at least 12 hours. Stir once after 4 hours and again 1 hour before serving.

Mrs. Charles Byron McDaniel
Dunedin, Fla.

LEMON-DILL FRIED SHRIMP

2 tbsp. salad oil
2 tbsp. butter or margarine
2 lb. raw shrimp, cleaned
½ tsp. salt
Coarsely ground black pepper
1 tsp. dill weed
3 tbsp. fresh lemon juice

Heat oil and butter in large skillet; add shrimp. Sprinkle with salt, pepper and dill weed. Fry until shrimp turn pink. Pour lemon juice over shrimp; cover skillet and steam for 4 to 5 minutes. May be served hot or cold. Yield: 10-12 servings.

Barbara Robinson
Los Angeles, Calif.

PICKLED SHRIMP

1 pt. cooking oil
1 pt. vinegar
½ bottle catsup
Pinch of salt
2 bay leaves
1 lge. onion, sliced
1 clove of garlic
1 ½ tsp. curry powder
1 tsp. Worcestershire sauce
Tabasco sauce to taste
Shrimp

Marinate shrimp for two days in refrigerator before serving. Yield: 40 servings.

Mrs. Elizabeth Sutter
Somerset, Tex.

PICKLED SHRIMP

1 ½ c. salad oil
¾ c. white vinegar
2 ½ tsp. salt
2 ½ tsp. celery seed
1 clove of garlic, mashed
6 sm. canned hot peppers, chopped
2 ½ tbsp. capers and juice
Dash of Tabasco sauce
1 tbsp. Worcestershire sauce
3 lb. cooked shrimp
Onion rings

Combine all ingredients except shrimp and onions. Pour over shrimp and onions. Cover; let stand at room temperature or refrigerate for 24 hours. Stir several times. Yield: 12 servings.

Ann S. Keith
Carbon Hill, Ala.

SHRIMP REMOULADE

2 c. cleaned cooked shrimp
1 c. olive oil
⅓ c. vinegar
1 c. finely chopped celery
2 tbsp. chopped green onion
1 tbsp. chopped parsley
½ c. chopped green pepper
½ tbsp. salt
½ tsp. pepper
Garlic (opt.)
2 tbsp. paprika
½ c. creole-style mustard

Combine all ingredients; let stand for 1 to 2 hours. Serve as hors d'oeuvres or over shredded lettuce as appetizer. Yield: 4-6 servings.

Mrs. Hilaire Ogden
Waveland, Miss.

SHRIMP CANAPES

18 shrimp
1 hard-cooked egg yolk
2 tbsp. butter
12 crisp crackers
¼ c. mayonnaise or French dressing
1 tbsp. finely chopped parsley

Finely chop 6 shrimp; chill remaining whole shrimp. Force egg yolk through a sieve; set aside. Spread butter mixture on crackers. Dip reserved shrimp into mayonnaise or French dressing; place on crackers. Sprinkle egg yolk and parsley over each cracker. Yield: 12 servings.

Nancy R. McGath
Fremont, Nebr.

HOT TUNA TEASERS

1 can tuna
1 tbsp. catsup
¼ tsp. Worcestershire sauce
¼ tsp. salt
Dash of cayenne
¼ c. mayonnaise

2 tbsp. dry wine
Canapo cutoutc

Combine all ingredients except cutouts. Spread on canape cutouts. Brown under broiler. May be sprinkled with paprika.

Cathryn Kosegi
Stockbridge, Mich.

SHRIMP COCKTAIL LOAF

1 pkg. lemon gelatin
½ c. hot water
1 can tomato soup
1 lge. or 3 sm. pkg. cream cheese
½ tsp. salad dressing
½ c. finely chopped onion
1 c. finely chopped celery
2 lb. cooked chopped shrimp
Salt
Monosodium glutamate

Soften gelatin in hot water. Bring tomato soup to boiling point; add cream cheese, gelatin and salad dressing. Beat until well blended; cool. Add onion, celery, shrimp, salt and monosodium glutamate. Pour into mold; chill until firm.

Mrs. Alta S. Moore
Morganton, N.C.

SEAFOOD COCKTAIL

1 pkg. frozen shrimp, cleaned, cooked and chopped
1 can crab meat, flaked
2 pkg. frozen lobster, cleaned, cooked and chopped

SAUCE:
1 tbsp. mustard
1 tsp. dry mustard
1 tsp. Worcestershire sauce
1 c. chili sauce
1 c. mayonnaise
Salt and pepper to taste
1 sm. onion, grated
Horseradish to taste

Blend all ingredients well; pour over seafood. Yield: 12 servings.

Mrs. Alan Kadet
Gary, Ind.

TUNA CANAPES

2 6 ½ or 7-oz. cans tuna in vegetable oil
2 tsp. packaged onion, classic or Bleu cheese salad dressing mix
½ c. finely chopped celery
½ c. mayonnaise

Combine tuna, salad dressing mix, celery and mayonnaise; mix until well blended. Place tuna mixture on toast rounds; broil for 2 to 3 minutes. May be used as filling for finger sandwiches. Yield: 36 canapes.

Photograph for this recipe above.

ANTIPASTO

½ c. catsup
½ c. olive oil
1 sm. can tomato sauce
1 bay leaf
2 2-oz. cans anchovies and oil
2 or 3 cloves garlic, impaled on toothpick
1 tsp. salt
½ tsp. pepper
1 tsp. monosodium glutamate
1 tsp. chili powder
Few dashes Tabasco sauce
½ c. thinly sliced cooked carrots
½ c. thinly sliced cooked celery
1 6-oz. can chunk tuna
1 5-oz. jar pickled onions
1 c. mixed sweet pickles
1 sm. jar stuffed green olives
1 sm. can mushroom buttons
¼ c. capers (opt.)
1 sm. can ripe olives, pitted
1 sm. can Norwegian sardines
1 sm. can baby artichokes
½ c. dry white wine (opt.)

Combine catsup, olive oil, tomato sauce, bay leaf, anchovies and oil, garlic and seasonings. Boil for 2 minutes, stirring constantly to prevent burning. Add all remaining ingredients except sardines, artichokes and wine; bring to a boil. Cool; add sardines and artichokes. Add wine if mixture is too thick. Chill. Yield: 3 pints.

Mrs. Brinton C. Carter
Broomall, Pa.

CHIPPED BEEF AND CREAM CHEESE CANAPES

1 lge. pkg. cream cheese
Milk

(Continued on next page)

2 spring onions and tops, chopped
¼ lb. chipped dried beef
Crackers or thin bread slices

Blend cream cheese with milk to obtain spreading consistency. Add onions and stalks to cream cheese with dried beef. Add more milk if necessary. Spread on crackers or bread.

Mrs. Helen H. Colbert
Alex, Va.

DRIED BEEF PINWHEELS

1 lgc. pkg. cream cheese
Garlic salt to taste
½ c. chopped almonds
1 pkg. sliced dried beef

Combine cheese, garlic salt and almonds; spread on beef slices. Roll up and slice into miniature pinwheels; refrigerate or freeze until ready for use. Yield: 6-8 servings.

Mrs. Clarence Wallner
Bedford, Ind.

DEVILED HAM PUFFS

1 ½-lb. pkg. cream cheese
1 tsp. onion juice
½ tsp. baking powder
1 egg yolk
Salt to taste
24 sm. bread rounds
2 2 ¼-oz. cans deviled ham

Blend cheese, onion juice, baking powder, egg yolk and salt. Toast bread rounds on one side; spread untoasted sides with deviled ham. Cover each with mound of cheese mixture; place on cookie sheet. Bake at 375 degrees for 10 to 12 minutes or until puffed and browned. Serve hot.

Mrs. Doris Wilson
Kentland, Ind.

FROSTED DEVILED HAM

2 4 ½-oz. cans deviled ham
1 tbsp. minced onion
1 8-oz. pkg. cream cheese
¼ c. sour cream
2 ½ tsp. sharp mustard

Blend deviled ham and onion; mound mixture on plate; Mix all remaining ingredients; frost ham mound with mixture. Refrigerate overnight. Serve with chips or crackers or use as sandwich spread. Yield: 10 servings.

Joyce Titus
New Knoxville, O.

PORCUPINE SPREAD

1 8-oz. pkg. cream cheese
2 4 ½-oz. cans deviled ham
1 tbsp. minced onion
1 tsp. caraway seed
1 3-oz. pkg. cream cheese
Milk
½ c. crushed pretzel sticks
Sliced olives
Thin pretzel sticks

Blend cheese with deviled ham, onion and caraway seed; chill. Mold mixture into an oval shape about 8 inches long, making one end pointed for a head. Soften remaining cheese with small amount of milk; spread over porcupine. Beginning at round end, cover three-fourths of porcupine with crushed pretzels; chill. Just before serving, insert pretzel sticks in crumbed portion. Make eyes of olive slices. Serve with assorted crackers. Yield: 12 servings.

Mrs. Dolores Holmberg
Fairhope, Ala.

CHICKEN LIVERS AND BACON

1 1-lb. pkg. chicken livers
Worcestershire sauce
12 slices bacon
Rye or melba toast

Coat chicken livers with Worcestershire sauce; drain. Wrap each with 1 strip of bacon. Fasten by threading liver and bacon onto a skewer. Grill about 2 inches above hot coals for 10 minutes or until bacon is crisp. Turn frequently to cook evenly. Serve on wooden picks with party rye bread, melba toast or crackers. Yield: 12 servings.

Mrs. Anita K. Stoker
Smyrna, Tenn.

CHOPPED CHICKEN LIVER

½ lb. chicken livers, halved and deveined
1 med. onion, chopped
2 hard-cooked eggs
1 stalk celery, finely chopped
Chicken fat or salad oil
Salt to taste
Dash of pepper
Thinly sliced onion rings (opt.)
Crackers (opt.)

Saute onion in small amount of fat until golden; add livers. Cook until done; cool. Finely chop livers, onion, eggs and celery in onion chopper or blender. Add salad oil to obtain good spreading consistency; season to taste. Serve on a lettuce leaf, topped with onion rings as a dip-appetizer or spread on crackers as a canape. Yield: 4-6 servings.

Mrs. Hilda R. Ferber
Oceana, Va.

PSEUDO PATE DE FOIE GRAS

½ lb. fresh or frozen chicken livers
½ c. butter, melted
¾ to 1 tsp. salt
Cayenne pepper to taste
½ tsp. nutmeg
1 tsp. dry mustard
¼ tsp. ground cloves
½ tsp. monosodium glutamate
2 tbsp. minced or 1 tbsp. dried onion

Cover livers with water and simmer for 20 minutes. Drain off all but about 1 tablespoon of water; add all remaining ingredients. Pour hot water into blender to heat it; drain. Pour liver mixture into blender and blend for about 1 minute at high speed. Pack into a crock and chill. NOTE: This paste freezes well. Yield: Spread for 30 crackers.

Mrs. Bradley Bennett
Washington, D.C.

RUMAKI

4 tbsp. butter or margarine
12 to 15 whole chicken livers
12 to 15 canned water chestnuts
12 to 15 strips bacon

Melt butter or margarine in skillet; add chicken livers. Saute until golden; cool. For each rumaki, wrap 1/2 chicken liver and 1/2 water chestnut with 1/2 slice bacon and fasten with toothpick; refrigerate. At serving time, broil until bacon is crisp. Serve very hot. NOTE: Broiling may be done in oven or on an outside barbecue grill; rumakis are served on toothpicks.

Mrs. Irma Clay Allen
Richlands, Va.

CHOPPED LIVER

1 lb. calves liver
½ to ¾ c. chicken fat or salad oil
1 lge. onion, diced
4 hard-cooked eggs
Salt and pepper to taste

Panfry liver slowly in small amount of chicken fat. Saute onion until lightly browned. Grind or chop liver, eggs and sauted onion together. Add remaining chicken fat, salt and pepper. Serve on rye or pumpernickel rounds or crisp crackers.

Mrs. Allen S. Lawrence
Sinton, Tex.

EXOTIC CHEESE-LIVER SPREAD

1 lb. liver
4 stalks celery
5 leeks
4 hard-cooked eggs, separated
¼ tsp. garlic salt
¼ tsp. pepper
¼ tsp. celery seed
½ tsp. salt
½ pkg. prepared onion flavored salad dressing mix
1 6-oz. pkg. cream cheese, softened
½ c. mayonnaise
1 2-oz. jar pimento

Bake liver at 375 degrees for 10 minutes. Grind baked liver, celery, leeks and whites of eggs; add seasonings, creamed cheese, mayonnaise and pimento. Mold into shape desired; sprinkle with crumbled egg yolks. Use paprika sparingly. May be used with hot rolls, crackers, chips or sandwiches. Yield: 2 cups.

Jackie Downs
Boulder, Colo.

LIVER PASTE

1 round roll soft liverwurst
2 hard-cooked eggs
1 tsp. dried parsley
1 tsp. chopped onion
¼ c. finely chopped celery
2 tbsp. mayonnaise

Blend liverwurst and eggs. Add all remaining ingredients. Use as spread on assorted crackers for appetizers.

Phyllis P. Nash
Berwyn, Pa.

QUICK KABOBS

1 No. 2 ½ can sliced pineapple
1 can luncheon meat, cut into ½-in. cubes
1 med. bottle Maraschino cherries

Cut each pineapple slice into six chunks. Place meat, pineapple chunks and cherries on toothpicks.

Mrs. Emaline Miller
Orosi, Calif.

SWEET AND SOUR FRANKS

1 6-oz. jar mustard
1 8 or 10-oz. glass currant jelly
1 1-lb. pkg. frankfurters, cut into bite-sized pieces

Combine mustard and jelly in electric frying pan; heat to 180 degrees, stirring occasionally, until mustard and jelly are well blended. Add frankfurters to sweet-sour sauce; mix gently until well heated. Serve in skillet on toothpicks. Yield: 60 appetizers.

Mrs. Jack Pinta
North Hollywood, Calif.

ARTICHOKE APPETIZERS

¾ c. olive oil
¼ c. wine vinegar
¾ tsp. salt
½ tsp. Tabasco sauce
1 clove of garlic, peeled
4 tbsp. lemon juice
1 15-oz. can artichoke hearts

Combine olive oil, vinegar, salt, Tabasco sauce, clove of garlic and lemon juice. Add artichoke hearts. Chill in refrigerator. NOTE: If fresh artichokes are used, wash artichokes thoroughly and cut off stem end. Boil in salted water for 20 to 45 minutes or until tender and outside leaf is easily pulled off. Drain upside down. Garnish appetizer with artichoke leaves if desired. Yield: 2 cups.

Photograph for this recipe on page 77.

BONTONA HORS D' OEUVRES

Canned refried beans
Tostados
Jalapenos pepper, sliced
Sliced sharp cheese

Spread beans on tostados. Top with slices of pepper and cheese. Place under broiler until cheese melts. Serve hot.

Mrs. Ann Dezsy
Alamogordo, N.M.

CHILI BEAN CANAPE

1 doz. corn tortillas, quartered
½ c. shortening
1 8-oz. can refried beans
1 4-oz. can chopped green chili peppers
¼ lb. Longhorn cheese

Fry tortilla pieces quickly in very hot shortening, turning each piece once. Place on ungreased cookie sheet. Top with 1 teaspoonful of beans, 1/2 teaspoonful chili peppers and a 1-inch square slice of cheese. Place under broiler until cheese has melted. Serve hot. Yield: 48 servings.

Mrs. Donald Spoth
Alamogordo, N.M.

CAULIFLOWER APPETIZER

1 cauliflower
1 ½ c. Italian dressing

Wash cauliflower; break into bite-sized pieces. Place in casserole; cover with dressing. Marinate, covered, for 24 hours in refrigerator. Occasionally drain dressing and pour slowly over cauliflower. Yield: 6 servings.

Mrs. Marjorie F. Rendulic
Orlando, Fla.

EGGPLANT APPETIZER

1 sm. eggplant
⅓ c. olive oil
½ tsp. Tabasco sauce
½ tsp. salt
¼ c. lemon juice
1 sm. purple onion (opt.)

Wash and peel eggplant. Slice into fine strips about 2 inches long. Combine olive oil, Tabasco sauce, salt and lemon juice. Add eggplant strips. Chill. Garnish with finely chopped onion if desired. Yield: 2 cups.

Photograph for this recipe on page 77.

LIMA BEAN APPETIZER

1 sm. white onion, chopped
¼ c. olive oil
¾ tsp. salt
½ tsp. Tabasco sauce
2 tbsp. lemon juice
1 1-lb. can lima beans, drained
Red pepper or pimento (opt.)

Combine onion, olive oil, salt, Tabasco sauce and lemon juice. Add beans to marinade and chill for at least 2 hours, turning occasionally. Garnish with strips of pepper or chopped pimento. Yield: 2 cups.

Photograph for this recipe on page 77.

BAKED STUFFED MUSHROOMS

24 lge. mushrooms
Lemon juice
Butter
¼ c. grated Swiss cheese
½ c. plus 2 tbsp. bread crumbs
Salt and pepper to taste
¼ c. minced parsley
1 clove of garlic, minced
2 tbsp. minced onion
¼ c. Sherry

Wash mushrooms and remove stems; leave caps intact. Sprinkle a few drops of lemon juice in each cap; set aside. Finely mince stems; saute in butter. Combine with cheese, 1/2 cup bread crumbs, salt, pepper, parsley, garlic, onion and Sherry. Pile filling into mushroom caps; sprinkle with 2 tablespoons bread crumbs. Dot with butter. Bake at 350 degrees for 15 minutes. Yield: 12 servings.

Mrs. Jo Anne Sandager
Stillwater, Minn.

HI-HAT MUSHROOMS IN WINE SAUCE

16 med. fresh mushrooms
½ lb. ground sausage
1 c. tomato sauce
1 c. white wine
½ clove of garlic, crushed
⅛ tsp. oregano

Wash mushrooms; remove and chop stems. Add stems to sausage. Stuff caps, rounding meat mixture into high crown. Bake at 350 degrees for 30 minutes. Heat tomato sauce, wine, garlic and oregano in chafing dish. When blended, add mushrooms. Cover and let sauce bubble. Spear mushrooms with toothpicks and serve. Yield: 4-6 servings.

Mrs. Katheryn Chambers
Wayne, Nebr.

MUSHROOM APPETIZERS

½ lb. small mushrooms
⅓ c. olive oil
3 tbsp. wine vinegar
2 tbsp. lemon juice
¾ tsp. salt
½ tsp. Tabasco sauce
Pinch of thyme
2 c. water
3 tbsp. finely chopped parsley

Wipe mushrooms with a damp cloth. Trim off bottom of stem and cut into halves lengthwise.

(Continued on next page)

Combine olive oil, wine vinegar, lemon juice, salt, Tabasco sauce, thyme and water in a small saucepan. Bring to a boil and simmer for 5 minutes to blend flavors. Add mushrooms to boiling liquid. Cook slowly for 5 minutes or until barely tender. Let cool in liquid. Sprinkle with chopped parsley. Chill. Drain before serving. Yield: 3 cups.

Photograph for this recipe on page 77.

SWEET AND SOUR ZUCCHINI

1 pkg. dehydrated onions
1/8 c. wine vinegar
3/4 c. sugar
1 tsp. salt
1/2 tsp. pepper
1/3 c. salad oil
2/3 c. cider vinegar
1/2 c. chopped green pepper
1/2 c. sliced celery
5 zucchini, thinly sliced

Soak onions in wine vinegar. Add sugar, salt, pepper, oil and vinegar. Combine with vegetables; marinate for 6 hours or overnight. Drain and serve. Yield: 12 servings.

Luella Blankenship
Biggs, Calif.

PEPPER APPETIZER

12 green or red peppers
3 c. vinegar
1 c. salad oil
1 tbsp. salt
1 c. pickling onions, peeled

Wash peppers; remove seed and centers. Cut into serving pieces. Bring vinegar, oil and salt to a boil. Add a few peppers and onions at a time, turning in boiling liquid until peppers change color. Do not overcook. Cool and store in refrigerator if to be served within a few days. Peppers may also be canned. Yield: 25 servings.

Odessa L. Carlson
Wakefield, Mich.

WATER CHESTNUT HORS D'OEUVRES

2 cans water chestnuts, cut into thumb-sized pieces
1 to 1 1/2 lb. bacon
1 bottle catsup
8 tbsp. (heaping) sugar

Wrap chestnuts with 1/2 slice bacon; fasten with toothpick. Place in 9 x 6 x 2-inch pan. Bake at 350 degrees until bacon is almost done but not crisp. Remove from oven; pour off grease. Combine catsup and sugar; pour around but not over chestnuts. Bake at 350 degrees for 30 to 45 minutes. Serve immediately. Yield: 15-18 servings.

Mrs. John R. Swan
Indianapolis, Ind.

SAUERKRAUT APPETIZER

1 med. onion, chopped
1 green pepper, chopped
1 c. chopped celery
1 qt. sauerkraut, drained
1 c. sugar
1/4 c. vinegar

Combine onion, pepper, celery and sauerkraut. Heat sugar and vinegar until dissolved. Pour over sauerkraut mixture. Let stand for 24 hours. NOTE: May be stored in refrigerator until used. Yield: 20 servings.

Mrs. Paul Vetter
Carleton, Mich.

GLAZE FOR HORS D'OEUVRES AND CANAPES

4 tsp. unflavored gelatin
1/3 c. cold water
1 c. boiling water or consomme

Combine gelatin and cold water; let stand until thickened. Pour boiling water or stock over gelatin-water mixture; chill until thickened. Place hors d'oeuvres on cake rack with drip pan underneath. Pour glaze over hors d'oeuvres; remelt any glaze that drips off. Glazed hors d'oeuvres may be prepared a day in advance and stored in refrigerator in waxed paper-lined boxes.

Mrs. June Patchett
Metcalf, Ill.

GLAZED PEANUTS

2 c. raw unskinned peanuts
⅓ c. water
1 c. sugar
Dash of salt

Place all ingredients in 9-inch heavy iron frying pan. Cook until sugar crystallizes on nuts. Reduce heat and stir constantly with heavy spoon as sugar melts onto nuts. Turn onto marble slab or large greased platter. Separate into small clusters or individual nuts when cool enough to handle. Yield: 1 pound.

Mrs. E. Carlyle Lynch
Broadway, Va.

NUTS AND BOLTS

1 c. bacon drippings
1 stick margarine
1 tbsp. garlic salt
1 tbsp. Worcestershire sauce
1 tsp. red pepper
1 tsp. chili powder
1 tsp. monosodium glutamate
1 box Wheat Chex
1 box Cheerios
1 box Pretzel sticks
1 can peanuts
1 can mixed nuts

Melt drippings and margarine; stir in seasonings. Pour over cereal and nuts; mix well. Bake at 300 degrees until brown, stirring frequently. Cool; store in airtight containers.

Mrs. Mercer Scott
Natchitoches, La.

PARTY MIX

1 6-oz. pkg. semi-sweet chocolate
½ c. peanut butter
½ stick margarine
1 box Rice Chex
1 box confectioners sugar

Combine chocolate, peanut butter and margarine. Melt over low heat. Fold in Rice Chex gently until all are coated; add sugar. Fold until all are coated. NOTE: May be stored in sealed glass jar for weeks. Yield: 60 servings.

Mrs. Ann M. Braswell
Laurinburg, N.C.

RAISIN-NUT SNACK

2 boxes seedless raisins
2 c. black walnuts
1 pt. grape juice

Grind raisins and nuts together. Add grape juice to obtain spreading consistency. Chill. Serve on Ritz crackers. NOTE: Peanuts may be substituted for part of walnuts. Yield: 2 quarts.

Doris Ann Pyle
Marion, Va.

CHEESE SANDWICH SPREAD

1 8-oz. pkg. cream cheese
1 3-oz. bottle of stuffed olives, chopped
1 or 2 tbsp. olive juice

Beat cheese until creamy; add olives and juice.

Mrs. Harold Robison
Memphis, Tenn.

DELICIOUS NUTTY CHEESE SANDWICHES

18 slices white or whole wheat bread with crusts removed
Grape or plum jelly
Butter or margarine
2 3-oz. pkg. cream cheese, softened
Chopped nuts

Spread six slices of bread with jelly. Spread six slices with butter or margarine and place on top of jelly slices. Spread remaining slices with cream cheese and sprinkle with nuts. Place on top of other slices. Cut sandwiches into quarters diagonally and arrange on plate with points upward. Yield: 12 servings.

Mrs. F. L. Berry
North Sacramento, Calif.

INDIVIDUAL PIZZAS

1 lge. onion, chopped
½ green pepper, chopped
½ clove of garlic, minced

(Continued on next page)

½ c. oil
1 lb. grated Longhorn cheese
1 sm. can tomato sauce
1 sm. jar olives, sliced

Brown onion, green pepper and garlic in oil. Add all remaining ingredients; cook until cheese melts. Spread on hamburger bun halves or English muffin halves; place under broiler until lightly browned.

Dolly J. Voss
Benton Harbor, Mich.

MERRY MELBA GO ROUNDS

2 3-oz. pkg. cream cheese
1 tsp. chili powder
1 tsp. grated onion
¼ tsp. salt
½ c. pitted ripe olives, chopped
Melba toast

Combine all ingredients except toast; chill until needed. Spread on toast; serve. Yield: 30-36 servings.

Mrs. Eugene Cook
Washington Courthouse, O.

MEXICAN CHEESE SANDWICHES

3 lb. cheese, grated
½ lb. green peppers, finely chopped
1 lb. onions, minced
1 pt. stuffed olives, minced
16 hard-cooked eggs, chopped
4 tsp. Worcestershire sauce
1 ½ c. catsup
¼ c. margarine

Blend all ingredients. Serve as open-faced sandwiches. Yield: 90 sandwiches.

Mrs. Lois Gray
Bloomington, Ind.

PIMENTO CHEESE SPREAD

1 lge. can evaporated milk
1 lb. American cheese, grated
2 tbsp. vinegar
½ tsp. dry mustard
1 7-oz. can pimento, drained and chopped
1 tsp. salt
Dash of cayenne

Scald milk in double boiler; add all remaining ingredients. Stir until smooth; remove from heat. Cool; store in covered jars. Use spread on sandwiches, crackers or for celery stuffing.

Mary M. Cornwell
Waynesville, N.C.

TOASTED CHEESE SANDWICH

1 lb. strong store cheese, grated
1 recipe thin white sauce
Paprika
Toast

Blend cheese into white sauce; cook until cheese melts and sauce is smooth. Sprinkle with paprika; serve on toast.

Mrs. Franklin D. Roosevelt

COTTAGE CHEESE-PINEAPPLE SANDWICHES

1 c. creamed cottage cheese
½ c. crushed pineapple, well drained
⅛ tsp. salt
¼ c. toasted chopped almonds
½ tsp. curry powder
Bread, cut into 3 x 2 ¼-inch diamonds
Sliced radishes
Minced parsley

Combine cottage cheese with pineapple, salt, almonds and curry powder; blend well. Spread on bread; garnish with radish slices and parsley. Yield: 40 servings.

Mrs. LuRae Phillips
Cambria AFS, Calif.

LADIES' FAVORITE

½ lb. sharp cheese, grated
¼ lb. diced raw bacon
1 egg, beaten
2 tbsp. chili sauce
Dash of pepper
8 slices bread

Combine cheese, bacon, egg, chili sauce and pepper. Lay bread on cookie sheet. Spread cheese mixture on bread. Bake at 400 degrees for 15 to 20 minutes. Yield: 8 servings.

Mrs. F. M. Davison
Des Moines, Iowa

MEAT SANDWICH FILLING

Left-over roast beef
Chopped pickles
Chopped celery
Salt to taste
Mayonnaise to taste

Grind meat; add pickles, celery and salt. Blend well with mayonnaise.

Mrs. M. K. Goulding
Mineral Wells, Tex.

BACON AND OLIVE SANDWICH FILLING

½ c. chopped ripe olives
½ c. chopped nuts
1 c. cooked bacon, crumbled
1 ½ c. mayonnaise or salad dressing

Combine all ingredients; spread on bread. Yield: 4-6 servings.

Ruth Stevens
Aberdeen, O.

BACON-PEPPER SANDWICH FILLING

3 lb. bacon
3 green peppers, chopped
1 3-oz. pkg. cream cheese, softened
Mayonnaise
Salt and pepper

Cook bacon until crisp; crumble. Blend bacon and peppers into cream cheese. Add enough mayonnaise to moisten. Season to taste. Spread on whole wheat bread.

Mrs. Lena Milam
Beaumont, Tex.

LIVER AND BACON SANDWICH FILLING

½ c. chopped fried bacon
½ c. ground cooked liver
Salt and pepper to taste
1 tbsp. chopped parsley
¼ c. cream

Mix bacon and liver with seasonings; add cream. Blend until smooth. Yield: 6 servings.

Beatrice M. Jefferson
Cassadage, N.Y.

LUNCHEON SANDWICH

Tomato slices
8 strips bacon, partially cooked
4 slices cheese
4 slices bread, slightly toasted

Put tomato slices, bacon and cheese on bread; broil until cheese is melted. Serve hot. Yield: 4 servings.

Mrs. John Hostvedt
Wisconsin Rapids, Wisc.

DEVILED HAM SPREAD

½ tsp. Tabasco sauce
1 tsp. mustard
1 tbsp. minced onion
⅓ c. mayonnaise
1 tsp. lemon juice

(Continued on next page)

½ tsp. salt
½ c. diced celery
6 hard-cooked eggs, chopped
1 4½-oz. can deviled ham

Blend Tabasco sauce, mustard and onion with mayonnaise. Stir in lemon juice and salt. Combine celery, eggs and deviled ham; add mayonnaise mixture and mix thoroughly. Yield: 8 servings.

Mrs. J. T. Jinright
Troy, Ala.

HAM AND ANCHOVY SANDWICHES

1 ¼ c. chopped ham
1 tsp. onion juice
Paprika
Few drops of Tabasco sauce
Anchovy paste
Creamed butter

Combine all ingredients; spread on toast or bread.

Mrs. Earl F. Briggs
Corning, N.Y.

HAM SANDWICH FILLING

1 c. ground baked ham
2 hard-cooked eggs, finely chopped
Dash of salt and pepper
½ tsp. celery salt
¼ tsp. garlic salt
Mayonnaise to taste

Blend all ingredients; spread on slices of bread. Yield: 4 servings.

Mrs. J. Y. Morgan
Nacogdoches, Tex.

HAM SANDWICH FILLING

2 lb. baked ham
4 hard-cooked eggs, mashed
¼ c. mayonnaise
4 tbsp. pickle relish
2 tbsp. prepared mustard

Trim fat from ham; put meat through food chopper. Add all remaining ingredients; blend. Spread on bread slices. Yield: 10-12 servings.

Mrs. J. P. Thompson
Stephenville, Tex.

HAM SPREAD

½ c. cooked ground ham
½ c. ground bologna
1 hard-cooked egg
2 tbsp. chopped green pepper
2 tbsp. chopped pickle
Mayonnaise
Salt and pepper

Combine meats, egg, pepper and pickle; moisten with mayonnaise to spreading consistency. Season to taste. Spread thin rounds of white bread with butter; cover with filling. Garnish with slices of sweet pickles or paprika. Yield: 8 servings.

Mrs. Dora M. Hopkins
Blanchester, O.

OPEN-FACED SANDWICHES

1 can chopped ham
½ lb. Cheddar cheese, grated
½ green pepper, chopped
½ onion, chopped
Chopped green olives (opt.)
8 sesame rolls
1 tsp. salad mustard
¾ c. mayonnaise

Blend all ingredients; spread on split sesame rolls. Heat in 375 degree oven for 15 minutes. Yield: 8 servings.

Mrs. F. Alfred Berger, Jr.
St. Louis, Mo.

PARTY SANDWICH LOAF

FILLINGS:
2 c. ham salad
2 c. cottage cheese mixed with pineapple
2 c. egg salad
2 c. chicken salad
1 unsliced loaf bread
½ lb. butter

(Continued on next page)

2 3-oz. pkg. cream cheese
1 tbsp. cream
Pickle and olive slices

Prepare fillings. Remove crusts from bread; cut lengthwise into five slices. Spread each slice with softened butter. Spread ham salad between first and second slices of bread; spread cottage cheese mixture between second and third slices of bread. Spread egg salad between third and fourth slices. Spread chicken salad between fourth and fifth slices. Press loaf firmly together. Wrap in waxed paper; chill for 1 hour. Frost top and sides of loaf with cream cheese softened with cream. Arrange pickle and olive slices on top. Yield: 8-10 servings.

Mrs. Alta Jo Hazard
Midway Island, Calif.

CHICKEN AND PINEAPPLE SANDWICHES

1 8-oz. can crushed pineapple, drained
1 c. chopped cooked or canned chicken
1 c. chopped pecans
½ c. salad dressing

Combine all ingredients; mix well. Spread between buttered slices of bread. Cut each sandwich into quarters, diagonally. Yield: 2 dozen sandwiches.

Eila Davis
Valdosta, Ga.

CHICKEN SANDWICH FILLING

1 hen
1 onion
1 clove of garlic (opt.)
6 hard-cooked eggs
½ to 1 c. mayonnaise
Salt and pepper to taste

Stew hen with onion and 1 clove of garlic until tender. Reserve 1/2 cup fat-free broth. Grind hen and eggs together with 1/2 clove of garlic. Moisten with mayonnaise and broth; sprinkle with salt and pepper. Make into sandwich. NOTE: Chopped celery, sweet pickles and olives may be added.

Tillie Gemar
San Joaquin, Calif.

MOCK CHICKEN SANDWICH FILLING

½ lb. pork
½ lb. beef
½ lb. veal
Salt and pepper to taste
Mayonnaise
Meat stock

Half cover meats with water and cook in pressure cooker for 20 minutes or boil until meats fall apart; drain. Add salt and pepper; cool. Run through food chopper. Blend with enough mayonnaise and meat stock to moisten; serve on light or dark bread.

Mrs. John C. Adams
Del Rey, Calif.

DEVILED TONGUE SANDWICH SPREAD

1 lb. boiled smoked tongue, chopped
2 hard-cooked eggs, chopped
1 tbsp. chopped mustard pickle
1 lge. dill pickle, chopped
1 tbsp. prepared mustard
Mayonnaise to taste

Combine all ingredients; spread on toast. Yield: 8 servings.

Mrs. Lawrence Bundy
Clarence Center, N.Y.

TONGUE SANDWICH FILLING

1 fresh tongue
1 lge. sweet apple, finely chopped
2 med. sweet pickles, chopped
Mayonnaise to taste
Salt to taste

Cover tongue with cold salted water; boil until tender. Cool; remove tissue, bones and skin. Grind with medium fine blade. Combine all ingredients. NOTE: Finely chopped onion and celery may be added. Yield: 8 servings.

Mrs. R. E. Bradfield
Lometa, Tex.

OPEN-FACED SANDWICHES

2 tbsp. catsup
4 tbsp. melted butter
4 tbsp. milk
1 can luncheon meat, ground
4 tbsp. ground onion
3 tbsp. ground green pepper
1 c. ground Velveeta cheese
4 tbsp. ground sweet pickle
Hamburger buns

Combine catsup, butter and milk with ground ingredients. Mix well; spread mixture on buns. Place under broiler until light brown and bubbly. Yield: 10 servings.

Mrs. Ernest Lehman
Middleton, Wisc.

PARTY SANDWICH WHEELS

Butter
1 round loaf pumpernickel or rye bread, sliced
Cream cheese
1 green pepper, chopped
Cream
Chopped pimento
Liverwurst
Mayonnaise
Minced onion
Salt and pepper
Chopped hard-cooked eggs
Lemon juice

Butter each slice of bread. Combine cream cheese, green pepper and cream. Spread a small circle in center of bread; surround with narrow border of pimento. Combine liverwurst, mayonnaise, onion, salt and pepper. Spread 1-inch circle around pimento. Combine eggs, mayonnaise, lemon juice, salt and pepper; spread to edges of bread. Cut into wedges. Yield: 4-6 servings.

Elsie F. Holt
Topsham, Me.

VEAL-HEART SANDWICH

1 veal heart
3 peppercorns
1 bay leaf
Bread
Margarine
Mustard

Simmer veal heart, peppercorns and bay leaf for 2 hours in water to cover. Cool in water; remove. Slice; brown in margarine. Spread bread with margarine; fill with heart. Spread with mustard. Serve warm or cold. Yield: 6-8 servings.

Marian Brown
Horseheads, N.Y.

CANAPE SUPREME

White bread
Fillets of anchovy or anchovy paste
1 lge. tomato, sliced
1 lge. Bermuda onion, sliced
Sour cream
Olive slices
Parsley
Paprika

Trim and toast bread; cover each slice with 4 or 5 anchovy fillets. Place 1 tomato slice and 1 onion slice over anchovies. Cover with sour cream; chill. Garnish with olives and parsley; sprinkle with paprika.

Beatrice Freede
Clearwater, Fla.

CRAB MEAT ON HOLLAND RUSK

1 8-oz. pkg. cream cheese
1 can crab meat
Juice of 1 lemon
Salt and pepper to taste
1 tsp. onion, grated
5 or 6 Holland rusks
6 tomato slices
6 Cheddar or American cheese slices

Blend softened cream cheese, crab, lemon juice, seasonings and onion. Spread on Holland rusks; add a slice of tomato and a slice of cheese. Bake slowly at 300 degrees until cheese melts or at 400 degrees for 20 minutes. Yield: 6 servings.

Mrs. Rae M. Cavaleri
Augusta, Ga.

CRAB ROLLS

4 slices bread
1 sm. can crab meat or 1 lb. fresh crab
2 stalks celery, finely chopped
4 whole green onions, chopped
1 sm. can mushrooms, drained (opt.)
1 tsp. mayonnaise
8 slices bacon, fried
8 slices Cheddar cheese

Toast bread on one side. Combine crab meat, celery, onions, mushrooms and mayonnaise on untoasted side. Cover with bacon; top with a slice of cheese. Broil until cheese is bubbly. Yield: 4 servings.

Mrs. R. K. Gallagher
Sherman, Tex.

PINK SANDWICH CIRCLES

6 or 8 hard crust rolls
1 ½ tsp. unflavored gelatin
2 ½ tbsp. cold water
1 c. salmon or 1 c. tuna, flaked
¾ c. soft bread crumbs
¼ c. chopped sweet pickles
2 ½ tbsp. cream cheese
1 ½ tbsp. mayonnaise
1 ½ tbsp. catsup
1 ½ tbsp. chopped pimento
½ tsp. prepared mustard
Dash of pepper

Cut ends off rolls; reserve. Hollow out crusts with apple corer or knife. Soften gelatin in cold water; dissolve over boiling water. Drain salmon; combine with all remaining ingredients. Stir in gelatin. Fill rolls with salmon mixture; replace ends. Wrap in waxed paper; chill for 8 hours. Cut into 1/4-inch slices when ready to serve. Yield: 50 circles.

Mrs. John M. Frazier
Hattiesburg, Miss.

SHRIMP SURPRISES

1 5-oz. can shrimp or ¾ c. cooked fresh shrimp
½ c. soft butter
2 tbsp. lemon juice
⅛ tsp. minced garlic

Combine all ingredients; spread on tiny crackers or tea sandwiches. NOTE: Add 1/8 cup chopped walnuts, 1/8 cup chopped pimento or parsley or 1/16 teaspoon chili powder for variation. Yield: 1 1/2 cups.

Mrs. Joy Vandeway
Petaluma, Calif.

TASTY SANDWICH FILLING

1 can white tuna, flaked
4 hard-cooked eggs, chopped
4 whole carrots, shredded
1 sm. onion, chopped
½ celery stalk, chopped
Parsley
Salt
¾ c. mayonnaise
¼ green pepper, chopped

Combine all ingredients; serve on bread. Yield: 15-20 servings.

Mary A. Hays
Guymon, Okla.

TUNA-CHEESE SANDWICH SPREAD

½ lb. process cheese, grated
1 sm. can pimento, chopped
1 can tuna, flaked and drained
Juice of ½ lemon
Salt to taste
Mayonnaise to taste

Blend all ingredients; spread on sandwiches or serve with assorted crackers or potato chips. Yield: 10-12 servings.

Elizabeth S. Thornton
Toney, Ala.

TUNA SANDWICHES DELUXE

2 cans tuna, flaked
4 hard-cooked eggs, chopped
3 med. sweet pickles, chopped
½ med. onion, chopped
½ med. apple, chopped
¼ c. chopped nuts
4 tbsp. mayonnaise
2 lge. loaves sandwich bread

Blend all ingredients except bread. Spread bread with additional mayonnaise, then with sandwich mixture. Yield: 24 servings.

Mrs. A. R. Sanders, Jr.
Tornillo, Tex.

RAISIN SANDWICH SPREAD

1 c. sugar
1 egg
Juice and grated rind of 1 lemon
1 c. raisins
1 c. nuts, ground
1 c. mayonnaise

Combine sugar, egg, lemon juice and rind; cook until thickened. Cool. Add all remaining ingredients. Store in refrigerator. Use on any type bread. Yield: 20 servings.

Mrs. Charles Sain
Williamsburg, Va.

CUCUMBER SANDWICHES

2 med. cucumbers, peeled and chopped
1 tsp. onion juice
¼ tsp. salt
⅓ c. mayonnaise
2 tbsp. butter
8 thin slices whole wheat bread

Press water from cucumbers; combine with onion juice, salt and mayonnaise. Spread butter and cucumber mixture on four slices bread. Top with remaining bread; cut into halves. Yield: 8 servings.

Mrs. Donna Walker
Moffett Field NAS, Calif.

VEGETABLE SANDWICHES

3 hard-cooked eggs
5 carrots
1 lge. green pepper
1 med. onion
3 sour pickles
5 sweet pickles
1 lge. can pimento
½ pt. mayonnaise

Coarsely grind all ingredients except mayonnaise; add salt and drain. Fold in mayonnaise. Spread on slices of bread.

Viola DuPuis
Lake Linden, Mich.

RECIPE FOR CHILI CON QUESO ON PAGE 64

ALWAYS-A-FAVORITE DIP

DIP BASE:
1 8-oz. pkg. cream cheese
¼ c. evaporated milk
1 tbsp. lemon juice
1 tbsp. onion flakes or minced onion
Dash of paprika

Soften cream cheese; blend in milk. Add lemon juice, onion and paprika; blend.

VARIATIONS:
1 can smoked clams or oysters
1 c. pimento cheese
½ to 1 c. small shrimp
¼ c. grated carrots
¼ c. grated green pepper

Add any one of the above ingredients to the dip base. Blend well. Yield: 6-8 servings.

Mrs. Elsie Strum Hutchinson
Jacksonville Beach, Fla.

ANCHOVY DIP

1 8-oz. pkg. cream cheese
2 tbsp. cream
2 tsp. grated onion
½ tsp. celery seed
1 tbsp. lemon juice
2 tsp. anchovy paste

Soften cream cheese with electric mixer until smooth. Beat in all remaining ingredients until fluffy.

Mrs. Flo Brame
Waco, Tex.

BLEU CHEESE DIP

Bleu cheese dressing
Sour cream

Combine equal amounts of dressing and cream. Serve with crackers or chips.

Mrs. Nancy W. Darden
Durham, N.C.

CHILI CON QUESCO

½ c. minced onion
2 tbsp. butter
1 8-oz. can tomato sauce
1 4-oz. can green chilies, chopped
1 tsp. salt
¼ or ½ tsp. Tabasco sauce
1 c. large curd cottage cheese
8 oz. sharp Cheddar cheese, grated

Saute onion in butter until tender but not brown. Add tomato sauce, chopped chilies and salt. Simmer for 10 minutes. Stir in Tabasco sauce, cottage cheese and Cheddar cheese; cook slowly until cheese melts. Serve warm as dip for raw carrot sticks, cauliflowerets, cucumber slices, pepper strips and cherry tomatoes or tomato wedges. Texture and flavor are best if served immediately. Yield: 3 cups.

Photograph for this recipe on page 63.

CHILI CON QUESCO DIP

2 onions, chopped
1 clove of garlic
2 tbsp. cooking oil
2 No. 2 cans tomatoes, well drained
2 cans small green chilies, chopped
½ tsp. salt
½ tsp. oregano
1 lb. Velveeta cheese, cubed

Saute onions and garlic in oil; add tomatoes, chilies, salt and oregano. Simmer for 30 minutes. Remove from heat; add cheese. Serve warm with corn chips or crackers. Yield: 25 servings.

Mary L. Harris
Patagonia, Ariz.

CHILI DIP OR SAUCE

12 lge. tomatoes, chopped
1 red pepper, chopped
1 green pepper, chopped
4 onions, chopped
2 tbsp. salt
1 tsp. ginger
1 tsp. cloves
1 tsp. cinnamon
3 c. sugar
3 c. vinegar
4 apples, finely chopped
Cream cheese

Cook all ingredients except apples and cream cheese for at least 2 hours or longer if a

(Continued on next page)

What's in a salad? Practically everything. A salad may be a main dish, a side dish, an appetizer or a dessert. No matter what salad you choose, its success will depend to a large extent on your choice of dressing. It's the dressing that gives a salad character and personality.

SILHOUETTE SALAD DRESSING

1⅔ c. evaporated milk
⅓ c. vinegar
1 pkg. desired salad dressing mix
1 tsp. sugar

Put milk in 1-quart container. Gradually add vinegar, stirring constantly. Add mix and sugar; shake or stir until blended. Refrigerate. Serve over mixed greens, vegetables, seafood, meat, poultry, fruit salads or with cabbage for coleslaw. Yield: 2 cups dressing.

CURRY SALAD DRESSING

1⅔ c. evaporated milk
½ c. salad oil
½ c. lemon juice
4 tsp. curry powder
1 tsp. each sugar and salt
¼ tsp. ginger
2 tbsp. chopped chutney (opt.)

Beat evaporated milk and oil until blended. Beat in lemon juice until smooth. Mix in remaining ingredients. Refrigerate. Serve over fruit, poultry or seafood salads. Yield: 2½ cups dressing.

MONTEREY SALAD DRESSING

1⅔ c. evaporated milk
½ c. vinegar
1 pkg. dehydrated onion soup mix
½ c. catsup or chili sauce
1 tsp. Worcestershire sauce

Put evaporated milk in 1-quart container. Gradually add vinegar, stirring constantly. Add remaining ingredients; shake or stir until blended. Chill. Serve over mixed greens, vegetable, meat or seafood salads. Yield: 2½ cups dressing.

STEAK HOUSE SALAD DRESSING

¾ c. evaporated milk
½ c. salad oil
3 tbsp. vinegar or lime juice
1 pkg. Bleu cheese salad dressing mix

Beat milk and oil until blended. Add vinegar or lime juice; beat smooth. Stir in mix. Refrigerate. Serve over mixed greens, vegetables, meat, poultry or seafood salads or toss with cabbage for coleslaw. Yield: 1½ cups dressing.

See photograph on reverse page.

thicker sauce is desired. Add apples; cook for 30 minutes longer. If a sweeter dip is desired, vinegar may be reduced. Blend with cream cheese for a chip dip or cracker spread. Yield: 5 pints.

Mrs. Carol Paynter
Mineral Point, Wisc.

DIP

1 3-oz. pkg. cream cheese
½ c. Catalina dressing
¼ tsp. salt

Soften cream cheese with fork; stir in dressing until dip is light and fluffy. Add salt. Serve with corn or potato chips or crackers. Yield: 4 servings.

Martha Wooton
Nebo, Ky.

DIP MIX

1 sm. clove of garlic
4 onions and tops, finely chopped
2 tbsp. dry parsley
Salt and pepper to taste
1 c. sour cream
1 c. mayonnaise
1 pkg. Bleu cheese, cut up

Combine all ingredients with mixer except cheese. Fold in cheese or mix lightly with mixer. Yield: 2 1/2 cups.

Mrs. Loren Davis
Lake Preston, S.D.

GARLIC DIP

1 3-oz. pkg. cream cheese
1 tsp. Worcestershire sauce
¼ tsp. pepper
1 tsp. catsup
½ tsp. garlic powder
⅛ tsp. salt
Evaporated milk

Combine all ingredients except milk. Blend with electric mixer, adding milk gradually until mixture is of desired consistency. Serve with potato chips as a dip or as an appetizer with crackers.

Mrs. Betty Lou Archambault
Merrimack, N.H.

HOLIDAY DIP

1 8-oz. pkg. cream cheese
1 tbsp. mayonnaise
2 tbsp. evaporated milk
½ tsp. salt
1 sm. onion, minced
½ tsp. celery salt
5 slices crisp bacon, crumbled
¼ c. finely chopped salad olives

Cream cheese with mayonnaise and milk until smooth. Add all remaining ingredients. Add milk until dip is of desired consistency. Chill for 1 hour before serving. This may also be used as a sandwich spread. Yield: 10 servings.

Beth Bell
Barnsdall, Okla.

HOT CHEESE DIP

½ lb. sharp Cheddar cheese, grated
2 slices bacon, cooked and crumbled
½ bunch green onions and tops, thinly sliced

Combine all ingredients; place in casserole. Bake at 350 degrees for 20 minutes or until bubbling. Serve surrounded with crisp crackers or bread sticks. May be served in a chafing dish. Yield: 6 servings.

Maxine Garrigan
Stockton, Calif.

JOAN'S FAVORITE DIP

1 8-oz. pkg. cream cheese, softened
3 bouillon cubes
1 clove of garlic, minced
1 tsp. minced onion
2 tsp. mustard
Cream

Combine cheese, bouillon cubes dissolved in water, garlic, onion and mustard. Thin to desired consistency with cream. Serve with chips or crackers.

Mrs. Joan Kunde
York, Nebr.

ONION-DILL DIP

1 8-oz. pkg. cream cheese
¼ c. cream
2 tsp. grated onion
½ tsp. mustard
1 tsp. dill seed
2 tsp. Worcestershire sauce
1 tbsp. lemon juice

Blend cream cheese with cream until smooth. Add all remaining ingredients; stir well. Serve with celery and carrot sticks. Yield: 8 servings.

Mrs. Rochelle Heider
Brillion, Wisc.

PISTACHIO-CHEESE DIP

1 8-oz. pkg. cream cheese
3 tbsp. crumbled Bleu cheese
½ c. light cream
1 tbsp. lemon juice
½ c. chopped salted pistachio nuts

Blend cheeses; combine with all remaining ingredients. Chill. Serve with crackers and chips. Yield: 1 1/2 cups.

Mrs. Homer Lovejoy
Monterey, Calif.

QUICK 'N' EASY DIP

½ c. milk
2 tbsp. evaporated milk
1 8-oz. pkg. cream cheese, softened
1 ½ tsp. garlic salt

Gradually stir milk and evaporated milk into cream cheese; add garlic salt. Chill for at least 30 minutes. Remove from refrigerator at least 20 minutes before serving. NOTE: Dip will keep in refrigerator at least 10 days and may be freshened by stirring and adding drops of milk. Yield: 8 servings.

Mrs. Evelyn K. Hood
Carswell AFB, Tex.

SMOKY CHEESE DIP

2 3-oz. pkg. cream cheese
1 6-oz. roll smoky cheese
1 sm. clove of garlic, minced
⅓ c. pineapple juice
¼ tsp. Tabasco sauce
1 tsp. Worcestershire sauce

Combine all ingredients in blender; blend for about 20 seconds or until smooth. Chill and serve. Yield: 1 1/2 cups.

Mrs. Glenda Ballinger
Chattanooga, Tenn.

SNAPPY CHEESE DIP

1 3-oz. pkg. cream cheese
¼ lb. Bleu cheese
1 tbsp. grated onion
1 tbsp. Worcestershire sauce

Mash cream cheese with a fork. Add crumbled Bleu cheese, onion and Worcestershire sauce; mix well. Sprinkle with chopped parsley if desired. Serve with crackers or chips. Yield: 1 1/2 cups.

Mrs. Katherine M. Simons
Cross, S.C.

SWISS FONDUE

1 clove of garlic, cut
1 wine glass white wine
¼ lb. Emmental cheese, grated
¼ lb. Gruyere cheese, grated
1 clove of garlic, chopped
Dash of nutmeg
Dash of salt
1 ½ jiggers cherry brandy
1 tsp. cornstarch
Cubed French bread

Rub earthenware casserole with cut garlic; place over alcohol burner. Pour in wine; add cheeses, stirring constantly with wooden spoon until cheeses are melted. Add chopped garlic, cornstarch mixed with cherry brandy and seasonings. Spear bread cubes; swirl through fondue. Yield: 4 servings.

Mrs. Irene M. Rodden
Los Altos, Calif.

CREAMY CHEESE DIP

1 ½ oz. Roquefort cheese
4 ½ oz. cream cheese
1 tbsp. beer or ale
¼ tsp. Tabasco sauce
½ tsp. Worcestershire sauce

Cream cheeses; stir in beer, Tabasco sauce and Worcestershire sauce, mixing well. Serve with crisp crackers. Yield: 2/3 cup.

Photograph for this recipe above.

CURRY CHEESE DIP

1 c. cottage cheese
1 tbsp. chopped raisins
½ tsp. curry
1 tsp. grated onion
¼ tsp. Tabasco sauce
½ tsp. salt
1 tbsp. milk

Combine cottage cheese and raisins. Stir in curry, grated onion, Tabasco sauce, salt and milk. Yield: 3/4 cup.

Photograph for this recipe above.

EGG DIP

6 hard-cooked eggs, chopped
¼ c. chopped celery
2 tbsp. minced onion
1 tbsp. minced parsley
1 ½ tsp. salt
¼ tsp. pepper
1 3-oz. pkg. cream cheese
½ c. salad dressing
1 tbsp. catsup

Combine eggs, vegetables and seasonings. Blend cream cheese with salad dressing and catsup; add to egg mixture. Blend; chill. May be molded for salads or used as a sandwich spread or dip.

Mrs. Kay Reeves
McKinney, Tex.

EGG-OLIVE DIP

4 hard-cooked eggs, chopped
1 sm. can black olives, chopped
Salt to taste
Dash of lemon juice
Mayonnaise

(Continued on next page)

Blend eggs, olives, salt and lemon juice with enough mayonnaise to obtain dip consistency. NOTE: With less mayonnaise this makes a delicious sandwich filling.

Mrs. Loyd Breakey
Cody, Wyo.

SMOKED EGG DIP

12 hard-cooked eggs, diced
2 tbsp. soft butter
2 ½ tsp. liquid smoke
1 tbsp. lemon juice
2 tsp. mustard
1 tbsp. Worcestershire sauce
2 drops Tabasco sauce
½ tsp. salt
1 tsp. dried minced onion
¼ tsp. ground pepper
¾ c. mayonnaise

Combine all ingredients; blend until smooth. Refrigerate for at least 4 hours. Before serving, whip to soften and fluff. Yield: 1 quart.

Mrs. F. L. Brumback
Butler, Mo.

AVOCADO DIP

2 med. avocados, peeled and pitted
½ c. sour cream
2 tbsp. lemon juice
1 tsp. grated onion
1 tsp. salt
4 slices bacon, cooked and crumbled

Mash avocados with a fork or force through sieve. Add sour cream, lemon juice, onion and salt; chill. Just before serving, stir in bacon, reserving a few bits for garnish. Serve with chips. Yield: 1 1/2 cups.

Mrs. Jolene Hartman
Lancaster, Tex.

AVOCADO DIP

2 lge. avocados
1 tbsp. minced onion
⅛ tsp. garlic salt
⅛ tsp. pepper
¼ tsp. chili powder
⅓ c. salad dressing
6 slices bacon

Mash avocados; blend in onion, garlic salt, pepper and chili powder. Cover mixture with salad dressing to seal out air. Fry bacon until crisp; crumble. Stir avocado mixture when ready to serve; top with bacon. Yield: 12 servings.

Verdie B. Jones
McAlester, Okla.

AVOCADO-ROQUEFORT DIP

1 pt. sour cream
1 ripe avocado, mashed
¼ lb. Roquefort cheese, cubed
1 tsp. Worcestershire sauce

Fold sour cream into avocado. Add cheese and Worcestershire sauce. Serve with chips. Yield: 8 servings.

Mrs. Hazel C. Jacobsen
Ault, Colo.

GREEN DRAGON DIP

1 ripe avocado
1 3-oz. pkg. cream cheese
3 tbsp. mayonnaise
Dash of lemon juice or vinegar
¼ tsp. seasoned salt
⅛ tsp. pepper

Peel, pit and mash avocado. Blend with all remaining ingredients. Refrigerate until serving time. Serve with potato chips.

Mrs. Sarah Strawbridge
Westover AFB, Mass.

GREEN GODDESS DIP

1 ripe avocado
1 c. sour cream
¼ c. mayonnaise

(Continued on next page)

½ tsp. salt
½ tsp. seasoned salt
½ c. finely chopped parsley
¼ c. finely chopped green onions

Mash avocado well. Add sour cream and mayonnaise and mix well. Add salt and seasoned salt and mix well. Fold in chopped parsley and chopped green onions. Serve cold with chips or crackers. Yield: 2 1/2 cups.

Mrs. Marie Lovil
McLeod, Tex.

BACON AND SOUR CREAM DIP

1 8-oz. pkg. cream cheese
3 tbsp. finely cut chives
1 c. sour cream
1 tsp. horseradish
Dash of garlic salt
Dash of cayenne
6 slices crisp bacon

Soften cheese at room temperature. Blend with chives, sour cream, horseradish, garlic salt and cayenne. Add 4 slices crumbled bacon. Top with remaining bacon slices. Yield: 3 cups.

Mrs. Esther Cain
Brodhead, Wisc.

BEEF PICADILLO

½ lb. ground beef
½ lb. ground pork
1 tsp. salt
¼ tsp. pepper
4 tomatoes, peeled and diced
3 green onions, finely diced
3 med. potatoes, diced
¾ c. pimento, diced
¾ c. almonds, toasted
2 ½ cloves of garlic, minced
1 6-oz. can tomato paste
2 jalapeno peppers, chopped
¾ c. seedless raisins
¼ tsp. oregano

Cover meats with water; add salt and pepper. Simmer, covered, for 30 minutes; add all remaining ingredients. Cook until potatoes are tender; drain off excess liquid. Serve in chafing dish with corn chips. Yield: 20 servings.

Mrs. John E. Mitchell, Jr.
Memphis, Tenn.

CHICKEN-CHEESE DIP OR SPREAD

1 8-oz. pkg. cream cheese
¾ c. cooked chicken, finely ground
¼ c. olives, ground
2 tsp. grated onion
1 c. grated celery
1 tsp. Worcestershire sauce
Mayonnaise

Blend all ingredients with enough mayonnaise to moisten. NOTE: Ground dates, figs, raisins or crushed, drained pineapple or 1/4 cup mashed Bleu cheese and 1/4 cup sour cream or 1/3 cup ground ham and 2 hard-cooked eggs, finely diced, may be used instead of chicken. Yield: 2 cups.

Shirley Mae Griffiths
Easton, Pa.

DEVILED DIP

1 5-oz. jar pimento cheese spread or cream cheese
1 2 ¼-oz. can deviled ham
½ c. mayonnaise or salad dressing
2 tbsp. minced parsley
1 tbsp. minced onion
4 drops Tabasco sauce

Thoroughly combine all ingredients with electric mixer; chill. Yield: 1 1/3 cups.

Mrs. Joan Vella
Eglin AFB, Fla.

DEVILED HAM DIP

¼ lb. Velveeta cheese, grated
1 2 ¼-oz. can deviled ham
½ c. mayonnaise
Dash of garlic salt

Place cheese in top of double boiler; add all remaining ingredients. Heat and stir until blended. Serve hot or at room temperature. Yield: 6-8 servings.

Mrs. Carol Horne
Lorena, Tex.

DEVILED HAM-CHEESE DIP

1 4 ½-oz. can deviled ham
¼ c. grated Swiss cheese
2 tsp. pickle relish
¼ tsp. Tabasco sauce
1 tbsp. plus 1 tsp. mayonnaise

Combine deviled ham and cheese. Stir in pickle relish, Tabasco sauce and mayonnaise. Yield: 2/3 cup.

Photograph for this recipe on page 67.

DEVILED HAM-CHIP DIP

2 8-oz. pkg. cream cheese
½ c. sour cream
½ c. mayonnaise
1 2 ¼-oz. can deviled ham
2 tbsp. chopped chives or onion
½ tsp. Worcestershire sauce
Dash of salt and pepper

Soften cream cheese to room temperature. Blend in sour cream and mayonnaise. Add all remaining ingredients; mix well.

Mrs. William McDonald
Niles, Mich.

HOT DIP

1 2 ¼-oz. can deviled ham
¼ lb. Velveeta cheese
½ c. salad dressing
½ tsp. grated onion

Combine all ingredients; heat until cheese is melted. Serve hot in chafing dish. Yield: 12 servings.

Mrs. Paul McFall
Sparta, Mich.

HOT CHEESE DIP

1 lb. Velveeta cheese
1 onion, minced
½ c. butter
2 canned or cooked tomatoes, mashed
1 tbsp. Worcestershire sauce
¼ lb. dried beef, finely shredded

Melt cheese in double boiler; add all remaining ingredients. Serve in a chafing dish. Yield: 20 servings.

Mrs. Don Josephson
Polo, Ill.

CHICKEN LIVER PATE

12 slices bacon, cut up
4 tbsp. butter
1 lb. chicken livers
½ c. coarsely diced onion
2 sm. cloves of garlic, sliced
½ tsp. rubbed sage
½ tsp. marjoram
½ tsp. basil
½ c. chicken stock
4 hard-cooked eggs
1 tsp. salt
¼ tsp. pepper
½ tsp. rubbed thyme

Fry bacon until crisp; remove drippings. Add butter to pan with livers and bacon; saute for about 5 minutes. Add onion and garlic; cook for 2 minutes longer. Remove from heat. Put all ingredients in electric blender. Blend until smooth; chill. Serve with crackers. Yield: 8 servings.

Sylvia V. Hess
Westchester, Ill.

LIVER DIP

1 pkg. chicken livers or ½ lb. calves liver
2 lge. onions
1 c. butter
5 hard-cooked eggs
1 c. mayonnaise

Saute liver and onions in butter. Put liver, onions and eggs through food chopper. Add mayonnaise; stir.

Catherine S. Bradley
Aliquippa, Pa.

LIVERWURST-BEER DIP

1 lb. liverwurst, mashed
1 8-oz. pkg. cream cheese, softened
1 tbsp. Worcestershire sauce
½ c. sour cream
½ tsp. salt
¼ tsp. garlic powder
½ c. beer

Bring all ingredients to room temperature; combine all ingredients except beer. Gradually add beer for desired consistency. Serve with chips, crackers, raw vegetables or sliced party rye. Yield: 3 cups.

Mrs. Alvin F. Fowl
Glendale, Ariz.

TANGY TONGUE DIP

1 6-oz. can finely chopped tongue
1 c. grated sharp Cheddar cheese
¼ c. beer or ale
½ tsp. Tabasco sauce
¼ tsp. salt
¼ tsp. prepared horseradish
¼ c. mayonnaise

Combine tongue and cheese. Stir in beer, Tabasco sauce, salt, horseradish and mayonnaise. Yield: 1 cup.

Photograph for this recipe on page 67 .

CLAM DIP

1 8-oz. pkg. cream cheese
3 to 4 tbsp. mayonnaise
¼ c. finely diced celery
2 tbsp. finely cut canned pimento, drained
1 tsp. horseradish
1 sm. can clams, drained
Salt to taste
1 tsp. grated onion or onion juice

Cream cheese with mayonnaise; add all remaining ingredients. Serve with chips or crackers. Yield: 12 servings.

Mrs. Jane Golden
New Caney, Tex.

CLAM DIP

1 can clams
1 8-oz. pkg. cream cheese
1 ½ tsp. lemon juice
½ tsp. salt
Dash of pepper
Garlic powder to taste

Drain clams; reserve 1/3 cup juice. Soften cheese; add all remaining ingredients. Heat. Serve with crackers, potato or corn chips.

Mrs. Frank T. Gamec
Jonesboro, Ark.

CLAM DIP OR SPREAD

1 10-oz. can minced clams
1 8-oz. pkg. cream cheese
½ tsp. onion salt
⅛ tsp. pepper

Drain clams; reserve 2 to 4 tablespoons juice. Soften cream cheese in small bowl; add clam juice until mixture is of desired consistency; Add onion salt and pepper; beat until smooth. Stir in clams. Yield: 2 cups.

Dana Ray Owens
Eldorado, Tex.

BROILED CRAB DIP

1 egg white
½ c. salad dressing
1 7-oz. can crab meat
Salt and pepper to taste

Beat egg white until stiff; add all remaining ingredients. Pour into baking dish. Broil for 3 minutes or until light brown. Stir. Repeat process until desired consistency is obtained.

Jane Cline
Okanogan, Wash.

HOT CRAB-CHEESE DIP

2 lb. chilled Velveeta cheese, grated
1 ½ c. mayonnaise
½ c. sour cream
¾ c. chopped chives
3 cans crab meat

Melt cheese in a double boiler with mayonnaise and sour cream; add chives and crab. Serve hot in chafing dish with assorted crackers or toasted rounds. Yield: 20 servings.

Mrs. Theodore Peters
La Canada, Calif.

CRAB-CHEESE DIP

1 8-oz. pkg. cream cheese
⅓ to ¼ c. light cream or milk
2 tsp. lemon juice
1 to 1 ½ tsp. Worcestershire sauce
1 clove of garlic, minced
Salt and pepper to taste
1 6 ½ to 7 ½-oz. can crab or 1 c. flaked crab meat

Whip cream cheese; gradually add cream. Beat until smooth. Add lemon juice, Worcestershire sauce, garlic, salt and pepper. Remove bony bits from crab meat; snip into fine pieces. Stir into creamed mixture; chill. Yield: 1 1/2 cups.

Mrs. Sally Hildebrand
Enumclaw, Wash.

SNAPPY CRAB DIP

1 6 ½-oz. can crab meat
½ c. dairy sour cream
½ tsp. Tabasco sauce
1 tsp. lemon juice
¼ tsp. prepared horseradish
½ tsp. salt

Combine crab meat and sour cream. Stir in Tabasco sauce, lemon juice, horseradish and salt. Yield: 1 cup.

Photograph for this recipe on page 67.

DEVILED CRAB DIP

1 6 ½-oz. can crabmeat
2 hard-cooked eggs, chopped
½ c. mayonnaise
1 tbsp. lemon juice
½ tsp. mustard
Dash of Tabasco sauce (opt.)

Drain, bone and flake crab meat; may be cut finer with scissors. Add eggs. Blend all remaining ingredients; add to crab mixture. Serve as dip with potato chips or crackers or spread on small rounds of buttered bread. Yield: 1 cup.

Mary Alice Foster
Gary, Ind.

SEAFOOD DIP

1 can lobster, shrimp or crab
1 8-oz. pkg. cream cheese
2 tsp. chili sauce
2 tsp. horseradish
⅓ c. mayonnaise
1 tsp. lemon juice
Salt to taste

Cut seafood into small pieces; add to softened cream cheese with all remaining ingredients. Mix well.

Mrs. Hugh C. Higley
Menominee, Mich.

COTTAGE CHEESE-SHRIMP DIP

½ lb. cooked or 1 5 ½-oz. can shrimp
1 pkg. cottage cheese
3 tbsp. chili sauce
½ tsp. onion juice
½ tsp. lemon juice
¼ tsp. Worcestershire sauce
4 tbsp. milk or cream

Finely chop shrimp; combine with cottage cheese. Stir in chili sauce, onion juice, lemon juice and Worcestershire sauce. Gradually beat in milk until mixture reaches desired dipping consistency. Yield: 1 3/4 cups.

Mrs. G. L. Melody
Jasper, Ala.

SHRIMP DIP

1 can tomato soup
2 3-oz. pkg. cream cheese
1 tbsp. unflavored gelatin
1 tbsp. water
1 tbsp. chopped onion
1 tbsp. chopped green pepper
1 lge. can shrimp, mashed
Dash of garlic salt
1 pt. mayonnaise

Heat soup until bubbly. Add cream cheese; stir until well blended and smooth. Dissolve gelatin in water; add to soup mixture. Add onion, pepper and shrimp; cool. Add garlic salt and mayonnaise. This also makes a delicious sandwich filling which may be frozen. Yield: 16 servings.

Mrs. C. O. Littleton
Jackson, Miss.

CURRIED SHRIMP DIP

1 8-oz. pkg. cream cheese, softened
Pinch of salt
⅓ c. sour cream
1 tbsp. mayonnaise
½ tsp. onion juice
2 tsp. lemon juice
½ tsp. Worcestershire sauce
¾ c. cooked chopped shrimp
Curry powder to taste

Blend cream cheese, salt, sour cream and mayonnaise. Add all remaining ingredients; chill. Yield: 2 cups.

Mrs. Margaret Green
Edwards AFB, Calif.

SHRIMP DIP

1 c. sour cream
¾ c. canned drained shrimp
1 tbsp. mayonnaise
1 tsp. Tabasco sauce
2 tbsp. catsup
Dash of salt and pepper

Blend all ingredients thoroughly. Chill slightly and serve with assorted crackers. Yield: 2 cups.

Mrs. Nancy Murphy Mashburn
Paris, Tex.

HOT SHRIMP-CHEESE DIP

12 oz. cream cheese
¾ c. light cream
Juice of 2 cloves of garlic
2 tbsp. catsup
Dash of cayenne pepper
Dash of Tabasco sauce
1 tsp. paprika
2 sm. cans shrimp, drained and shredded
Juice of ½ lemon

Moisten cheese with cream. Add all remaining ingredients; serve bubbling hot from chafing dish. Yield: 50 servings.

Mrs. Tom Gartman
Brookhaven, Miss.

ALBUQUERQUE DIP

1 qt. cottage cheese
¼ c. milk
1 pkg. dry onion soup mix

Mix all ingredients in blender or with electric mixer until cheese is smooth. Yield: 6 servings.

Mabel Moorhouse
Belen, N.M.

CARROT DIP

3 med. carrots
3 med. dill pickles
1 sm. jar pimento
2 green peppers
1 sm. onion
3 hard-cooked eggs, chopped
Salt and pepper to taste
Mayonnaise

Grind carrots, pickles, pimento, peppers and onion together. Drain on paper towels or cheesecloth. Add eggs, salt and pepper and enough mayonnaise to hold mixture together.

Mrs. Jane Wisdom
Hillsboro, Ill.

CONFETTI SNACK DIP

1 pkg. dry onion soup mix
1 pt. sour cream
¼ c. finely chopped green pepper
¼ c. finely chopped cucumbers
¼ c. finely diced pimento

Combine all ingredients. Chill for at least an hour to blend flavors. Serve with assorted crackers or chips. Yield: 2 1/4 cups.

Mrs. Vada Belle Zellner
San Antonio, Tex.

COPONATINI

2 med. eggplants, cubed
Cooking oil
1 can tomato sauce
1 lge. onion, finely chopped
2 stalks celery, finely chopped
1 clove of garlic, finely chopped
10 green olives, quartered
1 tsp. vinegar
Sugar and salt to taste

Soak eggplants in 1 tablespoon salt for about 30 minutes; squeeze out lightly. Saute in hot oil until tender; add tomato sauce. Saute onion, celery, garlic and olives in a small amount of oil; add vinegar. Combine all ingredients with sugar and salt; cook until flavors are blended. Serve on crackers or with meats. Yield: 50 servings.

Mrs. Ted Trotter
Independence, La.

CUCUMBER DIP

1 8-oz. pkg. cream cheese
¼ to ½ c. unpeeled shredded cucumber, drained
¼ tsp. Worcestershire sauce
Dash of garlic salt

Blend cream cheese and cucumber until smooth. Add Worcestershire sauce and garlic salt; mix well. Serve with potato chips.

Mrs. Grace E. Kukuk
Negaunee, Mich.

DIET DIP

1 pt. cottage cheese
1 envelope French onion soup mix
1 tbsp. lemon juice
Few drops of Tabasco sauce (opt.)

Cream cottage cheese with electric mixer or in blender; add all remaining ingredients. Cover and chill for several hours to soften the onion bits. Serve with crackers, fresh vegetables or potato chips.

Nelle G. Tramp
Merino, Colo.

DILL DIP

12 oz. sour cream
¼ c. mild salad dressing
1 ½ tsp. sugar
1 tsp. salt
¼ tsp. garlic salt
1 tsp. chopped parsley
1 tbsp. plus 1 tsp. dill weed

Blend all ingredients thoroughly. Let season in refrigerator for at least 2 hours. Serve with potato chips, crackers or raw vegetables. Yield: 1 3/4 cups.

Mrs. C. Rodney Stoltz
Watertown, S.D.

DILL DIP

⅔ c. mayonnaise
⅔ c. sour cream
1 tbsp. shredded green onions
1 tbsp. whole parsley
1 tsp. dill weed
1 tsp. Beau Monde seasoning

Blend all ingredients. Set aside for several hours so flavors will blend. NOTE: Do not use fresh onions and parsley.

Mrs. Joan Ragan
Danville, Calif.

HOMAS BI THINEH

1 1-lb. 3-oz. can garbanzo peas, well drained
1 tsp. salt
1 clove of garlic, crushed
½ c. olive or salad oil
1 tbsp. lemon juice
Chopped parsley
Paprika

Put peas, salt and garlic into a blender and thoroughly blend. Add a little oil at a time until mixture is the consistency of soft mashed potatoes; add lemon juice. Garnish with parsley and paprika. Serve with crisp crackers. Yield: 12 servings.

Mrs. Jeanne Bundi
Van Buren, O.

HOT MUSHROOM DIP

1 lb. fresh mushrooms
1 clove of garlic, crushed
1 sm. onion, grated
2 tbsp. butter
¼ tsp. monosodium glutamate
⅛ tsp. mustard
½ tsp. soy sauce
⅛ tsp. paprika
⅛ tsp. salt
⅛ tsp. pepper
1 tbsp. flour
1 c. sour cream

Brown mushrooms, garlic and onion in butter. Combine monosodium glutamate, mustard, soy sauce, paprika, salt, pepper and flour with a small amount of cream to make a paste; add to mushroom mixture. Blend in remaining cream; stir over low heat until thickened. Do not boil. Serve with crackers or chips. Yield: 2 cups.

Annie Lillian Brewton
Pensacola, Fla.

MOCK OYSTER ROCKEFELLER

1 onion, finely chopped
Margarine
1 lge. can mushrooms, drained and finely chopped
1 can cream of mushroom soup
1 pkg. chopped broccoli, cooked
1 roll garlic cheese
Hot sauce to taste

Saute onion in margarine; add all remaining ingredients. Serve hot on crackers. Yield: 25-30 servings.

Mrs. Lucille Gelpi
Hahnville, La.

ONION SOUP DIP

½ pt. sour cream
1 pt. cottage cheese
½ c. mayonnaise
1 pkg. dry onion soup mix
2 tbsp. chopped parsley

Combine sour cream, cottage cheese and mayonnaise; mix well. Blend in soup mix and parsley. Chill and serve with crackers, melba toast or potato chips. Yield: 3 1/2 cups.

Mrs. Eleanor Zbornik
Arlington, Iowa

SPAGHETTI SAUCE DIP

1 pt. sour cream
1 pkg. dry spaghetti sauce mix

Blend cream and sauce mix. Serve with corn or potato chips.

Mrs. Nancy W. Piner
Smyrna, N.C.

PRAIRIE FIRE DIP

1 qt. pinto beans, cooked and sieved
½ lb. Provalone cheese
4 jalapeno peppers, chopped
1 clove of garlic, chopped
½ lb. butter
1 tsp. jalapeno pepper juice
2 tbsp. minced onion

Blend all ingredients; heat over hot water until cheese is melted. Serve hot from chafing dish with fried tortillas or potato chips.

Mrs. Troy Fort
Lovington, N.M.

CAPER SAUCE FOR COLD LOBSTER

½ c. small curd cottage cheese
⅓ c. milk
½ c. mayonnaise
Few grains of salt
⅛ tsp. paprika
⅛ tsp. dry mustard
3 tbsp. caper liquid
1 tbsp. anchovy paste
Whole capers

Blend cottage cheese in blender with milk until mixture is consistency of whipped cream. Add all remaining ingredients except capers. Blend for 2 minutes on high speed. Pile into a bowl and chill. Garnish with whole capers. Cut lobster into bite-sized pieces; insert toothpick into each piece. Serve on chipped ice centered with the sauce bowl. Yield: 12 servings.

Willie B. Barry
Laredo, Tex.

CUCUMBER SAUCE

1 c. peeled finely chopped cucumbers
½ tsp. salt
1 tbsp. sugar
1 tbsp. cider vinegar
⅛ tsp. ground white pepper
½ c. heavy cream, whipped

Combine cucumbers and salt; cover. Refrigerate for at least 1 hour. Drain; add sugar, vinegar and white pepper. Fold in cream just before serving. Yield: 1 1/2 cups.

Mrs. Lou John
Clarissa, Minn.

LOBSTER SAUCE

1 c. lobster meat
½ tsp. salt
⅛ tsp. pepper
1 tsp. Worcestershire sauce
2 tbsp. cooking Sherry
2 c. medium cream sauce

Combine lobster, salt, pepper, Worcestershire sauce and Sherry with cream sauce. Heat thoroughly. Serve with rolls or as a dip for toast. Yield: 4 servings.

Barbara A. West
Portsmouth, Va.

REMOULADE SAUCE

2 c. mayonnaise
2 hard-cooked eggs, sieved
4 tbsp. apple cider vinegar
1 tsp. mustard
½ tsp. salt
1 tsp. parsley flakes

Blend all ingredients; chill. Sauce may be stored for several weeks if covered and refrigerated. Serve with boiled shrimp or crab meat. NOTE: Two tablespoons apple cider vinegar and 2 tablespoons tarragon vinegar may be used in place of 4 tablespoons apple cider vinegar. Yield: 8 servings.

Ruth Bailey
Houston, Tex.

REMOULADE SAUCE

¼ c. vinegar
1 ½ tbsp. mustard
Horseradish to taste
½ tsp. salt
¼ tsp. cayenne pepper
1 ½ tsp. paprika
1 tbsp. catsup
½ clove of garlic, crushed
½ c. salad oil
¼ c. finely minced green onions and tops
¼ c. finely chopped celery

Combine vinegar, mustard, horseradish, salt, pepper, paprika, catsup and garlic. Add salad oil; beat vigorously. Add green onions and celery; pour over boiled seasoned shrimp and serve. Yield: 6-8 servings.

Mrs. Evelyn B. Fontenot
Church Point, La.

GARNISHES AND ACCOMPANIMENTS

RECIPE FOR ATHENIA MUSHROOMS ON PAGE 88

BAKED BROWN BREAD

1 pt. milk
½ tsp. salt
½ c. sugar
½ c. dark molasses
1 tsp. (heaping) soda
½ c. white flour
2 c. graham flour

Combine all ingredients except graham flour; beat until smooth. Add graham flour; beat again. Pour into prepared loaf pan. Bake at 350 degrees for 45 minutes.

Shirley Morrill
Dekalb Junction, N.Y.

BROWN BREAD

1 pkg. seeded raisins
2 c. boiling water
2 tbsp. soda
3 c. sifted flour
1 c. sugar
Pinch of salt
1 egg

Soak raisins in boiling water; let stand overnight. Add soda to raisin liquid. Combine all ingredients; mix well. Pour into two prepared loaf pans. Bake at 325 degrees for 1 hour.

Mrs. Watson Castle
Williamstown, N.Y.

PLAIN BROWN BREAD

2 c. whole wheat flour
⅔ c. brown sugar
1 ⅔ tsp. soda
⅔ c. white flour
⅔ tsp. salt
1 ½ tsp. cream of tartar
2 c. sour milk

Combine dry ingredients; stir in milk. Turn into oiled bread pan. Bake at 350 degrees for 50 to 60 minutes. NOTE: Sweet milk with 2 tablespoons vinegar added may be used for sour milk. Yield: 12 servings.

Mrs. Henry Erdmann
Little Valley, N.Y.

CRUSTY CHEESE BREAD

1 pkg. active dry yeast
¼ c. warm water
3 c. sifted flour
1 tbsp. sugar
1 tsp. salt
⅔ c. warm mashed potatoes
⅓ c. melted butter or margarine
1 c. shredded Cheddar cheese
2 eggs
¼ c. scalded milk

Dissolve yeast in warm water. Sift flour, sugar and salt. Combine potatoes, butter, cheese, eggs and milk and beat until well blended; add yeast mixture and dry ingredients. Turn dough onto well floured surface; knead for 8 minutes or until smooth and satiny. Place in greased bowl and cover; let rise for 1 hour or until doubled. Punch down and knead gently on floured surface for 2 minutes. Shape into 20-inch roll and place in well greased 9-inch ring mold. Pinch edges to seal. Cover; let rise until doubled in size. Bake at 375 degrees for 25 to 30 minutes. Yield: 25-30 servings.

Mrs. Mode Gregory
Jonesboro, Ark.

GARLIC BREAD

Sliced rye bread
Butter
Garlic salt
Paprika

Place rye bread on baking sheet; spread with butter. Sprinkle with garlic salt and paprika. Toast under broiler.

Gail Marie Boleng
West Stockbridge, Mass.

DILL BREAD

1 pkg. dry yeast
½ c. warm water
2 tbsp. sugar
1 tsp. salt
½ tsp. soda
2 tbsp. dill seed
1 tbsp. instant minced onion
1 c. warm creamed cottage cheese,
1 egg
3 c. flour

(Continued on next page)

Dissolve yeast in warm water. Combine all dry ingredients except flour. Blend cottage cheese and egg; add dry ingredients. Combine mixture with yeast. Add a little flour at a time; mix well. Let rise until doubled in bulk. Punch dough down; divide into two parts. Place in greased loaf pans; let rise. Bake at 350 degrees for 35 to 40 minutes. Brush warm bread with butter and sprinkle with salt. Yield: 2 loaves.

Kitty Steele Williamson
Beckley, W. Va.

OLIVE-NUT BREAD

2 ½ c. sifted flour
⅓ c. sugar
4 tsp. baking powder
½ tsp. salt
1 egg, beaten
1 c. milk
1 c. sliced stuffed green olives
1 c. broken walnuts

Sift dry ingredients. Combine egg and milk; add to flour mixture, stirring just until moistened. Stir in olives and nuts. Turn into greased 8 x 1 1/2-inch round baking dish. Bake at 350 degrees for 45 minutes or until done. Remove from pan; cool on rack. NOTE: Add 1 or 2 tablespoons chopped pimento to batter for holiday color.

Catherine Tatum
Hampton, Ark.

ONION BREAD

1 pkg. yeast
¼ c. warm water
1 c. cottage cheese
2 tbsp. sugar
1 tbsp. onion flakes
1 tbsp. soft butter
1 ½ tsp. dill seed
1 tsp. salt
¼ tsp. soda
1 egg
2 ¼ to 2 ½ c. flour

Dissolve yeast in warm water. Heat cottage cheese thoroughly. Combine all ingredients; beat well. Let rise in bowl until doubled in size. Stir down; place in well greased pans. Let rise again. Bake at 350 degrees for 55 to 60 minutes. Butter top and sprinkle with salt while hot. Sprinkle with caraway seed,if desired.

Mrs. David W. Phelps
Walworth, N.Y.

PEANUT BUTTER BREAD

2 c. sifted flour
⅓ c. sugar
3 tsp. baking powder
1 tsp. salt
¾ c. peanut butter
1 egg, slightly beaten
1 c. milk

Sift dry ingredients; cut in peanut butter. Combine egg and milk; stir into first mixture lightly. Turn into well greased 9 x 5 x 3-inch loaf pan. Bake at 350 degrees for 1 hour or until done. Yield: 1 loaf.

Rose Collier
Elwood, Ind.

SHREDDED WHEAT BREAD

2 ¼ c. lukewarm water
3 shredded wheat biscuits, crumbled
1 pkg. dry yeast
2 tsp. salt
3 tbsp. shortening
½ c. dark molasses
5 c. flour, sifted

Pour 2 cups water over shredded wheat. Dissolve yeast in remaining water. Add yeast, salt, shortening and molasses to wheat biscuits; mix well. Add flour and mix thoroughly. Knead lightly on well floured board. Place in greased bowl; cover bowl with clean cloth. Let rise in warm place for 2 hours. Divide into two parts; shape into loaves. Cover and set in warm place. Let rise for 2 hours longer. Bake at 350 degrees for 45 minutes. Yield: 2 loaves.

Mrs. Frank V. Young
Columbia, Ky.

RUSKS

2 c. milk
½ c. sugar
Butter
6 c. flour
1 cake yeast
2 eggs, beaten
½ c. sugar

Scald milk; add sugar and small piece of butter. Cool to lukewarm. Stir in flour and yeast; let rise overnight. Blend in eggs, 1 pat of butter and sugar. Let rise again; form into small biscuits. Bake at 350 degrees for 30 minutes.

Ruth Colburn
Fredonia, N.Y.

HERB BUNS

1 pkg. dry yeast
⅓ c. warm water
2 tbsp. sugar
¾ tsp. salt
1 tsp. caraway seed
½ tsp. crumbled leaf sage
¼ tsp. nutmeg
¾ c. lukewarm water
2 ½ c. flour
1 egg
2 tbsp. shortening, softened

Dissolve yeast in warm water. Add sugar, salt, caraway seed, sage, nutmeg, lukewarm water and one-half the flour. Beat until smooth; add egg, shortening and remaining flour. Beat until smooth. Cover with damp cloth and let rise in warm place until doubled in bulk. Stir down; spoon into muffin pans. Let rise until dough reaches top of muffin pans. Bake at 400 degrees for 15 to 20 minutes. Yield: 12 servings.

Mrs. Marten Schutte, Sr.
Watersmeet, Mich.

SCOTCH SCONES

2 c. sifted flour
2 tsp. baking powder
¼ tsp. soda
½ tsp. salt
⅓ c. butter
1 egg
½ c. buttermilk

Sift dry ingredients; cut in butter. Combine egg and buttermilk; add to dry ingredients. Stir until moistened; knead ten times. Divide dough in half; roll each piece into 6-inch circle. Cut into six wedges. Place on greased cookie sheet. Bake at 425 degrees for 12 to 15 minutes.

Mrs. Lola M. Wright
Fredonia, Kans.

CHEESE BISCUITS

½ lb. butter or margarine
½ lb. grated cheese
2 c. flour
¼ tsp. salt
¼ tsp. baking powder

Blend butter and cheese. Add flour, salt and baking powder; knead slightly. Roll out; cut into desired shapes. Bake at 400 degrees for 7 to 8 minutes.

Mrs. Mae R. Dowless
Aberdeen, N.C.

ORANGE TEA BISCUITS

20 sugar cubes
½ sm. can frozen orange juice
1 pkg. prepared dinner biscuits

Soak sugar cubes in orange juice until well saturated. Place biscuits in greased 8 x 8 x 2-inch baking dish. Press 2 sugar cubes into center of each biscuit. Bake in preheated 375 degree oven for 10 to 12 minutes or until orange syrup is golden brown. Yield: 5 servings.

Mrs. Ruth H. Methvin
McArthur, Calif.

SAUSAGE BISCUITS

½ lb. sausage
2 c. self-rising flour
¼ c. shortening
¾ c. buttermilk

(Continued on next page)

Fry sausage; drain and crumble. Place flour in mixing bowl; cut in shortening. Add buttermilk; stir until blended. Stir in crumbled sausage. Knead on floured board ten times; roll out to 1/2-inch thickness. Cut into desired shapes. Place on ungreased cookie sheet. Bake at 450 degrees for 10 minutes or until golden brown.

Annie Johnston
China Grove, N.C.

SWEET POTATO BISCUITS

3 c. flour
¾ c. sugar
4 ½ tsp. (rounded) baking powder
1 ½ tsp. (rounded) salt
½ c. shortening
2 ¼ c. cooked mashed sweet potatoes

Sift dry ingredients; cut in shortening. Add potatoes with enough water to obtain consistency of dough; shape into biscuits. Bake at 400 degrees until done.

Eleanor O'Day
Seaford, Del.

TOMATO-CHEESE BISCUITS

2 c. sifted flour
3 tsp. baking powder
1 tsp. salt
3 tbsp. shortening
1 c. grated American cheese
3 tbsp. chopped parsley or dry parsley flakes
¾ c. tomato juice

Sift flour, baking powder and salt; cut in shortening. Add cheese and parsley; mix well. Add tomato juice. Knead lightly on floured board for 30 seconds. Roll 1/2-inch thick; cut. Bake at 450 degrees for 10 to 12 minutes.

Mrs. Patricia Runyon
Washington, D.C.

BLINTZES

1 loaf white bread
1 lb. cottage cheese
Salt and pepper or sugar

Trim crusts from bread. Roll each slice with rolling pin until it becomes dough-like. Place 1 heaping tablespoon of cottage cheese on each piece; sprinkle with salt and pepper or sugar. Roll bread; secure firmly by pressing with finger. Fry in fat until golden brown. Serve hot. NOTE: Cooked chopped liver may be substituted for cottage cheese if desired. Yield: 10-12 servings.

Mrs. Frances Aikin
Long Beach, N.Y.

BREAD STICKS

2 c. self-rising flour
1 tbsp. sugar
½ tsp. soda
⅓ c. shortening
¾ c. buttermilk

Sift dry ingredients; add shortening and milk. Dough will be stiff. Roll out onto floured board to 1/2-inch thickness. Cut into slices 1 inch wide and 2 inches long. Deep fry at 375 degrees until brown, turning only once.

Mrs. Addy Pell
Patrick AFB, Fla.

BREAD STICKS

½ pkg. yeast
2 tbsp. warm water
½ c. shortening
6 tbsp. scalded milk
2 c. flour
¾ tsp. salt
½ tsp. sugar

Dissolve yeast in warm water. Melt shortening in scalded milk; cool to lukewarm. Add to yeast. Sift flour, salt and sugar into large bowl. Form well in center; add all liquid at once and beat until dough comes away from sides of bowl. Cover with cloth; set in warm place until doubled in bulk. Punch down; pinch off walnut-sized pieces. Roll between hands into pencil-like strips about 6 inches long. Lay on ungreased baking sheet; let dry for 10 minutes. Bake at 325 degrees for 25 minutes.

Fern Erickson
Eagle, Colo.

CARAWAY SALT STICKS

2 c. sifted flour
1 tsp. baking soda
¼ tsp. salt
⅓ c. shortening
½ c. milk
¼ c. vinegar
1 c. crumbled Rice Krispies
1 ½ tsp. caraway seed
1 tsp. salt
Evaporated milk

Blend dry ingredients with shortening, milk and vinegar; knead lightly. Roll dough into 16-inch roll; divide into sixteen 1-inch balls. Roll each ball into 6-inch stick. Dip each stick into evaporated milk; coat with crumbs. Place on greased cookie sheet. Bake at 450 degrees for 15 minutes. Yield: 16 sticks.

Mrs. Katherine Niemi
South Range, Mich.

SAVORY CHEESE LOAF

1 1-lb. loaf unsliced bread
½ lb. cheese, grated
1 ½ tbsp. chopped onion
1 tsp. Worcestershire sauce
¼ tsp. celery seed
4 tbsp. butter, melted

Trim all crusts except bottom from bread. Slice into 1 1/2-inch squares, cutting almost to bottom crust. Combine remaining ingredients. Spread between bread squares; brush tops and sides of bread with butter. Place on cookie sheet. Bake at 350 degrees for 20 to 25 minutes or until lightly browned. Serve hot. Yield: 8 servings.

Mrs. Clyde Davis
Williamsburg, Va.

PEANUT BUTTER STICKS

1 loaf white bread
1 ½ c. peanut butter
1 ¼ c. salad oil
½ c. sugar

Trim crusts from bread; cut each slice into five strips. Place crust and strips on baking sheet. Toast at 250 degrees for 2 hours, turning frequently. Blend peanut butter with salad oil and sugar. Remove crust and strips from oven; roll crust out into crumbs. Dip strips into peanut butter mixture; roll in crumbs. Yield: 8-10 servings.

Mrs. Jane C. Minge
Columbus, Miss.

SESAME-BREAD STICKS

1 can prepared biscuits
¼ c. butter, melted
Sesame seed

Roll biscuits into 7-inch strips; brush with butter and roll in sesame seed. Bake at 400 degrees for 10 minutes. Yield: 5-6 servings.

Mrs. Henry Steely
Cedartown, Ga.

SLAP STICKS

¼ c. butter or margarine
3 tsp. dry minced onion
⅔ c. grated sharp cheese
1 tsp. celery seed
Dash of salt
2 c. prepared biscuit mix
⅔ c. milk

Melt butter in shallow baking pan; sprinkle evenly with 2 teaspoons onion. Stir remaining onion, cheese, celery seed and salt into biscuit mix; add milk. Mix to a soft dough; stir vigorously, about 30 strokes. Knead lightly on floured board; roll into rectangle. Cut in half lengthwise; cut into 3 x 1-inch strips. Coat strips in butter mixture evenly; arrange in pan. Bake at 425 degrees for 15 minutes. Yield: 20 servings.

Mrs. Juanita Drescher
Ft. Polk, La.

CHEESE BUDS

½ lb. sharp Cheddar cheese, shredded
½ lb. margarine

(Continued on next page)

2 c. sifted flour
¼ tsp. red pepper
1 egg white, slightly beaten
Pecan halves

Blend cheese and margarine with mixer. Sift flour and pepper; gradually work into cheese mixture with spoon. Roll out to 1/2-inch thickness; cut into 1-inch rounds. Brush with egg white; top with pecans. Place on ungreased baking sheet. Bake at 425 degrees for 10 to 15 minutes. Yield: 8 dozen.

Mrs. C. C. Barnes
Lafayette, La.

CHEESE TIDBITS

1 c. flour
½ c. margarine
1 c. grated Cheddar cheese
⅛ tsp. salt
Dash of paprika
½ tsp. baking powder

Place all ingredients in bowl; blend well. Form into tiny balls; flatten slightly. Bake at 350 degrees for 15 minutes. NOTE: Watch carefully as cheese tends to burn.

Eve E. Ellis
Lafayette, La.

CHEESE STRAWS

1 lb. New York State aged cheese, grated
1 stick butter, melted
1 ½ c. flour
1 ½ tsp. baking powder
1 tsp. salt
¼ tsp. red pepper

Blend all ingredients; put through cookie press. Bake at 350 degrees for 12 minutes.

Mrs. Katrine Rogers
Fort Deposit, Ala.

FRIED CHEESE CANAPES

Fat
¼ lb. American cheese
2 tbsp. butter
½ c. flour
½ tsp. cayenne pepper
25 stuffed olives

Heat fat in fryer to 350 degrees. Combine cheese with butter; blend in flour and pepper. Flatten about 1 tablespoon mixture in palm of hand; place olive in center. Fold edges together; seal well. Fry for about 3 minutes; drain. Yield: 25 servings.

Mrs. John C. Foy
High Point, N.C.

CORN MEAL-CHEESE STRAWS

½ c. corn meal
1 c. flour
1 tsp. salt
½ c. butter
1 c. grated cheese
2 to 4 tbsp. milk

Sift meal, flour and salt; cut in butter. Stir in cheese. Add enough milk to combine mixture; knead gently. Roll to 1/8-inch thickness; cut into strips or shapes. Bake at 350 degrees for 12 minutes or until delicately browned. NOTE: One-fourth teaspoon ground red pepper and more cheese may be added for more spice. Yield: 3 dozen.

Mrs. Jean M. Hubbard
Carthage, N.C.

CHEESE PUFFS A LA CONVERSATION

1 3-oz. pkg. cream cheese
¼ lb. sharp Cheddar cheese
½ c. butter
2 egg whites, stiffly beaten
1 loaf firm unsliced bread

Combine cheeses and butter; cook in double boiler until blended. Fold in egg whites. Trim crust from bread; cut into cubes. Dip cubes into cheese mixture; place on baking sheet. Bake at 400 degrees for 12 to 15 minutes. NOTE: These puffs may be made ahead of time and frozen. Yield: 42 servings.

Mrs. George Flack
Metamore, O.

EGG AND CHEDDAR PUFFS

4 eggs, beaten
1/3 c. flour
1 tsp. baking powder
1/2 tsp. salt
1 tbsp. chopped onion
1/2 lb. Cheddar cheese, cut into 1/4-in. cubes
Shortening

Combine eggs with dry ingredients; add onion and cheese. Drop from spoon into hot shortening forming 3-inch patties. Brown slowly over low heat for about 2 minutes on each side.

Mrs. Richard Hall
Paramount, Calif.

PUFFED CRACKERS

Crackers
Ice water
Melted butter

Soak crackers in ice water for 8 to 10 minutes; drain. Place in greased pan; brush with seasoned melted butter. Bake at 450 degrees for 10 minutes. Reduce heat to 350 degrees; bake for 20 minutes longer. NOTE: Crackers may be sprinkled with grated cheese, nuts or caraway seed before baking.

Mrs. Mildred Lawson
Lander, Wyo.

CANDIED APPLE SLICES

6 apples, pared and cored
1/2 c. red cinnamon candies
2 c. sugar
1 c. water
Red food coloring

Slice apples 1/3-inch thick. Cook candies and sugar in water until melted; add coloring and apples. Cook slowly for 10 minutes or until transparent but not soft. Chill.

Mrs. Joe Ynfante
Kirbyville, Tex.

FRIED APPLE RINGS

Tart apples
Butter
Cooking oil
Brown sugar

Wash apples; core and slice crosswise into 1/4-inch pieces. Fry slowly in skillet until tender and lightly browned on both sides, using about 1 tablespoon butter and 1 tablespoon cooking oil for each apple. Sprinkle with brown sugar. Serve around platter with pork roast or duck.

Mrs. Leonard Klug
Barnesville, Minn.

GLAZED APPLES

5 med. cooking apples, pared and cored
1/2 c. light corn syrup
1 c. sugar
3/4 c. water
Few drops of red food coloring

Place apples in cooking utensil large enough for all apples to sit flat. Pour mixture of remaining ingredients over apples. Simmer until liquid is syrupy and apples are soft, turning once. Serve with turkey and dressing. Yield: 5 servings.

Patricia Fulford
Clanton, Ala.

GLAZED APPLE SLICES

2 lb. cooking apples
2 c. brown sugar
Juice and grated rind of 1 lemon
1/4 tsp. ground nutmeg
1/8 tsp. ground cloves
1/2 tsp. ground cinnamon
1 1/2 c. water

Pare, core and slice apples; arrange in shallow baking dish. Combine 1 cup sugar, lemon juice, rind and spices with water; pour over apples. Bake at 375 degrees for 25 minutes. Sprinkle top with remaining sugar. Broil under low heat for 5 minutes. Serve warm or chilled. Yield: 6 servings.

Mrs. Paul Bishop
Roan Mountain, Tenn.

APRICOT BALLS

1 lb. dried apricots
Rind of 1 orange
Rind of ½ lemon
Juice of 2 oranges
Juice of ½ lemon
2 c. sugar
2 c. chopped pecans or canned coconut (opt.)
1 lb. box powdered sugar

Grind apricots, orange and lemon rinds; place in saucepan. Add juices and stir; add granulated sugar. Cook over low heat, stirring constantly, until sugar is dissolved. Boil for 10 minutes, stirring constantly; cool. Add nuts; form into balls and roll in sifted powdered sugar. Yield: 50 balls.

Hal Johnson Douglas
Memphis, Tenn.

BANANAS AU RHUM

¼ c. butter
6 ripe bananas, halved
¼ c. (packed) brown sugar
Cinnamon
Rum

Melt butter in top pan of chafing dish over direct heat; add bananas. Sprinkle with one-half of sugar and a dash of cinnamon. Cook until bananas are lightly browned. Turn and sprinkle with sugar and cinnamon. Cook until soft; add rum and ignite. Serve with the liquid as accompaniment for pork or other meats. Yield: 4 servings.

Mrs. Cathy Farly
Tempe, Ariz.

CURRIED FRUIT BAKE

1 No. 2 ½ can mixed fruit, cut and drained
½ c. Maraschino cherries
2 bananas, cut into large pieces
1 c. black pitted cherries
¼ c. melted margarine
½ c. brown sugar
2 tbsp. cornstarch
1 tbsp. curry powder

Combine fruits and melted margarine. Combine sugar, cornstarch and curry powder; add to fruits and mix lightly. Pour into buttered 2-quart casserole. Bake at 350 degrees for 40 minutes. Yield: 8-10 servings.

Mary C. Riley
Seagoville, Tex.

STUFFED DILL PICKLES

4 lge. dill pickles
1 3-oz. pkg. cream cheese
Cream
Worcestershire sauce to taste
Crisp bacon bits or chopped pimento (opt.)

Cut ends from pickles; remove centers with apple corer or potato peeler. Soften cheese with cream; add Worcestershire sauce and bacon or pimento. Stuff pickles with cheese mixture. Chill for 2 to 4 hours. Cut into 1/2-inch slices.

Mrs. Juanita Goss
Avoca, Tex.

MARINATED FRUIT

1 cantaloupe, peeled and cubed
1 honeydew melon, peeled and cubed
2 pears, peeled and sliced
2 peaches, peeled and sliced
1 c. lemon juice concentrate
1 c. sugar
2 bananas, peeled and sliced

Combine cantaloupe, melon, pears, peaches and lemon concentrate; let stand for 30 minutes. Drain; reserve concentrate. Pack into a 1/2-gallon milk carton; sprinkle with sugar as it is packed. Marinate in refrigerator overnight. Cover bananas with concentrate; add to marinated fruit. Serve immediately. Yield: 10 servings.

Mrs. Alliene Allen
Fairfield, Tex.

CARAMELIZED PEACHES

½ c. crushed corn flakes
¼ c. chopped pecans
2 tbsp. brown sugar
2 tbsp. melted margarine
4 peach halves

Combine corn flakes, nuts, sugar and margarine; fill centers of peach halves. Place under broiler for 3 to 5 minutes. Yield: 4 servings.

Mrs. Kenneth J. Moore
Thomaston, Ga.

COCONUT PEACHES

3 tbsp. powdered sugar
Dash of nutmeg
½ c. sour cream
6 peach halves
Coconut flakes

Add sugar and nutmeg to sour cream. Place peaches in shallow baking dish; spoon mixture into peach halves. Sprinkle with coconut flakes. Broil until lightly browned. Yield: 6 servings.

Mrs. Dorothy West
Littlefield, Tex.

FILLED PEACHES

½ c. confectioners sugar
4 tbsp. sour cream
¼ tsp. nutmeg
4 peach halves
⅛ c. broken pecans
¼ c. flaked coconut

Blend sugar with sour cream and nutmeg; fill peach halves in casserole. Sprinkle with pecans and coconut. Broil until slightly brown. Yield: 4 servings.

Mrs. Jimmy E. Smith
Kress, Tex.

CURRIED PEARS

6 canned pear halves, drained
1 tbsp. curry powder
¾ c. brown sugar

Place pears on broiler pan rack. Combine curry powder and brown sugar; place in hollows of pears. Broil until sugar is bubbly; serve immediately. Yield: 6 servings.

Mrs. Betty Kirk Thomas
Arlington, Tex.

FERMENTED PRUNES

1 lb. prunes
Fruit juice
1 3-oz. pkg. Cream cheese
Salt
Chopped nuts (opt.)

Place prunes in 1/2-gallon jar; add water to cover one-third of the prunes. Cover entirely with fruit juice; let stand for 10 days in refrigerator. When ready to serve, split prunes and remove seed. Fill with cream cheese softened with a small amount of cream and salt; roll in chopped nuts. Yield: 35-45 servings.

Mrs. Frances Baker Bishop
Denton, Tex.

GOLDEN STUFFED PRUNES

24 lge. prunes
1 c. flaked coconut
½ c. crushed pineapple
2 tbsp. grated carrot
Salad dressing

Steam prunes; remove pits. Combine coconut, pineapple and carrot with enough salad dressing to hold together. Stuff prunes. Serve as a garnish. Yield: 6 servings.

Velma P. Ellis
Opp, Ala.

PICKLED PRUNES

12 lge. dried prunes
12 English walnut halves
⅔ c. vinegar
½ c. granulated sugar
1 stick cinnamon, 2-in. long
6 whole cloves

Partially cook prunes as directed on package; reserve juice. Cool. Remove pits; insert a walnut half. Press cut edges together. Combine vinegar, 1/3 cup prune juice and sugar. Boil for 5 minutes. Add cinnamon, cloves and prunes. Simmer until prunes are moderately soft. Cool; remove prunes from liquid. Refrigerate until ready to use. Place one prune on each fruit salad or use as a garnish on a dinner or luncheon plate. Yield: 12 servings.

Lucile K. Lawson
Hayfork, Calif.

PICKLED PRUNES

2 c. prunes
½ c. sugar
¼ c. cider vinegar
8 whole cloves
½ tsp. mustard seed
1 stick cinnamon

Cook prunes in water until boiling; reduce heat and simmer for 10 minutes. Add sugar, vinegar, cloves, mustard seed and cinnamon; cook for 5 minutes or until prunes are tender. Yield: 8-10 servings.

Mrs. Ella Adair
Tropie, Utah

DILL-ONION RINGS

1 lge. onion, thinly sliced into rings
½ c. sugar
2 tsp. salt
½ tsp. dill weed
½ c. white vinegar
¼ c. water

Place onion in small bowl or pack into a 2-cup jar. Combine sugar, salt, dill weed, vinegar and water in small saucepan; heat to boiling. Pour liquid over onion rings. Cover tightly and chill overnight. Yield: 2 cups.

Mrs. Andrew Calabrese
West Orange, N.J.

CREAM CHEESE PINEAPPLES

1 8-oz. pkg. cream cheese
½ c. thinly sliced stuffed olives
6 1 ½-in. sections celery, cut into thin strips

Divide cheese into six equal portions. Use a knife or spatula to mold each portion into the shape of a miniature pineapple; chill. Gently press olive slices into cream cheese shapes. Insert celery pieces in top. Yield: 6 servings.

Marina Economos
Sandstone, Minn.

FRENCH-FRIED ONIONS

½ lb. onions, sliced
1 egg
¾ to 1 c. flour
½ tsp. salt
½ c. milk
¼ tsp. baking powder (opt.)

Separate onions into rings. Combine egg, flour, salt and milk; blend well. Dip onions into batter; fry in hot fat for 2 minutes or until brown. Yield: 4-6 servings.

Mrs. Shirley Ann Boddie
Calvin, La.

STUFFED CELERY

2 ½ c. grated Cheddar cheese
2 tbsp. mayonnaise
1 sm. clove of garlic, finely chopped
1 can pimento, chopped
1 bunch celery

Blend cheese, mayonnaise, garlic and pimento. Clean celery stalks and remove some of the leaves from the outer stalks; trim off very wide stalk ends. Cut into 3-inch pieces, leaving end leaves for trimming. Chill in ice water for 1 hour if time permits. Drain and fill centers. Yield: 15-30 servings.

Mrs. D. J. Dear
Bay Springs, Miss.

GINGER ONIONS

1 No. 2 ½ or 3 can white onions or 16 uniform onions, cooked
4 tbsp. honey
2 tbsp. butter
1 tbsp. paprika
½ tsp. salt
¼ tsp. ginger

Place onions in buttered shallow baking dish. Cook honey, butter, paprika, salt and ginger for 5 minutes; pour over onions. Bake at 325 degrees for 10 minutes or until well glazed. Yield: 8 servings.

Mrs. Velma Shaffer
Little Rock, Ark.

SAVORY GOURMET ONIONS

5 or 6 med. onions, sliced
½ tsp. monosodium glutamate
½ tsp. sugar (opt.)
½ tsp. salt
½ tsp. pepper
¼ to ⅓ c. butter
¼ to ½ c. cooking Sherry (opt.)
2 to 4 tbsp. shredded Parmesan cheese

Season onion slices with monosodium glutamate, sugar, salt and pepper. Cook in butter for 5 to 8 minutes or until onions are barely tender. Stir to separate into rings. Add Sherry; cook quickly for 2 to 3 minutes. Sprinkle with cheese. Yield: 6 servings.

Mrs. Dora R. Wray
Richmond, Va.

ATHENIAN MUSHROOMS

½ lb. small mushrooms
½ c. lemon juice
⅔ c. olive oil
½ tsp. Tabasco sauce
1 tsp. salt
1 tsp. crushed tarragon leaves

Wipe mushrooms with a damp cloth; trim off bottom of stem and cut into halves lengthwise. Combine remaining ingredients; pour over mushrooms. Marinate in refrigerator overnight. Drain before serving. Yield: 2 cups.

Photograph for this recipe on page 77.

TOMATO ROSES

1 8-oz. pkg. cream cheese
1 tbsp. mayonnaise
6 sm. tomatoes, peeled

Thoroughly blend cream cheese with mayonnaise. Use a teaspoon to form petals with cheese mixture around each tomato to resemble a rose. Yield: 6 servings.

Dorothy Maltby
Muskegon, Mich.

APPLE SLICES

2 ⅔ c. sugar
2 c. vinegar
⅔ c. water
1 tsp. whole cloves
1 stick cinnamon
½ tsp. salt
6 drops red food coloring
6 lge. apples, pared and quartered

Combine all ingredients except apples; bring to a boil. Add apples; cook just until tender. Do not overcook. Seal in sterilized jars. Yield: 2 pints.

Mildred Christensen
Boscobel, Wisc.

CRAB APPLE PICKLES

2 c. sugar
2 c. water
1 stick cinnamon, broken
6 to 8 cloves
Red crab apples

Boil sugar and water in electric frying pan; add cinnamon and cloves. Boil for 5 minutes. Add layer of crab apples; boil carefully until tender. Place in pint jars; pour syrup over apples and seal.

Karen Jodock
Cooperstown, N.D.

CANTALOUPE PICKLES

2 med. cantaloupe
2 c. water
1 qt. white vinegar
2 sticks cinnamon, broken up
½ tsp. mace
15 whole cloves
4 c. sugar

Remove rind and seed from cantaloupe; cut flesh into 1 x 3-inch chunks. Bring water and vinegar to a rolling boil; add cinnamon. Put mace and cloves in cheesecloth bag; add to solution. Pour over cantaloupe. Let stand in refrigerator overnight. Drain solution from cantaloupe and bring to a rolling boil; add sugar, stirring until dissolved. Add cantaloupe chunks; cook for 20 to 30 minutes or until transparent. Remove spice bag; pack cantaloupe into sterilized jars. Add hot syrup; seal. Yield: 3 1/2 pints.

Mrs. Sallie Beville Fisher
Mechanicsville, Va.

SALAD CROUTONS

¼ c. butter or margarine
¼ tsp. celery salt
3 c. ready-to-eat cereal

Melt butter in large frypan. Blend in celery salt. Add cereal; stir lightly until well mixed. Cook for 5 minutes over low heat, stirring occasionally. Drain on absorbent paper. Serve warm sprinkled over chicken salad, served in petaled tomatoes. Yield: 3 cups.

Photograph for this recipe above.

CHERRY OLIVES

2 lb. fresh Bing cherries
1 c. vinegar
1 tbsp. sugar
3 c. water
3 tbsp. salt

Wash and pack cherries into sterilized jars. Combine remaining ingredients; heat just enough to dissolve salt and sugar. Cool; pour over cherries and seal jars. Yield: 6 pints.

Mrs. Patsy Howsley Mayer
Kermit, Tex.

CRANBERRY-APPLE RELISH

4 c. cranberries
2 apples, pared and cored
2 oranges, quartered and seeded
1 lemon, quartered and seeded
2 ½ c. sugar

Put cranberries, apples, oranges and lemon through food chopper. Add sugar; blend. Chill in refrigerator for several hours before serving. Will keep well in refrigerator for several weeks.

Mrs. Frances Detmer
Weeping Water, Nebr.

TEXAS PICKLED FIGS

3 qt. firm ripe figs
1 c. apple cider vinegar
6 c. sugar
1 c. water
2 tbsp. cinnamon sticks
1 tbsp. whole cloves

(Continued on next page)

Leave 1/4-inch stem on figs; cover figs with boiling water and let stand for 5 minutes. Mix vinegar, sugar and water. Break sticks into small pieces and tie loosely in small bag with cloves. Place spices with sugar mixture; bring to a boil. Add figs and bring to a boil; boil for 10 minutes. Remove from heat; let stand until next day. Boil for 10 minutes; let stand until next day. Boil for 10 minutes; remove spice bag and pack while hot into sterilized jars. Seal.

Mrs. Mary Carroll
Greenville, Tex.

BRANDIED PEACHES

Peeled peaches
Sugar

For every pound of peaches, use a pound of sugar. Layer peaches and sugar in jars; seal. Place jars in dark place; let stand for three months.

Ruth D. Jordan
Alexander City, Ala.

BAKED PEACH PICKLES

Whole cloves
Peeled peaches
1 pkg. stick cinnamon
5 pt. sugar
1 pt. vinegar

Stick 1 clove into each peach; break cinnamon over peaches. Pour sugar and vinegar over peaches. Bake at 375 to 400 degrees for 15 minutes or until bubbly. Reduce heat to 325 degrees; bake for 45 minutes longer. Fill 2-quart crock three-fourths full of peaches and juice; cover and let stand.

Mrs. Sue Chapman
Washta, Iowa

PEACH PICKLES

8 lb. small or medium peaches
2 tbsp. cloves
8 sticks cinnamon
4 c. sugar
1 c. vinegar
½ c. water

Wash and pare peaches. Tie cloves in thin white cloth; cook spices, sugar, vinegar and water for 5 minutes. Add layer of peaches; cook slowly for 5 to 10 minutes or until peaches change color. Remove peaches from syrup. Repeat until all peaches have been heated; return peaches to syrup and cook again for 5 to 10 minutes after syrup begins to boil. Do not overcook. Pack peaches into clean, sterilized jars; add a stick of cinnamon to each jar. Pour syrup over peaches, leaving 1/2-inch headspace. Seal jars and store in cool place.

Mrs. D. W. Cabiness
Polkville, N.C.

PICKLED PEACHES

1 c. sugar
1 c. vinegar
1 c. water
Cloves
10 Indian peaches, peeled

Combine sugar, vinegar and water; heat to boiling. Boil until sugar dissolves. Stick 2 cloves into each peach. Add peaches to syrup mixture; cook until soft. Pack peaches into jars; cover with syrup. Seal.

Mrs. C. T. Spigner
Foreman, Ark.

QUICK PICKLED PEACHES

1 No. 2 ½ can cling peach halves
¾ c. brown sugar
½ c. vinegar
2 sticks cinnamon, 3-in. long
1 tsp. whole cloves
1 tsp. allspice

Drain syrup from peaches; combine syrup with all remaining ingredients. Boil for 5 minutes. Add peaches to syrup; simmer for 5 minutes. Chill for several hours or overnight.

Mrs. J. J. Baughman
Newport News, Va.

PEACH MANGO

1 ½ gal. peaches
½ gal. vinegar
3 lb. brown sugar
1 c. white mustard seed
½ c. celery seed
1 tsp. allspice
2 lge. onions, thinly sliced
3 tsp. horseradish

Dip peaches into hot water; peel and cut into halves. Let peaches stand in salt water overnight. Boil vinegar, sugar and spices; drop peaches into boiling syrup. Boil until tender. Do not overcook. Cool; add onions and horseradish. Pack into jars and seal.

Mrs. Patricia Holden Leete
Chesapeake, Va.

BARTLETT PEAR AND TOMATO CHUTNEY

1 No. 2 can Bartlett pears
1 No. 2 can tomatoes
1 green pepper, coarsely chopped
1 med. onion, coarsely chopped
1 c. sugar
½ c. cider vinegar
1 tsp. salt
½ tsp. ginger
½ tsp. dry mustard
⅛ tsp. cayenne pepper
1 can pimento, coarsely chopped

Combine all ingredients except pimento. Bring to a boil; boil for 1 hour, just at the boiling point. Stir occasionally. Break pears with spoon; add pimento. Boil for 3 minutes longer. Fill sterilized glasses and seal. Yield: 4 glasses.

Mrs. Mildred Pirgan
St. Petersburg, Fla.

PEAR CHUTNEY

6 c. chopped pears
1 ½ c. raisins
1 onion, chopped
1 sm. cabbage, ground
4 stalks celery, ground
1 ½ c. brown sugar
3 tbsp. salt
1 tsp. mustard
½ tsp. turmeric
1 qt. vinegar

Combine pears, raisins, onion, cabbage, celery, sugar, salt and spices. Pour vinegar over all. Simmer for 45 minutes; pack while hot into sterilized jars.

Mrs. Eva Herbert
Beaumont, Tex.

PICKLED SICKEL PEARS

1 pt. vinegar
1 pt. water
3 ½ lb. sugar
1 tbsp. cinnamon
1 tbsp. allspice
1 tbsp. cloves
1 oz. ginger root
7 lb. sickel pears

Combine vinegar, water and sugar. Tie spices in bag; add to vinegar mixture. Boil mixture for 5 minutes. Pare pears, leaving on stems; add pears, a few at a time, to syrup. Cook until tender and clear. Place pears in hot sterilized jars. Pour in syrup to cover and seal. Yield: 5 pints.

Mrs. Shirley E. Crossby
Bloomsburg, Pa.

PEAR RELISH

12 lge. pears, ground
6 green sweet peppers, ground
6 red sweet peppers, ground
6 med. onions, ground
4 hot peppers, ground
2 c. vinegar
2 tbsp. salt
1 tsp. cloves
1 tsp. allspice
1 ½ c. sugar

Combine all ingredients; cook for 30 minutes. Pack into sterilized jars. Yield: 5 pints.

Mrs. Mary Sue Dunkin
Texarkana, Tex.

PINEAPPLE PICKLES

1 No. 2 ½ can pineapple chunks
½ c. pineapple syrup
½ c. vinegar

(Continued on next page)

1 ½ c. sugar
⅛ tsp. salt
6 to 8 cloves
1 3-in. stick cinnamon
1 No. 2 ½ can pineapple chunks

Drain pineapple; reserve 1/2 cup syrup. Combine pineapple syrup, vinegar, sugar, salt, cloves and cinnamon stick; bring to a boil. Reduce heat and simmer for 15 minutes longer. Remove from heat and add pineapple chunks. Place in jar and refrigerate.

Mrs. Elaine S. Washburn
Mayville, Wisc.

ROSY WATERMELON PICKLES

4 to 5 qt. watermelon rind
4 qt. water
3 tbsp. salt
3 c. vinegar
2 c. cold water
10 c. sugar
1 tbsp. whole cloves
3 sticks cinnamon
2 tsp. whole black pepper
½ c. Maraschino cherries

Trim outer green skin and pink flesh of rind, leaving a very thin line of pink; cut into 1 1/2 x 1 x 3/4-inch pieces. Soak melon cubes in water and salt for 24 hours; drain. Cover with boiling water and boil gently for 1 hour and 30 minutes; drain. Place rind in ice water until thoroughly chilled; drain. Combine vinegar, cold water, sugar and spices tied in cloth bag; bring to a boil. Add rind and boil gently for 30 minutes; remove spices. Let stand for 24 hours. Add Maraschino cherries; bring to a boil. Pack into hot sterilized jars; process in boiling water bath for 10 minutes. Yield: 6 pints.

Mrs. George House
Monroe, Wisc.

SPICY WATERMELON PICKLES

2 lb. watermelon rind
¼ c. salt
1 qt. water
2 tbsp. cinnamon bark
1 tbsp. whole cloves
4 c. sugar
2 c. white vinegar
1 lemon, thinly sliced
2 c. water

Trim dark green and pink portions from rind; cut rind into 1-inch cubes. Soak overnight in salted water. Drain; rinse and cover with cold water. Cook just until tender; drain. Tie spices in small cheesecloth bag. Combine sugar, vinegar, lemon, water and spice bag; simmer for 10 minutes. Add rind; simmer until clear. Fill sterilized jar to 1/2 inch from top.

Mrs. Margaret R. Luedtke
Sandusky, O.

ARTICHOKE RELISH

4 to 5 qt. artichokes
1 c. coarse salt
¾ tbsp. turmeric
1 tbsp. pepper
1 tbsp. dry mustard
½ c. flour
1 c. brown sugar
4 c. white sugar
1 c. water
6 to 8 lge. red and green peppers, ground
7 onions, ground
3 qt. vinegar

Wash artichokes carefully; cut into small bits. Sprinkle with salt; let stand overnight. Rinse and squeeze out water. Make a paste of turmeric, pepper, dry mustard, flour, brown sugar, 1 cup white sugar and water. Boil until thick. Grind peppers and onions; mix with artichokes, paste, vinegar and remaining sugar. Simmer for 20 minutes; seal in hot jars. Yield: 10 pints.

Mrs. Roy Young
White Stone, Va.

DILL BEAN STICKS

3 lb. fresh green beans
½ c. chopped fresh dill
2 cloves of garlic, peeled and halved
2 c. vinegar
2 c. water
4 tsp. sugar
4 tbsp. salt
½ tsp. cayenne

Wash beans; snip tips, but leave whole. Cover and parboil beans in unsalted water for 5 to 10 minutes or until tender-crisp. Lift beans out with slotted spoon; place at once in large bowl of ice water. Pack beans upright into hot sterilized jars; place 2 tablespoons dill and 1/2 clove of garlic in each

(Continued on next page)

jar. Heat vinegar, water, sugar, salt and cayenne to boiling; pour into jars to fill to rim. Seal.

Mrs. Wallace Tupper
Battle Creek, Mich.

DILLY BEANS

2 lb. fresh green beans
Red pepper
Cloves of garlic
Dill
2 c. cider vinegar
2 c. water
¼ c. salt

Pack washed and stemmed raw beans lengthwise into clean pint jars; add 1/2 teaspoon red pepper, 1 clove of garlic and 1 head of dill to each jar. Beans should not come above base of jar neck. Combine remaining ingredients; bring to a boil. Pour over beans and seal. Allow to cure for six weeks. Chill before serving.

Enid Hedrick
Garden Grove, Calif.

SWEET-SOUR GREEN BEANS

⅓ c. sugar
½ tsp. salt
½ tsp. pepper
½ c. white vinegar
½ c. oil
1 No. 2 ½ can green beans, drained
2 tbsp. finely chopped pimento
½ lge. onion, thinly sliced

Blend sugar, salt, pepper, vinegar and oil. Fold in beans, pimento and onion. Chill, covered, for at least 4 hours. May be kept for several days. Yield: 4-6 servings.

Jeanette Haas
Phoenix, Ariz.

BEET PICKLES

1 gal. fresh beets
2 c. water
2 c. cider vinegar
3 c. sugar
1 tbsp. mixed pickling spices

Cook whole unpeeled beets in water to cover until tender; drain and peel. Place in jars. Combine remaining ingredients; bring to a boil. Pour over beets; seal hot. Yield: 8 pints.

Mrs. Jean Maurer
Coggon, Iowa

SPICED PICKLED BEETS

24 small beets
1 c. cooking liquid
1 pt. vinegar
2 tbsp. salt
1 ¼ c. sugar
6 whole cloves
1 stick cinnamon, 3-in. long
3 med. onions, sliced

Remove beet tops, leaving roots and 1-inch stems; cover with boiling water. Cook until tender; drain, reserving 1 cup cooking liquid. Remove skins; slice. Combine cooking liquid, vinegar, salt and sugar; add spices tied in cheesecloth bag. Heat to boiling point; add beets and onions. Simmer for 5 minutes; remove spice bag. Continue simmering while quickly packing beets and onions into hot pint jars. Fill to 1/2-inch of jar top. Adjust lids; process in boiling 212 degree water bath for 30 minutes. Remove jars from canner; place on towel in warm dry place. Yield: 8 pints.

Shirley E. Mitchell
Townville, Pa.

BEET RELISH

6 c. ground beets
6 c. sugar
3 c. vinegar
1 tsp. cinnamon
1 tsp. cloves

Blanch beets and peel; grind and add sugar, vinegar, cinnamon and cloves. Cook for 30 to 35 minutes or until tender.

Mrs. William Hadler
Denton, Mont.

CARROT RELISH

3 med. carrots
1 lge. lemon, seeded
½ c. (scant) sugar

Finely grind carrots and lemon; add sugar. Store, covered, in refrigerator for several hours or overnight to develop flavor. Serve with meat salads.

Dorothy E. Kinsman
Ishpeming, Mich.

FLORIDA PICKLED BEETS

½ tsp. dry mustard
2 tbsp. sugar
¼ tsp. salt
½ tsp. ground cloves
1 1-lb. can Florida grapefruit sections
¼ c. vinegar
1 1-lb. can sliced beets, drained

Combine dry mustard, sugar, salt and cloves in saucepan. Drain grapefruit sections; stir syrup into sugar mixture with vinegar. Stir over medium heat until sugar is dissolved. Remove from heat. Add beets and grapefruit sections. Chill thoroughly before serving. Yield: 6 servings.

Photograph for this recipe above.

CABBAGE RELISH

1 med. cabbage
4 med. carrots
4 med. green peppers
4 med. red peppers
6 med. onions
¼ c. salt
3 c. sugar
1 pt. vinegar
¾ tbsp. celery seed
⅛ tsp. dry mustard

Grind cabbage, carrots, peppers and onions in medium grinder. Add salt; let stand for at least 2 hours. Drain well. Combine sugar, vinegar, celery seed and dry mustard; bring to a boil. Cool thoroughly; add to vegetables. Place in container; cover and let stand for at least 24 hours. Yield: 8 servings.

Mrs. Mary E. Miller
Hilliard, O.

CAULIFLOWER PICKLES

2 qt. caulifloweret s
1 ½ c. sugar
2 ½ c. white distilled vinegar
2 tbsp. salt
1 tbsp. white mustard seed
1 tbsp. celery seed
2 green peppers, cut into ¼-in. strips
2 sweet red peppers, cut into ¼-in. strips
1 ½ lb. onions, quartered

Cook cauliflower in small amount of water for 5 minutes; drain. Combine sugar, vinegar, salt and spices; cover and heat to boiling. Add all vegetables; boil, uncovered, for 2 minutes.

(Continued on next page)

Place in clean hot jars and seal. Yield: 5 pints.

Melba Lee Moore
Little Rock, Ark.

CELERY RELISH

4 ¾ qt. diced celery
⅓ c. chopped celery leaves
4 sweet red peppers, seeded and chopped
4 sweet green peppers, seeded and chopped
4 med. onions, chopped
6 c. sugar
4 c. white vinegar
¼ c. salt
1 tsp. turmeric
⅓ c. mustard seed

Combine vegetables; cover with boiling water. Let stand for 10 minutes; drain well. Combine sugar, vinegar, salt, turmeric and mustard seed; bring to a boil. Add vegetables and simmer for 5 minutes. Pack boiling hot into sterilized jars and seal. Yield: 3 quarts.

Mrs. Sally A. Kmon
Manchester, N.H.

CHOW CHOW

8 qt. green tomatoes
Salt
2 qt. green and red sweet peppers
2 qt. onions
2 lge. cabbages
4 tbsp. white mustard seed
2 tbsp. allspice
2 tbsp. celery seed
2 tbsp. ground cloves
1 sm. box yellow mustard
1 lb. brown sugar
3 to 4 c. sugar
1 can pimento, chopped
1 sm. hot pepper, chopped
½ gal. vinegar

Cut tomatoes into halves; sprinkle with salt. Place tomatoes in layers; let stand overnight. Drain. Grind tomatoes, peppers, onions and cabbages; mix with remaining ingredients. Cook for 4 hours. Seal in sterilized jars.

Mrs. Vivian Bain
San Antonio, Tex.

PENNSYLVANIA DUTCH CHOW CHOW

1 qt. lima beans
1 qt. chopped green beans
1 qt. corn beans
1 qt. chopped small pickles
1 qt. chopped small onions
1 qt. chopped celery
1 qt. sliced carrots
1 lge. cauliflower
8 sweet peppers, chopped and scalded
2 c. vinegar
2 c. water
¼ c. salt
3 tbsp. celery seed

Cook each vegetable except peppers separately until just tender; drain well. Mix vegetables with remaining ingredients; bring to a boil. Place in sterilized jars and seal. Yield: 8 quarts.

Lucy M. Bamberger
Myerstown, Pa.

CHUTNEY

12 apples, ground
12 green tomatoes, ground
12 onions, ground
3 green peppers, ground
2 red sweet peppers, ground
3 c. sugar
3 tbsp. salt
3 c. vinegar
3 tbsp. allspice
1 tsp. (scant) cloves
1 tsp. (scant) red pepper

Combine all ingredients, putting allspice in cloth bag. Cook for 30 minutes or until thickened. Pour into jars and seal.

Mrs. Peggy Hendrickson
Fourmile, Ky.

SOUR CREAM-VEGETABLE CHUTNEY

1 c. sour cream
1 c. yoghurt
¼ c. chopped chives
¼ c. chopped onion
1 c. chopped celery
1 med. cucumber, chopped
1 lge. tomato, chopped
¼ c. chopped ripe olives
1 tbsp. horseradish
1 tsp. sugar
1 tsp. salt
1 tsp. pepper

Mix all ingredients; chill and serve with corned beef brisket or as a dip for vegetables or potatoes. Yield: 3 cups.

Mrs. Maureen O'Neill
Belmont, Wisc.

CIDER RELISH

1 envelope unflavored gelatin
1 ½ c. cider
¼ c. sugar
½ c. ground carrots
1 c. chopped celery
½ c. ground cranberries

Soften gelatin in 1/2 cup cider. Heat remaining cider; do not boil. Add sugar to hot cider. Pour over softened gelatin and stir until dissolved. Chill until slightly thickened. Add carrots, celery and cranberries; pour into 1-quart mold. Chill until firm. Yield: 6-10 servings.

Mrs. Annette B. Tramm
Bradley, Ill.

CORN RELISH

¼ c. sugar
½ c. vinegar
½ tsp. salt
¼ tsp. Tabasco sauce
½ tsp. celery seed
¼ tsp. mustard seed
1 12-oz. can whole kernel corn
2 tbsp. chopped green pepper
1 tbsp. chopped pimento
1 tbsp. minced onion

Combine sugar, vinegar, salt, Tabasco sauce, celery and mustard seed in saucepan. Bring to a boil; boil for 2 minutes. Remove from heat. Combine with remaining ingredients; chill. Yield: 1 2/3 cups.

Mrs. Evelyn W. Newsom
Mt. Vernon, Tex.

BREAD AND BUTTER PICKLES

2 qt. unpeeled sliced cucumbers
1 pt. sliced onions
½ c. salt
1 pt. cider vinegar
1 c. water
2 c. brown or white sugar
1 ½ tsp. turmeric
1 ½ tsp. mustard seed
½ tsp. celery seed

Place cucumbers and onions in large bowl; sprinkle with salt. Let stand for 2 hours; drain. Boil vinegar, water, sugar and spices in large pot for 3 minutes. Add drained cucumbers and onions; bring to boil. Cook for 5 minutes; pour into four hot sterilized pint jars. Fill to overflowing with hot liquid; seal. Yield: 4 pints.

Rita Lariviere
Morris Plains, N.J.

CHOPPED PICKLE RELISH

12 lge. cucumbers
8 green peppers
10 med. onions
4 tbsp. salt
5 c. sugar
5 c. vinegar
3 tbsp. celery seed
6 tbsp. mustard seed

Slice cucumbers lengthwise and remove seed. Grind cucumbers, peppers and onions with coarse grinder; add salt. Let stand overnight. Drain. Combine remaining ingredients. Pour over vegetable mixture. Heat to a boil; simmer for 20 minutes. Seal in hot sterilized jars. Yield: 8 pints.

Mrs. Revia C. Munch
Branford, Fla.

REFRIGERATOR PICKLES

1 lge. cucumber, thinly sliced
1 ½ tbsp. salt
¼ c. water
¼ c. vinegar

Place cucumber in pint jar. Add water to cover; sprinkle in salt. Place in refrigerator for 3 hours; drain. Add 1/4 cup water and vinegar; let stand for 1 hour.

Mrs. Julia J. Stegall
Sallisaw, Okla.

SPANISH PICKLES

1 qt. large dill pickles
½ c. vinegar
1 ½ c. sugar
1 can pimento, cut up

Slice pickles crosswise and drain. Combine vinegar and sugar in saucepan; boil for 2 to 4 minutes. Heat pimento in vinegar-sugar solution. Alternate layers of pickles, pimento and solution in 1-quart jar. Use as needed. Yield: 1 quart.

Mrs. Ruth Garside Lindhart
Rochester, Ind.

GARDEN RELISH

6 ears corn
6 green peppers, finely cut
1 pt. chopped cucumbers
1 pt. chopped onions
1 ¼ pt. cider vinegar

(Continued on next page)

Full of surprises is the South of the Border dish, Escabeche Peruano. The fruit, fish, and vegetable combination has an exotic appeal long to be remembered. Though it must be started at least 12 hours before serving, it is simple to prepare.

ESCABECHE PERUANO

2 lb. fillet of sole
24 raw shrimp, cut into halves
1 c. flour
Salt and pepper to taste
6 tbsp. butter
¾ c. lime juice
¼ c. orange juice
½ c. white wine
1 head lettuce
20 orange sections
16 grapefruit sections
1 tsp. chopped parsley
1 Spanish onion, finely chopped
6 scallions, finely chopped
1 green pepper, thinly sliced
1 c. olive oil

Dip sole and shrimp in flour with salt and pepper to taste. Sauté very quickly in butter until half cooked. Arrange in deep pan; add lime juice, orange juice, white wine, salt and pepper. Marinate for 12 hours. Cover bottom of serving plate with lettuce leaves; place fillet of sole on top of lettuce. Place 6 pieces of shrimp on each fillet, leaving room between each fillet. Alternately arrange orange and grapefruit sections in spaces between fillets. Sprinkle parsley, onion and scallions over all; place green pepper around edge of platter. Add olive oil to marinade; pour over fish. Yield: 8 servings.

See photograph on reverse side.

2 c. sugar
2 tsp. celery seed
3 tbsp. salt
½ tbsp. pepper
1 tbsp. turmeric

Cut corn from cob. Place all ingredients in large kettle; mix. Cook for 1 hour just at boiling point. Wash six pint jars in soap and water; fill with boiling water and let set. Set screw tops and lids in boiling water. Pour relish into jars 1/2 inch from top; seal. Yield: 6 pints.

Mrs. Carol Ralston
Novi, Mich.

TEXAS PICKLED OKRA

2 c. white vinegar
1 c. water
¼ c. salt
1 tbsp. dill seed
1 tbsp. mustard seed
1 tbsp. celery seed
2 red hot peppers
2 garlic pods
5 lb. okra

Combine vinegar, water and salt; bring to a boil. Add all remaining ingredients except okra. Wash and drain whole okra; place in jars. Pour hot liquid over okra. Tighten lids; let stand for at least three to four weeks. Yield: 6 pints.

Mrs. Duane J. Kimbrel
Fort Sam Houston, Tex.

PICKLED SWEET PEPPERS

1 c. sugar
1 c. vinegar
1 tsp. salt
Yellow banana peppers

Place sugar, vinegar and salt in saucepan. Heat and stir until sugar dissolves. Slice peppers lengthwise; remove seed and caps. Place in sterilized jars; pack tightly. Pour syrup over peppers; seal. Let set for several weeks; serve. NOTE: Green peppers may be used.

Mrs. Dorothy S. Bienski
Waller, Tex.

RED PEPPER RELISH

7 c. finely chopped sweet red peppers
2 tbsp. salt
5 c. sugar
3 c. cider vinegar
¼ tsp. citric acid
½ tsp. ground ginger
½ tsp. onion powder

In a non-metallic container, mix peppers with salt; let stand for several hours. Pour pepper mixture into kettle. Mix sugar, vinegar, citric acid, ginger and onion powder; add to pepper mixture. Boil for 1 hour or until thick. Yield: 3-4 pints.

Mrs. Eugene S. Turner
Lexington, Tenn.

PICKLED PIMENTOS

30 pimento peppers
1 pt. vinegar
1 pt. water
¼ c. salt
6 tbsp. sugar

Remove stem ends and seed from peppers. Cover three times with boiling water, allowing water to stand for 3 minutes each time. Drain. Pack whole or sliced into sterilized jars. Combine remaining ingredients and boil for 10 minutes; pour over peppers. Seal. Let stand for three weeks before using.

Mrs. Mary Jean Earl
Commerce City, Colo.

PICCALILLI

2 qt. sliced green tomatoes
1 pt. chopped onions
1 pt. sliced green peppers
1 qt. shredded cabbage
1 pt. thinly sliced carrots
1 pt. chopped celery
2 oz. mustard seed
1 tsp. turmeric
4 tbsp. salt
2 lb. sugar
2 qt. white vinegar

Place all ingredients in large kettle; mix well. Cook slowly for 1 hour, stirring occasionally. Pour into hot sterilized jars; seal at once. Yield: 12 pints.

Mrs. Pauline Moxley
McAllen, Tex.

SQUASH PICKLES

Hot peppers
Cloves of garlic
Dill
Sliced sm. squash
Alum
1 c. water

(Continued on next page)

1 c. salt
8 c. white vinegar

Place 1 pepper, 2 cloves of garlic and dill in bottom of each of four pint jars. Wash and pack uncooked squash into jars. Add pinch of alum to each jar. Mix water, salt and vinegar; bring to a boil. Pour hot liquid over squash in jars; seal. Let stand for eight to ten weeks to season. Yield: 4 pints.

Carolyn Wajmack
Pine Bluff, Ark.

GREEN TOMATO COCKTAIL PICKLES

4 c. water
4 c. vinegar
4 qt. tiny green tomatoes, washed and drained
1 c. sugar
1 ½ tbsp. salt
2 or 3 cloves of garlic
2 tbsp. mixed pickling spices
Hot peppers
Dill
Bay leaves
Mustard seed

Combine water and vinegar in large heavy kettle. Add tomatoes, sugar, salt, garlic and pickling spices tied in cheesecloth bag; bring to a boil. Reduce heat and simmer for 15 minutes. Pack tomatoes loosely into hot quart jars. To each quart add 1 hot green pepper, 1 head dill, 1 small bay leaf and 1/2 teaspoon mustard seed. Pour hot pickling liquid over tomatoes. Process quarts for 30 minutes at simmering temperature or 15 minutes in boiling water. Yield: 4 quarts.

Mrs. Linda Knutson
Casselton, N.D.

RIPE TOMATO RELISH

24 ripe tomatoes, peeled and chopped
6 sweet green peppers, ground
6 hot peppers, ground
8 onions, ground
2 ½ c. sugar
¼ tsp. allspice
1 pt. vinegar
3 tsp. salt
2 tsp. celery salt
½ tsp. cinnamon
¼ tsp. cloves

Combine all ingredients; mix well. Cook, stirring often, until thick. Put into sterilized jars and seal. Yield: 6 pints.

Mrs. Dean Bradley
Hereford, Tex.

TOMATO-CUCUMBER RELISH

1 pkg. French dressing mix
¼ c. water
¼ c. winegar
¼ c. salad oil
2 tomatoes, sliced into thin wedges
2 onions, chopped
1 med. cucumber, peeled and sliced

Empty contents of French dressing package into pint jar; add water, vinegar and oil. Shake well. Place vegetables in shallow bowl; pour dressing over top. Mix lightly. Chill thoroughly. Yield: 2 cups.

Mrs. Jo Anne Davis
Oakdale, Calif.

TWENTY-DAY RELISH

1 c. vinegar
1 c. sugar
1 c. cooking oil
1 tsp. salt
1 tsp. pepper
1 tsp. celery seed
1 pkg. unflavored gelatin
¼ c. water
2 lb. cabbage, finely chopped
1 green or red pepper, chopped
1 onion, chopped (opt.)
½ c. finely chopped celery

Boil vinegar with sugar, oil, salt, pepper and celery seed. Cool. Dissolve gelatin in water. Add all remaining ingredients and liquid mixture. Mix well. Store in covered jar in refrigerator. NOTE: All vegetables may be ground in food grinder. Yield: 15-20 servings.

Mrs. John Sperling
Empire, Oreg.

VEGETABLE PICKLES

1 pt. lima beans
1 pt. sliced carrots
1 pt. sliced onions
1 pt. chopped green tomatoes
1 pt. chopped celery
1 pt. cauliflowerets
3 or 4 green peppers, sliced
1 pt. sweet pickles
1 qt. vinegar
1 ¾ lb. sugar
3 tsp. dry mustard
1 tsp. turmeric
½ c. flour

Precook vegetables. Combine all ingredients in large pan; boil slowly until slightly thickened. Use canning process for storing pickle. Yield: 4-6 quarts.

Mrs. Robert Kier
Northfield, N.J.

SALAD DRESSINGS

RECIPE FOR SOUR CREAM-BLEU CHEESE DRESSING ON PAGE 104
RECIPE FOR SOUR CREAM-FRUIT SALAD DRESSING ON PAGE 117

BIG SKY COUNTRY SALAD DRESSING

1 c. catsup
1 c. sugar
1 c. oil
1 c. vinegar
½ onion, grated
Juice and pulp of ½ lemon
Salt and pepper
2 tsp. horseradish

Combine all ingredients; refrigerate. Especially good on tossed salad. Yield: 1 quart.

Mrs. William B. West
Camas, Wash.

BUTTERMILK SPECIAL SALAD DRESSING

2 c. salad dressing
1 c. buttermilk
¼ c. catsup
¼ c. sugar
½ tsp. salt
1 tsp. paprika
2 tsp. vinegar
1 clove of garlic, mashed

Combine all ingredients in a 1-quart jar. Shake until thoroughly blended. Refrigerate. Yield: 1 1/2 pints.

Mrs. Charles W. Parton
Plainview, Tex.

CATALINA DRESSING

¼ tsp. pepper
¼ c. vinegar
½ c. catsup
1 sm. onion, grated
½ tsp. salt
½ c. sugar
1 c. salad oil

Beat all ingredients together except oil. Gradually add oil while beating. Refrigerate. Yield: 1 pint.

Mrs. Ina Luadtke
Fisher, Minn.

CATSUP DRESSING FOR SALAD

4 c. sugar
4 tsp. celery seed
4 tsp. salt
4 tsp. paprika
2 c. catsup
1 c. salad oil
1 c. vinegar
Juice of 3 lemons
2 med. onions, grated
Garlic (opt.)

Blend all ingredients well. May be stored indefinitely. Yield: 3 quarts.

Mrs. Thurman Banghman
Bladensburg, O.

CENTURY-OLD DRESSING

¼ c. sugar
½ c. water
¼ c. lemon juice
¼ c. vinegar
¼ tsp. salt
¼ tsp. paprika
1 c. salad oil
½ c. castup
1 sm. onion, grated

Boil sugar with water for 10 minutes. Add lemon juice; simmer for 5 minutes longer. Cool quickly by placing pan in ice water. Add vinegar, salt and paprika to cooled mixture. Beat with rotary beater to blend well. Mix oil, catsup and onion into cold syrup mixture; beat until thickened. Refrigerate. Shake well before serving. Yield: 1 1/2 pints.

Sarah A. McCreight
Morganton, N.C.

CHEF'S SALAD DRESSING

1 tsp. sugar
1 tsp. salt
⅛ tsp. pepper
2 tsp. grated onion
Dash of paprika
⅓ c. oil
2 tbsp. vinegar
2 tbsp. catsup

Combine all ingredients in jar; shake well. Yield: 6 servings.

Mrs. Genieve G. Royse
Corydon, Ind.

DELICIOUS SALAD DRESSING

¾ c. salad oil
½ c. catsup
½ c. vinegar
2 tsp. salt
⅓ c. sugar
Juice of 1 lemon
1 tsp. onion or garlic juice
1 tsp. mustard
1 tsp. paprika (opt.)

Combine all ingredients. Pour into bottle; shake well. Yield: 1 pint.

Rosa A. Holodynsky
Saginaw, Mich.

HEALTH DRESSING

⅔ c. salad oil
3 tbsp. sugar
⅓ c. catsup
1 tbsp. lemon juice
½ tsp. grated onion
½ c. vinegar
¾ tsp. salt

Combine all ingredients; shake well. Yield: 1 1/3 cups.

Lydia E. Griffin
Gatesville, N.C.

ITALIAN DRESSING

1 tsp. salt
½ tsp. dry mustard
½ tsp. paprika
½ tsp. garlic salt
½ tsp. oregano
2 tbsp. vinegar
½ c. catsup
½ c. salad oil
¼ c. finely chopped onion
½ c. wine vinegar

Combine dry ingredients in jar; add all remaining ingredients. Shake vigorously; chill. Serve on salad greens, sliced tomatoes or bean salad. NOTE: May be used as a marinade or basting sauce for meats. Yield: 1 2/3 cups.

Mrs. Dolan Shaler
Niles, Mich.

NEW YORK DRESSING

1 c. (scant) sugar
½ c. water
1 c. oil
½ c. catsup
3 tsp. vinegar
3 tsp. lemon juice
1 tsp. paprika
1 tsp. dry mustard
½ tsp. Tabasco sauce
1 tsp. celery salt
½ tsp. garlic salt

Bring sugar and water to a boil; cook until candy thermometer registers 226 degrees. Remove from heat; add all remaining ingredients and beat with electric mixer. NOTE: The secret of this dressing is the stage of cooking.

Esther Settle
Granger, Wash.

OLD GRIST MILL SALAD DRESSING

1 c. oil
¾ c. vinegar
½ c. sugar
2 tsp. salt
1 tsp. grated onion
1 tbsp. Worcestershire sauce
½ c. catsup

Blend all ingredients well. Store in refrigerator. NOTE: May be stored for weeks.

Mrs. Howard R. Branch
Waterbury, Conn.

RUSSIAN DRESSING

1 c. water
1 c. sugar
Juice of 2 lemons
2 c. salad oil
1 c. catsup
2 tsp. Worcestershire sauce
2 tbsp. grated onion
1 tsp. celery salt
1 tsp. paprika
Pinch of red pepper

Boil water and sugar; cool. Add all remaining ingredients; blend thoroughly. Chill.

Carol Van Sickle
Wells, Minn.

SALAD DRESSING

¾ c. catsup
¼ c. chili sauce
1 ½ c. salad oil
¾ c. vinegar
2 tsp. celery seed
1 tsp. paprika
1 tsp. salt
1 med. onion, grated
1 c. sugar
¼ tsp. garlic salt

Combine ingredients in blender. Store in refrigerator.

Mrs. Boyd Noftsger
Leesburg, O.

SCHOOL SALAD DRESSING

1 c. sugar
1 c. vinegar
1 c. catsup
1 tbsp. paprika
¼ tsp. salt
2 tbsp. salad oil

Combine all ingredients; shake well. Chill and keep refrigerated. Shake well before serving. Yield: 50 servings.

Rosella M. Ault
Sunbury, O.

TASTY SALAD DRESSING

¼ c. sugar
¼ c. vinegar
1 tbsp. lemon juice
½ c. catsup
½ c. salad oil
1 tsp. salt
1 tsp. pepper
1 tsp. paprika
1 clove of garlic (opt.)

Combine all ingredients in jar; shake well. Yield: 10 servings.

Mrs. Albert Tuber
Youngstown, O.

TOSSED SALAD DRESSING

1 c. salad oil
⅔ c. sugar
½ c. vinegar
⅓ c. catsup or chili sauce
Juice of 1 lemon
2 tbsp. paprika
2 tsp. salt
1 sm. onion, finely chopped

Combine all ingredients in 1-quart jar; shake well. Store in refrigerator.

Mrs. Joe C. Roberts
London, O.

CELERY SEED DRESSING

½ c. sugar
1 tsp. dry mustard
1 tsp. salt
⅓ c. vinegar
1 c. salad oil
¼ onion, grated
1 ½ tsp. celery seed

Combine sugar, mustard and salt; beat in one-half the vinegar. Gradually add salad oil, beating constantly. Add onion, remaining vinegar and celery seed. Mix well. Yield: 12 servings.

Caroline Lay
Otis AFB, Mass.

CELERY SEED DRESSING

1 ½ c. sugar
½ c. catsup
½ tbsp. minced onion or onion salt
½ tbsp. paprika
½ tbsp. celery seed
½ tbsp. salt
½ c. vinegar
1 c. salad oil

Combine all ingredients except oil. Add oil slowly, beating at high speed. Yield: 3 cups.

Sandra Weaver
LaFontaine, Ind.

CELERY SEED FRENCH DRESSING

½ c. sugar
1 tsp. dry mustard
1 tsp. salt
½ sm. onion, grated
6 tbsp. vinegar
1 c. salad oil
1 tbsp. celery seed

(Continued on next page)

Combine sugar, mustard, salt, onion and one-half the vinegar. Add oil gradually while beating; beat in remaining vinegar. Add celery seed. Yield: 1 1/2 cups.

Mrs. W. M. Piersall
Tarpon Springs, Fla.

CELERY SEED SALAD DRESSING

1 c. salad oil
½ c. sugar
⅓ c. catsup
⅓ c. vinegar
1 tsp. celery seed
1 tsp. paprika
1 tsp. salt
1 tbsp. grated onion

Blend all ingredients in glass jar or shaker; shake to blend. Shake well before pouring over salad. Dressing may be stored for several weeks in refrigerator. Yield: 1 pint dressing.

Mrs. Eva T. Warner
Frankfort, Ind.

CELERY SEED SALAD DRESSING

½ c. sugar
1 tsp. paprika
1 tsp. dry mustard
1 tsp. salt
½ tsp. celery seed
1 tsp. grated onion
3 tbsp. vinegar
¾ c. salad oil

Blend sugar, paprika, mustard, salt, celery seed and grated onion with 1 tablespoon vinegar; add oil slowly, alternating with vinegar. Dressing will keep indefinitely in refrigerator. Yield: 1/2 pint.

Nora Graham
Milton-Freewater, Oreg.

BLEU AND COTTAGE CHEESE SALAD DRESSING

1 c. cream-style cottage cheese
½ c. sour cream
½ c. crumbled Bleu cheese
2 tbsp. minced onion
2 tbsp. chopped pimento
2 tbsp. Worcestershire sauce
¼ tsp. salt
2 drops Tabasco sauce

Blend cottage cheese and sour cream. Blend all remaining ingredients; combine with cottage cheese mixture. Yield: 2 cups.

Mrs. Mary L. Burleson
Swan Quarter, N.C.

BLEU CHEESE DRESSING

½ c. evaporated milk
½ c. salad oil
3 tbsp. cider vinegar
1 tsp. salt
⅓ c. crumbled Bleu cheese
½ tsp. instant minced onion

Combine all ingredients in blender; blend for a few seconds or until smooth and thickened. Chill tightly covered. Yield: 1 1/2 cups.

Leona H. Harper
Oakland, Calif.

BLEU CHEESE DRESSING

4 oz. Bleu cheese
3 tbsp. mayonnaise
2 tbsp. lemon juice or vinegar
1 8-oz. carton sour cream

Bring cheese to room temperature; mash with fork. Add mayonnaise and lemon juice; blend well. Add sour cream; cover and refrigerate for at least 30 minutes. Yield: 6 servings.

Mrs. R. J. Crocker
Ft. Ord, Calif.

BLEU CHEESE DRESSING

1 8-oz. pkg. cream cheese
1 sm. onion, grated
2 sm. pkg. Bleu cheese
Salt and pepper to taste
Garlic salt to taste
2 tbsp. lemon juice
1 tbsp. Worcestershire sauce
1 pt. mayonnaise

Blend cream cheese, onion and Bleu cheese. Add seasonings, lemon juice, Worcestershire sauce and mayonnaise. Yield: 1 pint.

Mrs. Mary Ellen Servis
Smithland, Iowa

GOURMET BLEU CHEESE DRESSING

½ c. evaporated milk
½ c. salad oil
3 tbsp. cider vinegar
1 tsp. onion salt
2 oz. crumbled Bleu cheese

Combine all ingredients in container of electric blender. Cover; blend for a few seconds until smooth and thickened. Chill, tightly covered. Serve over tossed greens. Yield: 1 1/2 cups.

Photograph for this recipe above.

BLEU CHEESE SALAD DRESSING

1 c. salad dressing
¼ c. catsup
¼ c. sweet pickle relish
1 8-oz. pkg. Bleu cheese
2 hard-cooked eggs, finely chopped

Combine all ingredients; shake well. Yield: 12 servings.

Mrs. F. L. Quinones
Homestead, Fla.

BLEU CHEESE DRESSING

1 c. sour cream
1 c. mayonnaise
1 c. crumbled Bleu cheese
1 tbsp. onion juice
1 tbsp. Worcestershire sauce
1 tbsp. lemon juice

Combine all ingredients in blender; blend until smooth. Yield: 1 1/2 pints.

Athene Swanson
Vacaville, Calif.

SOUR CREAM - BLEU CHEESE DRESSING

1 3-oz. pkg. Bleu cheese
1 tsp. garlic salt
½ c. salad oil
¼ c. vinegar
1 c. dairy sour cream

Mash Bleu cheese with a fork; blend with garlic salt. Beat into oil and vinegar. Fold in sour cream. Cover and chill. Yield: 2 cups.

Photograph for this recipe on page 99.

EASY BLEU CHEESE DRESSING

1 c. buttermilk
1 c. vegetable oil
8 scallions, minced or 1 sm. onion, minced
1 tbsp. sugar
½ tsp. ground pepper
1 tsp. seasoned salt
¼ c. sweet pickle juice
½ lb. Bleu cheese
1 c. sour cream
1 c. mayonnaise

Combine all ingredients except sour cream and mayonnaise. Beat until well blended. Fold in sour cream and mayonnaise; refrigerate. Yield: 1 quart.

Mrs. Merritt R. Albin
Monrovia, Calif.

CREAM CHEESE DRESSING

1 8-oz. pkg. cream cheese, softened
⅛ tsp. salt
1 tbsp. lemon juice
2 to 3 tbsp. mayonnaise

Cream the cheese with an electric mixer. Add all remaining ingredients; mix well. Serve on fruit halves or lettuce. Yield: 6 servings.

Mrs. Deanna Patin Roy
Marksville, La.

FABULOUS ROQUEFORT DRESSING

3 oz. Roquefort cheese
2 c. mayonnaise
3 tsp. chopped chives
1 tsp. (heaping) pepper
1 tsp. garlic powder
½ tsp. Worcestershire sauce
1 c. sour cream
½ c. buttermilk

Blend all ingredients well, adding sour cream and buttermilk last. Chill. Dressing may be thinned with additional buttermilk at serving time. Yield: 1 quart.

Mrs. Winifred Robins
Fremont, Calif.

ROQUEFORT CHEESE DRESSING

¼ lb. Roquefort cheese
¼ c. boiling water
1 tsp. onion juice
1 tsp. garlic juice
½ tsp. Worcestershire sauce
Dash of hot pepper sauce
2 c. mayonnaise
1 c. buttermilk
½ tsp. salt

Dissolve cheese in boiling water; set aside for 30 minutes. Beat cheese mixture with rotary beater until smooth; add onion juice, garlic juice, Worcestershire sauce, pepper sauce, mayonnaise, buttermilk and salt. Blend well. Let stand for 24 hours before using. Yield: 1 quart.

Marciel W. French
San Francisco, Calif.

ROQUEFORT DRESSING

½ c. sour cream
¼ tsp. salt
1 c. buttermilk
3 tbsp. lemon juice
1 ½ c. mayonnaise
¼ tsp. dry mustard
⅓ c. crumbled Roquefort cheese

Blend sour cream, salt, 1/2 cup buttermilk, lemon juice, mayonnaise and mustard. Add Roquefort cheese and remaining buttermilk. Refrigerate for 24 hours before serving. Stir or shake well before using.

Mary Jones
Buena Park, Calif.

ROQUEFORT DRESSING

1 ½ qt. mayonnaise
2 c. buttermilk
2 3-oz. pkg. Roquefort cheese, crumbled
1 tbsp. white pepper
2 sm. cloves of garlic
2 tbsp. lemon juice
Chopped parsley
1 sm. onion, finely chopped
½ tbsp. monosodium glutamate
1 tsp. salt

Combine all ingredients. Mix with electric mixer.

Jean Medler
Moffett Field, Calif.

ROQUEFORT DRESSING

2 c. mayonnaise
1 ½ c. buttermilk
½ lb. Roquefort or Danish Bleu cheese, crumbled
2 tbsp. Worcestershire sauce
1 tsp. garlic powder

Blend all ingredients thoroughly but gently. Keep in tightly covered jar in refrigerator until ready to serve. Yield: 1 quart.

Mrs. Helen D. Greene
Asheville, N.C.

ROQUEFORT DRESSING

1 c. evaporated milk
¼ lb. Roquefort cheese
4 cloves of garlic, crushed
2 tsp. dried oregano
2 tsp. celery seed
1 tsp. salt
¼ tsp. pepper
2 c. mayonnaise
1 c. buttermilk

Heat evaporated milk until simmering; stir in cheese, garlic, oregano, celery seed, salt and pepper. Heat and stir until cheese is melted and blended; cool. Blend with mayonnaise and buttermilk. Refrigerate until used. NOTE: Mixture may be strained before refrigerating. Yield: 1 quart.

Janet M. Adkins
Troy, Mont.

CHEF'S SPECIAL SALAD DRESSING

1 ½ c. chili sauce
¼ c. finely ground celery
¼ c. finely ground sour pickles
2 c. mayonnaise
1 tsp. lemon juice
½ tsp. Worcestershire sauce
1 tsp. horseradish

Blend all ingredients well. Serve on any seafood salad. NOTE: Stores indefinitely in cool place but not in refrigerator. Yield: 1 quart.

Mrs. Robert C. Stewart
Gorham, Me.

CHILI SAUCE SALAD DRESSING

¾ c. sugar
½ c. water
1 tsp. grated onion
1 tsp. paprika
1 tsp. salt
1 tsp. vinegar
3 tbsp. lemon juice
1 c. chili sauce
1 c. salad oil

Combine sugar and water; cook for 5 minutes. Remove from heat; add all remaining ingredients. Beat well; refrigerate. Yield: 1 pint.

Angie T. Miller
Fredericksburg, Va.

HEAD LETTUCE DRESSING

1 sm. jar olives
½ lb. cheese
1 sm. onion
1 sm. can pimento
¼ c. chili sauce
Salad dressing

Grind olives, cheese, onion and pimento in food chopper. Add chili sauce and enough salad dressing to thin to desired consistency. Refrigerate. Yield: 1 pint.

Mrs. Jane Thurman
New Castle, Ky.

ROTISSERIE DRESSING

2 or 3 cloves of garlic, minced
1 c. mayonnaise
¼ c. chili sauce
¼ c. catsup
1 tsp. Worcestershire sauce
¼ to 1 tsp. pepper
½ c. salad oil
¼ tsp. Tabasco sauce
¼ tsp. paprika
1 sm. onion, grated
2 tbsp. water or juice of 1 lemon plus 1 tsp. water
1 tsp. mustard
Salt to taste

Blend all ingredients well. Keep refrigerated. Yield: 1 pint.

Mrs. Ruth J. Shaw
Umatilla, Fla.

SALAD DRESSING

½ c. salad oil
¾ c. chili sauce or catsup
¾ c. sugar
¼ c. vinegar
2 tsp. lemon juice
2 tsp. grated onion
¼ tsp. garlic salt
1 tsp. paprika
¼ tsp. salt

Combine all ingredients in jar; shake well. Will keep in refrigerator indefinitely. Yield: 1 pint.

Mrs. Earle L. Kimmel
Jewett, O.

BURGUNDY SALAD DRESSING

¾ c. sugar
1 c. wine vinegar
¾ c. peanut oil
½ tsp. salt
⅛ tsp. garlic salt
Dash of red pepper

Combine all ingredients except red pepper; bring to a boil. Remove from heat; add red pepper. Cool; do not store in refrigerator. Yield: 12-15 servings.

Mrs. Joan M. McGrail
Chanute AFB, Ill.

COOKED SALAD DRESSING

½ c. sugar
2 tsp. cornstarch
1 tsp. salt
1 tsp. mustard
1 egg
1 c. milk
1 tbsp. butter
1 c. hot vinegar

Sift dry ingredients. Add mustard and egg; blend well. Scald milk in double boiler. Stir in egg mixture. Add butter and vinegar. Beat well.

Elsie Hill Lord
Boston, Mass.

CREAM SALAD DRESSING

1 tbsp. dry mustard
3 eggs, beaten
½ c. sugar
1 tbsp. flour
½ c. water
⅓ c. vinegar
¼ tsp. salt

Combine all ingredients; cook until thickened, stirring constantly. NOTE: Especially good for potato salad. May be thinned with cream.

Mrs. Donald W. Swafford
Fortuna, Mont.

CREAM SALAD DRESSING

1 c. sugar
2 tbsp. flour
2 tbsp. dry mustard
½ tsp. salt
¼ tsp. cayenne pepper
2 eggs, beaten
1 c. sour cream or sweet milk
1 c. vinegar
Buttor or margarinc

Mix all dry ingredients; add eggs, milk and vinegar. Cook over double boiler until thickened. Remove from heat; add butter the size of a walnut. NOTE: Dressing may be thinned with cream or thickened with whipped cream to be used for fruit salads. Yield: 1 pint.

Anna B. Nickerson
Abington, Mass.

HOT ENDIVE DRESSING

2 tbsp. flour
1 egg
½ c. sugar
⅓ tsp. salt
Vinegar to taste
8 slices bacon

Combine flour, egg, sugar and salt; add vinegar and enough water to obtain smooth mixture. Fry bacon; crumble. Add water to bacon; heat. Stir in flour mixture. Pour over endive. Yield: 4 servings.

Mary E. Ziegler
Sarasota, Fla.

NON-OIL SALAD DRESSING

¾ c. sugar
1 tbsp. mustard
1 tbsp. cornstarch
1 tsp. salt
2 eggs, beaten
¾ c. hot vinegar
1 ½ c. milk

Blend sugar, mustard, cornstarch, salt and eggs in saucepan. Add vinegar and milk. Bring to a boil, stirring constantly. Cool.

Mrs. R. H. Gerken
New Carlisle, O.

OLD-FASHIONED BOILED DRESSING

¾ c. sugar
2 tsp. salt
2 tsp. dry mustard
½ tsp. paprika
4 tbsp. flour
4 eggs
¾ c. vinegar
1 ¼ c. water
3 tbsp. oil or butter

Blend sugar, salt, mustard, paprika and flour. Add eggs; beat until smooth. Add vinegar and water; cook over hot water until mixture thickens. Add butter; remove from heat. Chill before serving. Yield: 1 quart.

Mrs. H. Kieth Chambers
Delaware, O.

OLD-FASHIONED SALAD DRESSING

½ tsp. salt
1 tsp. (heaping) flour
1 tsp. dry mustard
2 tsp. sugar
2 tsp. butter
1 egg or 2 egg yolks
3 c. milk or cream
¼ c. vinegar

Combine dry ingredients; cream with butter. Add egg, milk and vinegar. Cook in double boiler until thickened. Yield: 1 pint.

Florence W. Harris
Concord, N.H.

OLD SOUTHERN BUTTERMILK SALAD DRESSING

½ c. sugar
1 tsp. dry mustard
1 tsp. salt
¼ tsp. celery seed
1 tbsp. flour
½ c. vinegar
1 c. buttermilk
1 tbsp. butter
2 eggs, beaten

Combine sugar, mustard, salt, celery seed and flour. Add vinegar, buttermilk and butter. Cook in double boiler until thickened. Pour mixture into beaten eggs, stirring constantly. Return to double boiler; cook until mixture reaches a consistency of soft custard. Cool; use with fruit salads or coleslaw. Yield: 15 servings.

Ruth C. Peabody
Sunnyside, Wash.

PENNSYLVANIA DUTCH SALAD DRESSING

5 slices bacon
½ c. sugar
½ tsp. salt
1 tbsp. cornstarch
1 egg, beaten
¼ c. vinegar
1 c. water
1 tbsp. bacon fat

Fry bacon until crisp; set aside. Combine all remaining ingredients in top of double boiler. Cook until mixture thickens, stirring constantly. Remove from heat; add crumbled bacon. Pour over tossed salad greens. Dressing can be reheated or kept hot over hot water. Do not put on the greens until just before serving. Yield: 6 servings.

Mrs. Donald Drought
Geneva, O.

POTATO SALAD DRESSING

1 tsp. salt
2 tsp. dry mustard
½ tsp. pepper
2 tsp. sugar
¾ c. vinegar
¼ c. water
1 tsp. butter
3 egg yolks, beaten

Combine all dry ingredients. Dilute vinegar with water; add to dry ingredients. Blend in butter and egg yolks. Bring to a boil; cook for 5 minutes, stirring constantly. Add hot dressing to potatoes and vegetables. Yield: 10 servings.

Mrs. Lucile Vaughn
Jackson, Mich.

SALAD DRESSING

3 tbsp. dry mustard
2 tbsp. salt
5 tbsp. sugar
2 tbsp. flour
6 tbsp. butter, melted
3 eggs
1 ½ c. milk
¾ c. vinegar

Combine dry ingredients with butter. Mix well. Add all remaining ingredients. Cook in double boiler until thickened. Yield: 1 quart.

Mrs. Hazel Riley
Quincy, Mass.

SALAD DRESSING

12 mangoes
12 green tomatoes
3 c. sugar
2 c. water
1 tbsp. salt
1 c. flour
1 c. vinegar
6 oz. prepared mustard
1 qt. salad dressing
Cream or milk

Grind mangoes and tomatoes; add sugar, 1 cup water and salt. Cook for 10 minutes. Make paste of flour, vinegar, mustard and 1 cup water. Cook until thickened; add to tomato mixture. Stir in salad dressing. Thin with cream. Pour into jars and seal.

Mrs. Phyllis Robinett
Edgertown, O.

SALAD DRESSING

⅔ c. sugar
1 egg
2 tbsp. flour
½ tsp. salt
½ tsp. dry mustard
¼ c. vinegar
1 c. hot water
Butter to taste

Combine sugar, egg, flour, salt and mustard; add vinegar and water. Cook until thickened; add butter. NOTE: This makes a delicious dressing for potato salad or head lettuce. Yield: 1 1/4 cups.

Mrs. Evelyn Thomas
Miami, Fla.

SWEET ONION DRESSING

1 c. sugar
1 tsp. salt
1 tsp. paprika
¼ c. onion juice
½ tsp. mustard
½ c. cider vinegar
1 ¼ c. corn oil
1 tbsp. celery seed

Dissolve sugar, salt, paprika, onion juice and mustard in vinegar; boil for 1 minute. Cool to lukewarm; beat until thickened. Gradually add oil, beating constantly until stiff. Fold in celery seed. Yield: 2 cups.

Mrs. Virginia Boyle
Ashland, Ill.

BEST FRENCH DRESSING

1 16-oz. can tomato paste
½ c. oil
½ c. white vinegar
¾ c. sugar
1 ½ tsp. Worcestershire sauce
¼ tsp. paprika
½ tsp. dry mustard
1 ½ tsp. salt
1 sm. onion, minced
¼ tsp. garlic powder or juice

Combine all ingredients; blend well.

Mrs. Laura DeLaBarre
Valley City, N.D.

BEST YET FRENCH DRESSING

½ c. sugar
2 tsp. salt
1 ½ tsp. dry mustard
½ tsp. paprika
1 can tomato soup
1 c. salad oil
1 c. vinegar
1 tsp. Worcestershire sauce
1 med. onion, grated
1 clove of garlic, grated or whole

Combine all ingredients; beat well. May be stored in refrigerator. Yield: 1 quart.

Mabel Pell
Brazil, Ind.

CREAMY FRENCH DRESSING

2 tsp. salt
½ tsp. pepper
1 tbsp. dry mustard
1 tsp. paprika
¼ c. sugar
1 3-oz. pkg. fruit pectin
1 can tomato soup
½ c. cider vinegar
1 tbsp. scraped onion
1 tbsp. Worcestershire sauce
1 ½ c. salad oil
1 clove of garlic

Combine all dry ingredients; sift three times. Combine soup and vinegar; add onion and Worcestershire sauce. Stir in dry ingredients. Slowly add oil, beating constantly. Fill 1-quart jar with dressing; add garlic. Dressing keeps indefinitely. Yield: 1 quart.

Suzanne Sanders
Burlington, Wash.

DELUXE FRENCH DRESSING

1 c. finely diced onions
½ c. sugar
1 tsp. salt
1 tbsp. dry mustard
1 tsp. white pepper
1 tbsp. paprika
1 c. corn oil
¾ c. vinegar
1 No. 1 can tomato soup
1 tsp. horseradish

Marinate onions and sugar for 30 minutes. Blend dry ingredients; add corn oil, vinegar, marinated onions and soup. Beat well; blend in horseradish. Let stand for 1 hour. Store in refrigerator. Yield: 1 1/2 pints.

Mrs. Dorothy Spayth
Findlay, O.

FRENCH DRESSING

3 tbsp. sugar
3 tbsp. catsup
1 tsp. salt
½ tsp. dry mustard
¼ c. evaporated milk
½ c. salad oil
3 tbsp. vinegar

Combine all ingredients except vinegar. Beat until well blended. Add vinegar; beat thoroughly. Yield: 1 1/4 cups.

Mrs. Margaret W. Lyles
Westminster, S.C.

EASY FRENCH DRESSING

⅔ c. sugar
⅔ c. catsup
1 tsp. salt
2 tbsp. paprika
1 c. vegetable oil
½ c. vinegar
2 tbsp. ground onion

Blend sugar, catsup, salt and paprika. Add oil, vinegar and onion; pour into bottle. Refrigerate. Shake well before using. Yield: 1 pint.

Mrs. Albert Aebersold
Lancaster, O.

FAVORITE FRENCH DRESSING

⅓ c. sugar
1 tsp. salt
½ tsp. dry mustard
Dash of cayenne pepper
1 tbsp. Worcestershire sauce
1 ¼ tsp. paprika
1 can tomato soup
½ c. wine vinegar
Juice of 1 sm. onion
1 ½ c. salad oil
Juice of ½ lemon
1 clove of garlic

Combine all ingredients in 1-quart jar. Let garlic stand in dressing for 24 hours; remove. Store in refrigerator. Yield: 1 quart.

Mrs. Donald B. Kendall
Malmstrom AFB, Mont.

FRENCH DRESSING

½ c. salad oil
1 can tomato soup
¾ c. sugar
¾ c. vinegar
½ tsp. salt
1 tsp. pepper
1 tsp. paprika
1 tsp. prepared mustard
1 tsp. onion or garlic salt

Combine all ingredients in 1-quart jar; shake well. Store in refrigerator; do not freeze. Yield: 1 1/2 pints.

Kathryn Obenour
Amherst, O.

FRENCH DRESSING

Juice of 1 lemon
½ pt. vinegar
¾ box confectioners sugar
1 tsp. paprika
1 tsp. Worcestershire sauce
½ tsp. red pepper
1 med. onion, finely grated
1 can tomato soup
1 pt. salad oil

Blend all ingredients in mixer, adding salad oil gradually. Yield: 1 quart.

Mrs. W. C. Games
Lebanon, O.

FRENCH DRESSING

1 c. olive or vegetable oil
¼ c. vinegar
¼ c. lemon juice
1 tsp. salt
½ tsp. dry mustard
½ tsp. paprika
Grated lemon rind (opt.)

Combine all ingredients. Shake well in tightly covered jar. Refrigerate until ready to use. Yield: 1 1/2 cups.

Mrs. Ann Beck
Antigo, Wisc.

GOLDEN FRENCH DRESSING

1 tsp. salt
¼ tsp. sugar
¼ tsp. pepper
1 tsp. paprika
⅔ c. olive or salad oil
3 tbsp. vinegar
1 ½ c. chopped onions

Combine dry ingredients; moisten with a small amount of oil. Add vinegar, onions and remaining oil; beat or shake vigorously. NOTE: A well beaten egg yolk may be added just before serving to give softness. Yield: 6 servings.

Mrs. Gene Stockstill
Sidney, O.

PIQUANT FRENCH DRESSING

½ c. salad oil
1 can tomato soup
¾ c. vinegar
¾ c. sugar
4 cloves of garlic, cut into pieces
1 tsp. salt
1 tsp. garlic salt
2 tsp. steak sauce
¼ tsp. celery salt
½ tsp. dry mustard
½ tsp. paprika
1 tsp. Tabasco sauce
1 tsp. Worcestershire sauce

Combine all ingredients in 1-quart jar; shake well. Store in refrigerator. Yield: 1 quart.

Mrs. A. H. Dahl
Brooklyn, N.Y.

SAVORY FRENCH DRESSING

1 c. sugar
½ c. vinegar
1 tsp. salt
2 tsp. paprika
2 tsp. celery seed
2 tsp. dry mustard
1 med. onion, finely grated
1 pt. oil

Combine all ingredients except oil. Add a little oil at a time, beating at medium speed with electric mixer. Yield: 35 servings.

Marian Henson
Sellersburg, Ind.

SWEET AND SOUR FRENCH DRESSING

1 can tomato soup
1 tsp. salt
1 tsp. grated onion
¼ c. cooking oil
¾ c. vinegar
½ tsp. paprika
1 c. sugar

Combine all ingredients except garlic with mixer or blender. Store in jar with garlic.

Lyda M. Jackson
Whitmore Lake, Mich.

TANGY FRENCH DRESSING

1 can tomato soup
1 tsp. salt
⅓ c. honey or sugar
1 tsp. paprika
2 tsp. prepared mustard or 1 tsp. dry mustard
¼ c. lemon juice
2 tbsp. vinegar
2 tbsp. grated onion
2 tbsp. Worcestershire sauce
1 c. salad oil
2 or 3 cloves of garlic (opt.)

Combine all ingredients except oil and garlic; beat with electric mixer until well blended. Add oil, beating until well blended. Add garlic. Pour into jar; cover and refrigerate. Yield: 1 1/2 pints.

Blanche Woerpel
Stanton, Mich.

ARGYLE DRESSING

1 tsp. butter
1 tsp. salt
1 tbsp. sugar
1 tsp. mustard
4 tbsp. vinegar
4 egg yolks, beaten
8 marshmallows
1 c. whipped cream
1 c. nuts (opt.)

Cream butter, salt and sugar. Dissolve mustard in small amount of the vinegar; add to butter mixture with egg yolks and remaining vinegar. Cook in double boiler. Add marshmallows to hot mixture. Chill; fold in cream and nuts.

Hazel S. Wilkinson
Ozark, Ala.

AVOCADO-DILL DRESSING

1 med. avocado, peeled and sliced
⅓ c. salad oil
1 tbsp. sugar
4 tbsp. lemon juice
½ tsp. salt
1 tsp. dill seed
½ c. water

Combine all ingredients except 1/4 cup water in blender; blend for 2 minutes. Add remaining water. Add more water to thin. Refrigerate. Serve on mixed fruit salad. Yield: 2 cups.

Mrs. E. Howard
Kent, Wash.

AVOCADO FRUIT DRESSING

1 lge. ripe avocado, peeled and mashed
½ c. orange juice
1 tbsp. lemon juice
1 tsp. honey
½ tsp. salt

Beat avocado until smooth. Gradually add all remaining ingredients; beat until smooth and fluffy. Chill; serve with orange and grapefruit salad garnished with fresh mint. Yield: 1 cup.

Marietta Twitchel
Martinez, Calif.

AVOCADO-OLIVE DRESSING

1 med. avocado
1 4-oz. can ripe olives, sliced or chopped
1 c. mayonnaise

Peel avocado; remove seed. Mash until soft and smooth. Blend in drained olives and mayonnaise. Serve on cottage cheese and pineapple. Yield: 6-8 servings.

Mrs. Evelyn Lewis
Wellton, Ariz.

GREEN GODDESS SALAD DRESSING

½ can anchovy fillets or to taste
½ med. avocado
2 tbsp. chopped parsley
½ pt. sour cream
Freshly ground black pepper to taste
Salt to taste

Mash anchovies and avocado to a pulp; add all remaining ingredients.

Nita P. Lowery
Phoenix, Ariz.

COFFEE-FRUIT DRESSING

1 ½ tsp. instant coffee
½ tsp. dry mustard
½ tsp. salt

(Continued on next page)

¼ c. butter, melted
⅔ c. sweetened condensed milk
¼ c. lemon juice
⅓ c. pineapple juice
1 egg yolk

Blend coffee, mustard and salt; stir into melted butter. Combine milk, juices and egg yolk. Stir into butter mixture; beat until thickened. Yield: 1 1/2 cups.

Mrs. Mary Jane Wilson
Fayetteville, Ark.

FRUIT DRESSING

10 marshmallows, cut up
½ pt. heavy cream
1 tbsp. mayonnaise
1 jar pimento cheese

Soak marshmallows in cream overnight. Beat until thickened; add mayonnaise and cheese. Yield: 8-10 servings.

Mrs. J. W. Frye
Rittman, O.

FRUIT DRESSING

2 eggs
¾ c. sugar
½ c. pineapple juice
⅓ c. lemon juice
½ pt. cream, whipped

Beat eggs until light and fluffy. Combine sugar and juices; add to eggs. Cook in double boiler over medium heat, stirring frequently until thickened. Cool overnight; fold into whipped cream. May be stored in refrigerator for several days. Yield: 15 servings.

Mrs. N. E. Copen
Somerset, O.

FRUIT SALAD DRESSING

1 egg
1 c. sugar
Juice and grated rind of 1 lemon
Juice and grated rind of 1 orange

Beat egg, adding sugar gradually. Add juices and rind. Cook over low heat or in double boiler for about 5 minutes or until desired consistency is obtained. Yield: 1/2 pint.

Florence Burman
Alameda, Calif.

FRUIT SALAD DRESSING

1 3-oz. pkg. cream cheese, softened
½ c. apricots and juice
1 tbsp. lemon juice
½ c. mayonnaise
Dash of Tabasco sauce

Mix softened cheese with small amounts of apricots and juice at a time. Add all remaining ingredients; mix well. Yield: 6 servings.

Gladys Olson
Seaside, Oreg.

FRUIT SALAD DRESSING

½ c. sugar
1 tsp. mustard
½ tsp. salt
3 tbsp. vinegar
1 c. salad oil
1 tsp. celery seed

Combine sugar, mustard, salt and vinegar. Gradually add salad oil; beat thoroughly at medium speed. Add celery seed. Yield: 8-10 servings.

Mrs. Robert C. Bakewell, Jr.
Custer, S.D.

FRUIT SALAD DRESSING

2 egg yolks
4 tbsp. sugar
½ tsp. salt

(Continued on next page)

½ tsp. mustard
Pinch of cayenne
4 tbsp. cream
2 tbsp. vinegar
½ pt. heavy cream, whipped

Beat egg yolks well. Blend sugar, salt, mustard and cayenne; stir into egg yolks. Add cream; cook in double boiler until thickened, stirring constantly. Add vinegar. Stir in whipped cream before serving.

Mrs. Judson Ballard
Barnesville, O.

GRANDMA'S FRUIT SALAD DRESSING

½ c. sugar
2 tbsp. flour
Dash of salt
½ c. pineapple juice
1 egg, beaten
½ c. evaporated milk (opt.)

Combine sugar, flour and salt; mix well. Add juice, egg and milk. Blend thoroughly. Simmer until thickened, stirring constantly. Spoon dressing over any desired fruit combination. NOTE: Dressing will keep in refrigerator for two weeks. Yield: 12 servings.

Flora White
Newark, O.

GOLDEN SALAD DRESSING

½ c. pineapple juice
½ c. lemon juice
⅔ c. sugar
1 tbsp. flour
¼ tsp. salt
4 eggs, slightly beaten
3 c. whipped cream

Heat juices in double boiler; blend in sugar, flour and salt. Add eggs; cook until thickened. Cool. Fold in whipped cream. Use on fruit salad. Yield: 12 servings.

Karen Pierson
John Day, Oreg.

GRAPEFRUIT SALAD DRESSING

⅓ c. sugar
1 tsp. salt
¼ tsp. paprika
¼ c. vinegar
¼ c. salad oil
2 tsp. grated onion
2 tbsp. minced celery
2 tbsp. minced green pepper
4 drops Worcestershire sauce

Combine all ingredients in jar; shake thoroughly. Serve on grapefruit, lettuce or cabbage salads.

Lorna Carswell
Spring Green, Wisc.

HONEY DRESSING

⅔ c. sugar
1 tsp. dry mustard
1 tsp. paprika
¼ tsp. salt
1 tsp. celery seed
⅓ c. honey
5 tsp. vinegar
1 tsp. lemon juice
1 tsp. grated onion
1 c. salad oil

Combine dry ingredients; add honey, vinegar, lemon juice and onion. Drizzle oil into mixture, beating constantly with electric mixer until well blended. Serve over fruit salads. Yield: 2 cups.

Mrs. Evelyn Stransky
Wallace, Nebr.

LEMONADE DRESSING

⅓ c. undiluted frozen lemonade concentrate
⅓ c. honey
⅓ c. salad oil
1 tsp. celery seed

Combine all ingredients; beat with rotary beater until smooth. Serve with fruit salads. Yield: 6 servings.

Helene Fanberg
Whitehall, Mich.

LIME-CHERRY DRESSING

¼ c. salad oil
¼ c. lime juice
¼ tsp. salt
⅛ tsp. paprika
3 tbsp. Maraschino cherry syrup
1 oz. soft cream cheese

Put all ingredients into blender; process on high until smooth. Yield: 3/4 cup.

Photograph for this recipe above.

FRUIT DRESSING

1 3-oz. pkg. cream cheese
¼ c. orange juice
2 tsp. lemon juice
⅛ tsp. almond extract

Cut cream cheese into three pieces. Put all ingredients into blender container. Blend at high speed until smooth. Yield: 1/2 cup.

Photograph for this recipe above.

HONEY-LIME DRESSING

3 tbsp. fresh lime juice
3 tbsp. honey
6 tbsp. salad oil

Combine all ingredients. Beat at medium speed with mixer until mixture looks creamy. Serve on fruit salads. Yield: 6 servings.

Mrs. Doris Dowell
Fort Worth, Tex.

HONEY-FRUIT DRESSING

½ c. creamed cottage cheese
¼ c. pineapple juice
1 tbsp. honey
¼ tsp. celery seed
½ tsp. salt

Combine all ingredients in blender container. Blend on high speed until smooth. Yield: 3/4 cup.

Photograph for this recipe above.

ONE-TWO-THREE FRUIT DRESSING

1 egg, well beaten
1 c. sugar
Juice and grated rind of 1 lemon
Juice and grated rind of 1 lime
Juice and grated rind of 1 orange

Combine all ingredients. Cook over medium heat, stirring constantly, for 1 minute. Cool; cover and refrigerate. Yield: 4 servings.

Irina Nikitin
Ramseur, N.C.

PINEAPPLE DRESSING FOR FRUIT SALAD

Syrup from No. 2 can pineapple
1 tbsp. flour
1 egg yolk

Cook ingredients in top of double boiler until mixture coats a spoon. Cool and use on fruit salads. NOTE: Do not use pineapple juice.

Mrs. Earl H. Martin
Hendersonville, N.C.

PEANUT BUTTER DRESSING

¼ c. peanut butter
⅓ c. salad oil
¼ c. vinegar
½ tsp. salt
5 tsp. sugar
½ tsp. prepared mustard
⅛ tsp. paprika

Beat all ingredients until smooth. Serve on fruit salads. Yield: 3/4 cup.

Pat Breidenbach
Elkton, S.D.

POPPY SEED DRESSING

1 ½ c. sugar
2 tsp. mustard
2 tsp. salt
⅔ c. vinegar
2 c. corn oil
1 tsp. poppy seed
½ med. onion

Combine sugar, mustard, salt, vinegar and oil; beat well. Add poppy seed; pour into jar. Drop in onion; let set overnight. Remove onion before using dressing.

Erma Shuey
Filley, Nebr.

PINEAPPLE DRESSING

1 egg, beaten
1 c. pineapple juice
1 c. sugar
1 tbsp. flour
Dash of salt (opt.)

Combine egg, pineapple juice, sugar, flour and salt in heavy pan or double boiler; bring to a boil over medium heat, stirring constantly. Serve over pineapple slices, bananas, apples or other fruit.

Alma Mae McCullough
Nichols, Iowa

POPPY SEED DRESSING FOR FRUIT SALAD

2 tsp. dry mustard
2 tsp. salt
1 ½ c. sugar
⅔ c. vinegar
3 tbsp. onion juice
2 c. cooking oil
3 tbsp. poppy seed

Mix mustard, salt, sugar and vinegar. Add onion juice; mix well. Slowly add oil, beating until thickened. Add poppy seed.

Ruby M. Carroll
Dallas, Tex.

RUBY RED DRESSING

½ c. currant jelly
¼ c. vegetable oil
2 tbsp. lemon juice
Dash of salt
Few drops onion juice

Beat jelly with fork until smooth. Add all remaining ingredients; beat until smooth. Use on citrus fruits. Yield: 3/4 cup.

Agnes Falkowski
Brussels, Wisc.

SALAD DRESSING FOR FRUIT SALAD

3 egg yolks
½ c. sugar
3 tbsp. butter
Juice of ½ lemon
½ c. pineapple juice
1 tsp. celery seed
1 c. heavy cream, whipped

Combine egg yolks, sugar and butter in top of double boiler. Cook until mixture begins to thicken; add lemon and pineapple juices. Stir in celery seed. Fold in whipped cream at serving time. Yield: 8-10 servings.

Bernice Booth
Montesano, Wash.

SOUR CREAM FRUIT SALAD DRESSING

1 tsp. grated orange rind
2 tbsp. orange juice
2 tbsp. lemon juice
1 tbsp. honey
½ tsp. dry mustard
1 tsp. salt
¼ tsp. paprika
1 c. sour cream

Blend all ingredients except sour cream; fold into sour cream. Chill thoroughly before serving. Serve with fruit salads. Yield: 1 1/4 cups.

Photograph for this recipe on page 99.

FRUIT MAYONNAISE

1 tsp. butter
2 tsp. flour
1 ½ c. pineapple or grapefruit juice
Juice of 1 lemon
Juice of 1 orange
½ c. sugar
2 eggs, separated
½ c. heavy cream, whipped

Melt butter; blend in flour. Add fruit juices and sugar. Cook over medium heat, stirring constantly, until thickened. Slowly pour over beaten egg yolks; stir vigorously. Cool; fold in stiffly beaten egg whites and whipped cream. Chill and serve over salads.

Grace Strutt
Bessemer City, N.C.

LOW CHOLESTEROL MAYONNAISE

2 egg yolks
¼ tsp. paprika
Dash of cayenne pepper
1 tsp. salt
½ tsp. dry mustard
2 tbsp. vinegar
2 c. corn oil
2 tbsp. lemon juice
1 tbsp. hot water

Bring eggs to room temperature. Combine dry ingredients. Blend in egg yolks. Add vinegar; mix well. Add 1 teaspoon oil at a time, beating at high speed until 1/4 cup has been added. Add remaining oil in increasing amounts, alternating last 1/2 cup with lemon juice. Add an additional tablespoon of lemon juice to vary the flavor. Beat in hot water to take away oily appearance. Yield: 1 pint.

Barbara Waybourn
Afton, Tex.

MAYONNAISE

1 egg yolk
1 tsp. mustard
1 tsp. confectioners sugar
Dash of cayenne pepper
2 tbsp. lemon juice or vinegar
1 c. salad oil

Beat egg yolk, mustard, sugar, pepper and 1 tablespoon lemon juice or vinegar with rotary beater. Continue beating while adding oil, drop by drop, then gradually increasing amount as mixture thickens until all is

(Continued on next page)

used. Slowly add remaining lemon juice or vinegar; beat well. Chill before serving. Yield: 1 1/2 cups.

Mrs. Jean Pearson
Del Rio, Tex.

MAYONNAISE

1 egg
3 tbsp. sugar
2 tsp. flour
1 tsp. dry mustard
1 tsp. salt
1 tbsp. butter
⅔ c. vinegar

Blend egg with dry ingredients; add butter and vinegar. Cook, stirring constantly, until mixture comes to a boil and thickens. Pour into jar; cover. Yield: 1 pint.

Mrs. Lucy Kosta
Sutherland, Iowa

MAYONNAISE DRESSING

1 egg
⅛ tsp. pepper
⅛ tsp. paprika
⅛ tsp. dry mustard
1 tsp. sugar
2 tbsp. lemon juice or vinegar
½ tsp. salt
1 c. salad oil

Combine all ingredients except oil in blender or mixer. Blend for a few seconds; add oil gradually. Blend thoroughly. Refrigerate. Yield: 1 1/4 cups.

Mrs. Mable Martens
Missouri Valley, Iowa

MINERAL OIL-MAYONNAISE DRESSING

1 egg
1 ¼ tbsp. sugar
¾ tsp. salt
1 tsp. mustard (opt.)
1 pt. mineral oil
3 tbsp. vinegar

Combine egg, sugar, salt and mustard; beat well. Slowly add 1 cup mineral oil, beating constantly. Add vinegar, beating constantly; slowly beat in remaining oil. NOTE: Lemon juice may be used for vinegar.

Mrs. D. H. Campbell
Sidney, O.

SOY MAYONNAISE

½ c. Soyalac
1 c. water
1 c. oil
½ tsp. salt
Juice of 1 lemon
Onion, garlic or paprika to taste

Blend Soyalac and water. Gradually add oil, salt and lemon juice. Season with onion, garlic or paprika. Yield: 2 1/2 cups.

Grace Smith
Dalton, Ga.

FRESH VEGETABLE THOUSAND ISLAND DRESSING

½ c. mayonnaise
1 can tomato soup
1 tsp. dry mustard
½ tsp. paprika
1 hard-cooked egg, chopped
½ c. chopped celery
1 lge. carrot, chopped
1 tsp. minced onion
4 med. sweet pickles, chopped

Blend mayonnaise with soup; add all remaining ingredients. Chill. Yield: 3 1/2 cups.

Betty Herrin
Albany, Tex.

THOUSAND ISLAND DRESSING

1 c. mayonnaise
½ tsp. dry mustard
2 tbsp. Worcestershire sauce
½ c. finely chopped onion
½ c. finely chopped green pepper
⅓ c. chopped sweet pickles
¾ c. chili sauce
½ c. catsup
1 tsp. paprika

Combine all ingredients. Refrigerate. Yield: 1 quart.

Mrs. Lynton Gerloff
Freedom, Okla.

THOUSAND ISLAND DRESSING

1 c. mayonnaise
1 tsp. paprika
¼ c. chili sauce
2 tbsp. vinegar
½ c. diced celery
1 sm. onion, slivered
2 tbsp. minced parsley
3 hard-cooked eggs, diced

(Continued on next page)

Combine all ingredients; blend thoroughly. Chill for 4 to 5 hours. Yield: 8 servings.

Mrs. G. W. Dill
Chandler AFS, Minn.

THOUSAND ISLAND DRESSING

1 1-in. square green pepper
8 stuffed olives
2 tsp. cut chives
½ clove of garlic
1 c. mayonnaise
2 hard-cooked eggs, quartered
1 sprig parsley
1 tsp. Worcestershire sauce
2 tbsp. dill pickle slices
¼ c. chili sauce

Place green pepper, olives, chives, garlic and mayonnaise in blender. Cover; blend at low speed. Add all remaining ingredients; blend at high speed until coarsely chopped. Chill before serving. Yield: 1 1/2 cups.

Mrs. James E. Anderson
Ludington, Mich.

THOUSAND ISLAND DRESSING

1 c. mayonnaise
½ c. chili sauce
⅓ c. pickle relish, drained
2 hard-cooked eggs, coarsely chopped
½ tsp. chopped onion
Dash of salt

Blend all ingredients; chill. Yield: 2 cups.

Mrs. Mary Maki
Negaunee, Mich.

THOUSAND ISLAND SALAD DRESSING

½ c. sugar
1 tsp. salt
1 qt. mayonnaise
6 hard-cooked eggs, finely chopped
½ c. chopped green pepper
½ c. chopped pimento
6 or 8 green onions, finely chopped
2 tbsp. chili sauce

Blend sugar and salt with mayonnaise. Add eggs, green pepper, pimento, onions and chili sauce; refrigerate until needed. Yield: 1 quart.

M. Kay Dailey
Piqua, O.

QUICK THOUSAND ISLAND DRESSING

Mayonnaise
Catsup
Piccalilli

Combine 4/5 cup mayonnaise, 3/5 cup catsup and 3/5 cup piccalilli; blend well. Yield: 1 pint.

Mrs. John Giese
Watervliet, Mich.

DELICIOUS SAUCE

1 can tomato soup
1 c. vinegar
1 c. oil
1 c. sugar
1 clove of garlic

Combine all ingredients in 1-quart jar. Refrigerate until ready to serve. Yield: 1 quart.

Mrs. Elaine Brannigan
Altoona, Pa.

GARLIC SALAD DRESSING

1 can tomato soup
½ c. salad oil
½ c. vinegar
½ tsp. salt
½ tsp. pepper
2 tsp. sugar or 8 drops artificial sweetener
3 or 4 cloves of garlic
¾ c. finely chopped onions

Combine all ingredients in 1-quart jar; let set overnight. Strain. Yield: 1 pint.

Mrs. Glenn Trowbridge
Parma, Mich.

HUBBELL HOUSE SALAD DRESSING

1 c. salad dressing
1 c. mayonnaise
1 c. tartar sauce or sandwich spread
1 c. tomato soup
1 sm. onion, grated
4 sweet pickles, finely chopped
1 tsp. dry mustard
2 tbsp. vinegar
2 tbsp. chili sauce
2 tbsp. sweet pickle juice

Blend salad dressing with mayonnaise. Add all remaining ingredients; mix well. Yield: 1 quart.

Gladys Severance
Huron, S.D.

MADDOX SALAD DRESSING

½ can tomato soup
¾ c. salad oil
⅓ c. vinegar
1 tbsp. Worcestershire sauce
¾ tsp. salt
⅛ tsp. paprika
¼ tsp. dry mustard
¼ c. sugar
1 ⅓ c. salad dressing

Blend all ingredients well. Refrigerate. NOTE: Excellent for tossed salads. Yield: 1 1/2 quarts.

LaRae Smith
Greybull, Wyo.

SALAD DRESSING

1 can tomato soup
½ soup can salad oil
½ soup can vinegar
½ tsp. salt
½ c. sugar
2 cloves of garlic, thinly sliced
1 tsp. garlic salt

Combine all ingredients; shake well. Shake before serving.

Mrs. Shirley Stevens
Concord, N.H.

SLAW DRESSING

1 qt. mayonnaise
1 c. vinegar
¾ c. sugar
1 can tomato soup
1 onion, grated
1 to 3 cloves of garlic (opt.)
1 tsp. salt
2 tsp. dry mustard
½ tsp. paprika
1 ¼ c. salad oil

Combine all ingredients; blend in electric mixer or blender. Refrigerate until ready to serve. Yield: 2 quarts.

Mrs. J. E. Maurer
Lemoncove, Calif.

SPECIAL CHEF SALAD DRESSING

1 can tomato soup
1 tsp. salt
1 tsp. pepper
1 tsp. paprika
½ tsp. dry mustard
1 tbsp. Worcestershire sauce
¾ c. sugar
½ c. vinegar
1 c. salad oil
1 med. onion, grated
1 clove of garlic (opt.)

Combine all ingredients. Shake well; chill for at least 24 hours before using.

Mrs. Laurin E. Detwiler
Hamilton, O.

TOMATO SOUP SALAD DRESSING

1 can tomato soup
1 c. salad oil
½ c. vinegar
1 tsp. salt
2 tsp. mustard
¼ c. sugar
2 tbsp. grated onion
½ tsp. paprika
¼ tsp. white pepper
¼ tsp. cloves

Place all ingredients in mixing bowl; beat slowly with electric mixer for 3 to 4 minutes. Keeps well in covered jar in refrigerator. Drop a clove of garlic into jar, if desired. Yield: 3 cups.

Mrs. R. M. Hickey
Palatka, Fla.

TOSSED SALAD DRESSING

1 10 ½-oz. can tomato soup
¾ c. cooking oil
½ c. white vinegar
½ c. sugar
1 tsp. Worcestershire sauce

(Continued on next page)

1 tsp. dry mustard
1 tsp. garlic salt
¼ tsp. pepper

Blend all ingredients well. Pour into 1-quart jar; store in refrigerator. Shake well before serving. Yield: 1 1/2 pints.

Mrs. Lela R. Ogburn
Raleigh, N.C.

LOW-CALORIE DRESSING

2 c. corn oil
1 c. vinegar
1 tbsp. salt
2 tbsp. sugar
2 tbsp. catsup
1 tsp. mustard
1 clove of garlic, chopped

Blend all ingredients; refrigerate for several hours. Yield: 1 quart.

Helen Hoffman
Lincolnton, N.C.

LOW-CALORIE FRENCH DRESSING

1 clove of garlic, sliced
¼ c. vinegar
¾ tsp. salt
⅛ tsp. pepper
¼ tsp. paprika
2 tsp. sugar
½ c. tomato juice
2 tbsp. water
2 tbsp. salad oil

Add garlic to vinegar; let stand for 20 minutes. Strain. Combine all ingredients in jar. Cover; shake vigorously. Store in refrigerator. Shake again before using. Yield: 1 cup.

Ann Friends Huh
Caledonia, Minn.

LOW-CALORIE PAPRIKA DRESSING

½ med. onion
1 c. vinegar
2 tbsp. paprika
2 tbsp. salt
15 ¼-grain sugar substitute tablets
¼ tsp. dry mustard
3 c. corn oil

Puree onion in blender or chop finely. Add all remaining ingredients except oil. Gradually add oil and continue blending. Shake well before using.

Mrs. Morris M. Campbell
Tavares, Fla.

LOW-CALORIE SALAD DRESSING

1 tsp. salt
1 tsp. powdered garlic
1 tsp. monosodium glutamate
1 tbsp. paprika
1 tsp. cumin powder
⅓ c. vinegar
⅔ c. light mineral oil

Combine salt, garlic, monosodium glutamate, paprika and cumin powder. Blend with vinegar and mineral oil until salt has dissolved. Shake well before serving. Yield: 8-10 servings.

Mrs. Paul R. McLane
Norwood, O.

CREAMY GARLIC DRESSING

4 eggs
1 tsp. salt
1 tsp. dry mustard
4 c. salad oil
⅔ c. blended lemon juice and vinegar
4 cloves of garlic
5 sprigs parsley, chopped (opt.)
4 green onions, chopped (opt.)
3 stalks celery, chopped (opt.)
4 hard-cooked eggs, chopped (opt.)

Place eggs in mixer; add salt and mustard while beating. Slowly add oil and continue beating. Add all remaining ingredients.

Josephine Curtiss
St. Louis, Mich.

CUCUMBER DRESSING

3 med. cucumbers
3 sm. onions
¼ c. sugar
¼ c. lemon juice
¼ tsp. monosodium glutamate
¼ tsp. garlic powder
2 tbsp. Worcestershire sauce
¼ tsp. green food coloring
1 qt. mayonnaise

Grind cucumbers and onions. Drain well. Add sugar, lemon juice, seasonings, coloring and mayonnaise. Stir until smooth.

Helen Hutchison
Jackson, Tenn.

EASY SALAD DRESSING

3 tbsp. sugar
3 tbsp. vinegar
1 ½ tbsp. oil
Sprinkle of paprika

Combine all ingredients in jar; shake well. Yield: 8 servings.

Mrs. Theresa Couvier
Sault Sainte Marie, Mich.

PURDUE SALAD DRESSING

1 med. onion, finely chopped
¼ c. vinegar
4 tbsp. sugar
¼ tsp. salt
2 tbsp. prepared mustard
2 tbsp. celery seed
1 ½ c. oil

Combine all ingredients except oil; mix at low speed for 1 minute. Add oil slowly; blend only until it becomes a little heavy and transparent. Use on hearts of lettuce or tossed salad greens. Yield: 6-8 servings.

Mabel R. Strite
Hershey, Pa.

RAIN WATER DRESSING

1 c. sugar
1 tsp. dry mustard
½ tsp. celery seed
½ tsp. salt
½ tsp. pepper
½ c. vinegar
½ c. water

Combine dry ingredients; add vinegar and water. Shake well. Serve over coleslaw. Yield: 12 servings.

Mrs. P. J. Pucci
Davenport, Iowa

RUSSIAN DRESSING

1 c. salad dressing
½ c. chili sauce
1 hard-cooked egg, chopped
2 tbsp. finely chopped green pepper
2 tbsp. finely chopped pimento
1 tsp. chopped chives
½ tsp. paprika
Salt to taste

Combine all ingredients; blend well.

Mrs. R. A. Graves
Woodward, Iowa

SALAD DRESSING

½ c. sugar
1 tsp. salt
1 tsp. dry mustard
¼ lge. onion, grated
⅓ c. vinegar
1 c. salad oil
1 tsp. celery seed

Combine all ingredients; beat well. Store; do not refrigerate.

Mrs. Virginia Hintz
Monticello, Iowa

SALAD DRESSING FOR COLESLAW

1 qt. salad dressing or mayonnaise
1 c. vinegar
1 c. oil
1 c. sugar
1 tsp. salt
1 ½ tbsp. mustard

Combine all ingredients; beat well.

Mrs. Celia L. Lego
Athol, Mass.

STATE FAIR SALAD DRESSING

¼ tsp. dry mustard
¾ tsp. salt
¼ tsp. paprika
1 ½ tbsp. sugar
1 tbsp. catsup
¼ tsp. thick meat sauce
¼ c. lemon juice
½ c. salad oil

Combine ingredients in jar; shake well. Chill; serve over vegetable salads.

Verna J. Erickson
Akron, O.

ZERO DRESSING

½ c. tomato juice
2 tbsp. lemon juice
1 tbsp. finely chopped onion
1 tbsp. chopped green pepper
⅛ tsp. salt
Dash of pepper

Combine all ingredients in jar with tight fitting cover. Store in refrigerator. Shake before using. Yield: 3/4 cup.

Mrs. Bernard Zerressen
Cambria AFS, Calif.

RECIPE FOR EGG CROWNED SUPPER MOLD ON PAGE 128

CHEESE DEVILED EGGS

6 hard-cooked eggs, chilled
1 tsp. mustard
1 tbsp. chopped parsley
¼ tsp. salt
⅛ tsp. pepper
½ c. finely crushed cheese crackers
½ c. mayonnaise
Paprika

Halve eggs lengthwise; remove yolks. Press yolks through a fine sieve; add mustard, parsley, salt, pepper and one-half the crumbs and mayonnaise. Refill centers of whites with yolk mixture; press two halves together. Dip one end of each egg into remaining mayonnaise and into crumbs. Sprinkle with paprika. Yield: 6 servings.

Barbara Widmyer
Conneaut Lake, Pa.

DEVILED EGGS

6 hard-cooked eggs
2 tbsp. mayonnaise
1 tsp. mustard
½ tsp. salt
¼ tsp. paprika
Dash of pepper
1 tbsp. chopped sweet pickle
1 tbsp. chopped stuffed olives

Halve eggs lengthwise with a wet knife. Remove yolks; mash with fork. Add all remaining ingredients; blend well. Stuff whites with yolk mixture. Garnish with a dash of paprika, additional olives or a sprig of parsley. Chill before serving.

Mrs. D. J. Dear
Bay Springs, Miss.

FATMA'S EGGS

6 hard-cooked eggs, halved
2 tsp. chopped onion
½ sm. chopped green pepper
¾ c. hamburger
2 tbsp. butter
½ tsp. salt
½ tsp. pepper
1 tomato, chopped

Remove egg yolks. Brown onion, green pepper and hamburger in butter. Combine with all remaining ingredients and one-half the egg yolks, mashed. Fill eggs. May be served on lettuce and grated onion and seasoned with salt, lemon juice and salad oil. Garnish with remaining egg yolk. Yield: 4-6 servings.

Mrs. Holman Egly
Berne, Ind.

FLUTED EGG SALAD

6 hard-cooked eggs
1 tsp. mustard
3 tbsp. relish spread
⅓ tsp. salt
Paprika
Mayonnaise

Flute eggs by cutting with end of knife in sawtooth fashion around egg, cutting through to yolk. Remove and mash egg yolks. Combine with all remaining ingredients. Refill whites with egg yolk mixture. Place in nest of lettuce, using three halves per serving. Sprinkle with paprika; garnish with mayonnaise. Yield: 6 servings.

Mrs. Minnie Lou Honeycutt
Monroe, N.C.

SHRIMP-STUFFED DEVILED EGGS

1 doz. hard-cooked eggs, halved
1 c. finely chopped cooked shrimp
1 tsp. mustard
3 tbsp. mayonnaise
Lemon juice
Salt and pepper
Russian or French dressing

Scoop out egg yolks; blend with all ingredients except whites. Fill egg whites. Serve on lettuce leaves with dressing.

Marion R. Eckert
Schwenksville, Pa.

STUFFED PINEAPPLE-EGG SALAD

1 No. 2 can crushed pineapple
1 doz. hard-cooked eggs, halved
Mayonnaise
½ tsp. salt

Drain pineapple; reserve juice. Remove egg yolks; combine yolks with a small amount of pineapple juice and mayonnaise to make a firm but smooth paste. Add salt and pineapple; stuff eggs with mixture. Chill if desired. Yield: 6 servings.

Dorcas Webster
Charleston, W. Va.

STUFFED EGGS CURRY

12 hard-cooked eggs
1 c. mayonnaise
1 tsp. chicken seasoned stock base
¼ tsp. instant onion powder
¼ tsp. white pepper
1 tsp. curry powder
½ tsp. salt
1 c. finely minced cooked chicken (opt.)
Anchovies
Olive slices
Capers

Cut eggs into halves, crosswise; slice a small cap off ends. Remove yolks; mash or force through sieve. Add mayonnaise, stock base, onion powder, pepper, curry powder, salt and chicken; mix thoroughly. Refill egg whites, piling yolk mixture high. Cap with smaller portion of white; top each with rolled anchovies, sliced ripe or stuffed olives and capers. Yield: 24 servings.

Photograph for this recipe above.

STUFFED EGGS

6 hard-cooked eggs, halved lengthwise
Cubed ham, olives or pimento
3 tbsp. butter, softened
1 tsp. Worcestershire sauce
2 tbsp. mayonnaise
Salt and pepper to taste

Remove egg yolks; force through a fine sieve. Place 1 cube of ham, olive or pimento in each egg white. Combine yolks with all remaining ingredients; beat until smooth. Force egg yolk mixture through a pastry tube onto egg whites. Yield: 6 servings.

Mrs. Bethel Schmidt
Vicksburg, Mich.

EASTER EGG SALAD

Salt
3 qt. boiling water
½ lb. elbow macaroni
½ c. salad dressing
2 tbsp. French dressing
3 drops Tabasco sauce
1 c. cooked kidney beans, drained
3 hard-cooked eggs, diced
¼ c. chopped sweet pickles
Watercress

(Continued on next page)

Combine 1 tablespoon salt, boiling water and macaroni. Cook for 8 minutes or until macaroni is tender; drain and rinse. Combine salad dressing, French dressing, 1 teaspoon salt and Tabasco sauce. Fold in kidney beans, eggs, pickles and macaroni. Serve on nests of watercress. Yield: 4 servings.

Mrs. Gloria J. Love
Mechanicsburg, Pa.

EGG AND CHEESE SALAD

6 hard-cooked eggs, mashed
¼ c. chopped chives
¾ c. small curd cottage cheese
½ c. salad dressing
3 tbsp. vinegar
1 tbsp. white sugar
Salt and pepper to taste

Combine eggs, chives and cottage cheese. Blend salad dressing, vinegar, sugar, salt and pepper. Combine the two mixtures. Serve on lettuce as a salad or use as a sandwich spread. Yield: 8 servings.

Dorothy Tenniswood
New Troy, Mich.

EGG AND LETTUCE SALAD

1 ½ c. chopped lettuce
3 hard-cooked eggs
1 tbsp. vinegar
3 tbsp. salad oil
¼ tsp. salt
¼ tsp. pepper

Place lettuce in bowl; add chopped egg whites. Mash egg yolks; add vinegar, salad oil and seasonings. Mix well; pour over lettuce. Toss and serve. Yield: 2 servings.

Mrs. Max Rose
Liberal, Mo.

EGG NEST SALAD

6 hard-cooked eggs
⅛ tsp. salt
Dash of pepper
3 tbsp. mayonnaise
6 crisp lettuce leaves
Paprika

Gently remove whole egg yolks; set aside. Mash the whites into small pieces with a fork. Add salt, pepper and mayonnaise. Place a rounded tablespoon of egg white mixture on lettuce leaf. Press mixture slightly with bowl of spoon for "nest" effect. Center egg yolk on nest; garnish with paprika. Yield: 6 servings.

Wilma Keeler
Cadillac, Mich.

EGG SALAD

4 hard-cooked eggs, mashed
½ c. ground carrots
½ c. ground celery
Salt and pepper to taste
2 tsp. mayonnaise
Sliced stuffed olives (opt.)

Combine all ingredients except olives; garnish with olives. Yield: 8 servings.

Elizabeth Barclay
Largo, Fla.

EGG SALAD

6 hard-cooked eggs, chopped
½ c. diced celery
¼ c. diced green pepper
1 tbsp. chopped pimento
½ c. mayonnaise
½ tsp. salt
¼ tsp. pepper

Combine all ingredients. Serve on lettuce. Garnish with additional pimento. Yield: 4 servings.

Winifred Blackwood
Hominy, Okla.

JERRY'S EGG SALAD

1 head lettuce
6 hard-cooked eggs, sliced
1 lge. onion, thinly sliced
1 ½ tsp. salt
¼ tsp. pepper
Dash of paprika
¼ c. salad oil
2 tbsp. vinegar
1 tsp. Worcestershire sauce
¼ c. grated sharp cheese

Break lettuce into bite-sized pieces. Alternate with layers of eggs and onion. Combine all remaining ingredients; pour over salad. Toss lightly. Yield: 6 servings.

Mrs. Arthur Holiman
Benton, Ark.

EGG SALAD

12 to 15 hard-cooked eggs, chopped
1 c. diced celery
1 tsp. Worcestershire sauce
Dash of Tabasco sauce
2 tbsp. grated onion
2 tbsp. chopped parsley
¼ c. pickle relish
2 tbsp. lemon juice
¼ c. chopped green pepper
1 envelope unflavored gelatin
½ c. cold water
2 c. mayonnaise
¾ tsp. salt
Pepper

Combine eggs, celery, sauces, onion, parsley, relish, lemon juice and green pepper. Soften gelatin in cold water; dissolve over boiling water. Beat in mayonnaise; combine egg mixture and mayonnaise mixture. Add salt and pepper. Place in mold; chill until firm. Yield: 12 servings.

Mrs. H. H. Hankins
Rogers, Ark.

LETTUCE-EGG SALAD

1 head lettuce, torn into sm. pieces
1 sm. onion, chopped
2 hard-cooked eggs, chopped
Salt and pepper to taste
Mayonnaise to taste
4 slices bacon, fried and crumbled

Combine lettuce, onion, eggs, salt and pepper with mayonnaise. Top with bacon. Serve immediately. Yield: 6 servings.

Beth White
Goliad, Tex.

OLD-FASHIONED EGG SALAD

1 head lettuce
1 lge. onion, sliced
6 hard-cooked eggs, sliced
1 ½ tsp. salt
¼ tsp. pepper
Dash of paprika
¼ c. salad oil
2 tbsp. vinegar
1 tsp. Worcestershire sauce
1 tbsp. chopped parsley
¼ c. grated sharp cheese

Break lettuce into bite-sized pieces. Alternate layers of lettuce, onion slices and egg slices. Blend all remaining ingredients; pour over layers. Toss lightly. Yield: 8 servings.

Mrs. M. S. Holley
Evergreen, Ala.

MOLDED EGG SALAD

8 hard-cooked eggs, coarsely chopped
1 c. finely diced celery
¼ c. salad dressing
1 tsp. Worcestershire sauce
1 tbsp. lemon juice
1 tsp. scraped onion
Salt and pepper to taste
6 thick tomato slices
Salad greens
Paprika
Celery curls

Combine eggs, celery, dressing and all seasonings except paprika. Press into molds and chill. Unmold on tomato slices placed in a bed of salad greens. Sprinkle with paprika; garnish with celery curls and additional seasoning. Yield: 6 servings.

Zelda Leigh Powell
Mandeville, La.

TASTY EGG SALAD

6 hard-cooked eggs, chopped
3 stalks celery, finely cut
1 med. onion, finely cut
½ c. cubed cream cheese
1 lge. dill pickle, finely cut
½ c. salad dressing

Combine all ingredients; blend well. Chill for 30 minutes. Serve on lettuce. Yield: 6 servings.

Idella I. Alfson
Woonsocket, S.D.

COSTAIN'S EGG RING SALAD

1 envelope unflavored gelatin
¼ c. cold water
½ c. boiling water
6 hard-cooked eggs, chopped
1 c. mayonnaise
1 tbsp. catsup
Juice of ½ lemon
½ c. chopped watercress or parsley
Salt to taste
¼ onion, chopped
½ clove of garlic, chopped
½ tsp. Worcestershire sauce

Soak gelatin in cold water; dissolve in boiling water. Combine all ingredients. Pour into mold; chill until firm. Yield: 8 servings.

Mrs. William T. Page
Stony Brook, N.Y.

DEVILED EGG-ASPIC SALAD

2 c. tomato juice
1 tsp. basil
1 tbsp. minced onion
1 tbsp. minced celery
1 tbsp. minced green pepper
1 3-oz. pkg. lemon gelatin
2 tbsp. chives or garlic vinegar
½ tsp. salt
3 hard-cooked eggs, sliced lengthwise and deviled

Combine tomato juice, basil, onion, celery and green pepper. Bring to a boil; remove from heat. Strain; add gelatin, vinegar or chives and salt. Stir until dissolved; chill until mixture begins to congeal. Arrange eggs, cut-side up, in a flat oblong bowl. Pour gelatin mixture over eggs; chill until firm. Cut so that yellow and white side of egg is centered in aspic. Serve with salad dressing or sour cream dressing. Yield: 6 servings.

Charlotte R. Turner
Hendersonville, N.C

EGG-CROWNED SUPPER MOLD

4 hard-cooked eggs
1 envelope unflavored gelatin
1 ¾ c. chicken broth
3 tbsp. prepared mustard
3 tbsp. sweet pickle relish
3 tbsp. diced green pepper
2 tbsp. instant minced onion
1 tsp. sugar
½ tsp. celery salt
2 ½ c. finely diced cooked potatoes
2 c. diced baked ham
Pepper
½ c. mayonnaise

Cut eggs into halves, crosswise; cut each piece in half. Soften gelatin in 1/4 cup broth. Heat remaining liquid; add gelatin, stirring to dissolve. Float a 6-cup ring mold in pan of ice and water. Pour 2 or 3 tablespoons gelatin mixture into mold; rotate to coat bottom of pan. Stand egg pieces on end in a circle on congealed gelatin. Spoon 1/2 cup gelatin mixture around egg pieces. Let stand long enough to set. Combine mustard, pickle relish, green pepper, onion, sugar and celery salt; add remaining gelatin mixture. Add potatoes, ham and any remaining eggs. Season with little pepper. Place pan in ice and water until slightly thickened; fold in mayonnaise. Spoon mixture over eggs in mold. Chill for several hours or until firm; unmold on tray. Fill center and around mold with crisp garden lettuce. Garnish with stuffed olives. Yield: 6 servings.

Photograph for this recipe on page 123.

DEVILED EGG SALAD

1 tbsp. gelatin
½ c. cold water
1 tsp. salt
2 tbsp. lemon juice
¼ tsp. Worcestershire sauce
⅛ tsp. cayenne pepper
¾ c. mayonnaise or salad dressing
1 ½ tsp. grated onion
½ c. finely diced celery
¼ c. diced green pepper
¼ c. chopped pimento
4 hard-cooked eggs, chopped

Soften gelatin in cold water; dissolve over boiling water. Add salt, lemon juice, Worcestershire sauce and pepper; cool. Stir in mayonnaise, onion, celery, pepper, pimento and eggs. Pour into mold; chill until firm. Yield: 6 servings.

Mrs. Newton V. Colston
Martinsville, Va.

EGG CURRY RING

2 c. clear chicken broth
1 tbsp. curry powder
1 ½ tbsp. gelatin
¼ c. cold water
1 ½ c. mayonnaise
3 hard-cooked eggs, chopped
6 stuffed olives (opt.)
½ tsp. salt

Bring broth to a boil; add curry powder. Soften gelatin in cold water for 5 minutes; dissolve in stock. Chill mixture until thickened. Blend in mayonnaise; fold in eggs, olives and salt. Pour into ring mold dipped into cold water; chill until firm. Yield: 8 servings.

Mrs. Charles F. Hunter
New Orleans, La.

EGG MOLD

1 envelope unflavored gelatin
⅓ c. cold water
12 hard-cooked eggs, chopped
3 tbsp. chopped green pepper
2 tbsp. sweet relish
½ c. finely chopped celery
1 tsp. salt
¾ c. mayonnaise

Soften gelatin in cold water; dissolve over hot water. Combine eggs, pepper, relish, celery and salt; add gelatin to mayonnaise. Add to egg mixture. Pour into mold. Chill until firm. Serve on endive or lettuce.

Mary H. Sargent
Minneapolis, Minn.

Nature's own colors need only a minor assist to present a sparkling tray of mixed fruits. Each may come from a different area, but all join in a rainbow of flavor. Pink Lemon Fruit Salad Dressing enhances the delightful freshness of each.

FRESH FRUIT SALAD TRAY

Honeydew melon slices
Cantaloupe slices
Watermelon balls
Honeydew melon balls
Fresh peach halves
Raspberries or strawberries
Banana slices
Honey
Toasted coconut
Orange sections
Frosted grapes
Pink Lemon Fruit Salad Dressing

Arrange melon slices and balls attractively on large tray. Top peach halves with raspberries. Dip banana slices in honey; roll in coconut. Place orange wedges and strawberries on toothpick. Place frosted grapes in clusters on tray. Garnish with mint sprigs and lettuce leaves. Serve with Pink Lemon Fruit Salad Dressing.

PINK LEMON FRUIT SALAD DRESSING

Juice of 2 lemons
1 tbsp. maraschino cherry juice
2 tbsp. honey
½ c. salad oil
1 tsp. celery seed

In small mixing bowl, combine lemon juice, cherry juice and honey. Beat with electric or rotary beater until thoroughly blended. Continue beating while adding oil very gradually, in a thin, steady stream. Stir in celery seed. Chill. Stir or shake before serving.

See photograph on reverse side.

EGG MOLD

1 ½ tbsp. gelatin
⅓ c. water
10 hard-cooked eggs, diced
½ tsp. salt
2 tbsp. catsup
Juice of 1 lemon
1 ½ c. mayonnaise
1 c. boiling water
2 c. tuna salad

Soften gelatin in water; combine with eggs, salt, catsup, lemon and mayonnaise. Add boiling water; mix well and chill. Place in mold; chill until firm. Unmold; spoon tuna salad over top and serve. Yield: 16 servings.

Elsie T. Hassel
Fayetteville, Ark.

EGG SALAD

1 tbsp. unflavored gelatin
½ c. cold water
1 tbsp. lemon juice
Salt
1 c. mayonnaise
4 hard-cooked eggs, diced
½ c. diced celery
2 tbsp. chopped pickle or 2 tbsp. sweet relish
2 tbsp. chopped pimento
2 tbsp. chopped green pepper

Soak gelatin in cold water; dissolve over hot water. Add lemon juice and salt; blend with mayonnaise. Stir in all remaining ingredients. Pour into buttered mold; chill. Top with small amount of mayonnaise.

Mrs. William T. Bates
Steubenville, O.

EGG SALAD

1 pkg. gelatin
¼ c. cold water
1 c. boiling water
12 hard-cooked eggs, chopped
Salt and pepper
1 sm. bottle stuffed olives, chopped
1 c. finely chopped celery
1 c. mayonnaise

Dissolve gelatin in cold water; add boiling water. Combine all ingredients; chill until firm. Yield: 10-12 servings.

Mrs. Ward Mitchell
Beaufort, S.C.

EGG SALAD MOLD

1 envelope unflavored gelatin
½ c. cold water
½ c. boiling water
¾ c. mayonnaise
10 hard-cooked eggs
¼ c. chopped stuffed olives
2 tsp. grated onion
2 tbsp. chopped parsley
¼ c. chopped celery
4 or 5 olives, sliced
Salad greens

Soften gelatin in cold water; dissolve in boiling water. Cool. Add mayonnaise, 8 chopped eggs, olives, onion, parsley and celery. Slice remaining eggs; arrange around sides and bottom of salad mold. Pour in part of gelatin mixture to hold slices in place. Chill until firm. Add remaining gelatin mixture. Chill until firm. Unmold on salad greens and press olive slices around sides. Serve cold. Yield: 8 servings.

Mrs. Grace B. Callaway
Greensboro, Ga.

EGG SALAD MOLD

1 family box unflavored or lemon gelatin
2 c. hot water
2 c. cold water
12 hard-cooked eggs, diced
5 sweet pickles, diced
5 sticks celery, diced
1 onion, diced
24 stuffed olives, sliced
½ c. mayonnaise
¼ tsp. salt

Dissolve gelatin in hot water; add cold water. Chill until thickened. Combine remaining ingredients; fold into gelatin. Chill until firm. Serve on lettuce; garnish with pickled crab apples, pickled beets and pickled onions. Yield: 8 servings.

Mrs. Juanita Eason
Bremen, Ky.

EGG SOUFFLE SALAD

1 pkg. lemon gelatin
1 c. hot water
½ c. cold water
2 tbsp. white vinegar
½ c. mayonnaise
3 hard-cooked eggs, finely chopped
½ c. diced celery
½ c. diced onion
½ c. diced green pepper
½ c. diced pimento
2 ½ oz. horseradish mustard

Beat gelatin, hot water, cold water, vinegar and mayonnaise; pour into ice tray for a quick chill. Beat again until fluffy. Fold in eggs, celery, onion, green pepper, pimento and mustard. Pour into mold and congeal. Top with additional mayonnaise or salad dressing. Yield: 6 servings.

Mrs. J. H. Jackson
Chicago, Ill.

GLENNA'S EGG SALAD

6 hard-cooked eggs, riced
1 pkg. lemon gelatin
1 c. hot water
1 tsp. mustard
1 tsp. celery salt
½ tsp. paprika
½ tsp. salt
⅓ c. vinegar
⅓ c. mayonnaise

Dissolve gelatin in hot water. Add all remaining ingredients; beat. Cool; serve on lettuce with additional mayonnaise.

Glenna A. Starbird
Norway, Me.

GRAHAM'S EGG SALAD

1 envelope unflavored gelatin
¼ c. cold water
1 c. mayonnaise
½ c. diced celery
6 hard-cooked eggs, sliced
⅓ c. chopped olives
Salt to taste
Dash of garlic salt
Tabasco sauce to taste

Soften gelatin in cold water; dissolve over hot water. Combine mayonnaise, celery, eggs, olives, salt, garlic salt and Tabasco sauce. Add gelatin. Chill until firm. Yield: 6 servings.

Mrs. Gavin G. Craig, Jr.
Alvaton, Ky.

MOLDED EGG AND SHRIMP SALAD

1 envelope unflavored gelatin
¼ c. cold water
1 bouillon cube
1 c. hot water
1 c. salad dressing
6 hard-cooked eggs, sliced
1 can small cocktail shrimp
1 c. diced celery
2 tbsp. chopped green pepper
2 tbsp. chopped pimento
2 tbsp. pickle relish
Salt and pepper

Soften gelatin in cold water; dissolve with bouillon cube in hot water. Cool; blend with salad dressing. Oil a ring mold; place slices of 2 eggs on bottom. Add all remaining ingredients; pour into mold. Chill until firm. Unmold; garnish edge with tomato wedges and watercress. Yield: 10-12 servings.

Mrs. H. W. Christensen
Salt Lake City, Utah

CHINESE EGG

12 hard-cooked eggs
1 qt. boiling water
3 tbsp. orange pekoe tea
1 tsp. anise seed
4 tbsp. soy sauce
1 ½ tbsp. salt

Shell eggs carefully so whites are not broken. Pour boiling water over tea; let steep for 5 minutes. Strain; combine with anise seed, soy sauce and salt. Add whole eggs; simmer for 1 hour. Store, covered, in refrigerator. Yield: 12 servings.

Lucile B. McGehee
South Decatur, Ga.

PENNSYLVANIA DUTCH RED BEET EGGS

5 med. beets
1 c. vinegar
1 c. water
½ c. sugar
1 tsp. salt
8 hard-cooked eggs

Boil beets until tender; remove skins and slice 1/2-inch thick. Blend vinegar, water, sugar and salt. Pour mixture over beets; refrigerate overnight. Next day remove one-half the beet slices; add whole shelled eggs. Refrigerate another day until eggs become rosy-red in color. Use sliced eggs as a salad garnish or serve with beets as a salad. Yield: 8 servings.

Lucy M. Bamberger
Myerstown, Pa.

PICKLED EGGS

2 No. 303 cans sliced or diced beets and liquid
1 beet can water
¾ c. vinegar
2 tbsp. sugar
1 doz. hard-cooked eggs, shelled

Blend all ingredients except eggs in bowl or large jar; stir until sugar is dissolved. Add eggs and set aside for 24 hours before serving.

Alice Mae Gabrielson
Red Bluff, Calif.

SMOKED EGGS

6 hard-cooked eggs
¼ c. vinegar
1 ¾ c. cold water
2 tsp. liquid smoke

Place hot eggs in a jar; add all remaining ingredients. Cover and refrigerate for several hours. Eggs may be kept in liquid smoke as long as desired. Yield: 6 servings.

Doris H. Schlumpf
Durand, Wisc.

RECIPE FOR FROZEN CITRUS SALAD ON PAGE 145

APPLE-CREAM SALAD

½ c. crushed pineapple, drained
3 eggs, beaten
½ c. sugar
⅓ c. lemon juice
¼ tsp. salt
½ c. shredded carrots
½ c. walnuts or pecans
½ c. diced celery
2 c. chilled applesauce
1 c. sour cream

Drain pineapple; reserve juice. Combine eggs, sugar, lemon juice, salt and pineapple juice; cook over slow heat until mixture coats spoon. Cool slightly; add all remaining ingredients. Pour into individual molds. Freeze for about 4 hours. NOTE: Salad will keep in freezer for one month. Yield: 12 servings.

Mrs. H. B. Copeland
Palmer, Tex.

APPLE-ORANGE FROST

1 No. 2 can applesauce
1 sm. can orange juice
2 or 3 tbsp. lemon juice
Artificial sweetener equivalent to 3 tbsp. sugar
3 egg whites, stiffly beaten

Combine applesauce, orange juice, lemon juice and sweetener. Fold in egg whites. Freeze until firm. Salad will keep from two to four weeks in freezer.

Mrs. Janet Krumme
Seymour, Ind.

FROZEN APPLE-PINEAPLE SALAD

1 9-oz. can crushed pineapple
2 eggs, beaten
½ c. sugar
¼ tsp. salt
3 tbsp. lemon juice
2 c. finely diced apples
½ c. finely diced celery
1 c. whipped cream

Drain pineapple, reserving syrup; add enough water to make 1/2 cup liquid. Combine eggs, sugar, salt, lemon juice and syrup-water mixture. Cook over low heat, stirring constantly until thick. Chill. Fold in pineapple, apples, celery and whipped cream. Pour into 2-quart refrigerator tray or salad mold; freeze.

Mrs. Barbara Deane
Hoxie, Kans.

FROZEN BANANA SALAD

4 med. bananas, mashed
2 tbsp. lemon juice
½ c. sugar
¼ c. mayonnaise
½ c. chopped Maraschino cherries
½ c. chopped walnuts
¾ c. heavy cream, whipped

Blend bananas with lemon juice, sugar, mayonnaise, cherries and nuts. Fold in whipped cream; place in freezing tray. Freeze. May be served on lettuce leaves and garnished with walnuts. Yield: 8 servings.

Bertha A. Achelpohl
Ellinwood, Kans.

FROZEN BANANA SALAD

1 3-oz. pkg. cream cheese, softened
½ c. mayonnaise
¼ c. sugar
3 tbsp. lemon juice
⅓ c. chopped nuts
⅓ c. coconut
¼ c. chopped Maraschino cherries
2 c. sliced bananas
⅔ c. evaporated milk, chilled

Blend cheese, mayonnaise, sugar and 2 tablespoons lemon juice. Stir in nuts, coconut and cherries. Add bananas. Whip milk until it holds a peak. Add remaining lemon juice; blend. Fold milk into cheese mixture. Freeze. Serve immediately after removing from freezer.

Charlotte Carter
Carpinteria, Calif.

RED AND WHITE CHERRY FREEZE

1 3-oz. pkg. cream cheese
1 9-oz. can crushed pineapple

(Continued on next page)

2 c. miniature marshmallows
1 9-oz. can pitted Royal Anne cherries, drained
⅓ c. quartered Maraschino cherries
1 c. heavy cream, whipped

Soften cream cheese, using creaming method; blend in pineapple, marshmallows and cherries. Fold in whipped cream; pile into 10 x 6 x 1 1/2-inch dish or tray. Freeze. May be garnished with whipped cream and whole Maraschino cherries. Yield: 9 servings.

Mrs. Astrid Ahrens
Delavan, Minn.

2 tbsp. mayonnaise
1 1-lb. can jellied cranberry sauce
1 c. drained crushed pineapple
½ c. heavy cream, whipped
½ c. chopped pecans

Cream softened cheese with sugar; stir in mayonnaise. Fold in cranberry sauce, pineapple, cream and nuts. Pour into 9 x 5 x 3-inch loaf pan; freeze until firm. Cut into squares; serve on lettuce. Yield: 8 servings.

Mrs. Edith Jolliff
Chariton, Iowa

BERRY-ICE CREAM SALAD

1 qt. vanilla ice cream
½ c. mayonnaise
1 c.canned pineapple, drained
1 c. drained blueberries
2 c. raspberries or strawberries

Soften ice cream; quickly blend in mayonnaise. Add fruit; mix. Freeze for 2 to 3 hours or until firm.

Mrs. Violet Moseley
Avon Park, Fla.

CRANBERRY FROZEN SALAD

1 can whole cranberry sauce
1 can pineapple chunks, drained
1 pkg. sour cream

Combine all ingredients. Pour into paper-lined muffin tins; freeze. Remove from tins; wrap in foil. Store in freezer until needed. Yield: 12-16 servings.

Mrs. George Donald Moore
Searcy, Ark.

ARTIC FREEZE

2 3-oz. or 1 8-oz. pkg. cream cheese
2 tbsp. mayonnaise
2 tbsp. sugar
1 sm. can crushed pineapple (opt.)
1 c. miniature marshmallow (opt.)
½ c. chopped nuts
1 lge. can whole cranberries
½ pt. heavy cream, whipped

Blend cream cheese, mayonnaise, sugar and pineapple; fold in remaining ingredients. Pour into greased loaf pan; freeze overnight. May be sliced and served on lettuce. NOTE: Remove from freezer about 15 minutes before slicing. Yield: 10 servings.

Mrs. Helen K. Coleman
Winnsboro, S.C.

CRANBERRY SALAD

2 3-oz. pkg. cream cheese, softened
2 tbsp. salad dressing
2 tbsp. sugar
1 can whole cranberry sauce
1 c. drained crushed pineapple
½ c. chopped walnuts
1 c. heavy cream, whipped

Whip cream cheese; add salad dressing, sugar, one-half of cranberry sauce, pineapple and walnuts. Fold in whipped cream. Line 8 x 8 x 2-inch baking pan with remaining cranberry sauce. Pour cream mixture over cranberries; freeze. Cut into squares; turn upside down to serve. Yield: 8 servings.

Mabel Taylor
Tomah, Wisc.

CRANBERRY ARTIC FREEZE

2 3-oz. pkg. cream cheese, softened
2 tbsp. sugar

CRANBERRY SLICES

1 No. 2 can crushed pineapple, drained
1 1-lb. can whole cranberry sauce

(Continued on next page)

FROZEN CRANBERRY MOLDS

½ pt. sour cream
¼ c. coarsely chopped pecans
Salad greens

Thoroughly combine pineapple, cranberry sauce, sour cream and pecans; turn into ice tray. Freeze until firm. Cut into slices and arrange on crisp greens. Yield: 8-10 servings.

Esther Hummel
Sterling, Colo.

1 lb. cranberries, ground
2 c. sugar
1 c. whipped cream

Combine pineapple and marshmallows; let stand overnight. Combine cranberries and sugar; let stand overnight. Combine mixtures; fold in whipped cream. Freeze.

June Stultz
Renton, Wash.

FROSTY CRANBERRY TIP TOPS

1 1-lb. can cranberry sauce
2 or 3 tbsp. lemon juice
1 c. whipped cream
1 3-oz. pkg. cream cheese, whipped
¼ c. mayonnaise
¼ c. sifted confectioners sugar
1 c. chopped nuts (opt.)

Crush cranberry sauce with fork; add lemon juice. Blend well. Pour into small paper cups. Combine remaining ingredients; spread over cranberry mixture. Freeze.

Mrs. Julian A. Raburn
McRae, Ga.

CRANBERRY-APPLE SALAD

1 qt. cranberries
6 apples, peeled and cored
1 ¼ c. sugar
1 sm. can crushed pineapple
¼ c. chopped nuts
1 pkg. miniature marshmallows
2 c. heavy cream, whipped

Grind cranberries and apples; add sugar. Let set for 15 minutes. Add remaining ingredients; freeze. NOTE: Chilled evaporated milk may be substituted for heavy cream. Yield: 12 servings.

Norma Stuart
Altoona, Iowa

CRANBERRY SALAD

1 No. 2 can crushed pineapple
1 lb. marshmallows, cut up

FROZEN CRANBERRY-APPLE SALAD

1 lb. whole cranberries
1 pkg. marshmallows
3 med. apples
½ c. nuts
1 c. sugar
1 c. heavy cream, whipped

Grind cranberries, marshmallows, apples and nuts together. Add sugar; let stand for 30 minutes. Fold whipped cream into cranberry mixture. Place in oblong pan; freeze. Yield: 12 servings.

Mrs. Phyllis Patton
Finley, N.D.

FROZEN CRANBERRY FRUIT SALAD

1 lb. cranberries
2 c. water
2 c. sugar
1 lemon, peeled and chopped
2 oranges, peeled and chopped
2 bananas mashed

Boil cranberries with water and sugar until done; strain while hot. Add remaining ingredients; freeze. Yield: 8 servings.

Mrs. Mildred M. Meier
Sterling, Nebr.

FROZEN CRANBERRY SALAD

1 qt. chopped cranberries
1 ¼ c. sugar
1 c. drained crushed pineapple
1 lb.miniature marshmallows
1 c. whipped cream

(Continued on next page)

Combine all ingredients; freeze.

Ira E. Grubl
Linton, N.D.

FROZEN CRANBERRY SALAD

1 1-lb. can cranberry jelly
Juice of 1 orange
1 c. heavy cream, whipped
¼ c. mayonnaise
¼ c. confectioners sugar
½ c. chopped walnuts

Mix cranberry jelly and juice; place in ice tray or similar container. Combine all remaining ingredients; spread over cranberry mixture. Freeze. Serve on lettuce leaf. Yield: 6 servings.

Mrs. John A. Wasson
Munster, Ind.

FROZEN CRANBERRY WALDORF SALAD

1 lb. cranberries, washed and drained
3 or 4 unpeeled apples, cored
20 lge. or 1 10-oz. pkg. miniature marshmallows
1 c. sugar
1 c. heavy cream, whipped

Grind cranberries, apples and marshmallows together. Stir in sugar. Fold in whipped cream; pour into mold. Freeze. Yield: 10 servings.

Mrs. Charles R. Bryant
Princeton, Ind.

FROZEN CRANBERRY-WALNUT SALAD

4 c. whole cranberries
3 tbsp. lemon juice
1 pt. whipped cream
1 c. finely chopped walnuts

Blend cranberries and lemon juice. Spread cranberry mixture in cake pan. Combine whipped cream and nuts. Spoon whipped cream mixture onto cranberries. Freeze.

Madeline Johnson
Pinehurst, Idaho

WALNUT-CRANBERRY RIBBON LOAF

1 1-lb. can cranberry sauce
¾ c. grated apple
½ pt. whipped cream
¼ c. confectioners sugar
1 tsp. vanilla flavoring
½ c. chopped English walnuts or pecans

Crush cranberry sauce with fork; stir in apple. Pour into freezing tray. Mix whipped cream, sugar, vanilla flavoring and 1/3 cup nuts. Spoon over cranberry layer; sprinkle with remaining nuts. Freeze until firm.

Mrs. Barbara Power
North Lewisburg, O.

FRUIT-CREAM CHEESE SALAD

1 3-oz. pkg. cream cheese
¼ c. mayonnaise
Pinch of salt
1 tsp. unflavored gelatin
2 tbsp. lemon juice
⅔ to 1 c. heavy cream
½ c. sugar
1 No. 2 ½ can fruit cocktail, drained
1 No. 1 can Royal Anne cherries, drained (opt.)
6 Maraschino cherries, chopped (opt.)
½ c. chopped pecans (opt.)

Blend cream cheese and mayonnaise; add salt. Soften gelatin in lemon juice; dissolve over hot water. Add to cheese-mayonnaise mixture. Whip cream until stiff, slowly adding sugar in last stage of beating. Add fruit, nuts and whipped cream to cheese mixture. Pour into waxed paper-lined refrigerator tray. Freeze. Yield: 8-10 servings.

Mrs. Olen Butts
Union, Miss.

FRUIT-CREAM CHEESE SALAD

1 pkg. cream cheese
2 tbsp. top milk or cream
⅓ c. mayonnaise
2 tbsp. lemon juice
½ c. sugar
1 lge. can fruit cocktail
½ pt. heavy cream, whipped

Soften cheese with milk; add mayonnaise, lemon juice, sugar and fruit. Fold in whipped cream; freeze. Yield: 8-10 servings.

Mrs. F. Raymond Gibson
Huntington, W. Va.

FROZEN FRUIT COCKTAIL SALAD

½ c. sugar
2 3-oz. pkg. cream cheese
Few drops of vanilla flavoring
½ c. heavy cream, whipped
1 lge. can fruit cocktail, drained
Maraschino cherries

Cream sugar, cream cheese and flavoring. Fold in whipped cream and fruit cocktail; pour into ice tray. Place Maraschino cherries on top, spacing evenly. Freeze until ready to serve. Yield: 8 servings.

Mrs. John C. McGill
Tuscon, Ariz.

FRUIT COCKTAIL SALAD

4 oz. marshmallows, cut into pieces
1 c. fruit cocktail
12 apricot halves, cut into pieces
12 Maraschino cherries, cut into pieces
3 slices pineapple, cut into pieces
½ c. boiled dressing
½ c. mayonnaise
½ c. heavy cream, whipped
Dash of salt

Combine all ingredients. Freeze until firm. Cut into squares; serve on lettuce with salad dressing. Yield: 12 servings.

Mrs. David O. Trauger
Philadelphia, Pa.

FROZEN FRUIT-CHEESE SALAD

1 tbsp. unflavored gelatin
2 tbsp. cold water
1 c. mayonnaise
3 c. fruit cocktail
½ lb. pkg. miniature marshmallows
¼ lb. cheese, grated
2 tbsp. confectioners sugar
1 c. whipped cream

Soak gelatin in cold water for 5 minutes; stir into mayonnaise. Mix in fruit, marshmallows and cheese. Mix sugar and whipped cream together; fold into fruit mixture. Pour into small ice trays. Freeze.

Suzanne H. Waldrop
Park City, Ky.

ROSY FRUIT COCKTAIL SLICES

2 3-oz. pkg. cream cheese
1 c. mayonnaise
1 c. whipped cream
1 No. 2 ½ can fruit cocktail, drained
½ c. Maraschino cherries, drained and quartered
2 ½ c. chopped marshmallows
Few drops red food coloring or Maraschino cherry juice

Blend cheese with mayonnaise. Fold in remaining ingredients. Freeze until firm. Thaw at room temperature for a few minutes before serving.

Mrs. John Leischner
DeLand, Ill.

FROZEN FRUIT- CREAM CHEESE SALAD

2 3-oz. pkg. cream cheese
⅓ c. mayonnaise
Salt to taste
½ c. whipped cream
3 ½ c. drained fruit cocktail
½ c. chopped nuts

Mash cheese; blend in mayonnaise and salt. Fold in whipped cream, fruit cocktail and nuts. Spoon into baking pan or refrigerator tray. Freeze for several hours or overnight. Yield: 8 servings.

Mrs. Christine Stewart
Jackson, Miss.

FROZEN FRUIT COCKTAIL SALAD

1 lge. pkg. cream cheese
1 lge. can fruit cocktail, drained
Miniature marshmallows
Maraschino cherries
Chopped nuts

Soften cream cheese; add all remaining ingredients. Place in 8 x 11-inch pan; freeze until firm. Serve in squares on lettuce. Yield: 8-12 servings.

Mrs. Robert E. Hockman
Winchester, Va.

FROZEN FRUIT COCKTAIL SALAD

1 tsp. unflavored gelatin
3 tbsp. lemon juice
1 3-oz. pkg. cream cheese
¼ c. mayonnaise
Dash of salt
⅔ c. heavy cream, chilled
½ c. sugar
½ c. chopped nuts
1 No. 2 ½ can fruit cocktail, drained

(Continued on next page)

Soften gelatin in lemon juice; dissolve over hot water. Blend cream cheese with mayonnaise and salt. Stir in gelatin. Whip cream until stiff, gradually adding sugar during last stages of beating. Fold in cheese mixture, nuts and fruit cocktail. Pour into refrigerator tray lined with waxed paper. Freeze until firm.

Mrs. Minnie G. Burke
Los Gatos, Calif.

FROZEN FRUIT-HONEY SALAD

2 tbsp. sugar
1 tbsp. flour
½ c. honey
1 egg
⅓ c. lemon juice
2 c. drained fruit cocktail
1 c. sliced bananas
⅓ c. diced orange slices
¼ c. Maraschino or Bing cherries, pitted and quartered
1 c. whipped cream

Combine sugar, flour and honey. Bring to a boil; cook for 1 minute, stirring constantly. Beat egg; gradually add lemon juice. Add a small amount of honey mixture to egg; mix well. Return mixture to heat; bring to a boil, stirring constantly. Remove from heat; cool. Combine fruits; add to honey mixture. Fold in whipped cream. Freeze.

Mrs. Georgia Balls
Pocatello, Idaho

FROZEN FRUIT SALAD

2 bananas, mashed
1 pkg. cream cheese
1 No. 2 can fruit cocktail, drained
1 jar Maraschino cherries
½ c. chopped nuts
½ pt. heavy cream, whipped

Mash bananas in cream cheese. Combine with remaining ingredients. Freeze for 1 hour. Cut into squares and serve. Yield: 8-10 servings.

Mrs. Robert B. Kotal
San Antonio, Tex.

FROZEN FRUIT SALAD

1 No. 2 can pineapple chunks
1 tbsp. butter
1 tbsp. flour
1 tbsp. sugar
1 tbsp. lemon juice
1 egg, slightly beaten
1 c. heavy cream, whipped
1 No. 2 ½ can apricots, diced
1 No. 2 ½ can fruit cocktail, drained

Reserve juice drained from pineapple. Melt butter in top of double boiler. Blend in flour. Add reserved pineapple juice, sugar, lemon juice and egg. Cook, stirring, until smooth. Cool. Fold cooked mixture into whipped cream and fruit. Freeze. Yield: 12 servings.

Hazel Tidmore
York, Ala.

FROZEN FRUIT SALAD

1 lge. can fruit cocktail
2 sm. pkg. cream cheese
2 tbsp. salad dressing
1 c. marshmallow cream

Drain fruit cocktail thoroughly. Blend cream cheese, salad dressing and cream; stir in fruit cocktail. Pack into round 1-quart ice cream container; freeze. Yield: 12 servings.

Mrs. C. B. Nance
Webb City, Mo.

FROZEN FRUIT SALAD

1 c. fruit cocktail, drained
3 c. diced peaches
½ c. mayonnaise
1 c. heavy cream, whipped

Combine all ingredients; freeze. Yield: 8-10 servings.

Mrs. James C. Harris
Warrenton, N.C.

FROZEN FRUIT SALAD WITH COCONUT

1 can fruit cocktail, drained
1 box flaked coconut
1 pkg. miniature marshmallows
1 No. 2 can pineapple chunks
1 c. heavy cream, whipped
½ c. salad dressing

Combine ingredients except whipped cream and salad dressing; toss lightly. Combine whipped cream and salad dressing; pour over fruit, mixing lightly. Freeze. Yield: 6 servings.

Bertha Carroll
West Plains, Mo.

FROZEN FRUIT SALAD

12 marshmallows, finely diced
1 No. 2 can fruit cocktail
1 pkg. cream cheese
½ c. mayonnaise
½ c. heavy cream, whipped
Pinch of salt
1 c. nuts
Maraschino cherries (opt.)

Combine marshmallows with fruit cocktail; let stand for a few hours. Add all remaining ingredients; freeze for 24 hours. Yield: 8 servings.

Mrs. Benzie T. Rice
Columbia, S.C.

FROZEN SUMMER SALAD

2 3-oz. pkg. cream cheese, softened
1 c. mayonnaise
½ c. chopped Maraschino cherries, drained
½ pt. heavy cream, whipped
1 c. miniature marshmallows
2 No. 303 cans fruit cocktail, drained

Combine all ingredients. Pour into 9 x 9 x 2-inch pan. Cover; place in freezer until frozen. Cut into 12 squares; serve on lettuce leaves. Yield: 12 servings.

Mrs. L. O. Day
West Palm Beach, Fla.

PARTY GELATIN SALAD

1 lge. can fruit cocktail
1 pkg. lemon gelatin
8 lge. marshmallows
2 pkg. cream cheese
¾ c.chopped celery
½ pt. heavy cream, whipped

Drain fruit, reserving juice. Heat juice; dissolve gelatin, marshmallows and cheese in heated juice. Cool. Add fruit and celery as mixture begins to congeal. Fold in cream. Freeze.

Mrs. Annie Stepanovich
East Liverpool, O.

PINK SNOW SALAD

1 ⅔ c. evaporated milk, chilled
2 tbsp. lemon juice
1 can fruit cocktail, drained
1 can sliced peaches or 2 c. fresh sliced peaches
¾ c. sugar
1 can pineapple chunks, drained
1 sm. bottle Maraschino cherries, drained
3 tbsp. cherry juice
1 c. miniature marshmallows
½ c. chopped pecans

Beat milk until stiff with electric mixer set at high speed. Add lemon juice. Fold in remaining ingredients. Freeze.

Mrs. Sudie Mitchell Bell
Isola, Miss.

ORANGE-CREAM MOLD

½ c. hot water
1 c. pineapple juice
1 pkg. orange gelatin
1 8-oz. pkg. cream cheese
¼ c. orange juice
2 tbsp. lemon juice

Combine hot water and pineapple juice; add gelatin. Stir until gelatin is dissolved. Combine gelatin mixture, cream cheese, orange and lemon juice. Blend well. Pour into paper-lined muffin pan. Freeze until firm.

Mrs. Jean Still
Tacoma, Wash.

HOLIDAY ORANGE SALAD

2 pkg. orange gelatin
1 11-oz. can Mandarin oranges, drained
2 c. mixed Mandarin orange juice and water, heated
1 pt. orange sherbet

Drain oranges, reserving juice; add enough water to make 2 cups juice. Dissolve gelatin in hot juice-water mixture. Immediately add sherbet; stir until melted. Chill until thickened; add oranges. Pour into 2-quart ring mold. Chill until firm. Wrap in moisture-proof paper. Freeze. To serve, unwrap and thaw in refrigerator for 3 to 4 hours or overnight. Unmold.

MANDARIN ORANGE FRUIT SALAD:
1 11-oz. can Mandarin oranges, drained
1 ⅔ c. crushed pineapple or chunks
1 c. flaked coconut
1 c. sour cream
1 c. miniature marshmallows

Combine all ingredients. Chill for several hours or overnight. Do not freeze. Fill center of mold.

Gudrun Harstad
Detroit Lakes, Minn.

FROZEN SPICED PEACH SALAD

1 1-lb. 14-oz. jar spiced peaches
1 3-oz. pkg. cream cheese
¼ c. sugar
⅓ c. evaporated milk
1 c. miniature marshmallows
½ c. chopped pecans
⅔ c. evaporated milk, partially frozen
1 tbsp. lemon juice

Drain peaches, reserving 1/2 cup liquid. Discard peach stones; chop peaches coarsely. Blend cream cheese and sugar until smoothly mixed. Slowly beat in 1/3 cup evaporated milk and reserved peach syrup. Stir in chopped spiced peaches, marshmallows and pecans. Whip partially frozen evaporated milk until very stiff. Beat in lemon juice to blend thoroughly. Fold in cheese mixture. Turn into two 1-quart ice cube trays; freeze until firm. Yield: 10-12 servings.

Photograph for this recipe above.

PEACH SALAD

2 c. chopped peaches
½ c. Maraschino cherries
1 tbsp. lemon juice
½ c. sugar
½ c. mayonnaise
1 c. whipped cream

Combine peaches, cherries, lemon juice and sugar; fold in mayonnaise and whipped cream. Freeze. May be served on lettuce. Yield: 8 servings.

Mrs. Mable H. Whisnant
Denver, N.C.

FROZEN PEACH SALAD

1 pkg. cherry gelatin
1 c. hot water
1 15-oz. can sliced peaches, drained
1 13 ½-oz. can crushed pineapple, drained
1 1-lb. can pears, drained and diced
½ c. miniature marshmallows
½ c. chopped nuts
1 c. heavy cream, whipped
¼ c. sugar
1 3-oz. pkg.cream cheese, softened
½ c. mayonnaise

Dissolve gelatin in hot water; chill. Add fruits with marshmallows and nuts to gelatin;

(Continued on next page)

chill. Combine whipped cream with sugar, cream cheese and mayonnaise; add to gelatin as soon as it begins to congeal. Pour into molds and freeze. Remove from freezer 10 minutes before serving. Yield: 16-18 servings.

Mrs. Janelle Farrell
Cleburne, Tex.

2 tbsp. pineapple syrup
24 marshmallows, quartered or 2 c. miniature marshmallows
1 No. 2 can pineapple chunks, drained
1 c. heavy cream, whipped
2 c. halved seeded red grapes

Soften cream cheese; blend with mayonnaise. Beat in pineapple syrup; add marshmallows and pineapple. Fold in whipped cream and grapes; pour into trays and freeze. Serve on lettuce leaves. Yield: 10 servings.

Mrs. Ward Kreider
Wadsworth, O.

FROZEN PEAR SALAD

1 No. 3 can pears, diced
1 pkg. lime or cherry gelatin
Juice of ½ lemon
2 3-oz. pkg. cream cheese
½ pt. whipped cream
½ c. almonds, slivered (opt.)

Drain pears, reserving 1 3/4 cups juice. Heat pear juice. Add gelatin, stirring to dissolve. Add lemon juice and cream cheese; mix well. Chill. Add pears, nuts and whipped cream. Pour into 9 x 9-inch pan. Freeze, stirring once or twice.

Mrs. Ruth DeFriese
Knoxville, Tenn.

FROZEN FRUIT SALAD

2 tbsp. lemon juice
1 pt. sour cream
¾ c. sugar
Pinch of salt
3 tbsp. chopped Maraschino cherries
1 can crushed pineapple, drained
Walnuts
3 or 4 bananas

Combine all ingredients. Mix well and freeze.

Mrs. James Barnhill
Gibsonburg, O.

FROZEN GRAPE SALAD

2 3-oz. pkg. cream cheese
2 tbsp. mayonnaise

FROZEN MARSHMALLOW-PINEAPPLE SALAD

½ lb. miniature marshmallows
1 c. crushed pineapple
¼ c. grated pimento or American cheese
¼ c. mayonnaise
½ c. heavy cream, whipped

Combine marshmallows, pineapple, cheese and mayonnaise; fold in whipped cream. Pour into 8 or 9-inch pan; freeze. May be served on lettuce with Maraschino cherry flower and mayonnaise. Yield: 6-7 servings.

Mrs. Anna S. Fronk
Mifflintown, Pa.

FROZEN PEPPERMINT DESSERT SALAD

1 No. 2 can crushed pineapple
1 pkg. strawberry gelatin
¼ c. cinnamon candies
1 10½-oz. pkg. miniature marshmallows
2 c. heavy cream
¼ lb. soft butter mints, crushed

Combine pineapple, gelatin, candies and marshmallows; mix well. Chill overnight. Set refrigerator control at lowest temperature. Beat cream, 1 cup at a time, in chilled bowl with chilled beaters until cream piles softly. Pour cream and mints into chilled pineapple mixture. Fold together thoroughly; pour into refrigerator trays. Freeze for 2 to 3 hours or until firm.

Ada Newell
Garden City, Kans.

FROZEN PINEAPPLE AND FRUIT SALAD

1 tbsp. mayonnaise
1 pkg. cream cheese
Pinch of salt
½ pt. heavy cream
¼ lb. soft marshmallows
1 No. 2 can sliced pineapple, drained and chopped
1 No. 2 can fruit cocktail, drained
16 Maraschino cherries

Blend mayonnaise with cream cheese; add salt. Whip cream; add marshmallows. Blend into cheese mixture. Combine pineapple with fruit cocktail; add to cheese. Place in ice tray; add cherries. Freeze until firm. Yield: 8-12 servings.

Mrs. Nellie F. Garrett
Lynchburg, Va.

FROZEN PINEAPPLE-MARSHMALLOW SALAD

4 egg yolks
½ c. sugar
½ c. water
¼ c. vinegar
1 pt. heavy cream, whipped
1 lb. marshmallows, cut up
1 c. Maraschino cherries, drained and chopped
1 can crushed pineapple, drained
1 No. 2 can pineapple chunks, drained

Combine egg yolks, sugar, water and vinegar; cook over low heat until thickened, stirring constantly. Cool. Fold in whipped cream, marshmallows and fruit; freeze. Yield: 15 servings.

Mrs. Carl Scott
Leavittsburgh, O.

FROZEN SALAD

2 tbsp. flour
1 c. pineapple juice
½ c. butter
⅛ c. sugar
Dash of salt
1 egg, slightly beaten
2 tbsp. lemon juice
4 slices pineapple, finely cut
2 oranges, finely cut
8 Maraschino cherries, chopped
10 marshmallows, finely cut
¼ c. nuts, chopped
1 pt. heavy cream, whipped

Blend flour and pineapple juice; cook in double boiler until thickened, stirring constantly. Add butter, sugar and salt; cook for 10 minutes. Stir in egg and lemon juice; cool. Stir in fruit, marshmallows and nuts; fold into cream. Freeze. Yield: 18-20 servings.

Mrs. Merle Rupert
Jeanette, Pa.

MINT SALAD

12 lge. marshmallows
1 tbsp. pineapple juice
⅛ tsp. green food coloring
⅛ tsp. peppermint flavoring
1 c. crushed pineapple
¼ c. salad dressing
¼ c. whipped cream

Melt marshmallows in pineapple juice over low heat. Add food coloring and peppermint flavoring; cool. Add pineapple, salad dressing and whipped cream. Freeze until firm.

Mrs. Carolyn Arthur
Mayville, Wisc.

PINEAPPLE SALAD

½ pt. sour cream
1 tbsp. lemon juice
¾ c. sugar
⅛ tsp. salt
½ pt. heavy cream, whipped
1 9-oz. can pineapple chunks, drained
⅓ c. Maraschino cherries
¼ c. nuts
2 bananas, diced
Salad dressing or whipped cream

Fold sour cream, lemon juice, sugar and salt into whipped cream; add all remaining ingredients except salad dressing. Spoon into paper muffin cups; freeze until firm. Unmold on lettuce; top with salad dressing. Yield: 18 small servings.

Mrs. Leona Dosland
New Hampton, Iowa

PINEAPPLE-SOUR CREAM SALAD

2 c. sour cream
2 tbsp. lemon juice

(Continued on next page)

FROZEN STRAWBERRY MOLDS

¾ c. sugar
¼ tsp. salt
⅓ c. coarsely chopped walnuts
3 tbsp. Maraschino cherries, drained and finely chopped
1 9-oz. can crushed pineapple, drained
½ c. miniature marshmallows

Blend sour cream, lemon juice, sugar and salt. Add all remaining ingredients. Spoon mixture into paper baking cups and set in muffin tins. Freeze. Before serving remove paper cups. Let stand at room temperature for a few minutes to soften. NOTE: Additional drained fruits may be added if desired. Yield: 10 servings.

Mrs. Harvey L. Noyes
Rouseville, Pa.

FROZEN STRAWBERRY GELATIN

½ pkg. lemon gelatin
1 8-oz. pkg. cream cheese
1 6-oz. can frozen lemonade
2 lemonade cans water
2 pkg. strawberry gelatin
1 sm. can crushed pineapple, drained
2 pkg. frozen strawberries, thawed
2 bananas, mashed
½ c. finely chopped nuts

Prepare lemon gelatin according to package directions; blend with cream cheese. Pour into mold; chill until firm. Blend frozen lemonade, water and strawberry gelatin; heat to boiling. Stir until gelatin is dissolved. Measure pineapple juice; add cold water to make 2 cups. Add to gelatin with strawberries, pineapple, bananas and nuts; chill until thickened. Pour gently over lemon-cream cheese gelatin; chill until firm. Garnish with mint leaves and Maraschino cherry halves. Yield: 8-10 servings.

Mrs. Lenice Chase
Clarksburg, Calif.

FROZEN STRAWBERRY SALAD

1 pt. frozen sweetened strawberries
1 c. drained crushed pineapple
½ c. chopped pecans
½ lb. miniature marshmallows
1 c. whipped cream
1 c. salad dressing
1 3-oz. pkg. cream cheese

Combine strawberries, pineapple, pecans and marshmallows. Combine remaining ingredients; beat until smooth. Add to fruit mixture; mix well. Freeze.

Irma Haley
Castleford, Idaho

STRAWBERRY-CHEESE SALAD

1 pt. strawberries
2 tbsp. sugar
2 3-oz. pkg. cream cheese
2 tsp. lemon juice
½ c. whipped cream

Crush strawberries; add sugar. Mix with cream cheese and lemon juice. Fold in whipped cream. Freeze.

Rony E. Bolton
Seaman, O.

STRAWBERRY SALAD

2 pkg. strawberry gelatin
1 c. hot water
1 c. cold water
2 10-oz. pkg. frozen strawberries, thawed
1 envelope dessert topping mix, whipped
2 tbsp. sugar
1 3-oz. pkg. cream cheese, softened

Dissolve gelatin in hot water; stir in cold water. Add 2 ice cubes; chill. Add strawberries. Pour one-half of mixture into oblong glass baking dish. Freeze. Chill remaining mixture until nearly set. Combine dessert topping mix, sugar and cream cheese. Beat until smooth. Spread dessert topping mixture on top of frozen layer; top with chilled gelatin. Chill for several hours.

Mrs. Fayma Drummond
Petersburg, Tex.

STRAWBERRY SALAD SUPERB

1 6-oz. pkg. cream cheese
2 tbsp. honey
1 c. sweetened crushed strawberries
½ c. diced canned pineapple
¼ c. lemon juice

(Continued on next page)

Blend cheese with honey; add strawberries, pineapple and lemon juice. Freeze.

Sister Del Rey
Dell Rapids, S.D.

FROZEN WALDORF SALAD

2 eggs, slightly beaten
½ c. sugar
½ c. pineapple juice
¼ c. lemon juice
⅛ tsp. salt
½ c. diced celery
½ c. crushed pineapple, drained
2 med. apples, diced
½ c. chopped English walnuts
1 c. heavy cream, whipped

Combine eggs, sugar, juices and salt. Cook over low heat until thickened, stirring constantly; cool. Add all remaining ingredients except whipped cream; mix well. Fold in whipped cream; freeze. Yield: 12 servings.

Mrs. Damon Brewer
Marshville, N.C.

FROZEN WALDORF SALAD

2 eggs
½ c. sugar
½ c. pineapple juice
¼ c. lemon juice (opt.)
⅛ tsp. salt
½ c. diced celery
½ c. crushed pineapple, drained
2 c. diced apples
½ c. chopped English walnuts
1 c. heavy cream, whipped

Combine eggs, sugar, juices and salt. Cook over low heat until thickened, stirring constantly. Cool; add celery, pineapple, apples and nuts. Gently fold in cream. Spoon into 8-inch square pan; freeze. Cut into squares; serve on lettuce leaves. Yield: 12 servings.

Margery W. Kearney
Elyria, O.

COTTAGE CHEESE SALAD

½ c. sliced Maraschino cherries
2 c. small curd cottage cheese, sieved
1 c. sour cream
3 tbsp. confectioners sugar
¾ tsp. salt
1 c. drained pineapple chunks
1 c. cooked chopped prunes
1 lge. banana, sliced
½ c. chopped blanched almonds
1 c. sour cream

Drain cherries, reserving 2 tablespoons juice. Combine all ingredients except sour cream and cherry juice. Pour into trays that have been rinsed in cold water. Freeze. Let stand at room temperature for a few minutes before serving. Serve with a mixture of sour cream and cherry juice.

Mrs. Trudy Fulmer
Springfield, S.C.

FROZEN FRUIT AND CHEESE SALAD

2 c. sm. curd cottage cheese
1 c. sour cream
3 tbsp. confectioners sugar
¾ tsp. salt
1 c. pineapple chunks, drained
1 c. diced orange sections
1 c. pitted cooked dates, chopped (opt.)
1 lge. banana, sliced
½ c. Maraschino cherries
½ c. blanched chopped almonds

Blend all ingredients; pour into refrigerator trays that have been rinsed in cold water. Freeze until firm. Allow to stand a few minutes before cutting into serving pieces. Serve on lettuce.

TOPPING:
1 c. sour cream
2 tbsp. Maraschino cherry juice
Red or green cherries
Orange sections

Combine sour cream with juice; pour over salad. Garnish with cherries and oranges. Yield: 6-8 servings.

Mrs. C. F. Livelsburger
Gary, Ind.

FROZEN FRUIT AND CHEESE SALAD

2 c. sm. curd cottage cheese
1 c. sour cream
½ c. mayonnaise

(Continued on next page)

3 tbsp. confectioners sugar
¾ tsp. salt
1 lge. banana, sliced
1 c. drained pineapple chunks
1 c. diced Mandarin orange sections
1 c. cooked chopped prunes
½ c. sliced Maraschino cherries
½ c. slivered blanched almonds

Press cottage cheese through sieve; blend with sour cream, mayonnaise, sugar and salt. Fold in fruits and almonds; pour into mold. Freeze. Remove from freezer 10 to 15 minutes before serving. May be served on salad greens and garnished with orange slices, cherries or mint sprigs. Yield: 12 servings.

Mrs. Mildred Summerlin
Lineville, Ala.

FLORIDA FRUIT SALAD

2 c. creamed cottage cheese
⅓ c. mayonnaise
2 tbsp. sugar
1 c. diced pineapple
1 c. diced orange sections
1 ½ c. chopped Maraschino cherries
2 tbsp. cherry juice
⅓ c. chopped pecans

Sieve cottage cheese. Blend with mayonnaise and sugar; fold in fruit, cherry juice and nuts. Freeze until firm. Serve on lettuce. Yield: 6 servings.

Mrs. Garland Hallman
Hollywood, Fla.

PINEAPPLE-CHEESE SALAD

16 lge. marshmallows
¾ c. pineapple juice
Juice of ½ lemon
1 c. crushed pineapple
1 pt. cottage cheese, drained
¾ c. whipped cream
1 banana, crushed

Heat marshmallows in 2 tablespoons pineapple juice until almost melted; fold over and over until smooth. Cool; fold in all remaining ingredients. Freeze until firm. Yield: 8 servings.

Louise Brumback
Strasburg, Va.

DATE-CHEESE SALAD

1 sm. can evaporated milk, chilled
¼ c. lemon juice
2 pkg. cream cheese, softened
½ c. mayonnaise
½ c. chopped pecans
½ c. slivered almonds
1 c. chopped dates
1 8 ½-oz. can crushed pineapple

Whip milk; gradually add lemon juice. Blend cheese and mayonnaise; blend into milk mixture. Fold in remaining ingredients. Freeze.

Carolyn Lutkemeier
Frankfort, Ky.

FESTIVE FROZEN SALAD

1 8-oz. pkg. cream cheese
½ c. light corn syrup
1 c. milk or light cream
½ c. pineapple preserves
½ c. toasted chopped almonds
½ c. chopped Maraschino cherries
Imitation rum flavoring to taste
Few drops of green food coloring

Blend cream cheese with syrup; stir in all remaining ingredients. Pour into refrigerator tray; freeze until firm. Yield: 8 servings.

Helen Stewart
Decatur, Ill.

FROZEN CHEESE SALAD

1 c. crushed pineapple
1 bottle Maraschino cherries
4 tbsp. confectioners sugar
1 pkg. cream cheese
¾ c. mayonnaise
1 c. heavy cream, whipped

Drain pineapple. Combine pineapple, cherries and sugar; chill for 1 hour. Drain. Mash cheese; blend in mayonnaise. Fold fruit into stiffly beaten cream; freeze.

Juanita Miller
Springfield, O.

FROZEN CHEESE SALAD

1 sm. pkg. cream cheese
¼ c. mayonnaise

(Continued on next page)

½ c. evaporated milk, chilled
½ c. drained crushed pineapple
½ c. chopped dates

Mix cheese and mayonnaise until soft and smooth. Whip milk until stiff; fold into cheese mixture. Add pineapple and dates; mix lightly. Freeze in refrigerator tray about 3 hours. Slice and serve on crisp lettuce without dressing. Yield: 6 servings.

Mrs. M. C. Simpson
Cleveland, Miss.

FROZEN FRUIT SALAD

1 lge. pkg. cream cheese
½ c. mayonnaise
1 sm. can crushed pineapple, drained
Halved Maraschino cherries
½ lge. box marshmallows, diced
¾ c. chopped nuts
1 pt. heavy cream, whipped

Blend cream cheese with mayonnaise; stir in remaining ingredients except whipped cream. Fold in whipped cream; freeze. Yield: 6 servings.

Mrs. Everett J. Harris
Grantsboro, N.C.

FROZEN CHEESE SALAD

½ c. mayonnaise
1 3-oz. pkg. cream cheese, mashed
½ c. canned chopped pineapple
3 tbsp. chopped green pepper
⅛ c. chopped Maraschino cherries
⅛ c. chopped nuts
¼ tsp. grated onion
½ c. whipped cream
3 tbsp. sugar

Stir mayonnaise into cream cheese. Add pineapple, pepper, cherries, nuts and onion. Mix in whipped cream sweetened with sugar. Freeze.

Mrs. D. E. Haugh
North Chicago, Ill.

FROZEN FRUIT SALAD

1 c. salad dressing
1 8-oz. pkg. cream cheese
2 tbsp. confectioners sugar
1 c. diced pineapple
1 c. diced apricots
1 c. heavy cream, whipped
½ c. chopped Maraschino cherries

Blend salad dressing with cheese until smooth; add sugar and fruits. Fold in whipped cream; pour into individual molds. Freeze until firm. Serve on lettuce; garnish with Maraschino cherries. Yield: 6-8 servings.

Mrs. Lorraine K. Kull
San Francisco, Calif.

FROZEN CITRUS SALAD

1 c. California orange pieces
1 c. miniature marshmallows
¼ c. sliced red or green Maraschino cherries
½ c. shredded coconut
1 3-oz. pkg. cream cheese
¼ c. mayonnaise
¼ tsp. salt

Mix orange pieces, marshmallows, cherries and coconut lightly. Cream cheese at room temperature until soft. Add mayonnaise and salt; blend with fruit mixture. Pour into refrigerator tray; freeze. Serve on lettuce leaves. Yield: 6-8 servings.

Photograph for this recipe on page 131 .

FROZEN FRUIT SALAD

1 sm. pkg. cream cheese
10 to 12 marshmallows, chopped
1 c. chopped pineapple slices
⅓ c. chopped pecans
10 Maraschino cherries
2 oranges, chopped
Juice of 1 lemon
1 c. heavy cream, whipped
½ c. mayonnaise

Combine all ingredients; freeze.

Mrs. F. S. Douglass
Chesterfield, S.C.

FROZEN FRUIT SALAD

1 3-oz. pkg. cream cheese
3 tbsp. mayonnaise
¼ c. sliced Maraschino cherries
¼ c. sliced bananas
¼ c. oranges, cut into small pieces
¼ c. pineapple
½ c. chopped nuts
1 c. heavy cream, whipped

Beat cheese with mayonnaise until smooth; combine with fruits and nuts. Fold in whipped cream; pour into freezing tray. Freeze for 2 hours and 30 minutes to 3 hours. Cut into squares; serve on lettuce with dressing. Yield: 4-6 servings.

Mrs. Betty Jardel
Port Clinton, O.

FROZEN SALAD

2 3-oz. pkg. cream cheese
¾ c. mayonnaise
1 c. heavy cream, whipped
1 c. crushed pineapple, drained
1 c. jellied cranberry sauce, cubed
1 c. chopped ripe olives
1 c. chopped celery

Blend cream cheese with mayonnaise. Fold in whipped cream; add all remaining ingredients. Freeze for 3 to 4 hours. Yield: 10-12 servings.

Mrs. M. G. Willey
Newport News, Va.

FROZEN SALAD

1 lge. pkg. cream cheese
1 c. salad dressing
1 lge. green mango, chopped and drained
1 lge. jar Maraschino cherries, drained
1 No. 2 ½ can crushed pineapple, drained
1 pt. heavy cream, whipped

Blend cream cheese and salad dressing; fold in mango, cherries, pineapple and whipped cream. Pour into 9-inch ring mold; freeze until firm. Slice and serve. Yield: 15 servings.

Mrs. M. McCrary
Mooresville, Ind.

FROZEN SALAD DELIGHT

2 3-oz. pkg. cream cheese
¼ c. maple syrup
½ lb. dates, chopped
1 ½ c. diced pineapple, drained
1 c. chopped nuts
1 c. heavy cream, whipped

Cream cheese until very soft; add syrup. Add dates, pineapple and nuts. Fold in whipped cream. Turn into mold or ice tray; place in freezer section of refrigerator until frozen. For a softer serving, remove from freezer 30 minutes before using. Yield: 8-10 servings.

Jean Gronendyke
Auburn, Ind.

FROZEN SPRING SALAD

1 1-lb. can sliced peaches
1 envelope unflavored gelatin
⅓ c. sugar
½ tsp. dry mustard
2 tbsp. lemon juice
1 c. sour cream
2 3-oz. pkg. cream cheese
1 lb. can pitted dark sweet cherries, drained
1 11-oz. can Mandarin oranges, drained
2 c. miniature marshmallows
½ pt. heavy cream, whipped

Drain peaches; reserve juice. Add water to peach juice to make 1 cup. Soften gelatin in juice. Heat, stirring constantly, until gelatin dissolves. Combine sugar, mustard, lemon juice, sour cream and cream cheese. Beat with mixer until well blended; stir into gelatin mixture. Chill until thickened; beat until smooth. Fold in well drained fruits, marshmallows and whipped cream; freeze.

Erma W. Meyer
Continental, O.

FRUIT SALAD FREEZE

1 No. 2 can pineapple chunks
12 marshmallows, cut up
1 pkg. cream cheese, softened
1 c. mayonnaise

(Continued on next page)

2 tbsp. confectioners sugar
1 c. pecans
2 c. chopped peaches, drained
2 c. apricots, drained
Juice of 1 lemon
1 c. flaked coconut
½ c. Maraschino cherries
1 c. heavy cream, whipped

Drain pineapple, reserving juice. Heat juice slightly; add all remaining ingredients. Pour into fruit cans; freeze. Cut out bottom of cans; push out salad. Slice and serve on lettuce leaves. Yield: 10-12 servings.

Mrs. Howard A. Bruce
Radford, Va.

NOEL SALAD LOAF

1 8-oz. pkg. cream cheese
⅓ c. mayonnaise
½ c. chopped celery
1 9-oz. can crushed pineapple, drained
½ c. cubed avocado
¼ tsp. salt
1 tsp. lemon juice
1 c. heavy cream, whipped
Dash of red food coloring
1 1-lb. can cranberry sauce

Blend cream cheese with mayonnaise; add celery, pineapple, avocado, salt and lemon juice. Fold in whipped cream. Tint pink with food coloring. Cube 3/4 can cranberry sauce; add to mixture. Freeze in loaf pan. Yield: 8 servings.

Kay Lebsock
Fairview, Mont.

SALAD SUPREME

3 pkg. cream cheese, softened
1 c. mayonnaise
3 bananas, diced
1 No. 2 can pineapple chunks
1 c. diced pecans
Juice of ½ lemon
1 c. miniature marshmallows
1 c. heavy cream, whipped or 1 pkg. dessert topping mix, prepared

Blend cream cheese with mayonnaise; add fruits, pecans, lemon juice and marshmallows. Fold in whipped cream; freeze for 3 hours. Yield: 8-10 servings.

Mrs. Philip Beatty
Kalamazoo, Mich.

FROSTY MINT CUBES

1 No. 2 can crushed pineapple
2 tsp. unflavored gelatin
½ c. mint jelly
Dash of salt
1 c. whipped cream
Green food coloring

Drain pineapple, reserving juice. Soften gelatin in juice; add jelly and salt. Heat, stirring constantly, until gelatin dissolves and jelly melts. Add pineapple. Chill until mixture is thick and syrupy. Fold in whipped cream; tint with few drops of food coloring. Freeze until firm. Cut into cubes or slices to serve.

JoAnn L. Bedore
Grand Blanc, Mich.

FROZEN FRUIT SALAD

1 c. crushed strawberries
1 banana, diced
1 sm. can crushed pineapple
¼ c. chopped walnuts
1 c. sugar
3 egg whites, stiffly beaten
¼ tsp. salt
1 c. heavy cream, whipped

Combine fruits with nuts and sugar; freeze until mushy. Fold in egg whites, salt and whipped cream; freeze. Yield: 10 servings.

Leatha Brown
Waynesburg, Pa.

FROZEN FRUIT SALAD

1 pt. heavy cream, whipped
2 c. salad dressing
½ c. sugar
¼ c. orange juice
½ c. grapes or cherries

(Continued on next page)

1 c. cubed peaches
½ c. canned pineapple
½ c. orange sections
½ c. diced bananas

Combine whipped cream and salad dressing; add sugar, orange juice and fruits. Freeze.

Opal Massey
Butte, Mont.

FROZEN SALAD

1 tbsp. gelatin
¼ c. cold water
3 tbsp. lemon juice
½ c. sugar
1 c. diced canned apricots
1 c. diced canned pineapple
1 c. diced canned peaches
2 bananas, diced
1 c. mayonnaise
1 c. heavy cream, whipped

Soak gelatin in cold water for 5 minutes; dissolve over boiling water. Add lemon juice, sugar and fruits; chill until thickened. Fold in mayonnaise and cream. Turn into mold. Freeze until serving time.

Mrs. G. Schrimsher
Alice, Tex.

FRUIT SALAD AND DRESSING

SALAD DRESSING:
1 egg, beaten
1 c. sugar
½ tsp. salt
½ tbsp. flour
¾ c. pineapple juice
2 tbsp. lemon juice

Combine egg, sugar, salt and flour. Blend in juices. Cook slowly over medium heat, stirring constantly, until thick. Cool.

SALAD:
1 c. heavy cream, whipped
3 bananas, diced
1 c. diced pears
1 c. diced pineapple
1 doz. red cherries, sliced thinly

Fold cream into fruits; add dressing. Pour into freezer trays; freeze for 6 to 8 hours. Yield: 8-10 servings.

Mrs. Burnett Weber
Sykesville, Pa.

RAINBOW FROZEN FRUIT SALAD

16 marshmallows, whole
1 c. canned crushed pineapple
½ c. mayonnaise
½ pt. heavy cream, whipped
6 marshmallows, quartered
3 bananas, sliced
1 c. diced peaches
1 c. raspberries

Heat whole marshmallows with pineapple until marshmallows are melted. Cool until slightly thickened. Add mayonnaise, whipped cream, quartered marshmallows and fruits. Pour into trays; freeze without stirring. Slice and serve on crisp lettuce. Yield: 8 servings.

Mrs. Richard A. Perry
Pasco, Wash.

SOUR CREAM-FRUIT SALAD

½ to 1 c. coarsely chopped nuts
3 tbsp. finely chopped Maraschino cherries
1 9-oz. can crushed pineapple, drained
1 pt. sour cream
¾ c. sugar
2 tbsp. lemon juice
⅛ tsp. salt
2 bananas, mashed

Combine all ingredients; blend well. Spoon into 12 paper-lined muffin cups. Freeze. Serve in lettuce cups or plain. Yield: 12 servings.

Mrs. Joseph D. Plummer, Jr.
New Castle, Ind.

RECIPE FOR CITRUS SALAD ON PAGE 155

APPLE SALAD

DRESSING:
1 egg, beaten
1 c. sugar
1 tbsp. butter
½ c. vinegar or lemon juice

Combine ingredients; cook over low heat until thickened, stirring constantly. Cool.

SALAD:
2 c. chopped apples
1 c. miniature marshmallows
1 c. nuts
1 c. finely chopped celery

Combine ingredients. Pour dressing over salad.

Mrs. Edna J. Rants
Indianapolis, Ind.

APPLE SALAD

1 egg, beaten
¼ c. cream
1 tsp. butter
1 tsp. flour
¼ c. sugar
¼ tsp. salt
¼ c. vinegar
6 apples, pared and finely chopped
2 stalks celery, finely chopped
½ c. chopped pecans

Combine egg, cream and butter in saucepan. Sift flour, sugar and salt; stir into egg mixture. Add vinegar. Cook slowly, stirring constantly, until thickened. Cool. Mix apples, celery and pecans. Add dressing mixture; mix well. Yield: 12 servings.

Mrs. L. H. DeWolf
Iowa, La.

APPLE SALAD

2 apples, diced
4 bananas, sliced
6 to 8 marshmallows, cut up
½ c. chopped nuts
1 ½ c. heavy cream, whipped
½ c. sugar

Combine apples, bananas, marshmallows and nuts. Fold in cream and sugar. Chill. Yield: 8-10 servings.

Mrs. Guy Gallinger
Union Star, Mo.

APPLE SALAD

4 apples, diced
1 c. diced celery
½ c. chopped nuts
¾ c. sugar
1 tbsp. flour
3 tbsp. water
1 tbsp. vinegar
1 egg, beaten
4 tbsp. cream

Combine apples, celery and nuts. Combine sugar, flour, water, vinegar and egg. Cook mixture until thickened. Cool; add cream. Add apple mixture just before serving. Yield: 4-6 servings.

Pauline Lindsey
Osceola, Mo.

APPLE SALAD WITH BLEU CHEESE DRESSING

2 c. unpared diced apples
1 c. sliced celery
1 ½ c. cantaloupe or honeydew melon balls
½ c. sour cream
⅓ c. mayonnaise
⅓ to ½ c. crumbled Bleu cheese

Mix apples, celery and melon balls. Blend sour cream and mayonnaise; stir in Bleu cheese. Add to apple mixture; toss lightly. Chill. Yield: 4-5 servings.

Mrs. Louise E. Frame
Coraopolis, Pa.

APPLE-FIG-CARROT SALAD

1 c. dried figs
2 c. unpeeled and diced red apples
1 c. diced celery
1 c. coarsely grated carrots

Pour boiling water over figs; let stand for 5 minutes. Drain and cool. Cut into chunks using scissors. Combine with remaining ingredients; toss with peanut butter dressing.

PEANUT BUTTER DRESSING:
4 tbsp. peanut butter
4 tbsp. lemon juice
½ c. mayonnaise

Blend peanut butter and lemon juice. Fold in mayonnaise.

Mary Ulrich
San Angelo, Tex.

BLEU CHEESE WALDORF SALAD

2 c. unpared diced tart apples
1 c. diced celery
½ c. broken walnuts
¼ c. crumbled Bleu cheese
¼ c. sour cream
¼ c. mayonnaise or salad dressing
Dash of salt

Combine apples, celery and walnuts. Mix remaining ingredients; add to first mixture. Toss; chill.

Elizabeth Davis Gibson
Detroit, Mich.

CINNAMON-APPLE SALAD

1 c. red cinnamon candies
2 c. sugar
1 c. water
6 apples, peeled and cored
Cottage cheese
Ground raisins
Lemon juice

Heat cinnamon candies and sugar in water until melted. Add apples; cook slowly until tondor, turning frequently. Fill with mixture of cottage cheese, raisins and a small amount of lemon juice.

Hazel Doak
Grundy Center, Iowa

CONFETTI SALAD

1 ½ c. diced unpeeled apples
1 ½ c. grated carrots
½ c. raisins
½ c. chopped peanuts
½ c. mayonnaise

Combine all ingredients. Serve on lettuce. Yield: 6 servings.

Mrs. Wilford Marrs
Roanoke, La.

EVELYN'S APPLE SALAD

4 apples, chopped
¼ c. diced celery
¼ c. chopped dates
¼ c. chopped nuts
3 tbsp. sugar
Maraschino cherries

Combine apples, celery, dates and nuts. Sprinkle with sugar. Toss. Chill. Garnish with cherries. Salad keeps for 4 to 5 hours.

Mrs. Mary Lou Demoise
Lancaster, Pa.

FAMILY FAVORITE SALAD

1 lge. carrot
1 lge. apple
2 lge. stalks celery
1 orange, peeled and diced
Dash of salt
1 tbsp. sugar

Grate carrot, apple and celery. Add orange, salt and sugar. Chill. NOTE: Artificial sweetener may be substituted for sugar. Yield: 3 servings.

Mrs. C. L. Fondoble
Washburn, Mo.

HOOSIER APPLE SALAD

3 c. diced apples
1 c. chopped dates
1 c. chopped celery
3 oranges, sectioned
Lettuce cups
Cheese balls
French dressing

Arrange mixed fruits and celery in lettuce cups; decorate with cheese balls. Serve with French dressing.

Sue Hornung
Milwaukee, Wisc.

PARTY SALAD APPLES

½ c. red cinnamon candies
½ c. water
6 sm. apples, pared and cored
1 pkg. cream cheese
6 walnut halves or olives

(Continued on next page)

Melt candies in water. Simmer apples in liquid until colored, turning occasionally. Drain and cool. Fill centers with cream cheese; top with walnut halves. Arrange in lettuce cups. Yield: 6 servings.

Mrs. Ann Wolfenbarger
Groton, Conn.

WALDORF SALAD

1 c. mayonnaise
1 c. sour cream
2 tbsp. honey
3 c. diced apples
2 c. diced celery
1 c. walnuts
2 c. red grapes, seeded and halved

Combine mayonnaise, sour cream and honey. Combine apples, celery, walnuts and grapes. Fold in dressing. Garnish with unpeeled apple slices. NOTE: For variation 1/2 cup sliced dates may be used.

Mrs. Ethel Moons
Artesia, Calif.

WALDORF SALAD

2 c. diced tart apples
2 c. diced celery
2 c. broken pecans or walnuts

Mix apples, celery and nuts.

COOKED DRESSING:
2 tbsp. flour
4 tbsp. sugar
¼ tsp. salt
3 c. milk
1 egg
½ c. vinegar
1 tbsp. butter

Make a paste of flour, sugar and salt. Add 1/2 cup of milk. Stir until smooth. Add egg and beat thoroughly. Add remaining milk. Bring vinegar and butter to a boil. Add milk mixture; cook slowly until thickened, stirring constantly. Mixture will curdle so keep cooking and stirring until smooth. Cool. Mix with salad. Yield: 12 servings.

Mrs. Juanita Walton
Duncan, Okla.

APRICOT SALAD

⅔ c. evaporated milk
⅔ c. salad oil
¼ c. vinegar
⅓ c. sugar
1 tsp. prepared mustard
⅛ tsp. salt
1 lge. can apricots, drained
1 med. can pineapple chunks, drained
3 c. miniature marshmallows
¼ lb. American cheese, grated
½ c. chopped pecans

Combine milk, oil, vinegar, sugar, mustard and salt in jar; shake until well mixed. Alternate layers of apricots, pineapple and marshmallows in 8 or 9-inch pan. Cover marshmallows with sauce; top with layers of cheese and pecans. Cover; refrigerate for 24 hours. Yield: 9 servings.

Mrs. Cleo Wheeler
Alvarado, Tex.

APRICOT SALAD GLAZE

1 can tropical fruit
2 bananas
1 can Mandarin oranges
½ c. apricot pie mix
1 c. miniature marshmallows (opt.)

Mix all ingredients; serve. Yield: 8-12 servings.

Mrs. Hazel Lockmon
Stuart, Nebr.

APPLACADO SALAD

2 red-skinned apples, diced
¼ c. chopped raisins
¼ c. chopped nuts
⅓ c. chopped celery
½ c. mayonnaise
½ tsp. salt
3 avocados

Combine all ingredients except avocados; toss lightly. Cut avocados lengthwise into halves; remove seed and skin. Fill with apple salad mixture. Yield: 6 servings.

Eugena Johnson
Centralia, Ill.

AVOCADO FRUIT SALAD

Chilled lettuce leaves
2 oranges, peeled and sectioned
2 grapefruit, peeled and sectioned
2 avocados, peeled and sliced lengthwise
French dressing

Arrange lettuce leaves on salad plates. Arrange sections of oranges, grapefruit and avocado slices alternately on lettuce leaves. Serve with French dressing. Yield: 4 servings.

Mrs. Joan Cameron
Tustin, Calif.

AVOCADO-ORANGE TOSSED SALAD

Lettuce
Ripe avocado, cut into small chunks
1 can Mandarin oranges
Bleu cheese dressing
1 can French-fried onion rings

Break lettuce into small pieces; add avocado and oranges. Toss with dressing; top with onion rings.

Dollie S. McCollum
Montgomery, Ala.

AVOCADO SALAD

1 apple, unpeeled
1 banana
½ avocado
1 No. 303 can fruit cocktail, drained
1 c. miniature marshmallows
¼ c. chopped nuts (opt.)
½ c. mayonnaise

Quarter and core apple; cut into small cubes. Slice banana; peel and cube avocado. Add fruit cocktail, nuts and marshmallows; mix well with mayonnaise. Yield: 6-8 servings.

Mrs. Norma Ballard
Sarasota, Fla.

AVOCADO SALAD

1 ripe avocado
¼ green pepper, finely minced
½ stalk celery, finely minced
1 tsp. pimento
½ tsp. salt
1 tbsp. mayonnaise
Lettuce
Sliced stuffed olives

Scoop out avocado; whip pulp until creamy. Add pepper, celery, pimento, salt and mayonnaise. Spoon onto lettuce. Garnish with olive rings. Yield: 6 servings.

Laura Bossier
Convent, La.

CHEESE-AVOCADO SALAD

1 c. sour cream
1 lge. pkg. cream cheese
2 tbsp. finely chopped onion
2 lge. avocados, peeled and pitted
Salt to taste

Mix sour cream, cheese, onion and salt with electric mixer. Add avocadoes; blend. Serve on lettuce.

Mrs. Lillian S. Ealy
Anthony, N.M.

GUACAMOLE

1 envelope exotic herbs salad dressing mix
1 to 2 tsp. chili powder
3 tbsp. chili sauce
4 dashes Tabasco sauce
¼ to ⅓ c. mayonnaise
1 tbsp. lemon juice
1 sm. onion, grated
2 lge. avocados, pureed

Combine all ingredients; mix well. Pour into 1-quart jar; seal tightly. Chill for 1 hour. For an appetizer salad, serve in small mounds on shredded lettuce or romaine. Yield: 8-12 servings.

Mrs. Milton Sanfor
Montross, Va.

GUACAMOLE SALAD

4 c. thickly sliced avocados
1 c. fresh pineapple wedges

(Continued on next page)

1/3 c. salad oil
1/3 c. vinegar
1 clove of garlic, finely minced
Salt and pepper

Toss avocados and pineapple. Combine remaining ingredients; pour over avocado mixture. Chill, turning occasionally. Serve on lettuce. Yield: 6 servings.

Anna Sprow
North Miami Beach, Fla.

BANANA-PEANUT SALAD

1 banana
Mayonnaise
Chopped salted peanuts
Lettuce leaf

Slice banana lengthwise; place on lettuce leaf. Spread generously with mayonnaise; sprinkle with peanuts. Yield: 1 serving.

Mrs. Sally McConnell
Punxsutawney, Pa.

BANANA-COCONUT SALAD

4 bananas
Lemon juice
1/2 c. mayonnaise
1/2 c. whipped cream (opt.)
1 c. toasted coconut or chopped nuts

Cut bananas lengthwise into halves and crosswise into halves. To prevent discoloring, prepare just before serving; coat bananas immediately with lemon juice. Combine mayonnaise and whipped cream. Roll bananas in mayonnaise mixture, then in coconut or chopped nuts. Serve on crisp salad greens.

Mrs. Shirley Leslie
Magazine, Ark.

BANANA SALAD

5 lge. bananas, sliced
1 5-oz. pkg. miniature marshmallows
3 tbsp. sugar
1 tbsp. mayonnaise
1 pt. heavy cream, lightly whipped
Red pepper
2/3 can peanuts, ground

Arrange layers of bananas and marshmallows in dish. Fold sugar and mayonnaise into cream. Top bananas with mixture. Sprinkle with red pepper and ground peanuts. Repeat layers until all ingredients are used. Yield: 6 servings.

Mrs. Dewey May Skinner
Tishomingo, Miss.

BANANA-NUT SALAD

1 c. sugar
2 tbsp. flour
1 egg, well beaten
2 tbsp. butter, melted
1/4 c. mild vinegar
3/4 c. water
6 or 8 bananas
1/2 c. chopped nuts

Combine sugar and flour; add egg, mixing thoroughly. Add butter, vinegar and water. Mix thoroughly. Cook over hot water, stirring constantly until thick and smooth. Cool. Dip bananas into dressing; roll in nuts.

Jean Cline
Morehead, Ky.

BANANA SALAD

1 1/2 c. pineapple chunks
2 tbsp. lemon juice
3 oz. cream cheese, mashed
4 bananas
Chicory or lettuce
Lemon French dressing

Drain pineapple, reserving 1/4 cup juice. Add lemon and pineapple juice to cheese gradually. Beat until creamy. Fold in pineapple chunks. Slice bananas lengthwise; arrange on salad greens. Top with cheese mixture. Serve with dressing.

Lavaughn Bouch
Sand Fork, W. Va.

ROLLED BANANAS

2 tbsp. mustard
2 ½ tbsp. sugar
½ to ⅔ can sweetened condensed milk
2 tbsp. (rounded) peanut butter
1 pt. cracker crumbs
24 firm ripe bananas

Combine mustard and sugar; add milk, beating slightly. Blend peanut butter and crumbs with fork. Peel bananas; cut into halves crosswise. Dip one piece at a time into milk mixture; roll in crumb mixture. Arrange on tray. Yield: 12-24 servings.

Mrs. Eva Jessup
Glenwood, Ark.

CITRUS SALAD

1 1-lb. can Florida grapefruit sections, chilled and drained
2 ½ c. mixed fresh fruit, chilled

Combine drained sections with mixed fresh fruit; serve on salad greens. Fruit may be arranged in groups on salad plate. Serve with French dressing. Yield: 4 servings.

Photograph for this recipe on page 149.

CITRUS SALAD WITH CRANBERRY DRESSING

CITRUS SALAD:
1 c. orange sections
1 c. grapefruit sections
2 c. melon balls
1 head lettuce
Maraschino cherries

Arrange orange, grapefruit and melon attractively on individual lettuce cups. Garnish with cherries.

CRANBERRY DRESSING:
1 c. jellied cranberry sauce
1 c. mayonnaise
2 tbsp. lime or lemon juice
1 c. whipped cream (opt.)

Blend cranberry sauce and mayonnaise with electric mixer. Add juice. For a richer dressing, fold in whipped cream.

Mrs. Thelma Hause
Claremont, N.H.

CITRUS SALAD WITH LEMON-MAYONNAISE DRESSING

2 grapefruit or 1 No. 303 can grapefruit sections
3 oranges
1 avocado
1 persimmon

Peel, section and remove membranes from citrus fruits. Peel avocado; slice lengthwise. Peel persimmon; cut into bite-sized pieces. Arrange fruits attractively on lettuce.

LEMON MAYONNAISE:
1 egg
¼ c. lemon juice
1 tsp. mustard
1 tsp. salt
1 tsp. sugar
¼ tsp. paprika
1 pt. salad oil

Combine all ingredients except salad oil. Slowly beat in salad oil. Continue beating until thick. Serve with salad.

Margarette C. Weeks
Highland, Calif.

GOLD COAST SALAD

1 grapefruit, sectioned
2 oranges
1 head lettuce, torn into bite-sized pieces

Pare grapefruit and oranges, cutting through white skin. Cut sections close to membrane; lift out. Arrange sections of grapefruit and orange on lettuce. Garnish with pomegranate seed or avocado slices. Pass fruit dressing.

DRESSING:
½ c. sugar
1 tsp. salt
1 tsp. dry mustard
1 tsp. celery salt

(Continued on next page)

1 tsp. paprika
1 tsp. grated onion
1 c. salad oil
¼ c. vinegar

Mix dry ingredients; add onion. Add oil, a small amount at a time, alternately with vinegar. Beat with fork; if mixture seems to separate use rotary or electric beater.

Frances Shipley
Coon Rapids, Iowa

CHRISTMAS CRANBERRY SALAD

4 apples
1 lb. cranberries
½ lb. marshmallows, cut up
2 c. sugar
1 pt. heavy cream, whipped

Core apples; do not peel. Put apples and cranberries through coarse food grinder. Combine with marshmallows and sugar. Cover; refrigerate overnight. Fold in whipped cream; serve. Yield: 12 servings.

Mrs. Ethel Belleau
Arlington Hall Sta., Va.

CRANBERRY DELIGHT

2 oranges
1 lb. cranberries
2 c. sugar
3 or 4 slices pineapple, chopped
3 or 4 apples, chopped

Peel oranges; reserve rind. Grind orange rind and cranberries; add sugar. Mix well. Mix in orange and pineapple pieces. Add apples just before serving. Serve in hollowed orange halves if desired.

Fay C. Patterson
Mohall, N.D.

CRANBERRY FLUFF

2 c. ground cranberries
3 to 4 c. miniature marshmallows
¾ c. sugar
1 to 2 c. unpared diced tart apples
½ c. seedless green grapes (opt.)
½ c. walnuts, broken (opt.)
¼ tsp. salt (opt.)
1 c. whipped cream
Pineapple slices (opt.)

Combine cranberries, marshmallows and sugar. Cover; chill overnight. Add apples, grapes, walnuts and salt. Fold in whipped cream. Chill. Turn into serving bowl or spoon onto pineapple slices in lettuce cups. Trim with a cluster of green grapes, if desired.

Mrs. Bessie Hutchins
Grady, N.M.

CRANBERRY SALAD

1 c. chopped cranberries
1 apple, diced
1 banana, diced
1 sm. can crushed pineapple, drained
⅔ c. sugar

Mix cranberries, apple, banana and pineapple. Stir in sugar until well blended. Refrigerate 2 or 3 hours before serving. Yield: 4 servings.

Mrs. Marilyn J. Fleener
Decatur, Ill.

CRANBERRY SALAD

4 c. cranberries
2 c. sugar
2 c. water
1 c. crushed pineapple, drained
1 c. chopped pecans
2 c. miniature marshmallows

Cook berries, sugar and water until berries pop; cool slightly. Add all remaining ingredients; stir until marshmallows melt. Pour into mold; chill until firm. Yield: 12 servings.

Mrs. Frankie L. Schaefer
Arnold AFS, Tenn.

CRANBERRY SALAD

1 c. water
2 c. sugar
1 qt. fresh cranberries
2 c. marshmallows, cut into pieces
2 apples, diced
3 bananas, sliced
3 c. orange sections
1 c. pecans, broken

Make a syrup of water and sugar. Add cranberries; cook until skins burst. Remove from heat; let stand, covered, for 10 minutes. Remove lid; cook for 5 minutes longer. Chill. Add marshmallows, apples, bananas, orange sections and pecans. Chill until ready to serve. Salad will keep in refrigerator for several days.

Pat Duncan
Fort Worth, Tex.

CRANBERRY SALAD SUPREME

1 c. chopped cranberries
1 c. sugar
2 c. seedless or Tokay grapes, chilled
½ c. canned diced pineapple, chilled (opt.)
½ to 2 c. chopped walnuts or pecans
1 c. whipped cream
½ c. marshmallows, quartered (opt.)

Combine cranberries and sugar. Blend. Refrigerate overnight. Drain liquid. Combine grapes, pineapple, nuts and whipped cream. Fold into cranberry mixture. Add marshmallows; stir until evenly distributed.

Nancy Lee
Cleburne, Tex.

FRESH CRANBERRY SALAD

1 lb. whole fresh cranberries, ground
1 ½ to 2 c. sugar
1 ½ c. applesauce
1 ½ to 2 c. crushed or chunk pineapple, well drained
½ pkg. miniature marshmallows
1 c. coarsely chopped nuts (opt.)
½ c. heavy cream
4 tbsp. sugar

Combine cranberries, sugar and applesauce. Let stand for several hours or overnight. Add pineapple, marshmallows and nuts; mix well. Whip cream; sweeten with sugar. Mix with cranberry mixture until just blended. Chill. Serve with poultry or pork.

Mrs. Mary Lou Michalewicz
Pierre, S.D.

CRANBERRY DELIGHT

1 lb. cranberries
1 ½ c. water
2 c. sugar
½ lb. Tokay grapes, halved and seeded
2 oranges, sliced
3 slices pineapple
Juice of 1 lemon

Cook cranberries in water until they pop. Force cranberries through a sieve; return to heat and stir in sugar until dissolved. Cool. Add grapes, oranges, pineapple and lemon juice. Chill and serve in sherbet glasses. Yield: 6 servings.

Mrs. Betty Barber
Warrens, Wisc.

STUFFED CRANBERRY-PEAR SALAD

4 c. fresh cranberries
1 whole orange, quartered and seeded
½ sm. grapefruit, sectioned and seeded
2 c. sugar or 1 c. sugar and 1 c. syrup
Pear halves

Put cranberries, orange and grapefruit through food chopper. Add sugar. Mix well. Chill for a few hours before serving. This relish will keep several days in refrigerator. Fill pear halves with mixture at serving time.

Mrs. Zella H. Mills
Sneedville, Tenn.

RAW CRANBERRY SALAD

1 lb. cranberries, ground
1 or 2 tart apples, ground (opt.)
Sugar
½ c. chopped celery
½ c. chopped nuts
½ c. diced marshmallows
1 c. chopped Tokay grapes
½ pt. whipped cream, sweetened

Cover cranberries and apples with an equal amount of sugar; let stand for several hours. Drain juice from cranberries until dry. Add remaining ingredients except whipped cream; mix with cream. Yield: 6 servings.

Willie Mae Cornwell
Waco, Tex.

DREAMY FRUIT SALAD

1 med. can fruit cocktail
1 8-oz. can chunk pineapple
1 11-oz. can Mandarin oranges
1 pkg. vanilla tapioca pudding
1 pkg. dessert topping mix, prepared
1 c. miniature marshmallows
Sliced bananas

Drain fruits, reserving 1 1/2 cups of combined juices. Prepare pudding as directed, substituting fruit juice for milk. Cool pudding thoroughly. Blend in prepared topping, fruit cocktail, pineapple, oranges and marshmallows. Mix well. Add bananas just before serving. NOTE: Other desired fruits or nuts may be added. Yield: 14 servings.

Mrs. Honora Bekke
Canton, S.D.

EASY FRUIT SALAD

1 can peach pie filling
1 can fruit cocktail, drained
1 can pineapple chunks, drained
1 can Mandarin oranges, drained
1 c. chopped apples (opt.)
1 can grapes, drained
1 c. miniature marshmallows
1 banana, sliced
1 c. chopped nuts

Combine pie filling, fruit cocktail, pineapple, oranges, apples and grapes. Add marshmallows, banana and nuts. Refrigerate for several hours before serving.

Mrs. Steve Nickisch
Napoleon, N.D.

FRUIT COCKTAIL SALAD

1 No. 2 ½ can fruit cocktail, drained
½ lge. bag miniature marshmallows
1 c. sour cream

Mix ingredients together. Cover; chill overnight.

Mrs. Betty Kandt
Herington, Kans.

FRUIT COCKTAIL IN SNOW

1 2-lb. box cottage cheese
1 lge. can fruit cocktail, drained
2 tbsp. sour cream
½ tsp. salt

Combine cottage cheese and fruit cocktail. Add sour cream and salt. Chill and serve. Yield: 6-8 servings.

Mrs. Jack E. Mathis
Fort Scott, Kans.

FRUIT-MARSHMALLOW SALAD

1 No. 2 can fruit cocktail, drained
1 No. 2 can peaches, diced and drained
1 No. 2 can pears, diced and drained
1 sm. can crushed pineapple, drained
3 or 4 bananas, diced
2 c. diced marshmallows
½ pt. sweetened whipped cream
Chopped nuts (opt.)

Toss all ingredients together. Chill for at least 2 hours before serving.

Mrs. Herman Marshall
Philadelphia, Miss.

FRUIT-MARSHMALLOW SALAD

1 can fruit cocktail
3 apples, diced
2 bananas, diced
½ c. raisins
½ c. miniature marshmallows
½ pt. heavy cream, whipped
3 tbsp. sugar

Drain fruit cocktail; combine all fruits and marshmallows. Whip cream; add sugar. Combine with fruit. Yield: 6 servings.

Mrs. Cecil Koberstein
Coos Bay, Oreg.

FRUIT SALAD WITH WHIPPED CREAM

1 can chunk pineapple
1 can fruit cocktail
2 tbsp. sugar
1 tbsp. cornstarch
1 egg
½ c. heavy cream, whipped
1 banana
3 apples, diced

(Continued on next page)

Drain fruits; reserve juice. Cook juice, sugar, cornstarch and egg until thickened; cool. Fold whipped cream into sauce and fruits. Chill until set.

Mrs. Avery L. Cox
McAlester, Okla.

Cook eggs, lemon juice, sugar and butter in double boiler, beating until thickened. Cool; fold in remaining ingredients. Chill; serve on lettuce. Yield: 8 servings.

Mrs. Addie M. Schneider
Olpe, Kans.

FRUIT SALAD WITH SOUR CREAM

1 med. can pineapple chunks
1 med. can fruit cocktail
½ pkg. miniature marshmallows
1 sm. can Mandarin oranges
½ c. chopped pecans
½ pt. sour cream

Thoroughly drain fruits in colander. Mix all ingredients. Chill before serving. Salad will keep for several days in refrigerator. Yield: 12 servings.

Mrs. Ralph Petty
Greenwood, Miss.

JUST FRUIT SALAD

1 lge. apple, diced
Salt
1 15-oz. can fruit cocktail, drained
1 11-oz. can Mandarin oranges, drained
2 sliced bananas
2 c. miniature marshmallows
Juice of ½ lemon
1 tbsp. brown sugar
½ c. heavy cream

Sprinkle apple with a dash of salt; combine all fruits and marshmallows. Sprinkle with lemon juice and brown sugar. Let set a few minutes. Whip cream and combine with fruit mixture. Yield: 10 servings.

Mrs. W. F. Penfield
Gearhart, Oreg.

MILLIONAIRE SALAD

2 eggs
3 tbsp. lemon juice
5 tbsp. sugar
2 tbsp. butter
1 No. 302 can fruit cocktail, drained
1 c. miniature marshmallows
1 c. evaporated milk, whipped

MILLIONAIRE SALAD

2 eggs
5 tbsp. lemon juice
5 tbsp. sugar
2 tbsp. butter, melted
½ lb. miniature marshmallows
1 c. pecans
3 bananas
1 No. 2 can crushed pineapple, drained
1 4-oz. bottle Maraschino cherries
1 c. heavy cream, whipped

Beat eggs slightly; add lemon juice, sugar, butter and marshmallows. Cook in double boiler, stirring constantly, until marshmallows melt. Cool; add pecans, bananas, pineapple and cherries. Fold in whipped cream. Pour into salad mold; chill for 12 to 24 hours. Yield: 8 servings.

Willa Dean Ormsby
Gorman, Tex.

SIX-CUP SALAD

1 c. large curd cottage cheese
1 c. sour cream
1 c. fruit cocktail
1 c. pineapple chunks
1 c. shredded coconut
1 c. miniature marshmallows

Combine all ingredients; refrigerate overnight. Yield: 10 servings.

Mrs. Harry J. Birt
Oak Hill, W. Va.

ANGEL SALAD

2 egg yolks, beaten
3 tbsp. pineapple syrup
1 tbsp. vinegar
2 tbsp. sugar
Dash of salt
2 c. seedless green grapes, halved
½ lb. marshmallows
1 c. whipped cream

(Continued on next page)

Combine egg yolks, pineapple syrup, vinegar, sugar and salt. Cook over hot water until thick, stirring constantly. Cool; pour over grapes and marshmallows. Mix well; let stand for several hours or overnight. Just before serving, fold in whipped cream.

Mrs. Miriam Erickson
Fish Creek, Wisc.

GREEN GRAPE SALAD

¼ c. mayonnaise
1 4-oz. pkg. cream cheese
Garlic salt to taste
1 lb. seedless green grapes, washed

Whip mayonnaise and cream cheese. Add garlic salt to taste. Fold grapes into cheese mixture. Serve in garnished bowl or as individual servings on salad greens. Yield: 4-6 servings.

Mrs. Emma L. Flake Van Laningham
Walnut Springs, Tex.

MOUNTAINEER SALAD

2 c. shredded cabbage
1 c. small marshmallows
1 c. fresh green grapes
½ c. raisins
½ c. shredded coconut
½ c. chopped nuts
¼ c. heavy cream

Toss all ingredients until well moistened. Chill. Yield: 6-8 servings.

Mrs. J. M. Allen
San Angelo, Tex.

MYSTERY GRAPE SALAD

1 3-oz. pkg. cream cheese
Mayonnaise
Garlic juice
1 sm. can crushed pineapple, drained
1 lb. seedless grapes

Thin cream cheese with mayonnaise; add garlic juice, pineapple and grapes. Cover; chill overnight. Yield: 8 servings.

Christine Thelen
Wichita, Kans.

TASTY SALAD

2 c. Concord grapes, halved and seeded
2 stalks celery, cut up
1 apple, diced
¾ c. whipped cream

Mix grapes, celery and apple. Add whipped cream; toss until fruits are coated. Yield: 4 servings.

Mary C. Shaw
Kress, Tex.

CANTALOUPE SALAD

1 med. cantaloupe
Lettuce leaves
2 c. seedless green grapes

Cut cantaloupe lengthwise into six sections; remove seed and shell. Place each section on crisp lettuce leaf. Pile grapes on each section.

DRESSING:
½ c. mayonnaise
2 tbsp. frozen orange juice concentrate

Mix well. Top each salad with desired amount of dressing.

Helen Hoermann
Jamestown, N.D.

CANTALOUPE CARNIVAL

Lemon juice
2 or 3 med. bananas, sliced

(Continued on next page)

1 med. cantaloupe, diced
1 c. miniature marshmallows
½ c. sliced almonds
½ c. sliced strawberries
⅓ c. salad dressing
½ c. strawberry ice cream, softened

Sprinkle lemon juice on bananas. Combine cantaloupe, bananas, marshmallows, almonds and strawberries. Chill. Just before serving, whip salad dressing and ice cream. Pour over salad.

Mrs. Jeanne Damhof
Manton, Mich.

COLORFUL-QUICK FRUIT AND MELON SALAD

¼ tsp. vanilla flavoring
2 tbsp. sugar
1 can fruit cocktail, drained
½ c. whipped cream
1 cantaloupe or honeydew melon, pared and sliced ½-in. thick
Maraschino cherries

Add vanilla flavoring and sugar to cream. Fold into fruit mixture. Place slice of melon on lettuce leaf. Fill hole with fruit mixture; top with a cherry.

Mrs. Geneva Gill Cooper
Monticello, Ky.

PARTY RAINBOW FRUIT SALAD

2 c. sliced fresh peaches
2 c. seedless grapes
2 c. diced watermelon
2 c. diced cantaloupe
2 bananas
1 c. red raspberries or blueberries

Arrange fruit except bananas and berries in layers in bowl. Chill. Just before serving, peel and slice bananas; place on fruit. Spoon onto lettuce; garnish with berries.

LEMON SWEET DRESSING:
1 egg
2 tbsp. sugar
¼ c. salad oil
2 tbsp. lemon juice
¼ tsp. salt
¼ c. heavy cream, whipped

Beat egg slightly in top of double boiler. Stir in sugar; cook until dissolved. Remove from heat; beat until thick and fluffy. Slowly beat in salad oil, lemon juice and salt. Chill. Fold in whipped cream just before serving. Serve on salad. Yield: 10-12 servings.

Nancy Blickenstaff
Nampa, Idaho

SEVEN-CUP FRUIT SALAD

1 c. pineapple chunks
1 c. Mandarin oranges
1 c. cantaloupe balls
1 c. watermelon balls
1 c. seedless grapes
1 c. coconut
1 c. miniature marshmallows
1 c. sour cream

Drain fruits thoroughly; add all ingredients. Mix well. Let stand for 24 hours. More cream may be added, if desired.

Doreen Nielsen
Murray, Utah

SUMMER AMBROSIA

2 c. cantaloupe chunks
2 c. pineapple chunks
2 c. white seedless grapes
2 c. miniature marshmallows
1 ½ c. shredded coconut

Toss ingredients together lightly; chill for several hours. Yield: 10-12 servings.

Mrs. Hobart Sell
Clinton, Mo.

SUMMER FRUIT MEDLEY

⅛ watermelon
½ cantaloupe
1 No. 2 can pineapple chunks
2 c. fresh strawberries
2 c. fresh blueberries
1 pkg. vanilla pudding
1 c. orange juice

(Continued on next page)

Remove seed and rind from watermelon; cut into 1-inch cubes. Remove seed and skin from cantaloupe; cut into 3/4-inch cubes. Drain pineapple, reserving 1 cup syrup. Wash and hull strawberries; wash blueberries. Toss fruits lightly; serve in glass bowl. Garnish with mint leaves or 5 strawberries which have their hulls on. Refrigerate until serving time. Place vanilla pudding mix in saucepan. Slowly stir in orange juice and pineapple syrup. Cook over medium heat, stirring constantly, until it begins to boil. Remove from heat; cool. Mixture will be thin and nearly clear in appearance. Pour over fruit.

Mrs. Jerrien Gunnink
Grand Haven, Mich.

SUMMER FRUIT TOSS

1 cantaloupe
1 bunch white seedless grapes
1 sm. can pineapple chunks, drained
2 lge. bananas, chopped

Scoop out melon with melon baller. Toss fruits together.

HONEY DRESSING:
¼ c. honey
⅛ c. lime juice
Dash of salt

Beat ingredients until completely combined. Pour over salad.

Mrs. Cilicia H. Burden
Morgantown, Ky.

FRESH PEACH SALAD

¼ c. sugar
1 c. sour cream
1 tbsp. mayonnaise
8 fresh peaches, peeled and sliced

Mix sugar, sour cream and mayonnaise; pour over peaches. Mix well; chill thoroughly. Serve on lettuce leaves. Yield: 6 servings.

Mrs. Crystal E. Durant
Pensacola, Fla.

PEACH BLUSH SALAD

1 3-oz. pkg. cream cheese
¼ c. mayonnaise
½ tsp. prepared horseradish
¼ tsp. salt
¼ c. chopped almonds
¼ c. chopped celery
¼ c. chopped green pepper
8 med. canned peach halves
Red food coloring
⅓ c. sour cream
2 tsp. cranberry jelly
1 ½ tbsp. peach syrup

Blend cheese, mayonnaise, horseradish and salt. Combine almonds, celery and green pepper; add to cheese mixture. Mix thoroughly. Fill each peach cavity with cheese mixture; press 2 peach halves together to form a whole peach. Chill. Dilute food coloring with water to make a pink color; brush color on each peach. Blend remaining ingredients; serve with peaches. Yield: 4 servings.

Mrs. Irene Fleshman
Quinwood, W. Va.

STUFFED PEACH SALAD

1 3-oz. pkg. cream cheese
½ c. chopped pecans
¼ c. Maraschino cherries
6 peach halves
Red food coloring
Whole cloves
½ c. mayonnaise
1 c. heavy cream, whipped

Cream cheese; add nuts and cherries. Fill centers of each peach half with cheese mixture. Place peach half on top of the cheese center, making a whole peach. Dilute red coloring with water; brush over one corner of the peach to produce a blush. Stick a clove in one end for stem. Combine mayonnaise and whipped cream; serve over peaches.

Mrs. Willie Fay Spurlock
Hazard, Ky.

FRESH PEAR SALAD AND DRESSING

DRESSING:
2 tbsp. flour
½ c. sugar
2 tbsp. lemon juice

Mix all ingredients; cook over low heat until flour is cooked and clear. Cool.

(Continued on next page)

SALAD:
1 c. diced celery
2 c. diced or sliced fresh pears
⅓ c. pecans
Salad greens
Maraschino cherries

Mix celery and pears with dressing; add nuts. Serve on salad greens. Garnish with cherries.

Mrs. Margaret Thornton
Thorndale, Tex.

PARTY PEAR SALAD

1 3-oz. pkg. cream cheese
½ No. 303 can red sour cherries, drained and chopped
1 tbsp. grated orange rind
1 No. 2 ½ can pear halves

Soften cheese at room temperature; mash. Add cherries and orange rind. Mix well. Arrange pear halves, hollow-side up, on lettuce leaves. Fill pear cavity with cream cheese mixture.

DRESSING:
3 eggs
⅓ c. sugar
1 ½ tbsp. butter
⅓ c. lemon juice
⅛ tsp. salt
½ c. heavy cream

Beat eggs in top of double boiler. Add sugar, butter, lemon juice and salt. Cook over boiling water, stirring constantly, until it coats spoon. Cool. Whip cream until stiff; fold into mixture. Pour dressing over pear halves. Yield: 6-10 servings.

Cecelia M. Murnane
St. Joseph, Mich.

PEAR-AVOCADO SALAD

1 No. 2 ½ can Bartlett pear halves, chilled
2 avocados, peeled and halved
Lettuce
Diced candied ginger

For each serving, arrange 2 pear halves and 1 avocado half on lettuce leaf. Place 2 or 3 pieces of ginger in each pear and avocado half. Serve with poppy seed dressing.

Mildred Williams
El Paso, Tex.

PINEAPPLE-GRAPE SALAD

2 c. chunk pineapple
½ c. sugar
2 tbsp. cornstarch
2 eggs, separated
1 tbsp. vinegar
1 tbsp. butter
1 c. white grapes
1 ½ c. marshmallows

Drain pineapple, reserving juice. Mix sugar, cornstarch, beaten egg yolks, vinegar and butter. Add pineapple juice; cook until thick. Pour juice mixture over fruits. Chill. Add marshmallows and stiffly beaten egg whites. Mix gently.

Mrs. Charles Reece
Warsaw, Ind.

PINEAPPLE OVERNIGHT SALAD

1 No. 2 can crushed pineapple
1 or 2 eggs, beaten
2 tbsp. flour
3 to 4 tbsp. sugar
½ tsp. salt (opt.)
2 tbsp. lemon juice
1 tsp. lemon peel (opt.)
8 oz. miniature marshmallows
1 c. whipped cream
¼ c. Maraschino cherries (opt.)

Drain pineapple, reserving 1 cup juice. Combine eggs, pineapple juice, flour, sugar and salt in double boiler; cook until thickened. Add lemon juice and peel. Cool. Fold in marshmallows, pineapple, whipped cream and cherries. Chill overnight.

Evangeline LaBarre
Belt, Mont.

PINEAPPLE SALAD

3 c. pineapple, cut into wedges
2 tbsp. cornstarch
2 eggs, well beaten
1 c. sugar
Juice of 2 lemons
1 c. nuts
½ lb. miniature marshmallows

Drain pineapple, reserving 1 cup juice. Combine cornstarch, eggs, pineapple juice and sugar. Cook until thick. Add lemon juice. Cool; add remaining ingredients.

Elizabeth L. Fox
Gustine, Tex.

PINEAPPLE SALAD

1 lge. can pineapple chunks
2 tbsp. cornstarch
5 tbsp. sugar
2 eggs, beaten
1 tbsp. butter
½ pkg. marshmallows
1 pt. whipped cream
Nuts (opt.)

Drain pineapple, reserving juice. Moisten cornstarch with pineapple juice; add sugar, eggs and butter. Cook until thick and cornstarch is thoroughly cooked. Cool. Add pineapple, marshmallows, whipped cream and nuts. Chill.

Mrs. Fern Todd
Bloomington, Wisc.

PINEAPPLE SANDWICH SALAD

4 tsp. Maraschino cherry juice
1 6-oz. pkg. cream cheese
4 tsp. chopped Maraschino cherries
8 pineapple slices
Bibb lettuce
Maraschino cherry wedges

Combine cherry juice and cream cheese; blend until smooth. Add cherries; mix well. For each serving, place a slice of pineapple on lettuce; spread with cream cheese mixture. Cover with a second slice of pineapple. Place a spoonful of cream cheese mixture in center of pineapple; garnish with cherry wedges.

Mrs. Myrtle Deranger
Sunset, La.

PINEAPPLE-WALNUT SALAD

1 No. 2 ½ can pineapple
2 eggs
2 tbsp. flour
1 c. sugar
½ lb. English walnuts
15 marshmallows, diced

Drain pineapple, reserving juice. Beat eggs; add flour, sugar and juice from pineapple. Cook until thickened; cool. Pour over diced pineapple, nuts and marshmallows. Chill at least 2 hours. Serve with whipped cream or on lettuce. Yield: 10 servings.

Mrs. Carrie Cassady
Belpre, O.

PINEAPPLE-WALNUT SALAD

3 tbsp. sugar
2 tbsp. cornstarch
1 egg, beaten
1 tbsp. butter
1 c. pineapple chunks
12 marshmallows, diced
1 c. chopped walnuts

Cook sugar, cornstarch and egg in double boiler until sauce is very thick; add butter, stirring well. Cool; mix pineapple, marshmallows and walnuts into sauce. Pour into serving dish; chill. Yield: 8-10 servings.

Mrs. Irene Marcusson
Allerton, Iowa

AMBROSIA SALAD

1 c. flaked coconut
1 c. miniature marshmallows
1 c. drained Mandarin oranges
1 8-oz. can pineapple chunks, drained
1 c. seedless green grapes
1 c. sour cream

Combine all ingredients. Chill for several hours. Serve on lettuce. Yield: 8-10 servings.

Margaret Stampfly
Okemos, Mich.

ANGEL HASH SALAD

1 No. 2 can pineapple chunks
2 tbsp. cornstarch
¼ c. sugar
2 egg yolks
1 c. whipped cream
¼ c. chopped walnuts
15 marshmallows, quartered
6 bananas, sliced

Drain pineapple, reserving juice; add enough water to make 1 cup. Combine cornstarch and sugar. Gradually add pineapple syrup, stirring to blend. Cook, stirring constantly, until thickened. Add part of mixture to egg yolks; blend well. Return to hot mixture. Cook, stirring constantly, for 2 minutes. Cool. Fold in whipped cream. Fold in pineapple, walnuts and marshmallows. Chill overnight. Add bananas just before serving. Garnish with Maraschino cherries; serve in lettuce-lined salad bowl.

Mrs. Marjorie Neilson
Arlington, S.D.

TANGERINE SALAD

6 tangerines
Crisp lettuce cups
2 3-oz. pkg. cream cheese
2 tbsp. top milk or cream
¼ c. cranberry jelly

Cut peel of tangerines part way down to form four sections; tuck peel under like flat petals. Separate tangerine sections but do not loosen from peel. Place each tangerine in a crisp lettuce cup. Soften cream cheese; blend in top milk. Add cranberry jelly; whip until smooth. Serve over tangerine salads. Yield: 6 salads.

Photograph for this recipe above.

CHERRY FRUIT SALAD

DRESSING:
4 eggs
1 c. (scant) sugar
4 tbsp. vinegar
1 c. whipped cream

Mix eggs, sugar and vinegar. Cook over low heat until thickened. Cool. Add whipped cream.

SALAD:
4 c. drained and pitted white cherries
4 c. drained and pitted dark cherries
4 c. drained pineapple cubes
4 c. diced marshmallows

Mix 1 cup of dressing with fruits. Refrigerate for 24 hours.

Janet Kohls
Waupun, Wisc.

CHILLED FRUIT SALAD

1 c. orange sections
1 c. pineapple chunks
1 c. miniature marshmallows
1 c. flaked coconut
1 c. sliced fresh peaches
1 c. sour cream

Drain fruits. Combine all ingredients; chill thoroughly. Yield: 6 servings.

Mrs. David R. Pyles
Williamstown, W. Va.

COCONUT-ORANGE SALAD

3 seedless oranges, peeled and sliced
Lettuce or romaine
½ c. coconut
French dressing

Arrange a circle of thick overlapping orange slices on crisp lettuce. Heap coconut in center. Serve with French dressing. Yield: 5 servings.

Loletta Pierce
Cumby, Tex.

CREAM CHEESE-CHERRY SALAD

1 8-oz. pkg. cream cheese, softened
¼ c. salad dressing
1 lge. can crushed pineapple, drained
1 sm. jar red Maraschino cherries, drained
1 sm. jar green Maraschino cherries, drained
18 marshmallows, cut into pieces
1 c. heavy cream, whipped

Mix cream cheese with salad dressing. Combine remaining ingredients; fold in cheese mixture. Spread into 9 x 13-inch pan. Chill until firm. Yield: 8 servings.

Mrs. Clifford Piner
Muncie, Ind.

FAIRY SALAD

1 c. milk
4 egg yolks
½ tsp. ground mustard
1 lge. can pineapple, diced
1 lb. marshmallows, diced
1 c. diced grapes
1 pt. cream, whipped

Heat milk, egg yolks and mustard. Cook until thick, stirring constantly. Cool. Add remaining ingredients. Let stand overnight. NOTE: Diced oranges may be substituted for grapes. Grated pecans may also be added for variety. Yield: 20 servings.

Billie Fenton
Tipton, Mo.

FIVE-CUP SALAD

1 c. miniature marshmallows
1 c. drained Mandarin oranges
1 c. crushed or chunk pineapple
1 c. sour cream
1 c. coconut

Combine all ingredients. Chill at least 1 hour or overnight. Yield: 6-8 servings.

Evalena Rossmann
Walnut, Iowa

FIVE-CUP SALAD

1 c. Mandarin orange sections
1 c. chopped bananas
1 c. miniature marshmallows
1 c. shredded coconut
1 c. sour cream
½ c. chopped pecans (opt.)

Combine all ingredients; chill for at least 1 hour before serving. Yield: 6 servings.

Mrs. C. S. Yelverton
Parris Island, S.C.

FRUIT PLATE AND DRESSING

Pear halves
Peach halves
Cantaloupe slices
Pineapple rings
Bananas

Arrange fruits on platter.

DRESSING:
2 eggs
3 tbsp. sugar
1 tbsp. cream
3 tsp. dry mustard
½ tsp. salt
3 tbsp. lemon juice
1 pt. whipped cream
1 c. diced marshmallows
1 c. chopped pecans

Combine eggs, sugar, cream, mustard, salt and lemon juice. Cook in double boiler until thick. Cool. Fold in remaining ingredients. Pour over fruit.

Mrs. Frances Morton
Tallulah, La.

COLUMBIAN FRESH FRUIT MELANGE

2 bananas, sliced
Lime or lemon juice
1 mango, sliced
½ c. flaked coconut
½ c. light corn syrup

Dip banana slices into lime or lemon juice. Arrange alternate layers of bananas, mango and coconut in serving dish until about one-half of fruits are used. Pour 1/4 cup corn syrup over fruits. Top with layers of fruits and coconut until all are used, ending with coconut. Pour remaining syrup over all; chill well. Garnish with extra coconut, cherries and strawberries. Yield: 4 servings.

Photograph for this recipe above.

FRUIT-COCONUT SALAD

1 can pineapple chunks, drained
2 oranges, cut into pieces
2 or 3 bananas, cut into pieces
1 c. miniature marshmallows
1 c. shredded coconut
1 c. sour cream
Chopped nuts (opt.)

Combine pineapple and oranges. Immediately stir in bananas to keep them from turning dark. Add coconut and marshmallows. Stir in sour cream and nuts if desired. Yield: 4-6 servings.

Mrs. Marvin Todd
Pontotoc, Miss.

FRUIT SALAD

1 c. pineapple chunks
1 c. sugar
3 tbsp. flour
2 eggs
¼ tsp. salt
1 ½ c. milk
Juice of 1 lemon
3 bananas diced
3 apples, peeled and diced
1 c. chopped pecans
Whipped cream

Drain pineapple, reserving 1/2 cup juice. Combine sugar, flour, eggs, salt, milk and pineapple juice. Cook in top of double boiler until thick. Stir in lemon juice. Cool. Add fruits and nuts. Serve with whipped cream. Yield: 12 servings.

Mrs. O. H. Lybrand
Birmingham, Ala.

FRUIT SALAD DELUXE

3 eggs
Juice of 1 lemon
¼ c. warm milk
1 tsp. cream of tartar
½ lb. marshmallows
1 can pineapple chunks
1 can white cherries, pitted and drained
1 c. nuts
½ pt. heavy cream, whipped

Combine eggs, lemon juice, milk and cream of tartar; cook until milk curdles. Remove from heat; cool. Fold in marshmallows, fruits, nuts and whipped cream. Refrigerate for 4 hours. Yield: 6 servings.

Mrs. Howard Rieck
Mac Dill AFB, Fla.

GRAPE, BANANA AND COTTAGE CHEESE SALAD

½ c. seedless green grapes, halved
2 bananas, diced
½ pt. small curd cottage cheese
¼ c. chopped pecans (opt.)
Maraschino cherries (opt.)

Combine all ingredients. A little cream may be added to make salad creamier. Serve on lettuce leaves; top with Maraschino cherries.

Mrs. Irene Miller Byrom
Brenham, Tex.

GUM DROP SALAD

1 No. 2 ½ can pineapple chunks
1 No. 2 can white grapes, drained
1 11-oz. can Mandarin oranges, drained
1 8-oz. pkg. miniature marshmallows
1 c. assorted gumdrops, no licorice
½ c. chopped nuts
½ c. sugar
¼ c. sifted flour
Pinch of salt
¼ c. lemon juice
1 ½ c. heavy cream, whipped

Drain pineapple, reserving 1 cup juice. Combine pineapple, grapes and oranges with marshmallows, gumdrops and nuts. Chill. Combine sugar, flour and salt in saucepan. Stir in lemon and pineapple juices; cook over low heat until thickened. Cool. Fold in whipped cream and fruit mixture. Chill in covered bowl for 24 hours. Yield: 8 servings.

Theresa F. Slusser
Bluffton, O.

GLORIFIED FRUIT SALAD

1 c. grapefruit segments
1 c. orange segments
½ c. Maraschino cherries
½ c. seedless grapes
1 c. canned diced pineapple
10 marshmallows, quartered
⅓ c. mayonnaise
⅓ c. whipped cream

Combine fruits and marshmallows. Chill for 1 hour. Blend mayonnaise and whipped cream together; serve in mounds over fruit mixture.

Meda Long
Franklin, Tenn.

HAWAIIAN FRUIT SALAD

1 c. fresh cubed pineapple or canned pineapple chunks
1 c. white seedless grapes
1 c. cubed cantaloupe or papaya
1 c. fresh shredded coconut or flaked coconut
½ c. whipped cream

Combine pineapple, grapes, cantaloupe and coconut. Toss lightly with cream.

Mrs. Daisy Massey
Fredericksburg, Tex.

HEAVENLY SALAD

3 ½ c. crushed pineapple
4 egg yolks
Juice and grated rind of 1 lemon
2 tbsp. sugar
3 ½ c. diced pears
1 lb. white grapes, halved
1 lb. miniature marshmallows
½ pt. heavy cream, whipped

Drain pineapple, reserving 1/3 cup liquid. Combine egg yolks, lemon juice and rind, sugar and pineapple juice. Cook in double boiler until thickened; cool. Pour dressing over fruits and marshmallows; refrigerate overnight. Fold in whipped cream. Yield: 20 servings.

Anna Richardson
Council Bluffs, Iowa

HOLIDAY SURPRISE SALAD

2 c. cranberries, ground
1 c. sugar
1 lb. marshmallows, finely cut
3 bananas, cut up
1 c. chopped nuts
1 c. crushed pineapple
1 c. heavy cream, whipped

Combine cranberries with sugar; fold in marshmallows. Refrigerate overnight. Add all remaining ingredients; chill and serve. NOTE: Leftovers may be used next day over short cake as dessert. Yield: 10 servings.

Mrs. Audre O'Melia
Fort Hamilton, N.Y.

HOT FRUIT SALAD

½ c. white raisins
1 can pears
1 can peaches,
1 can pineapple chunks
1 can white Queen Anne cherries
3 oranges, peeled and quartered
¼ tsp. salt
¾ c. sugar
3 tbsp. butter
3 tbsp. flour
½ c. cooking Sherry

Pour hot water over raisins to make them plump. Drain fruits, reserving 3/4 cup of mixed juice. Cut all fruit except oranges into large chunks. Cook oranges until tender; add salt. Drain well; add to mixed fruits. Add sugar. Combine butter, flour and fruit juice; cook until thick. Add Sherry. Fold sauce into fruit. Refrigerate overnight or freeze until needed. Bake at 350 degrees for 30 minutes or until mixture bubbles. Serve hot. Yield: 20 servings.

Mrs. Mineola Melton
Louisville, Miss.

HOT FRUIT SALAD

1 can sliced pineapple
1 can pear halves
1 can peach halves
1 bottle cherries
¼ c. butter, melted
⅓ c. (packed) brown sugar
2 tsp. curry powder

Drain fruits on paper towels. Mix butter, brown sugar and curry powder. Pour over fruit. Bake at 325 degrees for 1 hour. Yield· 6 servings.

Mrs. C. L. Broxton
New Brockton, Ala.

LUSCIOUS OVERNIGHT SALAD

3 egg yolks
2 tbsp. sugar
⅛ tsp. salt
2 tbsp. vinegar
2 tbsp. pineapple juice
2 tbsp. butter
2 c. white cherries
2 c. pineapple chunks
2 oranges, cut up
2 c. miniature marshmallows
1 c. heavy cream, whipped

Cook egg yolks, sugar, salt, vinegar, pineapple juice and butter, stirring constantly, until thickened. Cool. Drain all fruit; add remaining ingredients. Fold into cooked mixture. Chill overnight. Yield: 12 servings.

Mary Flowers
Olla, La.

MANDARIN ORANGE SALAD

1 c. marshmallows
½ pt. sour cream
1 can Mandarin oranges, drained
1 can Bing cherries, drained
1 can pineapple chunks, drained
½ c. grated coconut
¼ c. chopped pecans

Marinate marshmallows in sour cream for 30 minutes. Add remaining ingredients; mix well. Chill overnight. Serve on lettuce. Yield: 8 servings.

Mrs. J. C. Cason
Jena, La.

MARSHMALLOW DREAM

1 pkg. miniature marshmallows
1 c. Mandarin oranges
½ pt. sour cream
1 c. shredded coconut (opt.)

Combine marshmallows, oranges and sour cream. Refrigerate for at least 3 hours before serving.

Joan Brown
Farwell, Mich.

MARSHMALLOW SURPRISE

1 No. 2 can crushed pineapple
½ c. sugar
2 tbsp. flour
2 eggs, beaten
1 pkg. miniature marshmallows
2 oranges, sectioned
1 c. chopped pecans
1 c. evaporated milk, whipped

Drain pineapple, reserving juice. Combine juice with sugar, flour and eggs. Cook until thickened. Add marshmallows to hot mixture. Cool. Fold in pineapple, oranges, pecans and whipped milk. Refrigerate until firm.

Kathryn Williams
Ruidoso, N.M.

MIXED FRUIT SALAD

4 sm. bunches Tokay grapes
1 egg white
Confectioners sugar
1 banana
½ c. chopped pecans
4 orange slices, rind removed
4 lettuce leaf cups
4 canned figs
2 ½ c. fruit for salad

Wash and thoroughly dry grapes; dip into slightly beaten egg white. Roll in confectioners sugar. Place on waxed paper or in sieve to dry. Do not try to frost each grape in the cluster; coating the outside ones or the end ones is sufficient. Cut banana lengthwise into quarters and crosswise into halves. Dip into finely chopped nuts, coating well on all sides. Fill lettuce cups with orange slices. Place lettuce cups, canned fruits and figs on large plate. Fill corners of plate with grapes and banana fingers.

GOLDEN DRESSING:
2 tbsp. butter, melted
2 tbsp. flour
⅓ c. sugar
⅛ tsp. salt
1 c. pineapple juice
¾ c. orange juice
2 tbsp. lemon juice
2 eggs, slightly beaten
1 c. whipped cream

Blend butter and flour until smooth. Add sugar and salt. Stir in fruit juices; cook, stirring constantly, until smooth and thickened. Add small amount of hot mixture to eggs; return to pan. Cook for 3 minutes longer. Cool. Fold in whipped cream; serve with mixed fruit salad.

Mrs. Thomas H. Roach
Joliet, Ill.

OVERNIGHT SALAD

1 c. diced nuts
1 lb. white grapes, halved lengthwise
1 lb. miniature marshmallows
1 lge. can pineapple, diced
Juice of 3 lemons
4 egg yolks, beaten
½ tsp. powdered mustard
½ tsp. salt
1 pt. heavy cream, whipped

Combine nuts, grapes, marshmallows and pineapple in gallon crock or bowl. Combine lemon juice, egg yolks, mustard and salt in double boiler; cook until thickened. Cool. Mix with whipped cream. Stir into fruit mixture. Chill overnight, stirring two or three times. Yield: 15-20 servings.

Mrs. Faye E. Ringer
Dugger, Ind.

PINEAPPLE BEETS

1 13 ½-oz. can pineapple chunks
½ c. water
⅓ c. cider vinegar
4 tbsp. sugar
1 tbsp. cornstarch
½ tsp. salt
⅛ tsp. ground ginger
2 1-lb. cans sliced beets, drained

Drain syrup from pineapple; mix with water and vinegar. Mix sugar, cornstarch, salt and ginger; add vinegar mixture. Cook until thickened, stirring constantly. Add beets; heat to boiling. Stir in pineapple. Cool. Serve on lettuce. Yield: 8 servings.

Mrs. Arley A. Sarver
Crowley, La.

PINEAPPLE-LONGHORN CHEESE SALAD

1 can pineapple chunks
1 5-oz. pkg. Longhorn cheese, cut up
White peanuts (opt.)
1 c. miniature marshmallows
1 egg
1 tbsp. cornstarch

Drain pineapple, reserving juice. Combine pineapple, cheese, peanuts and marshmallows. Cook juice, egg and cornstarch until thickened. Add to pineapple mixture. Chill until ready to serve.

FROSTING:
1 c. milk
¼ c. flour
1 c. sugar
1 c. shortening
1 tsp. vanilla flavoring

(Continued on next page)

Cook milk and flour until thickened. Cool. Beat remaining ingredients together until creamy. Combine with milk mixture. Spread over salad when ready to serve. Yield: 6 servings.

Mrs. Tony Jeroski
Logansport, Ind.

PINEAPPLE AND TOMATO CUBE SALAD

Lettuce
Pineapple rings
Cubed tomato
Parsley

For each serving, make a bed of lettuce. Add a small amount of shredded lettuce and a pineapple ring. Arrange tomato cubes over pineapple. Garnish with parsley. Serve with honey French dressing.

Melba Dansie Stoffers
Hermiston, Oreg.

QUICK FRUIT SALAD

1 lge. can peach pie filling
1 lge. can pineapple chunks, drained
1 lge. can Mandarin oranges, drained
2 lge. or 2 sm. bananas, sliced
1 c. red grapes, cut into halves

Toss together all ingredients; chill thoroughly before serving. Yield: 8 servings.

Mrs. Alfred Daeffler
Waterloo, N.Y.

RADISH WING SALAD

6 pineapple slices
6 lettuce leaves
1 3-oz. pkg. cream cheese
Milk
6 radish roses
6 tbsp. French dressing

For each serving, place a slice of pineapple in a lettuce cup. Soften cream cheese slightly with a small amount of milk; place rounded tablespoonful of cheese in center of each pineapple slice. Press thin sliced radish roses into cheese to resemble wings. Place 1 tablespoon dressing on each serving.

Lois Slise
Woodrow, Colo.

ROYAL ANNE CHERRY SALAD

2 c. Royal Anne cherries
2 c. pineapple chunks
2 c. cubed orange sections
2 c. miniature marshmallows
¼ lb. almonds or other nuts
2 eggs
2 tbsp. sugar
¼ c. light cream
Juice of 1 lemon
1 c. whipped cream

Combine cherries, pineapple, oranges, marshmallows and nuts. Blend eggs, sugar, cream and lemon juice. Cook in double boiler until thickened; cool. Fold in whipped cream; add fruit mixture. Chill for 12 hours. Yield: 8-10 servings.

Mrs. Sue Christensen
Walker AFB, N.M.

SALAD ROYALE

1 qt. shredded cabbage
3 peach halves, diced
½ c. pineapple chunks
½ doz. Maraschino cherries, diced

Combine above ingredients; chill.

DRESSING:
½ c. (scant) mayonnaise
½ c. (scant) sugar
¼ c. heavy cream, whipped or evaporated milk

Combine ingredients; toss with salad just before serving.

Mrs. Emil W. Merritt
Guilford College, N.C.

SUPREME FRUIT SALAD

1 c. milk
3 egg yolks, beaten
2 tbsp. sugar
1 tbsp. cornstarch
1 lb. marshmallows, chopped
1 lb. white grapes
1 1-lb. can pineapple, drained
1 c. blanched almonds
1 pt. heavy cream, whipped

Combine milk, egg yolks, sugar and cornstarch. Cook, stirring constantly, until thickened. Cool. Add marshmallows, grapes, pineapple and almonds. Fold in whipped cream. Chill. Yield: 14 servings.

Mrs. Inez Cagle
Natchitoches, La.

TWENTY-FOUR HOUR SALAD

2 eggs, beaten
4 to 6 tsp. vinegar or lemon juice
4 to 6 tsp. sugar
2 tsp. butter (opt.)
1 c. whipped cream
2 c. diced Royal Anne cherries
2 c. diced pineapple
2 diced oranges
2 c. diced peaches (opt.)
2 c. miniature marshmallows

Cook eggs, vinegar and sugar in double boiler until thick and smooth. Cool. Fold in cream, fruits and marshmallows. Turn into ring mold or glass serving dish. Chill for 24 hours.

Mrs. Lora Hedegaard
Eagle Butte, S.D.

TWENTY-FOUR HOUR SALAD

½ c. milk
4 egg yolks, beaten
Juice of 1 lemon
1 pt. whipped cream
1 lb. miniature marshmallows
1 lge. can white cherries, drained
1 lge. can Bartlett pears, drained and cut
1 lge. can pineapple chunks, drained

Heat milk to boiling point; stir in egg yolks. Cook in double boiler until thickened. Add lemon juice. Cool. Fold in cream. Add marshmallows; fold in fruits. Chill for 24 hours.

Mrs. Dorothy E. Cobb
Sebring, O.

TWENTY-FOUR HOUR SALAD

DRESSING:
2 eggs or 3 egg yolks
2 tbsp. sugar
2 tbsp. lemon juice
2 tbsp. pineapple juice
1 tbsp. butter
Salt
1 c. whipped cream

Combine all ingredients except cream. Cook in saucepan over low heat, stirring constantly until boiling. Remove from heat. Cool. Fold in whipped cream.

SALAD:
2 c. drained Queen Anne cherries
2 c. drained pineapple chunks
2 oranges, pared or Mandarin
2 grapefruit, pared
2 c. miniature marshmallows
½ c. chopped pecans
½ c. Maraschino cherries
1 c. green grapes

Combine fruits; fold in dressing. Chill. Garnish with green grapes and mint leaves.

Beth Trotter
Morris, Ill.

VITAMIN SALAD

1 can chunk or crushed pineapple, drained
1 pt. cottage cheese
1 pkg. miniature marshmallows
1 c. grated carrots
½ c. mayonnaise

Mix and serve. Yield: 8-10 servings.

Mrs. Myron R. Brown
Cobleskill, N.Y.

WHITE FRUIT SALAD

1 1-qt. can diced pineapple
1 ½ lb. white cherries, diced
¾ lb. almonds, chopped
1 lb. marshmallows
½ c. hot milk
4 egg yolks
¼ tsp. mustard
Juice of 1 lemon
½ tsp. salt
1 pt. heavy cream, whipped

Combine fruit, nuts and marshmallows. Put milk, yolks, mustard, lemon and salt into double boiler; cook until thickened. Cool; add whipped cream. Stir custard into fruit; refrigerate for 24 hours. Yield: 12 servings.

Vera Rust
Richmond, Mo.

WINTER SALAD

1 No. 2 ½ can crushed or diced pineapple
½ c. sugar
1 egg
2 tbsp. cornstarch
1 10 ½-oz. pkg. miniature marshmallows
4 slices American cheese, diced
½ c. mayonnaise

Drain pineapple; reserve juice. Mix juice, sugar, egg and cornstarch. Cook until thickened; cool. Add remaining ingredients. Chill. Yield: 8-10 servings.

Mrs. G. P. Wheeler
Mountain Home, Ark.

RECIPE FOR BRANDIED CRANBERRY-PEACH GELATIN ON PAGE 181
RECIPE FOR CRANBERRY SALAD DESSERT GELATIN ON PAGE 181

AMBROSIA

8 to 10 juicy oranges, peeled and diced
1 c. moist coconut
½ c. chopped pecans
½ c. cherries, halved
¼ c. sugar
1 c. orange juice

Combine all ingredients. Chill. Yield: 4-6 servings.

Laverne Moore
Augusta, Ga.

AMBROSIA SALAD

1 can Mandarin oranges, drained
1 can pineapple chunks, drained
1 c. miniature marshmallows
1 can flaked coconut
½ pt. sour cream

Cut orange sections and pineapple chunks into halves. Mix all ingredients. Refrigerate overnight. Yield: 4 servings.

Frances McKelvey
Lindale, Ga.

AMBROSIA SALAD IN ORANGE CUPS

6 oranges
2 tbsp. grated orange rind
½ c. heavy cream
2 tbsp. lemon juice
3 tbsp. sugar
1 lb. seedless grapes
1 sm. can grated coconut
Nutmeg
6 Maraschino cherries

Remove a 1/2-inch slice from top of each orange. Remove pulp from oranges. Refrigerate orange cups. Remove seed and membranes from orange pulp. Add grated orange rind to cream; chill. Whip cream until it forms soft mounds; add lemon juice and sugar. Fold in orange pulp, grapes and coconut. Spoon into orange cups. Garnish each with nutmeg and a cherry. Yield: 6 servings.

Mrs. Ernestine A. McLeod
Wickes, Ark.

STUFFED APPLE-CINNAMON SALAD

½ c. red cinnamon candies
¼ c. sugar
2 c. water
6 apples, pared and cored
2 tbsp. pecans, broken
10 dates, pitted and chopped
½ c. crushed pineapple, drained
¼ c. mayonnaise
Grated cheese (opt.)

Dissolve candies and sugar in water over low heat. Add whole apples; cook slowly until transparent but not soft. Chill. Combine remaining ingredients; stuff apples. Serve on lettuce. Garnish with a small amount of grated cheese if desired. Yield: 6 servings.

Mrs. Freddie E. Taylor
Dierks, Ark.

STUFFED APPLE RING SALAD

5 red apples
Lemon or pineapple juice
1 8-oz. pkg. cream cheese
½ c. chopped dates
¼ c. chopped nuts

Wash apples but do not pare. Cut into 1/2-inch slices. Remove core with a small cutter, leaving a ring about 1/2 to 1-inch across. Brush with lemon or pineapple juice. Cream cheese until smooth; add dates, nuts and a dash of lemon juice. Blend well. Place apple rings on a tray; fill centers with cheese mixture. Chill. Yield: 8 servings.

Sharon L. Bickel
Liberty Center, Ind.

AVOCADO FRUIT SQUARES

1 lge. ripe avocado, halved and seeded
2 tbsp. lemon juice
1 3-oz. pkg. cream cheese, softened
2 tbsp. sugar
¼ c. mayonnaise or salad dressing
¼ tsp. salt
1 c. well drained diced canned peaches
¼ c. well drained chopped Maraschino cherries
½ c. heavy cream, whipped

Peel avocado; dice into bowl. Sprinkle with 1 tablespoon lemon juice. Blend cream cheese, remaining lemon juice, sugar, mayonnaise and salt; add fruits. Fold in whipped cream; pour into refrigerator tray. Freeze until firm for 6 hours or overnight. Before serving let stand at room temperature for about 15 minutes; cut into squares. Garnish with halves of cherries and avocado balls if desired. Yield: 6 servings.

Mrs. Wilda L. Haight
Portland, Oreg.

BUNCH OF GRAPES SALAD

3 oz. cream cheese, softened
Mayonnaise
6 pear halves
½ lb. green or red grapes, halved

Blend cream cheese with mayonnaise to consistency of frosting. Dry pear halves with paper towel; place on plate round-side up. Frost with cream cheese mixture. Place grape halves on cheese close together, so as to resemble a bunch of grapes. Insert a grape in wide end of pear. Serve. Yield: 6 servings.

Sara J. Gil
Falls Church, Va.

CANDLESTICK SALAD

8 pineapple rings, drained
8 lettuce leaves
4 bananas, cut into halves crosswise
8 strawberries, Maraschino cherries or candied cherries
Shredded coconut
½ c. whipped cream or fruit salad dressing

Arrange a slice of pineapple on lettuce for candle base or holder. Dip bananas into pineapple juice to prevent discoloration. Place a banana half in pineapple ring to make candle. Add cherry or strawberry for flame. Put coconut in cherry for wick. Dribble whipped cream down banana to make it look as if candle is melting. For a colorful Christmas salad, red or green candied apple rings may be used instead of pineapple. Yield: 8 servings.

Mrs. Lawrence A. Boyd
Vernon, Tex.

CHRISTMAS FRUIT SALAD

1 c. sliced fresh or frozen peaches
1 c. pineapple chunks
1 c. sliced bananas
1 c. orange sections
½ c. fresh grapefruit sections
½ c. seedless grapes
½ c. fresh or frozen strawberries
½ c. diced apple
1 c. chopped pecans
1 c. sugar
1 tsp. vanilla flavoring
1 tsp. lemon flavoring
1 c. heavy cream, whipped

Combine fruits, nuts and 1/2 cup sugar. Add remaining sugar and flavorings to whipped cream; fold in fruits and nuts. Chill thoroughly. May be garnished with Maraschino cherries. Yield: 12 servings.

Mrs. Harlan Hawkins
Waldron, Ark.

FLAMING CHRISTMAS CANDLE SALAD

1 4-oz. pkg. cream cheese
4 tbsp. pineapple juice
4 bananas
Lettuce
1 8 ½-oz. can sliced pineapple
4 cubes sugar
1 tbsp. lemon flavoring

Soften cream cheese at room temperature; whip until fluffy. Gradually add pineapple juice, continuing to beat until well blended. Cut ends from bananas so that bananas will be straight. Arrange lettuce leaves on four salad plates; place 1 slice pineapple on each lettuce leaf. Stand bananas in center of pineapple rings using cream cheese as support. Top bananas with 1 teaspoon cream cheese. Dip sugar cube into lemon flavoring; place on top cream cheese. Light sugar cube; serve flaming. NOTE: Cherries may be substituted for flaming sugar cubes. Yield: 4 servings.

Mrs. Robert P. Hunt
Williamsburg, Va.

FLIP FLOP SALAD

1 No. 2 can crushed pineapple
2 pkg. lemon gelatin
3 c. boiling water
1 8-oz. pkg. cream cheese
⅔ pkg. miniature marshmallows
½ pt. cream, whipped
5 tbsp. salad dressing

Drain pineapple, reserving 1 cup juice. Mix gelatin with water and juice; chill until partially congealed. Combine cream cheese, pineapple, marshmallows and cream. Grease 14 x 10-inch pan with salad dressing. Place cream mixture on bottom. Pour lemon gelatin on top; watch it flop. Let set; serve on lettuce leaf. Yield: 14 servings.

Helen Wragg
Amherst, O.

FRUIT BOATS

4 fresh pineapples
2 oranges, sectioned

(Continued on next page)

2 bananas, sliced diagonally
1 pt. whole strawberries, fresh or frozen
1 8-oz. pkg. cream cheese

Wash pineapples gently; halve lengthwise, keeping top intact. Scoop out insides leaving 1/2-inch shells. Discard core; dice pineapple. Combine with oranges, bananas and strawberries; fill shells. May be garnished with mint. Serve with cream cheese blended with juice from fruit. NOTE: Canned pineapple chunks may be used. Yield: 8 servings.

Harriett S. Reed
Milltown, Ind.

FRUIT SALAD

1 orange
6 peach halves
Lettuce
¾ c. finely diced celery
¼ c. finely diced apple
Mayonnaise
6 Maraschino cherries

Peel orange. Cut peel into strips. Place a peach half on lettuce. Stick orange strip into peach to form handle. Fill each with celery, apple and orange moistened with mayonnaise. Garnish with cherries.

Mrs. Fred Backus
Frost Proof, Fla.

FROZEN ORANGE BASKETS

4 oranges, cut into halves
1 c. drained fruit cocktail
¼ c. chopped blanched almonds
2 3-oz. pkg. cream cheese
¼ c. mayonnaise
1 tbsp. vinegar
¼ tsp. prepared mustard
⅛ tsp. salt
½ c. heavy cream, whipped
Orange sherbet

Carefully remove pulp from orange shells, leaving shell unbroken. Combine 1 cup chopped orange sections, fruit cocktail and almonds. Blend in cream cheese, mayonnaise, vinegar, mustard and salt. Fold in whipped cream. Heap mixture into orange shells; freeze. To keep for a longer time, wrap in airtight, moisture-proof paper. Let stand a few minutes before serving; top with a scoop of orange sherbet. Yield: 8 servings.

Mrs. Joseph W. Morel
West Palm Beach, Fla.

KRIS KRINGLE SALAD

1 ¼ c. water
½ c. sugar
¼ c. red cinnamon candies
2 apples, pared and cut into wedges
1 avocado, cut into wedges

Cook water, sugar and cinnamon candies until candies melt. Add apples; cook until tender. Chill. Alternate apples and avocado on lettuce. May be served with French dressing. Yield: 4 servings.

Mrs. Pecola L. Scott
Goodridge, Minn.

CANTALOUPE FRUIT SALAD

1 med. cantaloupe, peeled
Lettuce
3 oranges, peeled and sliced
3 fresh peaches, peeled and sliced
2 nectarines, peeled and sliced
Pineapple slices
1 c. strawberries
1 lge. bunch white grapes

Slice cantaloupe crosswise into five rings. Use pulp to make 1 cup cantaloupe balls. Place rings on lettuce. Arrange orange, peach, nectarine and pineapple slices on top. Add strawberries and cantaloupe balls. Place a small cluster of grapes by each ring.

YOGHURT DRESSING:
1 c. yoghurt
½ c. mayonnaise
½ c. Bleu cheese dressing

Combine ingredients; whip. Chill thoroughly. Serve with cantaloupe rings. Yield: 5 servings.

Helen Sergent
Gate City, Va.

MELON SALAD WITH DRESSING

Watermelon balls or cubes
Cantaloupe balls or cubes
Honeydew melon balls or cubes
Banana slices (opt.)
Pineapple slices (opt.)
½ watermelon shell, cut lengthwise

Combine fruits. Place in scooped out watermelon shell.

DRESSING:
½ c. oil
2 tbsp. vinegar
2 tbsp. lemon juice
½ tsp. salt
¼ tsp. dry mustard
¼ tsp. paprika
4 tbsp. confectioners sugar

Put all dressing ingredients in jar; shake well. Pour over fruits just before serving.

Darleen Pulkrabek
Mt. Iron, Minn.

(Continued on next page)

MELON AMBROSIA

2 nectarines, unpeeled
1 sm. cantaloupe
½ honeydew melon
1 c. grapes, halved and seeded
⅛ fresh pineapple, cut into chunks
1 orange, peeled and sectioned
1 c. flaked coconut
1 ½ c. dry Sherry or Sauterne
½ c. powdered sugar
Fresh mint

Cut nectarines into thin slices. Peel cantaloupe; cut into thin slivers. Cut honeydew melon into balls. Combine fruits; toss with coconut, wine and powdered sugar. Chill thoroughly. Serve in large compote or sherbet glasses; garnish with fresh mint. Yield: 10-12 servings.

Photograph for this recipe above.

MELON EN SURPRISE

1 whole cantaloupe
2 c. fresh raspberries or strawberries
2 c. fresh, frozen or canned pineapple chunks
2 c. peach slices
2 c. grapes
½ c. sugar
¼ c. Marsala wine or 1 tbsp. Kirsch
2 3-oz. pkg. cream cheese, softened
2 tbsp. milk
¼ c. chopped nuts

Pare whole cantaloupe; cut a 4 to 5-inch round opening in one end. Scoop out bite-sized pieces. Combine melon pieces with raspberries or strawberries, pineapple, peach slices and grapes; sprinkle lightly with sugar and wine. Fill melon with fruit; replace top. Frost with cream cheese blended with milk; sprinkle with nuts. Chill for 2 hours. Yield: 3-4 servings.

Mrs. Doris L. Watts
Scottsburg, Ind.

PINEAPPLE CUP

1 lge. pineapple
1 c. strawberries
1 c. honeydew balls
1 c. cantaloupe balls
1 c. cherry liqueur

Cut pineapple in half lengthwise. Scoop out center, leaving 1-inch shell. Remove core; cut

(Continued on next page)

fruit into cubes. Chill pineapple shells. Combine pineapple cubes with strawberries, melon balls and liqueur. Let stand at room temperature for 1 hour. Chill for at least 4 hours. To serve, spoon fruit and marinade into pineapple shells. Yield: 6 servings.

Mrs. Barbara Spears
Shafter, Calif.

SUMMER FRUIT BOUNTY

1 honeydew melon
2 tsp. fresh fruit juice or pineapple juice
2 tbsp. sugar
1 med. pear, diced
2 c. sliced peaches
1 banana, sliced
½ c. sliced strawberries
½ pt. orange sherbet
Sprig of fresh mint

Cut honeydew melon in half. Remove seed; scoop out meat. Cut into cubes. Scallop edges of shell. Turn melon halves upside down to drain; store in refrigerator. Combine fresh fruit or pineapple juice and sugar. Peel and slice pear, peaches and banana directly into sugar mixture. Add melon cubes and strawberries; toss well. Cover; store in refrigerator until ready to serve. Fill melon halves with fruit; top with tiny balls of orange sherbet and a sprig of mint. Yield: 2 servings.

Laoma D. Clevenger
Ohio City, O.

WATERMELON BASKET

1 watermelon, chilled
1 ½ c. cantaloupe and honeydew melon balls
1 c. whole fresh strawberries (opt.)
1 sm. can pineapple juice
Few grape leaves or mint (opt.)

Cut watermelon lengthwise, slicing off top third. Use larger piece for fruit holder. Scoop out melon balls with melon ball cutter or measuring teaspoon. Scallop top edge of shell. Fill with watermelon, cantaloupe and honeydew melon balls. Add strawberries. Pour pineapple juice over top. Tuck in grape leaves or mint. Yield: 10-15 servings.

Sharon Klickna
Tularosa, N.M.

WATERMELON DELIGHT

½ watermelon, chilled
3 cantaloupes, chilled
3 lb. white grapes, washed
4 lb. fresh peaches, sliced

Scoop balls from watermelon and cantaloupes; scallop edges of watermelon rind. Use rind as bowl. Combine all fruits and some of juice. Pour into watermelon bowl. Yield: 12-15 servings.

Millie Sanderson
LaCrosse, Kans.

POINSETTIA SALAD

Lettuce
Canned or fresh sliced pineapple
Pimento
Cream cheese
French dressing

Place a lettuce leaf on a salad plate; place pineapple slice in center. Cut a pimento into 1/2-inch strips; place one end in center of pineapple, letting other end extend to the rim. Arrange strips all around like the spokes of a wheel. Mix cream cheese with French dressing to moisten. Place a small ball of mixture in center of pineapple. Serve with French dressing.

Mrs. Walter Liller
Old Town, Fla.

THANKSGIVING SALAD

4 firm red apples, diced
½ c. pomegranate seed
½ c. seedless raisins
Mayonnaise or salad dressing

Combine apples, pomegranate seed and raisins; mix. Add mayonnaise or salad dressing. Yield: 6-8 servings.

Mrs. Myrtle Burnham
Lee, Me.

CANTALOUPE PARTY SALAD

1 tbsp. unflavored gelatin
¾ c. grapefruit juice
⅛ tsp. salt
⅓ c. sugar
½ c. cold water
⅓ c. lemon juice
2 c. cantaloupe balls
Cream cheese

(Continued on next page)

Soften gelatin in 1/4 cup grapefruit juice; melt over hot water. Add remaining grapefruit juice, salt, sugar, water and lemon juice. Chill until mixture begins to thicken. Fold in cantaloupe balls. Oil 2 1/2-cup mold and 1 1/2-cup mold; fill each with cantaloupe mixture. Refrigerate until firm. Unmold large salad onto serving plate. Center small salad on top of larger one. Garnish with cream cheese; serve with mayonnaise or fruit salad dressing. Yield: 4 servings.

Mrs. Gladys Evans
Camp Point, Ill.

FROSTED MELON SALAD

1 pkg. lime gelatin
1 med. cantaloupe, peeled
1 6-oz. jar cream cheese, softened

Dissolve gelatin according to package directions, using 1 3/4 cups water. Chill until slightly thickened. Cut open stem end of cantaloupe so edge of seed pocket is exposed. Scoop out seed and membrane. Fill pocket with gelatin. Secure lid with toothpicks. Place in refrigerator in upright position until gelatin is firm. Before serving, frost with cream cheese. Slice crosswise. Yield: 6-8 servings.

Lois Moss
New Plymouth, Idaho

AUNT TENA'S CHRISTMAS SALAD

1 pkg. lime gelatin
1 pkg. lemon gelatin
2 c. boiling water
1 qt. vanilla ice cream, softened
1 c. sliced red and green Maraschino cherries
1 c. pineapple chunks

Dissolve gelatins in boiling water. Immediately add ice cream; stir until melted. Add fruits. Pour into an oiled 1-quart mold. Chill until firm. Yield: 12 servings.

Mrs. Janet Jacobson
Saginaw, Mich.

CHRISTMAS RING SALAD

1 c. pineapple juice
1 lge. pkg. cream cheese
1 pkg. lime gelatin
1 or 2 pkg. unflavored gelatin
1 sm. bottle cherries
4 slices pineapple, finely cut
1 sm. bottle cherries
1 head lettuce
1 lge. bottle stuffed olives

Bring pineapple juice and cream cheese to a boil. Stir to dissolve cheese. Prepare lime gelatin according to package directions. Dissolve unflavored gelatin in cold water; add to lime gelatin mixture. Blend gelatin mixture into cheese mixture until smooth. Stir in pineapple and whole cherries. Mold in 9-inch ring mold. Chill until firm. Unmold on a bed of lettuce; fill center with olives. Yield: 10 servings.

Mrs. Ben Stanton
Red Springs, N.C.

CHRISTMAS TREES

1 c. crushed pineapple
1 pkg. lime gelatin
1 c. hot water
1 c. whipped cream
½ c. cottage cheese, drained
½ c. broken pecans
½ c. chopped Maraschino cherries
Mayonnaise
Whipped cream for garnish

Drain pineapple, reserving juice; add enough water to juice to make 1 cup. Dissolve gelatin in boiling water; add juice-water mixture. Chill until partially set. Fold in whipped cream. Fold in cottage cheese which has been put through a fine sieve, pineapple, nuts and cherries; blend well. Pour into pointed waxed paper cups to chill. Unmold on a bed of lettuce; garnish with mayonnaise and fluffed whipped cream. Let a small amount run down the sides of each tree. Top with a cherry wedge. Yield: 10 servings.

Mrs. Vera Troyer
Martin, S.D.

CHRISTMAS TREE SALAD

1 can cranberry sauce
¼ tsp. salt
¼ c. chopped celery
¼ c. finely cut dates
1 orange, finely cut
¼ c. chopped Maraschino cherries
½ c. chopped pecans
1 pkg. unflavored gelatin
1 pkg. cream cheese

(Continued on next page)

Heat cranberry sauce until softened. Add salt, celery, dates, orange, cherries and pecans. Soften gelatin in a small amount of water; add to cranberry mixture. Pour mixture into cone shaped paper cups. Chill until firm. Remove from cups to serve. Soften cream cheese. Using a decorator tube, make decorations on cone shaped salads to represent Christmas tree decorations.

Edna Burton
Okmulgee, Okla.

CHRISTMAS TREE SALAD

1 sm. can crushed pineapple
1 pkg. lime gelatin
16 marshmallows, chopped
1 c. whipped cream
8 lge. Maraschino cherries

Drain pineapple, reserving juice; add enough water to make 2 cups. Heat pineapple syrup to boiling; dissolve gelatin in hot liquid. Add marshmallows, stirring to dissolve. Add pineapple. Chill until very thick. Fold in whipped cream. Place a cherry in bottom of each cone mold. Pour mixture into each mold. Chill until set. Turn upside down and peel off paper mold before serving. Garnish around bottom with colored whipped cream or colored mayonnaise. Yield: 8 servings.

Alice Allison Kealhofer
Bentonia, Miss.

MERRY CHRISTMAS SALAD

1 pkg. lime gelatin
1 c. boiling water
1 No. 2 can crushed pineapple
1 c. small curd cottage cheese
½ c. finely sliced celery
1 tbsp. chopped pimento
½ c. chopped nuts
Jellied cranberry sauce
6 walnut halves
Maraschino cherries
Green pepper strips

Dissolve gelatin in boiling water; cool until syrupy. Stir in remaining ingredients; pour into round 8 or 9 x 1 1/2-inch waxed paper-lined cake pan. Chill until firm. Turn out onto waxed paper; cut into tree shape. To decorate, cut squares of cranberry sauce for base; trim with walnut halves, cherries and green pepper. Place curly endive around sides. Chill until serving time. Yield: 6 servings.

Lila Wilkins
Lubbock, Tex.

QUICK CHRISTMAS CRANBERRY CANDLES

1 3-oz. pkg. raspberry gelatin
1 No. 101 can whole cranberry sauce
Lettuce leaves
Salad dressing or whipped cream

Prepare gelatin according to package directions. Chill until mixture is consistency of egg whites. Add cranberry sauce; blend well. Pour into small frozen juice cans or small paper cups. Let set for several hours or overnight. Unmold on lettuce leaves; garnish with salad dressing or whipped cream. Yield: 4 servings.

Mrs. Martha F. Jenkins
Hildebran, N.C.

CRANBERRY-ICE CREAM SALAD

1 1-lb. can whole cranberry sauce
2 lge. oranges
1 tbsp. lemon juice
1 pkg. orange gelatin
1 pt. vanilla ice cream

Break cranberry sauce apart; drain well, reserving all syrup possible. Peel and dice orange sections, reserving orange juice. Combine cranberry syrup, orange juice and lemon juice with enough water to make 1 cup of liquid. Heat liquid to boiling; pour over gelatin and stir until dissolved. Add ice cream; mix until well blended. Chill until partially congealed. Fold in cranberry sauce and oranges; pour into mold. Chill until firm. Unmold and garnish with additional orange sections if desired. Yield: 8 servings.

Mary Jane Nash
Bay, Ark.

HOLIDAY CRANBERRY SALAD

2 c. cranberries
1 ½ c. cold water
1 c. sugar
1 tbsp. unflavored gelatin
Dash of salt
½ c. finely chopped nuts
1 c. diced celery
2 c. diced apples

Cook cranberries in 1 cup water until tender; add sugar. Cook for 5 minutes. Soften gelatin in remaining cold water; dissolve in hot cranberry mixture. Add salt. Chill until

(Continued on next page)

mixture begins to thicken; add nuts, celery and apples. Mix well; chill until firm. Yield: 8-10 servings.

Mrs. Wilson R. Kouba
Anamosa, Iowa

BRANDIED CRANBERRY-PEACH GELATIN

1 8-oz. can sliced peaches
⅓ c. brandy or 2 tsp. brandy flavoring
⅔ c. sugar
2 c. fresh cranberries
1 6-oz. pkg. strawberry gelatin
1 ½ c. boiling water
1 c. cold water
½ c. chopped celery
½ c. chopped nuts

Drain peaches and reserve syrup. Add brandy to syrup with enough water to make 1 cup liquid. Combine liquid, sugar and cranberries in small saucepan. Bring to a full boil, then remove from heat. Dissolve gelatin in boiling water; add cold water and cranberry mixture. Chill until thickened. Add peaches, celery and nuts; mix well. Pour into 1 1/2-quart mold. Chill until firm. Yield: 6-8 servings.

Photograph for this recipe on page 173 .

CRANBERRY SALAD DESSERT GELATIN

2 c. cranberries
1 c. water
1 c. sugar
2 sticks cinnamon
8 whole cloves
2 c. Port wine or black cherry carbonated beverage
2 envelopes unflavored gelatin
⅓ c. lemon juice
1 1-lb. can peach slices, drained

Combine cranberries, water, sugar and spices in saucepan. Bring to a boil; lower heat and simmer for 5 minutes. Cool. Remove cinnamon sticks and cloves. Add Port wine. Combine gelatin and lemon juice in saucepan; let stand for 5 minutes. Place saucepan over low heat; stir until gelatin is dissolved. Combine gelatin and cranberry mixtures; chill until slightly thickened. Fold in peach slices. Pour mixture into a 1 1/2-quart mold; chill until firm. Unmold and serve with sweetened whipped cream.

Photograph for this recipe on page 173 .

CUT GLASS SALAD

1 pkg. cherry gelatin
1 pkg. lime gelatin
1 pkg. lemon gelatin
1 pkg. unflavored gelatin
3 c. boiling water
2 c. cold water
1 c. pineapple juice
1 pkg. dessert topping mix
¼ c. sugar
½ c. chopped pecans

Prepare cherry, lime and lemon gelatin in separate containers by adding 1 cup boiling water and 1/2 cup cold water to each. Cool until firm; cut into cubes. Sprinkle unflavored gelatin on 1/2 cup cold water; stir into hot pineapple juice. Cool until partially set; add dessert topping mix, sugar and pecans. Fold gelatin cubes into pineapple mixture. Cool. Yield: 15 servings.

Virginia Kelley
Hartford, Kans.

GRAPEFRUIT BOATS

5 grapefruit
3 pkg. lemon gelatin
¾ c. boiling water
1 tbsp. gelatin
½ c. cold water

Cut grapefruit lengthwise; remove and cut up sections. Dissolve lemon gelatin in boiling water; dissolve gelatin in cold water. Combine all ingredients. Fill grapefruit shells; congeal.

DRESSING:
⅓ c. sugar
2 tbsp. flour
2 egg yolks
Juice of 2 lemons
8 marshmallows
⅔ c. chopped pecans
½ c. heavy cream, whipped

Combine all ingredients except pecans and whipped cream; cook until thickened. Cool; add nuts and whipped cream. Top each grapefruit with dressing. Yield: 20 servings.

Mrs. Victor McGee
Wadesboro, N.C.

LIME WREATH MOLD

1 No. 2 can crushed pineapple
1 pkg. lime gelatin

(Continued on next page)

½ c. grated American cheese
½ c. chopped pimento
½ c. chopped celery
⅔ c. chopped nuts
¼ tsp. salt
1 c. heavy cream, whipped
1 sm. bottle stuffed olives, sliced
Curly endive

Drain pineapple, reserving juice. Bring syrup, drained from pineapple, to a boil. Add gelatin; stir until dissolved. Cool. When slightly thick, add pineapple, cheese, pimento, celery, nuts and salt. Fold in whipped cream. Place a row of olive slices in 9-inch ring mold. Pour gelatin mixture into mold; chill until firm. Arrange endive on platter; unmold salad on top. Yield: 8-10 servings.

Mrs. Wesley Wade
Montgomery, Ala.

PEAR-GRAHAM CRACKER SALAD

4 lettuce leaves
4 lge. canned or fresh pear halves, drained
12 single graham crackers, crushed
4 tsp. mayonnaise
½ tsp. paprika

Wash lettuce leaves; place on individual plates. Roll pears in cracker crumbs; place on lettuce leaf. Top with mayonnaise; sprinkle with paprika. Yield: 4 servings.

Cathy Prihar
Bridgeport, Wash.

ROSY FRUIT COCKTAIL SLICES

2 3-oz. pkg. cream cheese, softened
1 c. mayonnaise
1 c. heavy cream, whipped
1 No. 2 ½ can fruit cocktail, drained
½ c. Maraschino cherries, drained and quartered
2 ½ c. chopped or miniature marshmallows
Few drops of red food coloring or cherry juice

Blend cream cheese with mayonnaise; fold in remaining ingredients. Pour into two 1-quart round ice cream or freezer containers. Freeze until firm. Remove from freezer; let stand for a few minutes. Remove from container; slice. May be served on salad greens and garnished with cherries. Yield: 10-12 servings.

Alice Cunningham
Hart, Mich.

ST. NICK SALAD RING

2 pkg. strawberry gelatin
3 ½ c. boiling water
2 tbsp. lemon juice
1 tbsp. vinegar
1 tbsp. grated onion
1 tsp. salt
2 3-oz. pkg. cream cheese
⅓ c. parsley, chopped
2 grapefruit, sectioned
1 c. diced celery
1 avocado, diced
1 med. unpared apple, diced

Dissolve gelatin in boiling water; stir in lemon juice, vinegar, onion and salt. Chill until syrupy. Form cream cheese into small balls about the size of marbles; roll in parsley. Lightly oil 1 1/2-quart ring mold. Alternate cheese balls and grapefruit sections around bottom of mold, rounded side of fruit down. Spoon syrupy gelatin around design to depth of about 1/4-inch. Chill until firm. Fold celery, avocado and apple into remaining syrupy gelatin. Pour into mold. Chill for several hours. Yield: 8-10 servings.

SOUR CREAM DRESSING:
1 c. sour cream
2 tbsp. mayonnaise
2 tsp. sugar
2 tsp. lemon juice
½ tsp. salt

Combine all ingredients. Chill to blend flavors. Serve with salad ring. Yield: 8-10 servings.

Mrs. Mildred R. Turner
Arcata, Calif.

SAINT PAT'S SALAD

1 c. crushed pineapple
1 pkg. lime gelatin
2 c. cottage cheese
1 c. whipped cream

Drain pineapple, reserving juice; add enough water to make 2 cups liquid. Dissolve gelatin in hot juice mixture; chill until partially set. Add cottage cheese and pineapple; fold in whipped cream. Pour into dish; chill until firm. Yield: 12 servings.

Jo Ann Brink
Circleville, O.

STUFFED NECTARINE SALAD

1 No. 2 ½ can peeled nectarines, drained
Juice of 4 lemons

(Continued on next page)

Juice of 2 limes
1 ½ c. sugar
½ c. water
2 ½ tbsp. unflavored gelatin
2 3-oz. pkg. cream cheese
½ c. chopped pecans
Mayonnaise

Blend nectarine syrup with lemon and lime juice and sugar. This should measure about 1 quart. Bring to a boil; remove from heat. Pour 1/2 cup water over the lemon and lime peels; rub with hands. Strain; add to gelatin. Pour hot mixture over the gelatin mixture; cool. Stuff nectarine halves with mixture of cream cheese, pecans and mayonnaise; place in individual molds with smooth side down. Fill molds with gelatin; chill until firm. May be served on lettuce with mayonnaise.

Mrs. Joe H. Rainey
Henderson, Tenn.

STUFFED PEAR SALAD

6 pear halves
1 c. fresh or frozen red raspberries, partially thawed
1 pkg. raspberry gelatin
Lettuce
⅓ c. mayonnaise
Cream

Drain fruits, reserving 1 3/4 cups juice. Heat juice; add gelatin. Stir until gelatin is completely dissolved. Pour a 1/8-inch layer of gelatin into glass baking dish that has been rinsed with cold water. Chill until gelatin layer is firm. Place pears with hollow side up on gelatin; fill hollows with raspberries. Carefully pour remaining gelatin over berries. Chill until firm. Cut into squares with stuffed pears in the center. Serve on lettuce with mayonnasie and whipped cream. Yield: 6 servings.

Mrs. Helen L. Ware
Salem, N.J.

THANKSGIVING FRUIT SALAD

1 c. diced canned peaches
1 c. pineapple chunks
1 c. green grapes, halved
¼ c. chopped Maraschino cherries
1 tsp. unflavored gelatin
2 tsp. lemon juice
1 3-oz. pkg. cream cheese
¼ c. mayonnaise
¼ tsp. salt
⅔ c. heavy cream
½ c. sugar
½ c. chopped nuts

Drain fruits. Soak gelatin in lemon juice; dissolve over hot water. Blend cream cheese with mayonnaise and salt; stir in gelatin. Whip cream until stiff, adding sugar gradually during last stages of beating. Fold in cheese mixture, nuts and fruits. Pour into oiled individual molds or refrigerator tray lined with waxed paper. Freeze until firm. Turn out onto salad plates or platter and garnish with watercress or salad greens. Yield: 8 servings.

Mrs. Ina A. Pierce
Middleboro, Mass.

YULETIDE SALAD

1 pkg. lime gelatin
2 c. boiling water
1 bottle Maraschino cherries
1 c. cottage cheese
1 c. crushed pineapple
¼ c. chopped nuts
¼ tsp. salt

Dissolve gelatin in boiling water; cool. Reserve 8 whole cherries; chop remaining cherries. Add cottage cheese, pineapple, nuts, chopped Maraschino cherries and salt to gelatin mixture. Place a whole cherry in bottom of cone paper cup; add gelatin mixture. When unmolded, cherry will be at top of tree. Serve on lettuce leaf with dressing. Yield: 8 servings.

Mrs. Olga J. Leonard
Lennox, S.D.

APPLE- LIME MOLDED SALAD

1 pkg. lime gelatin
2 c. boiling water
1 ¼ c. cold water
3 or 4 apples, quartered and diced
1 stalk celery, diced
½ c. chopped pecans
1 pkg. lime gelatin
1 3-oz. pkg. cream cheese, softened
½ c. crushed pineapple, drained
½ c. whipped cream

Dissolve 1 package of gelatin in 1 cup boiling water; add 3/4 cup cold water. Chill until partially set. Fold apples, celery, and nuts into gelatin; pour into 6-cup ring mold.

(Continued on next page)

Chill until firm. Dissolve remaining gelatin in remaining boiling water; add cold liquid. Chill until firm. Whip until foamy. Combine cream cheese and pineapple; fold into whipped gelatin. Fold in cream. Pour over first layer; chill until firm. Yield: 12 servings.

Mrs. Rosalynn Mickelson
Fithian, Ill.

MOLDED CINNAMON-APPLE SALAD

½ c. red cinnamon candies
1 pkg. lemon gelatin
2 c. hot water
2 tbsp. lemon juice
1 ¼ c. unpeeled diced apples
¼ c. broken toasted walnuts or filberts
1 3-oz. pkg. cream cheese
¼ c. cream
⅛ tsp. salt

Dissolve candies and gelatin in boiling water. Cool. Add lemon juice. Chill until syrupy. Fold in apples and nuts. Pour one-half of gelatin mixture into 8 x 8-inch square cake pan; chill until firm. Blend cream cheese with cream and salt. Spread on firm gelatin layer. Carefully pour remaining gelatin over cheese layer. Chill until firm. Yield: 6 servings.

Mrs. Eleanor Hatch
Joseph, Oreg.

APPLE SALAD

3 c. thick unsweetened applesauce
⅓ c. red cinnamon candies
2 c. hot water
2 pkg. lemon gelatin
2 8-oz. pkg. cream cheese
1 c. mayonnaise
1 c. chopped celery
1 c. chopped walnuts

Cook applesauce until thick. Dissolve cinnamon candies in hot water; add gelatin and dissolve. Add applesauce. Pour one-half of mixture into mold; chill until firm. Blend cream cheese and mayonnaise; stir in celery and walnuts. Spread over congealed gelatin; chill. Pour remaining applesauce mixture over filling; chill until firm. Cut into squares and serve on lettuce with mayonnaise.

Ruby Keyes
Anaconda, Mont.

APRICOT NECTAR SALAD

2 pkg. lemon gelatin
4 c. apricot nectar
1 sm. can crushed pineapple
1 8-oz. pkg. cream cheese
½ c. chopped nuts
½ c. chopped celery

Dissolve 1 package gelatin in 1 cup hot apricot nectar; add 1 cup cold water. Chill until thick. Add one-half of pineapple. Pour into 9 x 9-inch pan; allow to set. Soften cream cheese with a little nectar; blend in nuts and celery. Frost firm gelatin layer. Make second layer same as the first; allow to thicken slightly before pouring onto frosted layer. Chill thoroughly before serving. Yield: 8 servings.

Luella V. Henderson
Old Washington, O.

APRICOT RIBBON RING

1 c. crushed pineapple
2 envelopes unflavored gelatin
¼ c. cold water
1 ½ c. apricot nectar
¼ tsp. salt
¼ c. lemon juice
1 7-oz. bottle 7-Up

Drain pineapple, reserving syrup. Soften gelatin in cold water and pineapple syrup. Heat apricot nectar to boiling; stir in softened gelatin until completely dissolved. Add salt, lemon juice and pineapple. Cool to room temperature. Carefully add 7-Up, stirring as little as possible. Fill a 5 1/2-cup ring mold one-third full; chill until firm.

FILLING:
1 3-oz. pkg. cream cheese, softened
Dash of salt
3 tbsp. mayonnaise or salad dressing
⅓ c. chopped celery
¼ c. chopped pecans

Blend all ingredients. Spread evenly over chilled gelatin layer. Add remaining gelatin. Chill until firm. Serve on crisp lettuce. Yield: 8-10 servings.

Verna Buerge
Turlock, Calif.

AVOCADO-GRAPEFRUIT SALAD

2 3-oz. pkg. lime gelatin
2 fresh grapefruit, peeled and sectioned
2 avocados, sieved
½ c. mayonnaise

(Continued on next page)

Dissolve gelatin according to directions on package. Cool until partially set. Remove membranes from grapefruit sections. Arrange sections in 8 x 12-inch pan. Pour one-half of gelatin mixture over grapefruit. Chill. Pour remaining gelatin mixture into a bowl; add avocado and mayonnaise. Beat with electric or rotary beater until light and foamy. Pour over grapefruit layer. Chill until firm. Cut into squares; serve foamy-side up on a lettuce leaf. Garnish with whipped cream and a Maraschino cherry. Yield: 10 servings.

Mrs. Helen D. Andrus
Dillon, Mont.

BLUEBERRY-CREAM CHEESE SALAD

2 No. 2 cans blueberries
1 3-oz. pkg. lemon gelatin
1 ¼ c. hot water
1 lge. pkg. cream cheese
1 to 3 tbsp. sugar
1 tsp. vanilla flavoring
½ pt. cream or evaporated milk, whipped
2 3-oz. pkg. red gelatin

Drain blueberries, reserving juice; add enough water to make 3 cups liquid. Dissolve 1 package gelatin in hot water; cool. Cream cheese; slowly mix in gelatin. Add sugar and vanilla flavoring to whipped cream; fold into cheese mixture. Chill until firm. Heat juice-water mixture; pour over remaining gelatin to dissolve. Chill until slightly thickened. Add blueberries. Pour on firm gelatin-cheese mixture. Chill until firm. Yield: 8-12 servings.

Mrs. Mayme W. Day
Refrigio, Tex.

BLUEBERRY SALAD

1 envelope unflavored gelatin
½ c. cold water
1 c. milk
1 c. sugar
2 cartons sour cream
1 pkg. raspberry gelatin
1 c. boiling water
1 No. 2 can blueberries

Soften unflavored gelatin in cold water for 5 minutes. Scald milk with sugar; add gelatin, stirring until dissolved. Cool. Add sour cream to gelatin mixture; pour into 1 1/2-quart mold. Chill until firm. Dissolve raspberry gelatin in boiling water. Add blueberries; cool. Pour over firm sour cream mixture; chill for 12 hours. Unmold and serve. Yield: 12 servings.

Mrs. Si Swalheim
Arlington, Wisc.

BLUEBERRY SALAD

3 pkg. raspberry gelatin
5 c. boiling water
1 envelope unflavored gelatin
½ c. cold water
1 c. light cream
1 c. sugar
1 tsp. vanilla flavoring
1 8-oz. pkg. cream cheese
½ c. chopped nuts
1 can blueberries

Dissolve 2 packages raspberry gelatin in 4 cups boiling water; pour into 8 x 12-inch pan. Chill until firm. Sprinkle unflavored gelatin over cold water; add cream and sugar. Beat in vanilla flavoring and cream cheese; stir in nuts. Pour over firm gelatin. Chill. Dissolve remaining raspberry gelatin with remaining boiling water; add blueberries. Pour over cheese layer; chill. Yield: 15 servings.

Mrs. George Biehl
Lexington, Nebr.

BLUEBERRY SALAD

1 No. 2 can crushed pineapple
1 No. 303 can blueberries
3 3-oz. pkg. raspberry gelatin
2 c. hot water
2 pkg. dessert topping mix
1 c. chopped nuts

Drain pineapple and blueberries, reserving juice; add enough water to make 4 cups liquid. Dissolve gelatin in hot water; add juice-water mixture. Reserve 2 cups of gelatin mixture. Add pineapple and blueberries to remaining gelatin. Chill until firm. Prepare dessert topping mix according to package directions; add nuts. Chill reserved gelatin mixture to egg white consistency; combine with dessert topping. Spread over firm gelatin layer. Chill until firm. Yield: 16 servings.

Mrs. Beuford Rook
Clay Center, Kans.

BOYSENBERRY SALAD

2 lge. cans boysenberries
2 pkg. raspberry gelatin
1 tbsp. vinegar
⅛ tsp. salt
1 lge. pkg. cream cheese
½ pt. heavy cream, whipped

(Continued on next page)

Drain boysenberries, reserving juice. Dissolve 1 package gelatin in hot juice. Add vinegar, salt and 1 cup cold juice; place in refrigerator until firm. Dissolve remaining package of gelatin in remaining hot juice. Refrigerate until syrupy. Beat cheese until fluffy. Beat syrupy gelatin until fluffy. Add cream cheese; beat until blended. Add boysenberries; fold in whipped cream. Pour on firm gelatin; refrigerate. Yield: 8 servings.

Mrs. John W. King
Cape Girardeau, Mo.

BING CHERRY SALAD

1 30-oz. can crushed pineapple
1 30-oz. can Bing cherries, pitted
3 pkg. black cherry or cherry gelatin
2 1/3 c. boiling water
1/3 c. lemon juice
1/3 c. whipping cream
1/3 c. mayonnaise
2 3-oz. pkg. cream cheese, at room temperature
Dash of salt
1/2 c. coarsely broken nuts

Drain pineapple and cherries, reserving 3 cups of combined juices. Dissolve gelatin in boiling water. Chill one-half of gelatin mixture until partially set. Fold in pineapple. Spread evenly in a 9 x 13 x 2-inch pan; chill until firm. Whip cream, mayonnaise, cream cheese and salt together until light and fluffy; spread evenly over firm gelatin. Chill until firm. Chill remaining gelatin until partially set. Fold in cherries and nuts; spread over cheese layer. Chill until firm. Yield: 15 servings.

Mrs. Shelba W. Barnes
Waynetown, Ind.

CHERRY-MINCEMEAT MOLD

2 pkg. cherry gelatin
4 c. water
1 pt. brandied mincemeat
1/2 c. chopped pecans

Dissolve gelatin in water. When mixture thickens, pour a small amount in bottom of greased 6-cup mold. Chill until firm. Mix remaining gelatin with mincemeat and pecans; pour over firm gelatin. Chill until firm. Yield: 8-10 servings.

Mrs. Carolyn Rose
Gettysburg, O.

CHERRY-PINEAPPLE LAYER SALAD

1 pkg. lemon gelatin
2 1/2 c. boiling water
1 No. 2 can crushed pineapple
1 8-oz. pkg. cream cheese
Milk
2 No. 2 cans dark sweet cherries
2 pkg. cherry gelatin

Dissolve lemon gelatin in 1 cup boiling water. Cool until slightly thickened. Add pineapple. Pour into 8 x 11-inch pan; chill until firm. Whip cream cheese with a little milk until it reaches consistency of frosting. Spread over firm gelatin layer. Chill until set. Drain cherries, reserving 1 1/2 cups juice. Dissolve cherry gelatin in remaining boiling water; add cherry juice. Chill until slightly thickened. Add cherries; pour carefully over cheese layer. Chill until firm. Yield: 12-15 servings.

Mrs. Louise S. Ventura
Arnold, Pa.

DOUBLE-DECKER CHERRY SALAD

1 No. 2 can sliced pineapple
1 3-oz. pkg. cherry gelatin
1 3-oz. pkg. cream cheese
2 to 3 tbsp. light cream or top milk
1 No. 2 can Bing cherries, pitted and drained
1/3 c. lemon juice
1 pkg. orange gelatin
1/2 c. stuffed olives, sliced

Drain pineapple, reserving juice; add enough water to make 1 3/4 cups liquid. Heat pineapple juice to boiling. Add cherry gelatin; stir to dissolve. Chill until partially set. Cut pineapple slices into 1/8-inch pieces; add to cherry gelatin mixture. Pour into an oiled 8-inch square pan. Chill until firm. Soften cheese with cream; spread over firm gelatin. Drain cherries, reserving juice. Combine cherry juice and lemon juice; add water to make 1 3/4 cups liquid. Heat liquid to boiling; add orange gelatin, stirring to dissolve. Chill until partially set. Add cherries and olives. Spread over cheese. Chill until firm. Yield: 9 servings.

Virginia B. Dotson
Buffalo, W. Va.

CHRISTMAS LAYER SALAD

LIME LAYER:
1 pkg. lime gelatin
1 c. hot water

(Continued on next page)

1 c. pineapple chunks, drained
⅓ c. pineapple juice

Dissolve gelatin in hot water. Add pineapple and juice. Chill until firm.

CHEESE LAYER:
1 ½ tsp. unflavored gelatin
2 tbsp. cold water
1 8-oz. pkg. cream cheese
¼ c. milk

Sprinkle gelatin over cold water to soften. Add cream cheese softened with milk. Spread over firm lime layer.

CRANBERRY LAYER:
2 pkg. strawberry gelatin
2 c. hot water
1 can whole cranberries

Dissolve gelatin in hot water. Add cranberries. Cool. Pour over cheese layer. Chill until firm. Yield: 9-10 servings.

Mrs. Linda G. Wallace
York, Pa.

CHRISTMAS SALAD

1 pkg. red gelatin
1 pkg. lemon gelatin
1 pkg. lime gelatin
1 sm. pkg. cream cheese
1 c. drained pineapple
½ c. nuts
1 c. whipped cream

Prepare gelatin mixes according to package directions in separate containers. Pour red gelatin into 13 x 9 x 2-inch pan; chill until firm. Pour lemon gelatin into mixing bowl; chill until thickened. Beat with mixer; whip in cream cheese. Fold in pineapple, nuts and whipped cream; pour over red gelatin. Chill until firm. Pour lime gelatin over lemon layer; chill until firm. Yield: 12 servings.

Mrs. Shirley Casey
Lakeside, Mont.

CHRISTMAS SALAD

1 ¼ c. crushed pineapple
1 3-oz. pkg. lime gelatin
½ 3-oz. pkg. lemon gelatin
½ c. hot water
¼ c. finely chopped marshmallows
1 4-oz. pkg. cream cheese
½ c. mayonnaise
½ c. heavy cream, whipped
1 3-oz. pkg. cherry gelatin

Drain pineapple, reserving 1/2 cup juice. Prepare lime gelatin according to package directions; chill until thickened. Dissolve lemon gelatin in hot water in double boiler. Add marshmallows; heat until melted. Remove from heat; add pineapple juice and cream cheese. Beat with mixer until well blended. Stir in pineapple; cool. Fold in mayonnaise and whipped cream. Chill until thickened; pour over lime gelatin. Chill until almost set. Prepare cherry gelatin according to package directions; chill until thickened. Pour over pineapple layer. Chill until firm. Serve on crisp lettuce. Yield: 10 servings.

Mrs. Mary Lou Glass
Clawson, Mich.

MOLDED COTTAGE CHEESE-PINEAPPLE SALAD

1 pkg. lemon gelatin
2 c. boiling water
1 c. whipped cream
1 ½ c. cottage cheese
1 pkg. lime gelatin
1 c. pineapple juice
1 c. chopped pineapple
⅓ c. stuffed olives, sliced
⅓ c. broken walnuts

Dissolve lemon gelatin in 1 cup boiling water; cool slightly. Beat with egg beater until light; add cream and cottage cheese. Pour into round mold. Chill until firm. Dissolve lime gelatin in remaining water and pineapple juice; cool. Add pineapple, olives and walnuts. Pour over firm layer. Chill until firm. Yield: 12 servings.

Mrs. Charlotte Brainerd
Fennimore, Wisc.

GELATIN RIBBON SALAD

2 pkg. cherry gelatin
1 pkg. lemon gelatin
1 ½ c. pineapple juice
1 c. small curd cottage cheese
1 c. whipped cream

Dissolve 1 package cherry gelatin according to package directions; let set. Dissolve lemon gelatin in pineapple juice; let set until syrupy. Add cottage cheese and whipped cream. Pour lemon mixture over cherry gelatin. Let set until firm. Dissolve remaining cherry gelatin according to package directions; pour over lemon-cherry layer. Chill. Yield: 8-10 servings.

Carolyn S. Howard
Brigham City, Utah

EGGNOG CHRISTMAS SALAD

2 c. crushed pineapple with juice
1 envelope unflavored gelatin
3 tbsp. fresh lime juice
1 ½ c. eggnog
¾ c. chopped celery
1 3-oz. pkg. raspberry flavored gelatin
1 ½ c. boiling water
1 10-oz. pkg. frozen cranberry-orange relish
Salad greens

Drain pineapple juice into saucepan; heat to boiling. Soften gelatin in lime juice; dissolve in boiling pineapple juice. Cool. Add eggnog; chill until partially set. Fold in pineapple and celery. Pour into mold; chill until firm. Dissolve raspberry gelatin in boiling water; add cranberry-orange relish, stirring until relish is thawed. Chill until slightly thickened; pour over eggnog mixture. Chill until firm. Unmold on salad greens. Yield: 8-10 servings.

Photograph for this recipe above.

FOUR-CUP SALAD

1 box orange gelatin
3 c. boiling water
1 c. miniature marshmallows
1 c. cottage cheese
1 c. mayonnaise
1 c. heavy cream, whipped
1 box lime gelatin

Dissolve orange gelatin in 1 cup boiling water; add marshmallows, stirring until partially dissolved. Stir in cottage cheese and mayonnaise; blend. Cool; fold in whipped cream. Dissolve lime gelatin in remaining water; pour one-half into ring mold. Chill until firm; add marshmallow-mayonnaise mixture. Chill until firm. Add remaining lime gelatin; chill.

Mrs. John C. Geerdes
Hoxie, Kans.

GREEN AND WHITE SALAD

1 pkg. lime gelatin
2 ½ c. boiling water
1 No. 303 can crushed pineapple
1 pkg. lemon gelatin
1 c. whipped cream
½ c. cottage cheese or 1 3-oz. pkg. cream cheese combined with almonds

Dissolve lime gelatin in 1 1/2 cups boiling water; cool. Add pineapple. Pour into mold or 8 x 13-inch pan; chill until firm. Dissolve lemon gelatin in remaining boiling water;

(Continued on next page)

cool until partially set. Add whipped cream and cottage cheese; beat. Combine with partially set lemon gelatin. Pour lemon mixture over lime gelatin. Chill until firm. Yield: 8 servings.

Isabelle T. Staley
Huron, S.D.

GOLD 'N' MOLD

1 sm. can pineapple
2 envelopes unflavored gelatin
5 tbsp. sugar
2 tbsp. lemon juice
3 c. heavy apricot puree
3 drops almond flavoring
1 4-oz. pkg. cream cheese, softened
2 tbsp. minced green pepper

Drain pineapple, reserving juice. Soften gelatin in pineapple juice. Heat slowly until gelatin is dissolved and clear. Add sugar, lemon juice and apricot puree; blend well. Divide into three portions, making one portion larger than the other two. To the larger portion, add almond flavoring. Pour into a pyramid mold that has been rinsed in cold water. Chill in freezer until set, but not frozen. Whip cheese; fold cheese and green pepper into one of remaining gelatin portions. Spoon on top of chilled layer. Chill until set. Fold pineapple into remaining gelatin portion; spoon over chilled layers. Chill overnight. Yield: 8-10 servings.

Mrs. Pearl Wheaton
Moscow, Idaho

LAYER SALAD

2 pkg. lime gelatin
1 8-oz. bottle stuffed green olives, sliced
1 c. chopped nuts
1 pkg. lemon gelatin
1 ¾ c. hot water
1 No. 2 can crushed pineapple, drained
1 12-oz. pkg. cream cheese, softened
1 c. heavy whipping cream

Prepare lime gelatin according to directions on package; pour into large cake pan. Add olives and nuts, distributing evenly. Chill until firm. Dissolve lemon gelatin in hot water; add drained pineapple. Chill until partially congealed; fold in cream cheese whipped with cream. Pour over firm lime gelatin. Chill until set. Yield: 12-16 servings.

Mrs. Raymond Downing
Waverly, Iowa

LAYERED GELATIN SALAD

2 pkg. cherry gelatin
1 pkg. lemon gelatin
2 c. (scant) hot water
¼ lb. marshmallows
1 sm. can crushed pineapple
1 8-oz. pkg. cream cheese, softened
1 c. whipped cream

Prepare 1 package cherry gelatin according to package directions. Chill until firm. Dissolve lemon gelatin in hot water. Add marshmallows; stir until melted. Mix in pineapple. Whip cream cheese. Mix cheese and whipped cream; fold in lemon gelatin. Pour over firm cherry gelatin. Chill until firm. Dissolve remaining cherry gelatin according to package directions; pour over firm layer. Chill until firm. Yield: 12 servings.

Mrs. Jean Eliason
Mora, Minn.

LEMON RED HOT SALAD

2 pkg. red hot cinnamon candies
1 c. boiling water
1 pkg. lemon gelatin
2 c. applesauce
Pinch of salt
1 8-oz. pkg. cream cheese
Mayonnaise
½ c. chopped pecans

Dissolve candies in boiling water; pour over gelatin. Add applesauce and salt. Pour one-half of mixture into mold; chill until firm. Soften cream cheese with mayonnaise; add nuts. Spread mixture on firm gelatin; chill. Cover with remaining gelatin; chill until firm.

Mrs. C. A. Prewitt
Denver City, Tex.

LIME-WHIPPED CREAM SALAD

1 can crushed pineapple
1 can grapefruit sections
2 pkg. lime gelatin
1 c. boiling water
1 envelope unflavored gelatin
2 c. lemon-lime soft drink

Drain pineapple and grapefruit, reserving 1 cup of combined juices. Dissolve lime gelatin in boiling water. Soften unflavored gelatin in fruit juice; dissolve in hot gelatin mixture. Add soft drink; let jell. Add fruits. Pour one-half of mixture into a large flat pan; refrigerate until firm.

(Continued on next page)

FILLING:
1 3-oz. pkg. cream cheese
1 pkg. dessert topping mix
½ tsp. vanilla flavoring
½ c. powdered sugar

Let cream cheese come to room temperature. Prepare dessert topping mix according to directions. Beat cream cheese, vanilla flavoring and powdered sugar. Add dessert topping. Pour mixture over firm gelatin layer. Add remaining gelatin; let set. Yield: 12 servings.

Minnette Luebber
Cashmere, Wash.

MARTHA WASHINGTON SALAD

1 No. 2 can crushed pineapple
1 pkg. cherry gelatin
1 pkg. lemon gelatin
1 c. boiling water
½ lb. miniature marshmallows
1 12-oz. pkg. cream cheese, softened
1 c. mayonnaise
½ pt. cream, whipped
1 pkg. lime gelatin

Drain pineapple, reserving 1 cup juice. Dissolve cherry gelatin according to package directions. Pour into a 13 x 9 x 2-inch pan; chill until firm. Dissolve lemon gelatin in boiling water; add marshmallows, stirring to dissolve. Add pineapple juice; cool. Blend cream cheese and mayonnaise. Add to cooled lemon gelatin mixture. Add pineapple; fold in unsweetened whipped cream. Pour over firm cherry gelatin; cool to room temperature. Dissolve lime gelatin according to package directions. Cool; pour over lemon layer. Chill until set. Yield: 12 servings.

Eva Markin
Eureka, Calif.

ORANGE GELATIN SALAD

2 sm. pkg. orange gelatin
2 c. hot orange juice
1 pkg. dessert topping mix
1 6-oz. pkg. cream cheese
1 c. Mandarin oranges
1 sm. pkg. orange gelatin
1 c. water

Mix 1 package gelatin with 1 cup hot orange juice. Let set until slightly congealed. Beat dessert topping mix; add cream cheese. Mix cheese mixture with gelatin mixture. Add oranges. Chill until firm. Mix remaining gelatin with remaining hot orange juice and water. Pour over congealed layers. Chill until firm. Yield: 8 servings.

Mrs. Carolyn Weaver
Huntington, Ind.

ORANGE-PINEAPPLE MOLDED SALAD

2 pkg. orange gelatin
2 ½ c. hot water
1 3-oz. pkg. cream cheese, softened
¼ c. orange juice
2 tbsp. lemon juice
1 8-oz. can crushed pineapple

Dissolve 1 package orange gelatin in 1 1/2 cups hot water. Gradually blend into cream cheese. Add orange and lemon juice. Pour into mold. Chill until firm. Dissolve remaining gelatin in remaining hot water. Add pineapple. Chill until syrupy. Pour over firm layer. Chill until firm.

Mrs. Lena Brown
Tecumseh, Mich.

SUNNY SALAD SUPREME

2 boxes orange gelatin
1 No. 2 can crushed pineapple, drained
1 sm. can Mandarin oranges, drained
½ pt. sour cream
¼ to ½ c. coconut

Dissolve 1 package of gelatin according to package directions. Chill until partially set. Add pineapple. Spread mixture in 1 1/2-quart dish. Chill until firm. Dissolve remaining gelatin according to package directions. Chill until partially set. Add oranges. Spread sour cream over firm gelatin; sprinkle with coconut. Spread orange mixture over sour cream. Chill until firm. Yield: 8 servings.

Judith Ann Kostura
Windber, Pa.

PINK RIBBON SALAD

¼ c. red cinnamon candies
1 c. boiling water
1 pkg. lemon gelatin
1 c. applesauce
1 3-oz. pkg. cream cheese
2 tbsp. cream
2 tbsp. mayonnaise

Dissolve candies in boiling water. Pour liquid over lemon gelatin. Stir to dissolve. Add

(Continued on next page)

applesauce. Spoon one-half of mixture into loaf pan. Chill until set. Blend cream cheese, cream and mayonnaise; spoon over firm gelatin. Chill until set. Pour remaining gelatin over cheese layer. Chill until firm. Yield: 6-8 servings.

Beverly Schultz
Creston, Wash.

GREEN GAGE PLUM SALAD

1 1-lb. 4-oz. can green gage plums
1 3-oz. pkg. lemon flavored gelatin
Juice of 1 lemon
½ tsp. salt
¾ c. slivered almonds
Crisp lettuce cups
Salad dressing

Drain juice from plums; add water to make 2 cups liquid. Heat to boiling; pour over gelatin. Add lemon juice and salt; stir to dissolve. Cool until thickened. Pour 2 tablespoons gelatin into six individual molds. Chill until firm. Pit and chop plums. Fold almonds and plums into remaining gelatin. Spoon over gelatin in molds. Chill until firm. Serve in lettuce cups with dressing.

Mrs. Frank L. Martin
Canton, O.

RASPBERRY-FILLED GELATIN SALAD

1 sm. pkg. frozen raspberries
1 lge. stalk celery, finely diced
1 med. apple, pared and finely diced
1 3-oz. box raspberry gelatin
1 c. boiling water

Dissolve gelatin in boiling water. Add frozen raspberries; stir until raspberries are completely thawed. Add celery and apple; stir well. Pour one-half of mixture into mold. Congeal.

FILLING:
1 sm. pkg. cream cheese
⅔ c. sour cream
⅔ c. large marshmallows, cut up
1 lge. stalk celery, finely diced
½ c. chopped pecans (opt.)

Whip cheese with electric mixer. Blend in sour cream; fold in marshmallows, celery and nuts. Spread over firm gelatin mixture. Refrigerate until set. Add remaining gelatin mixture; refrigerate until firm. Yield: 10-12 servings.

Berniece M. Cobb
Westminster, Colo.

RASPBERRY LAYER SALAD

1 pkg. lemon gelatin
1 c. boiling water
16 lge. marshmallows
1 c. hot milk
1 c. crushed pineapple
1 8-oz. pkg. cream cheese
½ c. chopped nuts
1 pkg. dessert topping mix, whipped

Dissolve gelatin in water. Melt marshmallows in hot milk. Combine pineapple, cheese and nuts; add gelatin. Fold mixture into marshmallows. Fold in dessert topping. Chill until firm in 9 x 13-inch pan.

TOPPING:
2 pkg. raspberry gelatin
3 c. boiling water
3 c. fresh or 2 c. frozen raspberries

Dissolve gelatin in water; add berries. Cool and pour over firm gelatin. Yield: 12 servings.

Ella Cleland
Toledo, O.

RASPBERRY RIBBON SALAD

1 pkg. raspberry gelatin
2 c. hot water
1 pkg. frozen raspberries
1 c. cold water
Cultured sour cream
1 pkg. cherry gelatin
1 sm. can crushed pineapple, undrained

Dissolve raspberry gelatin in 1 cup hot water. Add frozen raspberries and 1/2 cup cold water. Chill until set. Spread firm gelatin with a layer of sour cream 1/2-inch thick. Dissolve cherry gelatin in remaining hot water. Add pineapple and remaining cold water. Cool until thick. Spoon cherry mixture onto sour cream layer. Chill until firm. Yield: 9 servings.

Deeanne Enders
Hebron, Nebr.

RED RASPBERRY SALAD

1 pkg. red raspberry gelatin
1 c. hot water
1 pkg. frozen red raspberries
½ c. heavy cream, whipped
5 lge. marshmallows, melted
1 pkg. cream cheese

(Continued on next page)

Dissolve gelatin in hot water. Add raspberries. Pour into 5 x 8-inch loaf pan. Chill until firm. Whip together cream, marshmallows and cream cheese until stiff. Spread over gelatin mixture; chill. Yield: 6 servings.

Mrs. Lowell Somers
Knightstown, Ind.

RED TOP SALAD

1 pkg. strawberry gelatin
4 c. hot water
1 pkg. lemon gelatin
10 marshmallows
1 c. crushed pineapple
½ c. chopped celery
½ c. grated cheese
¼ c. salad dressing
1 c. whipped cream
½ c. chopped nuts

Dissolve strawberry gelatin in 2 cups hot water. Pour into large mold. Chill until firm. Dissolve lemon gelatin and marshmallows in remaining hot water. Cool. Whip until frothy. Add pineapple, celery and cheese. Whip salad dressing into whipped cream; stir in nuts. Add to marshmallow mixture. Pour over firm strawberry layer. Chill until firm. Yield: 9-12 servings.

Marilyn Peterson
St. Paul, Minn.

RED AND WHITE GELATIN SALAD

1 pkg. orange gelatin
3 c. boiling water
1 5-oz. glass pineapple-cheese spread
½ c. salad dressing
½ c. marshmallow creme
1 c. heavy cream, whipped
1 c. crushed pineapple
1 pkg. cherry gelatin

Dissolve orange gelatin in 1 cup boiling water; cool. Mix pineapple-cheese spread with salad dressing, marshmallow creme, whipped cream and pineapple. Combine pineapple mixture with orange gelatin; let stand until firm. Dissolve cherry gelatin in remaining water. Cool; pour over orange gelatin mixture. Chill. Yield: 12 servings.

Mrs. Lillian Roberts
Kansas City, Mo.

RUBY SALAD

16 marshmallows
1 ½ c. Milnot
1 pkg. lemon gelatin
3 tbsp. cold water
1 8-oz. pkg. cream cheese
1 c. crushed pineapple
½ c. chopped blanched almonds
2 pkg. strawberry or cherry gelatin
2 c. hot water
2 c. cold water

Melt marshmallows and 1 cup Milnot over low heat. Mix lemon gelatin and cold water; add to marshmallow mixture. Stir in cream cheese, remaining Milnot, pineapple and almonds; let set. Dissolve strawberry or cherry gelatin in hot water; add cold water. Pour over lemon mixture. Chill until firm. Yield: 15-18 servings.

Dorothy Kimbley
Jeffersonville, Ind.

LAYERED STRAWBERRY AND CHEESE SALAD

1 pkg. strawberry or cherry gelatin
1 pkg. lemon gelatin
1 3-oz. pkg. cream cheese
¼ c. chopped black walnuts

Prepare strawberry or cherry gelatin according to package directions. Chill until firm. Prepare lemon gelatin in same manner. Let stand until the consistency of jelly. Beat until foamy. Beat in softened cream cheese and nuts. Spread over firm gelatin. Chill until firm. Cut into cubes. Yield: 6-8 servings.

Ruth I. Schwarz
Galesburg, Ill.

STRAWBERRY SALAD

2 3-oz. pkg. strawberry gelatin
2 c. boiling water
1 pkg. frozen strawberries
1 No. 2 can crushed pineapple
2 lge. bananas, diced
1 carton sour cream

(Continued on next page)

Tuna goes Hawaiian in a blend of fruits nested in pineapple shells. Tuna also goes cool when heaped in a lime-sour cream ring mold.

HAWAIIAN TUNA SALAD

1 med. pineapple
2 7-oz. cans tuna, drained
¾ c. sliced peaches
1 med. banana, sliced
½ c. flaked coconut
1 med. apple, cored and diced
½ c. mayonnaise
¼ c. orange juice
1 tsp. aromatic bitters
¼ tsp. salt
Stemmed red Maraschino cherries
Parsley

Cut pineapple in half; remove fruit, leaving ½-inch shell. Reserve shells; dice pineapple. Combine pineapple, tuna, peaches, banana, coconut and apple; mix lightly. Chill. Blend mayonnaise, orange juice, bitters and salt. Chill. Add dressing to tuna salad; toss lightly but well. Fill shells with salad. Garnish with cherries and parsley. Yield: 4 servings.

TUNA-LIME RING

2 3-oz. pkg. lime gelatin
2 c. boiling water
2 c. cold water
1 c. dairy sour cream
2 7-oz. cans tuna, drained
½ c. chopped celery
¼ c. chopped canned pimento
1 tbsp. dehydrated minced onion
3 tbsp. vinegar
Cucumber slices
Parsley

Dissolve gelatin in boiling water. Add cold water; chill until slightly thickened. Beat in sour cream until smooth. Turn into an 8-inch ring mold. Chill until firm. Combine tuna, celery, pimento, onion and vinegar; mix well. Unmold lime ring onto serving platter. Fill center with tuna mixture. Garnish with cucumber and parsley. Yield: 6 servings.

See photograph on reverse page.

Dissolve gelatin in boiling water. Add strawberries; break apart with a fork as they melt. Do not mash berries. Add pineapple and bananas. Pour one-half of gelatin mixture into a long baking dish. Chill until firm. Spread with sour cream; spoon remaining gelatin over sour cream. Chill until firm. Cut into squares; serve on lettuce. Yield: 8 servings.

Mrs. John S. Eason
Rome, Ga.

STRAWBERRY SALAD

1 pkg. raspberry gelatin
1 c. hot water
1 c. drained crushed pineapple
1 pt. frozen strawberries
½ pt. sour cream

Dissolve gelatin in hot water. Add fruit. Pour one-half of mixture into a small square pan; chill until firm. Spread sour cream over firm gelatin. Pour remaining mixture over sour cream. Chill again until firm. Cut into squares; serve on lettuce. Yield: 8 servings.

Mrs. Janie Lee Toole
Enid, Miss.

THREE-LAYER SALAD

1 pkg. strawberry gelatin
3 c. boiling water
1 No. 2 can crushed pineapple
1 8-oz. pkg. cream cheese
1 med. banana, mashed
½ c. chopped nuts
½ c. coconut
1 tbsp. sugar
1 tbsp. mayonnaise
½ pt. heavy cream, whipped
1 pkg. lime gelatin

Dissolve strawberry gelatin in 1 cup boiling water; add pineapple with juice. Chill until firm. Combine remaining ingredients except lime gelatin and hot water; mix well. Spread on firm gelatin; refrigerate overnight. Dissolve lime gelatin in remaining boiling water; cool. Pour over mixture; chill until firm. Yield: 8-10 servings.

Mrs. J. S. Childress
Radford, Va.

UNDER THE SEA SALAD

1 pkg. lime gelatin
1 ½ c. boiling water
½ c. pear juice
¼ tbsp. salt
1 tsp. vinegar
1 3-oz. pkg. cream cheese
⅛ tsp. ginger
2 c. diced pears

Dissolve gelatin in boiling water. Add pear juice, salt and vinegar. Pour 1/2-inch layer in loaf pan; chill until firm. Chill remaining gelatin until syrupy; beat until fluffy. Cream the cheese with ginger; beat into gelatin. Fold in pears; pour over first layer of gelatin. Chill until firm. Yield: 4 servings.

Mrs. Eunice M. Melzer
Cambria AFS, Calif.

CHRISTMAS BEETS

2 c. cooked cubed beets
½ c. French dressing
1 c. sour cream, whipped
½ c. finely chopped green onions

Blend hot beets with French dressing; place in serving dish. Top with whipped sour cream; sprinkle with onions. Yield: 4-6 servings.

Mrs. Marjory Fuller
Wyandotte, Mich.

CELERY RINGS

3 tbsp. butter
1 3-oz. pkg. cream cheese
3 tbsp. tomato paste
Salt and red pepper to taste
1 bunch celery

Cream butter; add cheese and tomato paste. Mix well. Add salt and red pepper. Stuff celery stalks with mixture. Put celery hearts together; place remaining pieces of celery around to make the stalk into its original shape. Wrap in waxed paper; chill. Slice into rings. Yield: 8 servings.

Evelyn Ford
Berryville, Va.

CHINA DOLL-STUFFED TOMATO AND LIMA SALAD

4 lge. firm tomatoes
1 6 ½-oz. can chunk tuna
1 c. cooked limas
½ c. diced cucumber
¼ tbsp. lemon juice
¼ tsp. curry powder
3 tbsp. mayonnaise
Salt to taste
Salad greens

Turn tomatoes upside down; cut into eighths for petals, cutting almost all the way through. Separate petals slightly. Combine remaining ingredients; heap into salted tomatoes. Chill; serve on salad greens. Garnish with parsley. Yield: 4 servings.

Mrs. Claude Wilson
Stuttgart, Ark.

FILLED TOMATO CUPS

6 lge. firm tomatoes
½ c. chopped ham
2 tbsp. finely chopped onion
3 tbsp. finely chopped olives
2 tbsp. finely chopped pimento
1 c. diced celery
1 c. diced hard-cooked eggs
¼ tsp. salt
1 c. mayonnaise thinned with whipped cream

Wash and peel tomatoes; scoop out centers. Chill. Combine remaining ingredients. Fill tomatoes with mixture. Chill before serving.

Mrs. Victor H. Weipert
Monroe, Mich.

STRIPE SALAD

3 peeled tomatoes
1 unpeeled cucumber, scored and sliced
Lettuce

Make four slashes at regular intervals in each tomato. Place cucumber slice in each slash. Place tomatoes on lettuce. Serve with favorite dressing.

Mrs. Ernest Constable
Robeline, La.

TOMATO PETAL SALAD

6 med. tomatoes
1 c. frozen or fresh peas, cooked
1 c. frozen or fresh diced carrots, cooked
1 c. diced celery
1 tsp. grated onion
¼ c. mayonnaise or salad dressing
1 tsp. sugar
1 tsp. lemon juice
Salt and pepper to taste
Lettuce leaves

Scald and peel tomatoes; remove core. Cut a slice off the bottom; scoop out seed cavities. Refrigerate until ready to use. Combine remaining ingredients except lettuce. Cut tomatoes in six places almost to the bottom; spread the petals. Arrange on lettuce leaves; fill centers with pea and carrot mixture. Yield: 6 servings.

Mildred Bartosh
Dodge, Nebr.

TOMATO PINWHEEL SALAD

2 or 3 lettuce leaves
1 med. tomato
1 cucumber, peeled, scored and sliced
1 hard-cooked egg, sliced
Mayonnaise
Grated cheese or paprika

Line salad plate with lettuce leaves. Remove core from tomato. Slice into six or eight wedges, but do not cut through to bottom of tomato. Place cucumber slices between tomato wedges to give pinwheel effect. Place cucumber and egg slices around the tomato. Fill tomato with mayonnaise. Garnish with cheese or paprika.

Mrs. Dianna Armentrout
Schertz, Tex.

TOMATO ROSE SALAD

¼ lb. cream cheese
Milk
1 firm tomato, peeled and chilled
1 hard-cooked egg yolk, strained
Salad greens
French dressing

Slightly soften cheese with milk. Form two rows of petals on each tomato by pressing level teaspoons of cream cheese against the side of tomato, then drawing the spoon down with a curving motion. Sprinkle center of tomato with egg. Serve on salad greens with French dressing. Yield: 1 serving.

Una Seeley
Superior, Mont.

RECIPE FOR PINEAPPLE-CHEESE SALAD WITH CREAMY TOPPING ON PAGE 214

APPLE-CUCUMBER SALAD

2 Delicious apples, peeled and diced
½ cucumber, peeled and diced
1 tsp. onion, grated
1 tbsp. mayonnaise

Combine all ingredients; chill for 1 hour before serving. Yield: 4 servings.

Elsie Kelling
Hartland, Wisc.

CONGEALED APPLE AND CHEESE SALAD

1 pkg. cherry gelatin
1 ½ c. boiling water
1 3-oz. pkg. cream cheese
1 sm. can crushed pineapple
1 ¼ c. grated apples
½ c. chopped nuts

Dissolve gelatin in boiling water; cool. Mix cream cheese with a small amount of the pineapple juice. Add pineapple, apples and nuts. Add to gelatin mixture. Chill until firm. Yield: 8 servings.

Mrs. Earl Laster
Pell City, Ala.

CONGEALED APPLE SALAD

1 envelope unflavored gelatin
¼ c. sugar
½ tsp. salt
1 ½ c. water
¼ c. lemon juice
2 c. diced tart apples
½ c. diced celery
¼ to ½ c. chopped pecans

Mix gelatin, sugar and salt thoroughly. Add 1 cup water. Cook over low heat, stirring constantly until gelatin is dissolved. Remove from heat; stir in remaining water and lemon juice. Chill mixture until it reaches the consistency of an unbeaten egg white. Fold in apples, celery and nuts. Chill until firm. Yield: 6 servings.

Myra J. Cannon
Pelzer, S.C.

SPICY APPLE SALAD

2 tsp. sugar
¼ c. red cinnamon candies
1 c. hot water
1 pkg. cherry gelatin
1 c. cold water
1 c. diced apples
¼ c. chopped walnuts

Dissolve sugar and candies in hot water. Heat to boiling; pour over gelatin. Add cold water. Chill until partially set. Add apples and nuts. Chill until firm. Yield: 9 servings.

Anna Mae Strickler
Chino, Calif.

SOUFFLE SALAD

1 pkg. lime gelatin
1 c. hot water
½ c. cold water
½ c. mayonnaise
2 tbsp. lemon juice
¼ tsp. salt
1 c. peeled diced apples
¾ c. seeded red grapes
¼ c. chopped walnuts

Dissolve gelatin in hot water. Add cold water, mayonnaise, lemon juice and salt. Blend well with rotary mixer. Pour into ice cube tray; freeze 15 to 20 minutes or until firm around edges but soft in center. Pour mixture into bowl; whip until fluffy. Fold in apples, grapes and walnuts. Pour into 1-quart mold; chill until firm. Unmold; garnish with grapes, pears and plums. Yield: 4-6 servings.

Catherine R. Carlson
West Palm Beach, Fla.

WALDORF SALAD

½ c. crushed pineapple
2 eggs, slightly beaten
½ c. sugar
½ c. lemon juice
⅛ tsp. salt
1 envelope unflavored gelatin
¼ c. cold water
½ c. diced celery
2 med. apples, diced
½ c. broken English walnuts
1 c. heavy cream, whipped

Drain pineapple, reserving 1/2 cup juice. Combine eggs, sugar, pineapple juice, lemon juice and salt. Cook over low heat until thickened, stirring constantly. Add gelatin which has been softened in cold water. Chill until partially set. Add celery, pineapple, apples and walnuts. Gently fold in whipped cream. Spoon into pan; chill.

Mrs. Gordon Hollifield
Jerome, Idaho

WALDORF WHIP

1 3-oz. pkg. lemon gelatin
1 c. hot water

(Continued on next page)

3 tbsp. lemon juice
½ c. mayonnaise
1 c. chopped celery
½ c. chopped walnuts
1 ½ c. chopped apples
⅔ c. evaporated milk, whipped

Dissolve gelatin in hot water; cool. Add 1 tablespoon lemon juice, mayonnaise, celery, nuts and apples. Mix well. Chill until mixture is the consistency of unbeaten egg whites. Chill evaporated milk in refrigerator tray until soft ice crystals form around edges. Whip milk until stiff. Add the remaining lemon juice; whip for 1 to 2 minutes or until very stiff. Fold whipped milk into gelatin mixture. Chill for 2 hours. Yield: 6-8 servings.

Mrs. Virginia J. Darling
Olivet, Mich.

APPLE CIDER DELIGHT

4 c. (scant) apple juice or cider
2 pkg. lemon gelatin
3 c. applesauce, drained
Green food coloring

Heat cider. Add gelatin and stir until dissolved. Add applesauce and a few drops of green food coloring. Pour into a ring mold; chill until firm.

DRESSING:
1 c. cottage cheese
1 ½ c. whipped cream
24 marshmallows, chopped
½ tsp. almond flavoring
2 tsp. lemon juice

Combine ingredients; refrigerate for 2 hours. Heap in center of molded salad. Yield: 10-12 servings.

Mrs. Eleanore M. Dahl
Belgrade, Minn.

APPLESAUCE-CINNAMON CROWN

⅓ c. cinnamon candies
½ c. hot water
1 pkg. lemon gelatin
1 16-oz. can applesauce
1 c. crushed pineapple
2 tbsp. lemon juice
¼ tsp. salt
¼ tsp. nutmeg

Dissolve candies in water over low heat. Remove from heat. Add gelatin; stir until dissolved. Blend in remaining ingredients. Chill until firm. Yield: 8 servings.

Mrs. Leo Hoffpauir
Lake Charles, La.

APPLESAUCE RING

½ c. red cinnamon candies
2 c. hot water
2 pkg. raspberry gelatin
4 c. applesauce

Simmer cinnamon candies in hot water until dissolved. Add gelatin; stir well. Add applesauce. Pour into a ring mold. Chill until firm. Yield: 12 servings.

Mrs. Bertha Leidahl
Willow River, Minn.

APPLESAUCE SALAD

1 pkg. lime gelatin
¾ c. boiling water
2 c. thick applesauce
1 c. cottage cheese
Crisp lettuce leaves
Mayonnaise
Paprika

Dissolve gelatin thoroughly in water. Fold in applesauce and cottage cheese. Pour into individual molds; chill until firm. Unmold onto lettuce leaves and top with mayonnaise. Garnish with paprika. Yield: 6-8 servings.

Fern A. Soderholm
Willmar, Minn.

LIME-APPLESAUCE DELIGHT

1 ¼ c. applesauce
1 pkg. lime gelatin
½ to 1 c. sugar
1 c. evaporated milk
1 tbsp. lime or lemon juice

Heat applesauce. Add gelatin and sugar. Stir until dissolved. Chill milk until very cold; whip until stiff. Add lime or lemon juice. Fold whipped milk into gelatin mixture. Chill. Yield: 8 servings.

Mrs. Doris E. Gregory
Mill City, Pa.

TEABERRY SALAD

¼ c. teaberry candies
¾ c. boiling water
1 pkg. red gelatin
1 c. applesauce
Minted pineapple chunks

(Continued on next page)

Dissolve candies in boiling water. Add gelatin, stirring to dissolve. Chill until slightly thickened. Fold in applesauce. Pour into ring mold; chill until firm. Serve on lettuce with pineapple chunks in the center of mold. Yield: 4-5 servings.

Mrs. H. E. Wagner, Jr.
New Cumberland, Pa.

APRICOT SALAD

2 1-lb. cans apricot halves
2 3-oz. pkg. orange gelatin
1 6-oz. can frozen orange juice
2 tbsp. lemon juice
1 7-oz. bottle lemon-lime carbonated beverage

Drain apricots, reserving 1 1/2 cups liquid. Puree apricots in blender or put through sieve. Heat apricot liquid to boiling; dissolve gelatin in hot liquid. Add apricot puree, orange juice and lemon juice. Stir well. Slowly pour carbonated beverage down side of pan to keep down bubbles. Mix gently with up and down motion. Pour into mold; chill for several hours. Yield: 12 servings.

Esther Nething
Washington, Mo.

APRICOT BOUFFANT SALAD

1 No. 2 ½ can apricots
1 c. crushed pineapple
2 pkg. orange gelatin
2 c. hot water
1 c. orange juice
¾ c. miniature marshmallows

Mix all ingredients; chill until set in 9 x 13-inch baking dish.

TOPPING:
½ c. sugar
3 tbsp. flour
1 egg, beaten
1 c. orange juice
2 tbsp. butter
1 c. heavy cream, whipped
Grated cheese

Mix sugar, flour, egg, orange juice and butter; cook until thickened. Cool; fold in whipped cream. Spread on gelatin mixture; garnish with cheese. Yield: 10 servings.

Mrs. Oliver Olson
New Underwood, S.D.

APRICOT-MARSHMALLOW SALAD

2 cans apricots
2 envelopes unflavored gelatin
½ c. cold water
18 marshmallows
Juice of 1 lemon
½ tsp. salt

Drain apricots, reserving juice. Dissolve gelatin in water. Heat apricot juice to boiling; add marshmallows. Remove from heat; stir until marshmallows are melted. Add lemon juice, salt and gelatin; cool. Add apricots. Chill until firm. Yield: 8-10 servings.

Janette Knox
Falkville, Ala.

APRICOT NECTAR SALAD

2 pkg. orange gelatin
1 ½ c. hot water
2 ½ c. apricot nectar
1 c. marshmallows
Mandarin oranges

Dissolve gelatin in hot water. Add apricot nectar, marshmallows and Mandarin oranges; let set.

TOPPING:
½ c. sugar
Salt
2 tbsp. flour
1 egg
1 c. apricot nectar
1 c. whipping cream

Combine sugar, salt, flour, egg and nectar. Cook until thickened. Fold in whipped cream; spread on set gelatin. Yield: 12-15 servings.

Norma Jean McCue
Coquille, Oreg.

COTTAGE CHEESE SALAD

1 No. 1 can apricot halves, chopped
1 pkg. lemon gelatin
¾ c. boiling water
1 ½ c. creamed cottage cheese
1 c. heavy cream, whipped
½ c. chopped nuts
½ c. chopped Maraschino cherries

Drain apricots, reserving 3/4 cup juice. Dissolve gelatin in boiling water; add apricot juice. Chill until partially set. Fold in apricots, cottage cheese, cream, nuts and cherries. Chill until firm. Yield: 6-8 servings.

Mrs. Frank Snyder
Scott City, Kans.

GELATIN-APRICOT NECTAR SALAD

2 pkg. orange gelatin
2 c. hot water
1 12-oz. can apricot nectar
1 lb. cottage cheese
Nutmeg

Dissolve gelatin in hot water. Add apricot nectar; mix well. Cool. Pour into 1-quart ring mold; chill until firm. Unmold onto plate of shredded lettuce; fill center with cottage cheese sprinkled with nutmeg. Yield: 8-9 servings.

Mrs. Ralph L. Perkins
Kailua, Oahu, Hawaii

AVOCADO AND GRAPEFRUIT SALAD

1 c. hot water
1 pkg. lime gelatin
2 avocados, pitted and peeled
2 tbsp. mayonnaise
2 tbsp. lemon juice
1 tsp. salt
1 pkg. cream cheese
¾ c. diced grapefruit sections
1 c. whole grapefruit sections

Add hot water to gelatin; stir until dissolved. Mash enough avocado to make 2/3 cup; slice remainder. Beat mashed avocado and remaining ingredients except grapefruit and avocado slices with rotary beater until creamy. Add thickened gelatin mixture; beat until blended. Fold sliced avocado and grapefruit sections into mixture; pour into mold. Chill until firm. Yield: 8 servings.

Helen C. Johnson
Bozeman, Mont.

AVOCADO MOLD

1 pkg. lime gelatin
1 c. boiling water
Juice of 1 lemon or 2 limes
½ c. mayonnaise or salad dressing
½ c. heavy cream, whipped
2 tbsp. finely chopped green pepper
Onion juice or chives
½ c. finely chopped celery
Salt to taste
1 to 2 drops Tabasco sauce
1 tsp. Worcestershire sauce
1 c. or more chopped avocado

Dissolve gelatin in water and lemon juice. Add remaining ingredients. Chill in ring mold until firm. Serve on lettuce. Yield: 8-10 servings.

Mrs. John L. Davidson
Livingston Manor, N.Y.

AVOCADO RING

1 tbsp. unflavored gelatin
¼ c. cold water
½ c. boiling water
¼ c. lemon juice
1 c. sieved avocado
½ c. mayonnaise
½ c. whipped cream
½ c. chopped celery
1 tbsp. grated onion or onion juice (opt.)

Soak gelatin in cold water; dissolve in boiling water. Cool until mixture begins to thicken. Add remaining ingredients. Turn into a ring mold; chill until firm. Fill center with ham, chicken or fruit salad if desired. Yield: 8 servings.

Augusta Jannett
Yoakum, Tex.

AVOCADO RING SALAD

1 pkg. lemon gelatin
1 c. boiling water
2 ripe avocados, mashed
¼ c. sour cream
2 tbsp. white wine
⅛ tsp. salt
1 c. heavy cream, whipped

Dissolve gelatin in boiling water. Add avocado pulp, sour cream, wine and salt. Beat until smooth and fluffy. Chill until mixture begins to set. Fold in whipped cream. Pour into a ring mold. Chill until firm. Unmold onto crisp dry salad greens. Yield: 6 servings.

Dorothy E. Brevoort
Trenton, N.J.

AVOCADO SALAD

1 pkg. lime gelatin
1 c. hot water
½ c. cold water
2 tbsp. vinegar
½ c. mayonnaise
½ tsp. salt
2 spring onions, chopped
½ c. minced celery
2 tbsp. cottage cheese
1 avocado, mashed

Dissolve gelatin in hot water; add cold water, vinegar, mayonnaise and salt. Blend with rotary beater. Chill until partially set. Blend in onions, celery, cheese and avocado; beat again. Pour into mold; chill until firm. Yield: 6 servings.

Mrs. N. VanMeter Hendricks
Short Hills, N.J.

MOLDED FRESH STRAWBERRY AND AVOCADO SALAD

2 envelopes unflavored gelatin
1 c. cold water
1 c. hot water
½ c. sugar
¼ tsp. salt
1 c. fresh orange juice
¼ c. fresh lemon juice
1 ½ c. sliced fresh strawberries
1 c. diced avocado
Whole uncapped strawberries
Mayonnaise

Soften gelatin in cold water. Add hot water, sugar and salt; stir to dissolve gelatin. Blend in orange and lemon juice. Chill until mixture slightly thickens; fold in strawberries and avocado. Pour into a 5-cup mold; chill until firm. Unmold onto serving plate; garnish with whole uncapped strawberries. Serve with mayonnaise. Yield: 6-8 servings.

Photograph for this recipe above.

FRUIT GELATIN

1 pkg. apricot gelatin
3 ripe bananas, thinly sliced
1 sm. can crushed pineapple, drained
Dessert topping mix
2 tbsp. sugar

Dissolve gelatin according to package directions; cool. Fold in bananas and pineapple. Chill until firm. Top with sweetened topping. Yield: 4 servings.

Mrs. Nancy York
Charleston, S.C.

BLUEBERRY SALAD

1 can crushed pineapple
1 can blueberries
1 pkg. black raspberry gelatin
1 c. chopped pecans

Drain pineapple and blueberries, reserving juice. Bring combined juices to a boil. Add gelatin; stir until dissolved. Add blueberries, pineapple and nuts. Chill until set.

Mrs. Martha L. Taylor
Algoma, Miss.

BLUEBERRY-GELATIN SALAD

2 3-oz. pkg. red gelatin
2 c. hot water
1 pt. sour cream
1 5-oz. can blueberries

(Continued on next page)

Dissolve gelatin in hot water. Chill until partially set. Blend in sour cream and blueberries. Chill until firm. Garnish with sour cream, dressing or pineapple chunks if desired. Yield: 8 servings.

Grace Lamusga
Robbinsdale, Minn.

BLUEBERRY-PINEAPPLE SALAD

1 sm. can crushed pineapple
1 14-oz. can blueberries
2 boxes raspberry gelatin
½ pt. heavy cream, whipped
1 ½ c. miniature marshmallows
½ c. chopped pecans

Drain pineapple and blueberries. Add water to juice to make 4 cups. Heat 2 cups liquid; add gelatin, stirring to dissolve. Add remaining liquid; cool until partially set. Fold in whipped cream, fruits, marshmallows and nuts. Cool until firm. Cut into squares and place on lettuce leaf. Yield: 8 servings.

Mrs. Randy Allio
Tulsa, Okla.

FRESH BLUEBERRY SALAD

2 3-oz. pkg. blackcherrygelatin
3 c. boiling water
1 8-oz. can crushed pineapple
¼ c. Maraschino cherries, halved
2 c. fresh blueberries

Dissolve gelatin in boiling water. Cool. Add pineapple; chill until thickened. Fold in cherries and blueberries. Chill until firm.

DRESSING:
1 c. miniature marshmallows
2 c. sour cream
1 tsp. mayonnaise
½ tsp. vanilla flavoring

Mix ingredients; let stand for several hours or overnight. Mix well; serve on salad. Yield: 12 servings.

Nora Peterson
Virginia, Minn.

LIME-BLUEBERRY MOLD

2 envelopes unflavored gelatin
1 c. cold water
1 ½ c. boiling water
½ c. sugar
¼ tsp. salt
¼ c. fresh lime juice
3 c. fresh blueberries

Soften gelatin in cold water. Add boiling water, sugar and salt; stir until gelatin dissolves. Add lime juice. Chill until mixture reaches the consistency of unbeaten egg white. Fold in blueberries. Yield: 6-8 servings.

Mrs. Carolyn Martin
Girard, Ill.

BING CHERRY SALAD

1 No. 2 can Bing cherries, pitted and halved
1 pkg. cherry gelatin
¾ c. hot water
½ c. Sherry
Pinch of salt
½ c. finely chopped pecans

Drain cherries, reserving 1/2 cup juice. Dissolve gelatin in hot water. Cool; add cherry juice and Sherry. Add salt, cherries and pecans. Whip with fork or mix well. Chill quickly; refrigerate for several hours before serving.

Ruth Wansley
Atlanta, Ga.

CHERRY SUPREME SALAD

1 pkg. lemon gelatin
1 c. hot cherry juice
2 c. drained cherries
1 c. whipped cream
⅓ c. mayonnaise
½ c. nuts

Dissolve gelatin in hot cherry juice. Chill until slightly firm; beat until fluffy. Fold in cherries, whipped cream, mayonnaise and nuts; chill until firm. Yield: 10 servings.

Mrs. Shirley Allen
Kaneoche Bay, Hawaii

CHERRY CONGEALED SALAD

1 No. 303 can pie cherries
1 c. sugar
½ c. water
2 sm. or 1 lge. pkg. cherry gelatin
1 sm. can crushed pineapple
1 c. pecans
1 sm. Coca-Cola

(Continued on next page)

Mix cherries, sugar and water; bring to a boil. Pour over gelatin, stirring to dissolve. Add pineapple, pecans and Coca-Cola. Chill until firm. Yield: 12 servings.

Mrs. Joe W. Washam
Blytheville, Ark.

DOUBLE TREAT BLACK CHERRY SALAD

1 pkg. black cherry gelatin
1 c. boiling water
1 1-lb. can dark sweet cherries, drained
2 tbsp. lemon juice
8 drops almond flavoring
1 c. heavy cream, whipped
1 banana, sliced

Dissolve gelatin in water. Drain cherries and reserve 3/4 cup syrup. Add lemon juice, almond flavoring and cherry syrup to gelatin. Chill until partially set. Divide gelatin. Fold cream and cherries into one-half of gelatin; pour into greased mold. Chill until almost firm. Fold banana into remaining gelatin; pour over cherry mixture. Chill; unmold and garnish with lettuce and cherries. Yield: 8 servings.

Mrs. Alice Boulanger
Tuthill, S.D.

MARION HOUSE SALAD

2 envelopes unflavored gelatin
½ c. cold water
2 egg whites
¾ c. sugar
1 c. cream
1 can Royal Anne cherries, pitted and halved
1 bottle Maraschino cherries, halved
1 c. drained crushed pineapple
1 c. chopped nuts
1 c. mayonnaise

Soften gelatin in cold water; dissolve over hot water. Beat egg whites with 1/2 cup sugar. Whip cream with remaining sugar. Combine all ingredients; chill until firm. Yield: 10-12 servings.

Mrs. James M. Rouse
Sylvester, Ga.

BEST-EVER CRANBERRY SALAD

1 pkg. strawberry gelatin
1 ½ c. hot water
1 7-oz. can jellied cranberry sauce
8 marshmallows
2 apples, chopped
½ c. chopped pecans
¼ pt. heavy cream, whipped

Dissolve strawberry gelatin in hot water. Add cranberry sauce and marshmallows; stir until dissolved. Refrigerate until partially congealed. Add all remaining ingredients; chill until firm. Yield: 8 servings.

Mrs. Dorothy Koliha
Pearl Harbor, Hawaii

CRANBERRY-APPLE SALAD

1 pkg. lemon gelatin
½ c. orange marmalade
1 c. boiling water
2 c. cranberries
2 apples, peeled and cored

Dissolve gelatin and marmalade in boiling water; chill until syrupy. Put cranberries and apples through food chopper; add to gelatin. Chill. Yield: 8-10 servings.

Mrs. Robt. S. Tomlinson
Elizabeth, N.J.

CRANBERRY SALAD

1 pkg. lemon gelatin
1 ½ c. boiling water
Juice of ½ lemon
½ c. finely cut celery
½ c. crushed pineapple
1 c. sweetened cranberry sauce

Dissolve gelatin in boiling water; chill until slightly thickened. Add lemon juice, celery, pineapple and cranberry sauce. Pour into mold; chill until firm. Yield: 6 servings.

Mrs. Hubert H. Humphrey

CRANBERRY- MARSHMALLOW SALAD

1 lb. cranberries
2 c. sugar
16 marshmallows
1 pkg. unflavored gelatin
½ c. cold water
1 c. diced apples
1 c. diced celery
½ c. chopped nuts

Cook berries and sugar as for cranberry sauce; add marshmallows. Stir until melted. Stir in gelatin and cold water; cool. Fold in apples, celery and nuts; refrigerate overnight. Yield: 4-6 servings.

Mrs. Ann Hill
Muskogee, Okla.

FRESH CRANBERRY SALAD

1 qt. cranberries
2 lge. apples
½ c. chopped celery
1 c. sugar
2 pkg. cherry gelatin
3 c. boiling water
1 c. crushed pineapple
½ c. chopped nuts

Grind cranberries, apples and celery; add sugar. Let stand overnight. Dissolve gelatin in boiling water; chill until partially set. Fold in cranberry mixture, pineapple and nuts. Pour into mold; chill until firm. Yield: 20 servings.

Mrs. Derrold Hartley
Soldiers Grove, Wisc.

GELATIN SURPRISE

2 pkg. red gelatin
1 can cranberry sauce
1 lge. can crushed pineapple, drained
1 c. chopped walnuts
¾ c. finely chopped celery
Jar of cherries (opt.)
Whipped cream (opt.)

Prepare gelatin according to package directions; chill until firm. Blend in cranberry sauce, pineapple, walnuts, celery and cherries. Chill. May be served plain or with whipped cream. Yield: 15 servings.

Mrs. Jean Stephenson
Willow Grove, Pa.

MOLDED CRANBERRY SALAD

2 c. cranberries
1 ¼ c. cold water
1 c. sugar
1 envelope unflavored gelatin
½ c. chopped celery
½ c. chopped nuts
½ tsp. salt

Cook cranberries in 1 cup water for 20 minutes. Stir in sugar; cook for 5 minutes longer. Soften gelatin in remaining 1/4 cup cold water; add to hot cranberries. Stir until dissolved. Set aside to cool. When mixture begins to thicken, add celery, nuts and salt. Rinse mold with cold water; pour cranberry mixture into mold. Chill until firm. Unmold onto serving plate; garnish with salad greens, if desired. Yield: 6 servings.

Mrs. Lyndon B. Johnson

ORANGE-CRANBERRY SALAD

1 qt. fresh cranberries
1 lge. orange, seeded
2 med. apples, cored
2 c. sugar
2 pkg. cherry gelatin
1 c. chopped nuts

Put cranberries, orange and apples through grinder using medium knife. Cover with sugar; let stand. Prepare gelatin as directed on package; chill until thickened. Add cranberry mixture and nuts. Pour into wet molds. Chill until firm. Yield: 20-24 servings.

Hilda Grace Rosett
Shreveport, La.

PINEAPPLE- CRANBERRY SALAD

1 pkg. cranberries
4 c. water
2 c. sugar
2 or 3 pkg. lime or lemon gelatin
1 c. chopped nuts
1 c. chopped celery
1 c. pineapple, drained

Simmer cranberries in water for 20 minutes. Remove from heat; stir in sugar and gelatin. Cool until slightly thickened. Add remaining ingredients; blend well. Refrigerate until firm. Yield: 15-20 servings.

Mrs. Clarence Creager
Linton, Ind.

QUICKIE CRANBERRY SALAD

2 pkg. raspberry gelatin
1 ½ c. hot water
1 can whole cranberry sauce
1 No. 2 ½ can crushed pineapple
3 lge. tart apples, diced
3 oranges, peeled and sliced crosswise
1 c. chopped pecans

Dissolve gelatin in hot water. Add cranberry sauce; stir until mixture is smooth except for berries. Add crushed pineapple, apples, oranges and nuts; stir thoroughly. Refrigerate overnight in desired mold. Yield: 10-12 servings.

Mrs. Carroll Lee
Clayton, Ga.

CARRY ALONG SALAD

1 lge. can fruit cocktail
1 pkg. celery gelatin
1 c. cottage cheese
½ c. finely diced celery
½ c. chopped nuts
1 3-oz. pkg. cream cheese
2 tbsp. sour cream
1 tsp. lemon juice

Drain fruit cocktail, reserving syrup; add enough water to syrup to make 2 cups. Heat 1 cup of syrup mixture to boiling; stir into gelatin. Add remaining syrup mixture; chill slightly. Fold in fruit cocktail, cottage cheese, celery and nuts. Pour into an 8-inch square pan; chill until firm. Beat cream cheese, sour cream and lemon juice until smooth. Spread over congealed mixture. Yield: 9 servings.

Mrs. Mary Sue Johnson
Pendleton, N.C.

SUNNY-SIDE SALAD

1 box lemon gelatin
2 c. boiling water
1 can fruit cocktail
Miniature marshmallows
½ c. heavy cream, whipped
Mayonnaise
½ lb. American cheese, shredded

Dissolve gelatin in boiling water; add fruit cocktail and enough marshmallows to cover top. Cool until firm; spread whipped cream and mayonnaise over salad. Garnish with cheese. Yield: 6 servings.

Mrs. E. F. Scheuerman
Bison, Kans.

WHITE SALAD

1 pkg. lime gelatin
2 c. water
½ c. evaporated milk
½ c. mayonnaise
1 lge. can fruit cocktail
1 c. pecans

Mix gelatin with water; chill. Combine milk and mayonnaise, whipping slightly. Add to gelatin mixture. Add fruit cocktail and nuts; congeal. Yield: 15 servings.

Mrs. Betty Ramey
Seneca, S.C.

GOOSEBERRY-ORANGE SALAD

1 pkg. lemon gelatin
2 c. hot water
¼ tsp. salt
1 c. diced marshmallows
1 c. sweetened gooseberries
1 c. chopped celery
½ c. chopped nuts
1 orange, peeled and diced

Dissolve gelatin in hot water. Add salt and marshmallows; stir until melted. Chill until partially congealed. Add remaining ingredients. Pour into mold; chill until firm. Yield: 15 servings.

Mrs. Harrison Miller
Orleans, Ind.

GOOSEBERRY SALAD

1 can gooseberries
½ c. sugar
2 boxes lemon gelatin
2 c. orange juice
2 c. diced celery
½ c. chopped nuts

Drain gooseberries, reserving liquid. Add water to liquid to make 1 1/2 cups. Heat liquid with sugar. Remove from heat. Dissolve gelatin in hot liquid. Add orange juice. Let stand until partially set. Add celery, nuts and gooseberries. Let set until congealed.

TOPPING:
1 8-oz. pkg. cream cheese
Mayonnaise
Lemon juice

Mix cream cheese, mayonnaise and lemon juice. Spread over salad. Yield: 14 servings.

Mrs. Rollin H. Smith
West Plains, Mo.

GRAPE SALAD

1 can crushed pineapple
1 pkg. unflavored gelatin
¼ c. cold water
1 pkg. lemon gelatin
1 ½ c. seedless grapes, washed
1 pt. sour cream
1 c. shredded almonds

Drain pineapple, reserving juice; add enough water to make 2 cups juice. Soak gelatin in cold water. Bring juice-water mixture to a boil; pour over lemon gelatin. Add soaked gelatin. Stir until dissolved. Cool. Add pineapple, grapes, sour cream and almonds. Place in refrigerator until set. Yield: 8 servings.

Irene H. Nelson
Talladega, Ala.

MOLDED GRAPE SUPREME

1 envelope unflavored gelatin
¼ c. cold water
1 c. boiling water
½ c. sugar
Dash of salt
1 6-oz. can frozen grape juice concentrate
3 tbsp. lemon juice
¾ c. seedless grape halves
2 med. bananas, diced
¼ c. chopped nuts

Sprinkle gelatin over cold water to soften. Add boiling water, sugar and salt; stir until dissolved. Stir in grape and lemon juice. Refrigerate until partially thickened. Fold in fruits and nuts. Pour into 1-quart mold. Refrigerate until firm.

Mrs. Beth Jones
Nashville, Tenn.

SPICED GRAPE SALAD

1 No. 2 can spiced white grapes
1 8-oz. can crushed pineapple
1 tbsp. unflavored gelatin
3 tbsp. cold water
1 tbsp. lemon juice
½ c. chopped celery
¼ c. nuts

Drain grapes and pineapple, reserving liquid; add enough water to make 1 3/4 cups liquid. Heat liquid. Soften gelatin in cold water and lemon juice. Combine gelatin with juice-water mixture. Chill until partially set. Add fruit, celery and nuts.

LEMON DRESSING:
1 egg
1 c. sugar
1 tbsp. butter
1 tbsp. lemon juice
1 c. whipped cream

Cook egg, sugar, butter and lemon juice until thickened. Cool. Stir cooked mixture into whipped cream. Serve over spiced grape salad. Yield: 6-8 servings.

Marian Joe Wilson
Odessa, Tex.

GRAPEFRUIT SALAD

1 pkg. lime gelatin
1 c. hot water
½ c. cold water
1 tbsp. vinegar
½ c. mayonnaise
¼ tsp. salt
Dash of pepper
¾ c. drained diced grapefruit
¾ c. diced celery
1 tbsp. grated onion

Dissolve gelatin in hot water. Add cold water, vinegar, mayonnaise, salt and pepper. Blend well with rotary beater. Pour into refrigerator tray. Quick-chill in freezer for 15 to 20 minutes or until firm 1 inch from edge. Turn mixture into bowl; whip until fluffy. Fold in grapefruit, celery and onion. Pour into 2-quart mold or individual molds. Chill until firm. Unmold and garnish with salad greens. Yield: 6-8 servings.

Mrs. Ernest N. Griffiths
Niagara Falls, N.Y.

GRAPEFRUIT SALAD WITH BUTTERCUP DRESSING

1 c. boiling water
1 pkg. lemon or orange gelatin
2 lge. fresh grapefruit, halved
1 No. 2 can crushed pineapple

Pour boiling water over gelatin. Cool until mixture begins to thicken slightly. Remove all sections from grapefruit rind. Combine grapefruit sections with crushed pineapple. Add to gelatin mixture. Pour into hollowed grapefruit halves. Chill until firm. If rind extends too far above firm gelatin, trim with a knife. When ready to serve, cut grapefruit in half again. Serve plain or with Buttercup Dressing.

BUTTERCUP DRESSING:
½ c. fruit juice
3 tbsp. flour
½ tsp. (heaping) salt
½ c. sugar
2 eggs, separated
3 marshmallows
¼ c. pecans, chopped (opt.)
⅛ c. lemon juice
½ c. whipped cream

Heat fruit juice. Combine flour, salt and sugar; blend with enough fruit juice to make a smooth paste. Add to remaining fruit juice; cook for 15 to 20 minutes or until thickened. Stir in slightly beaten egg yolks; cook for 5 minutes longer. Remove from heat; add marshmallows. Cool. Add nuts and lemon juice. Fold in stiffly beaten egg whites and whipped cream.

Mrs. Mary C. Dyches
Fort Mill, S.C.

FRUIT SALAD MOUSSE

2 envelopes unflavored gelatin
½ c. cold water
1 c. hot water
¼ c. sugar
¼ c. fresh lemon juice
⅛ tsp. salt
2 med. fresh peaches, peeled
½ c. mayonnaise
1 c. sour cream
1 c. green seedless grapes
1 c. fresh cantaloupe balls
1 c. diced fresh peaches
Salad greens

Soften gelatin in cold water; stir into hot water to dissolve. Blend in sugar, lemon juice and salt. Cut peaches into 1/2-inch slices. Dip slices into gelatin mixture; arrange as desired in oiled 1 1/2-quart mold. Chill gelatin mixture until slightly thickened. Combine mayonnaise and sour cream; fold into gelatin with remaining fruits. Turn into mold over sliced peaches. Chill until firm. Turn out onto a serving plate; garnish with additional grapes, cantaloupe balls and salad greens. Yield: 6-8 servings.

Photograph for this recipe above.

HONEYDEW SURPRISE

1 pkg. lime gelatin
1 c. boiling water
1 c. chunk pineapple, drained
1 c. Mandarin oranges
1 med. honeydew melon
Salad greens
Cottage cheese
French dressing

Dissolve gelatin in boiling water; cool until partially set. Add pineapple and oranges. Peel melon. Cut a slice from one end; remove seed. Fill center with fruit gelatin. Wrap in cellophane; refrigerate until gelatin is firm. Slice; place on bed of greens. Spoon cottage cheese on top. Serve with French dressing. Yield: 8 servings.

Rhoda M. Grushkin
Union, N.J.

MINT-MELON SOUFFLE MOLD

1 c. hot water
1 3-oz. pkg. lemon gelatin
2 or 3 sprigs fresh mint
½ c. cold water
2 tbsp. lemon juice
½ c. mayonnaise
½ tsp. salt
1 c. diced honeydew melon
1 c. diced cantaloupe
¼ c. slivered toasted blanched almonds

(Continued on next page)

Pour hot water over gelatin and mint sprigs; stir until gelatin is dissolved. Let set for 5 minutes. Remove mint; add cold water, lemon juice, mayonnaise and salt. Blend well with electric or rotary beater. Pour into refrigerator tray; quick-chill in freezer for 15 to 20 minutes or until firm about 1 inch from edge, but soft in center. Beat until fluffy. Fold in remaining ingredients. Chill until firm. Yield: 4-6 servings.

Mrs. Barbara Rawdon
Grants, N.M.

POLKA DOT MELON SALAD

1 pkg. lemon or lime gelatin
1 c. hot water
1 c. cold water
2 tsp. lemon juice
1 c. honeydew melon balls

Dissolve gelatin in hot water; add cold water and lemon juice. Let stand for 10 or 15 minutes. Chill until slightly thickened. Add melon balls. Pour into a 2 1/2-cup melon mold. Chill until firm. Yield: 4-6 servings.

Mrs. Nelda Shows Turner
Laurel, Miss.

RASPBERRY-MELON RING

3 10-oz. pkg. frozen raspberries, thawed
2 envelopes unflavored gelatin
½ c. lemon juice
1 ¼ c. boiling water
¾ c. sugar
¼ tsp. salt
¾ c. melon balls

Drain raspberries, reserving 2 cups syrup. Soften gelatin in lemon juice; dissolve in boiling water. Stir in sugar, salt and raspberry syrup. Chill until partially set. Add melon balls and raspberries. Chill until firm.

Mrs. Ruth L. West
Morgantown, Ky.

GOLDEN GLOW SALAD

2 pkg. orange gelatin
1 c. boiling water
1 can frozen orange juice
1 ½ c. cold water
1 can Mandarin oranges
1 sm. can pineapple chunks

Dissolve gelatin in boiling water. Add orange juice; stir until dissolved. Add cold water and fruits. Pour into mold; chill. Yield: 10-15 servings.

Mrs. Lelia E. Gish
Flora, Ind.

MANDARIN ORANGE SALAD

2 cans Mandarin oranges
1 lge. can pineapple chunks
1 pkg. lemon gelatin
1 pkg. orange gelatin
2 c. hot water
Miniature marshmallows

Drain oranges and pineapple, reserving 2 cups mixed juice. Dissolve gelatins in hot water; add juice. Cool. Add fruits. Cover top with marshmallows. Press them down slightly. Refrigerate for several hours.

TOPPING:
1 c. heavy cream, whipped
Sugar to taste
Vanilla flavoring
4 tbsp. mayonnaise
Grated cheese

Blend whipped cream, sugar, vanilla and mayonnaise. Spread over salad. Top with cheese.

Mrs. Joe Herron
Wabash, Ind.

MANDARIN ORANGE-PINEAPPLE SALAD

2 cans Mandarin orange slices
1 pkg. lemon gelatin
1 pkg. orange gelatin
2 c. hot water
1 pt. orange sherbet
1 ½ c. crushed pineapple

Drain oranges, reserving juice. Dissolve gelatins in hot water. Add enough water to juice from oranges to make 1 cup; stir into gelatin mixture. Chill until thickened. Fold in sherbet and fruits. Yield: 12 servings.

Mrs. Ida M. Tinnin
Bentonville, Ark.

ORANGE SHERBET RING

2 3-oz. pkg. orange gelatin
2 c. hot water
2 tbsp. lemon juice
1 pt. orange sherbet
2 11-oz. cans Mandarin orange slices, drained

(Continued on next page)

Thoroughly dissolve gelatin in hot water; add lemon juice. Cool to room temperature. Soften sherbet; fold into gelatin mixture. Add oranges. Pour into 6-cup ring mold; chill until firm. If desired, serve with whipped cottage cheese in center of mold; garnish with grated orange peel and mint sprigs. Yield: 8-10 servings.

Mrs. Harry Muenze
Elm Grove, W. Va.

SOUR CREAM-ORANGE SALAD

1 lge. pkg. pineapple-orange gelatin
½ pt. sour cream
1 can Mandarin orange segments

Make gelatin according to package directions. Allow to thicken. Whip in sour cream; add oranges. Chill thoroughly. Yield: 8 servings.

Mrs. E. R. Brashears
Evansville, Ind.

PEACH BUFFET SALAD

2 c. peach slices
8 to 10 Maraschino cherries
1 pkg. lemon gelatin
½ c. chopped celery
½ c. chopped pecans
1 c. cottage cheese
1 c. evaporated milk
2 tbsp. lemon juice

Drain peaches, reserving 1 cup juice. Arrange some peach slices and cherries in petal form around a 1 1/2-quart ring mold. Dissolve gelatin in hot peach juice; let set until thick. Fold in celery, pecans, remaining peaches and cheese. Chill milk in freezer until ice crystals form. Beat until stiff. Add lemon juice; beat until very stiff. Fold milk into gelatin mixture. Pour into mold. Chill until firm. Yield: 8-10 servings.

Mrs. George Raboin
Carney, Mich.

GINGER-PEACH MOLD

2 pkg. orange gelatin
2 c. hot water
2 sm. bottles ginger ale
1 to 1 ½ c. peaches, thinly sliced

Dissolve gelatin in hot water. Add ginger ale; chill until slightly thickened. Add peaches; place in 1 1/2-quart mold. Chill until firm.

TOPPING:
1 c. heavy cream, whipped
1 tsp. ground ginger

Combine ingredients; spread over salad. Yield: 6-8 servings.

Mrs. Kenneth Carter
Union, S.C.

PEACH ASPIC

1 No. 2 ½ can peaches
1 pkg. peach gelatin
1 3-oz. pkg. cream cheese, softened
1 tbsp. mayonnaise

Drain peaches, reserving juice; add water to make 2 cups juice. Reserve 1 peach half; dice remaining peaches. Heat peach juice to boiling; pour over gelatin. Stir until gelatin is dissolved. Chill until thick. Add peaches. Chill until firm. Blend cream cheese and mayonnaise together. Mash reserved peach half; stir it into the cheese mixture. Serve cheese mixture over gelatin. Yield: 8 servings.

Frances Rast
Covington, Tenn.

PEACH PICKLE SALAD MOLD

2 lge. jars or cans spiced peaches, diced
2 pkg. orange or lemon gelatin
2 cans white seedless grapes, drained
1 No. 2 can pineapple chunks, well drained
1 c. almonds or pecans, chopped

Drain peaches, reserving 2 1/2 cups juice; heat to boiling. Dissolve gelatin in peach juice. Cool. Combine peaches, grapes and pineapple. Add to gelatin. Add nuts. Chill until firm. Yield: 10-12 servings.

Myrtis L. McAlhany
St. George, S.C.

PEACH SALAD

1 1-lb. 1-oz. can sliced peaches
¼ c. vinegar
12 whole cloves
3 sticks cinnamon
1 pkg. orange gelatin

Drain peaches; reserve syrup. Add enough water to make 1 1/2 cups. Mix liquid with vinegar and spices; bring to boil. Lower heat; cook slowly for 10 minutes. Remove spices; add gelatin to hot liquid, stirring to dis-

(Continued on next page)

solve. Cool; add peaches. Pour into mold and chill. Yield: 6 servings.

Mrs. Irwin Perry
Cambridge, N.Y.

STUFFED SPICED PEACH SALAD

1 jar spiced peaches
1 pkg. lemon gelatin
1 pkg. lime gelatin
2 c. boiling water
1 sm. pkg. cream cheese
Lemon and orange juice
¼ c. pecans, chopped

Drain peaches, reserving juice; add enough water to make 2 cups liquid. Dissolve gelatins in boiling water; add juice. Chill until thickened. Soften cream cheese with orange and lemon juice. Add pecans. Take seed out of each peach and stuff with cream cheese mixture. Pour thickened gelatin into individual molds. Add a stuffed peach to each mold. Serve on lettuce; garnish with sprig of mint and cream cheese dressing. Yield: 6-8 servings.

Mrs. Ann Spencer
Chattanooga, Tenn.

GELATIN-PEAR SALAD

1 No. 2 ½ can pears, diced
1 pkg. lime gelatin
1 pkg. cream cheese
½ c. chopped pecans
1 pkg. dessert topping mix

Drain pears, reserving 1 3/4 cups juice. Bring pear juice to a boil; pour over gelatin, stirring to dissolve. Add cream cheese; mix thoroughly. Cool until partially set. Whip gelatin mixture; add pears, chopped pecans and dessert topping mix. Chill until firm. Yield: 12 servings.

Mrs. T. L. Lewis
Arvada, Colo.

LIME GELATIN-PEAR SALAD

1 can pears, mashed
1 pkg. lime gelatin
1 lge. pkg. cream cheese
2 tbsp. cream
1 c. heavy cream, whipped

Drain pears, reserving 1 cup juice; heat juice to boiling. Dissolve gelatin in pear juice. Mash cream cheese with cream; add to gelatin while hot. Cool until thick. Add pears and whipped cream. Chill. Yield: 8 servings.

Mrs. Gustav Perve
Juanita, N.D.

LIME-PEAR SALAD

1 med. can pears
1 c. cold water
1 lge. pkg. lime gelatin
1 sm. pkg. dessert topping mix or 1 c. heavy cream
1 lge. pkg. cream cheese

Drain pears, reserving 1 cup juice. Heat pear juice and cold water with gelatin; cool until partially congealed. Whip cream; fold in cream cheese. Mash pears; add to cooled mixture. Fold all ingredients together; chill until firm. Yield: 10-12 servings.

Mrs. Grayson Davis
Blunt, S.D.

MOLDED PEAR NECTAR SALAD

1 ½ c. pear nectar
1 pkg. unflavored gelatin
¼ c. lemon juice
⅓ c. sugar
¼ tsp. salt
2 egg whites
½ c. drained crushed pineapple
½ c. chopped nuts

Heat pear nectar to a full boil. Soften unflavored gelatin in lemon juice. Add sugar, salt and gelatin to hot pear nectar; stir until dissolved. Chill until mixture is slightly congealed. Beat egg whites until stiff; fold into gelatin mixture. Fold in crushed pineapple and nuts. Pour into a 1-quart mold or six individual molds. Chill until firm. NOTE: Green food coloring may be added to pear nectar. Yield: 6 servings.

Mrs. Pauline Morine
Burkburnett, Tex.

PEAR SALAD

1 lge. can pears
1 pkg. lime gelatin
1 8-oz. pkg. cream cheese
½ pt. whipping cream
Blanched chopped almonds
Whole almonds

Drain pears, reserving 1 cup juice. Puree pears; set aside. Bring pear juice to a boil;

(Continued on next page)

add gelatin, stirring until dissolved. Add pears and cream cheese; beat until smooth. Add more pear juice if too thick. Cool completely; fold in cream. Chill; fold in chopped almonds. Top with whole almonds; place in shallow mold. Chill until firm. Yield: 6 servings.

Gladys Lewis
Grass Valley, Calif.

PEAR-GELATIN SALAD

1 lge. can pears, cubed
1 pkg. lime gelatin
1 pkg. cream cheese, mashed
⅛ tsp. mustard
¼ tsp. salt
Nuts (opt.)

Drain pears, reserving liquid; add water to pear liquid to make 2 cups. Heat and pour over gelatin. Beat in cheese with egg beater. Add mustard, salt, pears and nuts. Pour into tray; freeze until firm. Place in refrigerator until ready to use. Yield: 8 servings.

Mrs. Gleneas Bessire
Pearl Harbor, Hawaii

PICKLED PEAR MOLD

½ c. bread and butter pickles
1 pkg. lemon gelatin
1 c. hot water
2 fresh pears, thinly sliced
2 tbsp. lemon juice
2 tbsp. sugar
1 c. fresh green grapes or canned green grapes

Drain pickles, reserving 1/2 cup juice. Dissolve gelatin in hot water; stir in pickle juice. Chill until beginning to set. Mix pears with lemon juice and sugar. Fold with remaining ingredients into gelatin. Pour into 1 1/2-quart mold; chill firm. Serve on lettuce garnished with additional pear slices and mayonnaise. Yield: 6 servings.

Mrs. Harry W. Collison
Winter Park, Fla.

WHIPPED PEAR SALAD

1 No. 2 ½ can pears
1 pkg. lime gelatin
2 3-oz. pkg. cream cheese, softened
2 tbsp. salad dressing
½ pt. heavy cream, whipped

Drain pears, reserving 1 cup juice; heat juice. Dissolve gelatin in pear juice. Cool until thickened. Mash pears; add to cream cheese mixed with salad dressing. Fold whipped cream and pear mixture into partially set gelatin. Cool until firm. Yield: 8 servings.

Donna Meier
Ovid, Colo.

SEAFOAM SALAD

1 lge. can pears, mashed
1 3-oz. pkg. lime gelatin
½ lb. cream cheese, softened
½ pt. cream, whipped
1 sm. bottle Maraschino cherries, chopped

Drain pears, reserving 1 cup juice. Dissolve gelatin in hot pear juice. Mix in pears and cream cheese. Cool. Fold in whipped cream and cherries. Turn into desired mold; chill until firm. Yield: 8 servings.

Anne Strang
Whitaker, Pa.

BAVARIAN SALAD

20 marshmallows
2 c. water
1 pkg. lime gelatin
1 c. grated American cheese
1 c. chopped nuts
1 No. 2 can crushed pineapple
½ c. heavy cream, whipped

Melt marshmallows in water over low heat. Remove from heat; add gelatin. Refrigerate to cool but do not let set. Whip gelatin until all large bubbles disappear. Add cheese, nuts, pineapple and cream. Chill until firm. Yield: 8-10 servings.

Mrs. Harvey Tenberg
Muskogee, Okla.

CONGEALED MOLD

1 pkg. lime gelatin
½ pkg. lemon gelatin
2 ¾ c. boiling water
½ c. chopped pecans
½ c. chopped celery
1 c. cottage cheese
1 c. crushed pineapple
¼ c. mayonnaise

(Continued on next page)

Dissolve gelatins in boiling water; chill until mixture starts to thicken. Mix remaining ingredients; add to slightly thickened gelatin. Turn into molds; chill until firm. Yield: 6 servings.

Mrs. George P. Allen
Atlanta, Ga.

CONGEALED SALAD

1 sm. can crushed pineapple
1 3-oz. pkg. orange-pineapple gelatin
1 c. grated Cheddar cheese
½ c. mayonnaise
1 c. milk
1 c. chopped nuts

Heat pineapple and gelatin until gelatin is completely dissolved. Add cheese, mayonnaise and milk. Continue to heat until cheese is dissolved, stirring constantly. Remove from heat; cool until thickened. Add nuts. Turn into molds. Chill until firm. Yield: 8 servings.

Mrs. Marvin Canington
Lumpkin, Ga.

COTTAGE CHEESE-PINEAPPLE MOLD

2 envelopes unflavored gelatin
1 c. cold water
1 No. 2 ½ can crushed pineapple
1 c. sugar
2 c. cottage cheese
4 pt. heavy cream, whipped

Soak gelatin in 1/2 cup water. Drain pineapple, reserving juice. Boil remaining water with pineapple juice and sugar until sugar is dissolved. Pour over gelatin. Mix in pineapple. Cool; add cottage cheese and whipped cream. Chill. Yield: 8 servings.

Dorothy Smith
Huntington, Ind.

COTTAGE CHEESE-PINEAPPLE SALAD

1 pkg. lemon gelatin
1 c. boiling water
1 pt. cottage cheese
1 c. crushed pineapple, drained
½ c. diced Maraschino cherries
½ c. chopped nuts
½ c. salad dressing
1 c. heavy cream, whipped

Dissolve gelatin in hot water. Cool; carefully add remaining ingredients except cream. Let mixture thicken slightly; fold in whipped cream. Pour into large pan; chill until firm. Yield: 12 servings.

Alice Krallman
Wakarusa, Ind.

GELATIN-FRUIT SALAD

1 pt. vanilla ice cream
3 pkg. lemon gelatin
5 c. liquid
1 med. can crushed pineapple
1 c. chopped celery

Combine all ingredients; chill until firm.

Mrs. William Smith
Athens, O.

GELATIN SALAD

2 tbsp. unflavored gelatin
½ c. cold water
1 No. 2 can crushed pineapple
½ c. sugar
Juice of 1 lemon
¾ c. pimento cheese, grated in long curls
1 c. whipped cream

Dissolve gelatin in cold water. Heat pineapple and sugar to boiling point; add lemon juice. Remove from heat. Add gelatin; stir until dissolved. Cool until partially set; whip until light and fluffy. Fold in cheese and whipped cream. Let set until firm.

Mrs. C. H. Simpson
Athena, Oreg.

GINGER ALE-PINEAPPLE SALAD MOLD

2 tbsp. gelatin
¼ c. cold water
1 tbsp. lemon juice
1 No. 2 can crushed pineapple
1 seedless orange, pared and diced
1 c. ginger ale
⅓ c. mayonnaise
2 tbsp. cream or Maraschino cherry juice

Soften gelatin in cold water; place over hot water until gelatin is dissolved. Add to lemon juice. Stir in pineapple with juice, orange and ginger ale; turn into 4-cup mold which has been rinsed with cold water. Chill until firm. Unmold. Serve with mayonnaise, thinned with cream. Yield: 5 servings.

Mrs. Clara Poole
Hill AFB, Utah

GOLDEN GLOW SALAD

1 c. diced pineapple
1 pkg. lemon gelatin
1 c. boiling water
½ tsp. salt
1 tbsp. vinegar
1 c. ground carrots
⅓ c. nuts (opt.)

Drain pineapple, reserving 1 cup juice. Dissolve lemon gelatin in boiling water; add pineapple juice, salt and vinegar. Mix well. Let stand until it starts to jell. Add pineapple, carrots and nuts. Mix well. Chill until firm. Yield: 8 servings.

Robena Smith
Manset, Me.

GREEN GELATIN SALAD

½ c. crushed pineapple
1 pkg. lime gelatin
½ c. water
1 c. cottage cheese
1 c. marshmallows
1 c. dessert topping mix, prepared

Drain pineapple, reserving 1/2 cup juice. Combine gelatin, water and juice. Boil for 5 minutes; cool. Add pineapple, cheese and marshmallows. Allow mixture to thicken slightly. Fold in topping mix. Chill.

Janet Mulder
Thorntown, Ind.

GELATIN SALAD

2 pkg. lemon gelatin
2 c. hot water
1 can crushed pineapple
½ c. cold water
½ pt. heavy cream, whipped
2 c. grated Cheddar cheese

Dissolve gelatin in hot water. Chill until thickened; add pineapple and cold water. Beat cream and cheese; add to mixture. Refrigerate in mold.

Mrs. Otto Betke
Ravenna, Nebr.

GOOD SALAD

1 6-oz. pkg. lime gelatin
2 c. boiling water
1 8-oz. pkg. cream cheese, softened
2 pt. vanilla ice cream, softened
1 No. 2 can crushed pineapple, drained

Dissolve gelatin in hot water. Chill until slightly thickened. Combine cream cheese and ice cream; mix in pineapple. Mix with gelatin. Turn into a 9-inch square pan. Chill until firm.

Mrs. Pearl M. Turner
Mann's Choice, Pa.

HORSERADISH-PINEAPPLE SALAD

2 pkg. lime gelatin
2 c. hot water
12 oz. cream cheese
⅓ c. mayonnaise
1 tsp. salt
2 tbsp. tarragon vinegar
2 tbsp. lemon juice
2 tbsp. sugar
1 No. 2 can crushed pineapple, drained
5 to 6 tbsp. horseradish

Dissolve gelatin in hot water; chill. Blend cream cheese and mayonnaise. Add salt, vinegar, lemon juice, sugar, pineapple and horseradish. Combine with gelatin, blending well. Turn into individual molds. Yield: 12 servings.

Mrs. Arthur H. Rose
Greensboro, N.C.

LEMON-PINEAPPLE SALAD

1 pkg. lemon gelatin
2 c. hot water
8 to 10 marshmallows, diced
1 sm. can crushed pineapple
½ pt. heavy cream, whipped
1 c. grated American cheese

Dissolve gelatin in hot water. Add marshmallows; stir until dissolved. Add pineapple; chill. Garnish with sweetened, whipped cream and cheese. Yield: 9 servings.

Mrs. Wm. C. Clothier
Pittsburg, Kans.

LIME-FRUIT SALAD

¼ lb. marshmallows
1 c. milk
1 pkg. lime gelatin
2 3-oz. pkg. cream cheese
1 No. 2 can crushed pineapple
1 c. heavy cream, whipped
⅔ c. mayonnaise

Melt marshmallows in milk; add gelatin, stirring until dissolved. Stir in cream cheese until blended. Add pineapple; cool until slightly thickened. Blend in whipped cream and mayonnaise. Chill until firm. Yield: 12 servings.

Mrs. Ralph Schroeder
Elwood, Nebr.

LIME-PINEAPPLE MOLD

¼ lb. marshmallows
1 c. milk
1 pkg. lime gelatin
1 6-oz. pkg. cream cheese
1 No. 2 can crushed pineapple
1 c. heavy cream, whipped
⅔ c. mayonnaise
12 cherries

Melt marshmallows in milk in top of double boiler. Pour hot mixture over gelatin, stirring until dissolved. Add cream cheese; stir until dissolved. Add undrained pineapple; cool mixture. Blend in whipped cream and mayonnaise; chill until firm. Top with a cherry. Yield: 12 servings.

Mrs. R. K. Wicker
Whiteman AFB, Mo.

LIME-PINEAPPLE GELATIN SALAD

1 pkg. lime gelatin
1 ½ c. water
12 marshmallows
1 c. crushed pineapple
½ c. chopped pecans
2 tbsp. mayonnaise
1 c. heavy cream, whipped

Dissolve gelatin in 1 cup water; chill until thickened. Melt marshmallows in 1/2 cup water. Add to gelatin. Stir in all remaining ingredients. Pour into mold; chill until firm. Yield: 12 servings.

Mrs. Lorayne Puckett
McCoy AFB, Fla.

LIME AND PINEAPPLE SALAD

1 can crushed pineapple
2 pkg. lime gelatin
3 ¾ c. water
3 eggs
1 c. sugar
3 tbsp. flour
¾ 8-oz. pkg. cream cheese
1 pkg. dessert topping mix, prepared

Drain pineapple, reserving 1 cup juice. Dissolve gelatin in water. Allow to thicken. Add pineapple; let gelatin set. Combine eggs, sugar, flour and juice. Cook over moderate heat until thickened. Add cheese; blend until smooth. Cool. Add mixture to gelatin. Fold in prepared topping mix. Chill. Yield: 8-10 servings.

Tona Huff
Burkett, Ind.

LIME SALAD WITH PINEAPPLE

¼ lb. marshmallows
1 c. milk
1 pkg. lime gelatin
2 3-oz. pkg. cream cheese
1 No. 2 can crushed pineapple
1 c. heavy cream, whipped
⅔ c. mayonnaise

Melt marshmallows and milk in top of double boiler. Pour hot mixture over lime gelatin; stir until dissolved. Stir in cream cheese until cheese dissolves. Add undrained pineapple; cool. Fold in whipped cream and mayonnaise. Chill and serve. Yield: 4 servings.

Mrs. Bonita Kirby
Ft. McClellan, Ala.

MOLDED FRUIT 'N' VEGETABLE SALAD

1 pkg. lemon flavored gelatin
1 c. boiling water
1 9-oz. can crushed pineapple
1 c. diced cooked carrots
Lettuce
Mayonnaise

Dissolve gelatin in boiling water. Add pineapple; chill until thickened. Add carrots. Pour into one large mold or five individual ones; chill until firm. Unmold on lettuce; serve with mayonnaise. Yield: 5 servings.

Mrs. Edith Mahoney
Fort Jay, N.Y.

MOLDED ICE CREAM-PINEAPPLE SALAD

1 3-oz. pkg. lime gelatin
¾ c. boiling water
1 pt. vanilla ice cream
1 c. crushed pineapple, drained (opt.)
½ c. nuts (opt.)

Dissolve gelatin in water. Add ice cream; stir until melted. Add pineapple and nuts if desired. Stir until well mixed. Pour into mold that has been greased with salad dressing. Chill for 2 hours. Yield: 6 servings.

Mrs. Vera Edgren
Lanse, Pa.

MOLDED PINEAPPLE SALAD

1 pkg. lemon gelatin
2 c. boiling water
½ c. grated American cheese
½ c. heavy cream, whipped
1 c. chopped nuts
1 c. crushed pineapple
½ c. sliced stuffed olives

(Continued on next page)

Dissolve gelatin in boiling water. Chill until mixture begins to thicken. Whip gelatin until fluffy; fold in remaining ingredients. Pour into ring mold or flat baking dish. Yield: 8 servings.

Mrs. Lawrence Anderson
Portage, Ind.

MOLDED SALAD

1 pkg. lemon gelatin
1 pkg. lime gelatin
2 c. hot water
1 c. crushed pineapple
1 c. evaporated milk
2 tbsp. lemon juice
1 c. sm. curd cottage cheese
1 c. mayonnaise
1 c. chopped walnuts
1 pkg. cherry gelatin

Dissolve lemon and lime gelatins in hot water; cool until thickened. Add pineapple, evaporated milk, lemon juice, cottage cheese and mayonnaise; mix with egg beater. Add walnuts. Pour into 8-inch square pan; chill until firm. Prepare cherry gelatin; pour over firm layer. Chill until set.

Mrs. Hugh Duffield
Kailua, Hawaii

NIPPY SALAD

1 pkg. lime gelatin
1 ¼ c. hot water
1 pt. cottage cheese
½ c. mayonnaise
1 sm. can crushed pineapple
2 tbsp. grated horseradish

Dissolve gelatin in hot water. Cool until syrupy. Add cheese, mayonnaise, pineapple and horseradish. Mix well; pour into mold. Serve on lettuce. Yield: 10-12 servings.

Mrs. Gabriel Raba
New Underwood, S.D.

PINEAPPLE-CARROT MOLD

1 No. 2 can crushed pineapple
1 pkg. lemon gelatin
½ c. sugar
¼ tsp. salt
3 tbsp. lemon juice
1 c. finely grated carrots
½ pt. heavy cream, whipped

Drain pineapple; reserve juice. Add enough water to pineapple syrup to make 1 1/2 cups; heat to boiling. Add gelatin; stir until dissolved. Add sugar, salt and lemon juice; chill until slightly thickened. Fold in pineapple, carrots and whipped cream. Pour into 1 1/2-quart mold. Chill until firm.

Mrs. William T. Allen
Brookley AFB, Ala.

PINEAPPLE-CHEESE SALAD

2 3-oz. pkg. orange gelatin
3 c. boiling water
4 tbsp. mayonnaise
1 8-oz. pkg. cream cheese
1 No. 2 can crushed pineapple
2 med. carrots, finely grated

Dissolve gelatin in hot water; chill until slightly thickened. Beat mayonnaise and cream cheese together until smooth. Combine all ingredients. Chill until firm. Yield: 6-8 servings.

Mrs. Roger C. Wagner
Bellefonte, Pa.

PINEAPPLE-CHEESE SALAD WITH CREAMY TOPPING

2 c. boiling water
2 3-oz. pkg. lemon flavored gelatin
2 c. cold water
1 1-lb. 4 ½-oz. can crushed pineapple
2 c. shredded sharp Cheddar cheese
6 med. ripe bananas, sliced
Crisp salad greens

Pour boiling water over gelatin; stir until gelatin is dissolved. Add cold water; chill until mixture begins to thicken. Drain pineapple, reserving syrup for creamy topping. Sprinkle cheese in 13 x 9 x 2-inch pan. Fold pineapple and bananas into thickened gelatin; spoon over cheese. Chill until firm. Cut into squares; serve on crisp salad greens with creamy topping.

CREAMY TOPPING:
½ c. sugar
2 tbsp. flour
1 c. pineapple syrup
1 tsp. lemon juice
2 eggs, slightly beaten
2 tbsp. butter
1 c. heavy cream, whipped

Combine sugar and flour; mix well. Stir in pineapple syrup, lemon juice and eggs. Cook over low heat until smooth and thickened, stirring constantly. Stir in butter. Chill; fold in whipped cream. Serve over pineapple cheese salad. Yield: 12 servings.

Photograph for this recipe on page 195.

PINEAPPLE-COTTAGE CHEESE SALAD

1 pkg. lime gelatin
1 pkg. lemon gelatin
2 c. hot water
¼ tsp. salt
½ No. 2 can crushed pineapple, drained
1 sm. can evaporated milk
1 c. salad dressing
1 tbsp. horseradish
1 c. broken pecans

Dissolve gelatins in water; add salt. Chill. Combine remaining ingredients; fold into gelatin. Chill until firm. Serve on lettuce. Yield: 12 servings.

Mrs. G. E. Snuggs
El Dorado, Ark.

PINEAPPLE-CREAM CHEESE MOLD

1 lge. can crushed pineapple
1 c. sugar
2 envelopes unflavored gelatin
Juice of 1 lemon
1 8-oz. pkg. cream cheese
⅓ c. milk
1 pt. cream, whipped
1 c. chopped pecans
1 c. chopped Maraschino cherries

Heat pineapple to boiling point; add sugar. Soak gelatin in lemon juice for 5 minutes; add to pineapple. Cool until mixture is partially thickened. Cream cheese, adding milk a little at a time. Add whipped cream to cheese mixture. Add cream-cheese mixture to gelatin. Add nuts and cherries. Chill until firm. Yield: 15 servings.

Mrs. Ferrell Gibson
Troy, Ala.

PINEAPPLE-CREAM CHEESE SALAD

1 c. boiling water
1 pkg. lemon gelatin
1 pkg. raspberry gelatin
1 sm. can pineapple
1 12-oz. pkg. cream cheese
½ c. mayonnaise
1 lge. can evaporated milk
Chopped pecans

Pour boiling water over mixed gelatins; mix well. Cool. Add pineapple. Combine cream cheese and mayonnaise. Gradually add milk to cheese mixture. Add nuts. Add cheese mixture to gelatin. Chill until firm.

Mrs. Margaret T. Rayfield
Weogufka, Ala.

PINEAPPLE AND GELATIN SALAD

1 pkg. orange gelatin
15 lge. marshmallows
1 3-oz. pkg. cream cheese
2 c. boiling water
½ c. mayonnaise
1 sm. can crushed pineapple, drained

Combine gelatin, marshmallows and cheese. Pour boiling water over mixture; blend until marshmallows are melted. Chill until thickened; add mayonnaise and pineapple. Chill until firm.

Mrs. Earl Kitterman
Hartford City, Ind.

PINEAPPLE-LIME DELIGHT

1 pkg. lime gelatin
½ pt. heavy cream, whipped
1 c. crushed pineapple, drained
1 4-oz. pkg. cream cheese, grated
½ c. pecans, chopped

Dissolve gelatin according to package directions; chill until slightly firm. Combine whipped cream with pineapple, cream cheese and pecans; fold into gelatin. Pour into molds; chill until firm. Yield: 6-8 servings.

Mrs. Dean Braselton
Oxnard AFB, Calif.

PINEAPPLE-MANGO SALAD RING

1 lge. ripe pineapple
Cooked mango pulp
1 pkg. apple or peach gelatin
1 pkg. orange gelatin
Cottage cheese

Peel and cut pineapple into small pieces. Puree pineapple; rub through strainer to remove all fiber. Add enough mango to make 5 cups of fruit pulp. Heat pulp to full boil; pour over combined gelatins; stir until dissolved. Pour into oiled ring mold; chill until firm. Unmold; fill center with cottage cheese.

Jane Camp
Honolulu, Hawaii

PINEAPPLE MOLD

1 med. can crushed pineapple
1 box lime gelatin
1 pt. vanilla ice cream
1 sm. glass pimento cheese spread
Diced Maraschino cherries

Drain pineapple, reserving juice. Add enough water to juice to make 1 cup. Heat juice and

(Continued on next page)

water to boiling; pour over lime gelatin. Stir until dissolved. Add ice cream, pineapple, cottage cheese and Maraschino cherries. Pour into mold; chill until firm. Yield: 8 servings.

Mrs. Alvan Ewers
Richland Center, Wisc.

PINEAPPLE-PIMENTO CHEESE SALAD

1 pkg. lemon gelatin
½ c. sugar
1 c. boiling water
1 glass pimento cheese spread
1 sm. can crushed pineapple
1 pkg. dessert topping mix

Dissolve lemon gelatin and sugar in boiling water. Cool until syrupy; beat in pimento cheese spread and pineapple. Let congeal to syrupy stage; fold in prepared dessert topping mix. Refrigerate until completely set. Yield: 8 servings.

Mrs. Louise Stricker
Montrose, Mo.

PINEAPPLE RELISH RING

1 No. 2 can crushed pineapple
1 ¼ c. hot water
1 pkg. lemon gelatin
¼ c. diced celery
½ c. diced unpared apple
¼ c. chopped walnuts or pecans
2 tsp. pickle relish

Drain pineapple, reserving 1/2 cup juice. Pour hot water over gelatin; stir until dissolved. Add juice. Chill, stirring occasionally, until consistency of unbeaten egg white. Fold in pineapple, celery, apple, nuts and relish. Pour into four or six individual molds; chill until firm. Unmold on crisp salad greens; serve with favorite salad dressing. Yield: 4-6 servings.

Mrs. Rogene H. Kilpatrick
Milton, Fla.

PINK PINEAPPLE SALAD

1 can crushed pineapple
2 pkg. strawberry gelatin
3 c. hot water
1 8-oz. pkg. cream cheese
1 6-oz. can evaporated milk

Drain pineapple, reserving juice. Dissolve gelatin in hot water; chill until slightly thickened. Soften cheese with pineapple juice. Blend cheese and pineapple. Whip chilled milk. Mix pineapple with gelatin; fold in whipped milk. Chill until firm. Yield: 15-18 servings.

Mrs. Clarence Musselman
Telford, Pa.

RASPBERRY-PINEAPPLE DELIGHT SALAD

1 pkg. raspberry gelatin
1 c. hot water
1 c. vanilla ice cream
2 tbsp. orange juice
1 9-oz. can crushed pineapple, drained
1 med. banana, sliced
½ c. chopped nuts

Dissolve gelatin in hot water; stir in ice cream and orange juice until blended. Chill until partially set; add fruits and nuts. Pour into 1-quart mold; chill until set. Yield:8 servings.

Mrs. Harold Birky
Cedar Rapids, Iowa

RECEPTION SALAD

1 med. can crushed pineapple
1 pkg. lemon gelatin
1 c. hot water
1 sm. can pimento
2 3-oz. pkg. cream cheese
½ to 1 c. finely chopped celery
⅔ c. nuts, chopped
½ pt. whipped cream
⅛ tsp. salt

Drain pineapple, reserving juice. Heat pineapple juice and water to boiling. Dissolve gelatin in juice. Cool. Mash pimento and cream cheese together. Add celery, nuts, pineapple and gelatin. Add cream and salt. Allow to chill before serving. Yield: 6-8 servings.

Sammie Saulsbury
Odessa, Tex.

REFRESHING SALAD

1 3-oz. pkg. lime gelatin
1 c. hot water
2 tbsp. lemon juice
1 sm. can crushed pineapple
1 c. cottage cheese
12 Maraschino cherries, sliced
¼ c. chopped nuts

Dissolve gelatin in hot water. Add lemon juice and pineapple. Blend in cottage cheese.

(Continued on next page)

Let mixture thicken; stir well. Pour into 9 x 9-inch dish or individual molds. Garnish with cherries and nuts. Chill. Yield: 9 servings.

Mrs. C. K. Reid
Bluffton, Ind.

7-UP SALAD

1 pkg. lemon gelatin
1 c. boiling water
1 8-oz. pkg. cream cheese
1 sm. can crushed pineapple, drained
1 tsp. sugar
4 drops green food coloring
1 bottle 7-Up
½ c. chopped pecans

Dissolve gelatin in boiling water; add cheese, pineapple, sugar, food coloring and 7-Up. Stir in pecans. Chill until partially congealed; pour into individual molds. Chill until firm. Yield: 6-8 servings.

Mrs. Elden Brunet
Oakdale, La.

TWENTY-FOUR HOUR FRUIT SALAD

1 ½ c. pineapple rings
30 marshmallows
1 c. Maraschino cherries
½ c. salad dressing
½ c. pimento cheese
1 pkg. unflavored gelatin
¼ c. cold water
2 c. heavy cream, whipped

Cut up pineapple rings, marshmallows and cherries. Mix salad dressing and pimento cheese. Dissolve gelatin in water; add to salad dressing and cheese mixture. Fold in whipped cream; add pineapple, marshmallows and cherries. Let set for 24 hours before serving. Yield: 8-10 servings.

Mrs. Betty Claiborn
Kimberly, Idaho

TEXAS SALAD

1 No. 2 can crushed pineapple
2 pkg. lemon or lime gelatin
1 sm. can pimento
1 c. chopped nuts
1 lb. cottage cheese
1 c. heavy cream, whipped

Bring pineapple to a boil; add gelatin. Stir until dissolved. Chill until thickened; fold in remaining ingredients. Pour into mold; chill until firm. Yield: 12 servings.

Mrs. F. A. Boutwell
Celeste, Tex.

YUM YUM CONGEALED SALAD

2 envelopes unflavored gelatin
½ c. cold water
1 lge. can crushed pineapple, drained
Juice of 2 lemons
¾ c. sugar
¼ c. mayonnaise
1 c. grated American cheese
1 pt. cream, lightly whipped

Soften gelatin in cold water. Heat pineapple, lemon juice and sugar. Add to gelatin; mix well. Chill until partially congealed. Fold in mayonnaise, cheese and cream. Chill until firm. Cut into squares; serve on lettuce. Yield: 15 servings.

Mrs. Jean C. Peavy
Gordon, Ga.

RASPBERRY-APPLE MOLD

1 pkg. raspberry gelatin
1 c. hot water
1 can applesauce
1 tart red apple, chopped
1 can pineapple chunks, drained
¼ c. chopped nuts
1 tbsp. mayonnaise
½ c. heavy cream, whipped

Dissolve gelatin in hot water; add applesauce. Chill in ring mold until firm. Toss remaining ingredients together; fill center of ring. Yield: 15 servings.

Mrs. Maurice Stewart
Marshalltown, Iowa

RED RASPBERRY MOLDED SALAD

2 boxes raspberry gelatin
2 c. boiling water
1 box frozen raspberries
1 3-oz. pkg. cream cheese
¼ c. ground nuts

Dissolve gelatin in boiling water. Add frozen berries; stir until berries have thawed. Chill until thickened. Make small cheese balls; roll in nuts. Arrange balls in bottom of mold. Pour gelatin over balls; place mold in refrigerator to congeal. Yield: 10 servings.

Mrs. S. J. McMeen
Gregory, S.D.

RASPBERRY SALAD

2 pkg. raspberry gelatin
2 ½ c. boiling water
1 ½ c. strained applesauce
Dash of salt
2 tsp. lemon juice
1 pkg. frozen raspberries, thawed
½ pkg. miniature marshmallows
1 sm. carton sour cream

(Continued on next page)

Dissolve gelatin in water; chill until partially set. Add applesauce, salt, lemon juice and raspberries. Chill until firm. Soak marshmallows in sour cream overnight; whip and spread over gelatin. Yield: 8 servings.

Mrs. Shirley Sandstedt
Hastings, Nebr.

CONGEALED RHUBARB SALAD

2 c. rhubarb
½ c. boiling water
2 c. pineapple juice
2 pkg. strawberry gelatin
Few drops red food coloring
1 c. pared chopped apples
½ c. chopped nuts

Cook rhubarb in boiling water for 5 minutes or until tender. Add 1 cup pineapple juice; bring to a boil. Add gelatin; stir until dissolved. Add remaining pineapple juice and food coloring. Chill until mixture begins to congeal; add apples and nuts. Chill until firm. Yield: 8 servings.

Mrs. Cecil C. Clem
Springfield, Va.

RHUBARB-PINEAPPLE SALAD

2 c. diced rhubarb
1 c. sugar
1 pkg. strawberry gelatin
1 sm. can crushed pineapple
½ c. broken nuts

Cook rhubarb until tender. Add sugar; stir until thoroughly dissolved. Add gelatin; stir until dissolved. Add pineapple and nuts. Chill until firm.

Mrs. Wanda McDonald
Cherokee, N.C.

RHUBARB SALAD

2 pkg. lime or lemon gelatin or 1 pkg. of each
2 c. hot water
16 lge. marshmallows, finely cut
1 c. cold water
1 pt. chopped cooked rhubarb, sweetened

Dissolve gelatin and marshmallows in hot water. Add cold water and rhubarb. Chill.

TOPPING:
¾ c. sugar
Juice of 1 lemon
2 eggs, beaten
1 pt. heavy cream, whipped

Combine sugar, juice and eggs in double boiler. Cook until mixture thickens. Cool. Fold in whipped cream; spread over salad. Sprinkle with nuts, if desired. Yield: 8 servings.

Juanita Crane
Shoals, Ind.

AMBROSIA MOLD

1 pkg. orange-pineapple or orange gelatin
1 tbsp. sugar
1 c. boiling water
¾ c. cold water
1 c. whipped heavy cream or 1 c. prepared dessert topping mix
¾ c. diced orange sections
1 ¼ c. seeded red grapes, halved or 1 banana, sliced and quartered
⅔ c. coconut

Dissolve gelatin and sugar in boiling water; add cold water. Chill until slightly thickened; fold in whipped cream. Add remaining ingredients. Chill in mold until firm. Yield: 8 servings.

Mrs. C. Wade Ferguson
Emporia, Va.

AMBROSIA GELATIN SALAD

2 pkg. orange gelatin
2 ½ c. hot water
1 can frozen orange juice
1 sm. can crushed pineapple, well drained
1 can Mandarin oranges, well drained
1 pkg. lemon chiffon pie filling
1 c. whipped cream

Dissolve gelatin in hot water; add frozen orange juice. Cool until slightly thickened. Add fruit. Pour into 8 x 12-inch pan; chill until almost firm. Mix pie filling according to directions on box; add whipped cream. Spoon mixture over gelatin. Chill until firm. Cut into squares to serve. Yield: 12 servings.

Mrs. Guy T. Roberts
Los Altos, Calif.

APPLESAUCE-PINEAPPLE SALAD

1 pkg. raspberry gelatin
1 c. hot applesauce
Grated rind and juice of 1 orange
1 sm. can crushed pineapple
1 sm. bottle 7-Up

Combine gelatin and applesauce. Mix in remaining ingredients. Stir occasionally until slightly cool. Refrigerate until firm. Yield: 6 servings.

Mrs. Opal Brovillard
Barnard, S.D.

BING CHERRY SALAD MOLD

1 c. pitted Bing cherries
1 pkg. cherry gelatin
1 c. cherry wine
1 c. chopped pecans
1 c. crushed pineapple, drained

Drain cherries, reserving 1 cup juice; heat juice to boiling. Dissolve gelatin in hot liquid; add wine. Fold in nuts, pineapple and cherries. Rinse mold with cold water. Chill until firm. Yield: 8 servings.

Mrs. Nathan Zeller
Newark, N.J.

BLACK BING FRUIT SALAD

1 No. 2 can black cherries, chopped
2 boxes cherry gelatin
1 c. hot water
1 pkg. cream cheese (opt.)
2 bottles Coca-Cola
1 c. chopped nuts
1 can crushed pineapple

Drain cherries, reserving juice. Dissolve gelatin in hot water. Add cream cheese; cool. Add Coca-Cola and cherry juice; congeal slightly. Add cherries, nuts and pineapple. Pour into mold; chill until set. Yield: 8 servings.

Ann Childers
Blountsville, Ala.

BLUEBERRY-PINEAPPLE SALAD

1 can blueberries, drained
1 can pineapple, drained
2 pkg. black raspberry gelatin
1 c. sour cream

Drain blueberries and pineapple; reserve juices. Add enough water to combined juices to make 3 2/3 cups liquid. Heat to boiling. Pour over gelatin; stir to dissolve. Cool slightly. Add sour cream and fruit. Pour into mold; chill overnight. Yield: 10 servings.

Mrs. Doyle Moore
Pickering, Mo.

CHERRY-BANANA SOUFFLE

1 pkg. cherry gelatin
1 c. hot water
½ c. cold water
½ c. mayonnaise or salad dressing
¼ tsp. salt
1 c. canned pitted dark cherries, drained
1 c. bananas, thinly sliced
⅓ c. chopped almonds, slivered and toasted or pecans

Dissolve gelatin in hot water. Add cold water, mayonnaise and salt; blend with rotary beater. Quick-chill in refrigerator freezing tray for 15 to 20 minutes or until firm, about 1 inch from edge. Turn into bowl; whip with rotary beater until fluffy. Fold in remaining ingredients. Pour into 1-quart mold. Chill until firm. Do not freeze. Unmold; serve on salad greens. Garnish with fluted banana slices if desired. Yield: 4-6 servings.

Mrs. W. Wayne Nichols
Tuscaloosa, Ala.

CHERRY-PINEAPPLE SALAD

1 can frozen cherries
1 c. sugar
2 pkg. cherry gelatin
1 c. red wine
1 sm. Coca-Cola
1 No. 2 can crushed pineapple, drained
1 c. chopped pecans

Bring frozen cherries and sugar to a boil; remove from heat. Drain well, reserving 2 cups juice. Reheat juice; pour over gelatin. Add wine and Coca-Cola. Cool slightly; add cherries, pineapple and pecans. Chill; stir several times while chilling to mix fruit. Yield: 12 servings.

Mrs. Louise Lawhon
Wichita, Kans.

CHUTNEY MOLDS

1 8½-oz. can crushed pineapple
1 11-oz. can Mandarin oranges
1 6-oz. pkg. lemon gelatin
1 c. hot water
¼ c. lemon juice
1 c. Sauterne
1 9-oz. bottle chutney, finely chopped

Drain pineapple and oranges, reserving 1/2 cup juice from each. Dissolve gelatin in hot water, stirring until completely dissolved. Add fruit juices, wine and pineapple; chill until mixture begins to thicken. Stir in oranges and chutney. Spoon into individual molds or one large mold; chill until firm. Thin mayonnaise with sour cream to serve as dressing, if desired. Yield: 8-10 servings.

Mrs. Cumi Birchmore
Colbert, Ga.

BLACK CHERRY SALAD

2 bottles Coca-Cola
2 pkg. cherry gelatin
1 jar black cherries
1 No. 2 can crushed pineapple
1 c. broken nuts
1 c. chopped celery

(Continued on next page)

Heat Coca-Cola; pour over gelatin. Drain cherries and pineapple; reserve juices. Add to gelatin. Add all remaining ingredients. Pour into mold; chill until firm. Yield: 6 servings.

Mrs. Berniece Gradine
Amarillo, Tex.

CRANBERRY-APPLE SALAD

1 1-lb. can jellied cranberry sauce
1 envelope unflavored gelatin
2 tbsp. cold water
2 tbsp. lemon juice
1 c. ginger ale
¾ c. diced apple
¾ c. diced celery
½ c. chopped nuts (opt.)

Crush cranberry sauce with fork. Soften gelatin in cold water and lemon juice; dissolve over hot water. Stir into cranberry sauce; cool. Add ginger ale; mix well. Chill until mixture begins to thicken. Fold in apple, celery and nuts; chill until firm. Serve on lettuce leaves with mayonnaise. Yield: 6 servings.

Helena F. McCormick
Wollaston, Mass.

CRYSTAL SALAD

1 pkg. lemon gelatin
1 ¼ c. hot water
½ c. pineapple juice
½ c. heavy cream, whipped
½ c. salad dressing
½ c. unpeeled diced apples
½ c. diced pineapple
½ c. diced celery
6 marshmallows, finely chopped

Dissolve gelatin in hot water. Add pineapple juice. Chill until thickened; fold in whipped cream. Combine remaining ingredients; fold into gelatin mixture. Pour into mold. Chill until firm. Yield: 12 servings.

Mrs. Joe Wunder
Bison, S.D.

FRUIT-CELERY SALAD

2 pkg. cherry or raspberry gelatin
4 c. hot water
1 pkg. cranberries
3 apples, chopped
Rind of 3 oranges, grated
3 c. sugar
½ c. chopped celery (opt.)
1 c. crushed pineapple (opt.)
½ c. chopped nuts (opt.)

Dissolve gelatin in water. Chill until slightly thickened; add remaining ingredients. Chill until firm. Yield: 16 servings.

Mrs. Harold Leap
Cicero, Ind.

FRUIT SALAD

1 No. 2 can pineapple, cut into sm. pieces
1 No. 2 can dark Bing cherries, cut into halves
2 pkg. cherry gelatin
3 c. Coca-Cola
½ c. finely chopped nuts

Drain pineapple and cherries, reserving 1/4 cup juice from each. Dissolve gelatin in hot juice mixture; add Coca-Cola. Chill until partially congealed. Fold in pineapple, cherries and nuts. Place in mold or baking dish; chill until firm. Yield: 12 servings.

Mildred Haney Harris
Dallas, Tex.

FRUIT SALAD DELIGHT

¼ c. chopped Maraschino cherries
1 envelope unflavored gelatin
½ c. cold water
1 c. mayonnaise
1 8-oz. pkg. cream cheese
2 tbsp. confectioners sugar
1 c. drained crushed pineapple
1 c. drained coarsely chopped apricots
1 c. heavy cream, whipped

Drain cherries, reserving 1/4 cup juice. Soften gelatin in water. Blend mayonnaise and cream cheese. Add cherry juice, sugar and gelatin. Chill until slightly thickened. Add fruits; fold in whipped cream. Chill until firm. Serve on lettuce. Yield: 16 servings.

Mrs. Marvin Pruett
Latah, Wash.

FRUIT SALAD PARFAIT

2 envelopes unflavored gelatin
½ c. cold water
1 c. salad dressing
1 8-oz. pkg. cream cheese
1 c. Maraschino cherry juice
2 tbsp. powdered sugar
1 c. crushed pineapple, drained
1 c. chopped apricots, drained
¼ c. chopped cherries, drained
1 c. heavy cream, whipped

Soften gelatin in cold water over hot water; cool. Add salad dressing to cheese; blend. Add juice, sugar and gelatin to cheese; mix

(Continued on next page)

well. Chill until slightly thickened. Add fruits; fold in whipped cream. Pour into 1 1/2-quart ring mold. Chill until firm. Unmold; surround with lettuce. Yield: 8-10 servings.

Helen Forehand
St. Bernice, Ind.

FROSTED SALAD

1 pkg. lemon gelatin
1 c. boiling water
1 c. cold water
2 bananas, sliced
1 sm. can diced pineapple
1 pkg. miniature marshmallows
½ c. sugar
2 tbsp. flour
1 egg, well beaten
1 tbsp. butter
1 c. pineapple juice
1 c. heavy cream
1 tsp. lemon juice
½ tsp. vanilla flavoring

Dissolve gelatin in boiling water; add cold water. Stir in bananas, pineapple and marshmallows; chill until firm. Cook sugar, flour, egg, butter and pineapple juice together until thickened. Cool. Whip cream with lemon juice and vanilla flavoring; fold into cooled egg mixture. Pour over firm gelatin. Cool. Yield: 12 servings.

Mrs. Herman N. Hall
Bridgeport, Nebr.

GOLDEN SALAD

1 pkg. lemon gelatin
2 tbsp. sugar
1 sm. can crushed pineapple, drained
2 bananas, sliced
8 marshmallows, finely cut

Prepare gelatin according to package directions; add all remaining ingredients. Chill until firm.

TOPPING:
1 egg, beaten
½ c. sugar
2 tbsp. flour
1 c. pineapple juice and water
2 tbsp. butter
½ pt. heavy cream, whipped

Combine egg, sugar and flour in top of double boiler. Add pineapple juice and water and butter; cook until thickened. Cool; fold in whipped cream. Spread over gelatin. Yield: 6 servings.

Mrs. Bobby W. Burrow
Cottonwood, Idaho

HARVEST FRUIT RING

1 pkg. apple gelatin
1 ¾ c. hot cider
½ tsp. salt
1 ½ c. diced unpared apples
1 c. Tokay grapes or seedless white grapes, halved
1 9-oz. can pineapple chunks
8 to 10 marshmallows, diced

Dissolve gelatin in cider; add salt. Chill until partially set. Add remaining ingredients. Pour into 5-cup ring mold. Chill until firm. Garnish with apple wedges if desired. Yield: 8 servings.

Mrs. Marian G. Craddock
Colorado City, Tex.

JELLIED AMBROSIA SALAD

1 envelope unflavored gelatin
¼ c. cold water
¼ c. boiling water
2 tsp. sugar
1 ¼ c. fresh orange juice
2 tsp. fresh lemon juice
3 med. oranges
1 lge. banana
3 tsp. grated or shredded coconut

Soften gelatin in cold water. Dissolve in boiling water. Add sugar; stir until completely dissolved. Add orange and lemon juices. Cool. Peel oranges; cut into sections. Peel and slice banana. When orange mixture is syrupy, fold in fruit and coconut. Pour into 3-cup mold or four individual molds; chill until firm. Serve garnished with orange sections and shredded coconut. Yield: 4 servings.

Emma Bybee
Glasgow, Ky.

LEMON-FRUIT SALAD

1 pkg. lemon gelatin
2 c. hot water
1 sm. can crushed pineapple, drained
1 c. miniature marshmallows
2 bananas, sliced

Dissolve gelatin in hot water; cool. Add all remaining ingredients; Chill until firm.

TOPPING:
2 tbsp. margarine
2 tbsp. flour
1 egg, beaten
½ c. sugar
¾ c. pineapple juice and water
½ c. Milnot

Blend margarine, flour, egg, sugar, pineapple juice and water; cook until thickened. Whip

(Continued on next page)

chilled Milnot until thickened; fold into mixture. Spread over gelatin. Yield: 6-8 servings.

Mrs. Shirley Talley
Gila Bend, Ariz.

LEMON - FRUIT SALAD

1 pkg. lemon gelatin
½ c. boiling water
1 sm. carton cottage cheese
1 c. heavy cream, whipped
2 tbsp. salad dressing
1 c. Mandarin oranges, drained
1 can pineapple chunks, drained
½ tsp. salt

Dissolve gelatin in hot water; cool. Combine cottage cheese, cream and salad dressing. Add fruits and salt. Fold into cooled gelatin. Refrigerate. Yield: 8 servings.

Verna J. Larson
Valley City, N.D.

TANGY FRUIT SALAD

1 1-lb. can Bing cherries
1 No. 2 can crushed pineapple
1 6-oz. pkg. cherry gelatin
2 sm. bottles Coca-Cola

Drain cherries and pineapple, reserving juices. Add water to juices to make 2 cups. Heat juices; pour over gelatin. Cool; add Coca-Cola and fruit. Pour into 1 1/2-quart mold. Chill until set. Yield: 8 servings.

Mrs. Raymond Gillming
Kearney, Nebr.

TWENTY-FOUR HOUR SALAD

4 egg yolks, beaten
1 c. milk
1 envelope unflavored gelatin
Juice of 1 lemon
1 lb. marshmallows, diced
1 pt. heavy cream, whipped and sweetened
1 No. 2 can sliced pineapple, drained
1 No. 2 can white cherries, drained
½ lb. blanched almonds, chopped

Mix egg yolks with 3/4 cup milk; scald. Add gelatin soaked in remaining milk to egg mixture. Cool. Add lemon juice, marshmallows, whipped cream, fruits and nuts. Refrigerate for 24 hours before serving. Yield: 15-20 servings.

Mary E. Callahan
Las Vegas, Nev.

CHEESE RING

1 c. milk
2 tbsp. gelatin
2 pkg. cream cheese
1 c. grated yellow American cheese
Dash of salt
1 c. heavy cream, whipped

Heat milk. Dissolve gelatin in cold water; add to hot milk. Mash cream cheese; blend in grated cheese and salt. Fold into gelatin mixture; chill until thickened. Fold in whipped cream; chill until firm. Salad may be used as a base for fruit gelatin salad or served plain with fresh fruit.

Mrs. Harry S. Truman
Wife of former President of the United States

CHEWY GELATIN SALAD

1 pkg. lemon gelatin
½ c. raisins
½ c. pineapple
¼ c. chopped green pepper
1 c. chopped celery

Mix gelatin according to directions on package; cool. Add remaining ingredients. Serve on lettuce.

HONEY DRESSING:
⅔ c. sugar
1 tsp. paprika
1 tsp. dry mustard
¼ tsp. salt
1 tsp. celery salt
⅓ c. strained honey
1 tbsp. lemon juice
5 tbsp. vinegar
1 tbsp. grated onion
1 c. salad oil

Combine sugar and dry seasonings. Add honey, lemon juice, vinegar and onion. Slowly pour in salad oil, beating constantly. Serve over salad. Yield: 8 servings.

Mrs. Kay Murphy
Holloman AFB, N.M.

MOLDED VEGETABLE SALADS

RECIPE FOR MOLDED KIDNEY BEAN SALAD ON PAGE 224

ASPARAGUS OR BROCCOLI MOLD

1 tbsp. unflavored gelatin
¼ c. cold water
1 can asparagus or 1 pkg. frozen broccoli, cooked
½ c. whipped cream
½ c. mayonnaise
1 tsp. salt
2 to 4 tbsp. lemon juice
1 c. almonds

Dissolve gelatin in cold water; let stand until partially set. Drain hot liquid from vegetable; add enough water to make 1 cup liquid. Combine liquid and gelatin mixture. Fold in whipped cream, mayonnaise, salt and lemon juice. Add vegetable and almonds. Congeal. Serve with mayonnaise whipped with a small amount of lemon juice. Yield: 8-10 servings.

Mrs. J. W. Gant
Sparta, Tenn.

ASPARAGUS SALAD

¾ c. sugar
Pinch of salt
½ c. vinegar
1 c. cold water
2 envelopes unflavored gelatin
½ c. hot water
1 c. chopped celery
½ c. chopped toasted pecans
1 can asparagus, cut into bite-sized pieces
1 can pimento, cut into strips
Juice of ½ lemon
1 tbsp. onion, scraped

Combine sugar, salt, vinegar and cold water; bring to a boil. Continue boiling for 5 minutes. Dissolve gelatin in hot water. Remove boiling mixture from heat; add gelatin. Cool. Combine remaining ingredients; add to liquid mixture. Chill until firm.

Mrs. Mary J. Higgins
Marietta, Ga.

CONGEALED ASPARAGUS SALAD

1 box lime gelatin
1 c. boiling water
1 c. mayonnaise
½ c. milk
¼ tsp. salt
½ c. grated cheese
1 tbsp. grated onion
1 tbsp. vinegar
Dash of red pepper or a few drops Tabasco sauce
1 No. 300 can green cut asparagus, drained

Dissolve gelatin in boiling water. Cool until syrupy. Mix mayonnaise, milk, salt, cheese, onion, vinegar and pepper. Fold into thickened gelatin. Add asparagus. Turn into oiled molds. Congeal.

Elizabeth Heard
Jackson, Miss.

JELLIED ASPARAGUS SALAD

¾ c. sugar
1 ½ c. water
½ c. white vinegar
2 pkg. gelatin
Cold water
½ tsp. salt
2 pimentos, chopped
1 sm. can asparagus tips
Juice of ½ lemon
2 tsp. grated onion
1 c. chopped celery

Mix sugar, 1 cup water and vinegar; bring to a boil. Dissolve gelatin in remaining water; add to hot mixture. Cool; add remaining ingredients. Congeal.

DRESSING:
1 c. sour cream
¼ c. lemon juice
2 tbsp. sugar
1 tsp. salt
Cayenne pepper
½ tsp. celery salt (opt.)
½ tsp. paprika (opt.)
1 tsp. dry mustard (opt.)
¼ tsp. garlic salt (opt.)

Combine all ingredients; blend with rotary beater until smooth and thick. Serve with salad. Yield: 6-8 servings.

Jimmie Garvin Harris
Aiken, S.C.

MOLDED KIDNEY BEAN SALAD

2 tbsp. lemon juice
2 tbsp. water
1 envelope unflavored gelatin
1 1-lb. can kidney beans, drained
½ c. chopped celery
½ c. sweet pickle relish
2 hard-cooked eggs, chopped
½ c. mayonnaise
1 tbsp. grated onion
¼ tsp. salt
1 c. evaporated milk

(Continued on next page)

Place lemon juice and water in custard cup. Sprinkle gelatin over top; let stand for 5 minutes to soften. Place custard cup in small saucepan with small amount of water. Place over low heat; heat until gelatin is dissolved. Mix beans with remaining ingredients except milk. Stir in gelatin; blend in evaporated milk. Ladle into 5-cup oiled ring mold. Chill until firm. Yield: 6-8 servings.

Photograph for this recipe on page 223 .

BEET-RASPBERRY SALAD

1 pkg. raspberry gelatin
2 c. cooked shoestring beets
½ c. finely chopped celery

Prepare gelatin according to package directions. Let partially thicken. Add remaining ingredients. Chill. Yield: 6 servings.

Hilma R. Davis
Pittsburg, Kans.

BEET-GELATIN SALAD

1 c. cooked chopped beets
1 pkg. lemon gelatin
1 c. hot water
2 tbsp. vinegar
2 tbsp. finely chopped onion
1 c. chopped celery

Drain beets, reserving 3/4 cup juice. Dissolve gelatin in hot water; add beet juice and vinegar. Chill until partially set. Add remaining ingredients; pour into mold. Chill until firm. Unmold on lettuce; serve with cream cheese dressing or mayonnaise. Yield: 6-8 servings.

Mrs. S. T. Barkman
Berlin, Wisc.

BEET-RASPBERRY SALAD

1 sm. can crushed pineapple
1 c. diced beets
⅛ tsp. salt
⅛ tsp. cinnamon
1 tbsp. vinegar
1 tbsp. sugar
1 pkg. black raspberry gelatin
1 c. hot water

Drain pineapple and beets, reserving juices. Combine pineapple and beet juice; add enough water to make 1 cup liquid. Add salt, cinnamon, vinegar and sugar. Heat liquid; add gelatin. Add hot water; stir until dissolved. Cool until gelatin begins to set; add pineapple and beets. Chill until firm.

Mrs. Mildred von Schausten
Honolulu, Hawaii

BEET-PINEAPPLE SALAD

1 pkg. strawberry gelatin
1 pkg. raspberry gelatin
1 pkg. cherry gelatin
4 c. boiling water
1 No. 303 can julienne beets
1 No. 2 can crushed pineapple
½ c. sweet pickle juice

Dissolve gelatins in boiling water. Drain beets and pineapple. Add 1 1/2 cups of liquid to pickle juice; stir into gelatin. Chill until syrupy. Stir in beets and pineapple. Pour into 3-quart mold. Chill until firm.

DRESSING:
1 c. mayonnaise
1 tbsp. chopped green onion and top
1 tbsp. diced celery
1 tbsp. chopped green pepper
Light cream (opt.)

Combine all ingredients; thin dressing with light cream if too thick. Let stand for several hours to blend flavors. Serve with salad.

Mrs. George W. Fox
Concord, Calif.

BEET-RASPBERRY SALAD

½ c. cider vinegar
⅓ c. sugar
6 to 8 whole cloves
6 to 8 whole allspice
1 pkg. raspberry gelatin
1 can shoestring beets

Boil vinegar, sugar and spices for 2 minutes. Strain. Dissolve gelatin according to package directions, substituting beet liquid for part of the water. Cool. Add beets; chill until firm. Serve on lettuce with mayonnaise. Yield: 6 servings.

Mrs. J. Coulter Qua
Sherrill, N.Y.

BEET SALAD

1 1-lb. can shoestring beets
1 3-oz. pkg. lemon gelatin
¼ c. sugar
¼ c. vinegar
1 tbsp. horseradish

(Continued on next page)

Drain beets; measure stock. Add water to measure 1 1/2 cups liquid; bring to a boil. Remove from heat; stir in gelatin, sugar, vinegar and horseradish. Stir until sugar and gelatin have dissolved; add beets. Turn into 1-quart mold; chill until firm. Yield: 6 servings.

Louise M. Jasken
White Bear Lake, Minn.

BEET SALAD

1 1-lb. can shoestring beets, drained
2 tbsp. vinegar
1 sm. onion, grated
1 tsp. prepared horseradish
½ tsp. celery salt
1 3-oz. pkg. lemon gelatin
1 ½ c. boiling water
1 c. thinly sliced celery

Marinate beets in mixture of vinegar, onion, horseradish and celery salt. Dissolve gelatin in boiling water. Let thicken slightly. Add celery and beet mixture. Turn into individual molds; chill until firm. Serve with mayonnaise seasoned with curry. Yield: 6 servings.

Mrs. Florence Lenox
Big Springs, Tex.

BEET SALAD

1 No. 2 can shoestring beets
1 pkg. lemon gelatin
1 ½ tbsp. vinegar
1 tsp. salt
1 ½ tbsp. grated onion
¼ c. sliced stuffed olives
2 tbsp. horseradish
1 ¼ c. chopped celery
½ c. nuts (opt.)

Drain beets, reserving juice; add enough water to make 1 1/2 cups juice. Heat water-beet juice mixture to boiling; add gelatin. Stir until clear. Add vinegar and salt. Chill until partially set. Stir in remaining ingredients. Pour into mold. Chill until firm. Yield: 6-8 servings.

May Lohmann
Miami, Okla.

BEET SALAD RING

1 No. 2 can diced beets
1 pkg. lemon gelatin
2 c. orange juice
2 tsp. vinegar
1 tbsp. scraped onion
1 tsp. salt
2 tsp. horseradish
1 c. chopped celery
Cottage cheese

Drain beets, reserving 1 cup juice. Add gelatin to boiling beet juice; stir until dissolved. Combine juice, vinegar, onion, salt and horseradish; chill until partially set. Add beets and celery; pour into ring mold. Refrigerate until firm; unmold on lettuce. Garnish with cottage cheese. Yield: 8 servings.

Myrtle Ruppert
McCook, Nebr.

BEET SALAD RING

1 qt. canned diced beets
2 pkg. lemon gelatin
⅓ c. vinegar
1 tsp. grated onion
2 tbsp. grated horseradish
1 c. chopped celery

Drain liquid from beets. Measure liquid; add water to make 3 cups. Heat to boiling. Add lemon gelatin; stir until dissolved. Add vinegar, onion and horseradish. Chill until mixture begins to thicken. Add beets and celery. Pour into 9-inch ring mold or into individual molds. Chill until firm. Unmold on platter; surround with salad greens. Yield: 8 servings.

Mrs. Kenton Broach
Murray, Ky.

CARDINAL BEET SALAD

1 can shoestring beets
1 pkg. lemon gelatin
1 c. boiling water
3 tbsp. white vinegar
2 tbsp. onion juice or grated onion
¾ c. diced celery
½ tsp. salt
2 tbsp. horseradish

Drain beets, reserving 3/4 cup juice. Dissolve gelatin in boiling water; add mixture of beet juice and vinegar. Cool. Add remaining ingredients; pour into mold or square pan. Chill until firm. Yield: 10 servings.

Mrs. Ruth M. Grace
Wallingford, Conn.

JELLIED BEET SALAD

1 1-lb. can julienne beets
1 pkg. raspberry gelatin
2/3 c. orange juice
Salt
2 tbsp. vinegar
2 tsp. grated onion
1 tbsp. horseradish
1/2 c. shredded carrots
1/2 c. finely diced celery

Drain beets, reserving 1 cup juice. Dissolve gelatin in beet juice. Add orange juice, salt, vinegar, onion and horseradish. Cool until slightly thick; add vegetables. Pour into mold. Chill until firm.

LaVergne Wilken
Burlington, Colo.

MOLDED BEET SALAD

1 c. chopped beets
1 tbsp. unflavored gelatin
1/4 c. lemon juice
2 tbsp. sugar
1 c. diced celery
1/4 c. chopped pecans
1/2 tsp. salt
Dash of pepper

Drain beets, reserving 1 cup juice. Soak gelatin in lemon juice for 5 minutes. Dissolve in hot beet juice. Cool. Add remaining ingredients. Chill until firm. Yield: 9 servings.

Mrs. C. F. Hammer
Nashville, Tenn

MOLDED BEET SALAD

1 c. cooked chopped beets
1 pkg. cherry gelatin
1 c. hot water
1/4 c. vinegar
1/2 tsp. salt
1 tbsp. horseradish
1 c. chopped celery
1/2 c. chopped nuts

Drain beets, reserving 3/4 cup juice. Dissolve gelatin in hot water. Add beet juice, vinegar, salt and horseradish. Cool. Add beets, celery and nuts. Place in mold; refrigerate until set. Serve on lettuce; top with mayonnaise, if desired. Yield: 8 servings.

Miss Anna M. Zinn
Clarksburg, W. Va.

BROCCOLI SALAD

1 envelope unflavored gelatin
2 c. hot beef consomme
2 pkg. broccoli, cooked and mashed
4 hard-cooked eggs, chopped
1/2 c. mayonnaise
Dash of Tabasco and Worcestershire sauce

Dissolve gelatin in hot consomme. Cool slightly. Add remaining ingredients. Pour into oiled molds; chill. Yield: 6-8 servings.

Dionetta K. Talley
Demopolis, Ala.

BROCCOLI SALAD

1 pkg. frozen broccoli spears
1 envelope unflavored gelatin
1/4 c. cold water
1 can hot beef consomme
1 c. mayonnaise
6 hard-cooked eggs
1/2 tsp. salt
1 tsp. onion juice
1 tsp. Tabasco sauce
Juice of 1 lemon
1 tsp. Worcestershire sauce

Cook broccoli according to package directions. Cool; cut into small pieces. Soak gelatin in cold water; dissolve in hot consomme. Cool completely. Add remaining ingredients. Pour into individual molds. Chill until firm.

Mrs. Frances E. Poole
Forsyth, Ga.

BROCCOLI SALAD MOLD

3 pkg. frozen broccoli
1 envelope unflavored gelatin
1 can beef consomme
6 hard-cooked eggs, chopped
3/4 c. mayonnaise
2 tbsp. Worcestershire sauce
1/4 tsp. salt
Dash of Tabasco sauce

Cook broccoli for 3 to 5 minutes. Soften gelatin in 1/4 cup cold consomme. Heat remaining consomme to a boil; add gelatin and seasonings. Cool; add remaining ingredients. Grease mold with mayonnaise; fill with salad mixture. Chill. Yield: 8-10 servings.

Mrs. Howard Thomason
Cairo, Ga.

BROCCOLI SALAD MOLD

1 10-oz. pkg. frozen chopped broccoli
1 ½ pkg. unflavored gelatin
¼ c. cold water
2 tbsp. lemon juice
1 tbsp. garlic vinegar
1 10 ½-oz. can beef consomme, heated
⅔ c. mayonnaise

Partially cook broccoli, drain. Cool. Soften gelatin in cold water; add with lemon juice and vinegar to hot consomme. Stir until dissolved; chill until thickened. Beat; add mayonnaise. Beat again; fold in broccoli. Pour into 1-quart mold; chill. Yield: 4-6 servings.

Mrs. Hazel Speake
Albuquerque, N.M.

JELLIED BROCCOLI SALAD

2 tbsp. unflavored gelatin
½ c. cold water
2 c. chicken consomme
1 c. mayonnaise
2 sm. boxes frozen broccoli, cooked and chopped
4 hard-cooked eggs, grated
1 tsp. Worcestershire sauce
Juice of 2 lemons
Cayenne

Soak gelatin in cold water. Heat consomme to boiling; add gelatin, stirring to dissolve. Add mayonnaise; whip. Add remaining ingredients. Chill until firm. Serve on lettuce with mayonnaise. Yield: 12 servings.

Sue Jones
Decatur, Ala.

CABBAGE-BEET SALAD

1 3-oz. pkg. raspberry gelatin
1 ½ c. hot water
1 tbsp. vinegar
2 tsp. prepared horseradish
1 c. finely shredded cabbage
1 c. cooked beets, cut into ¼-in. strips

Dissolve gelatin in hot water. Cool. Add remaining ingredients; refrigerate until firm. Yield: 6 servings.

Minna Farrar
Butte City, Calif.

CABBAGE MOLD

1 pkg. lime gelatin
½ c. drained crushed pineapple
½ c. finely shredded cabbage
1 green pepper, chopped (opt.)
Chopped celery (opt.)
1 tbsp. salad dressing
½ c. shredded Cheddar cheese
½ c. grated carrots

Prepare gelatin as directed on package. Stir in salad dressing. Chill until thickened; add remaining ingredients. Chill until firm.

Mrs. Bessie Hackett
Danvers, Ill.

CABBAGE SALAD

2 c. crushed pineapple
1 12-oz. can evaporated milk
20 marshmallows, quartered
2 tbsp. vinegar
2 pkg. lime or lemon gelatin
1 ½ c. hot water
4 c. finely shredded cabbage
2 c. chopped celery
1 c. salad dressing

Drain pineapple, reserving 1/2 cup juice. Chill evaporated milk overnight. Soak marshmallows in vinegar. Disslove gelatin in water and pineapple juice; cool. Place cabbage, celery, pineapple and marshmallows in large bowl. Pour cool gelatin mixture over cabbage; set aside until mixture begins to thicken. Whip evaporated milk until stiff, gradually adding salad dressing. Fold into cabbage-gelatin mixture. Chill several hours before serving. Yield: 14 servings.

Mrs. Paul E. Gehman
Lititz, Pa.

CABBAGE SLAW

1 tbsp. unflavored gelatin
¼ c. cold water
1 ½ c. sugar
1 c. vinegar
1 tsp. celery seed
1 tsp. salt
¼ tsp. pepper
1 c. salad oil
8 c. shredded cabbage
3 carrots, shredded
1 green pepper, minced
1 sm. onion, grated

Soften gelatin in cold water. Heat sugar and vinegar until sugar is dissolved; add seasonings. Add gelatin; beat in salad oil. Combine vegetables; pour on only enough dressing to moisten. Chill overnight. Yield: 15 servings.

Mrs. Raymond Coe
Kensett, Iowa

CABBAGE SOUFFLE SALAD

1 pkg. lime gelatin
1 c. boiling water
½ c. cold water
2 tbsp. lemon juice or vinegar
½ c. salad dressing
2 c. shredded cabbage
¾ c. crushed pineapple

Dissolve gelatin in boiling water. Add cold water and lemon juice or vinegar. Cool until partially set; beat with a rotary beater until fluffy. Beat in salad dressing. Fold in cabbage and pineapple. Chill until firm. Yield: 8 servings.

Mrs. Phebe G. Walker
Lebanon, N.H.

COLESLAW PARFAIT SALAD

1 pkg. lemon gelatin
1 c. hot water
½ c. mayonnaise
½ c. cold water
2 tbsp. vinegar
¼ tsp. salt
1 ½ c. finely shredded cabbage
½ c. sliced radishes
½ c. diced celery
2 to 4 tbsp. diced green pepper
1 tbsp. diced onion
1 c. cottage cheese (opt.)

Dissolve gelatin in hot water. Blend in mayonnaise, cold water, vinegar and salt. Chill until partially set. Beat until fluffy. Add remainining ingredients. Pour into individual molds or 1-quart mold. Chill until set. Unmold on ruffles of lettuce; garnish with thin slices of radish and mint leaves. Yield: 6-8 servings.

Mrs. Ethel H. Hale
Hackberry, La.

COLESLAW SOUFFLE

1 pkg. lemon or lime gelatin
1 c. hot water
½ c. cold water
2 tbsp. vinegar
½ c. mayonnaise
¼ tsp. salt
Dash of pepper
2 c. chopped cabbage
2 c. chopped green peppers
1 tbsp. chopped onion
¼ tsp. celery seed

Dissolve gelatin in hot water; add cold water, vinegar, mayonnaise, salt and pepper. Blend well; pour into freezing tray. Freeze for 15 to 20 minutes; place in bowl. Whip with beater until fluffy; fold in vegetables and celery seed. Pour into 1-quart mold; chill until firm. Yield: 7-8 servings.

Edith P. Sterling
Fort Scott, Kans.

COOL PERFECTION SALAD

1 ½ c. ginger ale, water or pineapple juice
1 pkg. lemon gelatin
2 tbsp. vinegar
1 tsp. salt
½ c. finely shredded cabbage
½ c. finely cut celery
1 lge. pimento, cut into sm. pieces or 2 tbsp. finely chopped red pepper

Heat 1 cup liquid; add gelatin, stirring until dissolved. Add remaining liquid, vinegar and salt; chill until slightly thickened. Fold in cabbage, celery and pimento. Pour into individual molds; chill until firm. Yield: 4 servings.

Mrs. C. W. Carlson
Cape Charles, Va.

FROSTY MOUNTAIN SALAD

2 pkg. unflavored gelatin
½ c. lemon juice
½ c. lime juice
3 c. hot water
½ c. sugar
2 c. finely shredded cabbage
½ c. finely chopped green pepper
1 c. drained crushed pineapple
2 c. seedless green grapes

Soften gelatin in lime and lemon juice. Dissolve gelatin in hot water; add sugar. Cool until syrupy. Beat until frothy. Add remaining ingredients. Chill until firm. Serve with a fruit dressing. Yield: 8 servings.

Mrs. Gladys M. Dunkle
Ashton, Ill.

GELATIN DELIGHT

1 pkg. lime gelatin
1 c. boiling water
1 c. crushed pineapple
1 c. pineapple juice
1 c. finely shredded cabbage
1 c. finely chopped marshmallows
½ c. chopped nuts
½ pt. heavy cream, whipped

(Continued on next page)

Dissolve gelatin in boiling water. Add remaining ingredients except whipped cream. Chill until partially set. Fold in whipped cream. Chill. Yield: 12 servings.

Mrs. Zelma Goben
Lancaster, Calif.

GELATIN-VEGETABLE SALAD

6 tbsp. sugar
1 tsp. salt
2 pkg. lemon gelatin
3 ¼ c. hot water
4 tbsp. vinegar
2 c. shredded cabbage
½ c. finely chopped celery
½ c. finely chopped green pepper
4 tbsp. chopped sweet pickle

Add sugar and salt to gelatin. Dissolve gelatin in hot water; stir in vinegar. When partially set, add vegetables. Yield: 12 servings.

Mrs. Irena Fossell
Holstein, Iowa

MOLDED CABBAGE SALAD

1 c. crushed pineapple
1 pkg. lime gelatin
1 c. hot water
1 c. marshmallows
1 c. mayonnaise
1 ½ c. shredded cabbage
1 c. heavy cream, whipped
1 c. chopped nuts

Drain pineapple, reserving 2/3 cup juice. Dissolve gelatin in water; add marshmallows. Stir until melted. Add remaining ingredients except whipped cream and nuts; let stand until it begins to set. Fold in whipped cream and nuts; congeal. Yield: 8 servings.

Mrs. B. D. Pace
Hendersonville, N.C.

OLD-FASHIONED COLESLAW

1 pkg. lemon gelatin
1 c. hot water
½ c. cold water
½ tsp. salt
½ c. mayonnaise
½ c. sour cream
1 tsp. grated onion
1 tbsp. prepared mustard
2 tbsp. vinegar
1 tsp. sugar
2 c. finely chopped cabbage

Dissolve gelatin and salt in hot water; add cold water. Chill until syrupy. Fold in remaining ingredients except cabbage. Chill until slightly thickened. Fold in cabbage. Chill until firm.

Louisa Liddell
Lacey, Wash.

PERFECTION SALAD

1 sm. can crushed pineapple
½ c. cold water
1 pkg. unflavored gelatin
½ c. vinegar
1 ½ c. sugar
1 c. chopped sweet pickles
1 sm. jar pimento, chopped
1 c. coarsely chopped nuts
1 c. shredded cabbage

Drain pineapple, reserving juice. Add cold water to pineapple juice to make 1 cup; add gelatin, stirring until dissolved. Dilute vinegar with water; add sugar. Cook until mixture spins a thread. Pour over gelatin; add remaining ingredients. Chill until firm. Yield: 16 servings.

Gladys Telshaw
Guthrie Center, Iowa

PERFECTION SALAD

1 envelope unflavored gelatin
¼ c. cold water
1 c. hot water
¼ c. vinegar
1 tbsp. lemon juice
2 tsp. sugar
½ tsp. salt
1 c. chopped celery
½ c. shredded cabbage
1 pimento, chopped

Soften gelatin in cold water. Stir in hot water, vinegar, lemon juice, sugar and salt. Cool until syrupy. Fold in celery, cabbage and pimento. Spoon into individual salad molds. Chill. Yield: 6 servings.

Mrs. Donald Nix
Seymour, Mo.

TWENTY-FOUR HOUR CABBAGE SALAD

1 envelope unflavored gelatin
¼ c. cold water
1 c. vinegar
½ c. sugar

(Continued on next page)

¼ c. water
1 tsp. salt
1 tsp. celery seed
1 med. cabbage, shredded
1 med. onion, grated
1 green pepper, finely cut
2 lge. carrots, grated
1 c. chopped celery
Cauliflower, broken into pieces

Soften gelatin in cold water. Heat vinegar, sugar, water, salt and celery seed; stir in gelatin. Cool completely. Pour over vegetables. Place in covered container; refrigerate several hours or overnight. NOTE: This salad keeps well for several days. Yield: 8-10 servings.

Mrs. Roy E. Peterson
Wausa, Nebr.

CARROT AND CELERY SALAD

1 envelope unflavored gelatin
¼ c. sugar
½ tsp. salt
1 ½ c. water
¼ c. lemon juice
1 ½ c. grated carrots
¼ c. finely diced celery
¼ c. diced green pepper

Thoroughly mix gelatin, sugar and salt. Add 1/2 cup of water. Stir constantly over low heat until gelatin is dissolved. Remove from heat; stir in remaining water and lemon juice. Chill mixture to unbeaten egg white consistency. Fold in mixed vegetables. Turn into 3-cup mold or individual molds. Chill until firm. Unmold. Garnish with salad greens, scallions and radishes. Yield: 6 servings.

Mattie Mary Green
Neely, Miss.

CARROT DELIGHT SALAD

1 pkg. lime gelatin
2 c. boiling water
1 6-oz. pkg. cream cheese
1 c. grated carrots
½ c. chopped pecans
1 pkg. dessert topping mix, stiffly beaten

Dissolve gelatin in boiling water. Add cream cheese; stir until well mixed. Cool until partially congealed. Fold in carrots and nuts. Fold in whipped dessert topping mix. Chill until firm. Serve on lettuce. Yield: 6 servings.

Mrs. Stella Geiger
Columbus Grove, Ohio

CARROT-GELATIN SALAD

1 pkg. lemon or orange gelatin
1 c. hot water
¼ c. ground carrots
1 8-oz. pkg. cream cheese
1 tsp. vinegar
1 c. cream, whipped
1 sm. can pineapple
½ c. nuts
Salt

Prepare gelatin with hot water and vinegar. Chill until gelatin begins to congeal. Beat until stiff. Add remaining ingredients; chill until firm. Yield: 12 servings.

Mrs. Kenneth Clouser
Harrisburg, Pa.

CARROT MOLD

1 No. 2 can crushed pineapple
1 pkg. lemon gelatin
½ c. sugar
¼ tsp. salt
3 tbsp. lemon juice
1 c. finely grated carrots
½ pt. heavy cream, whipped

Drain pineapple; add enough water to pineapple syrup to make 1 1/2 cups. Heat to a boil. Add gelatin; stir until dissolved. Add sugar, salt and lemon juice. Chill until slightly thickened. Add pineapple and carrots. Fold in whipped cream. Pour into 1 1/2-quart mold; chill until firm.

Mrs. William T. Allen
Brookley AFB, Ala.

CARROT-GELATIN SALAD

1 pkg. unflavored gelatin
1 tbsp. cold water
2 ½ c. boiling water
1 pkg. lemon gelatin
1 pkg. orange gelatin
2 tbsp. vinegar or lemon juice
⅛ tsp. salt
1 c. grated carrots
1 c. finely chopped celery
1 sm. can crushed pineapple, apricots or peaches

Dissolve unflavored gelatin in cold water; add boiling water, lemon and orange gelatins, vinegar and salt. Cool. Add carrots, celery and fruit; mix well. Pour into an oiled ring mold; chill until firm. Yield: 12 servings.

Mrs. Dora L. R. Beyer
Honolulu, Hawaii

CARROT-PINEAPPLE SALAD

1 pkg. orange gelatin
2 c. hot water
1 c. grated carrots
1 c. drained crushed pineapple

Dissolve gelatin in hot water; chill until partially set. Add carrots and pineapple. Chill until firm. Yield: 6-8 servings.

Elizabeth M. Vail
Uriah, Ala.

CARROT SALAD

1 pkg. lemon gelatin
1 c. boiling water
¾ c. cold water
1 tbsp. cider vinegar
1 sm. can crushed pineapple, drained
3 or 4 carrots, grated

Dissolve gelatin in boiling water; add cold water and vinegar. Pour into ring mold; add pineapple. Top with carrots; chill until firm. Serve with dressing.

DRESSING:
¼ c. heavy cream
½ c. mayonnaise
½ c. chopped celery
Mix ingredients. Yield: 8 servings.

Leah E. Durmam
Middletown, R.I.

CARROT SALAD

1 c. diced pineapple
1 pkg. orange gelatin
1 c. warm water
1 c. ground carrots
1 c. ground apples

Drain pineapple, reserving 1 cup juice. Mix gelatin with water and pineapple juice. Chill until thickened; add pineapple, carrots and apples. Chill until firm.

DRESSING:
Evaporated milk
1 pkg. cream cheese
Pinch of salt
1 tbsp. sugar
1 tsp. vanilla flavoring

Add enough milk to cheese to moisten, beating until fluffy. Add salt, sugar and vanilla flavoring; blend well. Spoon dressing over salad. Yield: 8-10 servings.

June B. Marshall
Philadelphia, Pa.

COTTAGE CHEESE-CARROT SALAD

2 pkg. lemon gelatin
1 ½ c. boiling water
½ c. ground green pepper
1 med. ground onion
6 carrots, ground
1 pkg. cottage cheese
1 c. coffee cream or milk
1 c. salad dressing
1 tsp. salt

Dissolve gelatin in boiling water; cool. Add remaining ingredients. Chill.

Mrs. Joan Mattson
Ishpeming, Mich.

EMERALD SALAD

1 pkg. green gelatin
1 c. boiling water
½ c. cold water
3 carrots, grated
½ c. crushed pineapple
1 apple, unpeeled and finely cut
½ c. celery pieces

Dissolve gelatin in boiling water; add cold water. Add remaining ingredients. Pour into oiled mold. Chill until firm. Yield: 8 servings.

Mrs. Clifton E. Whitney
Northfield, Vt.

FOURTEEN CARROT GOLD SALAD

1 pkg. orange gelatin
1 ½ c. hot water
1 ½ tsp. vinegar
½ tsp. salt
Grated onion
1 ½ c. coarsely grated carrots
1 red apple, diced or a few radishes, chopped
¼ c. shredded cabbage
½ sm. can crushed pineapple

Dissolve gelatin in hot water. Add vinegar, salt and small amount of onion. Chill until consistency of unbeaten egg whites. Add remaining ingredients. Pour into oiled 1-quart mold or individual molds. Chill. Serve on greens. Yield: 6 servings.

Mrs. Doris Gustafson
Brethren, Mich.

MOLDED CARROT SALAD

1 pkg. lime gelatin
2 tbsp. lemon juice
1 ½ c. grated carrots
Salad greens
Salad dressing

(Continued on next page)

Dissolve gelatin according to package directions. Add lemon juice; blend. Chill until partially set. Add carrots. Let stand until partially set. Pour into ring mold; chill until firm. Garnish with salad greens. Serve with desired salad dressing. Yield: 8-10 servings.

Mrs. Joyce Miller
Berlin, O.

MOLDED FRUIT 'N' VEGETABLE SALAD

1 pkg. lemon flavored gelatin
1 c. boiling water
1 9-oz. can crushed pineapple
1 c. diced cooked carrots
Lettuce
Mayonnaise

Dissolve gelatin in boiling water. Add pineapple. Cool until thick and syrupy. Add carrots. Pour into one large mold or five individual ones. Chill until firm. Unmold onto lettuce; serve with mayonnaise. Yield: 5 servings.

Mrs. Edith Mahoney
Fort Jay, N.Y.

SUNSHINE SALAD

1 pkg. lemon gelatin
½ tsp. salt
1 ½ c. hot water
1 can crushed pineapple
1 tbsp. lemon juice or vinegar
1 c. grated raw carrots
⅓ c. chopped pecans

Dissolve gelatin and salt in hot water. Add pineapple and lemon juice; chill until slightly thickened. Fold in carrots and nuts. Pour into molds; chill until firm. Yield: 6 servings.

Mrs. Joyce Canada
Bergstrom AFB, Tex.

COOL AS A CUCUMBER SALAD

1 pkg. lime gelatin
¾ c. hot water
¼ c. lemon juice
1 c. chopped cucumbers
1 c. sour cream, whipped
Tomato wedges

Dissolve gelatin in hot water; add lemon juice. Chill until partially set. Add cucumber; fold in sour cream. Pour into oiled molds; chill until firm. Unmold on crisp lettuce. Garnish with tomato wedges. Yield: 6 servings.

Mrs. Jean Wollum
Eagle River, Wisc.

COOL AS A CUCUMBER SALAD

1 pkg. lime gelatin
1 c. boiling water
¾ c. cold water
¼ c. lemon juice
½ c. non-fat dry milk
½ c. sour cream
¼ c. chopped green pepper
2 c. thinly sliced unpeeled cucumber
1 tsp. onion juice (opt.)
⅛ tsp. salt

Dissolve gelatin in boiling water. Add cold water and lemon juice. Chill until mixture begins to thicken. Add dry milk; beat until fluffy. Fold in remaining ingredients. Turn into molds; chill until firm. Yield: 8 servings.

Marie Green
Newton, Ill.

COTTAGE CHEESE RING

CUCUMBER LAYER:
1 pkg. lime gelatin
1 c. boiling water
¼ c. lemon juice
¼ tsp. salt
¼ tsp. dry mustard
⅓ c. instant non-fat dry milk
¼ c. sour cream
¼ c. chopped green pepper
¾ c. chopped cucumber
1 tsp. finely chopped onion

Dissolve gelatin in boiling water. Add lemon juice, salt, mustard and milk; stir well. Chill until firm; beat gelatin mixture for 5 minutes or until light and fluffy. Fold in sour cream. Add pepper, cucumber and onion; mix well. Pour into oiled mold. Chill until firm.

PINEAPPLE LAYER:
1 pkg. lime gelatin
1 c. boiling water
1 c. crushed pineapple
Cottage cheese
Salad greens

Dissolve gelatin in boiling water. Add pineapple; cool. Add to cucumber layer; chill until firm. Garnish with mounds of cottage cheese and salad greens if desired.

Mrs. Nina B. Moore
Sharpsville, Ind.

CREME D'CUCUMBER SALAD

2 c. boiling water
1 lge. pkg. lime gelatin
1 tbsp. vinegar
1 c. mayonnaise
1 c. grated cucumbers
1 tbsp. grated onion
1 tbsp. horseradish

Pour boiling water over gelatin. Add vinegar and a small portion of mayonnaise. Add remaining ingredients. Chill in mold. If desired, cooled gelatin may be whipped before remaining ingredients are added.

Mrs. Renwick W. Speer
DeKalb, Ill.

CUCUMBER MOLD

1 ½ pkg. lemon gelatin
½ c. boiling water
1 tbsp. vinegar
1 pt. cottage cheese
½ c. mayonnaise
1 med. unpeeled cucumber, ground
1 sm. onion, ground
¼ c. heavy cream

Dissolve gelatin in boiling water; add vinegar. Chill until partially set. Add cottage cheese, mayonnaise, cucumber and onion. Add whipped cream. Pour into mold; chill until firm. Yield: 4-6 servings.

Patricia Roppel
Ketchikan, Alaska

CUCUMBER MOLDED SALAD

1 pkg. lime gelatin
½ tsp. salt
1 c. boiling water
1 c. diced cucumbers
¼ c. chopped onion
¾ c. salad dressing
1 c. cottage cheese

Dissolve gelatin and salt in boiling water. Cool until thickened; add remaining ingredients. Pour into molds; chill until firm. Yield: 6 servings.

Opal Pierce
Montebello, Calif.

CUCUMBER RING

1 pkg. lemon gelatin
1 pkg. lime gelatin
2 c. boiling water
½ c. cold water
1 ½ tbsp. vinegar
½ tsp. salt
2 c. seeded, unpared finely chopped cucumbers

Dissolve gelatins in boiling water. Add cold water, vinegar and salt; mix well. Chill until slightly thickened. Stir in cucumbers. Pour into 1 1/4-quart mold. Chill until firm. Yield: 8-10 servings.

Mrs. Charles A. Lattus
Hickman, Ky.

CUCUMBER SALAD

1 pkg. lime gelatin
1 c. hot water
½ c. mayonnaise
1 med. cucumber, grated
1 tbsp. grated onion
1 tbsp. vinegar

Dissolve gelatin in hot water; add remaining ingredients. Mix well. Chill until firm. Yield: 4-6 servings.

Mrs. Marion Carlson
Madrid, Iowa

CUCUMBER SALAD

1 pkg. lime gelatin
¾ c. boiling water
1 lge. cucumber, finely chopped
1 med. onion, finely chopped
1 c. cottage cheese
1 c. mayonnaise
1 tbsp. lemon juice
Chopped pecans or English walnuts (opt.)

Dissolve gelatin in boiling water; chill until syrupy. Whip. Gently add remaining ingredients. Chill until firm. Yield: 10-12 servings.

Mrs. Kathy Hoar
Rapid City, S.D.

CUMBER SALAD

1 pkg. lime gelatin
1 c. boiling water
1 tsp. salt
1 tsp. grated onion
2 tbsp. vinegar
¼ c. chopped celery
¼ c. chopped green pepper
½ c. sour cream
1 c. grated cucumbers
¼ c. mayonnaise

(Continued on next page)

Dissolve gelatin in boiling water; add salt, onion and vinegar. Chill until almost set. Add remaining ingredients; let set until firm. Yield: 6 servings.

Lydia T. Burrows
Salt Lake City, Utah

CUCUMBER SALAD MOLD

1 pkg. lime gelatin
¾ c. hot water
¼ c. lemon juice
1 tsp. onion juice
1 c. sour cream, whipped
1 c. unpeeled finely chopped cucumbers

Dissolve gelatin in hot water; add lemon and onion juices. Chill until partially set; fold in whipped sour cream and cucumbers. Pour into mold; chill until firm. Unmold; garnish with crisp lettuce, curly endive or watercress. Yield: 6 servings.

Mrs. Herbert Hindin
Lakewood, N.J.

DELICIOUS CUCUMBER SALAD

2 pkg. lime gelatin
1 ½ c. hot water
1 ½ c. unpeeled and grated cucumbers
4 tbsp. grated onion
2 c. creamed cottage cheese
2 c. mayonnaise
⅔ c. chopped almonds or pecans

Dissolve gelatin in hot water. Cool; add remaining ingredients. Place in salad mold; chill until firm. Serve on lettuce leaf cup. Yield: 12 servings.

Mrs. Ray Bedsole
Ponce de Leon, Fla.

HAWAIIAN SALAD

1 pkg. lime gelatin
¾ c. hot pineapple juice
½ tsp. minced onion
⅔ c. crushed pineapple
1 c. diced cucumbers
4 tbsp. chopped green pepper
¾ c. mayonnaise

Dissolve gelatin in juice; set aside until partially jelled. Add remaining ingredients, folding in mayonnaise last. Chill; serve on lettuce or endive.

Betty Krell
Menomonee Falls, Wisc.

JELLIED CUCUMBER RING WITH COTTAGE CHEESE

2 pkg. lemon gelatin
1 ½ c. boiling water
¼ c. vinegar
½ tsp. salt
2 tbsp. grated onion
2 ½ c. grated cucumbers
4 c. cottage cheese
1 ½ tsp. chopped chives

Dissolve gelatin in boiling water; add vinegar and salt. Cool; add onion and cucumber. Pour into oiled ring mold; chill until firm. Fill center with cottage cheese seasoned with chopped chives. Garnish with sliced cucumbers and lettuce. Yield: 10-12 servings.

Mrs. H. A. Hoover
Roanoke, Va.

JELLIED CUCUMBER SALAD

1 pkg. lime gelatin
1 c. hot water
1 c. canned grapefruit juice
1 tsp. scraped onion
Dash of salt
1 c. diced cucumbers
½ c. thinly sliced radishes

Dissolve gelatin in hot water. Add grapefruit juice, onion and salt. Chill until slightly thickened. Fold in cucumbers and radishes. Turn into molds. Chill until firm. Unmold onto lettuce. Serve with mayonnaise. Yield: 6 servings.

Dorothy S. Giller
Harbor City, Calif.

MOLDED COTTAGE CHEESE SALAD

1 pkg. lime gelatin
1 c. boiling water
1 ½ c. cold water
1 pkg. unflavored gelatin
1 c. peeled and grated cucumbers
1 tbsp. grated onion
1 c. (heaping) cottage cheese
1 c. mayonnaise

Dissolve lime gelatin in boiling water; add 1 cup cold water. Soften unflavored gelatin in remaining cold water; stir in lime gelatin. Add remaining ingredients; stir well. Chill until firm; serve on lettuce. Yield: 10 servings.

Mrs. Jack W. Rich
Memphis, Tenn.

GREEN GROTTO SALAD

1 ¾ c. boiling water
1 pkg. lime gelatin
Dash of salt
3 tbsp. vinegar
1 c. chopped celery
¼ c. chopped olives
1 c. chopped cucumbers
1 7-oz. can tuna
¾ c. mayonnaise
Lettuce

Pour boiling water over gelatin. Add salt, vinegar, celery and olives. Pour one-half of mixture into mold; chill until firm. Stir cucumber, tuna and mayonnaise into remaining gelatin; pour over firm gelatin. Chill until firm. Unmold on salad greens. Serve with salad dressing or mayonnaise. Yield: 5 servings.

Mrs. Peggy McGuire
Tyndall AFB, Fla.

MOLDED LETTUCE SALAD

1 pkg. lime gelatin
2 c. lukewarm water
2 c. shredded lettuce
½ c. diced radishes
1 tsp. salt
½ tsp. white pepper

Dissolve gelatin in water. Chill until partially set. Fold in remaining ingredients. Refrigerate until set. Yield: 6 servings.

Margaret L. Jones
Armstrong, Ill.

GREEN ONION SALAD

1 pkg. lemon gelatin
1 c. hot water
1 c. cottage cheese
1 c. chopped celery
4 sm. whole green onions, chopped
⅔ c. salad dressing

Dissolve gelatin in hot water; set aside to cool. Combine all ingredients; pour into 9 x 9-inch dish. Chill until firm. Cut into squares; serve on lettuce leaves. Yield: 6 servings.

Ozada Graham
Dodson, Tex.

DILL PICKLE SALAD

1 pkg. lemon gelatin
1 sm. can crushed pineapple, drained
2 tbsp. chopped pimento
¼ c. chopped dill pickle
¼ c. chopped pecans

Prepare gelatin according to package directions. Let set until partially thickened. Add remaining ingredients. Let set until firm. Yield: 8 servings.

Mrs. Dorothy Faulk
Burkburnett, Tex.

PICKLE SALAD

1 tbsp. unflavored gelatin
¼ c. cold water
Hot water
½ c. sugar
¼ c. vinegar
1 can crushed pineapple
2 lge. pickles, finely chopped
1 jar pimento, chopped

Soak gelatin in cold water; add hot water to make 1 cup. Stir until dissolved. Add sugar, vinegar and pineapple. Cool; add pickles and pimento. Refrigerate.

Mrs. C. L. Allen
Axtell, Tex.

WALES SALAD

1 pkg. lemon gelatin
1 c. hot water
2 tbsp. vinegar
½ c. chopped nuts
½ c. chopped pimento
½ c. chopped olives
4 sweet pickles, chopped
1 c. heavy cream, whipped

Mix gelatin, water and vinegar; let stand until partially set. Fold in remaining ingredients. Chill until firm. Yield: 8 servings.

Mrs. Effie Reid
Milton-Freewater, Oreg.

ASHEVILLE SALAD

1 pkg. unflavored gelatin
½ c. cold water
1 can tomato soup
½ c. plus 2 tbsp. milk
Dash of red pepper
Dash of Worcestershire sauce
Salt to taste
1 c. chopped celery, nuts, green peppers or olives
1 tsp. finely chopped onion or onion juice

Soak gelatin in cold water. Combine and heat tomato soup and 1/2 cup milk. Add gelatin;

stir until dissolved. Add seasonings; chill slightly. Soften cheese with remaining milk; beat until fluffy. Stir into gelatin mixture; fold in remaining ingredients. Chill in mold until firm. NOTE: Chopped celery, nuts, green pepper or olives may be used in any combination to make one cup. Yield: 8 servings.

Mrs. Virginia D. Webb
Gordonsville, Va.

ASHEVILLE SALAD

1 tbsp. unflavored gelatin
½ c. water
1 can tomato soup
1 sm. pkg. cream cheese
1 c. chopped celery
1 lge. green pepper, chopped
½ c. mayonnaise

Dissolve gelatin in water; pour into hot soup. Mash cheese into soup; stir to dissolve. Add celery, green pepper and mayonnaise. Chill until firm. Yield: 6 servings.

Jean Palmer
Channelview, Tex.

JELLIED TOMATO-CHEESE SALAD

1 can tomato soup
3 3-oz. pkg. cream cheese
2 tbsp. unflavored gelatin
½ c. cold water
1 c. mayonnaise
1 c. chopped celery
¼ c. chopped green or red pepper
1 tbsp. minced onion
½ tsp. salt
Dash of cayenne pepper
Dash of black pepper

Heat soup to boiling; remove from heat. Add cheese; beat until blended. Soak gelatin in cold water for 5 minutes. Dissolve in hot soup mixture. Cool, but do not let mixture thicken. Stir in mayonnaise, vegetables and seasonings. Pour into mold. Chill until firm.

Mrs. Walter Edwards
Tulia, Tex.

JELLIED TOMATO SALAD

1 1-lb. can tomatoes
1 pkg. lemon gelatin
½ tsp. salt
½ tsp. dried onion flakes
½ tsp. dried parsley
Salad greens
Mayonnaise

Bring tomatoes to a boil; break larger pieces while heating. Add gelatin and seasonings, stirring constantly. Pour into large mold or six individual molds. Chill until firm; unmold. Serve on salad greens; garnish with mayonnaise. Yield: 6 servings.

Mrs. Eleanor J. Hayes
Alton, N.H.

JELLIED TOMATO SURPRISE

1 pkg. lemon gelatin
1 c. boiling water
1 can tomato soup or 1 c. tomato juice
1 sm. bottle olives, chopped
1 3-oz. pkg. cream cheese, cubed
3 or 4 stalks celery, finely diced
Few drops onion juice

Dissolve gelatin in boiling water; add tomato soup or juice. Cool until mixture is consistency of egg whites. Add olives, cream cheese, celery and onion juice. Spoon into individual molds or ring mold. Chill until firm. Yield: 8 servings.

Dorothy F. Kingsbury
Keene, N.H.

JELLIED TOMATO-VEGETABLE SALAD

1 envelope lemon gelatin
½ c. boiling water
1 No. 303 can stewed tomatoes
1 sm. onion, chopped
½ c. diced green pepper
2 tbsp. vinegar
½ tsp. salt

Dissolve gelatin in boiling water; add tomatoes. Chill until partially thickened. Fold in remaining ingredients; pour into 8 x 8 x 2-inch pan. Chill until firm. Yield: 6 servings.

Nancy Jo Kent
Dodge City, Kans.

ASPIC

1 tbsp. unflavored gelatin
2 tbsp. cold water
2 tbsp. hot water
1 can tomato soup
2 c. tomato juice
1 tsp. salt
2 tbsp. lemon juice
3 tbsp. chopped onion
2 tbsp. chopped celery
1 pkg. lemon gelatin

Soak unflavored gelatin in 2 tablespoons cold water; dissolve in 2 tablespoons hot water. Add tomato soup. Heat tomato juice; add lemon juice, onion and celery. Simmer for 10 minutes; dissolve lemon gelatin in mixture. Pour into ring mold; chill. Unmold onto bed of lettuce. Yield: 8 servings.

Mrs. Norman A. Button
Ft. Thomas, Ky.

EASY TOMATO ASPIC

1 envelope unflavored gelatin
1 ¾ c. tomato juice
¼ tsp. salt
½ tsp. sugar
½ tsp. Worcestershire sauce
⅛ tsp. Tabasco sauce
2 tbsp. lemon or lime juice

Sprinkle gelatin onto 1/2 cup tomato juice in saucepan to soften. Place over low heat until gelatin is dissolved, stirring constantly. Remove from heat; add remaining tomato juice, salt, sugar, Worcestershire sauce, Tabasco sauce and lemon juice. Pour into 2-cup mold or individual molds. Chill until firm; unmold onto platter. Garnish with avocado slices and salad greens. Yield: 4 servings.

Photograph for this recipe above.

LAYERED ASPIC RING

2 tbsp. gelatin
½ c. cold water
1 c. tomato juice
1 can tomato paste
2 tsp. grated onion
1 tsp. sugar
¼ tsp. paprika
½ c. light cream
2 c. cottage cheese

Dissolve 1 tablespoon gelatin in 1/4 cup cold water over boiling water. Combine with tomato juice, tomato paste, 1 teaspoon grated onion and sugar; stir well. Pour into 1-quart ring mold; chill until firm. Dissolve remaining gelatin in 1/4 cup cold water over boiling water. Combine with remaining ingredients; mix thoroughly. Pour over first layer in ring mold; chill until firm. Unmold onto lettuce; serve with small bowl of mayonnaise in center of mold. Yield: 10 servings.

Mrs. William H. Wetsel
Locust Dale, Va.

TOMATO ASPIC

1 envelope unflavored gelatin
1 ¾ c. tomato juice
¼ tsp. salt
½ tsp. sugar
½ tsp. Worcestershire sauce
⅛ tsp. Tabasco sauce
2 tbsp. lemon juice

Sprinkle gelatin into 1/2 cup tomato juice to soften. Place over low heat, stirring until gelatin dissolves. Remove from heat; stir in remaining tomato juice and seasonings. Turn into 2-cup mold or individual molds. Chill until firm. Unmold onto serving plate.

(Continued on next page)

Garnish with salad greens, cucumber slices and black olives. Serve with salad dressing. Yield: 4 servings.

Mrs. Clara B. Williams
Madisonville, Ky.

TOMATO ASPIC

3 ¾ c. tomato juice
2 cloves
1 bay leaf
1 sm. onion, chopped
Celery tops
Salt to taste
2 tbsp. vinegar
1 pkg. lemon gelatin
1 pkg. strawberry gelatin

Heat 2 cups tomato juice with remaining ingredients except gelatin. Strain; pour over gelatin powder, stirring to dissolve. Add remaining tomato juice. Pour into oiled mold; chill. Yield: 8-10 servings.

Mildred B. Ford
Glen Falls, N.Y.

TOMATO ASPIC

1 tbsp. unflavored gelatin
½ c. cold water
⅓ c. sugar
1 tsp. salt
1 10 ½-oz. can tomato soup
1 tbsp. tarragon vinegar
1 tbsp. vinegar
2 tbsp. lemon juice
¼ tsp. celery salt
1 c. chopped sweet pickles
1 c. sliced stuffed olives
1 sm. onion, grated
1 sm. green pepper, chopped
1 cucumber, finely chopped
½ c. chopped pecans

Soften gelatin in coldwater for 5 minutes. Add sugar and salt to soup; bring to boil. Add gelatin; stir until dissolved. Add vinegars, lemon juice and celery salt; stir until mixed. Chill until thickened. Add remaining ingredients. Pour into mold. Chill overnight.

Lela A. Tomlinson
Baton Rouge, La.

TOMATO ASPIC

1 pkg. lemon gelatin
1 c. hot water
1 8-oz. can tomato sauce
Dash of onion salt
Dash of celery salt
1 tsp. lemon juice
1 sm. can shrimp
½ c. sliced stuffed olives
½ c. chopped green pepper

Dissolve gelatin in hot water. Cool; add remaining ingredients. Pour into mold. Chill until firm. Yield: 6 servings.

Mrs. Henry Peach
Marshall, Okla.

TOMATO ASPIC

2 pkg. lemon gelatin
2 ½ c. boiling water
1 envelope unflavored gelatin
1 tbsp. cold water
1 can tomato paste
2 cans tomato sauce

Dissolve lemon gelatin in boiling water. Soften unflavored gelatin in coldwater; add to first mixture. Stir in tomato paste. Add tomato sauce; stir. Chill until firm. Yield: 8-10 servings.

Mrs. Blanche H. Wilt
Somerset, Pa.

TOMATO ASPIC ON SLAW

1 pkg. lemon gelatin
1 ¼ c. hot water
1 8-oz. can tomato paste
2 tbsp. vinegar
½ tsp. salt
Dash of pepper
Dash of celery seed

Dissolve gelatin in hot water. Add remaining ingredients. Pour into molds; chill until firm.

DRESSING:
1 egg
½ c. water
¼ tsp. mustard
1 tsp. sugar
1 tbsp. vinegar
Dash of salt
Dash of pepper
Dash of celery seed
3 c. shredded green cabbage

Mix all ingredients except cabbage; cook until thick. Cool. Mix cabbage with dressing. Make a nest of slaw on each salad plate; fill nest with aspic mold. Yield: 6 servings.

Mary Lynch Chesnutt
Knoxville, Tenn.

TOMATO CHIFFON SALAD

2 tbsp. unflavored gelatin
2 ¼ c. tomato juice
3 tbsp. chopped onion
3 tbsp. chopped green pepper
1 bay leaf
½ tsp. celery salt
½ c. instant non-fat dry milk powder
½ c. water
2 tbsp. lemon juice
Salad greens
Cottage cheese (opt.)

Soften gelatin in 1/2 cup tomato juice. Combine remaining tomato juice, onion, green pepper, bay leaf and celery salt in saucepan. Simmer for 10 minutes; remove bay leaf. Add gelatin; stir until dissolved. Cool until mixture reaches the consistency of jelly. Sprinkle non-fat milk powder over water; beat until stiff. Blend in lemon juice. Fold milk mixture into tomato mixture. Pour into mold rinsed with cold water. Chill until firm. Unmold onto salad greens; serve with cottage cheese, if desired. Yield: 6-8 servings.

Janet R. Stark
Blooming Prairie, Minn.

TOMATO AND CREAM CHEESE SALAD

1 pkg. lemon gelatin
1 c. boiling water
1 can tomato soup
3 3-oz. pkg. cream cheese
1 c. mayonnaise
1 c. diced celery
1 sm. onion, diced
1 green pepper, diced
2 cans shrimp
1 c. peas, drained

Dissolve gelatin in boiling water; cool to consistency of unbeaten egg whites. Heat soup until simmering. Remove from heat; beat in cream cheese. Cool; add mayonnaise. Combine all ingredients. Place in molds; chill. Yield: 12 servings.

Mrs. Mark Cochran
Passaic, N.J.

TOMATO RING MOLD

1 tbsp. unflavored gelatin
¼ c. cold water
1 c. hot tomato juice
¼ c. sugar
½ tsp. salt
¼ c. vinegar
1 tbsp. lemon juice
1 tbsp. finely chopped onion
½ c. finely chopped cabbage
½ c. finely chopped celery
3 tbsp. finely chopped green pepper

Soften gelatin in water. Add hot tomato juice, sugar and salt. Stir until dissolved. Add vinegar and lemon juice. Chill until partially congealed; fold in vegetables. Pour into oiled mold; chill until firm.

Mrs. Myrtle W. Reeve
Riverhead, Long Island, N.Y.

TOMATO SALAD

1 sm. can tomato soup
1 soup can water
2 pkg. lemon gelatin
2 3-oz. pkg. cream cheese
1 c. salad dressing
1 c. diced celery
2 tbsp. diced green pepper
1 tsp. minced onion
½ c. chopped walnuts

Heat soup and water; stir in gelatin, cream cheese and salad dressing. Heat until dissolved. Chill; add celery, green pepper, onion and walnuts. Yield: 8 servings.

Margaret Geraghty
Manhattan, Kans.

TOMATO SOUP SALAD

1 can tomato soup
2 pkg. cream cheese
2 tbsp. unflavored gelatin
¼ c. cold water
Pinch of salt
½ c. mayonnaise
1 c. chopped celery
1 c. chopped green pepper
1 sm. onion, chopped
1 cucumber, chopped
1 c. chopped nuts

Heat soup. Beat in cream cheese. Soften gelatin in cold water; beat into hot soup mixture. Cool. Add remaining ingredients. Turn into desired mold; chill until firm. Yield: 10 servings.

Mrs. Miller Kemp
McKeesport, Pa.

TOMATO SOUP SALAD

1 can tomato soup
2 tbsp. unflavored gelatin
⅔ c. cold water
1 8-oz. pkg. cream cheese, crumbled
1 c. mayonnaise
½ c. chopped celery
½ c. chopped green pepper

(Continued on next page)

Soak gelatin in water. Heat soup; add cheese and gelatin. Beat until smooth. Cool. Add remaining ingredients. Pour into mold; chill until firm. Yield: 6 servings.

Mrs. Raye L. Evers
McGregor, Tex.

TOMATO SOUP SALAD

1 pkg. lemon gelatin
1 can tomato soup, heated
1 3-oz. pkg. cream cheese
1 c. water
¾ c. chopped celery
¼ c. chopped onion
¼ c. chopped green pepper
½ c. chopped nuts
½ c. mayonnaise

Dissolve gelatin in hot soup. Add remaining ingredients. Chill. Yield: 8-10 servings.

Mrs. Glen Wuester
Beattie, Kans.

TOMATO SOUP SALAD

2 tbsp. unflavored gelatin
½ c. cold water
1 can tomato soup
2 pkg. cream cheese
1 c. chopped celery
1 c. chopped nuts
1 c. mayonnaise
1 can shrimp
Sliced stuffed olives (opt.)

Soak gelatin in cold water. Heat tomato soup. Add cream cheese; stir until smooth. Add softened gelatin. Remove from heat; stir in remaining ingredients. Chill until firm. Yield: 6 servings.

Mrs. Rush Valentine
Starkville, Miss.

TOMATO-VEGETABLE ASPIC

1 envelope unflavored gelatin
¼ c. cold tomato juice
1 tbsp. grated onion
1 tsp. salt
1 ¾ c. boiling tomato juice
¾ c. finely shredded cabbage
¼ c. chopped celery

Soften gelatin in cold tomato juice. Add gelatin, onion and salt to boiling tomato juice; stir. Chill until slightly thickened. Fold in cabbage and celery. Chill until firm. Yield: 5-6 servings.

Mrs. Frances Chappell
Apel, N.C.

V-8 ASPIC

1 can V-8 juice
1 pkg. lemon gelatin
2 tbsp. vinegar
½ c. diced celery and onion

Heat 1 cup V-8 juice; add gelatin, stirring until dissolved. Add remaining V-8 juice and vinegar. Chill until mixture begins to thicken; add celery and onion. Chill in mold until firm. Yield: 6-8 servings.

Mrs. C. B. Harris
Front Royal, Va.

ZIPPY TOMATO-CHEESE MOLD

2 envelopes unflavored gelatin
½ c. cold water
1 pkg. cream cheese
1 can tomato soup
1 c. mayonnaise
1 tsp. horseradish
1 ½ c. chopped celery
½ c. chopped pepper
½ c. diced onion

Soften gelatin in cold water. Combine with cheese and soup. Simmer over low heat until gelatin is dissolved. Remove from heat; cool. Stir in mayonnaise, horseradish, celery, green pepper and onion. Chill until firm. Yield: 8 servings.

Mrs. Virginia Watson
Albion, Nebr.

CELERY-PEPPER CONGEALED SALAD

1 pkg. lemon gelatin
1 c. hot water
1 c. mayonnaise
1 c. cottage cheese
Pinch of salt
1 c. chopped celery
2 tbsp. finely chopped onion
¼ c. chopped green pepper
Green food coloring (opt.)
Chopped pimento (opt.)

Dissolve gelatin in hot water. Let cool. Stir in mayonnaise, cottage cheese and salt. Add remaining ingredients. Let set for several hours. Yield: 6-8 servings.

Virginia L. Langston
Baton Rouge, La.

CONGEALED ONION SALAD

1 c. hot water
1 pkg. lemon-lime gelatin
1 c. ground celery
1 c. ground onions
1 c. sieved cottage cheese
1 c. mayonnaise

(Continued on next page)

Add hot water to gelatin; cool. Add remaining ingredients; chill.

Mrs. Wiley Breeding
Whitesburg, Tenn.

COOL AS A CUCUMBER SALAD

1 tbsp. unflavored gelatin
½ c. cold water
½ tsp. salt
3 c. cream-style cottage cheese
1 8-oz. pkg. cream cheese
1 med. cucumber, pared, seeded and grated
½ sm. onion, finely grated
½ c. mayonnaise
⅔ c. finely chopped celery
⅓ c. broken nuts, toasted

Soften gelatin in water; add salt. Stir over low heat until gelatin dissolves. Combine cheeses; beat until blended. Stir in gelatin. Add remaining ingredients. Pour into 6-cup ring mold. Chill until firm. Yield: 8-10 servings.

Mrs. Billy Marks
Pulaski, Tenn.

CORNFLOWER SALAD

2 No. 2 cans cream corn
1 tsp. grated onion
1 tsp. salt
Pepper to taste
2 tbsp. sugar
3 envelopes unflavored gelatin
½ c. water
6 cooked carrots
6 med. green peppers

Blend corn, onion, salt, pepper and sugar. Soften gelatin in water; dissolve over hot water. Add to corn mixture. Put a piece of carrot into each hollowed out pepper; fill with corn mixture. Set peppers in muffin pan to steady them while chilling. Slice; serve on salad greens with dressing. Yield: 10 servings.

Opal Pruitt
Buda, Ill.

COTTAGE CHEESE-VEGETABLE RING

2 envelopes unflavored gelatin
½ c. cold water
1 ½ c. creamed cottage cheese
1 ¼ c. salad dressing or mayonnaise
¾ c. whipped cream
2 tbsp. chopped parsley
2 tbsp. chopped pimento
2 tbsp. chopped onion
1 tbsp. lemon juice
½ tsp. Worcestershire sauce
Dash of Tabasco sauce
½ tsp. monosodium glutamate
Salt to taste

Sprinkle gelatin over cold water; dissolve over hot water. Cool slightly. Combine cottage cheese and salad dressing. Stir in dissolved gelatin. Fold in whipped cream. Add remaining ingredients. Turn into oiled 5-cup ring mold. Chill until firm. Unmold onto large platter.

VEGETABLE SALAD MEDLEY:
½ c. salad oil
2 tbsp. vinegar
½ tsp. garlic salt
Dash of Tabasco sauce
½ tsp. paprika
2 1-lb. cans mixed vegetables or 2 12-oz. pkg. frozen mixed vegetables, cooked and cooled

Combine salad oil, vinegar, garlic salt, Tabasco sauce and paprika. Beat with rotary beater. Pour over mixed vegetables. Chill. Fill center of mold with vegetables. Yield: 8 servings.

Mrs. Buford N. Irwin
Knoxville, Tenn.

COTTAGE CHEESE-VEGETABLE SALAD

1 pkg. lime gelatin
1 ½ c. boiling water
⅓ c. carrots, shredded
¼ c. chopped pepper
1 tbsp. minced onion
½ c. chopped celery
1 c. dry cottage cheese
½ c. crushed pineapple
½ tsp. salt
¼ c. heavy cream, whipped
½ c. salad dressing

Dissolve gelatin in boiling water; chill until partially set. Add vegetables, cottage cheese, pineapple and salt. Blend cream and salad dressing together; add to gelatin mixture. Chill. Yield: 6 servings.

Shirley Nasset
Regent, N.D.

CUCUMBER-CABBAGE SALAD

1 pkg. lime gelatin
1 c. hot water
½ c. mayonnaise
1 c. finely chopped cabbage

(Continued on next page)

½ c. finely chopped cucumber
2 tbsp. chopped green pepper
½ tsp. celery seed
2 to 4 tbsp. finely chopped onion

Dissolve gelatin in hot water; cool. Whip in mayonnaise. Add remaining ingredients. Chill until firm. Yield: 8 servings.

Janice Brown
Flagler, Colo.

GELATIN WHIP SALAD

1 pkg. lemon gelatin
2 c. boiling water
¾ c. Velveeta cheese
¾ c. finely chopped celery
¾ c. grated carrots
6 lge. marshmallows, chopped
Chopped Maraschino cherries (opt.)
2 c. heavy cream, whipped

Dissolve gelatin in boiling water. Add cheese to hot water; cool. Combine all ingredients except cream; chill until thickened. Fold in whipped cream; chill until firm.

Dorathea Sperling
Empire, Oreg.

GARDEN COTTAGE CHEESE MOLD

1 tbsp. unflavored gelatin
1 c. milk
⅔ c. French dressing
1 12-oz. carton cottage cheese
½ c. chopped celery
¼ c. green pepper strips
¼ c. thin radish slices
¼ c. shredded carrot
¼ c. shaved or thinly sliced cucumber
2 tbsp. minced onion

Soften gelatin in 1/4 cup cold milk. Heat remaining milk to lukewarm. Dissolve gelatin over hot water in saucepan or top of double boiler. Add gelatin to warm milk. Stir in French dressing and cottage cheese. Cool mixture until thickened. Fold in vegetables; pour into well oiled 1-quart ring mold. Chill until firm. Unmold on crisp lettuce; garnish with relishes. Serve plain or with salad dressing. Yield: 4-6 servings.

Anita June Story
Pikeville, Tenn.

MOLDED GARDEN SALAD

2 pkg. lemon gelatin
2 tbsp. lemon juice
½ c. finely sliced green onions
¾ c. diced cucumbers
½ c. thinly sliced radishes
½ c. thinly sliced celery
½ c. uncooked cauliflowerets
1 tsp. salt

Prepare gelatin according to package directions. Chill until partially set. Add remaining ingredients. Chill until firm. Yield: 4-6 servings.

Anne Cole
Livingston, Ky.

GELATIN SLAW

1 pkg. orange or lime gelatin
1 c. shredded cabbage
1 med. onion, finely chopped
2 carrots, shredded
8 to 10 radishes, finely sliced
⅓ cucumber, finely sliced
⅛ tsp. salt
⅛ tsp. garlic salt
⅛ tsp. celery salt or seed
Dash of pepper

Mix gelatin according to package directions; refrigerate. Mix all vegetables; add seasonings. Stir vegetable mixture into gelatin; chill until firm. Yield: 8 servings.

Mrs. Lillian J. Thompson
Moody AFB, Ga.

MOLDED RELISH SALAD

1 pkg. lime gelatin
1 pkg. lemon gelatin
3 c. boiling water
1 c. chopped celery
½ to 1 c. chopped nuts
1 green pepper, chopped
4 tbsp. chili sauce
4 tbsp. India relish
1 sm. bottle olives, chopped
1 sm. can pimento, chopped
Pinch of salt

Dissolve gelatins in boiling water. Chill until partially set. Combine remaining ingredients; fold into gelatin mixture. Chill until firm.

Virginia C. Lee
Memphis, Tenn.

JELLIED VEGETABLE LOAF

2 envelopes unflavored gelatin
3 c. water
½ c. sugar
½ tsp. salt
½ c. lemon juice
½ c. sliced radishes
½ c. grated carrots
2 c. finely shredded cabbage
½ c. diced green pepper

Sprinkle gelatin into 1 cup water in saucepan. Place over medium heat until gelatin is dissolved, stirring constantly. Remove from heat; add sugar and salt, stirring until sugar is dissolved. Stir in remaining water and lemon juice. Chill until mixture is slightly thickened; fold in remaining ingredients. Turn into 9 x 5 x 3-inch loaf pan; chill until firm. Unmold; serve with cucumber sauce.

CUCUMBER SAUCE:
⅓ c. mayonnaise or sour cream
⅔ c. finely diced cucumbers
¼ tsp. salt
⅛ tsp. Tabasco sauce

Mix all ingredients; serve with vegetable loaf. Yield: 8 servings.

Photograph for this recipe above.

MOLDED SALAD

1 pkg. lime gelatin
½ c. boiling water
½ c. salad dressing
½ c. evaporated milk
1 tbsp. chopped celery
2 tbsp. chopped green pepper
3 tbsp. shredded carrot
1 tbsp. grated onion
¼ tsp. salt
½ lb. cottage cheese or 1 pkg. cream cheese

Stir gelatin into boiling water until dissolved. Add remaining ingredients; pour into baking dish or mold. Chill thoroughly. Cut into slices and serve on lettuce. Yield: 8 servings.

Mrs. Arline MacDonald
Athol, Mass.

MOLDED VEGETABLE SALAD

1 pkg. lime gelatin
1 c. hot water
1 carrot, grated
1 green pepper, chopped
1 sm. onion, chopped
1 sm. cucumber, chopped (opt.)
1 c. diced celery
½ c. salad dressing
1 pt. cottage cheese
Salt to taste

(Continued on next page)

Dissolve gelatin in hot water. Add carrot, pepper, onion, cucumber and celery. Fold in salad dressing, cottage cheese and salt to taste. Pour into mold; chill until firm.

Mrs. H. E. Anderson
Newport, R.I.

NEAPOLITAN VEGETABLE SALAD

2 pkg. lemon gelatin
4 c. hot water
3 tbsp. vinegar
3 tsp. salt
1 ½ c. finely chopped carrots
1 ¾ c. finely chopped cabbage
1 tsp. minced onion
1 ½ c. finely chopped spinach

Dissolve gelatin in hot water; add vinegar and salt. Divide gelatin into three parts. Chill each part until partially thickened. Add carrots to one part of gelatin. Chill until firm. Combine cabbage and another part of gelatin. Pour over first layer. Chill until firm. Add onion and spinach to remaining gelatin. Pour over firmly chilled mixture. Chill until firm. Yield: 12 servings.

Pauline K. Fish
Pittsburgh, Pa.

PRIZE TOMATO-CHEESE SALAD

1 can tomato soup
3 sm. pkg. cream cheese
2 tbsp. unflavored gelatin
½ c. cold water
1 c. mayonnaise
¼ c. chopped onion
¼ c. chopped pimento
¼ c. chopped green pepper
¾ c. chopped celery

Bring tomato soup to a boil; add cheese. Beat with rotary beater until smooth. Soften gelatin in cold water; add to hot tomato-cheese mixture. Cool. Add remaining ingredients. Chill until firm. Yield: 10 servings.

Marguerite Goldsworthy
Sarasota, Fla.

SOUFFLE SALAD

1 pkg. lime gelatin
1 c. boiling water
½ c. cold water
2 tbsp. vinegar
½ c. mayonnaise
Salt
Pepper
1 ½ c. chopped celery and cabbage
1 tbsp. finely chopped onion
1 tsp. finely chopped cucumber
½ c. finely chopped green and ripe olives
½ c. tuna
Shredded lettuce

Dissolve gelatin in boiling water. Add cold water, vinegar, mayonnaise, salt and pepper. Mix well; chill until partially set. Turn mixture into bowl; whip until fluffy. Fold in vegetables, olives and tuna. Mix well; pour into mold. Chill. Serve on lettuce. Yield: 7 servings.

Margie Samson
Ovid, Colo.

SPRING SALAD

1 pkg. lime gelatin
1 c. boiling water
½ c. chopped green pepper
½ c. diced celery
3 tbsp. chopped onion
1 c. cottage cheese
½ c. mayonnaise

Dissolve gelatin in water; chill until partially set. Add remaining ingredients; stir until blended. Chill until firm. Serve on lettuce leaf. Yield: 6 servings.

Mrs. M. U. Burton
Falls City, Nebr.

SUNSET AND SOUR SALAD

1 pkg. lime gelatin
1 c. hot water
1 c. cottage cheese
½ c. mayonnaise
½ c. celery
½ c. chopped green pepper
½ c. chopped onion

Dissolve gelatin in hot water. Let set until partially congealed. Add remaining ingredients. Pour into molds rinsed with cold water. Let set until firm. Yield: 10 servings.

Earle H. Vallentine
Cordova, S.C.

TASTY SALAD

1 pkg. lemon gelatin
2 c. hot water
1 carton cottage cheese
1 c. salad dressing
1 c. diced celery
¼ c. diced green pepper
1 tbsp. grated onion

Dissolve gelatin in water. Cool slightly. Add remaining ingredients; mix. Pour into mold; chill. Yield: 8 servings.

Mrs. Marvin Bergstrom
Courtland, Kans.

TOMATO-ASPARAGUS SALAD

2 c. canned tomatoes or tomato juice
1 tsp. salt
Dash of pepper
1 sm. bay leaf
3 whole cloves
3 tbsp. minced onion
1 pkg. lemon gelatin
1 tbsp. vinegar
2 tbsp. cold water
1 ¼ c. cottage cheese
2 tbsp. minced green pepper
½ c. diced celery
1 c. cooked asparagus, cooled
Salt to taste
⅓ c. mayonnaise or salad dressing

Combine tomatoes or juice, salt, pepper, bay leaf, cloves and onion. Cook gently for 20 minutes. Remove bay leaf after 10 minutes of cooking. Force mixture through sieve. Measure; add hot water to make 1 1/2 cups. Dissolve gelatin in hot tomato mixture. Add vinegar. Measure 1/2 cup mixture; add cold water. Turn into ring mold or individual molds. Chill until firm. Chill remaining gelatin mixture until slightly thickened. Combine cottage cheese with remaining ingredients; fold into thickened gelatin mixture. Turn into mold over firm gelatin layer. Chill until firm. Unmold onto crisp lettuce. Yield: 8 servings.

Mrs. Virginia Vance
Central Lake, Mich.

VEGETABLE-GELATIN SALAD

2 pkg. lemon gelatin
1 c. boiling water
2 c. canned tomatoes
2 c. peas and carrots
¼ c. sour cream
¼ c. mayonnaise

Dissolve gelatin in water. Beat or cut tomatoes until shredded. Add to gelatin. Stir in peas and carrots. Chill until firm. Combine cream and mayonnaise. Serve with salad. NOTE: Diced cucumbers and celery may be substituted for peas and carrots. Yield:8 servings.

Mrs. Jessie Walther
Eugene, Oreg.

VEGETABLE SOUFFLE SALAD

1 pkg. lime gelatin
1 c. hot water
½ c. cold water
4 tsp. vinegar
½ c. mayonnaise
¼ tsp. salt
Dash of pepper
1 c. shredded carrots
1 c. shredded cabbage
¼ c. finely diced cucumber
1 tbsp. finely chopped onion

Dissolve gelatin in hot water. Add cold water, vinegar, mayonnaise, salt and pepper. Blend well with rotary beater. Pour into refrigerator tray. Chill in freezer for 15 to 20 minutes or until mixture is firm around edges but soft in center. Turn mixture into bowl; whip with rotary beater until fluffy. Fold in vegetables. Pour into 1-quart mold or individual molds. Chill until firm in refrigerator for 30 minutes. Unmold; garnish with salad greens. Yield: 4-6 servings.

Hazel Edberg
Denair, Calif.

GARDEN CHEESE SALAD

1 pkg. lemon gelatin
2 c. hot water
Salt and pepper
2 sm. tomatoes, peeled and chopped
1 sm. bunch green onions and tops, finely chopped
½ c. minced celery
1 carrot, grated
3 or 4 radishes, chopped
¾ c. left-over peas
1 ½ pkg. cream cheese

Dissolve gelatin in hot water; cool. Season vegetables with salt and pepper; add to gelatin. Chill until slightly thickened. Season cream cheese; roll into six balls. Pour part of thickened gelatin into six individual molds. Place a cheese ball in each. Cover with more gelatin mixture. Chill until firm. Yield: 6 servings.

Mrs. Ellen L. Canon
McClellandtown, Pa.

RECIPE FOR CALYPSO SALAD ON PAGE 250

ARTICHOKE-GRAPEFRUIT SALAD

1 head crisp green lettuce
1 bunch endive
1 can artichoke hearts
2 onions, sliced and separated into rings
2 grapefruit, sectioned
Garlic French dressing or Roquefort dressing

Make a nest of lettuce and endive. Place artichoke hearts, onion rings and grapefruit sections on nest. Season with dressing. Yield: 6 servings.

Monna S. Ray
Alexandria, Va.

STUFFED ARTICHOKE SALAD

2 c. cooked cubed chicken
¼ c. finely diced celery
1 6-oz. can water chestnuts, cut into strips
¾ c. tart mayonnaise
4 artichokes
1 tbsp. salt
2 tbsp. salad oil
½ lemon, cut up
1 clove of garlic
12 stuffed olives
1 tbsp. capers

Mix chicken, celery, water chestnuts and mayonnaise. Toss lightly with a fork. Refrigerate for several hours. Cut stems from artichokes. Cook about 1 hour in boiling water with salt, oil, lemon and garlic. Drain; cool and refrigerate for several hours. Carefully spread leafy spines of cooled artichokes from tip so the inner leaves can be removed. Use a spoon to remove the heart. Fill cavity with chilled chicken salad. Garnish with olives and sprinkle with capers. Yield: 4 servings.

Margaret Lopp
Chandler, Ariz.

ASPARAGUS-RADISH SALAD

3 tbsp. olive oil
1 tbsp. vinegar
1 tsp. salt
Freshly ground pepper
1 sm. clove of garlic, crushed
20 to 25 radishes, thinly sliced
Green asparagus, cooked and chilled
Salad greens

Mix oil, vinegar, salt, pepper and garlic. Add radishes; marinate for 2 to 3 hours. Place asparagus on salad greens. Arrange the radishes on top. Pour remaining marinade over radishes. Yield: 4 servings.

Mrs. Aussie A. Miller
Newton, Tex.

CHILLED ASPARAGUS LEMONETTE

1 med. onion, finely chopped
2 tbsp. lemon juice
¼ c. water
½ c. Sauterne
⅛ tsp. garlic salt
½ tsp. dried salad herbs
2 tbsp. salad oil
¾ tsp. salt
2 lb. fresh asparagus, cooked

Blend all ingredients except asparagus well. Pour over asparagus. Cover; refrigerate for several hours. Drain; serve on crisp salad greens. May be garnished with pimento strips.

Mrs. Marlys Garman
Lake Geneva, Wisc.

AVOCADO SALAD

2 tbsp. finely chopped dill pickle
2 tbsp. finely chopped sour pickle
¼ c. chopped onion
1 hot green chili pepper, seeded and chopped
1 tomato, diced
2 ripe avocados, diced
Dash of salt
2 tbsp. mayonnaise
Shredded lettuce
Sliced stuffed olives

Combine pickles and onion. Blend in pepper. Add tomato, avocados and salt. Toss lightly with mayonnaise. Serve on lettuce. Garnish with olives. Yield: 6 servings.

Mrs. Homer D. Shurbet
Katy, Tex.

AVOCADO SALAD SUPREME

1 lge. avocado
¼ lb. cheese, grated
1 sm. onion, finely chopped
1 canned green chili pepper
1 tbsp. mayonnaise
1 tbsp. vinegar
Dash of sugar
1 tsp. salt

Cream avocado. Add remaining ingredients; mix. Serve on lettuce.

Mrs. Leda Callahan
El Paso, Tex.

AVOCADO SALAD MONTEREY

2 avocados, halved lengthwise
Lemon juice
6 c. bite-sized salad greens
1 tomato, cut into wedges
1 3-oz. pkg. cream cheese, cut into ½-in. cubes
1 c. sliced cooked zucchini
2 green chili peppers, sliced
¼ c. salad oil
2 tbsp. vinegar
1 tbsp. finely chopped onion
1 tsp. salt
⅛ tsp. seasoned pepper
¼ tsp. chili powder
¼ tsp. sugar

Remove avocado seed; skin. Slice lengthwise again; sprinkle with lemon juice. Line salad bowl with greens. Arrange avocados, tomato, cheese, zucchini and peppers over greens. Combine remaining ingredients, beating or shaking well to blend. Pour over salad. Toss lightly just before serving. NOTE: One cup well-drained canned "pear" tomatoes and 1 cup cut Blue Lake green beans may be substituted for tomato and zucchini. Yield: 8 servings.

Photograph for this recipe above.

BEAN SALAD

1 lge. can whole green beans
1 lge. can cut wax beans
1 lge. can kidney beans
1 onion, minced
1 green pepper, diced
1 sm. can pimento
1 c. (scant) sugar
½ c. salad oil
⅔ c. white vinegar
¾ tsp. salt

Drain beans; add all remaining ingredients. Marinate salad for at least 12 hours. Yield: 6-8 servings.

Mrs. Bette Demmerle
Schilling AFB, Kans.

CHILLED BEAN SALAD

1 can red kidney beans
1 can yellow wax beans
1 can green beans
½ c. minced green pepper
½ c. minced celery
½ c. minced onion
½ c. sugar
1 tsp. salt
½ c. vinegar
½ c. salad oil

(Continued on next page)

Drain beans well; toss together with green pepper, celery and onion. Combine sugar, salt, vinegar and salad oil; pour over beans and toss well. Refrigerate for several hours before serving. Yield: 8 servings.

Mrs. Joan C. Pribble
McConnell AFB, Kans.

CALYPSO SALAD

1 1-lb. can cut Blue Lake green beans, drained
1 1-lb. 1-oz. can kidney beans, drained
1 c. sliced celery
½ c. chopped green pepper
¼ c. minced parsley
1 qt. torn iceberg lettuce
½ c. sliced onion rings

Combine all ingredients; toss lightly with dressing.

BASIL VINEGAR DRESSING:
¼ c. basil wine vinegar
2 tbsp. salad oil
⅛ tsp. garlic powder
¼ tsp. fines herbes
¼ tsp. salt

Combine all ingredients in jar with cover; shake to blend well. Pour over calypso salad. Yield: 6-8 servings.

Photograph for this recipe on page 247.

AVOCADO SALAD

3 cans red kidney beans, drained
1 lge. onion, chopped
1 c. salad oil
¼ c. red wine vinegar
1 tsp. salt
½ tsp. dry mustard
½ tsp. coarsely ground black pepper
½ tsp. sugar
3 or 4 cloves of garlic

Combine beans and onion. Blend salad oil, vinegar, salt and seasonings; pour over beans and mix well. Place each garlic clove on a toothpick; bury in beans. Cover tightly; marinate in refrigerator for a day or two for best flavor. Remove garlic before serving. Yield: 8-10 servings.

Mrs. Gloria Maylott
Tachikawa, Japan

COMBINATION BEAN SALAD

1 lge. can green beans
1 lge. can lima beans
1 lge. can kidney beans
1 lge. can yellow wax beans
1 lge. can chick peas
1 med. onion, chopped
1 celery heart, finely cut
1 c. cider vinegar
1 c. sugar
1 tbsp. salad oil
Salt to taste

Drain beans. Combine in large bowl with all remaining ingredients. Cover; marinate in cool place for 24 hours. Yield: 8-10 servings.

Mrs. Emelia Wilcox
Norfolk, Va.

ECONOMICAL PORK AND BEAN SALAD

1 lge. can pork and beans, drained and chilled
2 med. tomatoes, diced
½ green sweet pepper, diced
½ med. onion, diced
½ c. salad dressing

Combine beans, tomatoes, pepper and onion; add salad dressing. Chill for 1 hour. Yield: 8-10 servings.

Mrs. Margaret Ann Durham
Hereford, Tex.

GREEN BEANS BRAVO

1 No. 303 can cut green beans, drained
½ tsp. garlic salt
¼ tsp. dry mustard
2 tbsp. olive oil
1 ½ tbsp. cider vinegar
½ c. sliced celery
¼ c. sliced radishes
2 oz. dry salami
4 lettuce leaves
1 hard-cooked egg, sliced
2 green onions, sliced

Toss beans well with garlic salt, mustard, olive oil and vinegar; chill for several hours or overnight. Add celery and radishes. Arrange salami, lettuce, egg and onions in center. Yield: 6 servings.

Mrs. Mary Rosario
Oakland, Calif.

GREEN BEAN PARMESAN

2 lb. green beans
¼ c. minced onion
1 tsp. salt
½ c. salad oil
¼ c. wine vinegar
¼ tsp. pepper
½ c. grated Parmesan cheese
Lettuce cups
Radish slices

Wash beans; cut off ends. Cut into halves lengthwise. Cover; cook in 1-inch deep boiling salted water until tender. Drain; cool. Toss with onion, salt, oil, vinegar, pepper and cheese. Cover; chill thoroughly, stirring occasionally. Serve in lettuce cups; garnish with radish slices. Yield: 8-10 servings.

Swanie Smoot
Madison, W. Va.

GREEN BEAN SALAD

1 can green beans
½ c. mayonnaise
¼ c. minced onion
1 hard-cooked egg, chopped
1 to 2 tbsp. pickle relish
Salt and pepper

Cut beans into bite-sized pieces. Combine mayonnaise, onion, egg and relish; pour over beans. Mix thoroughly; season to taste. NOTE: Salad keeps well when refrigerated. Yield: 4-6 servings.

Mrs. Edna B. Mosteller
Waco, Tex.

HEARTY BEAN SALAD

1 No. 2 can garbanzo beans, drained
1 No. 2 can red kidney beans, rinsed and drained
1 No. 2 can French-cut beans, drained
1 c. diced celery
½ c. diced green pepper
¼ c. chopped green onions
1 c. French dressing

Lightly toss ingredients. Refrigerate for several hours before serving. Yield: 15 servings.

Ethel C. Glenn
Durango, Colo.

LIMA-DILL SALAD

1 pkg. frozen baby lima beans
2 tbsp. chopped parsley
½ c. chopped celery
¼ c. mayonnaise
1 tbsp. vinegar
1 tbsp. grated onion
½ tsp. whole dill seed
½ tsp. salt
¼ tsp. pepper

Cook limas until just tender. Drain and chill. Add parsley and celery. Mix together mayonnaise, vinegar, onion, dill seed, salt and pepper. Pour over bean mixture. Toss until well mixed. Serve in lettuce-lined bowl. Yield: 4-5 servings.

Wilma Garrity
North Vernon, Ind.

PATIO SALAD

1 28-oz. can pork and beans
1 c. chopped celery
1 c. thinly sliced cucumber
½ c. chopped green pepper
1 tbsp. vinegar
1 tsp. salt
Dash of pepper

Lightly mix all ingredients; chill. Serve on crisp greens. Yield: 6-8 servings.

Mrs. Pat Fortier
Fort Fisher, N.C.

PORK AND BEAN SALAD

1 sm. onion
1 lge. green pepper
1 lge. cucumber
½ c. celery
1 tsp. salt
½ tsp. pepper
1 can pork and beans, chilled

Chop onion, green pepper, cucumber and celery together; add salt and pepper. Stir in pork and beans. Prepare 30 minutes before serving. Yield: 6 servings.

Mrs. Ruby Quesenberry
Pulaski, Va.

PROSPERTY SALAD

2 No. 2 cans kidney beans, drained
1 c. salad oil
¼ c. wine vinegar
1 clove of garlic

(Continued on next page)

¼ c. thinly sliced onion
½ tsp. salt
Freshly ground pepper to taste

Combine all ingredients. Mix thoroughly. Refrigerate. Remove garlic bud from salad after two days. For improved flavor, store at least two days or as long as two weeks before serving. Yield: 8 servings.

Mrs. Georgia Waters Scott
Clarksville, Tex.

RED BEAN SALAD

1 c. diced celery
⅔ c. diced green peppers
⅔ c. diced onions
⅔ c. sweet pickle relish
⅔ c. green tomato relish
1 No. 300 can red kidney beans, washed and drained
⅔ c. Italian dressing

Combine all ingredients except dressing. Pour dressing over salad. Cover; marinate in refrigerator for several hours. Yield: 8-10 servings.

Mrs. Wilson Duncan
Rock Hill, S.C.

TANGY BEAN SALAD

2 cans pinto or kidney beans, drained
¼ c. mayonnaise
¼ c. tomato sauce
2 tbsp. mustard
¼ tsp. salt
¼ tsp. garlic salt
2 to 3 tsp. chili powder
¼ c. finely chopped onion
¼ c. finely chopped green pepper
3 hard-cooked eggs, diced
¼ lge. head lettuce

Combine all ingredients in large bowl and serve. Lettuce may be omitted and salad served on lettuce leaves. Yield: 6 servings.

Mrs. Helen Jo Jackson
Adak, Alaska

TEXAS CAVIAR

2 No. 2 cans black-eyed peas, drained
⅓ c. peanut oil
⅓ c. wine vinegar
1 clove of garlic
¼ c. finely chopped onion
½ tsp. salt
Cracked pepper

Place peas in bowl with remaing ingredients; store in refrigerator for 24 hours. Remove garlic; store for two days to two weeks before serving. Yield: 6-8 servings.

Mrs. Rachel Pearce
Fort Worth, Tex.

TRIPLE BEAN SALAD PIQUANT

1 1-lb. can wax beans, drained
1 1-lb. can green beans, drained
1 1-lb. can large kidney beans, drained
½ c. sliced celery
1 med. green pepper, cut into thin rings
1 med. onion, thinly sliced and separated
½ c. sugar
½ c. salad oil
¾ c. cider vinegar

Toss beans, celery, green pepper and onion in large bowl. Thoroughly blend sugar, oil and vinegar. Pour over vegetables; toss with a fork to coat evenly. Cover and refrigerate for at least 8 hours, tossing several times. Serve chilled. Yield: 8 servings.

Mrs. Eileen Christensen
Vandenberg AFB, Calif.

VEGETABLE OIL SALAD

1 8-oz. can cut green beans
1 8-oz. can yellow beans
1 8-oz. can lima beans
1 8-oz. can kidney beans
1 bunch celery, chopped
1 sm. onion, chopped
1 green pepper, chopped
1 can pimento
Water
¼ c. salt
1½ c. sugar
1 c. cider vinegar
½ c. vegetable oil

Drain beans in collander. Cover beans, celery, onion, pepper and pimento with cold water and salt. Let stand for 2 hours; rinse. Combine all remaining ingredients; pour over all. Mix well and serve. NOTE: Salad keeps well in refrigerator. Yield: 12-15 servings.

Mrs. LaVern Gough
Charleston, S.C.

WINTER'S SUPPER SALAD

2 10-oz. pkg. frozen lima beans
1 med. onion, chopped
2 stalks celery, sliced
6 slices bacon, cut into pieces
¼ c. wine vinegar
¼ tsp. pepper
½ lb. salami, cut into thin strips
1 8-oz. pkg. Swiss cheese, sliced
½ c. pitted ripe olives, halved
3 med. carrots, coarsely grated
3 sweet onion slices, separated into rings
Few romaine leaves
½ tsp. salt
Paprika
Salad oil and vinegar

Cook lima beans; drain. Place in salad bowl; add onion and celery. Saute bacon until crisp. Mix 1/4 cup bacon drippings with 1/4 cup wine vinegar and pepper. Pour over lima beans in bowl. Add bacon; toss lightly. Arrange salami, cheese, olives and carrots in separate piles on top; place onion rings in middle. Edge salad bowl with romaine. Sprinkle salt and paprika over all. Toss lightly. Add a little oil and vinegar, if needed. Yield: 6 servings.

Eloise W. Hadden
Auburn, Ky.

ZIPPY RED BEAN SALAD

1 1-lb. can red kidney beans, drained
6 slices bacon, cooked and crumbled
1 c. diced celery
½ c. diced dill pickles
2 hard-cooked eggs, diced
⅓ c. mayonnaise
2 tbsp. lemon juice
1 tbsp. minced onion
Salt and pepper to taste

Combine beans, bacon, celery, pickles and eggs in large bowl. Blend mayonnaise with lemon juice, onion, salt and pepper; pour over salad and toss lightly. Cover and chill thoroughly. Serve in lettuce lined bowl. Yield: 6 servings.

Mrs. Gladys Petterson
Chandler AFS, Minn.

BEET BORSCH

6 lge. fresh or canned beets
Water
3 tbsp. lemon juice
¼ c. sugar
1 tsp. salt
2 egg yolks
1 c. sour cream

Peel and grate or cut beets into shreds. Cook beets in 3 pints water in saucepan until tender. Add lemon juice, sugar and salt; simmer for 5 to 15 minutes longer. Beat egg yolks with 1 tablespoon cold water; gradually add hot beet mixture, stirring constantly. Chill thoroughly. Beat sour cream into mixture before serving. Yield: 6 servings.

Rebecca Fader
Shelbyville, Ind.

BEET AND ONION SALAD

Salad oil
Tarragon vinegar
1 No. 303 can sliced beets
5 pearl onions, sliced
Whole cloves (opt.)
Lettuce leaves
Chopped parsley
1 hard-cooked egg, chopped

Mix 3 parts salad oil and 1 part vinegar; toss beets and onions with oil-vinegar mixture. Add cloves if desired; drain mixture. Serve on lettuce leaves. Garnish with parsley and egg. Yield: 4 servings.

Mrs. Beverlee Williams
Campbell, Calif.

FLORIDIAN SALAD

1 1-lb. can julienne beets, drained
French dressing
Coleslaw
1 1-lb. can Florida grapefruit sections, drained

Marinate beets in French dressing. Arrange about two-thirds of the beets around edge of a salad bowl. Then make a row of coleslaw inside beets leaving center free for remaining beets. Arrange grapefruit sections on beets in center. Yield: 6 servings.

Photograph for this recipe on page 94.

BROCCOLI VINAIGRETTE

2 10-oz. pkg. frozen chopped broccoli
1 bottle Italian salad dressing
2 hard-cooked eggs, chopped
1 2-oz. jar pimento, chopped
8 black olives, chopped

(Continued on next page)

Cook broccoli according to package directions; drain and chill. Moisten broccoli with Italian dressing and garnish with combined eggs, pimento and olives just before serving. Yield: 6 servings.

Dorothy L. Anderson
Princeton, Minn.

CABBAGE AND APPLE SALAD

2 c. shredded cabbage
1 c. tart apples, cut into strips
¼ c. mayonnaise
Salt to taste
Lemon juice (opt.)
1 tsp. sugar (opt.)

Combine cabbage with apples. Add mayonnaise, salt, lemon juice and sugar. Yield: 5 servings.

Mrs. Verna L. Price
Duncanville, Tex.

CABBAGE-BANANA SALAD

5 tbsp. salad dressing
¼ tsp. salt
2 tbsp. pineapple juice
2½ c. finely shredded cabbage
½ c. diced banana
¼ c. cut up salted peanuts

Combine salad dressing, salt and pineapple juice. Pour over combined remaining ingredients. Toss lightly to mix.

Terri Reasor
Huntington, Va.

CABBAGE COLESLAW

¼ c. sugar
¼ c. vinegar
¼ c. salad dressing
¼ c. milk
Salt and pepper to taste
1 med. cabbage or 4 c. shredded cabbage

Combine sugar, vinegar, salad dressing, milk, salt and pepper in a jar. Cover and shake until well blended. Pour over shredded cabbage; mix well. Chill for 1 hour before serving. Yield: 6 servings.

Mrs. Leila J. Sylfest
Antigo AFS, Wisc.

CABBAGE SALAD

1 onion, finely chopped
1 cabbage, finely cut
½ c. sugar

Combine onion, cabbage and sugar.

DRESSING:
1 tbsp. sugar
½ tsp. salt
½ tsp. dry mustard
½ tsp. celery seed
⅓ c. oil
½ c. vinegar

Combine all dressing ingredients; bring to a boil. Pour over cabbage mixture. Refrigerate for 4 hours. Yield: 6-10 servings.

Mrs. Richard W. Hanes
Lambertville, Mich.

COLESLAW

½ c. sour cream
2 tbsp. sugar
2 tbsp. vinegar
1 tsp. salt
¼ tsp. pepper
4 c. shredded cabbage
½ c. chopped onion
2 tsp. celery seed

Blend sour cream, sugar, vinegar, salt and pepper. Combine all remaining ingredients; cover with sour cream mixture. May be sprinkled with paprika; chill before serving. Yield: 4-6 servings.

Mrs. Abbie Turnage
Boron AFS, Calif.

COOKED SLAW

1 med. cabbage, shredded
2 lge. onions, chopped (opt.)
1 can pimento, chopped
¾ c. sugar
½ c. vinegar
2 eggs, beaten
2 tbsp. flour
1 tsp. salt
1 tsp. turmeric
1 tsp. celery seed

Combine all ingredients; mix well. Bring to a boil; simmer for 10 minutes, stirring constantly. Yield: 12 servings.

Mrs. W. H. Capps
Maysville, Ky.

CREAM COLESLAW

4 c. shredded cabbage
½ c. finely sliced celery
¼ c. finely sliced green pepper
¼ c. finely sliced sweet red pepper or carrots
2 tbsp. finely sliced green onion
¾ c. sour cream
3 tbsp. vinegar
3 tbsp. sugar
1 tsp. salt
⅛ tsp. white pepper
1 tbsp. celery seed

Combine cabbage, celery, peppers and onion. Combine remaining ingredients; pour over cabbage mixture. Mix lightly. Yield: 6 servings.

Charlotte B. Love
Bells, Tenn.

CROCK SALAD

1 lge. cabbage, chopped
2 lge. carrots, chopped
Chopped celery
Chopped onion
1 red or green pepper, chopped
1 tbsp. salt
1 gal. water
2 c. vinegar
2 c. sugar
2 tbsp. celery seed
2 tbsp. white mustard seed

Combine vegetables. Dissolve salt in water; pour over vegetables. Refrigerate overnight. Heat vinegar and sugar until syrupy; add celery seed and mustard seed. Cool; pour over well drained vegetables. Will keep several days refrigerated.

Sue Junkins
Rosebud Circle, Iowa

HOT VEGETABLE SALAD

½ cabbage
1 green pepper
1 sm. bunch green onions
8 to 10 red radishes
4 or 5 carrots
1 tbsp. cooking oil

Slice all vegetables into long thin strips. Place in hot oil; cook over low heat until thoroughly heated. Do not saute. Vegetables should be tender yet crisp. Serve hot. Yield: 4-6 servings.

Carolyn Belanger
Tomball, Tex.

INDIAN COLESLAW

¼ c. mayonnaise
¼ c. sour cream
¾ tsp. salt
Dash of pepper
4 c. shredded cabbage
1 8-oz. can whole kernel corn, drained
¼ c. chopped green pepper
¼ c. chopped pimento

Combine mayonnaise, sour cream, salt and pepper. Pour over combined vegetables; toss lightly. Yield: 6-8 servings.

Mary J. Delich
Bethel, Kans.

NINE-DAY SLAW

1 qt. grated cabbage
3 med. onions, grated
2 green peppers, grated
1 ½ c. vinegar
1 ½ c. sugar
1 tsp. salt
½ tsp. celery seed
2 tsp. dry mustard
½ tsp. turmeric

Combine cabbage, onions and green peppers. Mix remaining ingredients; bring to a boil. Pour over cabbage mixture. Chill. Will keep for several days. Yield: 20 servings.

Pearl D. Oliver
Bradford, Tenn.

NON-WILT SLAW

1 med. cabbage, shredded
⅔ c. chopped celery
⅔ c. grated carrots
1 lge. onion, shredded
1 med. green pepper, chopped
½ c. honey
⅔ c. salad oil
1 c. white vinegar
2 tsp. salt
2 tbsp. sugar

Combine cabbage, celery, carrots, onion and green pepper. Mix remaining ingredients; bring to boil. Pour dressing over slaw while very hot; do not stir until cold. Let set until cool; refrigerate. Slaw will stay crisp for three or four days. Yield: 20 servings.

Inez Wells
Greenville, Ky.

PENNSYLVANIA DUTCH PEPPER CABBAGE

1 med. green pepper, finely chopped
1 med. cabbage, finely shredded
3 stalks celery, finely chopped
½ tsp. salt
½ c. sugar
½ c. apple cider vinegar
½ c. water

Mix vegetables. Combine remaining ingredients; pour over vegetables. Refrigerate. Yield: 12-14 servings.

Mrs. William M. Powell
Folsom, Pa.

PEPPER-CABBAGE SLAW

4 c. finely chopped cabbage
1 c. chopped celery
1 tsp. salt
½ c. sugar
½ c. vinegar
1 lge. pepper, chopped

Combine all ingredients. Chill at least 30 minutes before serving. Yield: 6-8 servings.

Mrs. Doris Weidemann
York, Pa.

SKILLET SALAD

4 slices bacon
¼ c. vinegar
1 tbsp. brown sugar
1 tsp. salt
1 tbsp. finely chopped onion
4 c. shredded cabbage
½ c. chopped parsley

Fry bacon until crisp; remove from skillet. Combine vinegar, sugar, salt and onion in bacon fat; add crumbled bacon. Heat thoroughly; toss cabbage and parsley in hot dressing. Yield: 4 servings.

Mrs. William D. Morris
Wadeville, N.C.

SUPPER SALAD

6 c. shredded cabbage
1 green mango, finely cut
1 red mango, finely cut
1 c. white vinegar
2 c. sugar
1 tsp. celery seed
1 tsp. salt
Horseradish to taste

Mix all ingredients; let stand overnight. Yield: 10 servings.

Mrs. A. Herb Baker
North Baltimore, O.

WINTER SALAD

4 qt. sliced cabbage
2 qt. sliced green tomatoes
6 lge. onions, sliced
6 red peppers, cut into thin strips
2 tbsp. mustard seed
1 tsp. turmeric
1 tbsp. celery seed
1 ¾ lb. sugar
⅓ c. salt
2 qt. vinegar

Combine ingredients; mix well. Let stand for 1 hour; simmer for 30 minutes. Store in sealed sterilized jars. Chill before serving. Use in place of fresh salad. Yield: 12 servings.

Esther Steiger
Mercersburg, Pa.

CARROT SALAD

1 c. flaked coconut
1 ½ c. shredded carrots
¼ c. seedless raisins
2 tbsp. lemon juice
½ tsp. ground ginger
¼ c. mayonnaise
Mandarin orange sections, drained

Combine all ingredients; mix well. Chill. Serve on crisp lettuce with additional mayonnaise. Garnish with orange sections if desired. Yield: 4-5 servings.

Sandra M. Cuchna
LaFarge, Wisc.

CARROT-COCONUT SALAD

¼ c. mayonnaise
2 tbsp. sour cream
1 ½ c. shredded carrots
½ c. flaked coconut
2 tbsp. lemon or orange juice
Mandarin orange sections, drained

Blend mayonnaise and sour cream. Combine all ingredients; mix well. Serve on crisp lettuce. Garnish with additional coconut and orange sections. Yield: 4 servings.

Bertha C. Stefan
Prophetstown, Ill.

The elegant avocado is now within reach of all. Rich and creamy, it adapts itself to spreads, soups, salads, and many other uses. Guacamole from Mexico is a favorite. Serve it with Mexican dishes for a very special meal.

GUACAMOLE

6 large avocados, chopped
2 med. onions, peeled and chopped
2 med. tomatoes, peeled and chopped (opt.)
2 tbsp. olive oil
2 tsp. vinegar
4 tsp. salt

Mix all ingredients until creamy. If made in advance, be sure to store in a cool place with the avocado seeds placed in the mixture to prevent its darkening. Remove seeds before serving. Serve on lettuce in cups or on lettuce leaves. Yield: 16 servings.

See photograph on reverse side.

CARROT CONCOCTION

⅓ c. raisins
1 ½ c. grated carrots
½ c. crushed pineapple, drained
¼ c. salted peanuts
½ c. cooked salad dressing
½ tsp. prepared mustard
1 tbsp. sugar
2 tbsp. sweet cream

Soak raisins in water until plump. Mix raisins, carrots, pineapple and peanuts together. Refrigerate for 1 hour. Combine dressing, mustard, sugar and cream. Whip until smooth. Combine salad and dressing about 15 minutes before serving. Yield: 6 servings.

Catherine Nelson
Jeffers, Minn.

CARROT AND LEMON SALAD

2 c. grated carrots
¼ c. sugar
Juice of 1 lemon

Mix ingredients; let stand for 1 hour. Serve on lettuce. Yield: 4 servings.

Mrs. Nettie Waller
Deer River, Minn.

CARROT-RAISIN SALAD

1 ½ c. shredded carrots
½ c. seedless raisins
1 ½ c. diced oranges
Mayonnaise

Toss carrots, raisins and orange pieces together; moisten with mayonnaise. Serve on lettuce. Yield: 6 servings.

Mrs. Jimmie Cain
Thrall, Tex.

CARROT SALAD

4 med. carrots, scraped and grated
2 tart apples, peeled and coarsely grated
½ c. white raisins
¼ tsp. salt
Pineapple (opt.)
4 tbsp. mayonnaise

Combine carrots and apples. Add raisins, salt and pineapple, if desired. Mix in mayonnaise. Chill. Yield: 6 servings.

Mrs. Nina T. Smith
Picayune, Miss.

CARROT SALAD MEAL

3 lge. carrots, shredded
4 strips bacon, cooked and diced
3 hard-cooked eggs
¼ c. salad dressing
¼ tsp. salt
½ c. grated cheese
¼ tsp. pepper

Combine all ingredients; mix thoroughly. Serve on lettuce. Yield: 4 servings.

Mildred Ellis
Newport News, Va.

LUNCHEON SALAD

6 fresh carrots, washed and scraped
6 hard-cooked eggs
1 c. pecans
1 sm. onion
Salt to taste
Mayonnaise
6 soda crackers, crumbled
6 lettuce leaves

Put carrots, eggs, pecans and onion through food chopper using medium blade. Combine ground ingredients with salt and enough mayonnaise to hold mixture together in salad bowl. Add crackers just before serving. Serve on lettuce leaves. NOTE: Egg yolks may be mashed instead of ground. Yield: 6 servings.

Mrs. Georgia M. Grissom
Cincinnati, O.

VITAMIN CARROT SALAD

2 c. grated carrots
2 tbsp. lemon juice
1 c. diced celery
¼ c. finely chopped nuts
Salad dressing

Lightly toss all ingredients with salad dressing. Chill. Serve on salad greens.

Mrs. Carolyn W. Yeatts
Farmville, Va.

GOOD CAULIFLOWER SALAD

¼ c. minced green onions
½ c. minced celery leaves
1 c. sour cream
½ c. French dressing
2 tsp. caraway seed (opt.)
Salt to taste
1 cauliflower, diced

Combine onions, celery leaves, sour cream, French dressing, caraway seed and salt.

(Continued on next page)

Dip cauliflower tidbits into dressing. Yield: 8 servings.

Mrs. Dwight R. Mann
Levelland, Tex.

COLIFLOR ACAPULCO

1 lge. cauliflower
French or desired sharp oil dressing
Iceberg lettuce
1 lge. cucumber, sliced
1 sm. can pickled beets, drained and sliced
Parsley
Radish roses
1 lge. avocado, mashed
1 tbsp. chopped onion
1 tbsp. chopped cashew nuts
Dash of salt, pepper and nutmeg
1 sm. jar stuffed olives
1 can garbanzo beans
1 sm. can pimento

Cook cauliflower in salted boiling water for about 10 minutes or until just tender. Drain and slightly loosen the flowerets at the base. Place cauliflower in a deep dish; pour dressing over the top. Chill for several hours. Place drained cauliflower head on lettuce-lined tray. Arrange cucumber and beet slices around base of cauliflower, tucking parsley and radish roses between base of cauliflower and vegetable slices. When ready to serve, mash avocado; add onion, nuts, seasonings and enough of the dressing to make a paste. Top cauliflower with mixture. Using toothpicks, make several skewers of olives, garbanzo beans and pimento to garnish top of cauliflower. NOTE: Do not mash avocado until ready to serve.

Photograph for this recipe on front cover.

BUFFET SALAD

1 sm. cauliflower, sliced crosswise
1 med. onion, cut into rings
½ c. sliced stuffed olives
½ to ⅔ c. French dressing
1 sm. head lettuce, broken into pieces
¼ to ½ c. Bleu or Roquefort cheese, crumbled

Combine cauliflowerets, onion, olives and French dressing. Let stand for 30 minutes. Just before serving, add lettuce and cheese. Toss lightly. Yield: 6-8 servings.

Mrs. Fern Gordon
Cheboygan, Mich.

CAULIFLOWER AND APPLE SALAD

1 sm. cauliflower, thinly sliced
3 unpeeled red apples, diced
1 c. sliced celery
3 sm. green onions, sliced
¾ c. chopped parsley or 1 sm. bunch watercress, chopped
1 clove of garlic
½ tsp. salt
¼ c. red wine vinegar
¼ c. salad or olive oil
Pepper to taste

Thoroughly chill cauliflower, apples, celery, onions and parsley. Rub salad bowl with garlic and salt. Shake vinegar, oil and pepper vigorously in a tightly covered jar. Pour over mixed fruit and vegetables; toss lightly. Yield: 6 servings.

Mrs. Ruth S. Park
Bend, Oreg.

CAULIFLOWER SALAD

1 c. oil
¼ c. vinegar
½ tsp. salt
1 tsp. sugar
¼ tsp. white pepper
Pinch of cayenne
2 tbsp. parsley flakes
1 head lettuce, broken into chunks
1 sm. cauliflower, thinly sliced
½ c. chopped stuffed olives
1 med. onion, chopped
1 6-oz. pkg. sharp cheese, grated

Combine oil, vinegar and seasonings; shake well. Toss all ingredients with dressing just before serving. Yield: 10-12 servings.

Mrs. Keith D. Morris
Oskaloosa, Iowa

CAULIFLOWER SALAD WITH SOUR CREAM

1 sm. cauliflower, chopped
3 tbsp. diced onion
1 lge. tomato, diced
¼ green pepper, chopped
½ c. sour cream
4 tsp. white vinegar
1 tbsp. sugar
Dash of salt

Mix cauliflower, onion, tomato and pepper. Stir sour cream and vinegar together; add sugar and salt. Add to cauliflower mixture. Yield: 4 servings.

Julie Gorman
Mound City, Kans.

CAULISLAW

½ fresh cauliflower, finely grated
¼ c. grated carrots
¼ c. finely chopped celery
¼ c. finely chopped green pepper
¼ tsp. vinegar
¼ tsp. sugar
Salt and pepper to taste
Mayonnaise
Hard-cooked eggs, sliced
Paprika

Combine all ingredients; mix well. Chill. Sprinkle with paprika or garnish with hard-cooked egg slices arranged in petal fashion if desired. Yield: 6 servings.

Carol Jean McConnell
Fredericktown, Pa.

CELERY SLAW

1 tsp. salt
1 ½ tsp. sugar
⅛ tsp. pepper
Dash of paprika
⅓ c. salad oil
2 tbsp. vinegar
¼ c. sweet or sour cream
2 c. thinly sliced celery
2 tbsp. pimento, slivered
Salad greens
Green pepper rings

Combine salt, sugar, pepper, paprika, oil and vinegar. Beat with a rotary beater. Add cream; continue to beat until smooth. Marinate celery in dressing for a few minutes. Add pimento; toss. Place greens in salad bowl; pile celery mixture in center. Garnish with green pepper rings. Yield: 6 servings.

Mrs. Dorothy Maxwell
Westville, Ill.

CELERY SLAW

1 ¾ tsp. salt
1 tbsp. sugar
½ tsp. pepper
Dash of paprika
⅓ c. salad oil
2 tbsp. wine vinegar
½ c. sour cream
3 c. diagonally cut, thinly sliced celery
½ c. shredded carrots

Blend salt, sugar, pepper, paprika, salad oil and vinegar; slowly stir in sour cream. Pour dressing over celery and carrots.

Mrs. Shirley Courtois
West Point, N.Y.

CORN SALAD

1 No. 2 can whole kernel corn, drained
1 pimento, chopped
1 sm. onion, chopped
1 sm. green pepper, chopped
1 sm. cucumber, chopped
½ c. French dressing

Combine all ingredients. Serve on lettuce cups. Mayonnaise may be substituted for French dressing and salad used for stuffing tomatoes. Yield: 4 servings.

Mrs. Judy Brumley
Kyle, Tex.

CORN RELISH SALAD

⅔ c. salad oil
2 ½ tbsp. vinegar
2 ½ tsp. salt
½ tsp. pepper
1 ¼ tsp. dry mustard
1 No. 2 can whole kernel corn
½ green pepper, chopped
2 ½ tsp. pimento, diced
5 sm. stalks celery, diced
1 med. onion, chopped

Combine salad oil, vinegar, salt, pepper and mustard. Mix vegetables; add mixture. Refrigerate for 24 hours. Yield: 8-10 servings.

Jessie Chambers
Cheyenne, Wyo.

CORN SALAD

2 large ears corn
1 med. cabbage, finely chopped
6 green peppers, finely chopped
2 Spanish onions, finely chopped
3 lge. stalks celery, finely chopped
1 tbsp. white mustard seed
1 tbsp. celery seed
1 ½ gal. vinegar
1 c. sugar

Cut corn from cob; add remaining ingredients. Simmer for 30 minutes. Place in sterilized fruit jars and seal. NOTE: This salad is excellent when served on a relish tray.

Marian P. Dickinson
Mason City, Iowa

COOKED CORN SALAD

¼ c. chopped onion
½ tsp. celery seed

(Continued on next page)

¼ tsp. ground turmeric
½ tsp. powdered dry mustard
½ tsp. salt
½ c. vinegar
⅓ c. sugar
1 12-oz. can whole kernel corn
¼ c. chopped green pepper
¼ c. chopped red pepper

Combine onion, celery seed, turmeric, mustard, salt, vinegar and sugar. Bring to a boil. Add vegetables; cool. Chill for 24 hours.

Marie F. Johnson
Satellite Beach, Fla.

EL TANGO SALAD

1 12-oz. can Mexicorn, drained
2 c. large curd cottage cheese
2 green onions with tops, minced
¾ c. lightly crushed corn chips

Combine corn, cheese and onions. Chill thoroughly. Toss with corn chips just before serving.

DRESSING:
¾ c. sour cream
½ c. salad mustard
Dash of hot sauce

Combine ingredients; whip thoroughly. Pour over salad. Serve on crisp lettuce leaves, if desired. Yield: 6-8 servings.

Mrs. Carl R. Payne
Denison, Tex.

CUCUMBER MARINADE

5 med. cucumbers
1 c. vinegar
2 tbsp. water
1 tbsp. salad oil
1 tbsp. sugar
1 tsp. salt
½ tsp. pepper
1 lge. onion, coarsely chopped
1 tsp. dried parsley flakes
½ tsp. dill seed

Peel and thinly slice cucumbers. Mix remaining ingredients except onion; pour over cucumbers and onion. Marinate at least 3 hours in refrigerator before serving. Yield: 8 servings.

Mrs. Bernard Lewis
Cleveland, Tex.

CUCUMBER SALAD

3 lge. cucumbers, diced
2 bunches red radishes, grated
2 bunches scallions, diced
½ pt. sour cream
Salt and pepper to taste

Combine all ingredients. Chill and serve. Yield: 6 servings.

Dorothy Winters
Newark, N.J.

CUCUMBERS IN SOUR CREAM

1 med. cucumber, sliced
1 tsp. salt
3 tbsp. sour cream
1 tsp. vinegar
1 tsp. sugar
¼ tsp. dill weed

Sprinkle cucumber with salt; cover with water. Soak. Combine sour cream, vinegar, sugar and dill weed. Drain cucumber; add dressing. Add a small amount of milk if dressing is too thick. Yield: 3 servings.

Mrs. Carol S. Johnson
Alexandria, Minn.

GRANDMA'S CUCUMBER SALAD

2 med. cucumbers, sliced
1 lge. onion, sliced
⅓ c. mayonnaise

Mix ingredients. Serve on lettuce; garnish with paprika or parsley. Yield: 4 servings.

Marjorie C. Gould
Kirkland, Wash.

YOGHURT-CUCUMBER SALAD

4 cucumbers, peeled and thinly sliced
1 ½ tsp. salt
1 clove of garlic, minced
2 tbsp. lemon juice
2 c. yoghurt
1 tbsp. finely chopped dill
¼ c. olive oil
2 tsp. chopped fresh mint

Sprinkle cucumbers with salt; set aside for 15 minutes. Mix garlic, lemon juice, yoghurt and dill; add drained cucumbers. Cover with oil; sprinkle with mint. Yield: 8 servings.

Evelyn Ann Farris
Beckley, W. Va.

EGGPLANT SALAD

1 med. eggplant
1 stalk celery, finely diced
3 tbsp. salad oil
2 tbsp. fresh lemon juice
Salt and pepper to taste
Sliced hard-cooked eggs

Slice eggplant in half or fourths, lengthwise. Broil until skin is crisp and stands away from pulp. Remove pulp; mash. Mix with remaining ingredients except eggs. Serve on lettuce with egg slices. Yield: 2-4 servings.

Elaine Smith
New York, N.Y.

STUFFED GREEN PEPPERS

6 medium-cooked eggs
1 pkg. American cheese
1 tsp. salt
1 tsp. mustard
2 tbsp. mayonnaise
Pepper to taste
Sweet pickle juice (opt.)
5 lge. sweet green peppers

Grate eggs and cheese. Add salt, mustard, mayonnaise and black pepper; mix well. Sweet pickle juice may be added to thin mixture if desired. Cut green peppers into halves lengthwise and clean out centers; wash and drain. Stuff with prepared mixture. Yield: 10 servings.

Harriet Mashburn Parker
Cullowhee, N.C.

HOT ENDIVE

1 lge. head endive, cleaned and chopped
1 tbsp. (heaping) flour
1 egg
½ c. vinegar
½ c. sugar
½ c. water
3 or 4 slices bacon, chopped
Salt and pepper to taste

Soak endive in salt water for 30 minutes; drain. Blend flour, egg, vinegar, sugar and water. Fry bacon crisp; add flour mixture. Cook until thickened, stirring constantly. Add water as needed. Add salt and pepper; pour over endive just before serving. Yield: 6 servings.

Mrs. Ruth Reich
Meyersdale, Pa.

CHEF'S SALAD

1 ½ lge. heads lettuce, broken into bite-sized pieces
5 lge. slices ham cut into med. pieces
2 4-oz. cans chicken, flaked
3 hard-cooked eggs, diced
2 tomatoes, diced
3 stalks celery, diced
½ green pepper, diced
2 carrots, thinly sliced
1 pkg. radishes, thinly sliced
3 med. sweet pickles, diced
1 med. onion, diced

Combine all ingredients; garnish with egg slices and green pepper slices, if desired. Serve with Casino dressing or other favorite dressing. Yield: 8 servings.

Mrs. Clyde E. Blevins
Paintsville, Ky.

DUTCH LETTUCE

1 lge. head lettuce, cut into sm. pieces
4 green onions, chopped
3 slices bacon, diced
4 tbsp. vinegar
4 tbsp. sugar
1 egg
2 tbsp. sour cream

Toss lettuce and onions together. Fry bacon; drain off most of drippings. Combine bacon and vinegar. Cream sugar, egg and sour cream; add to bacon mixture. Cook until thick; cool slightly. Pour over lettuce and onion while warm. Yield: 6 servings.

Marilyn L. Gies
East Wenatchee, Wash.

EGG AND LETTUCE SALAD

1 ½ c. chopped lettuce
3 hard-cooked eggs
1 tbsp. vinegar
3 tbsp. salad oil
¼ tsp. salt
¼ tsp. pepper

Place lettuce in bowl; add chopped egg whites. Mash egg yolks; add vinegar, salad oil and seasonings. Mix well; pour over lettuce. Toss and serve. Yield: 2 servings.

Mrs. Max Rose
Liberal, Mo.

LETTUCE--A MAN'S SALAD

1 clove of garlic
Olive oil
Lemon juice
⅛ tsp. dry mustard
Dash of salt
1 head lettuce

Rub garlic against the side of a wooden mixing bowl. Blend 2/3 part oil, 1/3 part lemon juice, mustard and salt. Add lettuce; toss gently.

Louise Blanton
Lewisville, Tex.

PENNSYLVANIA DUTCH COLD LETTUCE

¼ c. sugar
2 tbsp. mayonnaise
1 ½ tbsp. cream or evaporated milk
¼ c. (scant) vinegar
Salt to taste
1 med. head lettuce, torn into small pieces

Mix sugar and mayonnaise; blend in cream or evaporated milk. Add vinegar and salt. Immediately before serving pour dressing over lettuce. Toss so that every piece of lettuce is well coated. Yield: 6 servings.

Jane E. Spangler
Shippensburg, Pa.

STUFFED HEAD LETTUCE

1 3-oz. pkg. cream cheese
1 tbsp. Roquefort cheese
1 tbsp. chopped green pepper
1 tbsp. chopped carrot
1 tbsp. chopped tomato
1 tbsp. chopped onion
Salt and pepper to taste
1 solid head lettuce, cored

Thoroughly mix cheeses, green pepper, carrot, tomato, onion, salt and pepper. Stuff into lettuce. Wrap lettuce in a damp cloth and then in foil; let stand overnight. Cut into wedges to serve. Yield: 4-6 servings.

Mrs. Wetthalee G. Durham
Philadelphia, Pa.

STUFFED LETTUCE

1 sm. head lettuce
½ lb. Bleu cheese
1 3-oz. pkg. cream cheese
2 tbsp. milk
1 tbsp. chopped chives or green onion tops
1 pimento, chopped
French dressing

Hollow out center of lettuce, leaving a 1-inch shell. Beat cheeses and milk together until smooth. Add chives and pimento; mix thoroughly. Fill lettuce hollow with cheese mixture. Refrigerate until cheese is firm. Just before serving, cut across the lettuce making 3/4-inch slices. Serve with French dressing. Yield: 4 servings.

Mary S. Brisco
Prince Frederick, Md.

STUFFED LETTUCE

1 head lettuce
2 c. grated American cheese
¼ c. chopped pimento
2 tbsp. chopped green pepper
2 tsp. lemon juice
1 tbsp. sugar
Mayonnaise or salad dressing

Clean lettuce; cut out about 1/4 of the inside. Place in a plastic bag; refrigerate for 3 or 4 hours. Combine remaining ingredients with enough mayonnaise or salad dressing to moisten. Stuff filling into lettuce; chill. To serve, cut head into quarters. Yield: 4-6 servings.

Mrs. Doris J. Combs
Woodstock, Va.

WESTERN WILTED SALAD

4 slices bacon
3 tbsp. lemon juice
1 tbsp. sugar
1 tsp. salt
¼ c. chopped onion
1 head lettuce
2 or 3 med. oranges, peeled and cut into pieces
1 6-oz. pkg. Swiss cheese, cut into thin strips

Fry bacon until crisp; remove from skillet. Stir lemon juice, sugar, salt and onion into hot bacon drippings. Heat thoroughly. Tear lettuce into pieces; rinse and drain. Place in large salad bowl. Pour hot dressing over salad greens. Crumble bacon; add with orange pieces and cheese. Toss lightly. Yield: 6-8 servings.

Louise Barton
Herren, Ill.

WILTED LEAF LETTUCE

2 lge. bunches leaf lettuce
Salt and pepper to taste
2 tsp. sugar
2 green onions, chopped
4 slices bacon
¼ c. vinegar
2 tbsp. water
1 hard-cooked egg, chopped

Shred lettuce into hot bowl; add seasonings and onions. Fry bacon until crisp; chop. Add vinegar and water; heat. Pour over lettuce mixture; toss until wilted. Sprinkle with egg. Yield: 6 servings.

Mrs. Dolores Jones
Barksdale AFB, La.

WILTED LETTUCE

1 head lettuce
4 slices bacon
½ c. water
¼ c. cider vinegar
2 tbsp. sugar
⅛ tsp. salt

Wash and tear lettuce into pieces; set aside. Cut bacon into 1-inch pieces; fry very slowly until crisp. Drain on absorbent paper. Stir remaining ingredients into 1/4 cup bacon fat. Heat mixture to boiling; stir in bacon pieces. Immediately pour over lettuce; toss lightly. Garnish with slices of hard-cooked eggs and a dash of paprika. Yield: 6 servings.

Eula A Offenbacher
Casper, Wyo.

FRESH PARSNIP SALAD

2 to 4 parsnips, finely grated
⅓ c. crushed pineapple
½ c. marshmallows
⅓ c. salad dressing
1 tbsp. sugar
⅓ c. pineapple juice

Mix parsnips, pineapple and marshmallows. Mix salad dressing, sugar and pineapple juice. Pour dressing over parsnip mixture; blend. Chill. Yield: 4 servings.

Colleen Stevenson
Ripley, Okla.

PARSNIP SALAD

3 c. parsnips, shredded
1 ½ c. finely chopped celery
1 pimento, finely cut
½ c. olives
1 tsp. horseradish
½ tsp. salt
¼ tsp. pepper
½ c. mayonnaise
Lettuce

Combine all ingredients; toss. Serve on lettuce. Yield: 6 servings.

Mrs. Mari Hurley
El Centro, Calif.

WINTER SALAD BOWL

½ c. grated parsnips
2 tbsp. chopped sweet onion
¼ c. chopped celery
4 stuffed olives, chopped
¼ tsp. salt
French dressing
⅓ med. head lettuce, torn into bite-sized pieces
2 tbsp. mayonnaise

Marinate parsnips, onion, celery, olives and salt in French dressing for 1 to 2 hours. Just before serving, add lettuce. Toss lightly with mayonnaise. Yield: 2-3 servings.

Mrs. Bettie Lou Snapp
Albuquerque, N.M.

WINTER WONDER SALAD

1 ½ c. scraped and shredded parsnips
¾ c. diced celery
¼ to ⅓ c. minced onion
8 to 10 sm. stuffed olives, sliced
½ tsp. salt
Dash of pepper
¼ c. French dressing
¼ c. mayonnaise or salad dressing
1 sm. head lettuce
Sliced green pepper or stuffed olives

Combine parsnips, celery, onion, olives, salt and pepper. Add French dressing and mayonnaise; toss well. Arrange in lettuce nests; garnish with green pepper or stuffed olive slices. Yield: 4 servings.

Mrs. Zetta Forbes Robb
Napoleon, Mich.

ENGLISH PEA AND CHEESE SALAD

1 No. 2 can English peas, drained
1 med. tomato, diced

(Continued on next page)

1 c. cubed mild Cheddar cheese
1 tbsp. chopped pimento
4 tbsp. salad dressing or mayonnaise
Dash of seasoned salt
6 lettuce leaves
Dash of paprika

Combine English peas, tomato, cheese, pimento, salad dressing or mayonnaise and seasoned salt. Toss just enough to mix lightly. Serve on lettuce leaf; garnish with paprika. Yield: 6 servings.

Mrs. Winnie McQueen
Santa Anna, Tex.

ENGLISH PEA SALAD

1 15-oz. can English peas, drained
4 hard-cooked eggs, sliced
¾ c. chopped cheese
½ c. chopped pickles
½ c. chopped celery (opt.)
½ c. mayonnaise

Combine all ingredients except mayonnaise in medium bowl; lightly fold in mayonnaise. Yield: 4 servings.

Mrs. William T. Miracle
Seymour Johnson AFB, N.C.

ENGLISH PEA SALAD DELIGHT

1 1-lb. can English peas, chilled
½ c. drained, chopped sweet pickles
¼ c. chopped pecans
2 hard-cooked eggs, chopped
Mayonnaise and salt to taste

Mix ingredients. Serve on a lettuce leaf. Yield: 4 servings.

Mrs. J. H. Hellums
Batesville, Miss.

HEARTY PEA SALAD

2 c. drained cooked peas
½ c. diced mild Cheddar cheese
3 hard-cooked eggs, chopped
1 c. sliced celery
½ c. chopped sweet pickles
2 tbsp. cream
½ c. salad dressing
Salt to taste
Lettuce

Combine peas, cheese, eggs, celery and pickles. Mix cream and salad dressing. Stir dressing and salt into salad mixture. Chill. Spoon into lettuce cups. Yield: 6 servings.

Mrs. Christina Detrick
Ames, Okla.

PEA AND BACON SALAD

1 pkg. frozen peas
8 slices bacon, fried and cut into small pieces
1 c. sour cream
Pinch of salt

Thaw peas. Drain bacon on paper towel. Combine all ingredients. Yield: 4-6 servings.

Mrs. Lawrence Bymaster
S. San Gabriel, Calif.

PEA 'N' CHEESE SALAD

1 No. 303 can garden peas, chilled and drained
1 c. diced celery
1 tsp. grated onion
½ c. chopped sweet pickles
¼ lb. diced sharp cheese
½ c. mayonnaise
Salt and pepper to taste

Combine all ingredients; toss lightly. Serve on salad greens. Yield: 6 servings.

Mrs. Charles R. Vaughn
Macon, Ga.

PEA-PICKLE-PECAN SALAD

2 c. drained cooked English peas
6 tbsp. diced sweet pickles
½ tsp. salt
1 c. broken pecans
6 tbsp. mayonnaise

Combine peas, pickles, salt and pecans. Moisten with mayonnaise. Serve on lettuce leaf. Yield: 6 servings.

Gussie Mae Beard
Pelican, La.

PEA SALAD

1 egg
1 ½ tsp. sugar

(Continued on next page)

1 ½ tsp. pickle vinegar
2 tbsp. half and half cream
Dash of salt
1 tbsp. peanut butter
1 med. can peas, drained
3 sweet pickles, diced
½ sm. onion, diced
1 hard-cooked egg, diced (opt.)

Combine egg, sugar, vinegar, cream and salt. Cook over low heat until thickened, stirring constantly. Add peanut butter; mix. Pour cooked mixture over peas, pickles, onion and hard-cooked egg. Toss lightly. Yield: 6 servings.

Nevaleen Joy Selmat
Wakita, Okla.

PEA SALAD

1 can English peas, drained
1 sm. onion, diced
Cheese cubes
Chopped sweet pickles
Salad dressing
Lettuce

Combine peas, onion, cheese and pickles. Mix a small amount of pickle juice in salad dressing to thin. Add to pea mixture; toss well. Serve on lettuce leaf.

Mavis Benson
Denver, Colo.

BAKED GERMAN POTATO SALAD

1 c. diced bacon
1 c. sliced celery
1 c. chopped onions
3 tsp. salt
3 tbsp. flour
8 c. sliced cooked potatoes
⅔ c. sugar
⅔ c. vinegar
½ tsp. pepper
1 ⅓ c. water

Fry bacon; drain. Return 4 tablespoons of fat to skillet. Add celery, onions, salt and flour. Cook gently. Add sugar, vinegar, pepper and water. Bring to boil. Place potatoes and bacon in 3-quart baking dish. Pour hot mixture over potatoes and bacon. Cover. Bake at 350 degrees for 30 minutes. Yield: 12 servings.

Mrs. William A. Zang
Maineville, O.

BEST POTATO SALAD

6 slices bacon, chopped
1 c. sugar
1 egg, beaten
1 tbsp. flour
1 tsp. prepared mustard
½ c. water
½ tsp. salt
Dash of pepper
6 med. boiled potatoes, diced
6 med. boiled potatoes, diced
4 hard-cooked eggs, diced
2 stalks celery, chopped
1 sm. onion, chopped
1 tbsp. parsley, minced

Fry bacon. Mix sugar, beaten egg, flour, mustard, vinegar, water, salt and pepper. Add to bacon and drippings. Boil until slightly thickened, stirring constantly. Mix remaining ingredients. Add dressing. Serve cold. Garnish with parsley sprigs. Yield: 6 servings.

Mrs. Esther F. Zimmerman
Indiantown Gap, Pa.

COUNTRY-STYLE POTATO SALAD

10 potatoes, peeled
1 carrot, grated
1 cucumber, diced
½ green pepper, diced
1 stalk celery, diced or 1 tsp. celery seed
1 onion, diced

Cook potatoes until tender; dice. Combine all vegetables; mix well.

DRESSING:
1 egg
2 tbsp. flour
½ c. milk
¾ c. water
1 tbsp. salt
1 tbsp. sugar
⅓ c. vinegar
½ c. salad dressing
1 tsp. mustard

Combine all ingredients except salad dressing and mustard; mix well. Cook mixture until thickened. Blend in salad dressing and mustard. Serve over vegetables. Yield: 8 servings.

Martha Mongold
Brushy Run, W. Va.

EASY MASHED POTATO SALAD

8 potatoes, cooked and mashed
Salt and pepper to taste

4 hard-cooked eggs, chopped
¼ c. minced green pepper
¼ c. minced onion
1 tsp. minced parsley
1 c. (about) cooked salad dressing

Season potatoes with salt and pepper; add 3 eggs, green pepper, onion and parsley. Fold in enough salad dressing to moisten. Serve in crisp cold lettuce leaves garnished with remaining egg. Parsley and radish roses may also be used. Yield: 6 servings.

Mrs. Horace G. Cole
Fort Fisher AFS, N.C.

FAVORITE POTATO SALAD

6 med. potatoes, cooked and cubed
1 sm. onion, chopped
4 or 5 sprigs parsley
¼ c. vinegar
¼ c. salad oil
1 tsp. salt
1 tsp. pepper
½ c. mayonnaise
1 c. diced celery
2 hard-cooked eggs, chopped
3 tbsp. minced dill pickles

Combine warm potatoes with onion and parsley. Combine vinegar, oil, salt and pepper, Pour over potatoes; toss lightly with fork. Chill for 2 hours or overnight. Add all remaining ingredients; mix gently. NOTE: Add 3/4 teaspoon mustard to mayonnaise for extra zip. Yield: 12 servings.

Mrs. W. H. Coltrin
Denver, Colo.

GERMAN SOUR CREAM- POTATO SALAD

2 strips bacon
3 green onions, chopped
1 c. chopped celery
1 tsp. flour
½ tsp. dry mustard
1 ¼ tsp. salt
⅓ c. Sauterne
1 tbsp. white wine vinegar
2 c. diced boiled potatoes
6 hard-cooked eggs, diced
2 tbsp. chopped parsley
2 tbsp. chopped pimento
1 c. grated Cheddar cheese

Cook bacon until crisp. Remove bacon; crumble and set aside. Cook onions and celery in bacon fat until soft but not brown; stir in flour, mustard, salt and wine. Cook, stirring constantly until mixture boils. Blend in wine vinegar. Pour over potatoes and eggs; add bacon, parsley and pimento. Mix lightly. Pour into shallow baking dish; top with cheese. Bake at 375 degrees for 15 to 20 minutes until salad is heated and cheese is melted. Yield: 4-6 servings.

Gladys B. Harrison
San Pablo, Calif.

GERMAN POTATO SALAD

½ c. sugar
⅔ c. salad oil
⅔ c. vinegar
1 sm. onion, finely chopped
Parsley flakes
Salt to taste
5 boiled potatoes, finely chopped
Sliced hard-cooked eggs (opt.)

Combine all ingredients except potatoes and eggs. Place hot potatoes in dressing. Garnish with egg slices. Yield: 6 servings.

Mrs. Frances Vantassel
West Milton, Pa.

GERMAN POTATO SALAD

½ lb. bacon
2 med. onions, chopped
½ c. vinegar
½ c. water
½ c. sugar
2 tbsp. flour
Salt and pepper to taste
6 c. cooked cubed potatoes

Fry bacon and onions until golden brown. Combine vinegar, water, sugar, flour, salt and pepper. Add to bacon and onions; bring to a boil. Pour over potatoes; mix well. Serve warm. Yield: 6 servings.

Mrs. Joseph Nagle
Erie, Pa.

GREEK-STYLE POTATO SALAD

8 med. potatoes
1 lge. onion
1 lge. green pepper
1 c. mayonnaise
1 tbsp. parsley flakes
Salt and pepper to taste
10 whole lettuce leaves
2 stalks celery
1 bunch radishes
1 can pickled beet slices, drained
1 med. jar large stuffed green olives

(Continued on next page)

1 med. jar ripe olives, pitted and drained
1 bunch spring onions
1 8-oz. pkg. Coon cheese, cubed
½ c. corn oil
½ c. lemon juice
¼ c. wine vinegar
½ tsp. oregano

Boil potatoes in jacket; cool. Peel and slice crosswise. Slice onion and green pepper crosswise. Mix together with mayonnaise, parsley flakes, salt and pepper. Line platter with lettuce leaves. Mound potato salad on lettuce. Cover and refrigerate for at least 2 hours. Cut celery into sticks; clean radishes and make radish roses. Stack celery, radishes, beets, olives, spring onions and cheese over potato salad. Mix remaining ingredients. Pour over salad just before serving. Yield: 8 servings.

Mrs. James A. Leigh
Sarasota, Fla.

JUGOSLAW POTATO SALAD

4 lge. potatoes, cooked and thinly sliced
1 lge. onion, cut into long thin strips
5 slices bacon, cubed
½ c. white vinegar
½ c. water
Salt and pepper
2 tbsp. salad oil
1 tbsp. parsley

Combine potatoes and onion. Fry bacon until brown; pour over potatoes and onion. Blend vinegar, water, salt, pepper and salad oil; pour over potatoes and onion. Sprinkle parsley over salad. Mix gently. Yield: 5 servings.

Mrs. Mady Fulton
Ft. Polk, La.

MASHED POTATO SALAD

½ c. diced sweet onion or 3 green onions, diced
⅓ c. French dressing
3 c. hot potatoes, mashed and salted
½ c. diced celery
4 hard-cooked eggs, diced
¾ c. mayonnaise
Salt and pepper to taste
Paprika

Combine onions and French dressing; mix. Chill thoroughly. Add remaining ingredients about 1 hour before serving. Season to taste. Garnish with paprika. Yield: 6 servings.

Norma S. Howland
Tioga, Pa.

HANK'S FAVORITE POTATO SALAD

6 med. potatoes
1 lge. onion, finely chopped
1 c. mayonnaise
1 tbsp. celery seed
Salt and pepper to taste

Boil potatoes in skins until tender; while still warm, pare and dice. Add onion, mayonnaise, celery seed, salt and pepper to taste. Mix thoroughly; chill. Yield: 6 servings.

Mrs. Elanor Goodman
Baltimore, Md.

OLD-FASHIONED SKILLET SALAD

2 lb. potatoes
⅓ c. salad oil
3 or 4 tbsp. vinegar
1 tbsp. garlic salt
Dash of pepper
4 to 6 slices bacon
¾ c. finely chopped onions
1 tbsp. flour
1 tbsp. sugar
½ tsp. salt
1 tsp. celery seed
2 tbsp. coarsely chopped green pepper
1 tbsp. coarsely chopped parsley

Cook potatoes in salted water until tender. Drain; peel and cut into slices about 1/4-inch thick. Combine oil, vinegar, garlic salt and pepper. Set aside. Fry bacon until crisp. Drain on paper towel; crumble. Remove all except 2 tablespoons fat from skillet. Add 1/2 cup onions; saute until tender but not browned. Stir in flour, sugar, salt, celery seed and oil-vinegar mixture. Simmer until thickened. Add potatoes, remaining onions, green pepper and parsley. Stir together lightly. Garnish with bacon. Serve warm. Yield: 8 servings.

Mrs. Ardery Peery
Keota, Okla.

OLIVE-POTATO SALAD

6 med. potatoes
1 c. stuffed olives, quartered
2 hard-cooked eggs, chopped
¼ c. diced celery
2 tbsp. finely diced onion
⅓ c. thick cream
¼ c. vinegar
Salt

Boil potatoes until tender; drain and cool. Peel and cube. Add olives, eggs, celery and onion. Mix cream and vinegar; scald. Add to potato mixture; mix well. Salt to taste. Yield: 8 servings.

Ida Vivian Hrncir
Hallettsville, Tex.

POTATO SALAD

3 lb. potatoes
1 sm. onion, chopped
2 c. diced celery
2 tsp. salt
1 c. mayonnaise
2 tbsp. prepared mustard
2 tbsp. vinegar
½ tsp. Tabasco sauce

Cook potatoes in skins until tender. Peel and dice. Add onion and celery; sprinkle with salt. Mix mayonnaise, mustard, vinegar and Tabasco sauce; add to potato mixture. Mix lightly with a fork, being careful not to break potatoes; chill. Yield: 12 servings.

Photograph for this recipe above.

PERFECT POTATO SALAD

2 ½ c. cooked sliced potatoes
1 tsp. sugar
1 tsp. vinegar
½ c. chopped onion
1 ½ tsp. salt
1 ½ tsp. celery seed
¾ c. mayonnaise
2 hard-cooked eggs, sliced

Sprinkle potatoes with sugar and vinegar. Add onion, seasonings and mayonnaise; toss to blend. Carefully fold in eggs; chill. Serve in lettuce-lined bowl. May be garnished with parsley, sliced radishes, cucumbers and egg slices. NOTE: For extra crunch add 1/2 cup sliced celery and 1/4 cup sliced sweet pickles. Yield: 8 servings.

Mrs. Alexander P. Lezark
Ramey AFB, N.Y.

POTATO SALAD DELIGHT

2 c. diced cooked potatoes
1 lge. onion, finely chopped
2 hard-cooked eggs, diced
2 tbsp. water
¼ tsp. salt
Dash of pepper
2 tbsp. butter
2 tbsp. vinegar
½ c. minced parsley

Mix potatoes, onion and eggs lightly. Heat water, salt, pepper and butter until butter melts; add vinegar. Pour over potato mixture; mix thoroughly. Chill. Sprinkle with parsley. Yield: 4 servings.

Mrs. Curtis Crampton
Port Clinton, O.

POTATO SALAD SUPREME

1 lb. potatoes
¼ c. vinegar
Salt
1 sm. onion, sliced
1 pimento, finely chopped
2 hard-cooked eggs, diced
White pepper to taste
2 tbsp. parsley
⅔ c. mayonnaise

Boil potatoes in skins; cool. Peel and slice. Add vinegar; mix well and let soak. Pour salt over onion; squeeze out all juice. Rinse onion with cold water. Add onion to potatoes with 1 teaspoon salt and all remaining ingredients. Mix well; chill thoroughly. Yield: 6-8 servings.

Mrs. Edgar C. Jackson
McCoy AFB, Fla.

SPICY POTATO SALAD

5 c. cooked, diced potatoes
3 hard-cooked eggs, chopped
¼ c. diced green pepper
¼ c. diced celery
¼ c. diced sweet pickles
¼ c. chopped pimento
½ c. prepared salad dressing
1 tsp. mustard
1 tsp. salt
½ tsp. celery salt

Combine potatoes, eggs, green pepper, celery, pickles and pimento. Blend all remaining ingredients; add to potato mixture. May be served hot or cold. Yield: 8 servings.

Mrs. Chris Shaw
Corpus Christi, Tex.

TROPICAL POTATO SALAD

1 can sliced pimento
1 can ripe olives
5 med. potatoes, cooked and cubed
8 to 10 hard-cooked eggs, chopped
6 sweet pickles, chopped (opt.)
1 med. onion, chopped (opt.)
Mayonnaise
Salt and pepper to taste
1 tsp. sugar

Combine pimento, olives, potatoes, eggs, pickles and onion. Make dressing of mayonnaise, salt, pepper and sugar. Pour over vegetables; mix well.

Mrs. Leroy Webster
Haure AFS, Mont.

SWEET POTATO SALAD

3 or 4 med. sweet potatoes
1 tsp. salt
2 hard-cooked eggs, chopped
1 c. chopped sweet pickles
1 c. chopped celery
1 can luncheon meat, ham or frankfurters, cubed
2 or 3 apples, cubed
Mayonnaise or salad dressing
1 lge. onion, finely chopped

Peel potatoes; cut into bite-sized pieces. Boil until tender in salt water. Drain; add remaining ingredients. Toss lightly. Chill or serve immediately. Yield: 6-8 servings.

Mrs. John S. Grimes
Neshoba, Miss.

BEST SAUERKRAUT SALAD

⅓ c. salad oil
⅓ c. vinegar
1 lge. can sauerkraut
1 c. chopped onions
1 c. shredded carrots
1 c. diced green peppers
1 c. sugar

Bring oil and vinegar to a boil. Cool. Pour over remaining ingredients; refrigerate for 24 hours. Toss occasionally to mix. Yield: 20-25 servings.

Mrs. Virginia L. Noyes
Louisville, Ky.

EMMA'S SAUERKRAUT SALAD

1 No. 2 ½ can sauerkraut
1 c. chopped celery
1 c. diced green peppers
1 med. onion, chopped
1 c. sugar
½ c. vinegar
½ c. salad oil

Mix all ingredients; refrigerate at least 24 hours before serving. Yield: 8 servings.

Mrs. Emma Tussing
Baltimore, O.

GOOD SAUERKRAUT SALAD

1 qt. sauerkraut, drained
2 c. diced celery
1 green pepper, diced
1 med. onion, diced
1 sm. can pimento, chopped
1 tsp. salt
2 c. sugar
½ c. vinegar

(Continued on next page)

Combine all ingredients. Let stand for 24 hours before serving. Yield: 10 servings.

Myrtle Ziegler
Michigan Center, Mich.

KRAUT AND CORN SALAD

1 No. 2 ½ can kraut, drained
1 c. whole kernel corn, drained
2 c. chopped celery
1 sm. green pepper, chopped
1 red pepper, chopped
1 c. sugar
1 sm. onion, chopped

Combine all ingredients. Chill for 1 hour or longer; serve. Yield: 12 servings.

Mrs. Don O'Hara
Buckner, Mo.

OVERNIGHT SAUERKRAUT SALAD

1 c. sugar
¼ c. vinegar
½ c. chopped celery
½ c. chopped onion
½ c. chopped green pepper
2 c. drained sauerkraut
Pinch of celery seed

Heat sugar and vinegar until sugar is dissolved. Cool. Add remaining ingredients; let stand overnight. Yield: 8 servings.

Mrs. P. R. Evans
Casper, Wyo.

SAUERKRAUT SALAD

1 pt. sauerkraut, drained
1 lge. onion, sliced into rings
¾ c. sugar
¼ c. salad oil
¼ c. white vinegar

Drain sauerkraut in colander. Add onion rings. Combine remaining ingredients. Pour over sauerkraut; toss lightly. Refrigerate at least 1 hour before serving.

Mrs. Lester Bruder
Sandpoint, Idaho

SAUERKRAUT SLAW

1 lge. can sauerkraut
⅔ c. sugar
¼ c. finely chopped onion
⅔ c. diced celery
⅔ c. chopped green peppers
1 med. carrot, shredded (opt.)

Combine all ingredients; toss and let set overnight.

Elsie Elvidge
Peru, Ind.

VEGETABLE SALAD

1 lge. can sauerkraut
1 c. chopped celery
2 tbsp. diced onion
½ lge. green pepper, chopped
½ c. sugar

Chop sauerkraut. Do not drain. Mix with remaining ingredients. Let set at least 1 hour before serving. Yield: 10 servings.

Mrs. Millard Gowin
Casper, Wyo.

FRESH SPINACH SALAD

1 lb. fresh spinach
4 hard-cooked eggs, chopped
8 slices bacon, fried and crumbled
¼ c. chopped green onions
½ c. Italian salad dressing
Salt to taste

Remove large veins from spinach; tear into small pieces. Combine spinach, eggs and bacon. Add onions; toss lightly. Add dressing and salt just before serving. Yield: 6 servings.

Mrs. Jane Davis
Corpus Christi, Tex.

FRESH SPINACH WITH CHEESE SALAD

2 slices bacon, dried and crumbled
1 8-oz. pkg. cream cheese
1 med. onion, grated
1 8-oz. bottle French dressing
¼ c. vinegar
2 pkg. fresh spinach

Combine bacon, bacon drippings and cream cheese; mix well. Add onion, French dressing and vinegar; stir thoroughly. Just before serving, pour mixture over spinach.

Mrs. Frances Baker Bishop
Denton, Tex.

SPINACH-BACON SALAD BOWL

6 cloves of garlic, quartered
¾ c. French dressing
3 hard-cooked eggs
8 slices bacon
1 lb. crisp young spinach, washed

Add garlic to French dressing. Fry bacon until crisp;drain. Tear spinach into pieces in a large salad bowl; refrigerate. Chop eggs; crumble bacon. Sprinkle over spinach when ready to serve. Remove garlic from dressing; pour over spinach. Toss. May be garnished with slices of hard-cooked eggs. Yield: 6-8 servings.

Mrs. Denny Bergeman
Porte Clinton, O.

SPINACH SALAD

½ lb. spinach, shredded
1 med. onion, finely chopped
4 tbsp. diced celery
6 to 8 radishes, chopped
4 hard-cooked eggs, chopped
½ tsp. salt

Combine all ingredients. Toss and chill.

HOT FRENCH DRESSING:
4 tbsp. bacon fat
¼ c. vinegar
1 tbsp. sugar
2 slices bacon, fried crisp and chopped

Combine sugar, vinegar and bacon fat; bring to a boil. Add bacon. Pour over salad. Serve immediately. Yield: 8 servings.

Mary Martin
Cleburne, Tex.

TOSSED SPINACH SALAD

1 pkg. fresh spinach
Garlic salt to taste
3 tomatoes, quartered
2 tbsp. dry cottage cheese
Onion rings

Tear spinach into bowl; sprinkle with garlic salt. Place tomatoes on spinach; sprinkle with cheese. Garnish with onion rings. Serve with French dressing. NOTE: If dry cottage cheese is not available, rinse creamed cottage cheese with cold water; drain. Yield: 6 servings.

Margaret C. Jenkins
Upland, Calif.

TOSSED SPINACH AND ORANGE SALAD

FRENCH DRESSING:
1 tsp. salt
¼ tsp. pepper
1 tsp. sugar
3 tbsp. vinegar or lemon juice
¼ c. catsup
½ c. salad oil

Combine all ingredients. Blend or shake vigorously.

SALAD:
2 c. fresh spinach, cut or torn into sm. pieces
2 med. California oranges, sectioned
1 tbsp. sugar
Salt to taste

Combine all ingredients. Add 1/4 cup of French dressing. Toss together. Yield: 6-8 servings.

Mrs. Dorothy J. Clark
Tawas City, Mich.

BARBECUE SALAD

12 med. ripe tomatoes, chopped
8 med. onions, chopped
2 red peppers, chopped
6 green peppers, chopped
1 c. sugar
1 c. vinegar

Combine all ingredients in saucepan; cook for 1 hour or until thickened.

Henriette Tracy Schnelker
Chatsworth, Calif.

HERBED TOMATOES

⅔ c. salad oil
¼ c. tarragon vinegar
Few leaves fresh thyme or marjoram
1 tsp. salt
¼ tsp. pepper
6 tomatoes, peeled
⅓ c. finely chopped parsley
⅓ c. chopped chives

Combine salad oil, vinegar, thyme, salt and pepper. Place tomatoes in shallow bowl. Pour dressing over tomatoes. Chill for 2 to 3 hours, turning tomatoes occasionally. Remove from dressing; roll in parsley and chives. NOTE: A dash of dried thyme may be substituted for fresh leaves. Yield: 6 servings.

Mrs. Walter J. Nadolny
Fanwood, N.J.

MARINATED TOMATOES AND ONIONS

6 lge. tomatoes, peeled
3 onions
1 tbsp. parsley, chopped
¾ c. olive oil
¼ c. wine vinegar
Salt and pepper to taste

Thinly slice tomatoes and onions; arrange layers in serving bowl. Sprinkle each layer with parsley. Blend olive oil, vinegar, salt and pepper; pour over layers. Chill for at least 4 hours before serving. May be garnished with stuffed olive slices. Yield: 6 servings.

Nettie-Adelyn Landon
Fallon, Nev.

SUMMER VEGETABLE SALAD

4 tomatoes, chopped
1 cucumber, peeled and chopped
1 med. onion, chopped
1 med. mango pepper, chopped
1 tsp. salt
⅛ tsp. pepper
2 tbsp. sugar
2 tbsp. vinegar

Combine vegetables; add seasonings, sugar and vinegar. Let stand. Yield: 8 servings.

Mrs. Vernon Henninger
Arcanum, O.

TOMATO-CHEESE SALAD

1 c. tomato sauce
1 c. cottage cheese, drained
½ tsp. salt
½ tsp. horseradish
¼ to ½ tsp. onion juice
1 2 ¼-oz. can deviled ham
½ c. sliced stuffed olives
2 tbsp. catsup

Combine all ingredients except olives and catsup. Beat until well blended. Pour into 9-inch pie plate. Spread catsup on top; garnish with olive slices. Cover securely with aluminum foil. Freeze. Yield: 6 servings.

Mrs. Fred Beers, Jr.
McDonough, Ga.

TOMATO AND ONION SALAD

1 clove of garlic, minced
1 tsp. salt
1 tsp. sugar
¼ tsp. pepper
2 tsp. prepared mustard
¼ c. olive or salad oil
2 tbsp. tarragon vinegar
6 firm tomatoes, sliced
1 onion, thinly sliced
Chopped parsley

Combine garlic and salt; mash with a spoon. Stir in sugar, pepper, mustard, oil and vinegar. Pour over tomato and onion slices. Sprinkle with parsley. Chill. Serve without dressing. Yield: 6-8 servings.

Mrs. Pat Ashbrook
LaGrange, Ky.

TOMATOES A LA PEPPER ONION

Sliced tomatoes
Finely chopped onion
Finely chopped green pepper

Sprinkle tomato slices with onion and pepper. Sprinkle with dressing. Chill for 1 hour before serving.

Mrs. Irma B. Morley
Allegan, Mich.

TOMATO AND PEPPER SURPRISE SALAD

2 lge. tomatoes, diced
1 lge. green pepper, diced
1 med. onion, diced
¼ lge. box crackers, crumbled
Salt and pepper to taste
2 tbsp. (heaping) mayonnaise

Combine all ingredients. Toss lightly. Yield: 6 servings.

Anne G. Rollins
Coward, S.C.

TOMATO PLATTER

3 to 6 tomatoes
Salt and pepper
¾ c. finely chopped onions
½ c. finely chopped parsley
¼ c. vinegar
½ c. olive oil

Thickly slice tomatoes; arrange on platter. Sprinkle with remaining ingredients.

Norma Sue Evers
Willamina, Oreg.

TOMATO RELISH SALAD

½ tbsp. minced onion
1 tsp. salt
½ tsp. pepper
2 tsp. mustard
¼ c. salad oil
2 tbsp. tarragon vinegar
¼ c. chopped fresh parsley or ½ tsp. dried flakes
2 or 3 tomatoes, sliced

Combine all ingredients except tomatoes; spoon over sliced tomatoes. Yield: 8 servings.

Mrs. Edna Rich
Asheboro, N.C.

TOMATO SALAD

1 clove of garlic
6 med. tomatoes, cut up
1 tbsp. lemon juice
1 tbsp. olive oil
½ tsp. salt
1 tbsp. minced onion
10 leaves green mint

Pulverize garlic in salad bowl. Add remaining ingredients; stir from bottom of bowl. Let stand for 10 minutes. Yield: 6 servings.

Mrs. N. G. Nasif
Jonesville, La.

TOMATO SALAD DELIGHT

4 med. tomatoes
Salt
1 ½ tsp. lemon juice
1 3-oz. pkg. cream cheese
½ c. chopped cucumber, drained
½ tbsp. grated onion
1 tbsp. chopped parsley
2 tbsp. mayonnaise
2 tbsp. whipped cream
Onion slices
Parsley sprigs

Peel tomatoes; cut each into three slices. Sprinkle slices with salt and lemon juice. Combine cream cheese, cucumber, onion and parsley. Add mayonnaise mixed with whipped cream. Arrange 4 tomato slices on lettuce; top with cheese mixture. Place tomato slices on cheese mixture; top with cheese mixture. Top with remaining tomato slices. Garnish with onion slice and parsley sprig. Yield: 4 servings.

Mrs. John H. Cowan, Jr.
Allen Park, Mich.

TURNIP SALAD

2 med. turnips
⅛ tsp. salt
1 tsp. chopped red sweet pepper
1 tsp. chopped green sweet pepper
1 tbsp. salad dressing

Grate turnips. Add salt and peppers. Mix well. Stir in salad dressing. Serve at once. Yield: 4 servings.

Gladys LaForge
Seneca, Mo.

BOUQUET SALAD

1 clove of garlic
1 head crisp lettuce
2 or 3 tomatoes, sliced
3 hard-cooked eggs, sliced
1 sm. cucumber, sliced
½ green pepper, sliced
6 to 8 red radishes, sliced
1 carrot, cut into slivers
3 stalks celery, cut into slivers
1 or 2 slices Swiss cheese, cut into slivers
5 strips bacon, fried and crumbled
½ c. chopped olives
French dressing
Salt and pepper to taste

Rub wooden salad bowl with garlic clove. Toss all ingredients together. French dressing may be served separately. Yield: 8 servings.

Dianne J. MacPherson
New Holland, Pa.

CHEF'S SALAD

DRESSING:
½ c. vinegar
1 c. salad oil
1 tsp. onion juice
¼ tsp. dry mustard
2 tsp. sugar
Dash of pepper

Combine all ingredients in bottle; shake well.

SALAD:
½ head lettuce, torn into pieces
½ c. spinach or endive or both
¼ c. grated carrots
3 c. chopped celery
¼ c. chopped green pepper
½ c. chopped baked ham
¼ to ½ c. cubed sharp cheese
Thinly sliced radishes
Onion and cauliflower (opt.)

Combine all ingredients. Toss with dressing to coat greens just before serving.

Mrs. Mariguerite Crews
Lewisburg, Pa.

CORN AND PEA SALAD

1 can whole kernel corn, drained
1 can peas, drained
3 sweet pickles, finely chopped
1 tbsp. finely chopped onion
¼ c. salad dressing

Mix all ingredients; serve on lettuce leaf. Yield: 8 servings.

Flossie Hukel
E. St. Louis, Ill.

GREEN GODDESS SALAD BOWL

1 pkg. lime gelatin
1 ½ tsp. garlic salt
¾ c. hot water
Dash of pepper
¾ c. sour cream
¼ c. mayonnaise
1 tbsp. vinegar
1 2-oz. can anchovies, minced
1 9-oz. pkg. frozen artichoke hearts
1 grapefruit, sectioned
1 c. diced tomatoes
½ c. sliced olives
¼ c. chopped green onions
3 qt. salad greens, cut into bite-sized pieces
1 c. French dressing

Dissolve gelatin and garlic salt in hot water. Add pepper, sour cream, mayonnaise, vinegar and anchovies. Beat with egg beater until well blended. Pour into loaf pan; chill until firm. Cut into 1-inch squares. Cook artichoke hearts according to package directions; drain. Cut each artichoke in half; chill. Combine remaining ingredients except French dressing. Toss and chill. Mix artichokes and salad greens mixture. Toss lightly. Arrange anchovy squares on top. Yield: 10 servings.

Betty Pate
Clinton, Ark.

GREEN AND ORANGE SALAD

1 sm. head lettuce
½ head curly endive
2 oranges, sectioned
1 med. grapefruit, sectioned
½ c. orange juice

Toss greens with sectioned fruit. Pour over orange juice. Serve cold.

Dee Ann R. Breuer
Cambridge, Minn.

HODGE PODGE SALAD

6 lb. cabbage, finely shredded
3 lb. spinach, finely cut
2 lb. lettuce, finely chopped
1 lb. celery, thinly sliced
1 lb. raisins, plumped
2 lb. cheese, cubed
1 qt. bread crumbs, toasted and buttered (opt.)

Combine vegetables. Just before serving, add bread crumbs, if desired.

DRESSING:
2 c. vinegar
2 c. sugar
1 c. oil

Combine ingredients, mixing well. Toss salad with dressing just before serving. Yield: 100 servings.

Betty Deadman Shafer
Armada, Mich.

HOME GARDEN MARINADE

Radish slices
Sweet onion rings
Cucumber sticks
Thinly sliced tomatoes
Green pepper rings
Avocado slices
Carrot curls

Arrange vegetables on platter. Refrigerate for 1 hour.

DRESSING:
¾ c. fresh lime juice
6 tbsp. olive oil
1 sm. clove of garlic, crushed
1 ½ tbsp. sugar
1 ½ tsp. salt
½ tsp. pepper
1 tsp. aromatic bitters

Combine all ingredients in covered jar or blender; mix well. Pour over vegetable platter. Yield: 8 servings.

Mrs. Odell T. Lakeman
Haleyville, Ala.

HOT POTATO AND GREEN BEAN SALAD

8 c. thinly sliced cooked potatoes
1 tbsp. salt
Dash of pepper
⅔ c. salad oil
⅓ c. vinegar
3 c. cooked green beans
½ c. thinly sliced onion

(Continued on next page)

Combine all ingredients. Place in a greased 3-quart casserole. Cover; bake at 350 degrees for 45 minutes. Yield: 8 servings.

Mrs. Lawrence Norman
Jamesburg, N.J.

LETTUCE AND PEA SALAD

1 head lettuce, broken or cut
1 stalk celery, chopped
1 pkg. frozen peas, cooked, drained and cooled
1 Bermuda onion, chopped or sliced
1 c. mayonnaise
¼ to ½ c. sugar
½ lb. bacon, broiled, cooled and crumbled
Grated Parmesan cheese

Alternate layers of lettuce, celery, peas and onion. Cover with mayonnaise as if icing a cake. Sprinkle with sugar, bacon and cheese. Cover tightly; refrigerate for several hours. Yield: 12 servings.

Virginia N. Thompson
Ft. Lauderdale, Fla.

LOW-CALORIE BUTTERMILK SALAD

4 hard-cooked eggs, diced
4 cucumbers, peeled and sliced
1 sm. onion, minced
½ head lettuce, finely cut
1 tbsp. chopped celery (opt.)
1 tbsp. minced parsley (opt.)
3 c. buttermilk
½ tsp. salt
¼ tsp. pepper
¼ tsp. garlic salt
1 ½ tbsp. vinegar

Combine eggs, cucumbers, onion, lettuce, celery and parsley. Mix remaining ingredients; pour over egg mixture. Yield: 6-8 servings.

Mrs. Leah Jaeger
Beulah, N.D.

MANDARIN TOSSED SALAD

¼ c. sliced almonds
2 tbsp. sugar
½ head lettuce, shredded
1 c. chopped celery
1 tbsp. minced parsley
2 green onions and tops, chopped
1 can Mandarin oranges, drained

Sprinkle almonds with sugar; cook over low heat, stirring until sugar melts and collects on almonds. Cool. Combine lettuce, celery, parsley, onions, oranges and almonds.

DRESSING:
½ tsp. salt
Pepper
2 tbsp. sugar
2 tbsp. vinegar
¼ c. salad oil
Combine all ingredients in jar; shake vigorously. Serve with salad. Yield: 8 servings.

Mrs. E. E. Tuft
Stillwater, Minn.

ORIENTAL SALAD

1 can bean sprouts, drained
1 can mixed Chinese vegetables, drained
1 sm. can bamboo shoots, drained
1 sm. can water chestnuts, diced
1 canned pimento, diced
½ c. diced onion
½ c. diced green pepper
½ c. diced celery
8 slices bacon, chopped and fried
Bottled Italian dressing

Mix all ingredients except dressing in deep bowl. Cover with Italian dressing. Cover bowl tightly; refrigerate for 1 hour or more. Yield: 6-8 servings.

Mrs. Harry Earle
Middlesboro, Ky.

PATIO BEAN SALAD

1 No. 303 can ranch-style beans
1 No. 303 can French-cut beans
1 No. 303 can whole kernel corn
1 green pepper, chopped
1 onion, sliced into rings
½ c. vinegar
½ c. salad oil
1 c. sugar
½ tsp. salt
Dash of black pepper

Drain beans and corn; add green pepper and onion. Combine remaining ingredients; pour over vegetables. Toss lightly. Marinate in refrigerator for several hours. Serve garnished with spring onions, tomato wedges and celery hearts. Yield: 10-12 servings.

Mrs. R. L. Lemmons
Eads, Tenn.

PEA AND CABBAGE SALAD

1 can sweet peas
1 c. finely chopped cabbage
½ sm. onion, chopped
1 tbsp. salad dressing
Salt and pepper to taste

Combine all ingredients. Toss lightly until thoroughly blended. Yield: 4 servings.

Mrs. Robert F. Stasiak
Turner AFB, Ga.

QUICK AND EASY SALAD

1 1-lb. can red kidney beans
1 1-lb. can mixed vegetables
1 med. head lettuce
1 med. onion, diced
Salt and pepper to taste
Mayonnaise to taste

Drain beans and vegetables. Chop lettuce into bowl; add onion, beans, vegetables, salt, pepper and mayonnaise. Yield: 6 servings.

Mrs. C. D. Autrey
Gila Bend, Ariz.

RAINBOW SALAD

1 c. shredded cabbage
1 c. chopped green peppers
1 c. grated carrots
1 c. sliced celery
1 c. chopped lettuce
1 c. coarsely chopped tomato
1 c. cooked English peas
1 c. grated American cheese
½ c. chopped cucumbers
½ c. sliced onions, separated into rings

Combine all ingredients in large bowl.

DRESSING:
1 tsp. sugar
½ tsp. salt
⅛ tsp. pepper
½ c. vinegar

Combine ingredients; pour over salad. Toss lightly. Yield: 6-8 servings.

Mrs. R. A. Byrd
Tyler, Tex.

RELISH SALAD

1 lge. cucumber
2 med. tomatoes
1 green pepper, chopped
2 pimentos, chopped
2 tbsp. vinegar
2 tsp. sugar
Salt and pepper
Minced fresh onion or onion powder

Pare cucumber and dice. Cut tomatoes into halves; squeeze gently to get rid of most of juice and seed. Dice. Mix cucumber and tomato with green pepper, pimentos, vinegar and sugar; add salt, pepper and onion to taste. Serve on salad greens. Yield: 4-6 servings.

Bettie Watts
Madisonville, Ky.

SCANDINAVIAN SALAD

1 No. 303 can French-style beans, drained
1 No. 303 can sm. English peas, drained
1 sm. can pimento, chopped
1 bunch of celery, finely chopped
½ c. vinegar
¼ c. salad oil
¼ c. sugar
1 tsp. salt

Combine all ingredients. Refrigerate for 24 hours; drain. Yield: 12 servings.

Mrs. W. B. McDowell
Winnsboro, S.C.

SPINACH-CABBAGE SALAD

¼ lb. spinach, chopped
2 carrots, shredded
½ cabbage, shredded
French dressing

Combine all ingredients. Toss. Serve on lettuce leaves. Yield: 6 servings.

Anita Smith
Edinburg, Tex.

SPINACH, LETTUCE AND BACON SALAD

6 strips bacon, diced
4 c. spinach, torn into bite-sized pieces
2 c. lettuce, torn into bite-sized pieces
2 hard-cooked eggs, finely chopped
⅓ c. salad dressing

Fry bacon until crisp; drain. Combine spinach and lettuce; add bacon and eggs. Add salad dressing; toss lightly. Yield: 8 servings.

Judith Robertson
Athens, Ill.

SPRING SALAD

4 or 5 slices cucumber, unpeeled
1 green onion, chopped
2 radishes, cut circular
8 to 10 slices carrot, cut circular
5 or 6 bite-sized pieces lettuce, spinach or endive
2 tbsp. French dressing
Salt to taste

Combine all ingredients; toss lightly.

Mrs. Anna Mae Gausmann
Wolflake, Ind.

SPRING SALAD BOWL

1 bunch leaf lettuce, torn into bite-sized pieces
½ bunch watercress
1 ½ c. tiny spinach leaves
25 carrot curls
4 green onions with tops, chopped
12 ripe olives, pitted
12 almonds, blanched and toasted
Italian dressing

Combine greens, carrot curls and onions. Stuff olives with almonds. Add to greens. Toss with Italian dressing. Yield: 6 servings.

Mrs. Verna Eberhart
Cavalier, N.D.

SUMMER GARDEN SALAD

5 tomatoes, peeled and cut into wedges
1 sm. white onion, thinly sliced
2 or 3 med. boiled potatoes, peeled and sliced
2 or 3 oregano leaves, minced or ¼ tsp. dried oregano
½ tsp. salt
½ tsp. pepper
½ green pepper, chopped
2 or 3 tbsp. salad oil

Combine all ingredients. Toss gently. Chill before serving. Yield: 4 servings.

Virginia Martell
Johnston City, Ill.

SUPPER SALAD

1 No. 2 can cooked red kidney beans, drained
½ c. chopped salted blanched peanuts
1 tbsp. minced onion
½ c. diced celery
2 c. finely shredded cabbage
2 lge. carrots, shredded
¾ c. mayonnaise
¼ c. French dressing
Salt and pepper to taste

Combine all ingredients except mayonnaise, dressing, salt and pepper; chill. Mix remaining ingredients; pour over vegetables. Toss lightly. Garnish with sliced hard-cooked egg, olives or green pepper. Yield: 10-12 servings.

Mrs. O. E. Sponsler
North Baltimore, O.

SWEDISH VEGETABLE SALAD

1 ½ c. diced carrots
1 ½ c. sliced cooked cauliflower
1 ½ c. green peas, cooked
1 ½ c. sliced green beans, cooked
½ c. chopped onion
½ c. chopped celery
1 canned artichoke hearts
⅔ c. French dressing
¾ c. mayonnaise
¼ c. chili sauce
1 tsp. salt
2 tsp. ground dry dill
⅛ tsp. pepper
1 tbsp. lemon juice

Combine all vegetables; marinate in French dressing for 1 hour. Drain well. Mix mayonnaise, chili sauce, dill, salt, pepper and lemon juice; stir into vegetables. Chill. Yield: 12 servings.

Alma Betts
Southwick, Idaho

THREE-WAY SALAD

1 head lettuce
6 carrots, chopped
1 cucumber, chopped
1 tomato, sliced
1 c. croutons or ground crackers
3 stalks celery, diced
1 sm. onion, chopped
¾ c. diet dressing
½ c. grated Cheddar cheese
2 hard-cooked eggs, chopped (opt.)
2 6-oz. cans shrimp (opt.)

Combine all ingredients; toss lightly. Just before serving, add dressing and sprinkle cheese on top. Yield: 6 servings.

Judith McHugh
Ankeny, Iowa

VEGETABLE SALAD

1 c. sugar
1 c. vinegar
1 tsp. salt
1 tsp. mustard seed
½ tsp. celery seed
1 sm. can whole onions, drained
2 c. small whole carrots, cooked
1 No. 2 can whole green beans
French dressing
3 lge. cupped lettuce leaves

Combine sugar, vinegar, salt, mustard seed and celery seed. Heat to boiling point. Pour over onions. Let stand for 24 hours. Marinate carrots and beans in French dressing for several hours. Drain. Place onions, carrots and beans in individual lettuce cups. Yield: 6 servings.

Mrs. Lena Wood
Rockford, Mich.

WATERCRESS A LA DENNIS

2 eggs, beaten
2 c. salad oil
2 tbsp. horseradish
¼ c. tomato catsup
¼ lge. onion, grated
1 tbsp. salt
⅓ c. vinegar
2 tbsp. paprika
Dash of pepper
1 tbsp. Worcestershire sauce
Dash of red pepper
1 slice bacon per serving, crisply fried
Watercress

Thoroughly mix all ingredients except bacon and watercress. Toss watercress with bacon. Serve with dressing.

Mrs. J. D. Wigley
Huntsville, Ala.

MEXICAN SALAD

3 lge. green sweet peppers
1 med. onion
4 med. ripe tomatoes
1 tsp. chili powder
4 slices bacon
½ c. vinegar

Chop and mix vegetables. Cut bacon into small pieces; fry until crisp. Stir in remaining ingredients. When mixture bubbles, pour over vegetables. Place vegetables on lettuce leaves; serve immediately.

Mrs. Geneva Clements
Portales, N.M.

WALKING SALAD

Lettuce leaves
Peanut butter
Carrot sticks

Spread 1 large crisp lettuce leaf with peanut butter for each serving. Add 4 or 5 carrot sticks; roll lettuce leaf so that salad may be eaten from the hand. NOTE: Excellent for cook-outs.

Martha McNatt
Beech Bluff, Tenn.

WISCONSIN SALAD

½ tsp. horseradish
¼ tsp. salt
¼ tsp. pepper
½ c. sour cream
½ c. mayonnaise
7 hard-cooked eggs, chopped
½ lb. Swiss cheese, cut into ½-in. cubes
½ c. finely chopped green pepper
4 chilled tomatoes, peeled and sliced
Parsley sprigs

Combine horseradish, salt, pepper, sour cream and mayonnaise. Add eggs, cheese and green pepper. Chill. Just before serving put a tomato slice on lettuce leaf; cover with chilled mixture. Top with another tomato slice. Garnish with a sprig of parsley. For variety, French onion dip may be used instead of mayonnaise and sour cream.

Mrs. Vivian B. Barnes
Argyle, Wisc.

SWEET AND SOUR CABBAGE SALAD

DRESSING:
¾ c. sugar
½ tsp. salt
½ c. vinegar
½ tsp. celery seed
¼ tsp. pepper

Blend dressing ingredients; stir until sugar dissolves.

SALAD:
1 cabbage, finely chopped
6 celery stalks, diced
1 green pepper, diced
4 pimentos, diced

Combine all ingredients; add dressing. Refrigerate for at least 1 hour. Toss mixture before serving. NOTE: Salad may be made in smaller quantity; unused dressing may be stored in refrigerator. Yield: 20 servings.

Mrs. James J. Nelson
Fort Sheridan, Ill.

CEREAL AND PASTA SALADS

RECIPE FOR MACARONI SALAD PLATTER ON PAGE 282

CURLY RONI SALAD

1 box Curly-Roni
1 pt. peas
1 c. shredded cheese
1 med. can chunk pineapple, drained
½ c. salad dressing or to taste
1 tbsp. chopped red sweet pepper

Cook Curly-Roni according to directions on box; drain. Place in mixing bowl. Heat peas to boiling; drain. Add to Curly-Roni with cheese and pineapple. Toss with salad dressing and salt. Pour into covered dish. Top with red pepper. Yield: 10 servings.

Mrs. Mabel Vest
Polk, Mo.

GOOD MACARONI-FRUIT SALAD

1 c. macaroni
6 marshmallows
1 No. 2 can pineapple
½ c. sugar
2 tbsp. cornstarch
1 c. heavy cream, whipped
3 lge. bananas, sliced
Chopped nuts

Cook macaroni until tender; drain and cool. Finely cut marshmallows. Drain pineapple, reserving juice; cut pineapple coarsely. Pour over marshmallows. Cook pineapple juice, sugar and cornstarch until thickened. Cool; add whipped cream. Combine all fruit; add macaroni and dressing. Yield: 12-15 servings.

Mrs. Henry Elksnin
Yorktown, Va.

MACARONI-FRUIT SALAD DELIGHT

1 No. 303 can crushed pineapple
1 No. 303 can fruit cocktail
2 tbsp. lemon juice
2 tbsp. flour
½ c. sugar
4 eggs, beaten
1 pkg. macaroni rings, cooked and drained
1 pkg. miniature marshmallows
1 pt. heavy cream, whipped
2 c. Mandarin oranges

Drain pineapple and fruit cocktail, reserving juice. Combine lemon juice, flour, sugar and juice drained from pineapple and fruit cocktail. Cook until thickened. Remove from heat. Add eggs; heat again. Cool slightly. Add macaroni, pineapple and fruit cocktail. Chill several hours or overnight. Just before serving add marshmallows, whipped cream and remaining fruit. Yield: 25-30 servings.

Mrs. Melba Olverson
Clark, S.D.

MACARONI-FRUIT SALAD

1 No. 303 can crushed pineapple
1 No. 303 can fruit cocktail
2 tbsp. lemon juice
2 tbsp. flour
½ c. sugar
4 eggs, beaten
½ pkg. macarnoi, cooked and drained
1 pkg. miniature marshmallows
1 pkg. dessert topping mix, whipped
2 c. Bing cherries

Drain pineapple and fruit cocktail; reserve juices. Combine lemon juice, flour, sugar, pineapple and fruit cocktail juices; cook until thickened, stirring constantly. Remove from heat. Add eggs; cook until heated thoroughly. Add macaroni, pineapple and fruit cocktail. Chill for several hours or overnight. Add marshmallows, prepared topping and cherries just before serving. Yield: 25-30 servings.

Mrs. Bernice Cookson
Rawson, O.

MACARONI AND FRUIT SALAD

2 c. shellroni
Red and green food coloring
½ c. water
½ c. pineapple juice
2 eggs, beaten
Pinch of salt
2 tbsp. flour
½ c. sugar
1 ½ tbsp. vinegar
1 c. marshmallows
2 oranges, cut up
1 c. pineapple chunks
1 c. white grapes (opt.)

Prepare shellroni according to package directions. Cook 1 cup at a time, coloring one red and one green. Drain and cool. Combine water, pineapple juice, eggs, salt, flour, sugar and vinegar; cook until thickened, stirring constantly. Cool. Combine all remaining ingredients. Add shellroni and dressing; mix well. May be chilled before serving. Yield: 6 servings.

Mrs. Kathleen Bennett
Wheeler AFB, Hawaii

MACARONI-FRUIT SALAD

½ c. confectioners sugar
2 eggs, separated
¼ c. lemon juice
½ c. cooked alphabet macaroni
Chopped marshmallows
Chopped apples

(Continued on next page)

1 tall can fruit cocktail, drained
1 sm. can crushed pineapple, drained
1 c. whipped cream

Combine sugar, egg yolks and lemon juice; cook until thickened, stirring constantly. Cool. Fold into stiffly beaten egg whites; mix with all remaining ingredients except whipped cream. Chill; fold in whipped cream. Yield: 6 servings.

Mrs. Cecil G. McFarland
Dow AFB, Me.

MACARONI SALAD DELIGHT

4 eggs, well beaten
½ c. lemon juice
3 c. confectioners sugar
2 c. cooked macaroni
1 can pineapple chunks, drained
6 apples, diced
½ c. lemon juice
2 c. whipped cream

Combine eggs, lemon juice and sugar; cook until thickened. Cool; add all remaining ingredients except whipped cream. Chill overnight; add whipped cream.

Mrs. Lucille Speaks
Loami, Ill.

MACARONI SALAD SURPRISE

½ c. sugar
Dash of salt
1 tbsp. flour
2 egg yolks, beaten
1 c. pineapple juice
½ c. cream, whipped
1 box alphabet macaroni, cooked
1 sm. can crushed pineapple
2 oranges, sliced
½ lb. marshmallows

Add sugar, salt and flour to egg yolks. Mix. Add juice and equal amount of water. Boil until thick. Cool; add whipped cream. Pour over macaroni, pineapple, oranges and marshmallows. Chill and serve. Yield: 10 servings.

Mrs. Stanley Kotaska
Lankin, N.D.

BEST MACARONI AND CHEESE SALAD

1 3-oz. pkg. macaroni
1 12-oz. can ham, cut into strips
1 c. Cheddar cheese, cubed
½ c. cubed celery
¼ c. pickle relish
½ c. mayonnaise
1 tbsp. mustard
¼ tsp. salt

Cook macaroni according to package directions; drain and cool. Combine macaroni, ham, cheese, celery and relish. Blend mayonnaise, mustard and salt. Toss with macaroni mixture. Chill. Serve on greens. Yield: 6 servings.

Betty Canada
Munford, Ala.

CHICKEN-MACARONI SALAD

3 ½ qt. cooked elbow macaroni
1 ¾ qt. diced celery
1 qt. cooked diced chicken
2 c. diced green pepper
2 c. chopped pimento
2 c. mayonnaise or salad dressing
4 tsp. salt
1 tsp. pepper

Combine all ingredients; chill. Yield: 30-35 servings.

Mrs. O. J. Fry, Jr.
Willow Grove, Pa.

CHICKEN-MACARONI SALAD

1 5-oz. can boned chicken
3 hard-cooked eggs
1 c. cooked macaroni
2 tbsp. sweet pickle relish
1 tbsp. mustard
1 tsp. salt
1 tbsp. minced onion
Pimento (opt.)
Salad dressing to taste

Chop chicken and eggs; combine with macaroni. Add all remaining ingredients. Yield: 6 servings.

Josephine Pryor
Nevada, Iowa

CHILLED MACARONI SALAD

4 c. cooked shell macaroni, chilled
4 hard-cooked eggs, chilled and chopped
¾ c. diced or cubed ham
¾ c. cubed cheese
¼ c. diced green pepper
2 tbsp. diced onion

(Continued on next page)

3 tbsp. diced pickle
Dash of Worcestershire sauce
½ to ¾ c. mayonnaise
Lettuce
Paprika
Parsley

Combine all ingredients except paprika, parsley and lettuce. Toss lightly. Spoon onto lettuce cups. Garnish with paprika and parsley. Chill before serving. Yield: 6 servings.

Elizabeth Overley
Gueydan, La.

MACARONI AND HAM SALAD

2 c. uncooked macaroni
1 sm. onion, chopped
Salt to taste
Pepper to taste
1 c. diced ham or cheese
Mayonnaise or salad dressing

Cook macaroni according to package directions; drain and cool. Combine all ingredients using enough mayonnaise or salad dressing to moisten. Yield: 4 servings.

Phyllis Rae Horner
Severna Park, Md.

CUCUMBER CANOES

3 med. cucumbers
1 c. cooked elbow macaroni
1 12-oz. can luncheon meat, cubed
½ c. grated carrots
¼ c. chopped green pepper
½ c. mayonnaise
2 tbsp. vinegar
2 tbsp. horseradish
Salt and pepper

Cut cucumbers into halves lengthwise. Scoop out pulp from each half, leaving a shell 1/4-inch thick. Chop pulp; combine with macaroni, luncheon meat, carrots and green pepper. Blend mayonnaise, vinegar and horseradish. Add to meat mixture; toss lightly. Season to taste with salt and pepper. Pile salad into cucumber shells. Yield: 6 servings.

Mrs. Ruth Voigt
Monroeville, Pa.

MACARONI-CHICKEN SALAD BOWL

1 8-oz. pkg. elbow macaroni
4 c. water
½ tsp. salt
1 c. sliced celery
1 ½ c. diced cooked chicken
⅓ c. chopped sweet pickles
1 tbsp. scraped onion
¼ c. French dressing
Mayonnaise or salad dressing

Cook macaroni in water in a 2-quart saucepan. Add salt; bring to a rapid boil. Stir; cover and boil until tender. Drain and cool. Mix celery, chicken, pickles, onion and French dressing; blend with mayonnaise or salad dressing. Mix with macaroni. Chill. Garnish with sliced sweet pickles. Yield: 8 servings.

Mrs. Sarah Musgrave
Rattan, Okla.

MACARONI SALAD PLATTER

2 tbsp. plus 2 tsp. salt
4 to 6 qt. boiling water
4 c. uncooked elbow macaroni
2 c. chopped celery
¼ c. chopped onion
¼ c. sweet pickle relish
¾ tsp. dry mustard
2 tsp. vinegar
¾ to 1 c. mayonnaise
Western iceberg lettuce
Radish roses
1 12-oz. can luncheon meat, chilled and cut into strips
1 12-oz. can frankfurters, chilled and sliced
1 1-lb. can peas, chilled and drained

Add 2 tablespoons salt to rapidly boiling water. Gradually add macaroni so that water continues to boil. Cook, uncovered, until tender, stirring occasionally. Drain in colander. Rinse with cold water; drain again. Combine macaroni with celery, onion, pickle relish, remaining salt, mustard, vinegar and mayonnaise; toss lightly. Chill. Arrange on crisp lettuce leaves with radish roses, canned meats and peas. Serve with salad dressing if desired. Yield: 8 servings.

Photograph for this recipe on page 279.

MACARONI SALAD

1 6-oz. pkg. shell macaroni
⅓ c. mayonnaise
1 tsp. Worcestershire sauce
1 tsp. prepared mustard
Dash of salt
Dash of pepper
½ c. chopped celery
2 tbsp. minced onion
¼ c. chopped sweet pickles
1 c. cooked cubed ham

Cook macaroni in salted water; drain. Add mayonnaise, Worcestershire sauce, mustard,

(Continued on next page)

salt and pepper. Mix thoroughly. Add celery, onion, sweet pickles and ham. Serve warm or chilled. Yield: 6 servings.

Jane Baker
Paducah, Tex.

HAM SALAD

2 c. diced cooked ham
2 c. raw elbow macaroni, cooked
½ c. chopped green pepper
2 c. sliced celery
1 med. onion, diced
1 c. diced American Cheddar cheese
⅔ c. salad dressing
2 tbsp. vinegar
1 tsp. mustard
⅔ c. milk
1 tsp. salt
1 c. chopped ripe olives

Combine ham, macaroni, green pepper, celery, onion and cheese. Blend salad dressing, vinegar, mustard, milk, salt and olives; add to ham mixture. Toss lightly until well blended. Refrigerate. Yield: 8 servings.

Mrs. Clara David
Flint, Mich.

MACARONI SALAD

1 4-oz. pkg. elbow macaroni
1 lge. green pepper, chopped
4 sm. carrots, sliced or grated
1 sm. can pimento, chopped
3 stalks celery, finely cut
½ tsp. salt
Mayonnaise
2 hard-cooked egg yolks
¼ c. shrimp, diced ham or luncheon meat (opt.)
¼ c. cooked peas (opt.)
¼ c. cooked string beans (opt.)
¼ c. cooked butter beans (opt.)
¼ c. diced cheese (opt.)

Cook macaroni for 15 minutes; drain and cool. Add remaining ingredients except mayonnaise and egg yolks. Chill. Serve with combined mayonnaise and egg yolks. Yield: 6 servings.

Mrs. Catherine Richard
Destrehan, La.

MACARONI SALAD

3 c. cooked macaroni, drained
¾ c. chopped ham
¾ c. chopped chicken
¼ c. diced celery
¼ c. minced onion
¼ c. chopped green pepper
1 pimento, chopped
½ c. mayonnaise
Salt and pepper to taste
2 hard-cooked eggs, chopped

Combine all ingredients except eggs. Mix well. Garnish with eggs. Yield: 6-8 servings.

Judy Lennon
Achille, Okla.

MACARONI SALAD

1 8-oz. pkg. elbow macaroni
1 c. chopped celery
1 c. chopped sweet pickles
2 tbsp. grated onion
1 can Vienna sausage, thinly sliced
1 c. mayonnaise
2 tbsp. pickle juice
1 tsp. salt
¼ tsp. pepper

Cook macaroni until tender; drain. Rinse in cold water; drain thoroughly. Combine with celery, pickles, onion and sausage reserving a few for garnish. Blend mayonnaise with juice, salt and pepper; add to macaroni mixture. Arrange on salad plate; decorate top with sausage slices. May be garnished with deviled egg halves. Yield: 6 servings.

Ernestine Gresham
Bullard, Tex.

HAM AND MACARONI SALAD

1 12-oz. can ham, chopped
2 c. macaroni, cooked
4 hard-cooked eggs, diced
½ c. chopped celery
¼ c. minced onion
¼ c. chopped sweet pickles
½ c. salad dressing
1 tbsp. vinegar

Combine ham, macaroni, eggs, celery, onion and pickles. Blend salad dressing and vinegar. Pour over ham mixture; toss gently. Chill. Yield: 10 servings.

Mrs. Arnold Hantilman
Fenton, Iowa

HAM AND MACARONI SALAD

½ lb. cold boiled ham
3 hard-cooked eggs, chopped
4 sweet pickles, chopped

(Continued on next page)

1 tbsp. chopped pimento
1 c. diced celery
1 c. cooked macaroni
Salt and pepper to taste
Mayonnaise

Combine all ingredients, using enough mayonnaise to moisten. Mix lightly with two forks. Serve on crisp lettuce with mayonnaise. Yield: 8 servings.

Mrs. Goldie M. Bodine
St. Charles, S.D.

HEARTY MACARONI SALAD

1 8-oz. pkg. macaroni, cooked
1 c. chopped celery
½ green pepper, chopped
2 green onions, chopped
1 can luncheon meat, diced
¾ c. mayonnaise
1 4-oz. jar pimento
½ c. sour cream
2 tbsp. vinegar
¼ c. chopped parsley
½ c. diced Cheddar cheese
Salt and pepper to taste
Salad greens

Combine all ingredients except salad greens. Serve on bed of mixed salad greens. Yield: 10-12 servings.

Mrs. Donald Presson
Mammoth Spring, Ark.

HEARTY MACARONI SALAD SUPREME

½ c. uncooked macaroni
¼ lb. luncheon meat, cubed
½ c. canned green peas, chilled
½ c. chopped celery
¼ lb. Cheddar cheese, cubed
1 tbsp. chopped onion
1 tbsp. minced parsley
¼ c. chopped green pepper
Salt and pepper to taste
⅓ c. salad dressing
1 hard-cooked egg, sliced

Cook macaroni according to package directions; drain. Toss all ingredients together except egg. Chill. Garnish with egg slices. Yield: 6 servings.

Mrs. Stewart Knight
Hale Center, Tex.

HOT OR COLD MACARONI SALAD

1 4-oz. pkg. elbow macaroni
4 strips bacon, cut into ½-in. pieces
½ c. diced celery
¼ c. chopped green pepper
¾ c. chopped cucumber pickles
¼ c. chopped onion
2 tbsp. chili sauce
½ tsp. Worcestershire sauce
1 tsp. salt
⅛ tsp. pepper
1 tsp. sugar
¼ c. mayonnaise

Cook macaroni in boiling salted water about 12 minutes. Drain and rinse. Cook bacon until crisp. Fold all ingredients into macaroni. Heat in top of double boiler. Serve hot or chill overnight before serving. Yield: 8 servings.

Mrs. Mary C. Williamson
Hallsboro, N.C.

MAIN DISH SALAD

1 4-oz. pkg. elbow macaroni
1 c. cooked chopped chicken, turkey or tuna
2 hard-cooked eggs, diced
½ c. crushed pineapple, drained
¼ c. sliced radishes
¼ c. chopped nuts
1 tbsp. chopped onion
⅓ c. mayonnaise
1 ½ tbsp. pineapple juice
¼ tsp. celery seed
¼ tsp. salt
Dash of pepper

Cook macaroni as directed on package. Combine meat, eggs, pineapple, radishes, nuts and onion. Add macaroni; toss lightly. Combine mayonnaise and pineapple juice; mix until smooth. Stir in celery seed, salt and pepper. Pour over macaroni mixture. Toss until well blended. Chill. Serve on salad greens. Yield: 4 servings.

Mrs. Ruth A. Blomgren
Silver Springs, Md.

MACARONI SALAD

2 c. macaroni, cooked
2 c. diced cooked chicken or ham
1 lge. cucumber, finely chopped
1 c. mayonnaise
2 pimentos, chopped

Combine all ingredients; toss lightly. Yield: 8-10 servings.

Mrs. Frank Erts
Popejoy, Iowa

ZIPPY HAM AND MACARONI SALAD

½ lb. boiled ham, sliced ⅛-in. thick
4 tsp. salt
3 qt. boiling water
2 c. uncooked elbow macaroni
2 med. tomatoes, coarsely chopped
⅓ c. sliced scallions or green onions
⅓ c. salad oil
3 tbsp. vinegar
1½ tsp. dry mustard
2 tsp. sugar
⅛ tsp. pepper

Roll up ham slices tightly, jelly-roll fashion. Chill. Add 3 teaspoons salt to rapidly boiling water. Gradually add macaroni so that water continues to boil. Cook, uncovered, until tender, stirring occasionally. Drain in colander. Rinse with cold water; drain. Combine macaroni and remaining ingredients; mix well. Chill. Arrange ham rolls on macaroni salad. Garnish as desired.

Photograph for this recipe above.

VIENNA MACARONI SALAD

1 8-oz. pkg. elbow macaroni
1 c. chopped celery
1 c. chopped sweet pickles
2 tbsp. grated onion
1 c. thinly sliced Vienna sausage
1 c. mayonnaise
2 tbsp. pickle juice
1 tsp. salt
¼ tsp. pepper
6 lettuce leaves
3 deviled eggs, halved

Cook macaroni until tender. Drain; blanch in cold water. Drain again. Combine with celery, sweet pickles, onion and Vienna sausages. Blend mayonnaise with pickle juice, salt and pepper; add to macaroni mixture. Chill. Heap salad on lettuce in center of large serving plate. Arrange additional Vienna sausages over top to resemble spokes. Arrange deviled egg halves around salad. Yield: 6 servings.

Mrs. Dorothy Sue T. Hill
Oberlin, La.

CRAB-MACARONI SALAD

1 8-oz. pkg. elbow or shell macaroni
1 can crabmeat
½ c. shredded cabbage or 1 c. diced carrots
1 c. diced cucumbers

(Continued on next page)

1 c. diced celery
¼ c. chopped or thinly sliced onion
½ c. chopped or thinly sliced green pepper
1 sm. jar pimento, cut into strips
3 hard-cooked eggs, sliced
Salt and pepper to taste
Mayonnaise or dressing to taste

Boil macaroni according to package directions; drain well and chill. Flake crab; combine with macaroni, cabbage, cucumbers, celery, onion, green pepper, pimento and eggs. Season with salt and pepper. Blend with mayonnaise or boiled dressing. Garnish with thin slices of tomatoes and radishes. Chill for at least 30 minutes. Yield: 6 servings.

Mrs. Sally D. Pickering
Rumford Center, Me.

MACA-SALMON SALAD

2 c. macaroni
1 c. diced cheese
1 c. diced sweet pickle
1 c. diced celery
¼ c. diced pimento
¼ c. minced green pepper
¼ c. minced onion
4 c. canned salmon, drained and flaked
2 c. mayonnaise
2 tbsp. prepared mustard
6 tbsp. vinegar
2 heads lettuce

Cook macaroni according to directions on package; drain. Add cheese; toss until well mixed. Cool. Add pickles, celery, pimento, green pepper and onion. Add salmon. Blend mayonnaise, mustard and vinegar. Pour over salad; chill thoroughly. At serving time, use crisp outer leaves of lettuce to line big bowls or chop plates. Cut remaining lettuce; add to salad. Toss lightly. Yield: 14-18 servings.

Mrs. Ellen D. Feagan
Las Cruces, N.M.

MACARONI-SALMON SALAD

2 c. cooked macaroni, cooled
1 c. diced cucumbers
1 8-oz. can salmon, flaked
1 tbsp. grated onion
1 tbsp. minced parsley
¾ c. mayonnaise
½ tsp. salt
¼ tsp. pepper

Combine all ingredients; toss together until blended. Yield: 4-6 servings.

Mrs. Linda J. McCraw
Gaffney, S.C.

SALMON-MACARONI SALAD

2 c. cooked macaroni
1 1-lb. can salmon, drained and flaked
½ c. chopped celery
½ c. minced sweet pickles
2 tbsp. chopped green pepper
1 tsp. salt
1 tbsp. lemon juice
⅓ c. boiled dressing

Combine all ingredients; chill thoroughly. Yield: 8 servings.

Virginia Dale Rawls
Pearl River, La.

SALMON SALAD

2 c. flaked salmon
3 hard-cooked eggs, chopped
½ c. diced cheese
3 med. tomatoes, diced
1 ½ c. cooked macaroni
¼ c. diced sweet pickles
2 tbsp. sweet pickle juice
½ c. diced celery
Salt to taste
¾ c. mayonnaise

Mix thoroughly and chill. Yield: 6 servings.

Frances M. Watson
Millbury, O.

MACARONI SALAD DISH

2 c. cooked shrimp, sliced cold cuts, or frankfurters
French dressing
2 c. cooked macaroni
1 c. diced celery
½ c. diced cucumbers
3 tbsp. finely chopped green pepper
2 tbsp. grated onion
2 tbsp. chopped parsley
½ tsp. celery seed
Salt
Pepper
Mayonnaise or salad dressing
2 hard-cooked eggs, sliced

Sprinkle meat with a small amount of French dressing; chill for 30 minutes. Add macaroni, vegetables, seasonings, and enough mayonnaise to moisten. Toss; chill for 1 to 2 hours before serving. Garnish with egg slices. Yield: 6 servings.

Maud Cunningham
Exeter, Calif.

MACARONI-SHRIMP SALAD

2 c. macaroni
1 c. finely chopped celery
1 can shrimp
2 hard-cooked eggs, finely chopped
¼ c. pimento
¼ tsp. paprika
½ tsp. salt
1 c. mayonnaise
¼ c. French dressing

Cook macaroni according to package directions; cool. Add celery, shrimp, eggs, pimento, paprika and salt. Mix mayonnaise and French dressing and add to macaroni mixture.

Mrs. Sharon Nelson
Karlstad, Minn.

MACARONI AND SHRIMP SALAD

1 c. mayonnaise
3 tbsp. sweet pickle juice
¼ tsp. salt
Dash of pepper
Dash of cayenne
1 tsp. mustard
1 tsp. sugar
1 sm. onion, diced
¼ c. diced sweet pickles
3 hard-cooked eggs, sliced
1 c. shrimp
3 pimentos, diced
½ green pepper, diced
2 sticks celery, diced
½ c. diced Cheddar cheese
1 12-oz. pkg. macaroni, cooked

Combine all ingredients; add more mayonnaise if necessary. Chill for several hours. May be garnished with paprika, parsley and olives. Yield: 8-12 servings.

Mrs. Agnes E. Rogers
Milton, Fla.

SHRIMP DINNER SALAD

4 c. shell macaroni, cooked
½ c. French dressing
2 c. uncooked cauliflowerets
1 c. thinly sliced scallions
1 tsp. salt
¼ tsp. pepper
2 lb. cooked shrimp
1 c. sliced ripe olives
1 c. mayonnaise
½ c. chili sauce

Toss macaroni with French dressing; chill for 1 hour. Add cauliflowerets, scallions, salt, pepper, shrimp and olives. Blend mayonnaise and chili sauce; pour over salad. Toss to mix. Yield: 10 servings.

Mrs. Maranell Fleming
Honolulu, Hawaii

SHRIMP AND MACARONI SALAD

1 8-oz. pkg. elbow macaroni
1 can deveined shrimp
1 med. cucumber, diced
1 med. onion, chopped
2 hard-cooked eggs, cut up
Salt and pepper to taste
2 tbsp. mayonnaise

Boil macaroni until tender; drain. Let set in cold water until cooled; drain. Add shrimp, cucumber, onion, eggs, salt and pepper. Toss with mayonnaise; chill. Yield: 6 servings.

Mrs. Jessie Schulz
Parris Island, S.C.

SHRIMP AND MACARONI SALAD

2 c. fresh or frozen shrimp, cleaned and cooked
2 c. cooked salad macaroni
3 hard-cooked eggs, chopped
1 c. diced green pepper
1 c. diced celery
1 tbsp. mustard
1 c. salad dressing
½ tsp. cayenne pepper

Chop shrimp into medium pieces. Add all remaining ingredients. Chill; serve on lettuce. Yield: 8 servings.

Mrs. Richard Singleton
Requa, Calif.

SHRIMP-MACARONI SALAD

½ tsp. salt
¼ tsp. paprika
1 c. mayonnaise
¼ c. French dressing
1 ½ c. macaroni, cooked
1 c. chopped celery
1 med. onion, chopped
¼ c. chopped green pepper
¼ c. chopped pimento
1 7-oz. can shrimp
2 hard-cooked eggs, chopped

(Continued on next page)

Combine salt, paprika, mayonnaise and French dressing. Toss with remaining ingredients. Serve in crisp lettuce cup for individual servings. Yield: 6 servings.

Mrs. John Ramage
Langdon, N.D.

SHRIMP AND MACARONI SALAD

1 ½ tbsp. lemon juice
1 tbsp. oil
1 c. raw macaroni, cooked
1 ½ c. diced shrimp
2 hard-cooked eggs, diced
2 tbsp. chopped green pepper
1 tbsp. chopped onion
½ c. chopped celery
½ c. diced fresh tomato
¼ c. diced stuffed green olives
2 tbsp. sour cream
½ tsp. salt
¼ c. mayonnaise

Mix lemon juice, oil and macaroni; chill several hours. Fold in shrimp, eggs and vegetables. Combine remaining ingredients; fold into macaroni mixture. Toss; chill and serve. Yield: 6 servings.

Herman Keith Collins
Lucerne, Calif.

SHRIMP-MACARONI SALAD

1 ½ c. macaroni
¾ c. diced celery
¼ c. sliced green onions
3 radishes, sliced
½ c. sliced mushrooms
½ c. mayonnaise
1 tbsp. soy sauce
½ tsp. celery seed
1 c. shrimp, cooked and cleaned
Seasoned salt
Pepper to taste

Cook macaroni; drain and cool. Blend with all remaining ingredients; chill until ready to serve. Yield: 4-6 servings.

Mrs. Thomas Blastic
Adair, Oreg.

SHRIMP SALAD

3 c. cooked macaroni
½ c. shredded carrots
½ c. chopped celery
¼ c. finely chopped onion
2 cans salad shrimp
2 tbsp. sweet pickle relish
½ to 1 c. mayonnaise
Salt and pepper to taste

Combine all ingredients in large bowl. Cover and refrigerate until ready to serve. Yield: 6 servings.

Mrs. Patricia Pfleger
Ft. Benjamin Harrison, Ind.

SHRIMP SALAD

1 lb. shrimp, cooked and cleaned
1 pkg. shell macaroni, cooked
1 onion, chopped
1 green pepper, chopped
2 c. chopped celery
2 hard-cooked eggs, chopped
4 tbsp. salad dressing
Pepper to taste

Combine all ingredients; toss lightly to mix. Serve on salad greens. Yield: 8 servings.

Mrs. B. D. Thomas
Baytown, Tex.

SUMMER DELIGHT

1 14-oz. pkg. macaroni, cooked
4 hard-cooked eggs, chopped
1 c. finely chopped celery
1 c. finely chopped pickles
6 sm. green onions, chopped
1 4 ½-oz. can cocktail shrimp, drained
1 carrot, grated
Pimento (opt.)
Salad dressing to taste

Combine all ingredients; let blend for about 2 hours before serving. Yield: 8-10 servings.

Mrs. Carol C. Tone
Beaver Mtn., Oreg.

BEST MACARONI SALAD

4 c. cooked elbow macaroni
1 ½ c. sliced celery
½ c. chopped green onions
6 radishes, sliced
2 tbsp. snipped parsley
½ c. mayonnaise
½ c. French dressing
2 tbsp. vinegar
2 tbsp. salt
Pinch of pepper
1 c. diced Cheddar cheese
Lettuce
Pared cucumber

(Continued on next page)

Chopped green pepper
2 hard-cooked eggs, chopped
1 c. flaked salmon or tuna

Combine all ingredients; chill. Yield: 6 servings.

Mrs. Bertha Noe
Edwardsville, Ill.

FARMER'S SALAD GELATIN MOLD

2 envelopes unflavored gelatin
1 c. water
2 ½ c. tomato juice
2 tbsp. lemon juice
2 tsp. Worcestershire sauce
½ tsp. salt
¼ tsp. onion salt
2 7-oz. cans tuna, flaked and drained
½ c. diced celery
½ c. cooked peas
1 c. elbow macaroni, cooked and drained

Soften gelatin in water for 5 minutes over very low heat, stirring frequently. Combine with juices, Worcestershire sauce and seasonings. Chill until thickened; fold in all remaining ingredients. Turn into lightly oiled 9 x 5 x 3-inch pan; chill until firm. Yield: 6 servings.

Mrs. W. B. Nickell
Centerville, O.

FAVORITE TUNA-MACARONI SALAD

1 6-oz. can tuna
1 c. macaroni rings
3 hard-cooked eggs, chopped
½ c. chopped celery
1 tbsp. chopped onion
1 tbsp. chopped pickle or relish
½ c. salad dressing
2 tbsp. evaporated milk
2 tbsp. lemon juice or pickle juice
1 tbsp. mayonnaise

Cook macaroni rings according to directions on package. Combine tuna, eggs, celery, onion and pickle. Add macaroni. Combine salad dressing, evaporated milk and lemon or pickle juice. Fold dressing carefully into salad mixture; chill for several hours. Just before serving add mayonnaise. Garnish with egg slices, olives and paprika. Yield: 8 servings.

Mrs. Esther E. Smith
Westfield, Pa.

FISH AND MACARONI SALAD

1 lb. shell macaroni, cooked
1 c. mayonnaise
½ tsp. salt
¼ tsp. pepper
2 c. flaked fish
1 c. thinly sliced celery
1 c. thinly sliced onion
3 hard-cooked eggs, sliced

Chill macaroni. Blend mayonnaise, salt and pepper; add fish and macaroni. Add all remaining ingredients and toss. Chill before serving. Yield: 8 servings.

Ellen E. Kukkuck
Venice, Fla.

HOT TUNA-MACARONI TOSS

1 c. elbow macaroni
¼ c. Italian dressing
1 tsp. celery seed
¾ tsp. dry mustard
½ tsp. salt
Dash of pepper
1 6 ½-oz. can tuna
½ c. diced celery
½ c. diced green pepper
3 tbsp. salad dressing

Cook macaroni according to package directions; drain. Mix Italian dressing and seasonings; heat just to boiling. Add macaroni, tuna, celery and green pepper. Toss lightly; heat through. Stir in salad dressing. Serve immediately. Yield: 6 servings.

Mrs. Sarah Strange Martin
Tampa, Fla.

MACARONI SALAD

2 c. shell macaroni
1 c. Tokay grapes
1 c. diced celery
1 sm. onion, finely chopped
1 6 ½-oz. can chunk tuna
½ c. mayonnaise
3 tbsp. sugar

Cook macaroni in salted water until tender. Rinse and cool. Cut grapes in halves; remove seeds. Add grapes, celery, onion and tuna to macaroni. Mix mayonnaise and sugar; pour over macaroni. Mix well. NOTE: Fruit cocktail, drained, may be substituted for grapes. Yield: 10-12 servings.

Mrs. Albert Weber
Strandburg, S.D.

MACARONI-TUNA SALAD

1 sm. pkg. shell macaroni, cooked
1 sm. can tuna
1 sm. can green peas
½ c. chopped onion
½ c. chopped sweet pickles
½ c. chopped olives
½ c. chopped green pepper
½ c. mayonnaise
1 tbsp. mustard
Salt and pepper
1 sm. tomato, sliced
2 hard-cooked eggs, sliced

Combine all ingredients except tomato and egg slices. Mix well; top with tomato and egg slices. Yield: 6 servings.

Mrs. Jane Birley
Gila Bend, Ariz.

MACARONI-TUNA SALAD SUPREME

1 can tuna, flaked
½ c. diced celery
⅓ c. diced sweet pickles
½ c. chopped pimento
4 hard-cooked eggs, chopped
1 sm. can English peas
1 c. shell macaroni, cooked
Juice of 1 lemon
Salt and pepper to taste
Mayonnaise to taste

Combine all ingredients; chill thoroughly. Serve on lettuce leaf. Yield: 6 servings.

Mrs. J. D. Edmondson
Birmingham, Ala.

SALAD SUPPER

1 7-oz. pkg. shell or lge. elbow macaroni
1 7-oz. can tuna, drained
1 sm. onion, finely chopped
2 hard-cooked eggs, sliced
1 c. diced celery
½ c. sliced and pitted ripe olives
2 tomatoes, quartered
Mayonnaise
Salt to taste

Cook macaroni in small amount of water. Cool. Mix all ingredients except eggs and tomatoes, adding enough mayonnaise to moisten. Garnish with eggs and tomatoes. Chill before serving.

Mrs. Joe D. Gamble
Friendswood, Tex.

SPECIAL MACARONI AND TUNA SALAD

3 c. cooked macaroni
2 tsp. grated onion
¾ c. sliced celery
3 hard-cooked eggs, chopped
1 c. assorted cooked vegetables
¼ c. chopped green pepper
¼ c. chopped pimento
1 6½-oz. can tuna, flaked
¾ to 1 c. mayonnaise or salad dressing

Combine all ingredients; mix well. Pack into molds or mold; chill. Serve on salad greens; garnish with parsley.

Harriet R. Townsend
Altoona, Pa.

TUNA-CHEESE-MACARONI SALAD

1 7 or 8-oz. pkg. macaroni
1 6½-oz. can tuna
1 c. cubed Cheddar cheese
½ c. chopped sweet pickles
¼ c. minced onion
½ c. mayonnaise
2 tbsp. prepared mustard
1 tbsp. sugar
1 No. 303 can peas, drained

Drain cooked macaroni; rinse in cold water. Add tuna, cheese, pickles and onion. Mix mayonnaise, mustard and sugar. Combine with macaroni mixture. Add peas and salt to taste; mix well. Yield: 6 servings.

Mrs. Robert Berkner
Lamberton, Minn.

TUNA-MACARONI SALAD

1 8-oz. pkg. macaroni, cooked
1 lge. can tuna
2 hard-cooked eggs, chopped
Salt and pepper to taste
1 sm. onion, chopped (opt.)
Mayonnaise to taste

Combine all ingredients. Garnish with paprika. Yield: 5-6 servings.

Mrs. O. M. Baker
Key West, Fla.

TUNA-MACARONI SALAD

Garlic (opt.)
1 8-oz. pkg. macaroni shells, cooked
1 sm. onion, finely diced
1 sm. can tuna, drained and flaked
Mayonnaise to taste

(Continued on next page)

Rub salad bowl with garlic, if desired. Combine remaining ingredients; mix well. Yield: 4 servings.

Mrs. William H. Murphy
Youngstown, O.

TUNA-MACARONI SALAD

1 c. elbow macaroni
2 c. finely shredded cabbage
½ c. grated carrot
¼ c. julienne green pepper
2 tbsp. minced onion
1 7-oz. can tuna, drained and flaked
½ c. mayonnaise or salad dressing
2 tbsp. mustard
1 tsp. salt
2 tsp. vinegar

Cook macaroni in boiling salted water until tender; drain and rinse. Combine macaroni, cabbage, carrot, green pepper, onion and tuna. Blend mayonnaise with all remaining ingredients; pour over macaroni mixture and toss. Chill; serve on lettuce. Yield: 6 servings.

Mrs. Pauline Dilbeck
Section, Ala.

TUNA SALAD

1 6 ½-oz. can tuna
2 hard-cooked eggs, chopped
⅓ c. chopped sweet pickles
¼ c. chopped celery
1 box elbow macaroni, cooked and drained
2 tbsp. salad dressing or mayonnaise

Combine all ingredients; chill. Serve. Yield: 6-8 servings.

Mrs. J. W. Stanford
Forest Park, Ga.

TUNA RONI SALAD

½ c. shell macaroni
1 can tuna, flaked
1 No. 303 can English peas, drained
½ c. diced celery
1 c. cubed cheese
⅓ c. chopped sweet pickles
3 pimentos, chopped
¾ to 1 c. salad dressing
Salt and pepper to taste
Pimento strips, paprika or hard-cooked egg wedges

Cook macaroni in boiling salted water until tender; drain. Rinse with cold water. Combine all ingredients. Mix well. Garnish with pimento strips, paprika or egg wedges. Salad may be made the day before serving if desired. Yield: 8-10 servings.

Mrs. Thelma Cravy
Jacksonville, Tex.

TUNA SALAD FORTUNA

2 cans tuna
1 lge. can peas
½ pkg. macaroni, cooked
2 hard-cooked eggs, chopped
1 c. chopped Cheddar or American cheese
2 med. carrots, chopped
2 stalks celery, chopped
Mayonnaise to taste

Combine all ingredients. Arrange on lettuce. Yield: 6-8 servings.

Mrs. R. P. Shay
Westby, Mont.

BEST MACARONI SALAD

1 7-oz. pkg. macaroni, cooked
1 ½ c. shredded green cabbage
1 ½ c. cubed Cheddar cheese
1 lge. sweet green pepper, chopped
3 lge. tomatoes, cubed
1 sm. onion, chopped (opt.)
½ tsp. celery seed
Salt and pepper to taste
½ c. mayonnaise

Mix all ingredients. Serve on lettuce; garnish with stuffed olives and paprika if desired. Yield: 6-8 servings.

Mrs. Joalice Poehler
Big Lake, Tex.

CHEESE-MACARONI SALAD

2 c. cooked seasoned macaroni
1 c. diced celery
1 c. cooked peas
¼ c. shredded carrots
1 green pepper or pimento, shredded
Salt and pepper
Mayonnaise
Cheese balls or stuffed olives

Chill macaroni; combine with celery, peas, carrots and green pepper. Season to taste. Moisten with mayonnaise; mix lightly with two forks. Serve on crisp salad greens. Garnish with cheese balls or diced stuffed olives. Yield: 6 servings.

Mrs. Della Bradley
Wrightsboro, Tex.

EASY MACARONI SALAD

1 8-oz. pkg. shell or elbow macaroni
French dressing
3 hard-cooked eggs, chopped
½ c. chopped celery
½ c. chopped onion
½ c. chopped green pepper
½ c. sliced green stuffed olives
1 c. cooked green beans
½ c. salad dressing or mayonnaise
Salt to taste

Cook and drain macaroni. Combine with enough French dressing to coat macaroni; chill. Add all remaining ingredients; chill. Yield: 6-8 servings.

Mrs. Richard Wight, Jr.
Whittemore, Mich.

GOOD MACARONI SALAD

3 c. chilled cooked macaroni
½ c. cooked chilled peas
½ lb. cheese, cubed
1 c. chopped celery
2 tbsp. minced onion
¼ c. minced green pepper
3 hard-cooked eggs, chopped

Combine all ingredients reserving a small amount of eggs for garnish. Toss lightly with favorite salad dressing. Top with reserved eggs. Yield: 6 servings.

Mrs. R. B. Pearcy
Levelland, Tex.

MACARONI AND PEA SALAD

1 box macaroni
1 sm. can pimento
1 No. 2 can English peas
1 c. chopped celery
1 sm. onion, chopped
Mayonnaise to taste

Cook macaroni until tender; drain. Rinse with cold water. Add all remaining ingredients; chill. Yield: 6 servings.

Mrs. Toni Dillard
Cartersville, Ga.

MACARONI SALAD

1 7-oz. pkg. macaroni
½ c. French dressing
2 tbsp. grated onion
⅔ c. mayonnaise
1 c. diced cucumber
1 c. sliced radishes
½ c. finely chopped green pepper

Cook macaroni according to package directions. Rinse with cold water; drain well. Add French dressing and onion. Toss lightly with fork, mixing thoroughly. Cover tightly; refrigerate overnight. Stir in remaining ingredients to serve.

Mrs. Ralph Welch
Carmel, Ind.

MACARONI SALAD

DRESSING:
2 tbsp. salad dressing or mayonnaise
1 to 3 tbsp. vinegar
½ tsp. prepared mustard
2 tsp. sugar
Salt to taste

Combine all ingredients.

SALAD:
1 ½ c. macaroni
2 stalks celery, chopped or ½ tsp. celery seed
1 green pepper, chopped
1 cucumber, chopped
½ med. onion, chopped
2 med. tomatoes, cut into pieces
1 carrot, chopped

Cook macaroni in salted water until almost dry. Mix all ingredients with warm macaroni. Garnish as desired. Pour dressing over macaroni mixture; marinate for at least an hour before serving. Yield: 10 servings.

Mrs. Eileen Skaggs
Alderson, W. Va.

MACARONI SALAD

12 oz. shell macaroni
1 tbsp. seasoned salt
2 lge. onions, chopped
1 tsp. salt
8 hard-cooked eggs, sliced
2 c. chopped celery
½ c. sliced pimento
1 c. sliced green peppers
2 No. 2 ½ cans English peas, drained
1 ½ c. mayonnaise

Boil macaroni in salted water until tender. Drain; blanch with cold water and drain again. Add seasoned salt, onions, salt, eggs, celery, pimento and green pepper. Toss lightly. Add English peas; toss lightly. Gently

(Continued on next page)

mix in mayonnaise. Chill several hours before serving. Garnish as desired. Yield: 12 servings.

Mrs. Oleta M. Smith
O'Donnell, Tex.

MACARONI SALAD DELUXE

2 c. raw macaroni, cooked
6 hard-cooked eggs
1 c. diced celery
1 green pepper, diced
1 sm. onion, diced
2 carrots, shredded
Sliced olives
1 c. cooked drained peas

Drain macaroni; rinse under cold water. Peel eggs; reserve 2 whole yolks. Chop remaining eggs; combine with macaroni and all remaining ingredients.

DRESSING:
1 c. mayonnaise
¼ c. milk
1 tbsp. vinegar
1 tsp. salt
¼ tsp. pepper
Paprika
Parsley sprigs

Combine all ingredients except paprika and parsley. Mix well with salad. Force reserved egg yolks through sieve; sprinkle over top. Sprinkle with paprika; garnish with parsley sprigs. Yield: 12 servings.

Mrs. Betty Lou Kirkpartrick
Indianapolis, Ind.

SALAD SUPREME

1 c. macaroni
1 c. chopped celery
6 tbsp. chopped sweet pickle
3 tbsp. chopped pimento
6 tbsp. chopped green pepper
1 c. diced sharp cheese
½ c. cooked green peas
½ c. salad dressing

Cook macaroni according to package directions. Drain and chill for 2 hours. Add celery, pickles and pimento. Toss lightly. Add remaining ingredients; toss. Chill. Yield: 6 servings.

Mary Nan Fitch
Electra, Tex.

SUMMER MACARONI SALAD

1 7-oz. pkg. uncooked elbow, shell or ring macaroni
1 c. cubed Cheddar cheese
1 c. sliced gherkins
½ c. minced onion
½ c. mayonnaise
1 10 or 12-oz. pkg. frozen peas, cooked and drained
Salt and pepper to taste

Cook macaroni according to package directions. Drain; rinse with cold water. Drain again. Add remaining ingredients. Chill. Serve in lettuce cups. Yield: 6 servings.

Nelda Lowry
Caddo Mills, Tex.

MACARONI SALAD

½ lb. macaroni
1 green pepper, diced
1 sm. can pimento, diced
1 sm. onion, diced
4 tbsp. salad dressing
2 tbsp. sandwich spread
¼ c. catsup
Salt and pepper to taste
Celery seed (opt.)
Mustard seed (opt.)
Paprika

Cook macaroni as directed on package. Rinse and cool. Add green pepper, pimento and onion. Moisten with salad dressing, sandwich spread and catsup. Add seasonings; sprinkle with paprika. Yield: 8-10 servings.

Mrs. Dorothy M. Kelly
Lynn, Mass.

MACARONI-EGG SALAD

1 lb. macaroni
1 lge. cucumber
1 green pepper
6 hard-cooked eggs
2 ripe tomatoes
3 or 4 sweet pickles
2 tbsp. salad dressing
Salt and pepper to taste

Cook macaroni until tender; drain and cool. Chop cucumber, green pepper, eggs, tomatoes and pickles. Add to macaroni; mix well. Add salad dressing and seasonings. Yield: 8 servings.

Vivian Blankenship
Ocean, W. Va.

MACARONI SALAD

1 c. uncooked shell macaroni
½ c. salad dressing
2 hard-cooked eggs, chopped
1 green pepper, chopped
1 cucumber, chopped
1 med. onion, chopped

Cook macaroni according to package directions; drain. Add remaining ingredients. Chill. Garnish with additional hard-cooked egg and green pepper. Yield: 6 servings.

Lois Witt
Heber Springs, Ark.

MACARONI SALAD

1 10-oz. pkg. shell macaroni
4 hard-cooked eggs
½ c. mayonnaise
2 tbsp. mustard
1 ½ tbsp. vinegar
2 tbsp. sugar
½ c. chopped tomatoes
¼ c. chopped green pepper
¼ c. chopped onion
Salt
Paprika

Mix ingredients. Sprinkle with paprika; chill. Yield: 8 servings.

Mrs. Shirley Busch
Wichita, Kans.

MACARONI SALAD

2 c. cooked macaroni
½ c. chopped pickles
2 tbsp. onion
⅛ tsp. pepper
½ c. mayonnaise
1 c. chopped celery
3 tbsp. chopped green pepper
2 tbsp. chopped parsley
1 tsp. salt

Combine all ingredients; chill. Yield: 4 servings.

Mrs. Arvell Duncan
Whiteville, N.C.

MACARONI SALAD WITH TOMATOES

1 c. cooked shell macaroni
1 lge. tomato, diced
2 hard-cooked eggs, diced
3 med. sweet pickles, diced
¼ c. diced cucumber
¼ c. med. pepper, diced
1 sm. onion, diced
Salt and pepper to taste
Mayonnaise to taste

Combine all ingredients; mix well. Yield: 6 servings.

Christine McGlone
Grayson, Ky.

MAINLY MACARONI SALAD

8 oz. salad macaroni
¼ c. chopped green pepper
1 4 ½-oz. can chopped olives
1 med. onion, finely chopped
¼ c. chopped celery
3 hard-cooked eggs, sliced
Mayonnaise
Vinegar
Salt
Pepper
Paprika

Cook macaroni according to package directions; rinse. Combine green pepper, olives, onion, celery and eggs, reserving some egg slices for garnish. Add mayonnaise, vinegar, salt and pepper to taste. Garnish with egg slices and paprika. Let stand several hours before serving. Yield: 8 servings.

Helena Tidrow Raine
Morro Bay, Calif.

BUSY DAY SPAGHETTI SALAD

1 box spaghetti
½ lb. mild cheese, grated
1 sm. can pimentos, cut up
2 tbsp. sweet pickles
Salt to taste
2 tbsp. mayonnaise
4 hard-cooked eggs, cut up
2 tsp. lemon juice

Combine all ingredients, adding eggs and lemon juice last. Yield: 6 servings.

Mrs. Kate Nolen
Weaverville, N.C.

CONFETTI SPAGHETTI SALAD

1 1-lb. can mixed vegetables
½ lb. elbow spaghetti, cooked
3 med. tomatoes, quartered
3 hard-cooked eggs, sliced
2 stalks celery, ¼-in. slices
½ tsp. garlic or onion salt
⅓ c. mayonnaise

(Continued on next page)

Drain vegetables, reserving 2 tablespoons liquid. Drain spaghetti in colander; rinse with cold water. Add remaining ingredients except vegetable liquid and mayonnaise. Cream mayonnaise with liquid from mixed vegetables. Pour over spaghetti mixture; toss thoroughly. Chill; serve on lettuce leaf. VARIATION: Add 1 6 1/2-ounce can tuna. Substitute elbow macaroni for spaghetti. Yield: 4-6 servings.

Mrs. C. Van Spronsen
Ada, Mich.

EASY SPAGHETTI SALAD

1 16-oz. pkg. spaghetti
1 sm. head cabbage, shredded
1 sm. onion, minced
1 sprig celery
2 cans red kidney beans

Cook spaghetti according to package directions. Wash kidney beans; drain. Combine vegetables and spaghetti.

DRESSING:
3 eggs
1 ⅛ c. sugar
1 sm. jar prepared mustard
3 tbsp. butter

Combine all ingredients. Cook until mixture thickens slightly. Cool; add to salad. Yield: 12 servings.

Mrs. Margaret P. Samson
Lake Ariel, Pa.

GEORGE RECTOR'S SPAGHETTI-CHICKEN SALAD

½ lb. elbow spaghetti
2 c. diced cooked chicken
1 c. chopped celery
1 tbsp. grated onion
1 tsp. salt
½ c. mayonnaise or salad dressing
2 tbsp. chopped green pepper
1 tbsp. minced red pepper or pimento
Hard cooked eggs (opt.)

Cook spaghetti until tender; drain and chill. Add remaining ingredients, except eggs. Mix lightly. Yield: 6 servings.

Mrs. K. E. Sharp
Borger, Tex.

INEXPENSIVE SPAGHETTI-FRUIT SALAD

4 eggs, beaten
½ c. lemon juice
2 c. confectioners sugar
Dash of salt
2 c. spaghetti, boiled and blanched
6 med. apples, diced
1 can crushed pineapple or chunks
Bananas, diced (opt.)
Nuts, chopped (opt.)
Oranges, diced (opt.)
2 c. whipped cream, sweetened

Combine eggs, lemon juice, sugar and salt. Cook egg mixture until thick; cool. Add spaghetti and fruits. Let stand 12 to 24 hours. Add whipped cream. Yield: 30-40 servings.

Donna Mae Hurst
Brigham City, Utah

SPAGHETTI SALAD

1 8-oz. box spaghetti
1 pt. chopped cabbage
2 onions, chopped

Cook spaghetti in salted water until tender; drain. Rinse with cold water. Add cabbage and onions.

DRESSING:
½ c. evaporated milk
½ c. sugar
½ tsp. salt
½ c. vinegar
4 tsp. mustard
2 eggs
Butter

Combine milk, sugar, salt, vinegar, mustard and eggs. Cook over low heat, stirring constantly, until thickened. Add small piece of butter; remove from fire. Cool slightly; pour over cabbage mixture. Yield: 6 servings.

Lucille D. Gibson
Dayton, O.

SHRIMP SALAD

1 pkg. vermicelli spaghetti
1 can deveined shrimp, chopped
6 stalks celery, diced
3 hard-cooked eggs, chopped
2 tbsp. lemon juice
½ c. mayonnaise
Paprika

Break vermicelli into short lengths; cook for 4 minutes. Remove from heat; cover and let stand for 4 minutes. Drain; rinse in cold water. Add shrimp, celery and eggs. Mix lemon juice and mayonnaise. Add dressing to salad, blending well. Line salad bowl with lettuce and add salad; sprinkle with paprika. Chill. Yield: 6 servings.

Mrs. Earl Thome
Auburn, Calif.

TOMATO AND SPAGHETTI SALAD

1 c. elbow spaghetti
1 can chicken, turkey or tuna
1 c. diced celery
2 tsp. grated onion
¼ tsp. salt
Pepper to taste
½ c. mayonnaise or undiluted Cheddar cheese soup
5 tomatoes, peeled
Lettuce

Cook spaghetti according to package directions. Add meat, celery, onion, salt, pepper and mayonnaise or soup to cooked spaghetti. Cut tomatoes from flower end down to the stem end into four or eight sections. Place tomato on lettuce and fill with salad. Yield: 5 servings.

Mrs. Gloria Hixson
Scranton, Ark.

GELATIN-RICE SALAD

1 pkg. raspberry or lime gelatin
1 c. boiling water
2 c. cooked rice, drained and sweetened
1 sm. can crushed pineapple, drained
1 c. whipped cream

Dissolve gelatin in boiling water. Add rice. Chill for 2 to 3 hours so rice will take up flavor of the gelatin. Blend pineapple and whipped cream into gelatin mixture. Serve on crisp lettuce. Yield: 6-8 servings.

Mrs. Patsy Stemple
Gillham, Ark.

GLORIFIED RICE

1 can sliced pineapple
2 pkg. orange gelatin
3 c. hot water
2 c. cooked rice
20 marshmallows, quartered
2 tbsp. lemon juice
1 c. heavy cream, whipped

Drain pineapple; reserve juice. Dissolve gelatin in hot water; stir in rice and marshmallows. Add pineapple juice and lemon juice. Chill until partially thickened; stir in pineapple. Chill until nearly set; fold in whipped cream. Refrigerate. Yield: 12 servings.

Mrs. Roy Sheppard
Manchester, Iowa

MILLION DOLLAR RICE

1 8-oz. pkg. cream cheese
2 tbsp. sugar
1 tbsp. mayonnaise
2 c. cooked rice
12 Maraschino cherries
1 lge. can crushed pineapple, drained
1 pkg. marshmallows, diced
1 box dessert topping mix
½ c. chopped nuts

Cream cheese, sugar and mayonnaise until smooth; add rice, cherries, pineapple and marshmallows. Fold in whipped dessert topping. Add nuts; chill. Yield: 8-10 servings.

Joan Moseley
Wellington, Kans.

PINEAPPLE AND RICE SALAD

1 c. crushed pineapple
1 3-oz. pkg. lemon gelatin
½ c. cold water
1 c. cooked rice
1 c. chopped marshmallows
½ c. walnuts
¼ c. powdered sugar
1 c. heavy cream, whipped

Drain pineapple, reserving 1 cup juice. Dissolve gelatin in hot pineapple juice; add water. Chill until thickened. Add rice, pineapple, marshmallows and nuts. Add sugar to cream; fold into gelatin mixture. Chill until firm. Yield: 6 servings.

Alice Johnson
Bates, Oreg.

RICE MOLD

1 pkg. lemon gelatin
1 c. cooked rice, cooled
1 sm. can crushed pineapple
1 c. heavy cream, whipped
½ c. chopped nuts

Prepare gelatin as directed on package; chill until thickened. Add rice and pineapple. Fold in whipped cream and nuts. Chill until firm. Garnish with cherries or other fruit. Yield: 6 servings.

Mrs. Nina Forrester
Billings, Mont.

RICE-PINEAPPLE SALAD

1 c. rice
1 tsp. salt

(Continued on next page)

4 c. water
18 marshmallows, cut up
1 c. crushed pineapple
10 Maraschino cherries
½ c. heavy cream, whipped

Cook rice in salted water until tender; drain. Add marshmallows; cool. Fold in pineapple, cherries and whipped cream. Refrigerate for 1 hour. Yield: 6-8 servings.

Mrs. Leland M. Bohart
Maitland, Mo.

RICE SALAD

1 pkg. lime gelatin
1 c. boiling water
1 c. cooked rice
½ c. chopped nuts
¾ c. crushed pineapple
1 c. heavy cream, whipped
¼ c. confectioners sugar
¾ c. colored miniature marshmallows

Dissolve gelatin in boiling water; cool. Add rice, nuts and pineapple. Whip cream with sugar; add with marshmallows to gelatin. Chill until firm. Yield: 9 servings.

Mrs. Merrill E. Pike
Lisbon, Iowa

STRAWBERRY-RICE SALAD

2 pkg. strawberry gelatin
3 c. hot water
2 c. cooked rice
1 c. miniature marshmallows
1 c. crushed pineapple
1 c. whipped cream

Dissolve gelatin in hot water; cool. Add rice, marshmallows and pineapple. When mixture begins to congeal add whipped cream. Chill. Yield: 12-15 servings.

Elaine Crane
Mallard, Iowa

CURRY-RICE-NUT SALAD

1 ½ c. uncooked rice
2 c. cooked chicken or turkey chunks
1 No. 2 can crushed pineapple, drained
2 tbsp. salad oil
1 tsp. salt
½ tsp. curry powder
1 tbsp. lemon juice
⅓ can flaked coconut
1 c. chopped celery
¾ c. almonds
¼ c. chopped green pepper
½ c. mayonnaise
1 tbsp. red wine vinegar

Cook rice according to package directions. Combine chicken, rice, pineapple, salad oil, salt, curry powder and lemon juice; chill for 2 hours. Add remaining ingredients. Refrigerate for 2 days so flavors will have a chance to blend. Yield: 8 servings.

Mrs. William Hoting
San Gabriel, Calif.

HOT CHICKEN-RICE SALAD

⅓ c. uncooked rice
2 c. chicken broth
4 c. chopped cooked chicken
1 c. blanched almonds
1 c. mushrooms, chopped
1 sm. can pimento
1 sm. onion, chopped
1 sm. green pepper, finely cut
1 c. chopped celery
Salt and pepper to taste

Cook rice in chicken broth until tender. Combine all ingredients; place in buttered casserole. Sprinkle with buttered crumbs. Bake at 325 degrees for 1 hour. Yield: 8 servings.

Mrs. Clee Noyes
Lane, S.D.

HOT RICE SALAD

1 c. diced, cooked chicken
1 c. cooked celery
1 c. cooked rice
1 c. cream of chicken soup
¾ c. mayonnaise
3 tbsp. lemon juice (opt.)
2 to 3 tbsp. chopped onion
3 hard-cooked eggs, chopped (opt.)
½ c. slivered almonds
⅛ c. butter, melted (opt.)
1 c. crushed corn flakes or Rice Krispies

Combine chicken, celery, rice, soup, mayonnaise, lemon juice, onion and eggs; put in buttered casserole. Sprinkle with almonds which have been browned slightly in butter; top with crushed corn flakes. Bake at 350 degrees for 45 minutes. NOTE: Celery should be crisp, not soft; rice should be cooked in chicken stock. Yield: 6-8 servings.

Marjorie Schwacofer
Cleveland, O.

ORIENTAL SALAD

1 lb. bean sprouts
1 ¼ c. steamed rice
1 c. thinly sliced celery
2 tbsp. chopped green pepper
2 sm. carrots, finely grated
3 green onions and tops, sliced
½ c. slivered toasted almonds
2 c. cooked diced chicken or pork
Salt and pepepr to taste
Juice of ½ lemon
¾ c. French dressing
Soy sauce (opt.)

Cook bean sprouts in a small amount of salted water for 3 minutes or until tender. Drain; cool. Combine bean sprouts, rice, celery, green pepper, carrots, onions, almonds and chicken or pork. Chill thoroughly. Add salt, pepper and lemon juice. Add French dressing and toss lightly. Sprinkle with soy sauce, if desired. Yield: 6 servings.

Mrs. Luisa Pitchford
Los Banos, Calif.

RICE AND MEAT SALAD

1 ½ c. cooked rice, chilled
1 ½ c. diced chicken, tuna or turkey
1 c. English peas
1 c. shredded carrots
4 tbsp. chili sauce (opt.)
¼ tsp. curry powder
½ tsp. salt
½ c. French dressing

Mix rice with meat and vegetables; toss lightly. Mix chili sauce, curry powder, salt and French dressing. Pour over salad; toss lightly. Yield: 6 servings.

Mrs. Harriet Krause
Pasadena, Tex.

LOUISIANA CRAB MEAT SALAD

3 c. warm cooked rice
2 tbsp. bottled Italian-style salad dressing
1 5-oz. can crab meat, drained and flaked
1 c. finely chopped celery
2 pimentos, diced
2 tbsp. lemon juice
1 tbsp. chopped fresh dill
1 tbsp. grated onion
¼ tsp. salt
¼ c. mayonnaise

Marinate rice in salad dressing; chill. Combine all remaining ingredients. Mix with rice and serve. Yield: 8 servings.

Mrs. Joe D. Deason
Amarillo, Tex.

MAIN DISH RICE AND HAM SALAD

1 ⅓ c. instant rice
1 ½ tbsp. dry mustard
2 tbsp. cold water
1 ½ tbsp. sugar
1 ½ tbsp. wine vinegar
¼ c. vegetable oil
½ c. chopped green pepper
1 c. cooked diced ham
½ c. cooked peas
Chopped parsley
Salad greens

Prepare rice as directed on package. Blend mustard, water, sugar and vinegar; gradually beat in oil. Stir lightly into warm rice; cool. Add green pepper, ham and peas. Sprinkle with parsley and serve with greens. Yield: 4-6 servings.

Mrs. Jean Jordan
Spurger, Tex.

RICE AND SHRIMP SALAD

3 c. cold cooked rice
1 c. boiled shrimp
6 hard-cooked eggs
1 c. diced sweet or sour pickles
Salt and pepper to taste
1 c. diced celery
1 c. finely chopped stuffed olives
Salad dressing

Combine all ingredients. Garnish with additional hard-cooked eggs.

June Wright Curtis
Hamshire, Tex.

SEAFOOD-RICE RING

1 ½ c. rice
1 c. canned whole shrimp
1 c. canned or fresh crab
3 tbsp. lemon juice
¼ c. chopped green onions
¼ c. chopped green pepper
½ c. sliced stuffed olives
1 c.salad dressing
½ c. chili sauce
½ tsp. dry mustard
¼ tsp. pepper
¼ tsp. garlic salt
1 tsp. salt
1 tsp. Worcestershire sauce
1 tbsp. vinegar (opt.)

Steam rice according to package directions; cool. Sprinkle seafood with lemon juice; toss with rice. Add onions, green pepper and olives. Blend remaining ingredients; add to rice mixture. Pack into a 1 3/4-quart ring mold. Chill for several hours or overnight before serving. Yield: 8-12 servings.

Mrs. Ireta Lyngstad
Coeur d'Alene, Idaho

FRESH SPINACH AND RICE SALAD BOWL

¼ to ½ lb. fresh spinach
1 sm. onion, thinly sliced
½ c. thinly sliced celery
¼ c. sliced radishes
3 hard-cooked eggs, sliced
1 ½ c. cooked cold rice
¾ tsp. salt
¼ tsp. pepper

Wash spinach thoroughly. Break off stems; measure 1 quart. Tear leaves into bite-sized pieces if too large. Shake spinach in a towel to dry. Arrange attractively with other vegetables, eggs and rice in a salad bowl; season with salt and pepper. Chill. Add lemon dressing when ready to serve.

LEMON DRESSING:

1 tbsp. flour
⅓ c. salad oil
½ c. water
1 egg yolk, slightly beaten
½ tsp. salt
½ tsp. dry mustard
3 tbsp. lemon juice

Blend flour with 1 tablespoon oil; stir in water. Cook until thickened, stirring constantly. Gradually stir hot mixture into egg yolk. Blend in salt, mustard, remaining oil and lemon juice; beat until smooth. Chill. Pour dressing over salad; toss lightly. Yield: 5-6 servings.

Photograph for this recipe above.

CURRY-VEGETABLE SALAD

1 c. rice
½ c. peas
¼ c. French dressing
¾ c. mayonnaise
¼ c. minced onion
½ tsp. salt
¾ tsp. curry powder
½ tsp. dry mustard
⅛ tsp. pepper
½ c. cauliflowerets
½ c. thinly sliced radishes
½ c. diced celery

Cook rice and peas. Toss together with French dressing. Refrigerate. Mix mayonnaise, onion, salt, curry powder, dry mustard, pepper and cauliflowerets. Refrigerate. Just before serving, mix rice mixture and curry mixture with radishes and celery.

(Continued on next page)

Serve on lettuce. For additional dressing use equal parts of mayonnaise and French dressing. Yield: 8 servings.

Joann Parks
Wauseon, O.

GOLDEN RICE SALAD

¼ c. salad oil
2 tbsp. vinegar
2 tbsp. prepared mustard
1 ½ tsp. salt
Pepper to taste
4 ½ c. hot cooked rice
1 c. coarsely cut olives
2 hard-cooked eggs, diced
1 ½ c. sliced celery
¼ c. chopped dill pickle
¼ c. chopped pimento
1 sm. onion, minced
½ c. mayonnaise

Blend salad oil, vinegar, mustard, salt and pepper; pour over rice. Toss; set aside to cool. Add remaining ingredients; toss. Chill thoroughly. Serve on lettuce leaf; garnish with extra sliced eggs. NOTE: For rice, cook 1 1/2 cups rice in 3 cups chicken broth. Yield: 8 servings.

Ruth Jenkins
Elton, La.

RICE PICNIC SALAD

3 c. hot rice
¼ c. French dressing
¼ c. minced onion
1 tsp. salt
¼ tsp. pepper
½ c. minced celery
⅓ c. minced green pepper
¼ c. minced sour pickles
⅓ c. sweet relish
2 tbsp. minced pimento
2 hard-cooked eggs, chopped
⅔ c. mayonnaise

Combine rice, French dressing, onion, salt and pepper. Let stand while preparing remaining ingredients. Combine all ingredients. Toss lightly with a fork. Chill thoroughly. Yield: 6 servings.

Mrs. J. E. Clark, Jr.
Dayton, Tex.

RICE SALAD

1 c. rice
Paprika
4 hard-cooked eggs, chopped
½ c. chopped celery
½ c. chopped sweet pickles
¼ c. chopped onion (opt.)
¼ c. chopped green pepper
1 sm. can pimento, chopped (opt.)
½ c. salad dressing
Salt to taste

Cook rice according to package directions. Cool; sprinkle with paprika. Add eggs, celery, pickles, onion, pepper, pimento and salad dressing. Toss lightly to mix. Salt to taste. Yield: 8-12 servings.

Mrs. Christine Weems
Hazen, Ark.

RICE SALAD DELIGHT

½ c. salad dressing
1 tbsp. mustard
1 tbsp. pickle juice
2 c. cooked rice
4 hard-cooked eggs, chopped
4 sweet pickles, diced
1 tbsp. diced onion
¼ c. diced green pepper
¼ c. diced celery
1 tsp. salt
½ tsp. pepper
½ c. chopped pecans (opt.)

Mix salad dressing, mustard and pickle juice. Combine with remaining ingredients. Chill. Yield: 8 servings.

Mrs. Dorothy Weikal Bickerstaff
Marianna, Ark.

RICE SLAW

¼ c. grated carrots
¼ c. diced green pepper
1 hard-cooked egg, finely chopped
1 c. diced celery
1 med. tomato or one sm. jar of pimento
¼ c. diced pickles
2 c. cooked chilled rice
¾ c. salad dressing
Salt to taste

Combine all ingredients; mix lightly. Yield: 6 servings.

Mrs. G. D. Bell
Des Arc, Ark.

RECIPE FOR ANTIPASTO SALAD ON PAGE 319

ALL-IN-ONE SALAD

2 c. cooked cubed meat
¼ c. French dressing
1 c. diced celery
2 hard-cooked eggs
2 tbsp. chopped pimento
2 tbsp. chopped green onions
2 tbsp. chopped green pepper
Salt and pepper to taste
½ c. mayonnaise

Marinate meat in French dressing for 15 minutes; drain. Combine with all remaining ingredients. Place on lettuce leaves and serve chilled. Yield: 4 servings.

Mrs. Glenn E. Lemon
Navasota, Tex.

BASIC MEAT SALAD

2 c. cubed cooked meat
1 c. diced celery
1 tsp. salt
3 hard-cooked eggs, chopped
¼ c. chopped pickles
Mayonnaise

Combine all ingredients, moistening with mayonnaise. Toss lightly with two forks. Chill and serve. Yield: 6-8 servings.

Ethel Downs
Guntersville, Ala.

BEEF SALAD

1 3-lb. lean beef roast or boiling beef
1 c. chopped pickles
6 hard-cooked eggs, chopped
1 sm. can pimento, chopped
1 pt. salad dressing
Broth

Cook beef in moderate amount of water until very tender; cool. Remove fat and bones; grind in food chopper using fine plate. Mix pickles, eggs and pimento with ground meat, adding salad dressing and enough meat broth to make a moist mixture. Place in mold or serving dish; refrigerate until ready to serve. Yield: 12 servings.

Mrs. Max L. Suess
Booker, Tex.

COLD MEAT SALAD

2 c. diced leftover roast
1 c. diced celery
1 c. pared diced tart apples
¼ c. mayonnaise
1 tbsp. mustard
½ tsp. salt

Combine meat, celery and apples. Blend mayonnaise with mustard and salt; add to meat mixture. Serve on crisp lettuce leaves. Yield: 5 servings.

Mrs. Elizabeth R. Whisnant
Forest City, N.C.

COLD MEAT SALAD

2 c. cooked diced meat
1 c. diced celery
1 c. diced tart apples
¼ c. mayonnaise
1 tbsp. mustard
½ tsp. salt
Lettuce

Combine meat, celery and apples. Blend mayonnaise, mustard and salt; add to meat mixture. Toss lightly until all pieces are well coated with dressing. Serve on crisp lettuce. Yield: 5 servings.

Mrs. Frank Lorenz
Charlestown, Ind.

HOT MEAT SALAD

½ head lettuce, chopped
1 tomato, diced
1 onion, chopped
1 lb. ground beef
1 8-oz. can tomato sauce
2 tbsp. chili powder
Salt and pepper to taste
1 med. pkg. corn chips

Combine lettuce, tomato and onion. Brown meat; add tomato sauce, chili powder, salt and pepper. Cook until blended. Pour meat mixture over salad; toss. Add corn chips; toss lightly. Serve immediately. Yield: 6 servings.

Mrs. Allen Daggett
Houston, Tex.

LEFT-OVER MEAT SALAD

½ head lettuce
2 tomatoes, quartered
Cooked vegetables
Cooked cubed meat
Dash of salt and pepper
Vinegar and oil dressing

Cut lettuce into small pieces; add tomatoes and leftover vegetables, meat and salt and pepper. Add dressing just before serving. Yield: 4 servings.

Pat Hansen
Stockton, Calif.

BEEF AND ONION VINAIGRETTE

2 sweet Spanish onions, sliced
2 c. roast beef, cut into thin strips
¼ c. garlic-flavored red wine vinegar
½ c. olive oil
¼ c. capers, drained
2 tbsp. snipped parsley
¼ tsp. dry mustard
1 or 2 dashes Tabasco sauce
½ tsp. pepper
1 hard-cooked egg, chopped (opt.)

Combine onion rings and roast beef. Mix remaining ingredients; pour over onions and beef. Let stand for 1 hour at room temperature; chill until ready to serve. Mix again just before serving. NOTE: Roast lamb may be used instead of roast beef. Yield: 5-6 servings.

Photograph for this recipe above.

MEAT-POTATO SALAD

1 qt. cubed cooked meat, chilled
Salad dressing
4 cooked cold potatoes, diced
1 sm. onion, chopped
1 c. diced celery
½ c. slivered green or red pepper
6 hard-cooked eggs, chopped
Salt to taste

Marinate meat in salad dressing for 1 hour; drain well. Mix meat with vegetables, eggs and salt; toss with oil dressing.

OIL DRESSING:
⅔ c. vinegar
¾ c. sugar
⅓ c. salad oil
1 tsp. salt
1 tsp. celery seed

Combine ingredients in jar. Cover; shake a few times. Do not stir. Yield: 8-10 servings.

Mrs. S. C. Van Fossen
Pennsville, O.

MEAT SALAD

3 tbsp. salad oil
6 tbsp. lemon juice or vinegar
1 tsp. salt
½ tsp. pepper
½ tsp. onion juice
1 tsp. celery seed
3 c. cooked meat, chicken or fish
2 to 6 hard-cooked eggs, chopped
½ c. chopped sweet pickles
2 c. diced celery
¼ to ½ c. heavy cream, whipped
2 to 3 tbsp. mayonnaise

(Continued on next page)

Combine salad oil, lemon juice, seasonings, onion juice and celery seed; marinate chicken in mixture for 30 minutes. Add eggs, pickles and celery. Combine whipped cream with mayonnaise; add to mixture. Toss salad lightly; serve on lettuce. NOTE: Salad may also be used to stuff tomatoes.

Mrs. N. J. Rasmussen
Marshalltown, Iowa

MEAT SALAD

2 c. diced cooked meat
1 c. diced cooked potatoes
1 c. cooked peas
2 hard-cooked eggs, diced
1 med. onion, minced
½ c. chopped sweet pickles
Salt and pepper to taste
½ c. mayonnaise

Combine all ingredients; mix lightly. Chill. May be served on lettuce and garnished with paprika. Yield: 6 servings.

Mrs. Howard Thomas
Augusta, Mich.

MEAT SALAD

1 lb. ground chuck roast
3 c. water
1 tsp. salt
½ tsp. pepper
1 sm. onion, finely chopped
1 ½ c. chopped lettuce
1 sm. tomato, cut in small pieces
½ c. salad oil or dressing

Place meat in sauce pan with water, salt and pepper. Cook until meat is tender; drain off water. Place meat in large salad dish; add onion, lettuce and tomato. Pour salad oil or dressing over salad; mix well. Yield: 8 servings.

Mrs. W. W. Thorne
Jewett, Tex.

MEAT SALAD DELIGHT

2 c. diced or ground cold cooked meat
½ c. diced cucumbers
¼ c. diced green pepper
¼ c. diced red pepper
½ c. diced celery
½ tsp. salt
½ tsp. pepper
2 tbsp. mustard
2 tbsp. evaporated milk
Pimento
2 hard-cooked eggs, sliced
Sliced stuffed olives

Combine meat with vegetables; add salt and pepper. Blend mustard and milk; add to mixture and stir well. Serve on lettuce. Garnish with pimento rings, egg slices and olive slices. Yield: 8 servings.

Mrs. Mabel Watson
Bradenton, Fla.

MEXICAN BEEF SALAD

¾ c. salad oil
½ c. red wine vinegar
1 ½ tsp. salt
¼ tsp. pepper
½ tsp. chili powder
3 c. cooked beef, cut into strips

Blend oil, vinegar and seasonings. Add beef; marinate several hours. Drain; arrange on crisp salad greens. Garnish with onion and pepper rings, avocado slices and ripe olives. Serve marinade as dressing. Yield: 4 servings.

Jean Wydra
Jacksonville, Ill.

ONE-DISH MEAL

4 c. cubed cooked potatoes
2 tbsp. French dressing
½ c. finely chopped onion
½ c. finely chopped green pepper
½ c. sliced sweet pickles
1 c. diced celery
1 c. mayonnaise
1 tbsp. salt
¼ tsp. pepper
2 tsp. prepared mustard
½ tbsp. catsup
2 c. chopped meat
2 hard-cooked eggs, sliced
2 tomatoes, sectioned

Marinate potatoes in French dressing. Mix onion, green pepper, sweet pickles, celery, mayonnaise, salt, pepper, mustard and catsup; chill. Just before serving add potatoes, meat, eggs and tomatoes. Place in lettuce-lined bowl; garnish with eggs and tomatoes. Yield: 6-8 servings.

Marion G. Towle
Montgomery, Vt.

ROAST MEAT SALAD

1 head lettuce
1 c. cooked diced potatoes
1 onion, chopped
2 hard-cooked eggs, sliced
2 sweet pickles, chopped
2 c. cooked diced lean roast beef
½ c. diced celery
1 green pepper, cut into strips
2 tomatoes, quartered
Salt
⅔ c. mayonnaise
½ tbsp. catsup
⅛ tsp. pepper
2 tsp. mustard

Line salad bowl with lettuce leaves. Combine potatoes with onion; combine eggs with pickles. Arrange piles of meat, potato mixture, celery and egg mixture in bowl. Separate piles with green pepper strips; garnish with tomatoes. Sprinkle with salt. Blend all remaining ingredients; pour over salad. Chill. Yield: 6 servings.

Mrs. Richard Grudzinski
Grand Island, Nebr.

SOUP-MEAT SALAD

2 c. cooked chopped soup meat
2 onions, sliced
1 clove of garlic, finely chopped
1 c. chopped celery
1 c. chopped green pepper
½ c. French dressing

Combine meat, onions, garlic, celery and green pepper; marinate in French dressing. Serve on lettuce. Yield: 4 servings.

Mrs. Lucille R. Boyter
St. Bernard, La.

JELLIED MEAT MAIN DISH SALAD

1 ½ tbsp. unflavored gelatin
¼ c. water
1 c. meat or poultry broth or consomme, heated
1 tbsp. chopped onion
Salt to taste
1 tbsp. vinegar or lemon juice
1 c. chopped cooked meat or poultry
1 c. cooked peas
2 tbsp. chopped celery
2 tbsp. sliced cucumber pickle

Soften gelatin in cold water; dissolve in hot broth. Add onion, salt, vinegar or lemon juice and other seasonings to taste. Chill until thickened. Stir in meat, peas, celery and pickle. Pour into individual molds; chill until firm. Serve on lettuce. Yield: 4-6 servings.

Mrs. A. S. Feller
Occidental, Calif.

JELLIED MEAT SALAD

2 tbsp. gelatin
¼ c. cold water
2 c. hot broth or bouillon
2 tbsp. grated onion
Salt to taste
2 tbsp. vinegar or lemon juice
2 c. chopped cooked meat
½ c. cooked peas
¼ c. chopped celery

Soften gelatin in water; dissolve in hot broth. Add onion, salt and vinegar or lemon juice. Chill until thickened. Stir in meat, peas and celery. Pour into small loaf pan or individual molds; chill until firm. Yield: 6 servings.

Mrs. R. C. Boardwine
Saltville, Va.

FRUITED MEAT SALAD

2 c. cubed cooked veal
1 c. cubed pineapple
½ c. red grapes, halved and seeded
½ c. chopped celery
⅓ c. chopped pecans
3 tbsp. mayonnaise
2 tbsp. pineapple juice

Mix veal, pineapple, grapes, celery and pecans. Combine mayonnaise and pineapple juice; add to veal mixture. Toss lightly; chill. Serve in lettuce cups. Yield: 4-6 servings.

Pearl Nell
Hillsboro, Ill.

TENDERLOIN-VEAL SALAD

1 lb. lean tenderloin
1 lb. lean veal
1 c. diced celery
¼ c. diced olives
¾ lb. brick cheese, diced
Mayonnaise to taste

Boil meat; cool and dice. Combine all ingredients. Serve on lettuce. Yield: 12 servings.

Mrs. Russell Blankenship
Elwood, Ind.

VEAL LOAF

2 lb. lean veal
1 sm. onion
1 stalk celery
Salt and pepper to taste
1 tbsp. gelatin
1 c. broth
1 ½ c. bread crumbs

Cover veal, onion, celery, salt and pepper in water. Cook until done. Cool; grind with medium blade of food grinder. Dissolve gelatin in broth; add veal and bread crumbs. Pour into mold; chill until firm. Garnish as desired. Yield: 10 servings.

Mrs. Jocelyn Strader
Indianapolis, Ind.

JELLIED VEAL LOAF

1 can chicken soup
3 c. ground cooked veal
2 tsp. gelatin
2 tbsp. water
¼ tsp. salt
⅛ tsp. pepper
1 hard-cooked egg, sliced
5 stuffed olives, sliced

Strain chicken soup; heat broth. Mix rice, chicken and celery from soup with veal; put all through food chopper, using medium blade. Soften gelatin in water; dissolve in hot broth. Mix with ground meat mixture. Add salt and pepper. Arrange egg and olives in loaf pan; add meat mixture. Refrigerate until firm; unmold on shredded lettuce. Yield: 8 servings.

Mrs. R. R. Elliker
Fostoria, O.

MEAT SUPPER SALAD

1 box lemon gelatin
1 c. boiling water
½ tsp. salt
1 tbsp. grated onion
½ c. salad dressing
½ c. heavy cream
½ lb. cottage cheese, drained
3 hard-cooked eggs, chopped
2 tsp. finely chopped green pepper
3 c. thinly sliced celery
1 lb. cooked veal, chilled and ground

Dissolve gelatin in water; add salt and onion. Chill until thickened. Add salad dressing, cream and cottage cheese. Beat well. Combine eggs, green pepper, celery and veal; add to gelatin. Chill until firm. Yield: 6-8 servings.

Mrs. Ralph Knight
Belle Vernon, Pa.

TOWER VEAL SALAD

1 c. veal broth
2 cubes beef bouillon
2 pkg. unflavored gelatin
½ c. cold water
2 tbsp. lemon juice
1 c. mayonnaise
1 c. diced celery
1 c. green grapes
2 lb. cooked cubed veal
Salt to taste
½ c. toasted slivered almonds

Heat veal broth; add bouillon. Stir until dissolved. Soften gelatin in water; dissolve in bouillon mixture. Chill until thickened. Fold in all ingredients except almonds; mix well. Place in a 1 1/2-quart mold; chill until firm. Sprinkle salad with almonds. May be garnished with chilled cranberry sauce, sliced avocado strips, salad fruits and pineapple chunks. Yield: 8 servings.

Jessie Mae Jacobs
Apopka, Fla.

APPLE BALL AND HAM SALAD

8 tart apples, pared
2 tbsp. lemon juice
2 c. cooked cubed ham
1 c. diced celery
¼ c. mayonnaise
¼ c. light cream
2 oz. Bleu cheese, crumbled

Cut balls from apples with melon ball cutter or measuring spoon; sprinkle with lemon juice. Add to ham and celery. Blend mayonnaise and cream; add to apple mixture. Sprinkle with cheese. May be garnished with apple wedges and parsley. Yield: 6-8 servings.

Mrs. Sanders Cox
Prosser, Wash.

BEST HAM SALAD

1 sm. cabbage, grated
2 c. chopped ham
1 sm. onion, minced

(Continued on next page)

½ c. grated cheese
1 c. salad dressing
1 tsp. mustard

Combine cabbage, ham, onion and cheese. Blend salad dressing and mustard; add to salad. Yield: 6-8 servings.

Joan Paige
Bellevue, Mich.

CHEF'S SALAD

1 head lettuce
½ c. cooked chicken strips
½ c. cooked ham strips
⅓ c. chopped tomato
1 tbsp. chopped sweet pickle relish
1 tbsp. chives
1 hard-cooked egg, chopped
3 tbsp. whole marjoram
2 tbsp. vinegar
3 tbsp. olive oil
1 tsp. Worcestershire sauce

Tear lettuce into bite-sized pieces. Add chicken and ham with tomato and relish. Blend all remaining ingredients; pour over salad. Serve immediately. Yield: 4 servings.

Mrs. John L. Altshool
Las Cruces, N.M.

CHEF'S SALAD

1 lge. head lettuce
¼ c. minced onion
6 radishes, sliced
6 small tomatoes, cut into chunks
6 hard-cooked eggs, cut into wedges
1½ c. boiled ham or cold meat strips
1 ½ c. cheese strips
French or Russian dressing

Tear lettuce into bite-sized portions. Toss with onion, radishes and tomatoes. Divide into six portions and place in individual salad plates. Sprinkle with French or Russian dressing. Arrange eggs, meat and cheese in an attractive manner over the lettuce; sprinkle with salad dressing. Yield: 6 servings.

Mina F. Robinson
Perry, Kans.

CRUNCHY BAKE HAM SALAD

3 c. diced cooked ham
1 c. diced celery
½ c. chopped stuffed olives
2 hard-cooked eggs, diced
¼ c. chopped onions
1 tbsp. lemon juice
1 tbsp. mustard
Dash of pepper
¾ c. mayonnaise or salad dressing
1 c. crushed potato chips

Combine all ingredients except potato chips. Place in an 8 x 2-inch round baking dish. Sprinkle with potato chips. Bake at 400 degrees for 20 to 25 minutes. Yield: 6 servings.

Mrs. B. W. McPherson
Pine Bluff, Ark.

EASY HAM SALAD

2 c. cooked ground ham
2 or 3 hard-cooked eggs, chopped
2 tsp. ground onion
2 stalks celery, chopped
¾ c. ground sweet pickles
½ c. ground peanuts (opt.)
Mayonnaise to taste

Thoroughly blend all ingredients. Yield: 6 servings.

Mrs. William L. Jones
Ozona, Fla.

HAM AND CABBAGE SALAD

1 small cabbage, shredded
2 c. cooked diced ham
½ onion, chopped
1 sweet red pepper, chopped
1 green pepper, chopped
1 c. mayonnaise
Salt to taste

Combine cabbage, ham, onion and peppers; blend with mayonnaise. Salt to taste. Yield: 8 servings.

Clara M. Dayton
Cokeville, Wyo.

HAM-CHICKEN BOWL SUPREME

1 clove of garlic, cut
1 head lettuce
1 c. diced cucumbers
1 green pepper, cut into narrow strips
1 c. cooked ham cut into strips
1 c. cooked chicken cut into strips
3 hard-cooked eggs, sliced
2 tomatoes, cut into wedges
½ c. salad oil

(Continued on next page)

3 tbsp. vinegar
1 tbsp. horseradish
½ tsp. Worcestershire sauce
2 drops of Tabasco sauce
½ tsp. salt
⅛ tsp. pepper

Rub salad bowl with garlic. Break lettuce into bite-sized pieces in bowl. Arrange cucumbers, green pepper, ham, chicken, eggs and tomatoes on top. Combine all remaining ingredients to make dressing. Cover and shake thoroughly. Serve salad with dressing. Yield: 8-10 servings.

Mrs. R. W. Cogswell
Kirtland AFB, N.M.

HAM-KIDNEY BEAN SALAD

1 No. 2 can kidney beans
2 c. cooked cubed ham
3 hard-cooked eggs, chopped
½ c. chopped celery
¼ c. sweet relish
Salt and pepper
1 tsp. chopped onion
¼ c. chopped green pepper
½ c. mayonnaise

Place kidney beans in strainer; rinse with hot water to remove juice. Drain; combine with all remaining ingredients. Chill; serve on salad greens. Yield: 8 servings.

Edith Greenlee
Pittsburgh, Pa.

HAM AND POTATO SALAD

4 med. potatoes
1 ½ c. finely chopped celery
2 tbsp. finely chopped green pepper
½ tsp. prepared horseradish
1 ½ c. cooked diced ham
¼ c. mayonnaise or salad dressing
2 hard-cooked eggs, sliced

Cook potatoes in boiling salted water until tender; cool and dice. Add celery, green pepper, horseradish and ham; mix well. Fold in mayonnaise or salad dressing. Top with eggs; chill. Yield: 6 servings.

Mrs. Sara Anderson
Chesapeake, Va.

HAM SALAD

1 tsp. mustard
Salt to taste
Cayenne pepper to taste
½ c. heavy cream, whipped
3 tbsp. mayonnaise
2 tbsp. grated horseradish
2 c. chopped cooked ham
1 ½ c. diced celery
2 hard-cooked eggs, sliced
Paprika

Fold mustard, salt and cayenne into cream; beat in mayonnaise. Fold in horseradish, ham and celery. Place in loaf pan; garnish with eggs. Sprinkle with paprika; chill thoroughly. Serve on salad greens. Yield: 6-8 servings.

Mrs. James B. Ward
Bradenton, Fla.

HAM SALAD BOWL

2 c. cooked diced ham
1 c. diced celery
2 hard-cooked eggs, chopped
¼ c. mayonnaise
1 tbsp. chopped sweet pickles
1 tbsp. catsup

Combine ham, celery and eggs with mayonnaise, pickles and catsup. Place on lettuce cups; chill. May be served with crackers. NOTE: Turkey, salmon, chicken or roast beef may be substituted for ham. Yield: 4 servings.

Georgia Matthews
Oliver Springs, Tenn.

HAM SALAD FOR PICNICS OR SNACKS

2 cans ham or 1 sm. picnic ham, cooked
10 to 12 hard-cooked eggs
Onion or onion juice to taste
1 sm. carrot
2 sm. jars sweet relish
Salad dressing to taste

Grind ham, eggs, onion and carrot together. Stir in relish and salad dressing. Mix well.

Della Paugh Gainer
Glenville, W. Va.

HAM SALAD SPECIAL

1 lb. pressed ham, ground
½ c. sweet pickles, ground
1 c. salad dressing
¼ c. sweet pickle juice
1 tbsp. finely chopped onion or juice

(Continued on next page)

Combine all ingredients; mix well. Serve on lettuce as a salad or use as a sandwich spread. Yield: 4 servings.

Mrs. Nerine Kinsey
Gatesville, Tex.

HAM SALAD SUPREME

1 can chopped ham, diced
2 hard-cooked eggs, diced
3 tbsp. diced sweet pickle
3 tbsp. diced celery or 1 tsp. celery seed
1 sm. apple (opt.)
Salad dressing to taste

Combine all ingredients. Chill. May be served on lettuce leaf with cheese crackers. Yield: 4-5 servings.

Mrs. Margaret D. Randall
Tallulah, La.

HOT HAM SALAD

4 c. cooked cubed ham
1 c. finely chopped ripe olives
3 hard-cooked eggs, chopped
½ c. finely chopped celery
¼ c. finely chopped onion
½ c. chopped almonds (opt.)
½ c. mayonnaise
½ c. sour cream
Salt and pepper to taste
Italian herb seasonings
½ c. grated sharp Cheddar cheese
½ c. ground potato or corn chips

Combine all ingredients except cheese and potato or corn chips. Place in greased loaf pan; sprinkle with cheese and chips. Bake in pre-heated 350 degree oven for 30 minutes. Yield: 10 servings.

Helen G. Tellman
Sacramento, Calif.

MAIN DISH SALAD

1 can kidney beans, drained
½ c. chopped celery
½ c. diced green pepper
1 onion, cut into rings
½ c. chopped pickles
½ lb. cheese, chopped
1 lb. ham, cut into strips
2 eggs, sliced
Maynonaise

Combine all ingredients except mayonnaise; chill. Add mayonnaise just before serving. Place in lettuce cups; serve with hot bread or crackers. Yield: 6 servings.

Mrs. Mary Ann Lea
Vilonia, Ark.

MEAL-IN-ONE SALAD

6 c. shredded lettuce
4 ripe tomatoes
3 lge. green peppers
1 lge. onion, thinly sliced
1 c. diced cheese
1 c. diced celery
6 radishes, thinly sliced
1 c. diced cucumbers
1 c. cooked diced ham or chicken

Combine; toss lightly.

DRESSING:
¾ c. salad oil
⅓ c. vinegar
1 tsp. salt
1 tsp. pepper
1 tsp. sugar
1 tsp. catsup
2 tbsp. red cooking wine
1 tsp. onion powder
½ tsp. garlic powder

Combine all ingredients in fruit jar; shake well. Pour over salad and toss. Garnish with ripe olives. Serve with hot biscuits or crackers. Yield: 8 servings.

Mary Guydosh
Piney Fork, O.

PATIO SALAD WITH HAM

1 pkg. frozen green peas
½ tsp. salt
1 ½ c. boiling water
1 ⅓ c. instant rice
¾ c. mayonnaise
½ c. chopped dill pickles
1 tsp. grated onion
¼ tsp. pepper
1 c. cooked ham strips
1 c. Swiss cheese strips

Add frozen peas and salt to water; boil for 2 minutes. Add rice; stir to moisten. Cover; remove from heat. Let stand for 5 minutes. Stir in mayonnaise, pickles, onion and pepper. Mix lightly with fork; chill. Add ham and cheese; mix lightly. May be served on crisp salad greens and garnished with tomato wedges. Yield: 6 servings.

Betty McDonald
Marion, S.C.

HAWAIIAN HAM SALAD

2 c. ground cooked smoked ham
4 gherkins, ground or finely minced
¾ c. sour cream
1 ½ tsp. dry mustard
⅓ c. drained crushed pineapple

Combine all ingredients; mix until well blended. Cover; chill for 1 hour. Press one-fourth of mixture into a buttered custard cup to shape. Unmold onto lettuce cup. Arrange slices of Natural Swiss and American cheese, quarters of hard-cooked egg and tomato slices around ham molds. Garnish with radish rose, olives and watercress. Yield: 4 servings.

Photograph for this recipe above.

PORK AND APPLE SALAD

1 ½ c. diced cooked pork
2 c. diced apples
1 c. diced celery
½ c. chopped pecans
⅓ c. salad dressing
1 tsp. salt

Combine pork, apples, celery and pecans in bowl. Add salad dressing and salt; mix and chill. Serve in lettuce cups. Yield: 6 servings.

Mrs. William Gilbert
Blanchester, O.

QUICK HAM SALAD

1 c. cooked cubed ham
4 hard-cooked eggs, chopped
½ c. diced celery
½ c. diced cucumber pickles
Mayonnaise to taste
Lettuce

Combine ham, eggs, celery, pickles and mayonnaise. Serve in lettuce cups. Garnish with paprika. Yield: 4 servings.

Mrs. Stella Forrest
Wake Forest, N.C.

SKILLET HAM SALAD

¼ c. chopped green onions
¼ c. chopped green pepper

(Continued on next page)

2 c. diced cooked ham
1 tbsp. fat
3 c. cooked diced potatoes
¼ tsp. salt
⅛ tsp. pepper
¼ c. mayonnaise
½ lb. sharp American cheese, diced

Lightly brown onions, green pepper and ham in hot fat, stirring occasionally. Add potatoes, salt, pepper and mayonnaise; heat. Stir in cheese; heat until it begins to melt. Garnish with additional green onions. Yield: 4 servings.

Joyce Bradford
Raymond, Ill.

SUPER CHEF'S SALAD

1 head lettuce, chopped
1 c. cooked diced ham or other meat
½ c. dry packaged dressing mix
French dressing

Combine all ingredients. Add French dressing just before serving. Yield: 6 servings.

Catherine H. Maeder
Alva, Fla.

SWISS SALAD

2 c. cubed cooked pork
1 c. cooked peas
½ c. French dressing
½ c. diced celery
¼ c. broken walnuts
Paprika
Mayonnaise
2 hard-cooked eggs
6 stuffed olives

Marinate meat and peas in French dressing; chill. Add celery and nuts. Arrange on lettuce leaves; sprinkle with paprika; dot with mayonnaise. Cut each egg into 6 slices; remove yolks. Arrange white rings around salad. Cut each olive into 4 slices. Overlap 2 olive slices inside each ring. Sieve egg yolks; sprinkle over salad.

Mrs. Melvin Zack
Oglesby, Ill.

YUMMIE HAM SALAD

1 c. ham cut into thin strips
1 c. cheese cut into thin strips
1 c. canned peas, drained
½ onion, chopped
2 hard-cooked eggs, chopped
½ head lettuce, shredded
Mayonnaise to taste

Combine all ingredients. Serve on lettuce. Yield: 4 servings.

Mrs. Herbert Strand
Jackson, Mich.

CHOPPED HAM SALAD MOLD

1 tbsp. unflavored gelatin
¼ c. cold water
1 ½ c. tomato juice, heated
1 tsp. lemon juice
½ tsp. salt
1 c. cooked chopped ham
3 hard-cooked eggs, chopped
1 c. chopped celery
½ c. chopped cucumber
½ c. chopped bell pepper
1 tbsp. chopped onion
½ c. mayonnaise

Soften gelatin in cold water. Add hot tomato juice; stir until dissolved. Add lemon juice and salt; chill until partially set. Soak cucumbers in salted water; drain. Combine with all remaining ingredients; fold into thickened gelatin. Pour into mold; chill until firm. Yield: 6 servings.

Daphne Smith
Winnsboro, Tex.

COLD MEAT IN ASPIC

1 pkg. unflavored gelatin
¼ c. cold water
1 ½ c. heated highly seasoned consomme
½ c. cooked peas
1 hard-cooked egg, sliced
1 c. cooked sliced beets
Cubed ham, chicken or veal

Soften gelatin in cold water; stir into hot consomme. Pour a thin layer into greased pan; chill until thickened. Arrange peas, egg and beets on gelatin. Cover with another layer of gelatin; chill. Mix meat with remaining gelatin mixture; pour over cooled layer. Serve on lettuce garnished with radish roses. Yield: 6 servings.

Mrs. Elaine Petrik
Calmar, Iowa

HAM 'N' CHEESE MOLD

1 pkg. lemon gelatin
1 c. hot water
½ c. cold water
½ c. mayonnaise
1 to 2 tsp. vinegar
1 to 2 tsp. prepared horseradish
¾ tsp. salt
1 c. diced cooked or canned ham
½ c. shredded sharp process American cheese
¼ c. diced green pepper
2 tbsp. diced pimento
1 tsp. grated onion

Dissolve gelatin in hot water. Add cold water, mayonnaise, vinegar, horseradish and salt; blend well with electric or rotary beater. Pour into refrigerator tray. Chill in freezing unit 15 to 20 minutes or until firm 1 inch from edge, but soft in center. Turn into bowl; beat until fluffy. Fold in remaining ingredients; pour into a 1-quart mold. Chill until firm. Yield: 6 servings.

Mrs. Roy Spitnale
Cloverdale, O.

HAM AND CUKE

2 pkg. lime gelatin
1 c. hot water
1 hard-cooked egg, sliced
1 c. mayonnaise
1 ½ c. chopped ham
¼ c. sliced stuffed olives
1 tsp. grated onion
1 c. chopped celery
½ c. diced cucumber
½ tsp. dry mustard
½ c. dill pickles
8 strips pimento

Dissolve gelatin in hot water; chill until thickened. Put egg slices in bottom of mold. Pour one-third gelatin mixture over egg slices. Chill until firm. Combine all other ingredients; pour into mold. Chill until firm. Set in warm water to loosen salad from mold. Decorate with pimento strips and olives. Yield: 6 servings.

Lila Lill
Baytown, Tex.

HAM LOAF

1 pkg. unflavored gelatin
¼ c. cold water
½ c. chopped celery
1 green pepper
1 sm. onion
2 hard-cooked eggs
1 sm. can pimento
2 c. ground cooked ham
1 c. mayonnaise
1 tbsp. lemon juice
Sweet pickle juice

Soften gelatin in cold water; dissolve over hot water. Grind celery, pepper, onion, eggs and pimento together; add ham. Blend in mayonnaise, lemon juice and a small amount of pickle juice. Add gelatin; mix well. Place in mold; chill until set. Slice and serve. Yield: 6 servings.

Mrs. H. W. Ferguson
Venus, Tex.

HAM SALAD

2 tbsp. gelatin
¼ c. cold water
1 c. hot tomato juice
½ c. green pepper
2 c. cooked ham pieces
1 tbsp. vinegar
1 tbsp. lemon juice
1 tbsp. onion juice or 3 tbsp. grated onion
½ c. mayonnaise

Soak gelatin in cold water; dissolve in hot tomato juice. Grind green pepper and ham together; add with all remaining ingredients to gelatin mixture. Mix well; chill. Yield: 6 servings.

Mrs. Fred A. White
Port Arthur, Tex.

HAM SALAD

1 envelope gelatin
½ c. water
2 c. hot water or chicken broth
4 c. ground ham
3 hard-cooked eggs
1 c. cracker crumbs
1 c. mayonnaise
2 green peppers, chopped
2 pimentos, chopped
1 c. chopped celery
1 tbsp. minced onion
2 tsp. lemon juice

Soften gelatin in water; dissolve in broth. Add remaining ingredients. Pour into mold; chill until firm. Yield: 12 servings.

Mrs. Sheridan W. Bell
Harrisburg, Pa.

HAM SALAD MOLD

1 3-oz. pkg. lemon gelatin
1 c. hot water
3 tbsp. lemon juice
2 tsp. sugar
2 tbsp. chopped sweet pickle
1 c. chopped ham or tuna
1 c. chopped celery
2 tbsp. diced pimento
1 c. canned small peas
1 tbsp. grated onion
½ c. heavy cream, whipped
1 c. mayonnaise
¼ tsp. salt

Dissolve gelatin in water; add lemon juice and sugar. Cool. Add pickle, ham, celery, pimento, peas and onion. Fold in whipped cream, mayonnaise and salt. Mold in 8 x 8-inch pan or individual molds. Serve on lettuce. Yield: 6-8 servings.

Mrs. Jean Cummings
Kingsford, Mich.

HAWAIIAN HAM SALAD

3 pkg. pineapple gelatin
3 c. boiling water
1 ¼ c. mayonnaise
2 ¼ c. crushed pineapple and juice
3 ¾ c. cooked diced ham
1 ¼ c. chopped celery

Dissolve gelatin in boiling water; blend in mayonnaise. Add pineapple and juice; chill until slightly thickened. Fold in ham and celery; place in 2 1/2-quart mold. Chill until firm. Yield: 9 servings.

Mrs. Paul D. Miller
Mt. Pleasant, Iowa

JELLIED HAM SALAD

1 pkg. lemon gelatin
1 c. hot water
1 sm. can evaporated milk
3 tbsp. vinegar
¼ tsp. salt
¼ tsp. pepper
1 ½ c. chopped ham
1 c. chopped celery
1 ½ tbsp. chopped onion
½ c. mayonnaise

Dissolve gelatin in hot water; add milk and vinegar. Chill until mixture begins to thicken. Fold in remaining ingredients. Pour into 10 x 12-inch pan; chill until set. Cut into squares; serve on lettuce. Yield: 12 servings.

Mrs. C. H. Stahl
Loraine, Mich.

MOLDED HAM LOAF

2 tbsp. unflavored gelatin
½ c. cold water
1 c. boiling water
2 tbsp. lemon juice
1 tbsp. horseradish
2 tsp. Worcestershire sauce
½ c. mayonnaise
½ tsp. onion pulp
1 pimento, chopped
Dash of cayenne
Dash of cloves
Dash of nutmeg
2 ½ c. ground cooked ham

Soak gelatin in cold water. Dissolve in boiling water. Cool; stir in all remaining ingredients. Chill until thickened. Pour into a loaf pan; chill until firm. Yield: 6 servings.

Mrs. N. W. Berger
St. Petersburg, Fla.

MOLDED HAM SALAD

1 pkg. lemon gelatin
1 c. hot water
1 c. mayonnaise
2 hard-cooked eggs, chopped
½ c. diced cucumber
1 sm. onion, minced
1 c. ground cooked ham

Dissolve gelatin in hot water; cool until mixture begins to jell. Mix remaining ingredients; add to gelatin. Chill until set. Yield: 6-8 servings.

Mrs. Olive Williams
Bristol, Wisc.

MOLDED HAM SALAD

2 envelopes unflavored gelatin
1 ¾ c. cold water
1 can tomato soup
½ c. mayonnaise
2 hard-cooked eggs, diced
2 c. diced cooked ham
½ c. diced American cheese
1 3-oz. pkg. cream cheese
2 tbsp. lemon juice
1 tbsp. grated onion
2 tsp. prepared mustard

Soften gelatin in 1/4 cup cold water; dissolve over hot water. Add remaining water and soup; blend in mayonnaise. Chill until mixture begins to set. Combine eggs, ham and cheese. Combine cream cheese, lemon juice, onion and mustard; blend thoroughly.

(Continued on next page)

Blend gelatin mixture into cream cheese; add ham mixture. Pour into lightly greased 1 1/2-quart ring mold. Chill until firm. Garnish with watercress. Yield: 10 servings.

Mrs. T. U. Hill
Tifton, Ga.

CORNED BEEF AND POTATO SALAD

1 ½ c. cooked diced potatoes
½ c. finely cut celery leaves
¼ c. chopped sweet pickles
1 tsp. minced onion
1 c. chilled corned beef, cubed
½ c. mayonnaise
1 tsp. mustard
3 tbsp. chili sauce
Dash of salt
Dash of pepper
Lettuce

Combine potatoes, celery leaves, pickles, onion and corned beef. Mix mayonnaise, mustard, chili sauce, salt and pepper. Add to potato mixture and toss lightly. Chill well. Serve on lettuce. Yield: 4 servings.

Mrs. Thomas L. Noonan
Edison, N.J.

CORNED BEEF AND POTATO SALAD

6 med. potatoes, cooked
½ c. diced celery
2 tsp. salt
¼ tsp. pepper
⅓ c. mayonnaise
1 tbsp. vinegar
1 12-oz. can corned beef

Cut potatoes into small pieces; add celery, salt, pepper, mayonnaise and vinegar. Cut beef into cubes. Add to potatoes and mix. Yield: 6 servings.

Mrs. Dean Pratt
Mound City, Kans.

CORNED BEEF SALAD

1 c. salad dressing
2 tbsp. vinegar
1 tsp. sugar
Dash of salt and pepper
1 can corned beef, cubed
1 ½ tbsp. chopped onion
4 med. potatoes, cooked and diced
1 c. diced celery
3 c. grated cabbage

Combine salad dressing, vinegar, sugar, salt and pepper. Add all remaining ingredients; chill. Yield: 6 servings.

Mrs. Chase Adams
Taylor, Mich.

CORNED BEEF SALAD

4 med. potatoes, peeled
1 12-oz. can corned beef, chilled
4 med. dill pickles, finely chopped
½ c. chopped celery
¼ c. minced onion

Place potatoes in saucepan; cover with water and 1/2 teaspoon salt. Simmer until tender; chill. Cut into 1/2-inch cubes. Dice corned beef. Combine potatoes, corned beef and pickles with celery and onion.

DRESSING:
1 c. salad dressing
2 tbsp. lemon juice
2 tsp. mustard
1 tbsp. Worcestershire sauce
1 tsp. salt
Pepper to taste

Blend all ingredients; chill for 1 hour. Yield: 6 servings.

Nell P. Stevens
Isola, Miss.

BEST CORNED BEEF SALAD

1 box lemon gelatin
1 c. boiling water
1 can corned beef, shredded
2 c. diced celery
½ c. diced cucumber (opt.)
½ tsp. salt
3 hard-cooked eggs, diced
1 sm. onion, finely cut
1 c. salad dressing

Combine all ingredients except salad dressing; mix well. Add salad dressing. Turn into mold; chill until set. Yield: 9 servings.

Mrs. Roy Hooker
Steubenville, O.

BUSY DAY CORNED BEEF SALAD

1 tbsp. unflavored gelatin
¼ c. cold water
2 cubes beef bouillon

(Continued on next page)

1 ¾ c. boiling water
3 hard-cooked eggs, sliced
1 can corned beef
1 c. chopped celery
1 tbsp. minced onion
1 c. mayonnaise
⅛ tsp. salt

Soften gelatin in cold water; dissolve with bouillon in boiling water. Cool. Place sliced eggs in design in mold. Cover with thickened gelatin. Combine remaining gelatin and all remaining ingredients; pour into mold. Chill until firm. Yield: 8-10 servings.

Ethel Conn
Ovid, Mich.

CORNED BEEF-BOUILLON SALAD

2 envelopes unflavored gelatin
1 c. cold water
1 c. beef bouillon
1 c. salad dressing
1 can chilled corned beef, ground or finely cut
1 sm. green pepper, chopped
1 sm. can pimento, chopped
½ c. chopped celery
3 hard-cooked eggs, chopped

Soften gelatin in cold water. Bring bouillon to a boil; pour over gelatin. Mix salad dressing and beef. Add green pepper, pimento, celery and eggs. Mix with gelatin mixture; chill until firm. Yield: 12 servings.

Mrs. R. B. Stewart
Atlanta, Ga.

CORNED BEEF-EGG SALAD

1 can corned beef
2 c. diced celery
⅔ c. diced cucumber
3 hard-cooked eggs, diced
½ c. diced olives
Diced onion
Diced sweet pickle
Diced green pepper
1 pkg. lemon gelatin
¾ c. boiling water
1 c. salad dressing
½ pt. heavy cream, whipped

Combine corned beef, celery, cucumber, eggs, olives, onion, pickle and green pepper. Dissolve gelatin in boiling water; cool. Combine with meat mixture, salad dressing and whipped cream. Pour into dish; refrigerate. Yield: 8-12 servings.

Mrs. Ralph Cochran
Howard, O.

CORNED BEEF-GELATIN SALAD

1 pkg. lemon gelatin
1 c. hot water
1 can corned beef, shredded
1 ½ tsp. salt
½ onion, grated
5 hard-cooked eggs, chopped
1 c. chopped celery
1 c. mayonnaise

Dissolve gelatin in water; add all remaining ingredients. Pour into oblong pan; chill until firm. Yield: 8-10 servings.

Mrs. Irene Hackett
Barnesville, O.

CORNED BEEF-GELATIN SALAD

2 3-oz. pkg. lemon gelatin
1 qt. hot water
4 tbsp. vinegar
1 can corned beef, broken
2 c. chopped celery
4 tbsp. minced onion
1 green pepper, finely chopped
6 hard-cooked eggs, chopped
1 c. mayonnaise

Dissolve gelatin in hot water and vinegar. Chill until partially set; fold in mayonnaise and all remaining ingredients. Chill until firm. Yield: 10 servings.

Mrs. Wilda Carr
Holdrege, Nebr.

CORNED BEEF LOAF

1 pkg. lemon gelatin
1 c. boiling water
1 c. meat stock or 1 c. water plus 4 bouillon cubes
1 tbsp. Worcestershire sauce
¼ tsp. paprika
3 c. canned corned beef, ground
1 tbsp. grated onion
1 tbsp. prepared mustard

Dissolve gelatin in boiling water. Add meat stock, Worcestershire sauce and paprika; chill until slightly thickened. Fold in remaining ingredients. Pour into loaf pan; chill until firm. Unmold; slice and serve on crisp lettuce. Garnish with egg slices and tomato wedges. Yield: 10 servings.

Mrs. Robert W. Baker
Elmendorf, Alaska

CORNED BEEF LOAF

1 pkg. unflavored gelatin
½ c. water
2 tbsp. lemon juice
¼ tsp. salt
¾ c. mayonnaise
¼ c. minced onion
½ c. chopped sweet pickle
½ c. diced celery
3 hard-cooked eggs, sliced
1 12-oz. can corned beef, finely cut

Soften gelatin in cold water; dissolve over low heat. Remove from heat; stir in lemon juice and salt. Cool; gradually add mayonnaise. Add all remaining ingredients; place in a loaf pan. Chill until firm; unmold on lettuce. Yield: 6 servings.

Elizabeth McClary
Highland Park, Mich.

CORNED BEEF MOLD

2 tbsp. unflavored gelatin
½ c. cold water
1 ½ c. V-8 vegetable juice
1 tsp. lemon juice
½ tsp. salt
1 12-oz. can corned beef, shredded
3 hard-cooked eggs, chopped
½ c. chopped cucumber
1 c. chopped celery
2 tbsp. chopped onion
1 c. mayonnaise

Soften gelatin in cold water. Heat vegetable juice; add gelatin, stirring until dissolved. Add lemon juice and salt. Chill until partially set. Combine remaining ingredients; fold into gelatin mixture. Pour into 1 1/2-quart mold. Chill until firm; slice and serve. Yield: 8 servings.

Mrs. Ray Beard
Rome, Ga.

CORNED BEEF SALAD

1 pkg. lemon gelatin
1 ¼ c. boiling water
1 c. salad dressing
1 to 2 c. diced celery
½ cucumber, diced (opt.)
1 green pepper, chopped (opt.)
1 can corned beef
3 or 4 hard-cooked eggs, chopped
1 med. onion, chopped

Dissolve gelatin in boiling water; add salad dressing and mix well. Cool. Add all remaining ingredients; refrigerate until firm. Serve on lettuce leaf with crackers. Yield: 8 servings.

Mrs. Kenneth Wilson
Albany, Ind.

CORNED BEEF SALAD

1 pkg. lemon gelatin
1 c. boiling water
2 tbsp. vinegar or olive juice
1 can corned beef, fat removed
10 to 16 stuffed green olives, sliced
1 c. chopped celery
3 hard-cooked eggs, chopped
½ c. mayonnaise

Dissolve gelatin in boiling water with vinegar or olive juice. Break up corned beef; add with olives, celery, eggs and mayonnaise to gelatin. Pour in ring mold; refrigerate until firm. Serve on salad greens. Yield: 8-10 servings.

Frances Jones
San Marino, Calif.

CORNED BEEF SALAD

2 pkg. lemon gelatin
2 c. hot water
1 c. salad dressing
1 tsp. salt
¼ tsp. celery seed
2 c. chopped celery
1 tbsp. minced onion
2 tbsp. chopped green pepper
1 can corned beef, flaked
1 tbsp. vinegar

Dissolve gelatin in hot water; add all remaining ingredients. Blend well; pour into molds or bread pans. Chill until firm. Yield: 10-12 servings.

Margaret Bourcier
Otisville, Mich.

CORNED BEEF SALAD

2 envelopes plain gelatin
½ c. cold water
1 can tomato soup
1 c. mayonnaise
1 12-oz. can corned beef, ground
3 hard-cooked eggs, diced
2 tbsp. minced onion
2 c. diced celery
2 tbsp. chopped green pepper

(Continued on next page)

Dissolve gelatin in cold water. Heat soup; add gelatin. Stir until dissolved. Blend in mayonnaise. Add all remaining ingredients; pour into lightly oiled pans or molds. Chill until firm. Serve on lettuce. NOTE: Ham may be used for corned beef. Yield: 8-10 servings.

Mrs. M. A. Gorman
Detroit, Mich.

CORNED BEEF SALAD

1 tbsp. gelatin
¼ c. cold water
1 c. chopped corned beef
2 tbsp. minced onion
2 tbsp. minced green pepper
3 hard-cooked eggs, chopped
2 tbsp. vinegar
½ tsp. dry mustard
1 c. mayonnaise

Soften gelatin in cold water; dissolve over hot water. Combine with all remaining ingredients; place in a loaf pan. Chill until firm; slice into squares.

Velma Dean
San Dimas, Calif.

CORNED BEEF SALAD GELATIN

2 3-oz. pkg. lemon gelatin
3 c. hot water
1 can corned beef, minced
3 hard-cooked eggs, chopped
1 c. diced celery
1 tsp. chopped onion
1 med. green pepper, diced
3 tbsp. diced pimento
1 c. salad dressing

Dissolve gelatin in hot water; cool. Combine meat, eggs, celery, onion, green pepper, pimento and salad dressing. Place in mold or bowl. Pour gelatin over mixture; pierce with a knife so gelatin will work through. Chill. Yield: 6-8 servings.

Janice Hagemeister
Mott, N.D.

CORNED BEEF SALAD JELL

1 pkg. aspic gelatin
1 c. boiling water
1 can corned beef, crumbled
6 hard-cooked eggs
1 sm. green pepper
1 onion, grated
1 c. chopped celery
1 c. salad dressing
1 sm. bottle stuffed olives
1 c. peas

Dissolve gelatin in water; cool. Add remaining ingredients. Pour into 9 x 12-inch baking dish. Chill until firm. NOTE: 1 package unflavored gelatin dissolved with 1 bouillon cube may be substituted for aspic gelatin. Yield: 8 servings.

Josephine M. Kieseler
Lakewood, O.

CORNED BEEF SALAD

1 pkg. lemon gelatin
1 ⅓ c. hot water
1 c. mayonnaise
1 c. chopped celery
Chopped onion
Juice of 1 lemon
1 can corned beef, shredded

Dissolve gelatin in hot water; add mayonnaise and stir until smooth. Add celery and small amount of onion. Stir in lemon juice; add corned beef. Pour into 10 x 10-inch pan, chill. Flavor improves if made the night before serving. May be served on lettuce leaf with whipped cream or mayonnaise-horseradish dressing. Yield: 6-8 servings.

Mrs. Gifford Hoskins
Montebello, Calif.

CORNED BEEF SALAD MOLD

2 pkg. unflavored gelatin
¼ c. cold water
1 ½ c. hot tomato juice
1 tsp. lemon juice
½ tsp. salt
1 12-oz. can corned beef, shredded
3 hard-cooked eggs, chopped
2 c. chopped celery
½ c. chopped cucumbers
1 tbsp. chopped onion
1 c. mayonnaise

Soak gelatin in cold water. Add to heated tomato juice; stir until dissolved. Add lemon juice and salt; chill until partially set. Add all remaining ingredients; chill until firm. Yield: 8-10 servings.

Mrs. Al Gackowski
Bloomingdale, Mich.

CORNED BEEF SALAD MOLD

1 pkg. lemon gelatin
1 ½ c. boiling water
½ c. mayonnaise
½ c. sour cream
1 green pepper, chopped
1 tbsp. minced onion
2 hard-cooked eggs, chopped
1 can corned beef, crumbled

Dissolve gelatin in water; cool. Add remaining ingredients. Pour into lightly greased mold; chill until firm. Serve on salad greens. Yield: 8 servings.

Mrs. Norman F. Clarke
Hinsdale, Ill.

CORNED BEEF SALAD MOLD

1 envelope gelatin
¼ c. cold water
1 tbsp. lemon juice
½ tsp. salt
1 ½ c. hot tomato juice
1 12-oz. can corned beef, shredded
3 hard-cooked eggs, chopped
2 c. chopped celery
½ c. chopped cucumber (opt.)
1 tbsp. chopped onion
1 c. mayonnaise

Soften gelatin in cold water. Combine with lemon juice, salt and hot tomato juice; blend well. Add all remaining ingredients; spoon into 9-inch ring mold. Chill for 4 hours. Unmold. Yield: 8 servings.

Mrs. Carl Mayer
Rocky River, O.

CORNED BEEF SALAD

1 pkg. lemon gelatin
1 can consomme
1 consomme can cold water
1 can corned beef, broken into pieces
1 c. mayonnaise or ⅓ c. mayonnaise
combined with ⅓ c. sour cream
3 hard-cooked eggs
1 sm. onion, minced
1 c. chopped celery
½ c. chopped green pepper
Salt and pepper to taste

Dissolve gelatin in hot consomme; add cold water. Chill until thickened; add all remaining ingredients. Mold individually or in a loaf. May be served on lettuce with mayonnaise. NOTE: Eggs may be used as garnish rather than in the salad.

Louise T. Norcross
Portland, Oreg.

CORNED BEEF SALAD

1 pkg. lemon gelatin
1 can consomme
3 hard-cooked eggs, chopped
1 tsp. Worcestershire sauce
Juice of ½ lemon
1 can corned beef
1 sm. onion, grated
1 c. diced celery
1 c. mayonnaise

Dissolve gelatin in hot consomme; cool until partially set. Add remaining ingredients; pour into mold. Chill until firm. Yield: 6 servings.

Mrs. Louis Rathke
Reading, Kans.

CORNED BEEF SALAD

1 can corned beef, diced
1 c. diced celery
2 tbsp. grated onion
3 tbsp. chopped green pepper
4 hard-cooked eggs, diced
¾ c. salad dressing
2 pkg. unflavored gelatin
½ c. cold water
2 cubes beef bouillon
1 ½ c. hot water

Combine corned beef, celery, onion, green pepper, eggs and salad dressing. Soften gelatin in cold water; dissolve bouillon cubes in hot water. Add to gelatin; stir until dissolved. Cool; add to meat mixture. Chill for at least 24 hours. Yield: 8-10 servings.

Mrs. Sally Gegenheimer
Clawson, Mich.

EASY LUNCHEON SALAD

1 pkg. lemon gelatin
1 c. mayonnaise
1 can corned beef, shredded
1 tbsp. chopped green pepper
1 c. chopped celery
1 tbsp. chopped onion
2 hard-cooked eggs, chopped
½ tsp. salt

Prepare gelatin according to package directions. Chill until thickened. Beat until light; fold in mayonnaise. Add corned beef, the chopped ingredients and salt. Chill until firm. Serve on lettuce cups. Yield: 10 servings.

Mrs. Mildred E. Ready
Hartington, Nebr.

MOLDED CORNED BEEF SALAD

1 box lemon gelatin
1 c. boiling water
1 c. flaked corned beef
2 c. chopped celery
½ onion, diced
¾ c. chopped green pepper
1 c. mayonnaise

Dissolve gelatin in boiling water; cool. Add corned beef, celery, onion and green pepper. Stir in mayonnaise; mix well. Pour into a large mold or individual molds. Chill until firm. Serve on lettuce leaves. Yield: 4-6 servings.

Barbara Gaylor
Lansing, Mich.

MOLDED SALAD WITH CORNED BEEF

1 pkg. lemon gelatin
2 ¾ c. plus 1 tbsp. hot water
1 can corned beef
2 c. chopped celery
2 tbsp. chopped onion
2 tbsp. chopped green pepper
1 c. salad dressing
3 tbsp. vinegar

Dissolve gelatin in hot water; chill until thickened. Beat well; add all remaining ingredients. Place in 13 x 2 x 2-inch pan. Chill until firm. Yield: 16 servings.

Mrs. Margaret Veen
Marysville, Mich.

CORNED BEEF SALAD

2 3-oz. pkg. lemon gelatin
3 c. boiling water
¾ c. mayonnaise
1 12-oz. can corned beef, chopped
1 sm. onion, chopped
3 hard-cooked eggs, chopped
1 c. chopped celery
1 sm. can pimentos, chopped

Dissolve gelatin in water; allow to cool. Add remaining ingredients; chill until firm. Yield: 12 servings.

Mrs. Maurice Leeser
Cadiz, O.

ANTIPASTO SALAD

1 head romaine, washed and chilled
1 head lettuce, washed and chilled
6 oz. sliced Mozzarella cheese
6 oz. sliced salami
1 7-oz. can tuna
½ c. sliced green onions
½ c. sliced radishes
6 cherry tomatoes
6 ripe olives

Line a large salad bowl with romaine. Pull lettuce into bite-sized pieces; place in bowl. Cut cheese and salami into 1/2-inch strips. Drain tuna; break into chunks with a fork. Arrange cheese, salami, tuna, green onions and radishes in rows on top of greens. Arrange tomatoes and olives around side of salad bowl for garnish. Serve with chilled anchovy salad dressing.

ANCHOVY SALAD DRESSING:
1 c. evaporated milk
½ c. salad oil
¼ c. wine vinegar
1 tsp. salt
¼ tsp. pepper
Dash of garlic powder
¼ c. chopped parsley
2 2-oz. cans flat fillets of anchovies

Place all ingredients in container of electric blender. Cover; blend for a few seconds or until smooth. Chill; serve with "Antipasto" salad. Yield: 4-6 servings.

Photograph for this recipe on page 301.

BEEF TONGUE SALAD

1 lge. beef tongue
1 c. diced celery
½ c. diced apple
¼ c. chopped pecans
4 hard-cooked eggs, chopped
¼ c. diced sweet pickles
Salad dressing

Steam or boil tongue until tender; remove skin and roots. Finely chop or put tongue through food chopper. Add remaining ingredients, using enough salad dressing to moisten. Yield: 10 servings.

Mrs. Ed. C. Wallace
La Feria, Mich.

BOLOGNA SALAD

2 envelopes unflavored gelatin
2 ½ c. cold water
½ tsp. salt
½ c. vinegar
½ c. diced celery
½ c. chopped sweet pickles
2 c. grated American cheese
2 c. diced bologna
Mayonnaise thinned with sour cream
Tomato slices
Green pepper rings
Onion rings

Soften gelatin in 1 cup cold water. Dissolve over low heat, stirring constantly. Remove

(Continued on next page)

from heat; add remaining water, salt and vinegar. Chill until thickened. Fold in celery, pickles, cheese and bologna. Turn into a 6-cup mold; chill until firm. Unmold; serve with mayonnaise thinned with sour cream. Surround mold with tomato slices topped with green pepper and onion rings. Yield: 8-10 servings.

Mrs. Lamon Leon Bennett
George West, Tex.

DEVILED HAM MOUSSE

1 envelope unflavored gelatin
¼ c. cold water
¾ c. mayonnaise
2 3-oz. cans deviled ham
1 ½ tsp. grated onion
½ c. chopped celery
¼ c. chopped green pepper
¼ c. chopped sweet pickles

Soften gelatin in cold water; dissolve over hot water. Blend in all remaining ingredients. Pour into 1-pint mold. Chill until firm. Yield: 6 servings.

Mrs. Robert O. Roop
Highland Springs, Va.

FRANKFURTER-VEGETABLE SALAD BOWL

½ lb. frankfurters
2 lb. cooked pototoes, thinly sliced
⅓ c. cooked chopped vegetables
2 ½ tbsp. minced onion
2 ½ tbsp. minced parsley
⅓ c. salad dressing
½ tsp. celery seed
Salt and pepper to taste

Simmer frankfurters in boiling water for 5 minutes; cut into 1-inch pieces. Combine meat with all remaining ingredients; toss lightly to mix. Yield: 4 servings.

Mrs. Earl J. Conklin
McBrides, Mich.

HOT DAY SPECIAL

2 med. heads lettuce, chopped
½ med. carrot, grated
4 med. radishes, sliced
1 8-oz. pkg. Velveeta cheese, cubed
4 tomatoes, cut up
¾ lb. Honey Loaf, cubed
3 tbsp. diced onion

Combine all ingredients; toss. Serve with favorite dressing. Yield: 6-7 servings.

Patricia Richards
Nineveh, Ind.

HOT POTATO -FRANK SALAD

6 strips bacon, chopped
1 tbsp. flour
½ c. chopped green onions with tops
¼ c. vinegar
1 ½ tsp. salt
½ tsp. pepper
1 tbsp. sugar
½ c. water
1 lb. wieners, sliced
1 qt. sliced cooked potatoes, hot

Fry bacon until crisp. Blend in flour until smooth. Add onions, vinegar, seasonings, water and wieners; cook for 5 minutes. Pour over hot potatoes; mix lightly. Yield: 6 servings.

Mrs. George L. Walker
Haines City, Fla.

LIVER SALAD

1-lb. beef or pork liver
1 ½ c. water
½ tsp. salt
3 c. grated cabbage
1 tbsp. grated onion (opt.)
¾ c. salad dressing
⅛ tsp. pepper
1 tsp. celery seed
1 tsp. caraway seed
2 tbsp. vinegar
1 tbsp. sugar
2 tbsp. catsup
1 tsp. Worcestershire sauce

Boil liver in salted water for 10 minutes; drain. Grind liver; add cabbage and onion. Combine remaining ingredients; add to liver mixture. Chill and serve. Yield: 6 servings.

Lillian Johnson
Dayton, O.

MAIN DISH SALAD

1 ½ c. chopped cabbage
4 lge. carrots, chopped
3 c. cooked pinto beans, drained
3 hard-cooked eggs, chopped
1 can luncheon meat, chopped
1 sm. onion, chopped
3 tbsp. mustard
3 tbsp. mayonnaise
2 tbsp. milk
Salt and pepper to taste

Combine cabbage, carrots, beans, eggs, meat and onion. Blend mustard, mayonnaise, milk, salt and pepper. Pour over cabbage mixture; toss well. Chill for several hours before serving. Yield: 4 servings.

Mrs. Oral Cooper
Alamosa, Colo.

As fresh as the April breeze that blows away the last March chill, Molded Chicken Salad and Tomato Aspic Crown are: deal for a sit-down or buffet luncheon. You can prepare them ahead, and spend more precious moments with your guests.

MOLDED CHICKEN SALAD

2 envelopes unflavored gelatin
1 c. cold water
1 can cream of celery soup
½ tsp. salt
2 tbsp. lemon juice
1 tsp. instant minced onion
1 c. salad dressing
2 tbsp. diced pimento
1 c. diced celery
2 c. diced cooked chicken

Sprinkle gelatin over water in a 2½ quart saucepan to soften. Place over moderate heat for 3 minutes or until gelatin is dissolved, stirring constantly. Remove from heat; stir in soup, salt, lemon juice, minced onion and salad dressing. Beat with rotary beater until smooth. Chill until mixture mounds when dropped from a spoon, stirring occasionally. Add pimento, celery and chicken; turn into a 6-cup loaf pan or mold. Chill until firm; unmold on salad greens. Garnish with ripe olives and additional pimento if desired. Yield: 6 servings.

TOMATO ASPIC CROWN

2 envelopes unflavored gelatin
3¼ c. tomato juice
½ tsp. salt
1 tsp. sugar
1 tsp. Worcestershire sauce
¼ tsp. Tabasco sauce
¼ c. lemon or lime juice

Sprinkle gelatin over 1 cup tomato juice in a 2-quart saucepan to soften. Place over moderate heat for 3 minutes or until gelatin is dissolved, stirring constantly. Remove from heat; stir in remaining ingredients. Pour into 1-quart ring mold; chill until firm. Unmold; fill center with coleslaw. Yield: 6 servings.

See photograph on reverse side.

RECIPE FOR CELESTIAL CHICKEN SALAD ON PAGE 333

AUNTIE BESS'S SOUTHERN CHICKEN SALAD

1 5-lb. hen
Celery
1 tbsp. salt
½ onion
1 pt. mayonnaise
1 jar mustard chow-chow pickles, diced
Monosodium glutamate
Tabasco sauce to taste

Boil hen in water with 2 stalks celery, salt and onion until meat falls from bones. Cut meat and celery into small pieces. Combine 2 cups of chicken and 1 cup celery at a time. Continue until all are used. Add remaining ingredients; mix. NOTE: Salad is better if prepared a day in advance of serving. Yield: 12-16 servings.

Mrs. Faye C. Cochran
Fort Wainwright, Alaska

AVOCADO-CHICKEN-APPLE SALAD

2 lge. apples, cubed
1 ripe avocado, cubed
2 tbsp. lemon juice
½ c. mayonnaise
¼ c. cream
1 tsp. minced onion
2 c. cubed cooked chicken
¼ c. crumbled Bleu cheese

Sprinkle apples and avocado with lemon juice. Combine mayonnaise and cream; add onion. Toss avocado, apples, cheese and chicken with cream dressing. Serve on lettuce leaves.

Mrs. Katherine S. Hunter
Irving, Tex.

BEANS, BACON AND CHICKEN

4 tbsp. catsup
½ c. mayonnaise
2 tbsp. vinegar
½ tsp. salt
⅛ tsp. pepper
2 c. cooked string beans
4 tomatoes, diced
1 head lettuce, chunks
2 c. cooked cubed chicken
5 slices bacon, fried and crumbled
1 c. grated Swiss cheese

Combine catsup, mayonnaise, vinegar, salt and pepper. Pour over beans, tomatoes, lettuce and chicken. Toss lightly and chill. Garnish with bacon and cheese. Yield: 4 servings.

Mrs. Willis Moren
Wonewoc, Wisc.

BEST CHICKEN SALAD

2 hens, stewed and boned
2 cans whole mushrooms or 3 cans sliced mushrooms
1 c. sliced pimento
1 lge. onion, minced
3 c. diced celery
1 lge. green pepper, diced
1 ½ pkg. uncooked peas
1 ½ c. cashews
Salt and pepper to taste
1 qt. mayonnaise

Combine chicken, mushrooms, pimento, onion, celery and green pepper. Mixture may be stored up to four days in refrigerator. Just before serving add peas, cashews, salt, pepper and mayonnaise. Yield: 18 servings.

Mrs. William I. House
Pease AFB, N.H.

BUSY DAY CHICKEN SALAD

2 c. cooked cubed chicken
2 tbsp. chopped green olives
¾ c. chopped celery
½ c. almonds, toasted
2 tbsp. chopped ripe olives
2 tbsp. chopped sweet pickle
2 hard-cooked eggs, grated
¾ c. mayonnaise
Lettuce leaves

Combine all ingredients; toss lightly. Serve on lettuce leaves. Yield: 6 servings.

Mrs. T. C. Bedwell, Jr.
San Antonio, Tex.

CHICKEN-ALMOND SALAD

2 c. chopped chicken
1 c. diced celery
2 tbsp. chopped parsley
2 tbsp. capers
2 tbsp. chopped ripe olives
2 tbsp. lemon juice
½ c. fried almonds
⅛ tsp. pepper
1 tsp. salt
1 c. sour cream
1 c. mayonnaise

Combine all ingredients, reserving one-half of almonds for garnish. Chill and serve on lettuce. Garnish with reserved almonds. Yield: 8 servings.

Joyce Kincaid
Louisville, Ill.

CHICKEN-ASPARAGUS SALAD

1 ½ c. cooked diced chicken
1 c. asparagus tips
2 tbsp. minced green pepper
¼ c. shredded cabbage
¾ c. mayonnaise

Thoroughly blend all ingredients; serve. Yield: 6 servings.

Mrs. R. B. Gilbert
Lincolnton, N.C.

CHICKEN-FRUIT SALAD

2 c. diced cooked chicken
½ c. pitted white cherries
½ c. diced pineapple
1 pared orange, sliced
½ c. chopped nuts
1 c. mayonnaise

Combine all ingredients; mix well. Chill. Serve on lettuce. Yield: 6 servings.

Eugah Pearl Webster
Winfield, Ala.

CHICKEN-FRUIT SALAD

3 c. diced cooked chicken
1 c. diced celery
1 can Mandarin oranges, drained
1 can pineapple chunks, drained
Sliced ripe olives (opt.)
2 tbsp. salad oil
2 tbsp. wine vinegar
2 tbsp. frozen orange juice concentrate
½ c. mayonnaise
½ c. slivered almonds

Combine chicken, celery, oranges, pineapple and olives. Blend oil, vinegar and orange juice. Marinate chicken mixture in vinegar mixture for 1 hour or overnight. Add mayonnaise and almonds before serving. Yield: 8 servings.

Mrs. Frank Kiddoo
Coffeyville, Kans.

CHICK AND GRAPE SALAD

2 c. cubed cooked chicken
1 c. white grape halves
½ c. toasted, slivered slmonds
1 c. chopped celery
Salad dressing

Combine all ingredients, adding enough salad dressing to moisten. Fill lettuce cups with salad; garnish with grapes and watercress.

Mrs. Virginia Moore
Birmingham, Ala.

CHICKEN AND HAM SALAD

1 ½ c. diced cooked chicken
2 c. diced celery
½ tsp. salt
Mayonnaise to taste
1 ½ c. diced cooked ham
2 hard-cooked eggs, diced
¼ tsp. pepper

Combine all ingredients. Chill before serving. Yield: 6 servings.

Mrs. Robert Tyler
Monticello, Ind.

CHICKEN SALAD

2 c. diced cooked chicken
1 c. diced celery
3 hard-cooked eggs, diced
1 c. broken pecans
½ c. seeded Tokay grapes
¼ c. drained crushed pineapple
¾ tsp. salt
⅛ tsp. pepper
1 c. salad dressing

Combine all ingredients. Serve very cold on salad greens. Salad dressing may be combined with 1/2 cup whipped cream. Yield: 6 servings.

Harriet W. Smythe
Homer, O.

CHICKEN SALAD

1 c. cooked diced chicken
French dressing
⅛ c. crushed pineapple
½ c. diced celery
½ tsp. grated onion
½ c. chopped toasted almonds
Salad dressing

Marinate chicken in French dressing for 1 hour. Drain if necessary. Add remaining ingredients with enough salad dressing to moisten. Chill and serve in lettuce cups garnished with a few shredded almonds. Yield: 6 servings.

Mrs. Nicholas Mashlonik
Lancaster, N.Y.

CHICKEN SALAD

DRESSING:
2 eggs
½ c. sugar
1 tbsp. flour
1 tsp. mustard
½ c. vinegar
1 c. boiling water
Pinch of salt
1 tbsp. butter

Combine eggs, sugar, flour and mustard; beat until smooth. Add vinegar, water and salt. Cook in double boiler until thickened. Remove from heat and beat in butter. Cool.

SALAD:
6 c. diced cubed chicken
2 c. diced celery
1 c. chopped nuts
6 hard-cooked eggs, chopped
1 c. diced apples
1 sm. can diced pimento
½ c. diced sweet pickle
Mayonnaise

Combine all ingredients except mayonnaise; mix well. Mix equal parts of dressing and mayonnaise. Blend dressing into salad; chill. Yield: 10 servings.

Mrs. Ruth Reams
Greenville, Fla.

CHICKEN SALAD

Juice of 1 lemon
2 c. diced cooked chicken
½ c. diced apple
1 c. diced celery
2 hard-cooked eggs, chopped
½ c. chopped toasted almonds
⅓ c. mayonnaise
½ tsp. salt
Dash of pepper
¼ c. minced onion

Sprinkle lemon juice over chicken and apple; toss lightly. Add celery, eggs and almonds to chicken. Blend mayonnaise with seasonings and onion; fold into chicken. Garnish with apple wedges and parsley. Yield: 8 servings.

Mrs. J. W. Slay
Texarkana, Tex.

CHICKEN SALAD

3 c. chopped stewed chicken
1 c. white seedless grapes or 1 c. seedless raisins
1 c. chopped celery
½ c. sweet cream
½ c. mayonnaise

Combine all ingredients. Chill thoroughly. Serve on lettuce cups. Garnish with strips of pimento, if desired. Yield: 10 servings.

Mrs. D. E. Davis
Chillicothe, Tex.

CHICKEN SALAD DELIGHT

1 qt. cubed cooked chicken
1 qt. finely cut celery
1 pt. pecans, toasted
1 pt. salad dressing

Mix chicken, celery and pecans; add salad dressing. Serve in lettuce cup; top with additional salad dressing. Yield: 12 servings.

Sara Ridgway
Derby, O.

CHICKEN SALAD WITH FRUIT

⅔ c. raisins
2 c. diced chicken
½ c. chopped nuts
½ c. diced pineapple
1 c. diced celery
⅔ c. diced apples
Mayonnaise

Steam raisins until plump; cool. Add remaining ingredients, using enough mayonnaise to moisten. Yield: 6 servings.

Mrs. Belle Prey
Hot Springs, Ark.

CHICKEN SALAD WITH GRAPES

2 c. coarsely diced chicken
2 tbsp. lemon juice
Salt
1 c. diced celery
1 c. seedless white grapes
2 hard-cooked eggs, chilled and chopped
½ c. mayonnaise
¼ c. slivered blanched almonds, toasted

Sprinkle chicken with lemon juice and 1/2 teaspoon salt; chill for several hours. Add celery, grapes, eggs, mayonnaise and almonds. Toss lightly; season with salt to taste. Serve on lettuce cups. Yield: 4-5 servings.

Patricia McGee
Conrad, Mont.

CHICKEN SALAD

2 tbsp. lemon or lime juice
½ tsp. salt
¼ tsp. Tabasco sauce
½ c. mayonnaise
2 c. diced cooked chicken
1 c. diced celery
½ c. seedless grape halves (opt.)

Add lemon juice, salt and Tabasco sauce to mayonnaise; mix well. Place remaining ingredients in mixing bowl. Add mayonnaise mixture; toss lightly. Chill for 1 hour. Pile into lettuce cups. Yield: 6 servings.

Photograph for this recipe above.

CHICKEN SALAD IN PINEAPPLE

1 fresh pineapple
2 tbsp. sour cream
½ c. mayonnaise
1 tsp. salt
½ tsp. pepper
2 c. diced white chicken
1 c. diced celery

Cut pineapple in half; hollow out inside. Cut pineapple into bite-sized pieces, making 2 cups. Cut shell into eight pieces. Mix diced pineapple with remaining ingredients. Serve in pineapple shell. Yield: 8 servings.

Mrs. Jack Kelt
Vienna, Ga.

CHICKEN SALAD WITH PINEAPPLE

1 ½ c. diced cooked chicken
¾ c. drained crushed pineapple
½ c. chopped pecans
1 c. heavy cream, whipped
1 c. mayonnaise

Combine chicken, pineapple and pecans. Fold whipped cream into mayonnaise; add to chicken mixture. Freeze for 2 to 3 hours or until firm. Yield: 6 servings.

Mrs. Luella Robb
Covelo, Calif.

CHICKEN SALAD PLATE

3 c. coarsely diced cooked chicken
2 c. diced celery
½ c. mayonnaise
3 tbsp. lemon juice
1 tsp. seasoned salt
¼ tsp. pepper

(Continued on next page)

Combine chicken and celery. Blend mayonnaise with all remaining ingredients. Pour over chicken; let chill for 1 hour before serving in lettuce cups. May be garnished with tomato and hard-cooked egg wedges and ripe olives. Yield: 4-6 servings.

Rachael S. Goodman
Browns Summit, N.C.

CHICKEN SALAD SAN DIEGO

3 ½ c. cooked diced chicken
1 c. finely diced celery
1 c. sliced white grapes
½ c. shredded almonds
2 tbsp. minced parsley
1 tsp. salt
1 c. mayonnaise
½ c. heavy cream, whipped

Combine all ingredients. Yield: 6 servings.

Mrs. Gene C. Rosholt
San Diego, Calif.

CHICKEN SALAD FOR SANDWICHES

1 3-lb. chicken, cooked and chopped
½ c. salad dressing
1 tbsp. chopped onion
¼ c. chopped pickle
½ c. chopped celery
1 tsp. salt
Chicken broth

Mix chicken with salad dressing; add onion, pickle and celery. Season; moisten with chicken broth. Serve on lettuce or as a sandwich filling. Yield: 12-18 servings.

Margaret Knuteson
Blackstone, Ill.

CHICKEN SALAD SPECIALTY

1 c. cooked diced chicken
1 c. diced celery
3 hard-cooked eggs, diced
1 pimento, diced
½ c. chopped sweet pickles
1 c. seedless white grapes
1 can pineapple chunks, drained
Salt and pepper
Salad dressing

Mix all ingredients using enough salad dressing to moisten. Chill and serve on lettuce. Yield: 6 servings.

Mary A. Beaty
Martinsville, Ill.

CHICKEN SALAD SUPREME

1 chicken, cooked and diced
1 c. diced celery
3 hard-cooked eggs, chopped
1 lge. pimento, chopped
½ c. pecans
2 med. pickles, chopped
Juice of ½ lemon
Salt and pepper to taste
Salad dressing to taste

Combine all ingredients; serve on crisp lettuce. Yield: 6 servings.

Myrtle P. Teer
Hutto, Tex.

CHICKEN SALAD SURPRISE

1 c. diced green peppers
1 c. diced celery
3 tbsp. finely chopped onion
2 5-oz. cans chicken or 2 c. cooked chicken
⅔ to 1 c. mayonnaise
2 c. crushed potato chips
Salt to taste

Combine peppers, celery, onion and chicken. Chill. Just before serving add mayonnaise, potato chips and salt. Yield: 6 servings.

Mary J. Lewison
South Milwaukee, Wisc.

CHICKEN WALDORF SALAD

1 med. apple, diced
1 tbsp. lemon juice
2 c. cooked diced chicken
1 c. red grapes, cut and seeded
1 c. sliced celery
¼ c. finely cut onion
½ tsp. salt
Dash of pepper
½ c. chopped nuts
⅔ c. salad dressing

Lightly sprinkle lemon juice over apple to prevent browning. Mix all ingredients; chill. Serve on lettuce leaf. Yield: 6 servings.

Mrs. Peter Drenth
Escondido, Calif.

CHIP AND CHICKEN SALAD

1 ½ c. boned chicken
½ c. sliced celery
½ c. chopped green pepper

(Continued on next page)

2 tsp. minced green onion
⅓ c. mayonnaise
1 c. crushed potato or corn chips

Toss together all ingredients except chips; chill. Toss in chips; serve on crisp lettuce. Garnish with slices of honeydew melon and strawberries. Yield: 4 servings.

Mrs. Alfred Croix
Carthage, Tex.

COLD CHICKEN SALAD

½ c. slivered almonds
Butter
2 c. chopped cooked chicken
1 c. diced celery
1 tbsp. lemon juice
½ c. mayonnaise
3 hard-cooked eggs, diced
6 to 8 olives, sliced

Heat almonds in butter; combine all ingredients. Serve on lettuce leaf. Yield: 6 servings.

Mrs. Joe Gooley
New Holland, O.

CRUNCHY CHICKEN SALAD

4 c. diced cooked chicken
1 c. diced celery
½ c. diced green pepper
¾ c. chopped ripe olives
¾ tsp. salt
½ tsp. pepper
3 tbsp. lemon juice
Salad dressing
1 c. cashew nuts

Combine chicken, celery, green pepper, olives and seasonings; toss with lemon juice. Refrigerate until 20 minutes before serving time. Add enough salad dressing to moisten and hold mixture together. Add cashew nuts just before serving. Yield: 8 servings.

Mrs. Roy Reeb
Dwight, Ill.

CURRIED CHICKEN AND GRAPE SALAD

3 c. cooked diced chicken
1 ½ c. thinly sliced celery
1 c. green seedless grapes
2 tbsp. lemon juice
1¼ tsp. salt
¼ tsp. pepper, freshly ground
1 ½ tsp. curry powder
6 tbsp. mayonnaise
3 tbsp. toasted slivered almonds

Combine all ingredients; toss lightly. Chill. Serve on lettuce; garnish with almonds.

Lois Pullen
Baton Rouge, La.

DELIGHTFUL CHICKEN SALAD

1 c. cooked diced chicken
1 apple, chopped
½ c. chopped sweet pickles
¼ c. mayonnaise
Salt and pepper to taste
Paprika to taste

Combine all ingredients. Serve on lettuce leaves with crackers. Yield: 4-5 servings.

Mrs. Joyce Green Harrison
Sebastopol, Miss.

DOVER CHICKEN SALAD

1 8-oz. can pineapple chunks
3 c. cooked diced chicken
1 c. diced celery
½ c. sliced ripe olives
½ c. slivered almonds

Drain pineapple; reserve juice. Marinate all remaining ingredients in pineapple juice for 1 hour. Drain off juice; arrange salad on a bed of endive and top with mayonnaise. Yield: 6-8 servings.

Mrs. Jean Forsgren
Dover, Del.

EASY CHICKEN SALAD

1 c. shredded carrots
1 c. diced celery
2 tbsp. minced onion
1 can boned chicken or tuna
½ c. salad dressing
2 tbsp. cream
Pinch of dry mustard (opt.)
1 No. 2 ½ can shoestring potatoes

Combine carrots, celery, onion and chicken. Combine dressing, cream and mustard; add to vegetable mixture. Refrigerate; add potatoes before serving. Yield: 6 servings.

Cleo M. Sorenson
Alexandria, Minn.

EXOTIC CHICKEN SALAD

2 qt. cooked cubed chicken
1 No. 2 can water chestnuts, drained and sliced
2 lb. seedless grapes, halved
2 c. sliced celery
2 to 3 c. almonds, toasted
3 c. mayonnaise
1 tbsp. curry powder
2 tbsp. soy sauce
2 tbsp. lemon juice
Lettuce

Combine chicken, water chestnuts, grapes, celery and 1 1/2 cups almonds. Blend all remaining ingredients except lettuce; add to chicken mixture. Chill for several hours. Serve on lettuce; sprinkle with remaining almonds. Yield: 12 servings.

Mrs. Alfred F. Eaton
Wurtsmith, Mich.

FAVORITE CHICKEN SALAD

1 3-lb. chicken
1 tsp. salt
4 c. water
½ c. sweet pepper relish
1 onion, chopped
1 apple, chopped
4 radishes, chopped
½ c. chopped celery
¾ c. salad dressing

Cook chicken in salted water until tender; cool. Remove bones; chop meat. Combine chicken with remaining ingredients. Serve on lettuce or in tomato cups. Yield: 8 servings.

Mrs. Hope Cluff
Camden, Tenn.

FRUIT AND CHICKEN SALAD SUPREME

2 c. cubed cooked chicken
2 tbsp. chopped green olives
¾ c. chopped celery
½ c. toasted almonds
1 c. chopped apples
2 tbsp. chopped ripe olives
2 tbsp. chopped sweet pickle
2 hard-cooked eggs, diced
1 c. diced pineapple
½ c. raisins
¾ c. mayonnaise
1 c. potato chips

Combine all ingredients; toss lightly. May be served on lettuce and garnished with spiced apple rings, ripe olives and watercress. Sprinkle with 1 cup potato chips just before serving. Yield: 8 servings.

Betty Ann Augustad
Madison, S.D.

FRUITED CHICKEN SALAD

2 c. diced cooked chicken
White pepper to taste
1 c. pineapple chunks
½ c. grapes, halved and seeded
2 med. bananas, diced
¼ c. chopped pecans
1 c. mayonaise

Combine all ingredients; toss lightly to mix. Chill. Serve on lettuce or pineapple rings. Yield: 8 servings.

Mrs. William Collman
Bethalto, Ill.

GINGER-CREAM-CHICKEN SALAD

2 c. diced cooked chicken
1 c. diced celery
1 tsp. salt
⅛ tsp. pepper
2 tbsp. finely chopped ginger
1 tsp. honey
1 c. sour cream

Combine chicken, celery, salt and pepper; chill for 2 hours. Combine remaining ingredients just before serving. Stir one-half of dressing into chicken mixture. Serve salad on crisp greens; top with remaining dressing. Yield: 6 servings.

Mrs. Robert Adams
Union City, Tenn.

GOOD CHICKEN SALAD

2 c. cooked cubed chicken
1 c. chopped celery
2 tbsp. chopped ripe olives
2 tbsp. chopped sweet pickle
3 hard-cooked eggs, chopped
¼ c. crisp bacon, finely broken
2 tbsp. lemon juice
Salt and pepper to taste
½ c. mayonnaise

Combine all ingredients; toss lightly. Chill thoroughly. Yield: 4-6 servings.

Mrs. Clifford Beaver
Columbus, O.

LUNCHEON OR FRUITED CHICKEN SALAD

2 c. cooked cubed chicken or canned white meat
1 c. orange sections
¼ to ½ c. grapes, seeded and halved
¼ to ½ c. slivered toasted or salted almonds or pecans
1 or 2 bananas, sliced
¾ to 1 c. mayonnaise or salad dressing

Chill ingredients. Combine all ingredients, using enough mayonnaise to moisten. Serve on crisp lettuce or pineapple slices with watercress garnish. Salad may be garnished with whole strawberries if desired.

Elizabeth Chenoweth
Corpus Christi, Tex.

LUNCHEON CHICKEN SALAD

1 3-oz. pkg. softened cream cheese
½ c. sour cream
Dash of salt
1 c. drained pineapple chunks
¾ c. chopped celery
¼ c. chopped green pepper
½ c. English walnuts
1 ½ c. cubed cooked chicken
1 c. cranberry sauce, chilled and cubed

Blend cheese, sour cream and salt. Add pineapple, celery, green pepper and nuts. Mix well. Fold in chicken and cranberry cubes. Serve in lettuce cups. Garnish with additional cranberry cubes. Serve with hot rolls. NOTE: Cranberry sauce and nuts may be omitted and salad served in tomato roses. Yield: 4-6 servings.

Mrs. William Burns
Marysville, O.

MANDARIN-CHICKEN SALAD

3 c. cooked chopped chicken
1 tbsp. minced onion
1 tsp. salt
2 tbsp. fresh lemon juice
1 c. thinly sliced celery
1 c. seedless grapes
⅓ c. mayonnaise or cooked salad dressing
1 11-oz. can Mandarin orange segments or 1 c. tangerine sections, drained
6 to 8 lettuce leaves
½ c. slivered almonds, toasted
6 pitted ripe olives

Combine chicken, onion, salt, lemon juice and celery; refrigerate for several hours. Combine chicken mixture lightly with grapes and mayonnaise. Add orange sections and almonds, reserving a few for garnish. Line salad bowl with lettuce leaves; fill with chicken mixture. Garnish with reserved orange sections and almonds and ripe olives. Yield: 6 servings.

Mrs. Donald H. Swan
Homestead, Fla.

NUTTY CHICKEN SALAD

1 sm. can boned chicken, diced
Sweet pickles, chopped
½ sm. can crushed pineapple, drained
¼ c. chopped pecans
¼ c. chopped celery
½ sm. apple, chopped
Pinch of salt
Pepper to taste
Mayonnaise

Combine all ingredients, using enough mayonnaise to moisten. Chill before serving. Yield: 4 servings.

Rose Henley
De Funiak Springs, Fla.

OHIO CHICKEN OR TURKEY SALAD

4 to 5 c. cubed cooked chicken or turkey
2 tsp. grated onion
1 c. finely cut celery
1 c. minced green peppers
¼ c. light cream
½ c. mayonnaise
1 tsp. salt
⅛ tsp. pepper
2 tbsp. vinegar
1 c. seedless grapes, halved
1 c. pineapple chunks
Slivered almonds

Combine chicken, onion, celery and peppers. Mix cream with mayonnaise, salt, pepper and vinegar; toss with chicken. Refrigerate until time to serve. Arrange on crisp salad greens. Add grapes and pineapple in a circle. Sprinkle top with almonds. Yield: 8 servings.

Mrs. William J. Newill
Dayton, O.

OLD-FASHIONED CHICKEN SALAD

3 c. cooked diced chicken
1 ½ c. diced celery
1 tsp. salt

(Continued on next page)

3 hard-cooked eggs, diced
3 sweet pickles, chopped
Mayonnaise to taste

Combine chicken, celery, salt, eggs and pickles; moisten with mayonnaise. Chill. May be stuffed into tiny cream puffs for serving.

Mrs. Vernon Baldwin
Blacksburg, Va.

PARTY BUFFET CHICKEN SALAD

3 c. cooked diced chicken
1 ½ c. chopped celery
3 tbsp. lemon juice
1 ½ c. seedless white grapes
½ c. toasted chopped almonds
1 c. mayonnaise
¼ c. cream or milk
1 ½ tsp. salt
1 tsp. dry mustard

Combine chicken, celery and lemon juice; let stand for 1 hour. Combine all remaining ingredients; add to chicken mixture. May be served in tomato aspic ring garnished with small bunches of grapes. Yield: 8 servings.

Mrs. A. B. Hinerman
Huntington, W. Va.

PARTY CHICKEN SALAD

2 to 3 c. chopped chicken
1 tbsp. minced onion
1 tbsp. salt
2 tbsp. lemon juice
1 c. chopped celery
1 c. drained cut pineapple
1 11-oz. can Mandarin oranges
½ c. toasted almonds
Mayonnaise

Combine chicken, onion, salt, lemon juice and celery. Fold in pineapple, oranges and almonds. Refrigerate several hours. Fold in mayonnaise when ready to serve. Yield: 6-8 servings.

Mrs. Henry Rogers, Jr.
Odessa, Tex.

SALAD BOATS

PASTRY BOATS:
2 c. flour
1 tsp. salt
⅔ c. shortening
¼ c. water

Mix flour and salt. Cut in shortening. Sprinkle with water; mix with fork. Round into ball; divide into half. Roll each half 1/8-inch thick on heavy-duty foil with lightly floured cloth-covered rolling pin. Cut foil and pastry into 5 x 2-inch rectangles; prick well with fork. Bring long side of rectangle up; moisten and pinch ends firmly together. Place on baking sheet. Spread sides out like a canoe; balance to stand by themselves. Bake at 475 degrees for 10 to 12 minutes or until lightly browned. NOTE: If hydrogenated shortening is used, increase amount by 2 tablespoons.

SALAD:
4 c. finely diced cooked chicken
4 hard-cooked eggs, chopped
2 c. finely diced celery
4 sweet pickles, chopped
Salad dressing to taste

Combine all ingredients; serve in pastry boats.

Mrs. John O. Jackson
Birdseye, Ind.

TALK OF THE TOWN SALAD

1 sm. head lettuce, torn
2 tomatoes, cut as desired
¼ c. diced celery
1 4-oz. can mushrooms
⅛ c. diced Velveeta cheese
2 tbsp. diced Bleu cheese
⅔ c. canned peas or French-cut beans
8 stuffed olives, sliced
½ tsp. onion salt
Dash of garlic salt
1 ½ c. chicken, crab, lobster, shrimp or combination
1 tsp. lemon juice
French dressing
Salt and pepper to taste
1 c. cooked macaroni (opt.)

Toss all ingredients together in a large salad bowl.

Annabelle Wikkerink
Amery, Wisc.

TOMATOES STUFFED WITH CHICKEN SALAD

1 c. diced cooked chicken
⅔ c. diced celery
3 tbsp. diced cucumber
3 tbsp. French dressing
Mayonnaise
8 med. tomatoes

Mix all ingredients except tomatoes, adding enough mayonnaise to moisten. Chill for 30 minutes. Wash and peel tomatoes; cut out blossom end. Cut tomatoes from top to within a quarter inch of bottom into 5 or 6 wedge shaped sections. Salt and chill. Pull wedges apart to resemble petals of a flower; fill with salad which has been mixed with additional mayonnaise. Yield: 8 servings.

Mrs. Lola Holloway
Edwards AFB, Calif.

TURKEY-TOMATO SALAD

½ pt. sour cream
¼ c. mayonnaise or salad dressing
2 tbsp. lemon juice
1 tsp. sugar
½ tsp. curry powder
½ tsp. paprika
½ tsp. dry mustard
½ tsp. salt
2 c. diced cooked turkey or chicken
2 c. sliced celery
2 hard-cooked eggs, chopped
½ c. sliced almonds, toasted
6 to 8 lge. tomatoes, chilled

Combine sour cream, mayonnaise and seasonings; mix well. Combine turkey or chicken, celery, eggs and almonds; add dressing. Mix lightly to coat ingredients well. Chill for several hours before serving. Cut tomatoes into sixths three-fourths of the way through. Fill with salad mixture. Yield: 6-8 servings.

Photograph for this recipe above.

TURKEY SALAD

1 14-lb. turkey
Salt to taste
Celery, cut into large pieces
Onions, quartered
Parsley
1 pt. heavy cream, whipped
1 qt. salad dressing
¼ c. vinegar
¼ c. sugar
2 qt. diced celery
2 qt. seedless green grapes
18 hard-cooked eggs, diced
2 c. toasted slivered almonds

Clean turkey well; season with salt inside and out. Stuff with large pieces of celery, quartered onions and a little parsley. Place in a covered roaster; bake at 325 degrees until meat begins to leave bones. Remove from oven; cool. Cut into desired size pieces. Combine whipped cream, salad dressing, vinegar and sugar. Mix with turkey and remaining ingredients. Chill several hours before serving. Yield: 50 servings.

Marie Strand
Stillwater, Minn.

TURKEY SALAD

1 lb. breast of turkey, cooked and cubed
½ c. chopped celery
French dressing

(Continued on next page)

Lettuce cups
2 hard-cooked eggs, quartered
Tomato wedges
Mayonnaise
Toasted slivered almonds

Marinate turkey and celery in French dressing for 1 hour. Pack cup 3/4 full with salad; turn out on lettuce cups. Decorate each serving with eggs, tomatoes and 1 teaspoon mayonnaise; sprinkle with almonds. Yield: 4 servings.

Mrs. Clifford V. Davis
Chattanooga, Tenn.

BAKED CHICKEN SALAD

3 c. diced cooked chicken
1 c. sliced celery
1 c. shredded sharp Cheddar cheese
¼ c. chopped pitted ripe olives
1 tbsp. chopped onion
1 tsp. salt
Salad dressing to taste
1 c. crushed potato chips
Tomato wedges

Combine chicken, celery, 1/2 cup cheese, olives, onion, salt and salad dressing; toss lightly. Place in 1 1/2-quart casserole; sprinkle with remaining cheese and potato chips. Garnish with tomato wedges. Bake at 350 degrees for 25 minutes.

Edith Jacobson
Ironwood, Mich.

BAKED CHICKEN SALAD SUPREME

1 6-oz. can boned chicken or 1 c. chopped, cooked chicken
1 can cream of chicken soup
1 c. diced celery
2 ½ tsp. minced onion
½ c. chopped nuts
½ tsp. salt
¼ tsp. pepper
⅔ c. mayonnaise
3 hard-cooked eggs, thinly sliced
1 can peas (opt.)
1 can chow mein noodles

Combine chicken, soup, celery, onion, nuts, salt, pepper, mayonnaise, eggs and peas in a 9-inch baking dish. Top with noodles. Bake at 450 degrees for 15 minutes. Yield: 8 servings.

Mrs. Lois S. Hall
Clyde, O.

BEST HOT CHICKEN SALAD

2 ½ c. chopped cooked chicken
2 c. chopped celery
½ c. blanched salted almonds, chopped
2 tbsp. minced onion
¼ c. chopped green pepper
2 tbsp. chopped pimento
¾ tsp. salt
2 tbsp. lemon juice
½ c. mayonnaise
⅓ c. grated Swiss cheese
3 c. crushed potato chips

Blend chicken, celery, almonds, onion, green pepper, pimento, salt, lemon juice and mayonnaise. Turn into a buttered 1 1/2-quart casserole. Top with grated cheese and crushed potato chips. Bake at 350 degrees for 25 minutes or until cheese melts. Yield: 6 servings.

Betty Trout
Ames, Iowa

BROILED CHICKEN SALAD

2 c. diced cooked chicken
1 ½ c. diced celery
¼ c. French dressing
½ c. mayonnaise
⅓ c. sour cream
¼ c. almonds, toasted
2 c. crushed potato chips
1 c. grated cheese

Marinate chicken and celery in French dressing for 1 hour. Add mayonnaise, sour cream and almonds. Place in a baking dish. Mix potato chips and cheese; sprinkle on top of the salad. Place under broiler until cheese melts.

Mrs. Johnnie T. Broome
Blackshear, Ga.

CALIFORNIA HOT CHICKEN SALAD

3 c. diced cooked chicken
2 c. diced almonds
½ c. pimento
1 ¼ c. mayonnaise
3 tbsp. lemon juice
3 tbsp. grated onion
1 tsp. salt
¼ tsp. pepper
1 pkg. frozen peas, cooked
1 c. crushed potato chips
½ c. grated Cheddar cheese

Combine all ingredients except potato chips and cheese; place in a buttered casserole. Top with potato chip crumbs and cheese. Bake at 350 degrees for 1 hour. Serve immediately. Yield: 12 servings.

Eunice Houghton
Ventura, Calif.

CELESTIAL CHICKEN SALAD

4 c. diced cooked chicken
2 c. diced celery
1 4 ½-oz. jar whole mushrooms, drained
½ c. pecan halves, toasted
4 slices crisp fried bacon, crumbled
1 c. mayonnaise or salad dressing
1 c. sour cream
1 ½ tsp. salt
2 tbsp. lemon juice

Combine chicken, celery, mushrooms, pecans and crumbled bacon in a large bowl. Blend mayonnaise or salad dressing with remaining ingredients. Add to chicken mixture, tossing lightly to mix. Chill thoroughly. Serve in crisp lettuce cups if desired. NOTE: To toast pecans, place in shallow baking pan in preheated 350 degree oven for 15 minutes. Yield: 6-8 servings.

Photograph for this recipe on page 321.

EASY HOT CHICKEN SALAD

3 c. cooked diced chicken
1 ½ c. diced celery
½ c. chopped almonds
1 tbsp. minced onion
1 ½ tsp. grated lemon rind
1 ½ tbsp. lemon juice
⅛ tsp. pepper
¾ c. mayonnaise
1 ½ c. grated Cheddar cheese
1 ½ c. crushed potato chips

Combine all ingredients except cheese and potato chips. Place in baking dish; cover with cheese and potato chips. Bake at 350 degrees for 30 minutes. Yield: 8 servings.

Mrs. Thelma Land
Hickory, Miss.

GOOD HOT CHICKEN SALAD

2 c. cooked cubed chicken
2 c. thinly sliced celery
½ c. slivered toasted almonds
½ tsp. salt
2 tsp. grated onion
1 tsp. monosodium glutamate
1 tbsp. lemon juice
1 c. mayonnaise
½ c. grated American cheese
1 c. crushed potato chips

Combine chicken, celery, almonds, salt, onion, monosodium glutamate, lemon juice and mayonnaise; place in buttered baking dish. Combine cheese with potato chips; sprinkle over chicken mixture. Bake at 450 degrees for 30 minutes. Yield: 6 servings.

Mrs. Carolyn Palmer
Archibold, O.

HOT CHICKEN-NUT SALAD

2 c. stewed chicken
1 c. diced celery
3 hard-cooked eggs, diced
1 c. mayonnaise
1 tbsp. lemon juice
1 can cream of chicken soup
1 can water chestnuts or ⅓ c. almonds, slivered
Salt and pepper to taste
Potato chips, crushed

Mix all ingredients except potato chips. Cover with crushed potato chips. Bake at 400 degrees for 20 minutes.

Margaret Hefner Peden
Raeford, N.C.

HOT CHICKEN SALAD

3 c. chopped cooked chicken
1 ½ c. diced celery
½ c. chopped almonds
1 can water chestnuts (opt.)
1 to 3 tbsp. minced onion
1 ½ tbsp. lemon juice
⅛ to ½ tsp. pepper
1 c. mayonnaise
1 ½ c. grated Cheddar cheese
1 ½ c. crushed potato chips

Combine chicken, celery, almonds, water chestnuts, onion, lemon juice and pepper in mixing bowl. Add mayonnaise; toss. Divide mixture into individual casseroles or one baking dish. Sprinkle generously with cheese and potato chips. Bake at 375 degrees for 25 minutes. Yield: 8-10 servings.

Mrs. Robert Thompson
Hartley, Tex.

HOT CHICKEN OR TUNA SALAD

2 c. cubed cooked chicken or tuna
2 c. thinly sliced celery
½ c. chopped toasted almonds
½ tsp. salt
2 tsp. grated onion
1 c. mayonnaise
2 tbsp. lemon juice
2 c. toasted bread cubes
½ c. grated cheese

(Continued on next page)

Combine all ingredients except 1 cup bread cubes and cheese; toss lightly. Sprinkle with cheese and bread cubes. Bake at 450 degrees for 10 to 15 minutes. Yield: 6 servings.

Mrs. Bernard Silvrants
Heron Lake, Minn.

HOT CHICKEN SALAD CASSEROLE

2 c. cooked diced chicken
1 can cream of chicken soup
1 c. diced celery
1 tsp. onion (opt.)
½ to 1 c. almonds, whole or slivered
¼ to 1 tsp. salt
½ tsp. pepper
1 tbsp. lemon juice
3 hard-cooked eggs
½ to ¾ c. mayonnaise
2 c. potato chips, crushed

Combine all ingredients except potato chips. Place in baking dish. Top with potato chips. Bake at 400 degrees for 12 to 20 minutes. NOTE: Potato chips are very salty so salt to taste. Yield: 6 servings.

Mrs. Dorothy S. Satterwhite
Washington, D.C.

HOT CHICKEN SALAD DELIGHT

1 pkg. frozen peas
2 tbsp. diced onion
1 c. diced celery
2 c. cubed chicken
2 tbsp. diced onion
2 c. cubed chicken
½ c. salad dressing
¾ tsp. salt
1 c. crushed potato chips

Cook peas, onion and celery; drain. Combine all ingredients; top with potato chips. Bake at 325 degrees for 20 minutes. Yield: 4-6 servings.

Mrs. E. D. McKeown
Greensboro, N.C.

HOT CHICKEN SALAD SAULT STE. MARIE

4 c. cooked chopped chicken
3 c. chopped celery
4 tbsp. chopped onion
4 tbsp. pimento (opt.)
⅔ c. chopped green pepper
1 c. slivered almonds
4 tbsp. lemon juice
1 c. mayonnaise
⅔ c. grated Swiss cheese
6 c. potato chips, crushed
Salt to taste

Blend all ingredients. Pour into a greased loaf pan. Bake at 350 degrees for 25 to 30 minutes. Yield: 8-10 servings.

Mrs. Rita Siegman
Sault Ste. Marie, Mich.

HOT CHICKEN SALAD SUPREME

2 c. diced cooked chicken
2 c. chopped celery
1 c. nuts
1 c. mayonnaise
3 tbsp. chopped onion
2 tbsp. Worcestershire sauce
2 tbsp. lemon juice
½ c. crushed potato chips
½ c. crushed barbecued potato chips

Mix all ingredients except potato chips. Sprinkle potato chips over top. Bake at 350 degrees for 20 minutes.

Mrs. Myrtle G. Allen
Moncks Corner, S.C.

HOT TURKEY SALAD

1 c. mayonnaise
2 tbsp. lemon juice
½ tsp. salt
½ c. cream of mushroom soup
Dash of onion salt or 2 tbsp. grated onion
2 c. diced cooked turkey
2 c. chopped celery
½ c. slivered almonds
1 c. grated cheese
1 c. crushed potato chips or Chinese noodles

Blend all ingredients except cheese and chips or noodles. Pile into 8 x 12-inch baking dish. Sprinkle cheese and chips on top; bake at 350 degrees until bubbly. Yield: 8-10 servings.

Mrs. John Marvel
Camarillo, Calif.

CHICKEN-ALMOND SALAD

1 envelope unflavored gelatin
¼ c. cold water
1 c. mayonnaise
1 c. heavy cream, whipped
½ tsp. salt

(Continued on next page)

1 ½ c. diced cooked chicken
¾ c. blanched toasted almonds, chopped
¾ c. green seedless grape halves

Soften gelatin in cold water; dissolve over hot water. Cool slightly; combine with mayonnaise, whipped cream and salt. Fold in all remaining ingredients. Chill in individual molds until firm. Unmold on crisp lettuce. Yield: 6-8 servings.

Mrs. Agnes R. Mills
Montgomery, Ala.

CHICKEN AND AVOCADO SALAD

3 envelopes unflavored gelatin
¾ c. cold water
2 c. chicken stock, heated
2 tbsp. fresh lemon juice
1 ½ tsp. grated onion
2 tsp. salt
¼ tsp. white pepper
2 c. ripe avocado pulp, sieved
½ c. mayonnaise
3 c. cooked diced chicken
Salad greens
Cantaloupe balls

Soften gelatin in cold water; stir in hot stock. Add remaining ingredients except salad greens and cantaloupe balls, folding in chicken last. Turn into a lightly oiled 2-quart mold. Chill until firm. Serve garnished with salad greens and cantaloupe balls. Yield: 10-12 servings.

Mrs. Lucy Coggins
Oakwood, Ga.

CHICKEN BUFFET MOLDS

1 envelope unflavored gelatin
½ c. cold water
1 c. mayonnaise or salad dressing
1 ½ c. diced cooked or canned chicken
½ c. unpared chopped cucumber
⅓ c. diced celery
3 tbsp. minced onion
3 tbsp. chopped green olives
1 tbsp. chopped pimento
2 tbsp. lemon juice
½ tsp. salt
¼ tsp. paprika
1 c. heavy cream, whipped

Soften gelatin in cold water; dissolve over hot water. Add all remaining ingredients folding in whipped cream last. Pour into individual molds. Chill until firm. Yield: 8 servings.

Mrs. Jack L. Moore
APO, New York

CHICKEN-CRANBERRY MOLD

1 pkg. lemon gelatin
1 ½ c. hot water
2 c. cooked cubed chicken
1 hard-cooked egg, chopped
¼ c. chopped celery
⅓ c. salad dressing
1 can cranberry jelly
2 tbsp. orange juice

Dissolve gelatin in hot water. Combine chicken, egg, celery and salad dressing with 1/2 cup gelatin. Chill in 8-inch square pan. Beat cranberry jelly until smooth; add orange juice and pour over chilled gelatin. Cut into squares and serve on lettuce. Yield: 9 servings.

Mrs. M. L. Hostetter
Huntington, W. Va.

CHICKEN-CRANBERRY PARTY SALAD

3 envelopes unflavored gelatin
½ c. cold water
2 cans cream of chicken soup
¼ c. mayonnaise
½ c. whipped cream
1 c. diced cooked chicken
½ c. slivered almonds
½ c. chopped celery
1 1-lb. can jellied cranberry sauce
1 tsp. grated orange or lemon peel
1 tbsp. lemon juice

Soften 2 envelopes gelatin in 1/4 cup water. Heat 1/4 cup soup; add to gelatin. Stir until dissolved; add to remaining soup. Cool. Fold in mayonnaise, whipped cream, chicken, almonds and celery. Pour into greased mold; chill until firm. Crush cranberry sauce with fork. Soften remaining gelatin in remaining water. Set in pan of boiling water; stir until gelatin dissolves. Mix gelatin, cranberry sauce, orange peel and lemon juice. Pour over chilled layer. Chill until cranberry layer is firm. Serve on crisp salad greens. Yield: 6-8 servings.

Mrs. J. M. Christian
Dublin, Ga.

CHICKEN-CRANBERRY SALAD

CRANBERRY LAYER:
1 envelope unflavored gelatin
¼ c. cold water
2 c. whole cranberry sauce
1 9-oz. can crushed pineapple
½ c. broken walnuts
1 tbsp. lemon juice

(Continued on next page)

Soften gelatin in cold water; dissolve over hot water. Add cranberry sauce, pineapple, nuts and lemon juice. Chill until firm.

CHICKEN LAYER:
1 envelope unflavored gelatin
¾ c. cold water
1 c. mayonnaise
3 tbsp. lemon juice
¾ tsp. salt
2 c. cooked diced chicken
½ c. diced celery
2 tbsp. chopped parsley

Soften gelatin in 1/4 cup cold water; dissolve over hot water. Blend in mayonnaise, remaining water, lemon juice and salt. Add chicken, celery and parsley. Pour over firm cranberry layer. Chill until firm. Cut in squares. Yield: 25 servings.

Mrs. Oden White
Philadelphia, Miss.

CHICKEN MAYONNAISE

1 fat hen, cooked and diced
1 lge. bunch celery, diced
1 sm. can pimento, diced
1 sm. can tiny green peas, drained
Dash of cayenne
1 c. chicken stock
2 envelopes gelatin
1 ½ c. mayonnaise

Combine chicken, celery, pimento and peas. Season with cayenne. Heat stock in pan. Dissolve gelatin in 1/2 cup cold water; add to hot stock. Cool; add with mayonnaise to cut ingredients. Mix well; place in molds. Chill; serve on lettuce leaf. Yield: 12-15 servings.

Mrs. Obera B. Pruitt
Belton, S.C.

CHICKEN-MAYONNAISE SUPREME

2 envelopes unflavored gelatin
2 c. hot chicken broth
1 chicken, cooked and finely chopped
1 c. chopped nuts
1 No. 2 can English peas, drained
1 pt. salad dressing
2 c. diced celery
3 hard-cooked eggs, sliced
Salt and pepper to taste

Dissolve gelatin in 1/2 cup cold water; add chicken broth. Cool; add all remaining ingredients. Let stand overnight in refrigerator. Cut into squares; serve on lettuce leaves. Pimentos, garlic salt, red pepper and paprika to taste may be added.

Essie L. Stanley
Saltillo, Tex.

CHICKEN MOLD

3 c. chicken stock
1 box unflavored gelatin
1 hen, cooked and diced
2 c. chopped celery
2 tbsp. India relish
¾ c. English peas
4 hard-cooked eggs, diced
1 c. chopped nuts
Salt and pepper
Red pepper
Lemon juice
1 c. mayonnaise

Skim fat from chicken stock; dissolve gelatin in heated stock. Add all remaining ingredients except mayonnaise; cool. Add mayonnaise; chill overnight. Yield: 18 servings.

Mrs. Mary Frances Bigby
Greenville, S.C.

CHICKEN MOUSSE

½ pkg. lemon gelatin
1 c. boiling chicken broth
1 c. cooked chopped chicken
1 c. finely cut celery
1 pimento, finely chopped
1 tbsp. vinegar
Salt to taste
½ c. cream, whipped

Dissolve gelatin in skimmed broth; chill until partially set. Beat with rotary egg beater to consistency of whipped cream. Combine chicken, celery, pimento, vinegar and salt; fold into gelatin. Fold in cream. Pour into oblong mold; chill until firm. Unmold on lettuce and garnish with stuffed olives. Yield: 6 servings.

Mary L. Shelton
Alton, Ill.

CHICKEN MOUSSE

2 tbsp. unflavored gelatin
2 c. cooked chopped chicken
4 hard-cooked eggs, mashed
½ c. chopped celery
8 pickle chips, finely cut
Salt and pepper to taste
Dash of Worcestershire sauce
Dash of red pepper
1 sm. pimento, chopped
1 c. mayonnaise
Juice of ½ lemon

(Continued on next page)

Dissolve gelatin in 1/4 cup cold water; add 1/2 cup boiling water. Stir until melted. Cool; add all remaining ingredients. Congeal in loaf pan; serve in slices. Yield: 8 servings.

Elizabeth Heard
Jackson, Miss.

CHICKEN MOUSSE SPECIAL

1 4 to 5-lb. hen
2 c. water
Salt and pepper
Onion, sliced
Celery, diced
1 can cream of celery soup
1 8-oz. pkg. cream cheese
1 ½ pkg. unflavored gelatin
Chicken stock
¾ c. diced green pepper
2 tbsp. diced green onion

Cook hen in water seasoned with salt, pepper, onion and desired amount of celery for flavor until tender. Cut meat from bone. Reserve strained stock. Heat soup and cream cheese in top of double boiler. Stir occasionally until hot and well blended. Add gelatin and 1 1/2 cups of cold stock. Add stock mixture to cheese mixture; heat until gelatin is dissolved. Remove from heat; cool slightly. Add 3/4 cups celery, green pepper, green onion and chicken. Put in lightly greased ring mold; chill at least 4 hours. Serve with mayonnaise or salad dressing.

Dr. Mary E. Dichmann
Lafayette, La.

CHICKEN SALAD

2 pkg. lemon gelatin
3 c. boiling water
1 lge. pkg. cream cheese
1 ¾ c. salad dressing
½ pt. heavy cream, whipped
3 tsp. sugar
¾ c. chopped celery
¾ c. grated carrots
1 No. 2 can crushed pineapple
2 c. boned chicken

Mix gelatin and water. Refrigerate until thickened. Mix cream cheese, salad dressing, whipped cream and sugar. Add to gelatin. Mix celery, carrots, pineapple and chicken; add to gelatin mixture. Refrigerate overnight. Yield: 10 servings.

Mrs. Jerry E. Furlong
Florissant, Mo.

CHICKEN SALAD GEL

1 envelope unflavored gelatin
¼ c. water
2 c. chicken broth
1 tbsp. salt
¼ tbsp. paprika
1 tbsp. chopped onion
¼ c. lemon juice
¾ c. mayonnaise or salad dressing
1 c. diced cooked chicken
¼ c. chopped celery
¼ c. sliced stuffed olives
2 tbsp. chopped green pepper

Soften gelatin in 1/4 cup water; add 1 cup hot broth. Combine with salt, paprika, onion, lemon juice and remaining broth. Cool until it begins to thicken; beat in mayonnaise. Fold in chicken, celery, olives and green pepper. Chill in a shallow 7 x 9-inch container. Cut into squares; unmold on salad plate. May be garnished with deviled eggs, radish roses or parsley. Yield: 6 servings.

Pauline Waggener
Du Quoin, Ill.

CHICKEN SALAD MOLD

1 pkg. lemon gelatin
2 c. hot chicken stock
½ c. cooked peas
½ c. grated carrots
½ c. chopped celery
1 ½ c. diced cooked chicken

Dissolve lemon gelatin in chicken stock; chill until consistency of egg whites. Fold in remaining ingredients. Pour into mold; chill until set. Serve with mayonnaise on salad greens. Yield: 6 servings.

Mrs. E. C. Bailey
Moulton, Ala.

CHICKEN SOUFFLE SALAD

1 c. boiling water
1 pkg. lemon gelatin
2 chicken bouillon cubes
½ c. cold water
3 tbsp. vinegar
½ c. mayonnaise
½ tsp. salt
Dash of pepper
2 tsp. grated onion
¾ tsp. Worcestershire sauce
1 ½ c. chopped chicken
⅓ c. chopped celery
2 tbsp. diced pimento

Pour boiling water over gelatin and bouillon cubes; stir until dissolved. Add cold water, vinegar, mayonnaise, salt, pepper, onion and Worcestershire sauce. Blend well; pour into

(Continued on next page)

freezing tray. Chill for 15 to 20 minutes in freezing compartment until about 1 inch of outer edge is firm. Empty into bowl; beat with hand beater until fluffy. Fold in chicken, celery and pimento. Pour into 8 x 4 x 2-inch pan; chill until firm. Unmold; garnish with tomatoes and salad greens.

Mrs. Elmer Pohle, Sr.
Bloomington, Wisc.

MRS. EISENHOWER'S JEWEL RING SALAD

2 envelopes unflavored gelatin
1 c. cranberry juice cocktail
1 1-lb. can whole cranberry sauce
2 tbsp. lemon juice
¾ c. cold water
1 tbsp. soy sauce
1 c. mayonnaise
1 ½ c. diced cooked chicken
½ c. diced celery
¼ c. coarsely chopped toasted almonds

Sprinkle 1 envelope unflavored gelatin onto cranberry cocktail in saucepan to soften. Dissolve gelatin over low heat, stirring constantly. Break up cranberry sauce; stir into gelatin mixture with lemon juice. Pour into 6-cup ring mold; chill until almost firm. Sprinkle remaining gelatin in cold water in saucepan to soften. Dissolve over low heat, stirring constantly. Remove from heat; stir in soy sauce. Cool. Gradually stir gelatin mixture into mayonnaise until blended. Mix in remaining ingredients. Spoon over chilled cranberry layer. Chill until firm. Unmold onto salad greens. Yield: 8 servings.

Mrs. Dwight D. Eisenhower
Wife of former President of the United States

CHICKEN OR TURKEY CONGEALED LOAF

2 envelopes unflavored gelatin
½ c. plus 2 tbsp. hot water
2 bouillon cubes
½ onion, grated
1 c. chopped celery
1 c. seedless chopped grapes or ½ c. chopped black olives
1 ½ c. chopped chicken or turkey
1 c. mayonnaise
1 c. heavy cream, whipped
Salt and pepper
Monosodium glutamate

Dissolve gelatin in 2 tablespoons water; dissolve bouillon in remaining hot water. Add bouillon to gelatin; stir. Combine all ingredients. Place in refrigerator overnight or until congealed. Slice and serve. Yield: 8 servings.

Mrs. Jack Stegall
St. Petersburg, Fla.

CHILLED CHICKEN SALAD

4 c. cubed chicken
1 ½ c. diced celery
1 c. halved white grapes
½ c. mayonnaise
2 tbsp. lemon juice
Salt and white pepper to taste

Mix all ingredients; cover and refrigerate for several hours before serving. Serve on salad greens; garnish as desired. Yield: 6 servings.

Mrs. Lee McFarland
Quincy, Ill.

CONGEALED CHICKEN SALAD

1 tbsp. unflavored gelatin
¼ c. cold water
1 c. mayonnaise
1 c. heavy cream, whipped
½ tsp. salt
1 ½ c. diced cooked chicken
¾ c. chopped toasted almonds

Soften gelatin in cold water; dissolve over hot water. Cool. Combine mayonnaise, whipped cream and salt with gelatin. Fold in remaining ingredients. Chill in mold. Serve on lettuce. Yield: 6-8 servings.

Mrs. Leon Bender
Villa Grove, Ill.

CONGEALED CHICKEN SALAD

1 tbsp. unflavored gelatin
1 ¾ c. chicken stock
½ tsp. salt
1 tbsp. lemon juice
1 ¼ c. diced cooked chicken
½ c. diced celery
2 tbsp. chopped green pepper

Soften gelatin in 1/2 cup cold chicken stock. Heat remaining chicken stock with salt; pour over gelatin mixture. Add lemon juice; chill until thickened. Then fold in chicken, celery and green pepper. Chill until firm; unmold. May be garnished with salad greens, tomato wedges and stuffed olives. Yield: 8 servings.

Elsie Snellgrove
Warrior, Ala.

CONGEALED CHICKEN SALAD

1 pkg. lemon gelatin
1 c. hot water
2 tbsp. lemon or lime juice
½ tsp. salt
½ c. mayonnaise or salad dressing

(Continued on next page)

¼ c. finely diced green pepper
¼ c. chopped pimento
1 c. chopped celery
1 c. chopped chicken

Dissolve gelatin in hot water. Add lemon juice and salt; cool. Gradually blend in mayonnaise. Add remaining ingredients. Chill until firm. Yield: 6 servings.

Mrs. Ada Brookes
Miami, Fla.

CREAM OF CHICKEN SALAD

1 pkg. unflavored gelatin
¼ c. cold water
1 can cream of mushroom soup
2 tbsp. diced green pepper
2 pimentos, finely chopped
1 c. diced celery
¼ c. sliced ripe olives
½ c. salad dressing

Soften gelatin in cold water; add to soup. Heat until dissolved. Remove from heat; cool. Add remaining ingredients. Pour into 1-quart mold; chill. Unmold on salad plate; garnish with lettuce, radish roses, ripe olives, tomato wedges and carrot curls. Yield: 8 servings.

Lu Birks
Molino, Ill.

CREAM-CHICKEN SALAD LOAF

1 tbsp. gelatin
2 ½ c. chicken broth
2 c. cooked diced chicken
3 eggs, beaten
1 ½ tsp. salt
½ tsp. pepper

Soften gelatin in 1/2 cup cold broth. Combine chicken, eggs and remaining hot broth with seasonings; cook in top of double boiler for 10 minutes. Add gelatin; chill. Slice and serve with lettuce and mayonnaise. Yield: 6 servings.

Mrs. W. C. Mauldin
Dover, Del.

HAWAIIAN CHICKEN SALAD

3 pkg. lemon gelatin
4 c. boiling water
1 c. mayonnaise
1 c. heavy cream, whipped
1 No. 2 ½ can pineapple chunks, drained
2 c. sm. green grapes
1 c. chopped nuts
3 c. diced cooked chicken
½ tsp. salt

Dissolve gelatin in water; cool. Add remaining ingredients; mix well. Pour into a 9 x 13-inch pan. Chill overnight. Garnish with sliced olives. Yield: 15 servings.

Mrs. H. A. Berry
Manlius, Ill.

INDIVIDUAL CHICKEN SALAD MOLDS

1 tbsp. gelatin
¼ c. cold water
21 c. mayonaise
2 c. chopped chicken
½ c. chopped celery
¼ c. chopped pimento

Soak gelatin in cold water; add to mayonnaise. Fold in chicken, celery and pimento; add additional mayonnaise if necessary. Pour into individual molds; chill until firm. Serve on lettuce; garnish with stuffed olives. Yield: 4 servings.

Mrs. Ira H. McMillan
Pekin, Ill.

JENNIE'S CHICKEN LOAF

1 envelope gelatin
2 c. chicken broth
1 hen, cooked and chopped
1 c. chopped nuts
1 bunch celery, chopped
½ can pimento, chopped
½ can English peas, drained
1 tbsp. chow-chow
3 hard-cooked eggs, chopped
Juice of 1 lemon
Dash of cayenne
1 pt. mayonnaise

Dissolve gelatin in broth; add all ingredients except mayonnaise. Chill; add mayonnaise. Mix well; chill until ready to serve. Yield: 8 servings.

Jennie Thurston
Asheboro, N.C.

MOLDED CHICKEN SALAD

1 ¼ tbsp. gelatin
¼ c. water
2 ½ c. cooked cubed chicken
1 c. pitted white cherries
½ c. shredded almonds
2 tsp. diced parsley

(Continued on next page)

1 c. finely chopped celery
1 tsp. salt
Dash of pepper
½ c. chicken stock
½ c. cream
1 c. mayonnaise

Dissolve gelatin in water. Combine chicken, cherries, almonds, parsley, celery and seasonings. Add hot chicken stock to gelatin with cream. Slowly pour mixture into mayonnaise, stirring until smooth. Fold in chicken mixture. Pack into ring mold; chill for at least 12 hours. May be garnished with tomato wedges, avocado sections and watercress.

Mrs. Arthur W. Dew
Arlington, Va.

PRESSED CHICKEN MOLD

2 chickens, cut up
1 c. broth
¼ lb. butter
¼ tsp. (heaping) pepper
⅓ tsp. allspice
1 egg, beaten

Cook chicken slowly until tender. Remove chicken from broth; chop. Boil chicken broth until evaporated to 1 cup; add butter, pepper, allspice and egg. Mix thoroughly; add chicken. Press into mold; chill. Slice and serve with hard-cooked eggs on lettuce leaves with dressing. Yield: 6-8 servings.

Mrs. Ruth Edwards
Cullman, Ala.

MOLDED TURKEY SALAD

2 envelopes unflavored gelatin
⅔ c. water
1 c. salad dressing
1 6-oz. can Milnot
1 ½ tsp. monosodium glutamate
¾ tsp. salt
1 ⅓ c. turkey or chicken broth
2 ⅔ c. cooked diced turkey or chicken
1 c. chopped celery
⅓ c. sliced almonds
⅓ c. parsley

Sprinkle gelatin over cold water. Blend salad dressing and Milnot; add monosodium glutamate, salt, broth and gelatin. Let thicken for 1 hour; add remaining ingredients. Place in a mold or square glass dish. Refrigerate until serving time. Yield: 8 servings.

Jane McClary
Vincennes, Ind.

PRESSED CHICKEN SPECIAL

1 ½ c. cold chicken broth
2 envelopes unflavored gelatin
2 c. cooked diced chicken
2 c. cooked peas
½ c. blanched chopped almonds
2 tbsp. pickle relish
1 c. mayonaise

Skim fat from cold chicken broth; sprinkle gelatin over broth to soften. Dissolve over hot water; cool slightly. Stir in chicken and all remaining ingredients. Pour into 2-quart mold or 10 x 5 x 3-inch loaf pan. Chill until set. Remove from mold; slice and serve on greens. NOTE: Turkey may be substituted for chicken. Yield: 10 servings.

Mrs. Blanche Pike
Independence, Mo.

PRESSED CHICKEN

3 pkg. unflavored gelatin
½ c. cold water
4 c. chicken broth
1 lge. hen, cooked and cubed
1 c. finely chopped celery
½ c. chopped sweet pepper
½ c. chopped pecans
6 hard-cooked eggs, chopped
1 or 2 slices pimento, chopped
Juice of 1 lemon
Salt and pepper to taste

Soak gelatin in cold water; add to hot chicken broth. Simmer until dissolved. Add remaining ingredients. Pour in mold and congeal. Yield: 24 servings.

Mrs. Robert W. Davis
Laurens, S.C.

SPECIAL CHICKEN MAYONNAISE

2 envelopes unflavored gelatin
1 c. hot stock
1 hen, cooked and finely chopped
1 tsp. mustard
Salt and pepper
2 c. diced celery
2 tsp. chopped olives
2 tsp. chow-chow
3 sour pickles, chopped
1 can English peas, drained
1 c. pecans
1 pt. salad dressing

Dissolve gelatin in 1 cup hot stock. Cool; add all remaining ingredients. Mix well; place in 9 x 13 x 2-inch dish. Chill until firm; cut into squares. Serve on lettuce leaf. Yield: 20 servings.

Mrs. Chloe Thorp
Abilene, Tex.

RECIPE FOR BRUSSELS SPROUT AND TUNA MOUSSE ON PAGE 366

ARTICHOKE-CRAB MEAT SALAD

1 9-oz. pkg. frozen artichoke hearts
3 c. shredded lettuce
3 hard-cooked eggs, sliced
3 green pepper rings
3 tomatoes, quartered
1 6-oz. pkg. King crab meat, flaked
1 envelope Italian salad dressing mix
½ c. mayonnaise
3 tsp. capers

Prepare artichoke hearts according to package directions; drain and chill. Arrange lettuce on salad plates with egg slices in the center of each. Surround with a pepper ring. Alternate 4 artichoke hearts and 4 tomato quarters in a semi-circle around green pepper. Place a mound of crab meat on each salad. Prepare salad dressing according to package directions; blend in mayonnaise and pour over crab meat. Sprinkle with capers. Yield: 3 servings.

Mrs. Bert Gaither
Crane, Ind.

AVOCADO-CRAB MEAT SALAD

1 6 ½-oz. can crab meat, flaked
½ c. diced celery
1 tomato, diced
4 stuffed olives, chopped
½ c. mayonnaise
2 avocados, halved
1 tsp. lemon juice
1 hard-cooked egg
Watercress

Combine crab, celery, tomato, olives and mayonnaise. Sprinkle avocado halves with lemon juice. Pile crab mixture into avocado halves. Garnish with egg and watercress. Yield: 4 servings.

Mrs. Pat Folland
Rawson, O.

AVOCADO STUFFED WITH CRAB MEAT

½ c. crab meat
Mayonnaise
Chili sauce
Salt
Pepper
Lemon juice
1 avocado half
Shredded lettuce
Shredded carrot
Shredded radish
Tomato strips (opt.)

Mix crab meat with equal parts of mayonnaise and chili sauce. Season to taste with salt, pepper and lemon juice. Place avocado half on bed of shredded vegetables; fill with crab mixture. Top with mayonnaise and thin strips of tomato if desired. Yield: 1 serving.

Shirley L. Andersen
Enterprise, Oreg.

BAYLEY'S WEST INDIES SALAD

1 med. onion, finely chopped
1 lb. fresh lump crab meat
Salt and pepper
4 oz. salad oil
6 tbsp. cider vinegar
½ c. ice water

Place one-half of onion in bowl. Separate crab meat; place on onion. Spread remaining onion over crab meat. Salt and pepper to taste. Pour oil, vinegar and ice water over crab. Cover; refrigerate for 2 to 12 hours. Toss lightly just before serving. Yield: 6 servings.

Grace Lunsford
Foley, Ala.

CRAB DELECTABLE

1 c. crab meat
1 c. chopped celery
2 or 3 tomatoes, chopped
½ green pepper, chopped
1 sm. onion, chopped
Salt and pepper to taste
Vinegar to taste
Pinch of sugar
2 to 3 tbsp. mayonnaise

Combine all ingredients; chill. May be served on lettuce. NOTE: One cup cooked elbow macaroni may be added. Yield: 6 servings.

Mrs. Carl Legett
Gulfport, Miss.

CRAB LOUIS

LOUIS DRESSING:
1 c. mayonnaise
¼ c. sour cream
¼ c. chili sauce
¼ c. chopped green onion
1 tsp. lemon juice
Salt

Combine mayonnaise, sour cream, chili sauce, onions and lemon juice. Salt to taste. Chill. Yield: 2 cups.

(Continued on next page)

SALAD:
1 lge. head lettuce
2 to 3 c. cooked crab meat, chilled
2 lge. tomatoes, cut into wedges
2 hard-cooked eggs, cut into wedges

Line four large plates with lettuce leaves. Shred remaining lettuce; arrange on leaves. Arrange crab meat on lettuce. Circle with tomato and egg wedges. Sprinkle with salt. Pour 1/4 cup Louis Dressing over each salad. Sprinkle with paprika. Pass remaining dressing. Yield: 4 servings.

Betty Ann McCullough
Conneaut Lake, Pa.

CRAB LOUIS

1 to 1 ½ lb. crab meat
6 hard-cooked egg slices
4 fresh tomatoes, cut into wedges
1 avocado, sliced
Lettuce
1 c. mayonnaise
⅓ c. heavy cream
4 tbsp. chili sauce
1 tsp. Worcestershire sauce
1 tsp. prepared horseradish
1 tsp. minced parsley
1 green pepper, chopped
3 stuffed olives, chopped
3 stuffed onions, chopped
Salt and pepper to taste

Arrange crab, egg slices, tomato wedges and avocado slices in a bed of crisp lettuce. Combine remaining ingredients; pour over salad and serve cold. Yield: 8 servings.

Mona M. Bohn
Seattle, Wash.

CRAB SALAD

1 6-oz. can King crab meat, deboned and drained
Juice of 1 lemon
½ to ¾ c. mayonnaise
½ tsp. Tabasco sauce
½ tbsp. minced onion
½ c. chopped celery
1 c. shredded crisp iceberg lettuce
¼ tsp. freshly ground pepper
¼ tsp. salt

Flake crab; sprinkle with lemon juice. Refrigerate until needed. Combine mayonnaise and Tabasco sauce; toss with remaining ingredients. Serve immediately. Yield: 2 servings.

Mrs. J. E. Gibbs
Philadelphia, Pa.

CRAB SALAD

1 sm. head of lettuce
2 or 3 firm tomatoes
½ lb. crab, chilled
½ c. mayonnaise or salad dressing
¼ c. finely chopped celery
2 tbsp. chili sauce
1 tsp. horseradish
4 to 12 olives, sliced
4 hard-cooked eggs, sliced
1 sm. cucumber, sliced

Shred lettuce; place on four plates. Cut tomatoes into fourths or eighths. Place tomatoes, cut-side up, on lettuce. Top with crab. Combine mayonnaise, celery, chili sauce and horseradish; use as a dressing. Garnish with olives, eggs and cucumber. Yield: 4 servings.

Mrs. Fred Hart
Tillamook, Oreg.

CRAB SALAD SUPREME

1 ½ c. mayonnaise
1 tbsp. chopped green pepper
1 tbsp. grated onion
1 tsp. Worcestershire sauce or steak sauce
Juice of 1 lemon
Paprika
6 lge. ripe tomatoes
4 hard-cooked eggs
1 head lettuce, shredded
1 lb. crab meat
6 artichoke hearts

Combine mayonnaise, green pepper, onion, Worcestershire sauce and lemon juice. Peel tomatoes; scoop out centers. Marinate in dressing for 30 minutes. Press eggs through ricer or chop very fine. Arrange bed of lettuce on salad plate; sprinkle with egg. Place tomato in center; stuff with crab meat. Top with artichoke. Serve with remaining French dressing. Yield: 6 servings.

Mrs. Walter A. Kropp
Albany, Oreg.

FLUFFY CRAB SALAD

10 to 12 slices buttered white bread
Salt
4 hard-cooked eggs, cut up
1 sm. onion, minced
1 c. mayonnaise
1 c. salad dressing
1 16-oz. can flaked crab
Lemon juice to taste
Red food coloring (opt.)

Cut bread into 1-inch cubes; sprinkle with salt. Add eggs and onion; refrigerate for

(Continued on next page)

several hours. Add remaining ingredients; refrigerate for 3 to 4 hours. Yield: 6 servings.

Mrs. Robert Cooper
Salem, Oreg.

CRAB-MANDARIN ORANGE SALAD

2 envelopes unflavored gelatin
½ c. cold water
2 11-oz. cans Mandarin orange sections
½ tsp. salt
2 tsp. vinegar
1 tbsp. lemon juice
2 6½-oz. cans crab meat
1 c. diced celery
1 sm. onion, minced
1 c. mayonnaise
Dash of cayenne
Dash of paprika

Soften gelatin in water for 5 minutes. Strain syrup from Mandarin oranges. Heat syrup to boiling; pour over soft gelatin. Stir until dissolved. Add salt, vinegar and lemon juice. Cool until thick and syrupy. Drain, flake and remove bones from crab meat. Mix with celery, onion and all but 1/3 cup Mandarin orange sections. Mix in mayonnaise. Stir in gelatin mixture; add cayenne and paprika. Pour into mold or individual molds. Garnish with remaining Mandarin orange sections. Yield: 9 servings.

Helen Geraghty
Spokane, Wash.

CRAB MEAT MOLD

1 envelope unflavored gelatin
2 tbsp. cold water
2 6½-oz. cans crab meat, finely cut
3 8-oz. pkg. cream cheese, softened
6 tbsp. mayonnaise
¼ tsp. salt
¼ tsp. curry powder
1 tbsp. lemon juice
2 tbsp. grated onion
1 tsp. Worcestershire sauce

Soften gelatin in cold water; dissolve over hot water. Set aside to cool. Combine all remaining ingredients; add gelatin. Brush a 1 1/2-quart mold with oil; press crab mixture into it. Chill for several hours. Unmold onto flat tray; serve with crackers.

Mrs. George T. Seaman
Traverse City, Mich.

KING CRAB SALAD

1 pkg. lemon gelatin
1 can tomato soup
2 pkg. cream cheese
1 can crab meat
½ c. diced celery
1 tbsp. chopped green pepper
1 tbsp. minced onion
1 c. canned peas
1 c. mayonnaise
1 tbsp. vinegar
½ tsp. salt

Dissolve gelatin in 3/4 cup boiling water. Heat soup with cheese in double boiler; cool. Combine crab, celery, green pepper, onion, peas, mayonnaise, vinegar and salt. Add to gelatin mixture. Pour into buttered mold. Yield: 6-8 servings.

Ruth I. Lamb
Silverdale, Wash.

RED MOLDED CRAB SALAD

1 6-oz. can tomato paste
1 ½ c. water
1 3-oz. pkg. lemon gelatin
1 c. cottage cheese
½ c. finely chopped green onions and tops
½ c. mayonnaise or salad dressing
1 tbsp. Worcestershire sauce
1 c. flaked crab meat

Combine tomato paste and water in a saucepan; bring to a boil. Remove from heat; dissolve gelatin in hot liquid. Chill until mixture begins to thicken. Using a rotary beater, beat in cottage cheese, green onions, mayonnaise and Worcestershire sauce. Fold in crab meat; pour into a 1 1/2-quart mold or individual molds. Chill until firm. Unmold onto crisp greens. Yield: 6-8 servings.

Mrs. Bee Hoffman
Minot, N.D.

MOLDED CRAB SALAD

2 pkg. lemon gelatin
2 ¼ c. hot water
Onion flakes
2 cans tomato sauce
3 tbsp. vinegar
1 tsp. salt
Dash of pepper
1 or 2 cans crab meat
1 c. chopped celery
1 c. peas, cooked

Dissolve gelatin in water; sprinkle in a few onion flakes. Add tomato sauce, vinegar, salt

(Continued on next page)

and pepper. Cool until thickened. Add remaining ingredients. Chill until firm. Yield: 9 servings.

Mrs. David R. Gilkey
Mt. Vernon, Wash.

MOLDED CRAB SALAD

1 pkg. unflavored gelatin
½ c. cold water
½ c. hot water
1 c. chili sauce
1 c. cottage cheese
½ c. mayonnaise
1 can crab meat, flaked

Soften gelatin in cold water; stir in hot water. Add remaining ingredients. Pour into mold; chill until firm. Serve on crisp lettuce. Yield: 6-8 servings.

Aileen Schroeder
Shelton, Wash.

SALAD RING

1 pkg. lemon gelatin
2 c. hot tomato juice
2 tsp. lemon juice
1 c. mayonnaise
2 pkg. cream cheese
1 c. diced celery
2 tsp. onion juice
Salt to taste
1 can crab, shrimp or tuna
Hard-cooked eggs

Dissolve gelatin in tomato juice; add lemon juice. Chill until partially set. Add mayonnaise and cream cheese; beat until smooth. Add celery, onion juice, salt and crab, shrimp or tuna. Pour into ring mold. Serve with cole slaw in center. Garnish with hard-cooked eggs. Yield: 6 servings.

Mrs. F. A. Putney
Cumberland, Va.

SEAFOOD SPECIAL

1 6-oz. pkg. lemon gelatin
2 c. hot water
Juice of ½ lemon
2 c. whipped cream
½ lb. cheese, grated
1 c. chopped stuffed olives
6 hard-cooked eggs, chopped

Dissolve gelatin in hot water; cool until slightly thickened. Whip. Combine remaining ingredients; fold into gelatin mixture. Refrigerate until firm.

DRESSING:
1 c. mayonnaise
½ c. chili sauce
1 tsp. sweet relish
1 lb. crab meat or shrimp

Combine ingredients. Serve with salad. Yield: 6-8 servings.

Mrs. Jane Odell
Tempe, Ariz.

LOBSTER MOUSSE

1 tbsp. unflavored gelatin
¼ c. water
¾ c. minced celery
1 ½ c. canned or cooked lobster
⅔ c. minced apple
¾ c. mayonnaise
3 tbsp. lemon juice
Salt
Paprika
⅓ c. whipped cream
Watercress
Marinated cucumbers

Soak gelatin in water; dissolve over boiling water. Combine celery, lobster, apple, mayonnaise and lemon juice. Season with salt and paprika. Add gelatin; whip until mixture is stiff. Fold in cream. Place mousse in a wet mold; chill thoroughly. Unmold onto a platter; garnish with watercress and marinated cucumbers. Yield: 6 servings.

Gloria Shelton
Clarksville, Tenn.

LOBSTER SALAD

4 c. cooked cubed lobster
4 hard-cooked eggs, chopped
½ c. diced celery
¼ c. minced parsley
1 tsp. dry mustard
1 tsp. grated onion
1 tsp. Worcestershire sauce
½ tsp. salt
1 c. mayonnaise
Lettuce

Combine lobster, eggs, celery and parsley. Add mustard, onion, Worcestershire sauce and salt. Add mayonnaise; mix well. Serve on lettuce. Yield: 6 servings.

Mrs. Emily Porter
Savoy, Tex.

LOBSTER SALAD SPECIAL

2 c. diced lobster
1 c. finely diced celery
3 hard-cooked eggs, chopped
¼ tsp. salt
⅛ tsp. pepper
Mayonnaise

Combine all ingredients with enough mayonnaise to moisten. Chill. Serve on lettuce leaves. Yield: 6 servings.

Mrs. Genevieve Snyder
Denver, Pa.

TASTY LOBSTER SALAD

1 chicken breast, cooked
½ lb. lobster meat, cooked and diced
French dressing
3 hard-cooked eggs
1 c. finely chopped celery
1 c. mayonnaise
Salt to taste
1 tbsp. chopped chives
Salt to taste
½ c. whipped cream
Lettuce

Cut chicken into strips. Marinate lobster and chicken in a little French dressing with chopped egg whites and celery for 1 hour. Mash or sieve egg yolks; blend with mayonnaise, chili sauce, chives and salt. Fold in whipped cream. Chill. Mix chicken, lobster and dressing. Serve on lettuce. Yield: 4-6 servings.

Margaret K. Shollenberger
Girard, Pa.

OYSTER SALAD

DRESSING:
2 eggs, well beaten
¼ c. vinegar
4 tbsp. sugar
½ tsp. salt
1 tsp. prepared mustard
2 tbsp. water

Mix all ingredients. Cook over hot water or low heat until mixture is consistency of soft custard. Cool.

SALAD:
3 cans cove oysters
12 soda crackers, crumbled
8 hard-cooked eggs, diced
1 c. finely chopped sweet pickles
¼ tsp. pepper
1 c. finely cut celery

Mash oysters in their liquid. Add remaining ingredients; toss well. Add dressing. Chill for several hours before serving. Yield: 8 servings.

Kathryn Davis
Pinckneyville, Ill.

OYSTER SALAD SPECIAL

2 No. 1 cans oysters
1 med. can pimento
8 hard-cooked eggs
4 sour pickles
4 tbsp. margarine, melted
30 soda crackers
Salt
Vinegar

Grind oysters, pimento, eggs, pickles, margarine and crackers; mix well. Add salt and vinegar to taste. Yield: 12 servings.

Mrs. Joyzelle Sauls
Brownsville, Tex.

BANANA-SALMON SALAD

3 ripe bananas, chopped
½ c. canned pineapple
1 ½ c. canned flaked salmon
¼ c. diced celery
½ tsp. salt
1 tbsp. chopped sweet pickle
Mayonnaise

Mix bananas and pineapple; add salmon. Fold in remaining ingredients with enough mayonnaise to moisten. Garnish with lettuce and lemon slices. Yield: 4-5 servings.

Mrs. Margaret Rettke
Scottville, Mich.

CLUB PARTY SALMON SALAD

1 1-lb. can red salmon
½ c. chopped pimento
½ c. small peas
½ c. mayonnaise

Combine all ingredients; chill. Serve on crisp lettuce with peach half. May be garnished with stuffed olive. Yield: 10 servings.

Mrs. Leon Smith
Soperton, Ga.

LOMI SALMON

1 1-lb. can red salmon, flaked
1 lge. onion, minced
2 lge. ripe tomatoes, cubed

Mix salmon and onion until well blended. Add tomatoes; toss gently to prevent tomatoes from falling apart. Chill. Yield: 6 servings.

Mrs. Betty Kirk Thomas
Arlington, Tex.

MOLDED SALMON SALAD

1 pkg. lime or lemon gelatin
1 ¾ c. boiling water
3 tbsp. vinegar
¼ tsp. salt
1 tsp. sugar
¼ tsp. dry mustard
½ c. mayonnaise
1 c. chopped celery
1 c. diced cucumber
1 lge. can salmon, flaked

Dissolve gelatin in boiling water; add vinegar. Chill. Combine salt, sugar, mustard and mayonnaise. Fold mixture into partially thickened gelatin. Add all remaining ingredients. Turn into molds rinsed in cold water. Chill until firm. Serve on lettuce. Yield: 6 servings.

Dorothy Rae Percival
Riverton, Wyo.

SALMON AND EGG SALAD

1 8-oz. can salmon, drained
3 hard-cooked eggs, cut into eighths
1 c. diced celery
2 tbsp. minced onion
2 tbsp. minced parsley
Salt to taste
⅛ tsp. pepper
2 tbsp. lemon juice
¼ to ⅓ c. mayonnaise
Salad greens
1 lemon, quartered

Remove bones and skin from salmon; flake into large pieces. Combine salmon, eggs and celery. Blend all remaining ingredients except greens and lemon; stir into salmon mixture. Serve on crisp greens; garnish with lemon. Yield: 4 servings.

Mrs. Pat Starbuck
Angels Peak, Nev.

SALMON SALAD

1 1-lb. can salmon
2 c. cracker crumbs
½ c. chopped walnuts
½ c. salad dressing
1 c. sour cream
6 sweet pickles, chopped

Combine all ingredients; mix lightly. Chill; serve on lettuce. Yield: 6 servings.

Mrs. Paul Myers
Benedict, Nebr.

SALMON SALAD

½ c. tomato soup
1 tbsp. unflavored gelatin
2 tbsp. cold water
½ c. tomato soup
⅛ tsp. paprika
¼ tsp. Worcestershire sauce
Salt and pepper to taste
1 c. whipped cream
½ c. mayonnaise
1 tsp. lemon juice
2 drops red food coloring
⅓ c. minced celery
Dash of soy sauce
2 tbsp. minced green pepper
½ lb. red salmon

Bring soup to boiling point. Soften gelatin in cold water; add to soup. Add all remaining ingredients. Pile into individual molds; chill until firm. Serve on lettuce leaves. Yield: 4 servings.

Nancy Euren
Hope, N.D.

BEST SHRIMP SALAD

1 lb. boiled shrimp, cut into sm. pieces
3 hard-cooked eggs, chopped
1 tbsp. diced sweet pickle
Salt and pepper to taste
2 tbsp. mayonnaise
½ c. diced celery

Combine all ingredients. May be served in ripe tomato, cut into petals on lettuce. Yield: 6 servings.

Mrs. Jack Skinner
Augusta, Ga.

COLESLAW AND SHRIMP SALAD

1 can shrimp, drained and rinsed
¼ tsp. sugar
⅛ tsp. salt
⅛ tsp. pepper
1 sm. onion, finely chopped
½ lge. cabbage, finely cut
¼ green pepper, finely diced
1 stalk celery, finely cut

Combine all ingredients, mixing well.

TANGY DRESSING:
2 eggs
¼ c. sugar
1 tsp. salt
2 tsp. flour
1 tsp. dry mustard
¼ tsp. pepper
½ c. vinegar
2 tsp. butter
1 c. whipped cream

Combine all ingredients except butter and cream; cook until thickened. Add butter; chill. Add whipped cream. Pour over salad. Yield: 4 servings.

Mrs. A. D. Griffin
Sherman, Tex.

CURRIED SHRIMP AND PINEAPPLE SALAD

2 c. whole shrimp, cooked
2 hard-cooked egg yolks
½ tsp. curry powder
½ c. salad oil
3 tbsp. vinegar
2 c. diced pineapple

Chill shrimp. Mash egg yolks. Add curry powder; blend in a small amount of oil at a time, beating well after each addition. Add vinegar; continue beating until well blended. Combine shrimp, pineapple and dressing. Toss lightly to mix. Chill. Mix well; serve in lettuce cups, sea shells or on salad plates. Yield: 6 servings.

Mrs. William R. Scott
Sunnyside, Wash.

EASY SHRIMP SALAD

2 c. cleaned cooked shrimp
1 c. chopped celery
½ c. diced cucumbers
3 hard-cooked eggs, quartered
¼ tsp. salt
Dash of pepper
Juice of 1 lemon
Mayonnaise to taste

Combine all ingredients except lemon juice and mayonnaise. Sprinkle with lemon juice; moisten with mayonnaise. Chill; serve on crisp lettuce. Yield: 6 servings.

Sue Schimmelpfenning
Monmouth, Ill.

ORIGINAL SHRIMP LOUIS

½ pt. mayonnaise
1 tbsp. tarragon vinegar
3 tbsp. chili sauce
1 tsp. Worcestershire sauce
2 tbsp. chopped pimento
1 clove of garlic, pressed
1 tsp. salt
1 tsp. powdered sugar
1 tsp. paprika
¼ tsp. mustard
Lettuce leaves
Cooked shrimp
Quartered tomatoes
Quartered hard-cooked eggs

Combine mayonnaise, vinegar, chili sauce and Worcestershire sauce. Mix in pimento, garlic, salt, sugar, paprika and mustard. Mix well. Cover; refrigerate. Arrange lettuce leaves on plate. Place desired number of shrimp in center. Circle with tomato and egg wedges. Pour sauce over shrimp.

Mrs. James K. Dowling
Colorado Springs, Colo.

MARINATED SHRIMP

3 c. cooked shrimp
½ c. vinegar
¼ c. salad oil
1 tsp. salt
Few drops garlic juice
Dash of hot pepper sauce
2 tbsp. chopped chives
2 tbsp. chopped parsley
2 tbsp. chopped dill pickle

Put shrimp in a quart jar; add vinegar, salad oil, salt, garlic juice, hot pepper sauce, chives, parsley and dill pickle. Shake jar well; store in refrigerator. Do this a day in advance; shake jar often. Yield: 8 servings.

Elaine Anderson
Lynn Haven, Fla.

MOCK LOBSTER SALAD

4 hard-cooked eggs, chopped
1 green pepper, finely minced
1 med. onion, finely minced
1 c. finely minced celery
3 c. shrimp, broken into sm. pieces
½ c. chili sauce
1 c. mayonnaise

Combine all ingredients. Chill for at least 2 hours before serving. Serve on lettuce with crackers or toast. Yield: 6 servings.

Mrs. Carl T. Heath, Jr.
Topeka, Kans.

PINEAPPLE-SHRIMP OUTRIGGER

1 lb. fresh shrimp
1 tbsp. seafood seasoning
1 tbsp. salt
¼ c. vinegar
¼ c. water
1 ripe pineapple
Prepared French dressing

Wash shrimp. Add seasoning, salt, vinegar and water; mix. Place in saucepan; cover. Bring to boil; simmer for 25 minutes. Drain; remove shells and devein shrimp. Cool. Cut pineapple, including crown, in half. Hollow out, leaving shell about 1/4-inch thick. Remove core. Dice pineapple; mix with shrimp. Marinate with enough French dressing to coat mixture. Pile mixture into pineapple shell. Garnish with fresh flowers.

Mrs. Rose Marie Staley
Union Bridge, Md.

SATURDAY LUNCH SALAD

2 c. cooked diced potatoes
2 c. chopped cooked shrimp
½ c. finely shredded carrot
¼ c. grated onion
¾ c. diced tart apples
¾ c. mayonnaise
1 tsp. salt
½ tsp. pepper
2 tbsp. prepared mustard
1 tbsp. lemon juice

Mix all ingredients. Chill. Yield: 6 servings.

Mrs. Enid Beazley
Virginia Beach, Va.

SHRIMP-GREEN BEAN SALAD

2 c. boiled shrimp
1 No. 2 can green beans, chopped
1 med. onion, minced
½ c. diced green pepper
¼ c. diced drained mushrooms
¼ c. diced pimento
Iceberg lettuce

Combine all ingredients. Serve on iceberg lettuce leaves with a salad oil dressing. Yield: 8 servings.

Leo Williams Rushing
Joaquin, Tex.

SHRIMP-POTATO SALAD

6 med. potatoes, cooked and cubed
6 hard-cooked eggs, sliced
1 c. shrimp, broken into pieces
1 tsp. parsley
1 ½ tsp. salt
½ tsp. pepper
1 c. chopped celery
1 med. onion, chopped

Combine all ingredients except a few pieces of eggs and shrimp.

DRESSING:
3 tbsp. milk
3 tbsp. wine or tarragon vinegar
1 c. salad dressing
Paprika

Beat milk and vinegar with salad dressing. Pour over salad; mix well. Garnish with reserved eggs, shrimp and paprika. Chill for 2 to 3 hours. Yield: 6-8 servings.

Mrs. Lura Campbell
Toledo, O.

SHRIMP SALAD

½ c. vinegar
¼ c. salad oil
1 tsp. salt
½ tsp. sugar
¼ tsp. pepper
1 tsp. mustard
½ head lettuce, chopped
1 green pepper, chopped
1 cucumber, chopped
2 tomatoes, cubed
4 green onions, chopped
1 can shrimp, drained

Combine vinegar, oil, salt, sugar, pepper and mustard in a jar; shake well. Chill. Combine all remaining ingredients, tossing lightly. Chill. Serve with dressing. Yield: 6 servings.

Mrs. Wiley Roberts
Littlefield, Tex.

SHRIMP-BANANA SALAD SPLIT

⅔ c. mayonnaise
½ tsp. salt
¾ to 1 tsp. curry powder
Dash of pepper
2 lb. shrimp, cooked, shelled and cleaned
1 c. cooked rice
¾ c. chopped celery
¼ c. finely chopped onion
4 med. bananas, all yellow
Romaine lettuce
Lemon juice
Chopped nuts

Blend mayonnaise with seasonings in bowl; add shrimp, rice, celery and onion. Toss lightly; chill. Halve bananas lengthwise; brush with lemon juice. Arrange bananas on lettuce-lined oblong plates with salad in center. Sprinkle nuts on top. Yield: 4 servings.

Photograph for this recipe above.

SHRIMP SALAD

3 c. cleaned cooked shrimp
1 bottle French dressing
2 c. chopped celery
1 c. chopped green peppers
1 c. mayonnaise
3 hard-cooked eggs, diced
8 firm tomatoes, peeled

Marinate shrimp in French dressing for 1 hour. Combine celery, green peppers, mayonnaise, eggs and marinated shrimp. Cut stem end from tomatoes; scoop out part of center. Fill with salad; serve on salad greens. Yield: 8 servings.

Mrs. William Suckel
Martins Ferry, O.

SHRIMP SALAD ANITA

1 can cream of celery soup
½ c. mayonnaise
1 tsp. lime juice
1 tsp. curry powder
1 tsp. salt
½ tsp. monosodium glutamate
3 c. shredded cabbage
1 c. shrimp, cut into pieces
½ c. pineapple chunks
2 tbsp. slivered almonds

Combine soup, mayonnaise, juice and seasonings; chill. Toss all remaining ingredients

(Continued on next page)

except almonds with dressing. Sprinkle with almonds; serve on lettuce leaves. Yield: 4 servings.

Mrs. Eugene W. Shier
Randolph AFB, Tex.

SHRIMP SALAD BOWL

1 lb. cooked shrimp, cleaned
1 head lettuce
¼ head curly lettuce
12 stuffed olives, sliced
2 hard-cooked eggs, sliced

Chill shrimp. Combine well chilled greens, shrimp and olives in salad bowl. Toss lightly with Piquant Mustard Dressing. Garnish with eggs.

PIQUANT MUSTARD DRESSING:
1 c. cold evaporated milk
3 tbsp. lemon juice
1 tbsp. chopped chives
3 tbsp. mustard
½ tsp. salt
¼ tsp. cayenne pepper

Blend evaporated milk and lemon juice; stir in all remaining ingredients. Chill; serve over shrimp salad bowl. Yield: 4-6 servings.

Mrs. Nina T. Smith
Picayune, Miss.

SHRIMP SALAD SUPREME

1 7-oz. can shrimp, chilled
1 c. diced celery
1 tsp. minced onion
1 can Mandarin orange sections
Salad dressing to taste

Combine shrimp, celery, onion and orange sections; add salad dressing. Serve in lettuce cups. Yield: 6 servings.

Mrs. Edward E. Wanner
East Peoria, Ill.

SHRIMP SALAD SUPREME

2 c. cleaned cooked shrimp
½ c. sliced celery, chilled
1 tsp. minced onion
⅓ c. mayonnaise
¼ c. chili sauce
3 tbsp. fresh lemon juice
2 or 3 hard-cooked eggs, chopped
Salt and pepper to taste

Thoroughly combine all ingredients. Serve on chilled crisp lettuce. Yield: 6 servings.

Frances B. Kniceley
Winchester, Va.

SHRIMP-STUFFED CELERY

2 c. chopped shrimp
¼ c. mayonnaise
1 tsp. catsup
2 tsp. horseradish
⅛ tsp. monosodium glutamate
5 stalks celery, cut into 4 pieces
Paprika
3 stuffed olives, chopped

Combine shrimp, mayonnaise, catsup, horseradish and monosodium glutamate. Stuff celery stalks with shrimp mixture. Garnish with paprika and olives. Yield: 6 servings.

Marguerite Robson
Flora, La.

SHRIMP- VEGETABLE SALAD

2 ½ lb. shrimp
1 c. celery tops
5 tsp. salt
¼ c. pickling spice
2 med. onions, sliced
2 sm. cans mushrooms, sliced
1 ¼ c. salad oil
¾ c. cider vinegar
2 ½ tbsp. capers and juice
2 tsp. sugar
2 tsp. lemon juice
2 to 4 bay leaves
2 ½ tsp. celery seed
Dash of Tabasco sauce
Dash of Worcestershire sauce
½ c. chopped green pepper
2 avocados, diced
Carrot curls
Caulifloweret s

Cook shrimp in boiling water with celery tops, 3 1/2 teaspoons salt and pickling spice. Layer cleaned shrimp, onions and mushrooms in a shallow dish. Combine oil, vinegar, capers and juice, sugar, lemon juice and bay leaves; add celery seed, remaining salt, Tabasco sauce and Worcestershire sauce. Pour sauce over shrimp. Cover and refrigerate for 24 hours or up to five days. Add all remaining ingredients. Drain off sauce and serve on lettuce. NOTE: If used as an hors d'oeuvre, omit pepper, avocados, carrots and caulifloweret s. Serve shrimp, onion and mushrooms on toothpicks.

Mrs. J. L. Shipman
Sanford, Fla.

SPRINGTIME SHRIMP SALAD

1 c. cottage cheese
1 c. cooked shrimp
¼ c. chopped celery
¼ c. sweet pickle relish
Marjoram to taste
¼ c. mayonnaise
Tomato slices or cups

Combine all ingredients except tomato. Serve on tomato slices or cups in crisp lettuce. Garnish with paprika.

Mrs. Geraldine Cannady
Vandenberg AFB, Calif.

SUMMER SHRIMP SALAD

¼ tsp. crushed dill seed
1 c. lemon flavored mayonnaise
3 c. coarsely chopped cooked shrimp
1 c. finely chopped celery
⅛ tsp. garlic salt
⅛ tsp. cayenne

Blend crushed dill seed into mayonnaise; add all remaining ingredients. Chill well. May be served on bed of spinach leaves. Top with additional mayonnaise and whole shrimp. Yield: 4 servings.

Mrs. Reid A. Olson
Deerfield, Ill.

SHRIMP SALAD

1 c. chopped shrimp
1 c. diced celery
1 c. lettuce hearts, cut into sm. pieces
1 tsp. juice
1 tsp. finely minced onion
Salt and paprika to taste

Mix all ingredients lightly. Chill. Drain just before serving; toss with mayonnaise to moisten. Serve on crisp lettuce. Yield: 4 servings.

Meredith Hansen
Brigham City, Utah

BLUSHING SHRIMP SALAD

1 sm. pkg. cherry gelatin
2 c. tomato juice, heated
4 tsp. vinegar
1 c. cooked cleaned shrimp
½ c. finely chopped celery
1 tbsp. grated onion
⅓ c. grated carrots

Dissolve gelatin in tomato juice; add vinegar. Chill until thickened. Add all remaining ingredients; pour into mold. Chill until firm. Yield: 6 servings.

Mrs. Robert Savage
Pease AFB, N.H.

BRIGHT JEWEL SALAD

1 pkg. lemon gelatin
1 c. hot water
1 tsp. salt
¼ tsp. garlic salt
Dash of pepper
1 tbsp. vinegar
½ c. cold water
1 c. cooked shrimp, cut into ½-in. pieces
1 avocado, diced

Dissolve gelatin in hot water. Add seasonings, vinegar and cold water. Pour into an 8-inch square pan. Chill until slightly thickened. Add shrimp and avocado pieces arranged so they will be in small cubes when cut. Chill until firm. Cut into 1-inch squares.

SALAD BASE:
1 ½ c. grapefruit sections
1 c. diced tomato
1 c. cheese, cut into thin strips (opt.)
½ c. sliced ripe olives
¼ c. chopped green onions
3 qt. salad greens

Combine ingredients and toss lightly. Arrange shrimp and avocado squares on top. Serve with favorite salad dressing. Yield: 8 servings.

Mrs. Loretta Fowler Bennett
Annandale, Va.

CARROT AND SHRIMP SALAD

2 tsp. unflavored gelatin
1 tbsp. cold water
1 c. mayonnaise
½ tsp. salt
1 c. cooked diced shrimp
1 c. seedless raisins
1 c. sliced celery
2 c. shredded carrots
12 stuffed olives, sliced
1 c. cottage cheese

Soak gelatin in cold water; dissolve over hot water. Mix with mayonnaise and salt. Combine shrimp, raisins, celery, carrots, olives and cheese. Carefully fold into mayonnaise

(Continued on next page)

A profusion of seafood, dewy vegetables and a delectable sauce are the ingredients for this hearty main dish salad that's easy to prepare and a delight to behold. For an adventure in good eating, try this unusual salad.

FISHERMAN'S FEAST

2 10-oz. pkg. frozen California Brussels sprouts
1½ lb. shrimp, cooked, shelled and deveined
1½ c. cooked lobster pieces
1 c. small whole white onions, cooked
2 c. cooked, sliced potatoes
1 c. cherry tomatoes or tomato wedges

Cook Brussels sprouts according to package directions; drain. Combine sprouts with all remaining ingredients in large, shallow bowl.

GREEN SAUCE:

¾ c. olive or salad oil
⅓ c. wine vinegar
⅓ c. finely chopped parsley
1 clove garlic, crushed
2 tbsp. anchovy paste
1 tbsp. sugar
1 tsp. salt
¼ tsp. black or cracked pepper

Combine all sauce ingredients. Pour over Brussels sprout mixture. Chill for 2 hours, stirring occasionally.

See photograph on reverse page.

mixture with forks to prevent mashing. Pour into mold or individual molds; chill. Serve with additional salad dressing. Yield: 6-8 servings.

Carolyn M. Smet
Newmarket, N.H.

LIME-SHRIMP MOLD

1 No. 2 can crushed pineapple
1 6-oz. pkg. lime gelatin
2 c. hot water
1 ½ c. cold water
8 oz. cottage cheese
1 to 2 c. fresh cooked shrimp

Drain pineapple, reserving 1/2 cup juice. Dissolve gelatin in hot water; add cold water and pineapple juice. Cool. Add pineapple and cottage cheese. Mix well. Add shrimp. Chill. Yield: 8-10 servings.

Mrs. Elizabeth S. Richardson
Orangeburg, S.C.

MOLDED FISH SALAD

2 tbsp. unflavored gelatin
½ c. cold water
2 ½ c. mayonnaise
4 c. shrimp, lobster or crab
2 ½ c. finely chopped celery
½ c. sliced stuffed olives
¼ c. finely chopped green pepper
2 tbsp. chopped pimento
¼ c. finely chopped green onions
1 tsp. salt
Dash of red pepper

Soften gelatin in 1/2 cup cold water; dissolve over hot water. Cook; slowly add to mayonnaise. Combine all remaining ingredients; add to mayonnaise mixture. Pour into fish mold; chill. May be served with lemon gelatin cut into cubes. Yield: 10-12 servings.

Mrs. Harry R. Tevis
Park Ridge, Ill.

MOLDED SALAD SHRIMP

1 pkg. lemon gelatin
1 c. hot water
1 can tomato soup
½ c. chopped celery
¼ c. chopped green pepper
1 pkg. pecans, chopped
1 can shrimp, cleaned

Dissolve gelatin in hot water. Add soup; mix well. Stir in all remaining ingredients. Pour into mold; chill until firm. Yield: 4 servings.

Mrs. Henry G. Ehleringer
San Diego, Calif.

OLIVE-SHRIMP MOLD

4 envelopes unflavored gelatin
1 lge. can tomato juice
¼ tsp. Tabasco sauce
½ tsp. chili powder
½ tsp. paprika
½ c. lemon juice
1 8-oz. pkg. cream cheese, softened
⅓ c. mayonnaise
1 ½ lb. shrimp, cooked, cleaned and finely chopped
1 c. finely chopped stuffed olives
1 c. finely chopped celery
Sliced pimento-stuffed olives

Sprinkle gelatin over 2 cups tomato juice. Add remaining tomato juice, Tabasco sauce, chili powder and paprika; cook over boiling water until gelatin dissolves, stirring constantly. Add lemon juice; cool. Combine cream cheese and mayonnaise; beat until smooth. Gradually add juice mixture. Chill until slightly thickened. Fold shrimp, chopped olives and celery into tomato mixture. Turn into 2 1/2-quart mold. Chill until set. Unmold; garnish with olives. Yield: 6-8 servings.

Mrs. Evelyn V. Taylor
Atlanta, Ga.

OVERNIGHT SHRIMP SALAD

1 pkg. lemon gelatin
1 c. boiling water
½ tsp. salt
1 c. mayonnaise
½ c. whipped cream
1 tbsp. chopped green pepper
3 hard-cooked eggs, chopped
1 c. diced celery
2 cans shrimp or tuna
Chopped pimento
2 3-oz. pkg. cream cheese

Mix gelatin, water and salt; cool until it begins to thicken. Add mayonnaise, whipped cream, pepper, eggs, celery, shrimp or tuna and pimento. Mix cheese until creamy; fold into mixture. Pour into 10-inch ring mold; chill overnight. Serve in nest of endive with tomato, cucumber slices and radish roses for garnish. Yield: 8 servings.

Mrs. Donald Hoff
Grand Meadow, Minn.

SEAFOOD SALAD

4 tsp. unflavored gelatin
⅓ c. catsup
1 10½-oz. can tomato soup
1 3-oz. pkg. cream cheese
½ c. mayonnaise
½ c. cream or evaporated milk
1 tbsp. lemon juice
2 4½-oz. cans shrimp or lobster, drained
1½ c. diced celery
¼ c. chopped green pepper
1 tbsp. chopped pimento

Sprinkle 1 teaspoon gelatin over catsup. Heat catsup, stirring constantly to dissolve gelatin. Spoon catsup into any mold; place in refrigerator to congeal. Sprinkle remaining gelatin over tomato soup; heat soup to dissolve gelatin. Cool. Soften cream cheese with mayonnaise and cream; add lemon juice. Stir into tomato soup. Fold shrimp or lobster, celery, green pepper and pimento into tomato soup mixture. Pour over congealed catsup. Chill for several hours. Unmold; garnish with watercress or endive. Yield: 4-6 servings.

Mattie Finney
Burton, Wash.

SEAFOOD SALAD

1 pkg. lemon gelatin
1 c. hot water
1 jar pimento cheese
½ c. mayonnaise
1 c. shrimp, crab or tuna, drained
2 tbsp. chopped green pepper
2 tbsp. chopped celery
1 tbsp. grated onion
1 carrot, grated

Dissolve gelatin in water; chill until slightly congealed. Add remaining ingredients. Chill until firm. Yield: 6-8 servings.

Ella G. Moyer
Spokane, Wash.

SHRIMP ASPIC

3 c. V-8 juice
1 tsp. Worcestershire sauce
1 bay leaf
1 tsp. lemon juice
½ tsp. paprika
Dash of Tabasco sauce
2 pkg. unflavored gelatin
1 c. cold water
½ c. canned artichoke hearts, drained
½ lb. medium shrimp, cooked and cleaned

Boil V-8 juice, Worcestershire sauce, bay leaf, lemon juice, paprika and Tabasco sauce. Dissolve gelatin in cold water; add to mixture. Pour into a tube pan; arrange artichokes and shrimp in pan. Chill until set. Yield: 8 servings.

DRESSING:
2 lge. avocados, mashed
1 pt. sour cream
2 tbsp. mayonnaise
Dash of Tabasco sauce
Dash of lemon juice

Blend all ingredients well. Unmold aspic; fill center with dressing.

Mrs. Thad Wolinski
Woodland Hills, Calif.

SHRIMP ASPIC SALAD

1 lge. pkg. lemon gelatin
4 c. V-8 juice
⅓ c. horseradish sauce
2 lge. cans medium shrimp

Dissolve gelatin in 1 cup V-8 juice, heated to boiling point. Let mixture partially set; add remaining juice, horseradish and shrimp. Chill until set. Yield: 8 servings.

Mrs. Luella T. Hale
Dexter, N.Y.

SHRIMP CREME

1 pkg. lemon gelatin
1⅓ c. boiling water
1 sm. can shrimp
1 c. diced celery
½ c. chopped walnuts
½ tsp. grated onion
Juice of ½ lemon
1 c. salad dressing

Dissolve gelatin in boiling water. Cool until mixture reaches the consistency of egg white. Beat with a rotary beater until double in bulk. Add remaining ingredients. Pour into an oiled mold. Chill until firm. Yield: 8-10 servings.

Mrs. Doris Smith
Dayton, Wash.

SHRIMP MOLD

1 pkg. lemon gelatin
1 c. boiling water
½ c. chili sauce
1 tsp. vinegar
Dash of Tabasco sauce

(Continued on next page)

1 tsp. Worcestershire sauce
2 tbsp. horseradish
1 ¼ lb. diced cooked shrimp

Dissolve gelatin in boiling water. Combine chili sauce, vinegar, Tabasco sauce, Worcestershire sauce and horseradish; add cold water to make 1 cup. Add gelatin; chill until slightly thickened. Fold in shrimp; pour into mold. Chill until firm. Yield: 6 servings.

Mrs. H. A. Bergman
Roanoke, Va.

SHRIMP MOUSSE

3 pkg. unflavored gelatin
1 c. cold water
1 10-oz. can tomato soup
3 3-oz. pkg. cream cheese
1 c. mayonnaise
15 drops Tabasco sauce
1 ½ c. cooked cleaned shrimp
1 c. chopped celery
½ c. finely chopped green pepper
2 tbsp. grated onion
1 tsp. salt
3 tbsp. lemon juice
1 tbsp. Worcestershire sauce
Sliced stuffed olives
Black olives

Soften gelatin in cold water. Heat soup and cheese until cheese melts. Add gelatin; cool. Add all remaining ingredients except olives. Pour into greased 1-quart fish mold. Refrigerate for at least 24 hours. Serve on lettuce leaves. Garnish with stuffed and black olives. Yield: 6 servings.

Mrs. F. F. Shriner
Randolph AFB, Tex.

SHRIMP MOUSSE SPECIAL

1 can tomato soup
1 soup can milk
3 pkg. cream cheese
2 pkg. gelatin
⅓ c. chopped onion
⅓ c. chopped green pepper
⅓ c. chopped celery
2 lb. fresh shrimp, cooked
Finely chopped cucumber
1 c. mayonnaise

Heat soup and milk. Add cheese; beat until smooth. Dissolve gelatin in small amount of cold water; stir into hot cheese mixture. Cool. Add onion, green pepper, celery and shrimp. Pour into mold; chill until firm. Add cucumber to mayonnaise; serve with shrimp mold. Garnish with tomato and hard-cooked eggs.

Mrs. David Lamar McDonald
Washington, D.C.

SHRIMP SALAD

1 ½ pkg. lemon gelatin
2 c. V-8 juice
2 tbsp. vinegar
1 can small shrimp, deveined
2 tbsp. chopped onion
2 tbsp. chopped celery
2 tbsp. chopped green pepper

Add lemon gelatin to V-8 juice; simmer for 2 to 3 minutes. Stir in vinegar; pour into bowl. Chill until slightly thickened. Add shrimp, onion, celery and green pepper. Yield: 4 servings.

Mrs. Richard Werblow
Chilton, Wisc.

SHRIMP SALAD

2 pkg. unflavored gelatin
⅓ c. cold water
3 pkg. cream cheese
1 can tomato soup
3 cans shrimp
1 c. chopped celery
1 c. chopped green peppers
½ c. chopped sweet pickles
¾ c. mayonnaise

Soften gelatin in cold water. Heat cream cheese and tomato soup; add gelatin and stir until dissolved. Cool; add all remaining ingredients. Chill. Yield: 8-10 servings.

Mrs. C. R. Gilliland
Albuquerque, N.M.

SHRIMP SALAD DELIGHT

1 can tomato soup
3 3-oz. pkg. cream cheese, softened
1 c. mayonnaise
2 pkg. lemon gelatin
1 c. boiling water
1 c. cold water
1 bunch celery, diced
½ green pepper, diced
1 tbsp. grated onion
2 pimentos, chopped
2 cans shrimp

Heat tomato soup to boiling; add cream cheese and mayonnaise. Dissolve lemon gelatin in

(Continued on next page)

boiling water; add cold water. Add to soup mixture. Add celery, green pepper, onion, pimentos and shrimp. Chill until firm. Yield: 12 servings.

Mrs. Mary Witt
Buffalo, Wyo.

SHRIMP SALAD SPECIAL

1 envelope unflavored gelatin
2 tbsp. cold water
1 can tomato soup
1 c. mayonnaise
1 3-oz. pkg. cream cheese
2 tbsp. grated onion
1 sm. bottle stuffed olives
1 can shrimp

Soften gelatin in cold water. Heat soup; add gelatin, stirring until dissolved. Cream mayonnaise and cream cheese; add onion, olives and shrimp. Combine all ingredients; pour into mold. Chill. Yield: 24 servings.

Mrs. Homer Turner
Columbia, Miss.

SHRIMP SALAD BARBARA ANN

1 pkg. lemon gelatin
1 c. boiling water
1 tsp. salt
3 tbsp. grated onion
½ c. mayonnaise
½ c. light cream
3 hard-cooked eggs, chopped
1 tbsp. chopped green pepper
1 c. chopped pecans
½ lb. Old English cheese, grated
1 lb. cooked shrimp, cut into bite-sized pieces
Chopped parsley (opt.)

Dissolve gelatin in water; add salt and onion. Chill until thickened. Whip in mayonnaise and cream; add eggs, green pepper, pecans, cheese and shrimp. Garnish with parsley. Yield: 6 servings.

Mrs. John A. Watt
Mountain Home, Idaho

SHRIMP SALAD MOLD

1 pkg. lemon gelatin
1 c. boiling water
1 c. cooked chopped shrimp
2 hard-cooked eggs, chopped
½ c. chopped walnuts
1 tbsp. finely cut green celery
1 tbsp. finely cut green pepper
1 tbsp. minced fresh onion
1 tsp. salt
1 c. mayonnaise
½ c. heavy cream, whipped

Dissolve gelatin in boiling water; chill until thickened. Add all remaining ingredients except cream. Fold cream into the gelatin mixture. Pour into molds and chill overnight. Yield: 8 servings.

Mrs. A. P. Schaefer
March AFB, Calif.

SPRINGTIME SHRIMP MOUSSE

1 envelope unflavored gelatin
¼ c. cold water
1 can tomato soup
2 or 3 sm. pkg. cream cheese, crumbled
1 c. mayonnaise
¾ to 1 c. finely minced celery
¼ to ¾ c. finely minced green onions
¼ to ½ c. chopped green pepper (opt.)
Salt and white pepper to taste
2 sm. cans medium shrimp or ½ to 1 lb. boiled fresh or frozen shrimp

Soften gelatin in water. Bring soup to boiling point; do not boil. Melt cheese and gelatin in hot soup. Cool; add mayonnaise, celery, onions, green pepper, salt and pepper. Chill until thickened. Slice cleaned shrimp lengthwise; place in mold. Add gelatin and shrimp in alternate layers. Chill until firm. NOTE: This recipe may be varied by adding another envelope of gelatin and 1 more cup of water. Yield: 10-12 servings.

Mrs. Aline J. Owens
Norfolk, Va.

TANGY SHRIMP SALAD

½ lb. cooked fresh or frozen shrimp
1 3-oz. pkg. lemon gelatin
½ tsp. salt
1 c. boiling water
1 8-oz. can tomato sauce
1 ½ tbsp. vinegar
1 tsp. horseradish
1 tsp. grated onion
Dash of celery salt
Salad greens
1 avocado, sliced

Cut shrimp into 1/2-inch pieces. Dissolve gelatin and salt in boiling water. Add tomato sauce, vinegar, horseradish, onion, celery salt and shrimp; mix thoroughly. Pour into six individual 1/2-cup molds or custard cups; chill until firm. Unmold onto salad greens. Garnish with avocado slices.

(Continued on next page)

SOUR CREAM DRESSING:
⅓ c. sour cream
1 tbsp. lemon juice
½ tsp. horseradish
¼ tsp. salt

Combine all ingredients, mixing thoroughly. Chill. Top each salad with 1 tablespoon dressing.

Bobby Cork
Tuscaloosa, Ala.

AMERICAN NICOISE SALAD

1 sm. head lettuce, shredded
2 7-oz. cans solid pack tuna, drained
1 c. cooked sliced potatoes
1 c. cooked snap beans
3 hard-cooked eggs, quartered
3 sm. tomatoes, quartered
1 sm. red onion, thinly sliced and separated into rings
12 ripe olives, pitted

Place lettuce in large shallow bowl. Place large pieces of tuna in center of bowl. Surround with a ring of potatoes and a ring of beans. Alternate egg and tomato quarters around beans. Garnish with onion and olives.

SALAD DRESSING:
¾ tsp. salt
Dash of paprika
½ tsp. monosodium glutamate
⅓ c. lemon juice or vinegar
⅔ salad oil

Add salt, paprika and monosodium glutamate to lemon juice; stir with fork until dry ingredients are dissolved. Add oil; beat with fork until blended. Pour this dressing over salad just before serving. Yield: 6 servings.

Mrs. Irene Wells
Ulysses, Kans.

BOWL 'EM OVER SALAD

½ c. water
¼ c. butter or margarine
½ c. flour
⅛ tsp. salt
½ to 1 tsp. caraway seed
2 eggs

Preheat oven to 400 degrees. Bring water and butter to a boil in saucepan. Immediately stir in flour, salt and caraway seed. Stir vigorously over low heat for 1 minute or until mixture leaves sides of pan and forms a ball. Remove from heat; cool about 10 minutes. Add eggs, one at a time, beating until smooth after each addition. Spread batter evenly in greased 9-inch glass pie plate. Do not spread batter up sides of plate. Bake for 45 to 50 minutes. Cool away from drafts. The puff will form a bowl, high on the sides and flat in the center.

FILLING:
1 c. chopped tuna or crab meat
1 c. diced celery
1 c. lettuce hearts, broken into sm. pieces
1 tsp. lemon juice
1 tsp. finely minced onion
Salt and paprika to taste
Mayonnaise

Combine all ingredients, adding mayonnaise just before serving. Fill puff with mixture. Yield: 6-8 servings.

Mrs. Abbie Kehl
Waco, Tex.

MY FAMILY'S FAVORITE

1 sm. head lettuce, chopped
1 very sm. cucumber, chopped
2 tomatoes, chopped
1 6-oz. can tuna, flaked
1 8-oz. can fruit salad, drained
3 tbsp. salad dressing

Combine all ingredients; serve immediately. Yield: 4 servings.

Mrs. Charles Machamer
Cleveland, Miss.

PROTEIN SALAD BOWL

1 lge. head lettuce, torn into lge. pieces
4 hard-cooked eggs, quartered
4 tomatoes, peeled and quartered
4 thick slices American Swiss or Bleu cheese, cut into bite-sized chunks
6 dill pickles, sliced
½ c. halved walnuts
1 lge. red or white onion, sliced into rings
2 cans chunk-style tuna, drained
Salad dressing to taste

Toss all ingredients; serve chilled. Yield: 4-6 servings.

Mrs. Cecil Fuller
Washington, D.C.

SEAFOOD SALAD BOWL

1 head iceberg lettuce
1 cucumber, diced
1 sm. onion, diced
1 6-oz. can tuna or salmon
1 tbsp. lemon juice
1 c. salad dressing or mayonnaise
2 tbsp. milk

Break lettuce into bite-sized pieces; toss with cucumber, onion, tuna or salmon and lemon juice. Let stand for 10 minutes. Blend dressing with milk; add to salad. Chill; serve with crackers. Yield: 6-8 servings.

Mary C. Stapleton
Toledo, O.

SHOESTRING-TUNA SALAD

1 c. mayonnaise
1 tbsp. mustard
¾ c. milk
Dash of Tabasco sauce
2 7-oz. cans tuna, drained
1 ½ c. diced celery
1 4 ½-oz. can shoestring potatoes

Blend mayonnaise, mustard, milk and Tabasco sauce. Add tuna and celery. Chill. Immediately before serving add shoestring potatoes; mix just so they stick together. Serve on lettuce leaf. Yield: 8 servings.

Myrna E. Erickson
Cooperstown, N.D.

STUFFED TOMATO WITH TUNA

1 can tuna, flaked
2 hard-cooked eggs, chopped
6 to 8 crackers, crumbled
1 tsp. chopped onion
1 tbsp. chopped parsley
3 tbsp. chopped celery
2 tbsp. mayonnaise
6 med. tomatoes

Combine all ingredients except tomatoes. Cut top off tomatoes; scoop out inside. Fill each tomato with tuna mixture. Serve in lettuce cups. Yield: 6 servings.

Mrs. Pruda C. Prather
Carter, Ky.

SUSAN'S TUNA SALAD

1 head lettuce, torn into sm. pieces
2 to 4 tomatoes, cubed
1 green pepper, diced
Salt and pepper to taste
6 to 8 radishes, diced
1 13-oz. can chunk tuna
2 c. bite-sized cheese crackers
2 tbsp. mayonnaise

Combine all ingredients. Chill.

DRESSING:
1 clove of garlic
¾ tsp. salt
¼ tsp. Worcestershire sauce
4 c. mayonnaise
1 tbsp. vinegar

Crush garlic with salt; add remaining ingredients. Mix well. Chill. Serve with tuna mixture. Yield: 8 servings.

Mrs. Patricia Crouch Dabney
Columbia, S.C.

TUNA CRUNCH SALAD

1 7-oz. can tuna, drained
¼ c. chopped sweet pickles
1 tbsp. minced onion
1 to 2 tbsp. lemon juice
¾ c. salad dressing
1 ½ c. shredded cabbage
1 ¼ c. crushed potato chips

Combine tuna, pickles, onion, lemon juice and salad dressing. Cover; chill until ready to serve. Add cabbage; toss. Add 1 cup potato chips; toss lightly. Heap into shallow lettuce-lined bowl; sprinkle with remaining potato chips. Yield: 6 servings.

Arlene Lenort
Maynard, Minn.

TUNA-LETTUCE SALAD

1 med. head lettuce
1 can chunk tuna
1 can peas
½ c. chopped celery
¼ c. chopped onion
2 to 3 tbsp. salad dressing
Dash of salt

Core and wash lettuce. Combine tuna, peas, celery and onion. Add torn lettuce. Mix with salad dressing. Salt to taste. Yield: 6-8 servings.

Mrs. Martha Wilson
Jonesville, Mich.

TUNA-STUFFED TOMATOES

1 7-oz. can chunk tuna
1 tbsp. lemon juice
2 hard-cooked eggs, chopped
¼ c. thinly sliced sweet pickles
¼ c. finely chopped onion
2 tbsp. diced pimento
¼ tsp. salt
Dash of pepper
⅓ c. mayonnaise
4 tomatoes

Combine all ingredients except tomatoes; chill. Turn tomatoes stem-end down. Cut each almost through into six equal sections. Salt insides; fill with chilled tuna salad. Serve on lettuce. Yield: 4 servings.

Mrs. Philip N. Reger
Columbus, O.

TUNA-TOMATO STARS

1 tbsp. lemon juice
1 6 ½-oz. can chunk tuna
2 hard-cooked eggs, chopped
¼ c. chopped sweet pickles
¼ c. chopped onion
2 tbsp. chopped green pepper
¼ tsp. salt
⅓ c. mayonnaise
4 med. tomatoes

Sprinkle lemon juice on tuna. Add remaining ingredients except tomatoes; mix gently. Chill. Cut tomatoes partially through, with stem end down, into six equal sections. Spread apart; sprinkle with salt. Fill with tuna salad. Top with carrot curl. Yield: 4 servings.

Mrs. Gerald Elliott
Crete, Nebr.

TUNA WALDORF SALAD

1 red apple, chopped
1 tbsp. lemon juice
1 7-oz. can tuna, drained and flaked
1 c. cooked peas
1 tbsp. chopped pickle
½ c. chopped cooked carrots
⅛ tsp. salt
⅔ c. mayonnaise

Sprinkle apple with lemon juice; combine with all remaining ingredients. Chill. Yield: 4-6 servings.

Mrs. John J. Marlow
Andrews, Tex.

TUNA WALDORF SALAD

2 7-oz. cans tuna, drained and flaked
1 c. diced apples
½ c. chopped celery
1 c. chopped nuts
½ c. mayonnaise
Lettuce

Combine all ingredients; mix lightly. Serve on lettuce. Yield: 6 servings.

Mrs. Ralph Earhart
Elk City, Kans.

CONGEALED TUNA SALAD

2 pkg. lemon gelatin
2 c. hot water
¼ c. lemon juice
2 7-oz. cans tuna, cut into chunks
1 c. mayonnaise
1 ½ c. chopped celery
½ c. pickle relish
1 tbsp. minced onion
2 hard-cooked eggs, chopped

Dissolve gelatin in 1 cup hot water; add lemon juice. Chill until partially set. Pour 1 cup boiling water over tuna; drain. Fold in all remaining ingredients; chill until firm. Yield: 8-10 servings.

Mary Dean Bayles
Loda, Ill.

LUNCHEON SALAD

1 10 ½-oz. can cream of mushroom soup
2 pkg. unflavored gelatin
¼ c. vinegar
¼ c. cold water
2 3-oz. pkg. cream cheese
1 c. mayonnaise
1 sm. can minced pimento
2 cans tuna
1 med. onion, minced
½ c. sliced stuffed olives
½ c. sliced ripe olives
4 hard-cooked eggs, chopped
Dash of Tabasco sauce

Heat soup; soften gelatin in vinegar and water. Add to hot soup with cheese; stir until melted. Add all remaining ingredients; mix well. Chill for about 8 hours. NOTE: Chicken or turkey may be used for tuna. Yield: 6 servings.

Ginnie Ramsey
San Leandro, Calif.

TUNA MEAL IN ONE

½ head lettuce, broken into small pieces
1 9 ¼-oz. can flaked tuna
1 No. 303 can peas, drained
3 cooked potatoes, diced
2 sweet pickles, chopped
½ med. onion, chopped
½ c. chopped celery
Salt to taste
Salad dressing or mayonnaise

Reserve one-half of lettuce. Combine remaining lettuce with remaining ingredients. Toss lightly. Chill. Serve on reserved lettuce. Yield: 6 servings.

Mrs. Margaret C. Hoffman
Harrisville, Pa.

TUNA SALAD

1 can tuna
½ c. chopped cucumber
½ c. chopped celery
1 med. ripe tomato, chopped
1 sm. onion, finely chopped
2 hard-cooked eggs, chopped
½ tsp. salt
1 tbsp. mayonnaise
Lettuce or finely shredded cabbage

Combine all ingredients; mix lightly. Serve on lettuce or cabbage. Yield: 6-8 servings.

Berdie M. Hughes
Carmi, Ill.

TUNA SALAD

1 can tuna, flaked
2 hard-cooked eggs, diced
¼ c. diced onion
2 sweet pickles, diced
¼ c. mayonnaise
Salt and pepper to taste
4 lge. tomatoes

Gently blend all ingredients except tomatoes. Remove stem end from tomatoes; stuff with tuna salad. Yield: 4 servings.

Mrs. Winston Scott
Lacon, Ill.

TUNA SALAD

1 7-oz. can chunk-style tuna
½ c. diced celery
1 tbsp. minced onion
1 tbsp. lemon juice
½ c. chopped green pepper
¼ tsp. salt
Pepper to taste
3 hard-cooked eggs, quartered
2 tomatoes, chopped
¼ c. mayonnaise

Mix tuna, celery, onion, lemon juice, green pepper, salt and black pepper together. Add eggs, tomatoes and mayonnaise. Mix lightly until blended. Chill. Yield: 4 servings.

Sybil Widvey
Medford, Wisc.

LUAU TUNA SALAD

CURRIED MAYONNAISE:
¾ c. mayonnaise
¾ tsp. curry powder
1 tbsp. parsley flakes

Mix ingredients well.

SALAD:
1 13-oz. can tuna
1 c. pineapple chunks, drained
1 c. chopped celery
½ c. chopped walnuts

Combine tuna, pineapple, celery and walnuts. Fold in curried mayonnaise. Serve on lettuce leaves garnished with whole walnuts. Yield: 8 servings.

Mrs. Donald Young
Greenwood, Ark.

TUNA-SHOESTRING POTATO SALAD

6 carrots, shredded
½ c. diced celery
1 sm. onion, minced
1 7-oz. can tuna, drained
1 c. cooked salad dressing
3 tbsp. French dressing
2 tbsp. sugar
1 sm. can shoestring potatoes

Combine carrots, celery, onion and tuna in a bowl. In a separate bowl, combine dressings and sugar. Add dressing to salad mixture; stir until moistened. Add shoestring potatoes just before serving. Yield: 4 servings.

Mrs. Sandra Ericson
Stillwater, Minn.

MOLDED TUNA SALAD

3 7-oz. cans grated tuna
4 hard-cooked eggs, chopped
¼ c. chopped stuffed olives
2 tsbp. minced onion
1 c. diced celery
2 tbsp. gelatin
½ c. cold water
2 c. mayonnaise
Parsley
Celery curls

Combine tuna, eggs, olives, onion and celery. Sprinkle gelatin on cold water; dissolve over hot water. Stir into mayonnaise; add to tuna mixture. Blend well; turn into 9 x 5 x 3-inch loaf pan. Chill; unmold. Garnish with parsley and celery curls. Yield: 10 servings.

Mrs. Betty Temple
Fairfield, Ill.

MOLDED TUNA SALAD

2 tbsp. unflavored gelatin
½ c. cold water
1 can cream of chicken soup
¼ c. lemon juice
1 tbsp. mustard
1 tsp. salt
½ c. grated cucumber
¼ c. chopped green pepper
1 c. mayonnaise
1 c. coarsely chopped celery
2 6 ½-oz. cans tuna, drained and flaked

Soften gelatin in cold water. Heat soup until boiling. Remove from heat; add softened gelatin, stirring to dissolve. Blend in lemon juice, mustard and salt. Chill until partially set. Fold in all remaining ingredients. Pour into oiled 8 1/2 x 4 1/2 x 2 1/2-inch loaf pan or individual molds; chill until firm. Unmold; serve on salad greens. Yield: 8 servings.

Hazel Bussey
Alice, Tex.

MOLDED TUNA SALAD

1 pkg. lime gelatin
2 c. hot water
1 7-oz. can tuna, drained and flaked
1 tsp. lemon juice
½ tsp. salt
Dash of pepper
¼ tsp. paprika
1 c. chopped celery
1 hard-cooked egg, chopped
1 green pepper, chopped
1 sm. onion, chopped
1 cucumber, chopped
1 sprig parsley, chopped
1 c. chopped pecans

Dissolve gelatin in hot water; chill until slightly thickened. Combine all remaining ingredients; fold into gelatin. Pour into a 1 1/2-quart mold rinsed in cold water. Chill until firm. Unmold; serve. May be garnished with mayonnaise and pecan halves. Yield: 4-6 servings.

Mrs. Bob Patterson
Aberdeen, Miss.

MOLDED TUNA LOAF

1 pkg. lime gelatin
1 ½ c. boiling water
1 tbsp. vinegar
Dash of salt
½ c. diced celery
¼ c. mayonnaise
3 tbsp. minced onion
1 1-lb. carton cottage cheese
1 c. tuna, drained and flaked

Dissolve gelatin in boiling water; add vinegar and salt. Let cool until slightly thickened. Combine remaining ingredients with tuna. Fold into gelatin mixture; chill until firm. Yield: 4-6 servings.

Laura Howell
Ashley, Ill.

MONTEREY SOUFFLE SALAD

1 pkg. lemon gelatin
1 c. hot water
½ c. cold water
2 tbsp. lemon juice
½ c. salad dressing or mayonnaise
Salt to taste
1 6 ½-oz. can chunk tuna
¾ c. chopped celery or cucumbers
¼ c. sliced stuffed olives
2 tbsp. chopped pimento
½ tsp. grated onion

Dissolve gelatin in hot water. Add cold water, lemon juice, salad dressing and salt. Blend well with rotary beater. Pour into refrigerator freezing tray. Quick-chill in freezing unit for 15 to 20 minutes, or until firm about 1 inch from edge but soft in center. Whip with rotary beater until fluffy. Fold in remaining ingredients. Pour into 1-quart mold or individual molds. Chill until firm.

(Continued on next page)

Garnish with salad greens. Serve with more tuna and salad dressing, if desired. Yield: 4-6 servings.

Mrs. Doris Hybl
Bell, Fla.

SEAFOAM

1 pkg. lime gelatin
2 tbsp. mayonnaise
1 can tuna
1 c. chopped celery

Prepare gelatin according to package directions. Add remaining ingredients. Chill. Serve with crackers or chips. Yield: 6 servings.

Carolon Craft
Chalmette, La.

TUNA ASPIC SALAD

1 pkg. lime gelatin
1 c. boiling water
1 can tomato soup
1 bay leaf
1 can tuna, well drained
1 sm. can ripe olives, chopped

Dissolve gelatin in boiling water. Add soup and bay leaf; bring to a boil. Simmer for 5 minutes. Remove bay leaf. Pour into one large mold or four to six small molds; gently stir in tuna and olives until evenly distributed. Refrigerate for at least 4 hours or until firmly set. Yield: 4-6 servings.

Mrs. Virginia Gould
Belleville, Ill.

TUNA-CRANBERRY LOAF

TUNA LAYER:
2 envelopes unflavored gelatin
¼ c. cold water
2 cans cream of chicken soup
¼ c. mayonnaise
1 tbsp. minced parsley
1 c. white chunk tuna
¼ c. blanched almonds

Soften gelatin in water. Heat 1/4 can of soup; add gelatin. Stir until dissolved; add to remaining soup. Cool; fold in remaining ingredients. Pour into a 1 1/2-quart mold; chill until firm.

CRANBERRY LAYER:
1 can jellied cranberry sauce
1 envelope unflavored gelatin
¼ c. cold water
¼ c. chopped celery

Crush cranberry sauce with a fork. Soften gelatin in cold water; dissolve over boiling water. Mix into cranberry sauce; stir in celery. Pour over tuna layer; chill until firm. Yield: 8 servings.

Mrs. Lloyd R. Moses
Fort Sheridan, Ill.

TUNA GARDEN LOAF

2 tbsp. unflavored gelatin
½ c. cold water
1 can cream of celery soup
¼ c. lemon juice
1 tbsp. prepared mustard
1 tsp. salt
⅛ tsp. pepper
1 c. mayonnaise
2 7-oz. cans tuna
1 c. chopped celery
½ c. grated cucumber
¼ c. chopped green pepper

Soften gelatin in cold water. Heat soup to boiling. Add gelatin to soup; stir to dissolve. Stir in lemon juice, mustard, salt and pepper. Chill until partially set. Blend in mayonnaise. Fold in tuna, celery, cucumber and green pepper. Pour into 8 1/2 x 4 1/2 x 2 1/2-inch loaf pan. Chill until firm. Yield: 8 servings.

Mary Elizabeth Ball
Grand Rapids, Mich.

TUNA MOLD

1 envelope unflavored gelatin
½ c. cold water
½ c. hot water or pea stock
1 can tuna
½ c. chopped celery
1 sour pickle, chopped
½ c. chopped nuts
2 hard-cooked eggs, chopped
½ c. salad dressing
1 sm. can tiny English peas
1 tbsp. chopped onion
1 tbsp. Worcestershire sauce
2 to 3 tbsp. chopped pimento

Soften gelatin in cold water; dissolve in hot water. Rinse tuna in hot water; chop. Add tuna with all remaining ingredients to gelatin. Pour into individual molds or one large mold. Chill until set. Yield: 6 servings.

Mrs. Irvine Hurd
Brady, Tex.

TUNA MOUSSE

6 sm. cans tuna, flaked
2 green peppers, finely chopped
4 med. onions, finely chopped
1 can English peas
1 tbsp. gelatin
1 c. mayonnaise
1 c. heavy cream

Combine tuna, green peppers, onions and English peas. Soften gelatin in small amount of water; combine with mayonnaise and cream. Fold into tuna mixture; season to taste. Pour into a large lightly oiled mold; refrigerate.

SAUCE:
12 radishes, chopped
1 cucumber, chopped
1 jar capers
½ c. chives
2 tsp. lemon juice
Salt and pepper to taste
1 carton sour cream

Blend all ingredients well. Serve over tuna mousse. Yield: 12 servings.

Mrs. Robert W. Poellnitz
Tuscaloosa, Ala.

TUNA SALAD

1 can tuna, flaked
2 tbsp. lemon juice
1 envelope unflavored gelatin
¼ c. cold water
1 c. sour cream
2 tbsp. catsup
¾ tsp. salt
½ c. chopped green pepper
½ c. chopped celery

Marinate tuna in lemon juice. Soften gelatin in cold water; dissolve over hot water. Blend sour cream, catsup, salt, green pepper and celery; add to gelatin with tuna. Pour mixture into molds; chill thoroughly. Serve on lettuce. Yield: 6 servings.

Mrs. H. H. Watson
Dallas, Ga.

TUNA SALAD MOLD

2 envelopes gelatin
½ c. cold water
1 can cream of celery soup
1 tsp. mustard
½ tsp. salt
Dash of pepper
1 c. mayonnaise
2 6-oz. cans tuna, flaked
¼ c. chopped green pepper
1 tbsp. chopped pimento

Soften gelatin in cold water. Heat celery soup to boiling; add gelatin, mustard, salt and pepper. Mix well; chill until partially set. Blend in mayonnaise, tuna, green pepper and pimento. Pour into fish mold; chill until set. Unmold; define eyes with sliced stuffed olive and mouth with pimento strip. Yield: 6 servings.

Mildred Stoltzmann
Crystal Lake, Ill.

TUNA-TOMATO SALAD

1 1-lb. can tomatoes
1 3-oz. pkg. strawberry gelatin
3 tbsp. vinegar
1 7-oz. can tuna, drained and flaked
1 tbsp. chopped onion
2 tbsp. chopped green pepper (opt.)
½ c. chopped celery
½ tsp. salt

Heat tomatoes to boiling point; remove from heat. Add gelatin, stirring until dissolved. Fold in all remaining ingredients; chill until firm. Serve with mayonnaise. Yield: 6-8 servings.

Mrs. Albert L. Vandeveer
Troy, O.

TUNA-VEGETABLE SALAD LOAF

1 envelope unflavored gelatin
¼ c. cold water
¼ c. hot water
⅔ c. mayonnaise
2 tsp. prepared mustard
2 tbsp. lemon juice
1 7-oz. can tuna
¾ c. minced celery
½ c. canned peas
2 tbsp. minced pimento
1 tsp. salt
1 hard-cooked egg, chopped

Soften gelatin in cold water. Dissolve in hot water. Combine mayonnaise, mustard and lemon juice. Add dissolved gelatin. Mix tuna, celery, peas, pimento, salt and egg. Combine with gelatin mixture; pour into loaf pan and chill. Yield: 8 servings.

Mrs. Robbie Hanks
El Paso, Tex.

SCALLOP SALAD

½ pt. fresh sea scallops, washed and drained
2 tbsp. water
1 tbsp. plus ½ tsp. lemon juice
2 tbsp. mayonnaise
2 tbsp. tartar sauce
1 tsp. tarragon vinegar
⅛ tsp. salt
Dash of pepper
½ c. sliced celery
2 tbsp. diced pimento
Salad greens
Green pepper strips or rings
Celery strips

Combine scallops, water and 1 tablespoon lemon juice in saucepan. Bring to a boil; simmer, covered, for 2 to 5 minutes. Drain; chill. Cut scallops into quarters. Blend mayonnaise, tartar sauce, vinegar, remaining 1/2 teaspoon lemon juice, salt and pepper. Toss with scallops, sliced celery and pimento. Chill until serving time. Mound on salad greens. Garnish with green pepper and celery strips as desired. Yield: 3 servings.

Photograph for this recipe above.

FROZEN FISH SALAD

1 1-lb. pkg. frozen codfish
½ tsp. salt
4 tbsp. chopped pickle
4 tsbp. chopped onion
4 tbsp. chopped pimento
Salad dressing

Place fish in salted water. Cook for 15 to 20 minutes or until well done. Combine pickle, onion, pimento and fish. Add salad dressing to moisten. May be used as sandwich filling, cream cheese dip, or as spread for crackers. Yield: 8 servings.

Billie Lue Bosher
Amherst, Tex.

SARDINE SALAD

4 med. sardines
2 hard-cooked eggs, quartered
Lettuce leaves
½ c. mayonnaise

Drain sardines; cut each into four pieces. Place sardines and eggs on lettuce; top with mayonnaise. Yield: 4 servings.

Mrs. Hollis Corbin
APO, N.Y.

MIXED HERRING SALAD

3 fresh salted herring
1 sm. cooked beet, chopped
2 cooking apples, chopped
Chopped pickled onions and gherkins
8 cold cooked potatoes, diced
2 hard-cooked eggs
Shredded lettuce or curly endive
2 tbsp. salad oil
2 tbsp. vinegar
Salt
Mayonnaise

Soak herring for 24 hours in small amount of milk or water; cut into small pieces, reserving a few for garnish. Combine herring with beet, apples, onions, gherkins and potatoes. Chop an egg; add to herring mixture with lettuce. Blend with oil, vinegar and salt. Place salad on a flat dish; smooth top with wet spoon. Cover with mayonnaise; garnish with remaining egg, cut into quarters, and remaining herring pieces. Serve with toast and butter. Yield: 4-6 servings.

Mrs. Gail van den Doel
East Troy, Wisc.

BAKED SEAFOOD SALAD

1 med. green pepper, chopped
1 med. onion, chopped
1 c. chopped celery
Butter
½ lb. crab meat
1 c. cleaned shrimp
1 tsp. salt
¼ tsp. pepper
1 tsp. Worcestershire sauce
½ c. mayonnaise
½ c. sour cream
¼ to ½ c. Sherry
1 c. buttered crumbs

Saute green pepper, onion and celery in small amount of butter. Combine with all remaining ingredients except crumbs. Place in individual shells or greased casserole. Sprinkle with crumbs. Bake at 350 degrees for 30 minutes. Yield: 8 servings.

Mrs. Lawrence Anderson
Ft. Eustis, Va.

BAKED SEAFOOD SALAD

2 c. shrimp
2 c. crab meat
2 c. chopped green pepper
½ c. minced onion
2 c. mayonnaise
1 tbsp. Worcestershire sauce
Salt to taste
½ tsp. pepper
2 c. buttered bread crumbs

Combine all ingredients except 1 cup bread crumbs. Place in casserole or individual shells. Sprinkle with remaining bread crumbs. Bake at 350 degrees for 45 minutes. Let stand for 5 minutes before serving. NOTE: Salad may be mixed the day before baking. Yield: 8 servings.

Mrs. Joseph Higgins
New Orleans, La.

BAKED SEAFOOD SALAD

1 10 to 12-oz. pkg. frozen shrimp, peeled and deveined
1 6 ½-oz. can crab meat
1 ½ c. finely chopped celery
½ c. finely chopped green pepper
¼ c. finely chopped onion
1 c. mayonnaise
1 tsp. Worcestershire sauce
½ tsp. salt
1 ½ c. crushed potato chips
½ tsp. paprika
2 tbsp. butter or margarine

Drop shrimp into boiling salted water; cook for 1 minute after water returns to boil or until shrimp are pink. If shrimp are large, cut into 1/2-inch pieces. Combine with crab, celery, green pepper and onion. Mix mayonnaise with Worcestershire sauce and salt; fold in. Spread into 2-quart buttered baking dish or into six individual casseroles. Bake at 400 degrees for 10 minutes. Blend potato chips with paprika; sprinkle over mixture. Dot with butter; bake for 10 minutes or until potato chips are brown. Yield: 6 servings.

Mrs. Betty Mitchell
Monroe, Conn.

CRAB-TUNA SALAD

1 6 ½-oz. can crab meat
1 6 ½-oz. can tuna
½ tsp. salt
¼ tsp. pepper
Garlic powder to taste
½ tsp. Worcestershire sauce
¼ tsp. Tabasco sauce
⅛ onion, minced
⅛ green pepper, minced
1 stalk celery and leaves, diced
2 pieces pimento, diced
3 hard-cooked eggs, diced
2 or 3 tbsp. salad pickles, diced
½ c. mayonnaise
Lettuce leaves

(Continued on next page)

Sprinkle crab and tuna with salt, pepper, garlic powder, Worcestershire and Tabasco sauces. Refrigerate for a few hours or overnight. Mix with all remaining ingredients except lettuce leaves. Chill. Serve on crisp lettuce. Yield: 4-5 servings.

Mrs. James Codron
Eufaula, Ala.

HOT SEAFOOD SALAD

1 ½ pt. shrimp, halved lengthwise
1 ½ pt. lobster pieces
½ c. chopped pimento
1 pt. mayonnaise
3 lge. cans asparagus
4 hard-cooked eggs, sliced
2 or 3 stalks celery, chopped
Crumbled Ritz crackers (opt.)
Chopped almonds (opt.)

Combine all ingredients except crackers and almonds. Spread evenly in large casserole; top with cracker crumbs or almonds. Bake at 300 degrees for 40 minutes. Yield: 12 servings.

Mrs. Myra Lamar
Fort Worth, Tex.

HOT SEAFOOD SALAD

1 c. cooked crab
1 c. cooked shrimp
1 c. chopped celery
1 c. chopped green pepper
1 c. mayonnaise
½ c. chopped onion
1 tsp. Worcestershire sauce
½ tsp. salt
½ tsp. pepper
3 hard-cooked eggs, chopped
½ c. buttered almonds
Buttered bread crumbs

Combine all ingredients except bread crumbs. Pour into casserole; top with crumbs. Bake at 350 degrees for 30 minutes. Yield: 8 servings.

Mrs. Lauretta Koelper
Northbrook, Ill.

PINEAPPLE- SEAFOOD SALAD

2 tbsp. flour
1 tsp. salt
1 tsp. paprika
1 tsp. dry mustard
½ c. vinegar
3 tbsp. light molasses
¾ c. salad oil
1 tbsp. grated onion
1 tbsp. horseradish
1 tbsp. poppy seed

Combine dry ingredients in saucepan. Blend in vinegar, molasses and 1 tablespoon salad oil. Cook over low heat until thickened, stirring constantly. Add onion, horseradish and poppy seed. Cool. Add remaining oil gradually, beating constantly. Chill. Shake before using.

SALAD:

1 avocado
3 tbsp. lemon juice
1 can large shrimp
1 can crab
1 sm. head lettuce, cut up
2 grapefruit, sectioned
1 can pineapple chunks, drained
1 ½ c. chopped celery
¾ c. almonds

Chill all ingredients. Slice avocado; sprinkle with lemon juice. Place all ingredients in bowl; toss with dressing. Yield: 8 servings.

Mrs. Don G. Lewis
The Dalles, Oreg.

BRUSSELS SPROUT AND TUNA MOUSSE

2 10-oz. pkg. frozen California Brussels sprouts
3 envelopes unflavored gelatin
2 ½ tsp. salt
1 c. boiling water
¼ c. thin canned pimento strips
2 c. sour cream
4 c. chopped watercress
1 c. mayonnaise
3 tbsp. lemon juice
2 6 ½ to 7-oz. cans tuna, drained and flaked
½ c. boiling vegetable stock or bouillon

Cook Brussels sprouts according to package directions; drain, if necessary, and cool. Reserve 4 to 6 sprouts for garnish. Cut 18 sprouts in half crosswise. Using rounded halves of cut sprouts, place each half, rounded-side down, in bottom of well oiled 6 1/2 cup ring mold. Reserve remaining Brussels sprouts halves. Dissolve 1 envelope gelatin and 1/2 teaspoonful salt in boiling water; cool. Carefully pour 2/3 cup gelatin mixture over arranged Brussels sprout halves. Chill until set. Arrange pimento strips directly above sprouts against outside edge of mold. Pour remaining gelatin over pimento; chill until set. Combine remaining Brussels sprouts, sour cream, watercress, remaining salt, mayonnaise, lemon juice and tuna. Blend in electric blender or force through food mill. Dissolve remaining gelatin in vegetable stock. Cool slightly and blend into Brussels sprout mixture. Spoon into mold; chill until set. Unmold and garnish with reserved Brussels sprouts. Serve with mayonnaise. Yield: 6-8 servings.

Photograph for this recipe on page 341.

FOREIGN SALADS

RECIPE FOR ORIENTAL CRANBERRY SALAD ON PAGE 369

COLESLAW (AFRICA)

1 tsp. salt
¼ tsp. pepper
½ tsp. dry mustard
1 tsp. celery seed
2 tbsp. sugar
¼ c. chopped green pepper
1 tbsp. chopped red pepper or pimento
½ tsp. grated onion
3 tbsp. cooking oil
⅓ c. vinegar
3 c. finely chopped cabbage

Combine all ingredients in order given; mix well. Cover and chill thoroughly. Yield: 4 servings.

Beth Ann Dugal
Wilmot, Ark.

ASSYRIAN SALAD (ASSYRIA)

1 c. Assyrian wheat or wheat germ
1 head lettuce, broken into bite-size pieces
1 lb. tomatoes, finely diced
1 sm. bunch parsley, finely diced
1 onion, finely diced
1 cucumber, finely diced
Diced carrots (opt.)
Diced celery (opt.)
Juice of 2 lemons
3 tbsp. olive oil
Salt to taste
Sugar (opt.)

Cover wheat with warm water; let stand for 30 minutes. Combine vegetables; add soaked wheat. Combine all remaining ingredients; pour over salad. Serve immediately. Yield: 6 servings.

Mrs. Alma L. Graven
Blackwell, Okla.

CHINESE BEAN SALAD (CHINA)

1 lge. green pepper, chopped
1 onion, grated
1 can kidney beans, drained
1 can yellow beans, drained
1 can Garbanzo beans, drained
1 can bean sprouts, drained

Combine all ingredients in large bowl.

DRESSING:
½ c. vinegar
½ c. salad oil
½ c. sugar
1 tbsp. salt
Pepper to taste

Blend all ingredients. Pour over bean mixture. Marinate for 12 to 24 hours. Drain before serving. Yield: 12 servings.

Mrs. Porter Houghland
Springfield, Idaho

CHINESE SALAD (CHINA)

1 5-oz. can noodles
1 tsp. garlic salt
3 tbsp. butter, melted
1 tsp. curry powder
2 tsp. Worcestershire sauce
2 qt. salad greens
1 tbsp. vinegar
½ c. ripe olives
2 tbsp. salad oil

Combine noodles, garlic salt, butter, curry powder and Worcestershire sauce. Heat for 15 minutes at 200 degrees. Just before serving, toss noodle mixture with all remaining ingredients. Yield: 8-10 servings.

Joyce Tower
Braham, Minn.

CHINESE SALAD WITH HOT SAUCE (CHINA)

1 chicken breast
2 eggs, beaten
1 carrot, cut into 2-in. strips
1 cucumber, peeled and sliced lengthwise
1 stalk celery, cut into 2-in. strips
2 onions, cut into 2-in. strips
2 boiled ham slices, cut into 2-in. strips

Cook chicken in salted water. Cool and cut into 2-inch strips. Drop eggs by tablespoonfuls into lightly greased skillet. Fry on each side, similar to a pancake. Cool and cut into 2-inch strips. Boil carrot for 1 minute; cool. Combine all ingredients except chives. Garnish with chives.

HOT SAUCE:
2 tsp. (heaping) dry mustard
2 tsp. sugar
3 tbsp. soy sauce
3 tbsp. vinegar
Add enough warm water to mustard to make a paste; beat vigorously. Gradually add all remaining ingredients, mixing well after each addition. Just before serving, pour sauce over salad and toss. Yield: 4 servings.

Mrs. Douglas W. Stanton, Jr.
Fort Lee AFS, Va.

LENG P'EN SALAD DRESSING (CHINA)

3 tsp. vinegar or lemon juice
3 tsp. soy sauce
1 tsp. sugar
2 tsp. salad oil

Combine vinegar, soy sauce and sugar; add oil slowly, stirring constantly. Serve over vegetable salads. NOTE: Omit oil for low-calorie diet. This dressing may be made in advance, does not need refrigeration.

Mrs. Eileen A. Beaty
APO New York

ORIENTAL CRANBERRY SALAD (CHINA)

1 pkg. orange flavored gelatin
1 c. boiling water
½ c. cold water
1 tbsp. lemon juice
1 14-oz. jar cranberry orange relish
2 tbsp. crystallized ginger
1 5-oz. can water chestnuts, drained and chopped
½ tsp. celery seed

Dissolve gelatin in boiling water. Add cold water and lemon juice. Chill until slightly thickened. Fold in cranberry orange relish, ginger, water chestnuts and celery seed. Pour into molds. Chill until firm. Yield: 6 servings.

Photograph for this recipe on page 367.

SALAD A LA ORIENTAL (CHINA)

1 1-lb. 14-oz. can pineapple chunks, drained
1 1-lb. can bean sprouts, drained
2 c. shredded lettuce, chilled
¾ c. fresh orange sections or canned Mandarin oranges
½ c. chopped cashews
⅓ c. mayonnaise
¾ tsp. soy sauce

Drain pineapple, reserving syrup. Marinate bean sprouts in pineapple syrup for 15 minutes; drain. Toss together bean sprouts, pineapple chunks, lettuce, orange sections and cashews. Combine mayonnaise and soy sauce. Add to salad ingredients and toss gently to coat evenly. Yield: 6 servings.

Mrs. Winona J. Weikum
Patuxent NAS, Md.

SHANGHAI SALAD (CHINA)

1 tsp. soy sauce
¼ c. French dressing
1 lb. cooked diced veal
2 c. bean sprouts
½ c. sweet pickles
¼ c. shredded onion
1 tsp. salt
½ tsp. pepper
¼ tsp. monosodium glutamate
¾ c. mayonnaise

Blend soy sauce with French dressing. Cover veal with mixture; refrigerate overnight. Add bean sprouts, pickles, onion, salt, pepper and monsodium glutamate. Blend mayonnaise in gently; serve on lettuce. Yield: 4 servings.

Mrs. Agnes M. Hanson
White Sands, N.M.

SHANGHAI SALAD (CHINA)

½ pkg. fresh spinach
1 lge. head lettuce
1 can bean sprouts
1 can water chestnuts, sliced
1 green pepper, chopped
½ c. sliced toasted almonds
½ c. chopped celery

Tear lettuce and spinach into bite-sized pieces. Combine all ingredients in large wooden salad bowl.

DRESSING

1 pt. mayonnaise
1 ½ tsp. mustard
½ tsp. Tabasco sauce
2 tsp. chili powder
1 tsp. onion juice
2 tbsp. vinegar
1 ½ tsp. ground marjoram
¾ tsp. thyme
1 ½ tsp. minced garlic

Combine all ingredients in order listed; mix well. Add just enough dressing to salad to coat all vegetables. Yield: 8-10 servings.

June B. Keifer
Batavia, O.

SALATA BEDINGAN--EGGPLANT SALAD (EGYPT)

1 eggplant, peeled and cut into ½-in. slices slices
2 tomatoes, sliced

Saute eggplant in butter until soft; drain on absorbent paper. Alternate rows of eggplant and tomatoes on a platter. Serve with oil and vinegar dressing, seasoned to taste. Yield: 4 servings.

Ruth Metaweh
Villard, Minn.

ECUADORIAN SEVICHE (ECUADOR)

2 lb. striped bass
½ c. lime juice
1 tsp. salt
⅛ tsp. Tabasco sauce
½ c. orange juice
1 ½ tsp. minced onion
1 ½ tsp. minced pepper
1 tsp. snipped chives or cilantro
1 tbsp. catsup
1 Spanish onion, thinly sliced
4 scallions, finely chopped
½ fresh red pimento, finely chopped
12 orange sections

Cut bass into small slices; marinate for 12 hours in mixture of lime juice, salt and Tabasco sauce. Add orange juice, minced onion, pepper, chives and catsup to marinade. Arrange fish in deep dish; add marinade. Place Spanish onion slices in center of fish. Sprinkle with scallions and pimento; garnish with orange sections.

Photograph for this recipe above.

RHUBARB AND ONION PICKLE (ENGLAND)

1 qt. cubed rhubarb
1 qt. chopped onion
1 pt. vinegar
2 lb. brown sugar
1 tbsp. salt
1 tbsp. ginger
⅛ tsp. cayenne pepper
½ tsp. paprika
1 tsp. cloves
1 tsp. mace
1 tsp. allspice
1 tsp. nutmeg
1 tsp. pepper
1 tsp. cinnamon

Combine all ingredients; cook over medium heat to consistency of chili sauce, stirring often. Seal in sterilized jars. Yield: 2 quarts.

Mrs. Lois E. Pritchard
Susquehanna, Pa.

BEET SALAD (FINLAND)

1 c. cooked diced beets
2 c. cooked diced potatoes
¾ c. cooked diced carrots
2 tbsp. diced onion
¾ c. herring or anchovies
¼ c. vinegar
Salt to taste
Lettuce
Hard-cooked egg slices

(Continued on next page)

Combine all ingredients except lettuce and egg slices. Chill for 2 to 4 hours. Serve on lettuce; garnish with egg slices. Yield: 6 servings.

Mrs. Fred Lamppa
Chisholm, Minn.

SIENISALAATTI--MUSHROOM SALAD (FINLAND)

3 c. fresh or salted mushrooms
½ sm. onion, grated
1 ½ tsp. sugar
3 tbsp. cream
White pepper

Boil fresh mushrooms in salted water; slice very thin. Combine all ingredients; place in salad bowl. NOTE: If salted mushrooms are used, rinse thoroughly many times or soak overnight in fresh water. Yield: 4 servings.

Elma Ranta
Negaunee, Mich.

BEAN SALAD (FRANCE)

1 can French-style green beans, drained
1 can yellow French-style beans, drained
1 can bean sprouts, drained
½ c. chopped onion
½ c. chopped green pepper
¾ c. sugar
½ c. salad oil
½ c. vinegar
½ tsp. salt
½ tsp. pepper

Combine vegetables in large bowl. Blend sugar, salad oil, vinegar, salt and pepper. Pour over vegetables and toss. Refrigerate for 12 hours before using. Will keep for two weeks.

Mrs. Hulbert Clark
Bancroft, Wisc.

FRENCH SLAW (FRANCE)

10 c. vinegar
15 c. sugar
15 tsp. salt
15 tsp. celery seed
15 tsp. mustard seed
7 ½ tsp. turmeric powder
20 lge. cabbages, shredded
10 sweet onions, chopped
12 green peppers, chopped
2 bunches radishes, sliced
1 bunch carrots, sliced

Mix vinegar, sugar and seasonings. Pour over vegetables. Let stand for 2 hours before serving. Yield: 300 servings.

Mrs. Robert Mandeville
Troy, N.Y.

MARINADE DE TROIX LEGAMES (FRANCE)

1 No. 2 can cut green beans, drained
1 No. 2 can wax beans, drained
1 No. 2 can kidney beans, washed and drained
1 onion, cut into rings
1 green pepper, cut into rings
⅓ c. salad oil
⅔ c. vinegar
¾ c. sugar
1 tsp. monosodium glutamate
½ tsp. pepper
1 tsp. salt

Combine beans, onion and pepper. Mix remaining ingredients; add to bean mixture. Let stand for 24 hours.

Mrs. Doris C. Dunford
Flagstaff, Ariz.

SALADE NICOISE (FRANCE)

6 med. potatoes, boiled
½ c. finely chopped onion
1 tbsp. chopped fresh basil
3 tbsp. chopped parsley
1 tsp. salt
½ tsp. freshly ground pepper
¾ c. olive oil
¼ c. wine vinegar
3 ripe tomatoes, peeled and cut into sixths
1 can tuna in olive oil, broken into chunks
20 to 30 anchovy fillets
4 to 6 hard-cooked eggs, peeled and sliced
Green pepper, cut into rings
Pitted black olive
Romaine or Bibb lettuce

Toss potatoes and onion with basil, parsley, salt, pepper, oil and vinegar. Garnish with all remaining ingredients. Serve with an oil and vinegar dressing, sprinkled with additional chopped parsley and basil. Yield: 6 servings.

Mrs. J. H. Cochran, Jr.
Ft. Benning, Ga.

SHRIMP SALAD DEAUVILLE (FRANCE)

2 c. cooked cleaned shrimp
½ c. walnut halves

(Continued on next page)

1 apple, sliced
3 hard-cooked eggs, halved
1 c. canned mushrooms, drained
1 c. shredded iceberg lettuce
1 tbsp. vinegar
1 tsp. mustard
¾ tsp. salt
Pinch of cayenne pepper
2 tbsp. vegetable oil
1 tbsp. minced celery
1 tbsp. mayonnaise

Arrange chilled shrimp, walnut halves, apple, eggs, mushrooms and lettuce in a salad bowl. Thoroughly mix all remaining ingredients; pour over salad. Yield: 4-6 servings.

Gayle E. Mitchell
Quincy, Calif.

BAVARIAN SALAD (GERMANY)

2 c. hot water
1 3-oz. pkg. lime or orange gelatin
20 lge. or 2 c. sm. marshmallows
½ to 1 c. chopped nuts
½ pt. heavy cream, whipped
1 can crushed pineapple
1 to 1 ½ c. grated American or Cheddar cheese

Pour hot water over gelatin. Melt marshmallows in hot gelatin. Chill until firm. Add all remaining ingredients and refrigerate until serving time. Yield: 12 servings.

Mrs. Raymond Sealey
Red Oak, Tex.

BITTA POTUFFEL--SWEET POTATO SALAD (GERMANY)

4 med. sweet potatoes
¼ tsp. salt
1 tbsp. finely chopped onion
2 tbsp. vinegar
2 tbsp. brown sugar
2 tbsp. margarine

Cook potatoes in boiling salted water; drain and mash. Combine with all remaining ingredients; serve hot. Yield: 8 servings.

Mrs. Myrtle Wood
Rogers, Tex.

COLESLAW (GERMANY)

1 c. shredded cabbage
3 tbsp. chopped onion
¼ c. chopped parsley
1 tbsp. salad oil
2 tsp. salt
1 ½ tbsp. vinegar
1 ½ tbsp. sugar

Combine cabbage, onion and parsley. Add all remaining ingredients and toss lightly. Yield: 4 servings.

Mrs. Norman Little
Albuquerque, N.M.

HERRING AND APPLE SALAD

1 c. diced pickled herring
3 apples, diced
5 potatoes, cooked and diced
3 tbsp. minced onion
4 hard-cooked eggs, diced
1 ½ c. sour cream
3 tbsp. mayonnaise
1 tbsp. sugar
4 tbsp. vinegar

Mix all ingredients. Refrigerate for at least 3 hours before serving. Serve on lettuce leaves.

Grace A. Kurz
Shannon, Ill.

HERRING SALAD (GERMANY)

1 12-oz. glass herring fillets
1 lb. potatoes, cooked
2 apples
1 dill pickle
3 tbsp. salad oil
1 to 2 tbsp. vinegar
Dash of salt
1 tsp. mustard
1 sm. onion, diced

Dice herring fillets, potatoes, apples and dill pickle; place in dish. Beat oil, vinegar, salt, and mustard until mixture thickens; add onion and pour over herring mixture. Mix well. Let stand for several hours before serving. Yield: 4 servings.

Briggitte-Maria Theisen
Escanaba, Mich.

HOT GERMAN SALAD DRESSING (GERMANY)

1 tbsp. animal fat
Dash of salt
½ c. vinegar
1 egg
2 tbsp. sugar

Combine fat, salt and vinegar; bring to a boil. Beat egg and sugar well; pour into fat and vinegar. Cook to boiling point; stir well. Serve over potato salad or cole slaw. Yield: 6 servings.

Edith M. Keenan
Hopewell, Va.

HOT POTATO SALAD (GERMANY)

4 lge. potatoes
4 slices bacon
2 tsp. minced onion
½ c. vinegar
¼ c. water
¼ c. sugar
2 tsp. salt
¼ tsp. pepper
1 tsp. dry mustard
¼ c. chopped parsley

Cook potatoes with jackets on; salt lightly. Cover with cold water to hasten cooling. Peel; cut into cubes. Mince bacon; fry until crisp. Combine onion, vinegar, water, sugar, salt, pepper and mustard; heat. Add potatoes and bacon. Heat slowly and mix to flavor potatoes. Garnish with parsley. Yield: 8 servings.

Mrs. Joyce Carder
Madison, Wisc.

HOT SLAW (GERMANY)

3 c. chopped cabbage
½ tsp. salt
1 tbsp. butter
1 tbsp. flour
⅓ c. light cream
1 tbsp. vinegar
1 egg, well beaten

Cook cabbage in salted water until tender; drain or allow to cook dry. Melt butter; stir in flour. Add cream, vinegar and egg; cook until slightly thickened. Add to cooked cabbage and heat. Yield: 5-6 servings.

Hilda Rohlf
Tallmadge, O.

POTATO SALAD (GERMANY)

3 lb. potatoes
3 strips bacon, diced
¼ c. chopped onion
1 tbsp. flour
2 tsp. salt
1 ¼ tbsp. sugar
¼ tsp. pepper
⅔ c. vinegar
⅓ c. water

Simmer potatoes in jackets until tender; peel and thinly slice. Fry bacon until crisp; add onion. Cook for 1 minute. Blend in flour, salt, sugar and pepper. Stir in vinegar and water. Cook for 10 minutes, stirring occasionally. Pour bacon mixture over warm potatoes. Serve warm.

Mrs. Pauline Wattner
Seagoville, Tex.

POTATO SALAD (GERMANY)

8 potatoes
1 stalk celery, diced
2 hard-cooked eggs, sliced
1 onion, minced
1 tbsp. minced parsley
4 slices bacon, diced
2 eggs, well beaten
1 c. sugar
½ tsp. dry mustard
½ tsp. salt
¼ tsp. pepper
½ c. vinegar
½ c. cold water

Boil potatoes in jackets until soft; peel and dice. Add celery, eggs, onion and parsley. Fry bacon until crisp and lightly browned. Combine beaten eggs, sugar, mustard, salt, pepper, vinegar and water. Mix well. Pour egg mixture into hot bacon and fat; cook until mixture thickens, stirring constantly. Pour bacon mixture over potato mixture; mix lightly. Let stand in a cold place for several hours.

Lucile S. Brown
Hartland, Mich.

POTATO SALAD (GERMANY)

5 slices bacon, diced
½ c. chopped onion
1 tbsp. flour
⅔ c. water
½ c. vinegar
1 tbsp. sugar
1 ¼ tsp. salt
¼ tsp. pepper
2 c. sliced cooked potatoes

Brown bacon and onion. Add flour; stir until smooth. Combine water, vinegar, sugar, salt and pepper; slowly add to bacon-onion mixture. Add potatoes and mix lightly. Cover tightly and simmer for 20 minutes. Serve hot. Yield: 8 servings.

Mrs. Charles Scott
Indio, Calif.

SAUERKRAUT SALAD

1 c. sugar
½ c. vinegar
1 No. 2 ½ can sauerkraut, drained
½ c. chopped green pepper
½ c. chopped onion
½ c. sliced celery
2 tbsp. chopped pimento
1 tsp. dill seed
¼ c. salad oil

Bring sugar and vinegar to a hard boil. Combine all remaining ingredients. Pour sugar

(Continued on next page)

mixture over sauerkraut mixture. Place salad in covered container; let stand overnight in refrigerator. Yield: 6 servings.

Mrs. Robert H. Irion
Kingsville, Tex.

SENFGLEE--MUSTARD RELISH MOLD (GERMANY)

2 envelopes unflavored gelatin
½ c. cold water
1 ½ c. sugar
1 ½ tbsp. dry mustard
2 tsp. monosodium glutamate
1 ¼ tsp. salt
6 eggs, slightly beaten
2 c. vinegar
1 1-lb. can green peas, drained
1 c. grated carrots
1 c. chopped celery
1 tbsp. minced parsley

Sprinkle gelatin evenly over water; let stand for 5 minutes. Combine sugar, mustard, monosodium glutamate and salt; add eggs. Gradually add vinegar; cook over simmering water, stirring constantly, until thickened. Remove from heat; stir in softened gelatin. Cool until mixture begins to congeal; add peas, carrots, celery and parsley. Pour into an oiled mold; chill until firm. Yield: 12 servings.

June Kreutzkampf
Hawarden, Iowa

GREEK SALAD DRESSING (GREECE)

1 slice white bread
1 jar American lumfish or caviar
1 sm. pkg. cream cheese
1 tsp. chopped onion
Juice of ⅛ lemon
Dash of Tabasco sauce

Moisten bread with water; squeeze out. Place with remaining ingredients in blender; mix well. NOTE: Dressing improves with age. Yield: 6 servings.

Mrs. C. P. Mahaffey
Richland, Va.

CHICKEN SALAD HAWAIIAN (HAWAII)

2 c. diced cooked chicken
3 hard-cooked eggs, chopped
¼ tsp. salt
½ c. sliced celery
1 c. pineapple cubes, drained
¼ c. sliced stuffed olives
¼ c. diced sweet pickles
French dressing to taste

Combine all ingredients. Chill and serve with additional French dressing or mayonnaise. NOTE: Canned tuna may be substituted for chicken; salad may be served on pineapple rings. Yield: 6 servings.

Mrs. Helen A. Gerald
Hilo, Hawaii

DUTCH LETTUCE (HOLLAND)

3 slices bacon, cut into sm. pieces
¼ c. plus 1 ½ tsp. flour
½ tbsp. sugar
¼ c. water
¼ c. vinegar
½ head lettuce, torn into bite-sized pieces
2 onions, chopped
½ bunch green spinach

Fry bacon on medium heat until crisp and brown; drain off all fat except 1 tablespoon. Sift 1 1/2 teaspoons flour and sugar into reserved fat and bacon pieces. Cook over low heat, stirring constantly until smooth. Combine 1/4 cup flour, water and vinegar; add to bacon paste. Stir until thickened. Combine lettuce, onions and spinach. Pour warm bacon dressing over lettuce mixture. Yield: 2-4 servings.

Mrs. C. N. Davis
Felton, Minn.

HULD'S SHRIMP SALAD (ICELAND)

3 c. boiled shrimp
½ c. grated cheese
1 apple, cut into strips
1 sm. carrot, cooked and cut into strips
⅓ c. sweet peas
5 tbsp. mayonnaise
2 tbsp. sour cream
4 tbsp. grated carrots
4 tbsp. finely chopped cauliflower
4 tbsp. chopped onion

Arrange ingredients separately on the same platter; chill.

DRESSING:
1 to 2 tbsp. lemon juice
6 tbsp. olive or salad oil
6 tbsp. water
1 ½ tsp. honey

Combine all ingredients. Pour over shrimp platter just before serving. Yield: 6 servings.

Mrs. Jeannine K. Goethe
Savannah, Ga.

BOMBAY CHICKEN SALAD (INDIA)

2 c. cooked diced chicken
½ c. raw rice, cooked
½ c. India or sweet pickle relish
¼ c. mayonnaise
1 tbsp. sour or heavy cream
1 can pimento, chopped
1 c. shredded coconut
Paprika

Combine chicken, rice and relish; toss until well blended. Mix mayonnaise and cream; add to chicken mixture. Add pimento and coconut; garnish with mayonnaise and paprika. Serve at room temperature. Yield: 6 servings.

Mrs. Willard Johnson
Palestine, Tex.

INDIAN COLESLAW (INDIA)

¼ c. mayonnaise
¼ c. sour cream
¾ tsp. salt
Dash of pepper
4 c. shredded cabbage
1 8-oz. can whole kernel corn, drained
¼ c. chopped green pepper
¼ c. chopped pimento

Combine mayonnaise, sour cream, salt and pepper. Pour over combined vegetables and toss lightly. Yield: 6-8 servings.

Mary J. Delich
Bethel, Kans.

PACHADI (INDIA)

1 cucumber, sliced
3 green onions, sliced
½ green pepper, sliced
1 cauliflower, sliced
1 tomato, sliced
Yoghurt or buttermilk
Salt and pepper to taste

Arrange vegetables attractively in serving dish. Cover with yoghurt or buttermilk. Season to taste.

Mrs. Frank Charles Hodge
Dandridge, Tenn.

KOSHER SLAW (ISRAEL)

1 lge. cabbage, shredded
2 lge. onions, sliced
1 c. sugar
1 c. white vinegar
1 tsp. salt
1 tsp. dry mustard
1 tsp. celery seed
1 c. salad oil

Alternate layers of cabbage and onion rings; sprinkle with 7/8 cup sugar. Heat white vinegar, 1 tablespoon sugar, salt, mustard, celery seed and salad oil to boiling point; pour over cabbage mixture. Cover and refrigerate for 3 hours. When cool pour mixture into another bowl; serve. Yield: 8-10 servings.

Barbara Covalt
Liberal, Kans.

GREEN BEAN SALAD (ITALY)

2 lb. green beans
Salt and pepper to taste
½ c. olive oil
¼ to ½ c. wine vinegar

Cook green beans in small amount of boiling water just until crisply tender. Drain; add salt and pepper to taste. Combine olive oil and vinegar; add to beans and toss. Chill and serve cold. Yield: 4-6 servings.

Mrs. Reba Wilson
Chattanooga, Tenn.

INSALATA PICCANTE DE GAMBERTTI (ITALY)

SALAD
¾ c. mayonnaise
¼ c. sweet relish
2 tbsp. parsley flakes
2 tbsp. capers
1 ½ lb. cooked shrimp

Combine all ingredients except shrimp; mix thoroughly. Add shrimp and serve. NOTE: Dressing may be prepared ahead of time and refrigerated. Yield: 6 servings.

Mrs. Myra Terwilliger
Gainesville, Fla.

ITALIAN SLAW (ITALY)

1 med. cabbage, shredded
1 med. onion, thinly sliced
¾ c. plus 2 tsp. sugar
1 c. vinegar
¾ c. salad oil
1 tsp. salt
1 tsp. dry mustard
1 tsp. celery seed

Place cabbage in bowl alternately with sliced onion; sprinkle with 3/4 cup sugar. Combine all remaining ingredients and heat to boiling. Pour over cabbage. Cover and refrigerate for 4-6 hours. Yield: 8 servings.

Mrs. Richard McGlashon
Marshall, Minn.

COMBINACION DE ACEITUNAS--OLIVE-SHRIMP MOLD (SPAIN)

4 envelopes unflavored gelatin
1 1-qt. 14-oz. can tomato juice
¼ tsp. Tabasco sauce
½ tsp. chili powder
½ tsp. paprika
½ c. lemon juice
1 8-oz. pkg. cream cheese, softened
⅓ c. mayonnaise
1 ½ lb. shrimp, cooked, shelled, deveined and finely chopped
1 c. finely chopped pimento-stuffed olives
1 c. finely chopped celery
Sliced pimento-stuffed olives

Sprinkle gelatin over 2 cups tomato juice. Add remaining tomato juice, Tabasco sauce, chili powder and paprika; mix well. Cook over boiling water, stirring constantly, until gelatin dissolves. Add lemon juice; cool. Beat cream cheese and mayonnaise together until smooth. Gradually add tomato mixture, blending well. Chill until slightly thickened. Fold shrimp, 1 cup chopped olives and celery into tomato mixture. Turn into a 2 1/2-quart mold. Chill until set; unmold. Garnish with sliced pimento-stuffed olives. Yield: 6-8 servings.

Photograph for this recipe above.

CUCUMBER SALAD (SWEDEN)

6 thin onion rings
2 lge. cucumbers, peeled and thinly sliced sliced
⅓ c. vinegar
5 tbsp. water
5 tbsp. sugar
½ tsp. salt
Dash of pepper
Chopped dill or parsley

Mix onion and cucumbers. Combine vinegar, water, sugar, salt and pepper; mix well. Pour dressing over onion and cucumbers. Chill until cucumbers are wilted; garnish with dill or parsley. Yield: 6 servings.

Pat Coley
Magdalena, N.M.

HERRING SALAD (SWEDEN)

1 8-oz. jar fillet of herring in wine sauce
1 lge. sweet onion thinly sliced
1 tart unpeeled red apple, cored and thinly sliced
½ c. sour cream

(Continued on next page)

Remove herring and onions from wine sauce. Mix with fresh onion, apple and sour cream. Marinate for 10 or 15 minutes. Serve on lettuce cups. Yield: 6 servings.

Ruth E. Carlson
Donovan, Ill.

CHICKEN SALAD A LA SPANISH (SPAIN)

5 c. cooked diced chicken
6 scallions, thinly sliced
2 heads lettuce, shredded
5 tomatoes, cut into wedges
¾ c. olive oil
½ c. red wine vinegar
Salt and pepper to taste
6 ripe pitted olives, sliced
6 stuffed olives, sliced

Combine chicken, scallions, lettuce and tomatoes. Toss lightly with oil, vinegar, salt and pepper. Garnish with olives. NOTE: Turkey may be substituted for chicken. Yield: 12 servings.

Mrs. Dan M. Parker
Marietta, Ga.

GUACAMOLE (SPAIN)

2 avocados, peeled and mashed
1 med. tomato, peeled and diced
1 sm. onion, grated
1 tbsp. lemon juice
½ tsp. salt
Dash of chili powder

Combine avocados and tomato; mix well. Add all remaining ingredients; blend thoroughly. Serve on crisp lettuce. NOTE: If salad must stand a while before serving add avocado seeds to mixture to prevent discoloration. Yield: 8 servings.

Mrs. W. G. Owens
Kelens, Tex.

SPANISH SALAD (SPAIN)

1 slice bacon
½ head romaine lettuce
2 green onions, sliced
¼ c. chopped celery
1 tbsp. chopped green pepper
⅛ c. sliced cheese
¼ c. salami, sliced into 1-in. strips
¼ c. cucumbers, sliced into 1-in. strips
1 med. tomato, quartered

Fry bacon until crisp; drain and crumble. Combine all ingredients; toss lightly.

DRESSING:
½ c. hot bacon drippings
¼ c. hot wine vinegar
1 tsp. garlic salt
¼ tsp. pepper
¼ c. sliced black olives
1 hard-cooked egg, sliced

Combine bacon drippings, vinegar, garlic salt and pepper; pour over salad. Garnish with olives and egg slices. Yield: 4 servings.

Mrs. Penny Winchester
Munday, Tex.

SPANISH SOUP SALAD (SPAIN)

⅛ tsp. cominos seed
1 head lettuce, chopped
1 green pepper, diced
4 tomatoes, diced
1 c. chopped celery
1 bunch green onions, chopped
10 radishes, sliced
Salt and pepper
Cold water
8 ice cubes
Fresh bread, cut into 1-in. cubes
Stuffed olives, sliced

Crush cominos seed in wooden salad bowl with wooden spoon; add all fresh vegetables and seasonings. Mix well. Barely cover mixture with water; add ice cubes. Just before serving stir in bread cubes; garnish with olives. Serve in soup bowls. Yield: 12 servings.

Mrs. Earl C. Joslyn
Grand Forks AFB, N.D.

CHICKEN IN CURRY MAYONNAISE (SWEDEN)

2 to 2 ½ c. cooked diced chicken
1 c. peeled diced apple
1 c. diced celery
1 tbsp. chopped dill (opt.)
1 ½ to 2 tsp. curry powder
¾ c. mayonnaise
1 tbsp. lemon juice
Pinch of sugar
½ c. whipped cream
2 hard-cooked eggs, sliced
1 lge. tomato, cut into wedges

Combine chicken, apple, celery and dill. Stir 1 1/2 teaspoons curry powder into mayonnaise; add lemon juice and sugar. Add more curry powder if desired. Fold in cream. Spoon curry mayonnaise over chicken mixture, toss lightly. Chill thoroughly. Garnish with egg slices and tomato wedges. Yield: 6 servings.

Ardis A. Williams
Yuba City, Calif.

HERRING SALAD (SCANDINAVIA)

2 lge. salt herring
2 c. cubed canned beets
2 c. diced cold boiled potatoes
½ c. finely chopped onions
1 c. peeled, cored and cubed tart apples
½ c. diced dill pickles
½ c. chopped English walnuts
1 c. mayonnaise
1 tsp. prepared mustard
Salt to taste
½ tsp. pepper
5 tbsp. vinegar
½ tsp. sugar
½ c. sour cream
Red food coloring

Soak herring in cold water for at least 5 hours. Change water every hour. Skin fillets; cut into small pieces. Combine herring, beets, potatoes, onions, apples, pickles and walnuts. Toss thoroughly. Combine remaining ingredients. Add to herring mixture; toss. Let stand overnight. When ready to serve, add a mixture of additional mayonnaise and sour cream to moisten if necessary. Salad will keep three or four days if refrigerated. Yield: 6 servings.

Mrs. Inez K. Waechter
Anna, Ill.

SWEDISH BEAN SALAD (SWEDEN)

½ c. sour cream
⅓ c. mayonnaise
1 16-oz. can French-cut green beans, drained
1 med. cucumber, diced
6 green onions, finely chopped
1 tsp. dill
Salt and pepper

Blend sour cream and mayonnaise. Combine beans, cucumber, green onions, dill, salt and pepper. Pour sour cream mixture over vegetables and toss. Cover and chill for several hours. Serve on greens; garnish with chopped parsley. Yield: 4-5 servings.

Mrs. George Kehlenbrink
Ripon, Wisc.

SWEDISH SALAD (SWEDEN)

1 No. 2 ½ can chunk pineapple, drained
2 sm. cans Mandarin oranges, drained
1 lb. green grapes
1 c. slivered blanched almonds
¾ lb. minitaure marshmallows
1 tsp. salt
2 tbsp. water
2 eggs
2 tbsp. lemon juice
½ pt. heavy cream, whipped
1 c. sliced celery

Combine pineapple, oranges, grapes, almonds and marshmallows. Mix salt, water, eggs and lemon juice. Cook in double boiler until thick. Add to fruit mixture. Let stand for 24 hours. Just before serving, fold in whipped cream and celery. Yield: 8-10 servings.

Mrs. Sidney C. Smith
Fernandina Beach, Fla.

SWEDISH SHRIMP SALAD (SWEDEN)

⅔ c. diced ripe olives
2 c. cooked or canned shrimp
6 hard-cooked eggs
2 cooked potatoes, cubed
3 tbsp. wine vinegar
½ c. mayonnaise
¾ tsp. salt
⅛ tsp. paprika
Crisp lettuce
2 sm. slices American or Swiss cheese

Combine olives, shrimp, 2 coarsely chopped eggs, and potatoes with 2 tablespoons vinegar; chill for several hours. When ready to serve, blend mayonnaise, salt, paprika and remaining tablespoon vinegar; combine with shrimp mixture. Turn into lettuce lined salad bowl. Cut remaining eggs into halves, arrange over top. Cut cheese slices to form four triangles. Spear a toothpick through each cheese triangle into egg to resemble a sail. NOTE: Deviled eggs may be used for garnish in place of egg-cheese sail boats. Yield: 6 servings.

Mrs. Shelley Wilsor
Lincoln, Nebr.

SWEDISH VEGETABLE SALAD (SWEDEN)

1 ½ c. cooked diced carrots
1 ½ c. cooked sliced cauliflower
1 ½ c. cooked green peas
1 ½ c. cooked sliced green beans
½ c. chopped onion
½ c. chopped celery
1 c. canned artichoke hearts
⅔ c. very sharp French dressing
¾ c. mayonnaise
¼ c. chili sauce
1 tsp. salt
2 tsp. ground dry dill
⅛ tsp. pepper
1 tbsp. lemon juice

Combine all vegetables; marinate in French dressing for 1 hour. Drain well. Mix mayonnaise, chili sauce, salt, dill, pepper and lemon juice; stir into vegetables. Chill. Yield: 12 servings.

Alma Betts
Southwick, Idaho

INDEX

We wish to thank the following for supplying us with photographs and editorial material: Western Iceberg Lettuce; National Pickle Packers Association; McIlhenny Company (Tabasco); National Dairy Council; The R. T. French Company; Sunkist Growers; Florida Citrus Commission; Ocean Spray Cranberries, Inc.; California Foods Research Institute; National Macaroni Institute; Evaporated Milk Association; National Pecan Shellers and Processors Association; Brussels Sprout Marketing Program.

International Tuna Fish Association; Kellogg Company; John Oster Manufacturing Company; Best Foods, Division Corn Products Company; American Dairy Association; United Fresh Fruit and Vegetable Association; Knox Gelatine; Rice Council; The Borden Company; Idaho Onion and Potato Commission; National Banana Association; Spanish Green Olive Commission.